OXFORD
UNIVERSITY PRESS

Great Clarendon Street, Oxford OX2 6DP

rsity Press is a department of the University of Oxford.
iversity's objective of excellence in research, scholarship,
nd education by publishing worldwide in

Oxford New York

Cape Town Dar es Salaam Hong Kong Karachi
mpur Madrid Melbourne Mexico City Nairobi
New Delhi Shanghai Taipei Toronto

With offices in

Austria Brazil Chile Czech Republic France Greece
a Hungary Italy Japan Poland Portugal Singapore
a Switzerland Thailand Turkey Ukraine Vietnam

a registered trade mark of Oxford University Press
in the UK and in certain other countries

Published in the United States
by Oxford University Press Inc., New York

Delahunty, Sheila Dignen, and Penny Stock 2001, 2005

moral rights of the authors have been asserted
tabase right Oxford University Press (maker)

First published 2001

ished as an Oxford University Press paperback 2003

Second Edition 2005

itish Library Cataloguing in Publication Data

Data available

rary of Congress Cataloging in Publication Data

Typeset in Swift and Frutiger
by Interactive Sciences Ltd
Printed in Great Britain by
Clays Ltd, St Ives plc

ISBN 978-0-19-860919-3

3

The Oxford Dictionary of

Allusions

Andrew Delahunty, **Sheila Dignen**, and **Penny Stock**
are all freelance lexicographers with many years'
experience in writing dictionaries and other reference
works. Between them they have worked on a wide range of
books including dictionaries for adults, children,
and those learning English as a foreign language.

OXFORD
UNIVERSITY PRESS

The

A

Seco

Edite

AND
SHE
PEN

This b

OXI
UNIVER

Oxford Unive
It furthers the U

Auckland
Kuala l

Argentina
Guatema
South Kor

Oxford is

© Andrew

The

Da

First pub

All rights r
stored in a retr
without the
or as expressly p
reprographic
outside the sc

You must
and yo

B

Lib

Contents

Introduction

What is an allusion? When we make an allusion we mention the name of a real person, historical event, or literary character, not simply as a straightforward reference (as in 'Hercules was an ancient Greek hero') but in order to conjure up some extra meaning, embodying some quality or characteristic for which the word has come to stand. *The Oxford Dictionary of Allusions* aims to identify and explain such allusions used in English and to illustrate their use by quotations from a variety of texts.

Writers use allusions in a variety of ways. They can be used as a kind of shorthand, evoking instantly a complex human experience embedded with a story or dramatic event. For example, in this passage from *Jude the Obscure*,

> Arabella ascended the stairs, softly opened the door of the first bedroom, and peeped in. Finding that her shorn Samson was asleep she entered to the bedside and started regarding him.

Thomas Hardy's phrase 'shorn Samson' succinctly expresses Arabella's quiet triumph at finally having Jude in her power. Allusions can convey powerful visual images, as Robertson Davies does in his reference to the tangled limbs and snakes of the classical statue of Laocoön in *Leaven of Malice*:

> 'And seeing it's you, I'll give you a hint: the way the string's tied you can get loose at once if he lies down flat and you crawl right up over his head; then the string drops off without untying the knots. Bye now.' And she was off to encourage other strugglers, who lay in Laocoön groups about the floor.

It is often possible to pack more meaning into a well-chosen allusion than into a roughly equivalent descriptive term from the general language either because an allusion can carry some of the connotations of the whole story from which it is drawn, or because an individual's name can be associated with more than one characteristic. Some authors can even use a multiplicity of allusive terms to entertaining effect, as in this quotation from *The Scold's Bridle* by Minnette Walters:

> I watched Duncan clipping his hedge this afternoon and could barely remember the handsome man he was. If I had been a charitable woman, I would have married him forty years ago and saved him from himself and Violet. She has turned my Romeo into a sad-eyed Billy Bunter who blinks his passions quietly when no one's looking. Oh that his too, too solid flesh should melt. At twenty, he had the body of Michelangelo's David, now he resembles an entire family group by Henry Moore.

The majority of allusions in English derive from classical mythology and the Bible, particularly the Old Testament. These ancient stories — the

Wooden Horse of Troy, the protracted return home of Odysseus, David and Goliath, the banishment of Adam and Eve from the Garden of Eden — remain very much alive in our collective consciousness. Other fertile sources include folklore and legend (for example, Robin Hood, Lancelot, and Faust); Shakespeare (Romeo, Othello, and Lady Macbeth); Dickens (Micawber, Scrooge, and Pecksniff); the visual style of great artists (Rembrandt and Modigliani); and children's stories (Cinderella, Pinocchio, and Eeyore). Some individual works, such as *Gulliver's Travels*, *Alice's Adventures in Wonderland*, and *The Pilgrim's Progress*, are particularly rich sources. Modern allusions often derive from the visual media of cinema and television (Terminator, Norma Desmond, Del Boy, Archie Bunker), and from the worlds of the comic strip and the animated film (Bambi, Linus blanket, Mr Magoo, Roadrunner). And now we are starting to derive allusions from computer games (Lara Croft).

This second edition of *The Oxford Dictionary of Allusions*, like the first, is largely based on the evidence of the quotations collected as its source material. Unlike the first, it is fully alphabetical. The original edition had a thematic structure with entries grouped under themes such as 'Anger', 'Cunning', and 'Hypocrisy'. In the new edition this structure is preserved in the form of a thematic index, enabling readers to discover different allusions that can be used in similar contexts. The thematic index can be used in the same way as a thesaurus for finding different entries with a similar meaning or theme. For example, Judas is by far the most frequently cited exponent of betrayal, but the thematic index yields other allusions in the same semantic area such as Benedict Arnold, Delilah, and the 'lady in red'. It also reveals other juxtapositions such as changes in allusions over time. For example, in the nineteenth century Jack Sheppard represented the archetype of the person who successfully escaped. In the twentieth century he was replaced by Houdini.

We have added some 300 new entries for this new edition. A number of contemporary allusions have become well-established since the publication of the previous edition and take their place within these pages. These include Princess Diana, Frodo, Bill Gates, Guantanamo Bay, Jerry Springer, Teletubbies, and the X-Files.

The authors would like to thank Ruth Langley and Laurien Berkeley from Oxford University Press. We also thank again those who worked with us on the first edition of the dictionary, particularly Elizabeth Knowles, and the contributors to the reading programme which provided us with the basis of our original database of quotations: Kendall Clarke, Ian Clarke, Robert Grout, Mark Grout, Ruth Loshak, Jane McArthur, Duncan Marshall, Camilla Sherwood, Peggy Tout, and Brigit Viney.

Abaddon Abaddon, whose name is Hebrew for 'destruction' or 'abyss', is described in the book of Revelation as 'the angel of the bottomless pit' who presides over a swarm of tormenting locusts that 'have tails like scorpions, and stings' (Rev. 9: 10–11). He is sometimes identified with the Devil and also with Hell. His Greek name is Apollyon.

> And my father preached a whole set of sermons on the occasion; one set in the morning, all about David and Goliath, to spirit up the people to fighting with spades or bricks, if need were; and the other set in the afternoons, proving that Napoleon (that was another name for Bony, as we used to call him) was all the same as an Apollyon and Abaddon.
> ELIZABETH GASKELL *Cranford* 1851–3

> Some red-liveried, sulphur-scented imp of Abaddon.
> AUGUSTA J. WILSON *Vashti* 1869

Abdera Abdera was an ancient Greek city on the coast of Thrace whose inhabitants were proverbial for their stupidity.

Abednego *See* SHADRACH, MESHACH, AND ABEDNEGO.

Abelard and Héloïse Peter Abelard (1079–1142), French theologian and philosopher, became tutor to the young Héloïse (1098–1164) at the request of her uncle Fulbert, a canon of Notre Dame. They fell in love, and when the affair was discovered by Fulbert, the couple fled. Héloïse bore a son and they were secretly married in Paris. However, Héloïse's enraged relatives castrated Abelard, who then became a monk, and required Héloïse to become a nun. Abelard and Héloïse are buried together in Paris, and a book of their correspondence was published in 1616.

> Therefore the mooning world is gratified,
> Quoting how prettily we sigh and swear;
> And you and I, correctly side by side,
> Shall live as lovers when our bones are bare
> And though we lie forever enemies,
> Shall rank with Abelard and Héloïse.
> DOROTHY PARKER 'The Immortals' in *Enough Rope* 1926

> By the end of the winter I was pregnant, but with Albert's access to black-

market goods it was easy for us to find in Stuttgart a highly qualified obstetrician to help us out. Neither of us liked the idea, but Albert knew that if things were not arranged this way it was likely that some of father's huskier Staroviche cops would fall on him one night and at best leave him neutered. Pressure was perhaps increased by the fact that he called me Heloise, and even though he was no Abelard, he remembered what Heloise's uncle . . . had done to the body of that great philosopher out of jealousy and vengeance.
THOMAS KENEALLY *A Family Madness* 1985

Abraham Abraham was a biblical leader, considered to be the father of the Hebrews. All Jews claim descent from him (Gen. 11: 27 – 25: 10).

In the latter quarter of each year cattle were at once the mainstay and the terror of families about Casterbridge and its neighbourhood, where breeding was carried on with Abrahamic success.
THOMAS HARDY *The Mayor of Casterbridge* 1886

Wendell went on carefully, considerately, 'Let me propose this. Has she ever smoked pot?' 'Not with me around. I'm an old-fashioned father figure. Two parts Abraham to one part Fagin.'
JOHN UPDIKE *Bech: A Book* 1970

Abraham's bosom In the biblical parable of the rich man and Lazarus, when Lazarus dies he is 'carried by the angels into Abraham's bosom', whereas the rich man goes to Hell. 'And in hell he lift up his eyes, being in torments, and seeth Abraham afar off, and Lazarus in his bosom' (Luke 16: 23). Abraham's bosom is thus a place where the good rest in peace when they die. *See also* LAZARUS.

Absalom In the Bible, Absalom was the favourite son of King David, who led a rebellion against his father, chasing David out of Jerusalem. In the subsequent battle, David ordered his men to 'deal gently for my sake with the young man, even with Absalom' (2 Sam. 18: 5), but his commander Joab ignored this command and slew Absalom. According to the biblical account, Absalom was fleeing on a mule, but was caught by his long hair in the branches of an oak tree, and 'he was taken up between the heaven and the earth'. Joab took three darts in his hand 'and thrust them through the heart of Absalom, while he was yet alive in the midst of the oak'. On hearing of the death of his son, David wept, 'O my son, Absalom, my son, my son Absalom! Would God I had died for thee, O Absalom, my son, my son!' (2 Sam. 18: 33). Absalom is alluded to as the ultimate rebellious son. *See also* DAVID.

Sometimes, the worthy gentleman would reprove my mother for being over-indulgent to her sons, with a reference to old Eli, or David and Absalom, which was particularly galling to her feelings.
ANNE BRONTË *The Tenant of Wildfell Hall* 1848

Well, doctor, 'tis a mercy you wasn't a-drowned, or a-splintered, or a-hanged

up to a tree like Absalom—also a handsome gentleman like yerself, as the prophets say!
THOMAS HARDY *The Woodlanders* 1887

'This business of love between father and son sounds like something in the Bible.' 'The patterns of human feeling do not change as much as many people suppose. King David's estimate of his rebellious son Absalom was certainly in masculine terms. But I suppose you recall David's lament when Absalom was slain?' 'I have been called Absalom before, and it isn't a comparison I like.'
ROBERTSON DAVIES *The Manticore* 1972

Achates In Virgil's *Aeneid*, Achates is the companion of Aeneas whose fidelity to his friend is so exemplary as to become proverbial, hence the term *fidus Achates* ('faithful Achates').

'Friend!' replied Craigengelt, 'my cock of the pit? why, I am thy very Achates, man, as I have heard scholars say—hand and glove—bark and tree—thine to life and death!'
WALTER SCOTT *The Bride of Lammermoor* 1819

Acheron In Greek mythology, Acheron ('the river of woe') was one of the rivers in Hades over which the souls of the dead were ferried by Charon. The name can also be used to mean the underworld, or Hades. *See also* HADES.

Throughout that night Boldwood's dark form might have been seen walking about the hills and downs of Weatherbury like an unhappy Shade in the Mournful Fields by Acheron.
THOMAS HARDY *Far from the Madding Crowd* 1874

[They] then made their way across the river, which under the grey and growing light looked as desolate as Acheron.
G. K. CHESTERTON *The Man Who Was Thursday* 1908

Achilles Achilles was one of the greatest Greek heroes of the Trojan War. According to legend, he was the son of the mortal Peleus and the sea-nymph Thetis. During his infancy his mother dipped him in the waters of the river Styx, thus making his body invulnerable except for the heel by which she held him. This vulnerable spot would later prove fatal.

The *Iliad* relates how, during the Trojan War, Achilles quarrelled with his commander, Agamemnon, because of Agamemnon's slight in taking from him his war-prize, the concubine Briseis. Achilles retired in anger to his tent, refusing to fight any longer. Later, after the death of his beloved friend Patroclus at the hand of the Trojan hero Hector, he did emerge, filled with grief and rage. In revenge, Achilles killed Hector and dragged his body behind the wheels of his chariot round the walls of Troy. Achilles himself was wounded in the heel by a poisoned arrow shot by Paris, Hector's brother, and died of this wound.

The *Iliad* opens with the words: 'Sing, goddess, of the anger of Achilles, son of Peleus, that accursed anger which brought uncounted anguish on the

Achaians.' Achilles can typify anger, and in particular angry sulkiness. A person's 'Achilles heel' is their only weak or vulnerable point. *See also* AGAMEMNON, HECTOR, TROJAN WAR.

> There was every temporal reason for leaving: it would be entering again into a world which he had only quitted in a passion for isolation, induced by a fit of Achillean moodiness after an imagined slight.
> THOMAS HARDY *The Woodlanders* 1887

> It reveals a curious Achilles heel in the master spindoctor: brilliant as he is at selling Labour, he is strangely bad at selling himself. *The Observer* 1997

Achilles and Patroclus In Greek mythology, the Greek heroes Achilles and Patroclus were bosom friends. According to the *Iliad*, Patroclus, having prevailed on Achilles to lend him his armour, was killed by the Trojan hero Hector. Achilles returned to the battle and avenged his beloved friend's death by slaying Hector. *See also* TROJAN WAR.

> Close as Achilles and Patroclus, the two of us.
> JULIAN BARNES *Talking It Over* 1991

Bob Acres Bob Acres is a ridiculous but mild character in Sheridan's *The Rivals* (1775) who believes himself to be a rival for the hand of Lydia Languish. He is persuaded to fight a duel with her preferred suitor, but on his arrival at the location for the fight his courage disappears rapidly, 'oozing out at the palms of his hands'.

> 'If you are busy, another time will do as well', continued the bishop, whose courage like Bob Acres' had oozed out, now that he found himself on the ground of battle.
> ANTHONY TROLLOPE *Barchester Towers* 1857

Actaeon In Greek mythology, Actaeon was a hunter who, because he accidentally saw Artemis (the virgin goddess of the hunt) bathing naked, was changed into a stag and torn to pieces by his own hounds.

> 'Rash man!' she said; 'like Actaeon, thou hast had thy will; be careful lest, like Actaeon, thou too perish miserably, torn to pieces by the ban-hounds of thine own passions.'
> H. RIDER HAGGARD *She* 1887

> Further up they saw in the mid-distance the hounds running hither and thither, as if the scent lay cold that day. Soon members of the hunt appeared on the scene, and it was evident that the chase had been stultified by general puzzle-headedness as to the whereabouts of the intended victim. In a minute, a gentleman-farmer, panting with Actaeonic excitement, rode up to the two pedestrians, and Grace being a few steps in advance he asked her if she had seen the fox.
> THOMAS HARDY *The Woodlanders* 1887

Actium Actium, a promontory in ancient Greece, was in 31 BC the scene of a sea and land battle in which the forces of Mark Antony and Cleopatra were decisively defeated by the fleet of Octavian (the future Emperor Augustus).

> Soon he would be overtaken; but warm in the circle of Leila's arms, as if he were Antony at Actium, he could hardly bring himself to feel fear.
> LAWRENCE DURRELL *Mountolive* 1958

Adam and Eve According to the book of Genesis, Adam was the first man, created by God from the dust of the ground and God's breath, and Eve the first woman, formed from one of Adam's ribs. They lived together in innocence in the Garden of Eden, knowing nothing of good and evil and unashamed of their own nakedness. The tree of the knowledge of good and evil grew in the Garden of Eden, the only tree whose fruit Adam and Eve were expressly forbidden by God to eat. Tempted by the Serpent to eat the forbidden fruit, Eve did so and then in turn persuaded Adam to do the same. As a punishment for disobeying God's command, they were banished from Eden. Because Eve had eaten first and then tempted Adam, God told her that as a punishment women would henceforth always suffer in childbirth: 'I will greatly multiply thy sorrow and thy conception; in sorrow thou shalt bring forth children.' Man for his part would be forced to toil for his livelihood: 'In the sweat of thy face thou shalt eat bread, till thou return unto the ground.'

Adam and Eve can represent a state of utter contentment or innocence, particularly when preceding the loss or destruction of such happiness. *See also* EDEN, EVE, the FALL, FORBIDDEN FRUIT, SERPENT, TREE OF KNOWLEDGE.

> We are Adam and Eve, unfallen, in Paradise.
> GEORGE ELIOT *The Mill on the Floss* 1860

> But here . . . shut in by the stable hills, among which mere walking had the novelty of pageantry, any man could imagine himself to be Adam without the least difficulty.
> THOMAS HARDY *The Return of the Native* 1880

> So there they were, naked as Adam and Eve.
> PHILIP ROTH *Epstein* 1959

> 'At least in other nations,' Robbie Ross had fulminated, 'Adam and Eve arrived innocent. Here they arrived with their crimes already written all over their faces.'
> THOMAS KENEALLY *The Playmaker* 1987

Charles Addams Charles Samuel Addams (1912–88) was an American cartoonist whose cartoons about a group of bizarre people living in a decaying Gothic mansion became immortalized as the television series *The Addams Family*.

> The front door opened behind us. Sebastian entered, tapping along with a white cane. 'Neverman? Is that you in here?' 'Christ!' Neverman muttered.

'He's like something out of Charles Addams.'
MARCIA MULLER *Ask the Cards a Question* 1982

Beyond the tracks, standing alone in a neglected field, was a Victorian mansion like the one in the Charles Addams cartoons in the *New Yorker.*
BILL BRYSON *The Lost Continent* 1989

Addams family The Addams family was a television show derived from Charles Addams's *New Yorker* cartoon strip which was aired on ABC in the United States from 1964 to 1966 and on ITV in the United Kingdom from 1966 to 1968. Gomez and black-haired Morticia Addams and their daughter Wednesday and son Pugsley, with Uncle Fester, Grandmama, and butler Lurch, were the 'creepy, kooky, mysterious and spooky' family in the spoof horror sitcom, along with cousin Itt. Their furnishings included an electric chair kept by Pugsley in his room. The same characters were later played in a film, *The Addams Family* (1991), and a sequel, *Addams Family Values* (1993).

In fact, Marsha's office was filled with other souvenirs: a human skull, a large specimen bottle with a human fetus preserved in formaldehyde, framed color pictures of gruesome murder scenes. 'Who does your decorating?' I asked. 'The Addams family?'
STEVEN WOMACK *Dead Folk Blues* 1992

I haven't got anything to take with me—the cards in the newsagent's were all vile. They looked like the sort of thing the Addams family would send to each other on their birthdays.
NICK HORNBY *High Fidelity* 1995

Detective Escovedo was right, there was a distinctly Gomez and Morticia quality about my life, a thought that prompted me to return to Ms. Baljur's desousing program with greater vigor.
LINDSAY MARACOTTA *The Dead Celeb* 1997

Admah and Zeboiim According to the book of Deuteronomy (29: 23), the cities of Admah and Zeboiim suffered the same fate as Sodom and Gomorrah, namely destruction by God as a punishment for their citizens' sinfulness.

Admirable Crichton *See* CRICHTON.

Adonis In Greek mythology, Adonis was a beautiful youth who was loved by both Aphrodite and Persephone. He was killed by a wild boar, but Aphrodite begged Zeus to restore him to life. Zeus decreed that Adonis should spend the winter months of each year in the underworld with Persephone and the summer months with Aphrodite. As the quotations below suggest, a man described as an Adonis usually has not only a handsome face but also a gorgeous body.

I really can't see any resemblance between you, with your rugged strong face

and your coal-black hair, and this young Adonis, who looks as if he was made out of ivory and rose-leaves.
OSCAR WILDE *The Picture of Dorian Gray* 1891

I suppose a very calculating man would keep his shirt on to the last, getting rid of his socks and shorts as fast as possible, and then cast off the shirt, revealing himself as an Adonis. But I was a schoolboy undresser, and had never stripped to enchant.
ROBERTSON DAVIES *The Manticore* 1972

The funny thing about David was that though he was absolutely not an Adonis and pretty wet in most ways, he was rather good in bed—fairly simple, but enjoying himself a lot and seeing that you did too.
PETER DICKINSON *The Yellow Room* 1995

Adullam In the Bible, when David was fleeing from Saul because Saul wanted to kill him, he took refuge in the cave of Adullam. When others heard that he was there, they went to join him: 'And every one that was in distress, and every one that was in debt, and every one that was discontented, gathered themselves unto him' (1 Sam. 22: 2). Adullam can be mentioned in the context of a place where those in trouble can seek refuge.

Mixen Lane was the Adullam of all the surrounding villages. It was the hiding-place of those in distress, and in debt, and trouble of every kind.
THOMAS HARDY *The Mayor of Casterbridge* 1886

Aegeus In Greek mythology, Theseus had promised his father, Aegeus, that if he successfully destroyed the Minotaur he would signal this on his return to Athens by hoisting white sails, rather than the customary black ones. This he forgot to do and Aegeus, believing his son to be dead, threw himself to his death from a cliff.

Aeneas In Greek and Roman mythology, Aeneas was a Trojan leader, son of Anchises and Aphrodite, and legendary ancestor of the Romans. At the end of the Trojan War, when Troy was in flames, he carried his ageing father away upon his shoulders. The story of his subsequent wanderings is told in Virgil's *Aeneid*. *See also* DIDO AND AENEAS.

She shook her head, and he lifted her up; then, at a slow pace, went onward with his load. . . . Thus he proceeded, like Aeneas with his father.
THOMAS HARDY *The Return of the Native* 1880

Trouble was, though they shared great areas of social conscience in common, the spin that nature and/or nurture had put on hers made her regard the police force as a cure almost as bad as the disease. Peter, on the other hand, though not blind to its flaws, felt himself duty driven to work from within. A right pious little Aeneas, *Italiam non sponte sequor*.
REGINALD HILL *On Beulah Height* 1998

Aeolian According to Greek mythology, Aeolus was a mortal who lived on the floating island of Aeolia. He was a friend of the gods, and Zeus gave him control of the winds. Aeolus was later regarded as the god of the winds. He has given his name to the Aeolian harp, a musical instrument that produces sounds when the wind passes through it. Aeolian music is thus music produced by the effect of the wind.

> Time to drink in life's sunshine—time to listen to the Aeolian music that the wind of God draws from the human heart-strings around us.
> JEROME K. JEROME *Three Men in a Boat* 1889

Aeschylus Aeschylus (*c*.525–*c*.456 BC) was a Greek dramatist, best known for his trilogy dealing with the story of Orestes, the *Oresteia* (458 BC), consisting of *Agamemnon*, *Choephoroe*, and *Eumenides*. According to legend, an eagle, mistaking his bald head for a rock, dropped a tortoise on it (to break the shell), thus killing him.

Aesculapius Aesculapius (or Asclepius), the son of Apollo and Coronis, was instructed in the art of medicine by the centaur Chiron. He was said to have been killed by Zeus after Hades had complained that Aesculapius' skills were keeping mortals from the underworld. After his death, he was honoured as the god of medicine and healing. He was represented holding a staff with a serpent wreathed around it, now the emblem of the medical profession.

> Carl Moss might be willing to protect Merle with the mantle of Aesculapius, up to a point.
> RAYMOND CHANDLER *The High Window* 1943

> I looked round you see but I said, Wilmot, I said, this anatomy is not for you. No indeed, you have not the stomach for it. In fact as I said at the time, I abandoned Aesculapius for the Muse. Have I not said so to you, Mr Talbot?
> WILLIAM GOLDING *Rites of Passage* 1980

Aesop's fable Aesop (6th c. BC), who is believed to have come from Thrace and lived as a slave on the island of Samos, traditionally has all Greek fables ascribed to his authorship. The fable, a popular literary form in ancient Greece, is a morality tale in which the characters are animals. A typical example is the story of the hare and the tortoise, in which the hare is so confident that he can win a race with the tortoise that he takes a nap. When he wakes, he finds that the tortoise has plodded slowly but surely to the finishing line and the hare is unable to sprint fast enough to beat him. The moral of the story is 'Slow but steady wins the race'.

> I told you that capital thing I heard her say about Craig—that he was like a cock, who thought the sun had risen to hear him crow. Now that's an Aesop's fable in a sentence.
> GEORGE ELIOT *Adam Bede* 1859

Agag Agag was the king of the Amalekites, whom Saul defeated in battle. Although Saul wanted to spare Agag's life, the prophet Samuel ordered Agag to be brought to him: 'Then said Samuel, Bring ye hither to me Agag the king of the Amalekites. And Agag came unto him delicately' (1 Sam. 15: 32). Samuel then 'hewed Agag in pieces' as retribution for Agag's brutality. As can be seen from the quotations below, the word 'delicately' is forever associated with the name of Agag.

> So as I lay on the ground with my ear glued close against the wall, who should march round the church but John Trenchard, Esquire, not treading delicately like King Agag, or spying, but just come on a voyage of discovery for himself.
> J. M. FAULKNER *Moonfleet* 1898

> If they were not rendered completely immobile, they certainly walked as delicately as Agag, the King of the Amalekites, is supposed to have done according to 1 Samuel xv.32. *Independent on Sunday* 1997

Agamemnon In Greek mythology, Agamemnon was the king of Mycenae and brother of Menelaus. The *Iliad* refers to the wrath of Agamemnon on being told that he must return a captive Trojan girl to her father to appease the god Apollo: 'Then there stood up in the assembly the hero son of Atreus, wide-ruling Agamemnon, in deep anger: fury filled his dark heart full, and his eyes were like blazing fire.' Agamemnon agreed to return the girl, but demanded that Achilles hand over to him his concubine Briseis to take her place, which led to the furious quarrel between the two men. Agamemnon typically represents terrible wrath. *See also* ACHILLES, TROJAN WAR.

> The frogs and the mice would be nothing to them, nor the angers of Agamemnon and Achilles.
> ANTHONY TROLLOPE *Barchester Towers* 1857

Aganippe In Greek mythology, Aganippe was a spring sacred to the Muses on Mount Helicon, whose waters were believed to give inspiration to those who drank from them. *See also* MUSES.

> I never dranke of Aganippe well.
> PHILIP SIDNEY *Astrophel and Stella* 1586

Agincourt Agincourt (now Azincourt), a village in France, is close to the site of a battle between the French and the English in 1415 during the Hundred Years War. Although the English were heavily outnumbered, the terrain, a muddy valley, suited the English forces, largely archers, rather than the French, who had armoured cavalry and infantry fighting in massed formations. The English lost only about 200 men to French losses of over 5 000. The battle is remembered chiefly because of its prominence in Shakespeare's *Henry V*.

Aglaia *See* GRACES.

St Agnes St Agnes (d. *c*.304) was a Roman martyr and is the patron saint of virgins. Said to have been a Christian virgin who refused to marry, she was martyred during the reign of Diocletian. Her emblem is a lamb.

Ahab

king of Israel In the Bible, Ahab (c.875–854 BC) was the idolatrous king of
Israel who married Jezebel and introduced into Israel the worship of the
Phoenician god Baal. His name became associated with wickedness,
especially the offence of honouring pagan gods: 'There was none who sold
himself to do what was evil in the sight of the Lord like Ahab, whom Jezebel
his wife incited' (1 Kgs. 21: 25). When he was finally killed, 'the dogs licked
up his blood' (1 Kgs. 22: 38). Ahab can be alluded to for his wicked pride in
refusing to believe in God but choosing rather to worship Baal. See also BAAL,
JEZEBEL.

> 'Does Judith or either of the boys ever come down to hear you preach?' . . .
> 'Nay, they struts like Ahab in their pride, and their eyes drip fatness, nor do they
> see the pit digged beneath their feet by the Lord.'
> STELLA GIBBONS Cold Comfort Farm 1932

captain in *Moby Dick* Captain Ahab is the captain of the whaling ship *Pequod*
in Herman Melville's *Moby Dick* (1851). The monomaniacal Ahab obsessively
pursues Moby Dick, the huge white whale that on a previous voyage had cost
him his leg.

> I could feel the road some twenty inches beneath me, unfurling and flying and
> hissing at incredible speeds across the groaning continent with that mad Ahab
> at the wheel.
> JACK KEROUAC On the Road 1957

> Take Ky Laffoon. Anyone with a name like that has all the potential to be as
> loopy as Captain Ahab, and sure enough Laffoon was potty. The Guardian
> 1997

Ahasuerus

Persian king Ahasuerus was a Persian king who appears in the Old Testament
book of Esther, and is usually identified with Xerxes (486–465 BC). The wrath
of Ahasuerus was aroused when his first wife, Vashti, would not submit to
his commands. As a result of this, he banished Vashti, and in her place
married Esther, a Jew. Later, Haman, one of the courtiers of Ahasuerus,
angered by the refusal of the Jew Mordecai to bow down to him, persuaded
Ahasuerus to allow the extermination of all Jews. Haman prepared a gallows
50 cubits high on which to hang the Jews, including Mordecai, who was the
former guardian of Esther. On hearing of this, Esther went to Ahasuerus to
plead for the life of Mordecai and all the Jews: 'And Esther spake yet again
before the king, and fell down at his feet, and besought him with tears to put
away the mischief of Haman the Agagite, and his device that he had devised
against the Jews' (Esther 8: 3). Ahasuerus, realizing that Haman was wicked,
ordered him to be hanged on his own gallows. Ahasuerus is alluded to as a
man whose wrath is to be feared or appeased, or a man who should be
approached with trepidation. See also ESTHER, VASHTI.

> 'Utter it, Jane: but I wish that instead of a mere inquiry into, perhaps, a secret, it

was a wish for half my estate.' 'Now, king Ahasuerus! What do I want with half
your estate?'
CHARLOTTE BRONTË *Jane Eyre* 1847

Presently my mother went to my father. I know I thought of Queen Esther and
King Ahasuerus; for my mother was very pretty and delicate-looking, and my
father looked as terrible as King Ahasuerus.
ELIZABETH GASKELL *Cranford* 1851–3

Wandering Jew *See* WANDERING JEW.

Ahriman According to the dualistic cosmology of Zoroastrianism, Ahriman
is the supreme evil spirit who is perpetually in conflict with the supreme
good spirit Ahura Mazda (or Ormazd). This is Bunyan's description of him in
The Pilgrim's Progress: 'He was clothed with scales like a fish (and they are his
pride), he had wings like a dragon, and out of his belly came fire and smoke,
and his mouth was as the mouth of a lion.'

Ajax Ajax was a Greek hero of the Trojan War, proverbial for his size and
strength. When Agamemnon awarded the armour of the dead Achilles to
Odysseus and not to him, Ajax went mad with rage, slaughtered a flock of
sheep, and then committed suicide in shame. *See also* TROJAN WAR.

She sat as helpless and despairing among her black locks as Ajax among the
slaughtered sheep.
GEORGE ELIOT *The Mill on the Floss* 1860

It was like the siege of Troy the next morning. The rain had gone and left dark
concrete patches under the drying sun. Arrayed in all their panoply along
Hardens Lane, the gentlemen of the press stood in little knots, like so many
Ajaxes and Achilles, probing the weak spots of the citadel that was Leighford
High.
M. J. TROW *Maxwell's House* 1995

Aladdin's cave Aladdin, the hero of a story in *The Arabian Nights*, is born the
son of a poor tailor and is too lazy after his father's death to help his mother.
A magician tricks him into a cave filled with treasure, in order to retrieve a
magic lamp. When the magician discovers that Aladdin has stolen as much
of the treasure as he can hide in his clothes, he shuts him into the cave,
whereupon Aladdin discovers the secret of the lamp, a jinnee who must do
his bidding. He is able to escape the cave, and the 'slave of the lamp' makes
him and his mother rich. The term 'Aladdin's cave' is used to describe a place
full of treasures. *See also* ARABIAN NIGHTS.

She thought . . . of the Aladdin's cave she had perceived in the Pusey's suite,
with its careless deployment of pleasurable attributes.
ANITA BROOKNER *Hotel du Lac* 1984

Harry followed Leo downstairs into the Aladdin's cave that was Devaney

Records, but his mind was no longer on the record he had spent twelve months hunting for.
MARTIN EDWARDS *Yesterday's Papers* 1994

Ever since then the place has remained in my memory the Mecca of fashion, an Aladdin's cave of incomparable splendour.
ANDRÉ BRINK *Imaginings of Sand* 1996

Alamo The Alamo was a fort (formerly a Christian mission) in San Antonio, Texas, which in 1836 was besieged by the Mexican army during the war between Texas and Mexico. It was defended by a small group of soldiers and civilians, all of whom (including the frontiersman and politician Davy Crockett) died. The phrase 'Remember the Alamo' was later used as a rallying cry by the Texan army. 'The Alamo' can refer to a last stand that fails.

He still had what Donald once described as that 'last Texican at the Alamo look': ready, willing, and able to go down fighting.
TOM CLANCY and STEVE PIECZENIK *Op-Center* 1995

Alastor Alastor is a supernatural figure, 'the Avenger', in ancient Greece who seeks vengeance after a crime has been committed.

Their impulse was well-nigh to prostrate themselves in lamentation before untimely rains and tempests, which came as the Alastor of those households whose crime it was to be poor.
THOMAS HARDY *The Mayor of Casterbridge* 1886

albatross *See* ANCIENT MARINER.

Alberich's cloak In the German epic poem the *Nibelungenlied*, Alberich is a dwarf who guards the treasure of the Nibelungs, which includes a cloak of invisibility called 'tarnkappe'. He is robbed of it by Siegfried.

Albion In poetic or literary contexts, the name Albion (traditionally from Latin *albus* ('white'), in reference to Dover's chalk cliffs) is sometimes used to denote Britain or England, conceived of as a green paradise.

When their keepers departed, the 400-odd rodents escaped and set up home under the green trees of Albion. *Independent on Sunday* 1993

Alcatraz Alcatraz was a notorious American prison on the island of Alcatraz in San Francisco Bay. Built in 1868, it was originally a prison for military offenders, but was later used for civilian prisoners. From 1934 it held the most dangerous criminals, including the gangster Al Capone. Alcatraz was closed in 1963. Its name has come to symbolize a prison from which escape is impossible.

Conditions are awful inside a new £3m unit designed to hold the country's most dangerous prisoners, says Sir David Ramsbotham, the Chief Inspector of Prisons. The Close Supervision Centre at Woodhill Prison in Milton Keynes was labelled Britain's Alcatraz when it opened earlier this year. *The Independent* 1998

Alcibiades Alcibiades (*c*.450–404 BC) was an Athenian general and statesman who had a reputation for debauchery. He had been a student and perhaps a lover of Socrates.

> 'But I sometimes wonder if the Victorians didn't have more fun than we did,' she was saying. 'The more prohibitions, the greater the fun. If you want to see people drinking with real enjoyment, you must go to America. Victorian England was dry in every department. For example, there was a nineteenth century amendment about love. They must have made it as enthusiastically as the Americans drink whiskey. I don't know that I really believe in Athenian enlargements—that is, if we're one of them.' 'You prefer Pecksniff to Alcibiades,' Wille Weaver concluded.
> ALDOUS HUXLEY *Point Counter Point* 1928

Alexander Alexander the Great (356–323 BC), the son of Philip II of Macedon, became king at 19 when his father was assassinated (336 BC). He defeated the Persians in three major battles, at the river Granicus, at Issus in Cilicia, and at Gaugamela, freeing the Greek city states and Egypt from Persian rule, while in Egypt he founded Alexandria. He extended his empire eastwards as far as India before dying young of a fever. Alexander is often cited as one of the greatest generals of all time.

> Had Philip's warlike son been intellectually so far ahead as to have attempted civilization without bloodshed, he would have been twice the godlike hero that he seemed, but nobody would have heard of an Alexander.
> THOMAS HARDY *The Return of the Native* 1880

> Monday dawned, the sun rising into the inevitable blue sky with the radiant serenity of Alexander entering a conquered province.
> REGINALD HILL *On Beulah Height* 1998

Alfred Alfred (849–899), generally known as Alfred the Great, was the king of Wessex in 871–899, who led the Saxons to victory over Danish invaders. The most famous story associated with Alfred is the legend that, when in hiding in Somerset, he forgot to watch a peasant woman's cakes, as he had been asked to do, with the result that they burnt.

> My word, Miriam! You're in for it this time. . . . You'd better be gone when his mother comes in. I know why King Alfred burned the cakes. Now I see it! 'Postle would fix up a tale about his work making him forget, if he thought it would wash. If that old woman had come in a bit sooner, she'd have boxed the brazen things' ears who made the oblivion, instead of poor Alfred's.
> D. H. LAWRENCE *Sons and Lovers* 1913

Horatio Alger Horatio Alger (1832–99) was an American writer and clergyman who wrote adventure stories for boys. The stories were on the theme of rags to riches, with the hero's initial struggles with poverty eventually leading to fame and wealth. His most popular story was *Ragged Dick* (1867).

> Schliemann was the original Horatio Alger hero. He began his career as a stock boy, sleeping under the counter of the store at night, and ended up a millionaire merchant. Once he'd acquired his wealth, he dumped his business interests and turned to the subject that had obsessed him since his daddy had read to him from Homer. Unlike most historians of his time, naïve Heinrich believed the Homeric poems were literally true. The credulous merchant was right, and the historians were wrong. Schliemann found Troy.
> ELIZABETH PETERS *Trojan Gold* 1987

Muhammad Ali Born Cassius Clay in 1942, Muhammad Ali, the American boxer, won the world heavyweight title for the first time in 1964, regaining it in 1974 and 1978, to become the first boxer to be world champion three times. He retired in 1981. Ali frequently boasted 'I am the greatest'.

> Gimme a cup of coffee as strong as Muhammad Ali.
> CHESTER HIMES *Blind Man with a Pistol* 1969

> 'Scream, damn it!' He grabbed a handful of my nightie and tried to tear it. I defy Mohammad Ali to rend a wad of Dacron; it just stretches, interminably.
> ELIZABETH PETERS *Silhouette in Scarlet* 1983

Ali Baba In the story of 'Ali Baba and the Forty Thieves' (one of the stories in *The Arabian Nights*), the captain of the 40 thieves conceals his men in leather oil jars outside the house of Ali Baba, intending to kill him during the night.

> Blue Ali Baba oil jars were dotted around, big enough to keep tigers.
> RAYMOND CHANDLER *The Lady in the Lake* 1943

Alice in Wonderland Lewis Carroll's children's story *Alice's Adventures in Wonderland* (1865) is an account of a young girl's experiences in a surreal, illogical, dreamlike world. At the beginning of the story Alice follows a white rabbit down a rabbit-hole and finds herself apparently tumbling down a very deep well: 'Down, down, down. Would the fall never come to an end? "I wonder how many miles I've fallen by this time?" she said aloud.' She eventually lands with a thump in Wonderland. Alice finds a little door that is too small for her to fit through until she drinks from a bottle labelled 'Drink me' and immediately starts to shrink, becoming 10 inches high. Not long after this she is required to eat a cake labelled 'Eat me', to make her grow taller. Further strange incidents occur, with Alice greeting each development with the words 'Curiouser and curiouser!' In addition to the White Rabbit, Alice encounters a succession of other outlandish creatures, including the Cheshire Cat, the Mad Hatter, and the March Hare. At the end of the story Alice wakes from what has apparently been a dream. The phrase 'Alice-in-Wonderland' can be used to describe a puzzling, seemingly illogical situation. Alice is depicted in John Tenniel's illustrations with long blonde hair. In Carroll's sequel, *Through the Looking-Glass* (1871), the illustrations show Alice's hair held back with a wide hairband, now known as an Alice band. *See also* CHESHIRE CAT, DORMOUSE, FATHER WILLIAM, MAD HATTER, MARCH HARE, RABBIT-HOLE, RED QUEEN, WHITE RABBIT.

> The plane was unmistakably going down, down, down, like Alice in the rabbit hole.
> E SCOTT FITZGERALD *The Last Tycoon* 1941

> What would they make of the wedding photos stuck in the back of his bureau drawer? Of Vic, with her Alice-in-Wonderland hair and pale, innocent face.
> DEBORAH CROMBIE *All Shall Be Well* 1995

> 'Yes,' I admitted, feeling enormous, like Alice after she'd OD'd on Eat Me mushrooms. Size 2 women have that effect on me.
> LINDA BARNES *Cold Case* 1997

> It is easy, though, to lose the track in the confusion of tyre-marks and rough sign-posts, and when this happens the driver, a small wiry Londoner baked to the colour of burned custard, navigates by a combination of map-reading and guesswork. He drove a taxi before the war, it emerges, and treats the desert with contemptuous familiarity, as though it were some Alice-in-Wonderland inversion of London topography.
> PENELOPE LIVELY *Moon Tiger* 1998

Alsatia In the 17th century, Alsatia was an area around Whitefriars, London, which became a sanctuary for criminals and debtors. The name is taken from Alsace, the much disputed territory between France and Germany.

> But Maggie always appeared in the most amiable light at her aunt Moss's: it was her Alsatia, where she was out of reach of law—if she upset anything, dirtied her shoes, or tore her frock, these things were matters of course at her aunt Moss's.
> GEORGE ELIOT *The Mill on the Floss* 1860

Amalekite The Amalekites were a nomadic tribe of Canaan and the Sinai peninsula, reputedly descended from Esau's grandson Amalek. They waged war against the Israelites, for whom the Amalekites represented perpetual treachery and hostility: 'The Lord will have war with Amalek from generation to generation' (Exod. 17: 16).

> But he, sly fox, son of Satan, seed of the Amalekite, he saw me looking at him in the church.
> OLIVE SCHREINER *The Story of an African Farm* 1883

Amalthea In Greek mythology, Amalthea was a she-goat or goat-nymph, who provided the milk Zeus drank when he was first born. *See also* CORNUCOPIA.

Amazon In Greek mythology, the Amazons were a race of female warriors alleged to exist on the borders of the known world. Their name was explained by the Greeks as meaning 'without a breast', from a story that they cut off their right breasts to enable them to draw their bows more easily. An Amazon is thus any tall, strong, athletic, or aggressive woman, or a woman who becomes fierce once her anger has been roused. The corresponding adjective is 'Amazonian'.

> Save for a certain primness as she offered the tray to her sister, Sophia's demeanour gave no sign whatever that the Amazon in her was aroused.
> ARNOLD BENNETT *The Old Wives' Tale* 1908

> Sofia right about her sisters. They all big strong healthy girls, look like amazons.
> ALICE WALKER *The Color Purple* 1983

> The image I lingered on the longest was, unsurprisingly, of Francoise. Francoise as an Amazon, frozen, with a spear poised above her head, concentrating fiercely on the shapes beneath the water.
> ALEX GARLAND *The Beach* 1996

ambrosia Ambrosia was the food of the Greek gods and the source of their immortality. *See also* NECTAR.

> We feasted that evening as on nectar and ambrosia.
> CHARLOTTE BRONTË *Jane Eyre* 1847

> The rolls didn't taste quite as good as they had done in the cool of the morning, but as I ate I began to feel better. The tepid water was a benison, and the fruit was ambrosia itself.
> MARY STEWART *My Brother Michael* 1960

Idi Amin Idi Amin (1925–2003) was a Ugandan soldier and head of state 1971–9. In 1971 he overthrew President Milton Obote and seized power. He presided over a regime characterized by brutality and repression, during which Uganda's Asian population was expelled and thousands of his political opponents murdered. Amin was overthrown in 1979 and forced to flee the country.

> Don't forget what I told you in the motel room. About the world getting crazier and crazier. Besides, maybe the cultists were camera shy when your professor friend studied them but not anymore. Weirdos change, like anyone else. Jim Jones was everyone's hero until he turned into Idi Amin.
> JONATHAN KELLERMAN *Blood Test* 1986

Amos and Andy *Amos and Andy* was originally an American radio show, written and voiced by Freeman Gosden and Charles Correll, and first broadcast in 1928. In 1951 it became a television sitcom, the first with an all-black cast. The show's central character, the conman George Stevens, known as Kingfish, endlessly schemed to make money, and shared membership of the Mystic Knights of the Sea Lodge with the self-confident but gullible Andy Brown and Amos Jones, a hard-working taxi driver and the show's narrator. Andy and Amos originally came from rural Georgia, seeking work in the

North. The shows were made in the United States from 1951 to 1955 and
shown by the BBC in the United Kingdom in 1954. Reruns were broadcast
until the mid-1960s but came to an end after much pressure from black
groups and after being banned by Kenya.

> Del Rio did a movie Mexican accent when it pleased him to, though he spoke
> English without any accent at all. Hawk did some of the same thing. Amos and
> Andy one minute, Alistair Cooke the next.
> ROBERT B. PARKER *Thin Air* 1995

Anak In the Bible, Anak was a man of great stature who founded a race of
giants known as the Anakim. They were so huge they frightened the spies of
Moses: 'And there we saw the giants, the sons of Anak, which come of the
giants: and we were in our own sight as grasshoppers, and so we were in
their sight' (Num. 13: 33).

> By some naturalists who have vaguely heard rumors of the mysterious creature,
> here spoken of [giant squid], it is included among the class of cuttle-fish, to
> which, indeed, in certain external respects it would seem to belong, but only as
> the Anak of the tribe.
> HERMAN MELVILLE *Moby Dick* 1851

> Even without the backing of rational argument, Mirabelle was a fearsome
> disputant. With it, she towered like the sons of Anak, and Ursell became as a
> grasshopper in her sight.
> REGINALD HILL *Singing the Sadness* 1999

Ananias In the New Testament, Ananias was the husband of Sapphira who
lied in order to keep some money for himself. On being found out and
accused of lying to God as well as to men, he 'fell down, and gave up the
ghost' (Acts 5: 5).

> Suddenly, catching the surgeon's arm convulsively, he exclaimed, pointing down
> to the body, 'It is the divine judgement on Ananias! Look!'
> HERMAN MELVILLE *Billy Budd* 1924

Anansi Anansi is the trickster spider in West African folk tradition. In some
stories he tricks the supreme god into allowing disease to enter the world.

> Cautioning members about the 'Brer Anansi' arithmetic, Leacock asked them
> not to reduce the usefulness of the Federation because 'trade unions are
> becoming weaker in these parts.' *News (St Vincent)* 1994

Ancient Mariner The Ancient Mariner is the central character and narrator
in Samuel Coleridge's poem *The Rime of the Ancient Mariner* (1798). He stops a
wedding guest at the door of the church where a wedding is about to take
place, and insists on recounting his tale to the guest. The mariner relates
how he shot an albatross at sea and as a result of this 'hellish thing', killing a
bird of good omen, a curse fell on his ship. As a penance, he was forced to
wear the albatross hung round his neck. The ship was becalmed near the

Equator and everyone except the mariner perished. The term 'Ancient Mariner' can be used to describe either a compulsive speaker irresistible to his audience, someone boring a reluctant listener, or someone who insists on telling their tale of woe. In addition, the story can be mentioned in the context of an individual who seems to have invited a curse upon their head.

> In Oily's demeanour as he took another sip of his cocktail and prepared to speak there was a suggestion of that Ancient Mariner of whom the poet Coleridge wrote. Like him, he knew he had a good story to relate, and he did not intend to hurry it.
> P G. WODEHOUSE *Cocktail Time* 1958

> In my weaker moments I have often longed to cast myself on your mercy. How lucky, for both our sakes, that I have held out! You do not need an albatross from the old world around your neck.
> J. M. COETZEE *Age of Iron* 1990

> Like the Ancient Mariner, they cannot resist buttonholing strangers in order to inform them of the facts.
> LOUIS DE BERNIÈRES *Captain Corelli's Mandolin* 1994

> But, no such placard existing, he had instead the urge, the need, to speak to every man, and, like the Ancient Mariner, explain constantly, constantly wanting to reassert something, anything.
> ZADIE SMITH *White Teeth* 2000

Hans Christian Andersen Hans Christian Andersen (1805–75) was a Danish author and poet who is most famous for his fairy tales, which first appeared in 1835 and include *The Emperor's New Clothes*, *The Snow Queen*, *The Red Shoes*, *The Ugly Duckling*, and *The Little Mermaid*. There were three English translations of his stories in 1846 by Charles Boner, Mary Howitt, and Caroline Peachey. He epitomizes the great storyteller. *See also* EMPEROR'S NEW CLOTHES, LITTLE MATCH GIRL, RED SHOES, SNOW QUEEN, UGLY DUCKLING.

> 'Leave him, leave him,' Mr Biswas said. 'Leave the storyteller.' . . . Mr Biswas came in and presently walked into the room, saying in his rallying voice, 'Well, well. What happen to our Hans Andersen?'
> V. S. NAIPAUL *A House for Mr Biswas* 1961

> 'He says that according to the grapevine—alias his mates at Kensington—nobody's very anxious for the job. With the last two supers dying in harness, they reckon Shepherd's Bush is a poisoned chalice. That's why we've had the night watchman so long.' 'They're a right bunch of Hans Andersens down at Kensington,' said Slider.
> CYNTHIA HARROD-EAGLES *Blood Lines* 1996

Andersonville Andersonville is a village in south-west Georgia in the United States. It was the site of a notorious Confederate prison, where dreadful conditions led to the death of over 12 000 Union soldiers.

Andromeda In Greek mythology, Andromeda was the daughter of Cepheus and Cassiopeia, king and queen of Ethiopia. Cassiopeia boasted that her daughter was more beautiful even than the Nereids, or sea-nymphs, which angered Poseidon. As a punishment, Poseidon sent a sea-monster to destroy the land and agreed to end the punishment only if Andromeda was sacrificed to the sea-monster. Andromeda was therefore chained to a rock and left to her fate. She was saved by Perseus, who flew to her rescue on the winged horse Pegasus and slew the sea-monster. *See also* PEGASUS, PERSEUS.

> I mean, it's bad enough being forced to appear on a television programme in the first place, let alone chained to a series like Andromeda to a rock.
> JOHN MALCOLM *Into the Vortex* 1996

Angel of Death Death is sometimes personified as a winged messenger, often cloaked and in the form of a skeleton, called the Angel of Death. The term can also be applied to a number of angels including Apollyon, Azrael, and Michael. *See also* APOLLYON, AZRAEL.

> Some day soon the Angel of Death will sound his trumpet for me.
> BRAM STOKER *Dracula* 1897

> When Staunton died . . . his death was reported at some length in our *Neue Zurcher Zeitung*. That paper, like the London *Times*, recognizes only the most distinguished achievements of the Angel of Death.
> ROBERTSON DAVIES *World of Wonders* 1975

> Every so often I thought: What if the engine dies on us—what then? And saw a skinny man, like the Angel of Death, watching us from the rag of a cactus's shade.
> PAUL THEROUX *The Old Patagonian Express* 1978

Annie *See* ORPHAN ANNIE.

Antaeus In Greek mythology, Antaeus was a giant, son of the sea-god Poseidon and the earth-goddess Gaia. He forced all-comers to wrestle with him, and overcame and killed them until he was defeated by Hercules. Antaeus was invincible as long as he touched the earth (enabling him to draw new strength from his mother), but was lifted into the air by Hercules and crushed to death in his arms.

> Still I knew I hadn't come out to Westport just to escape the phone and the doorbell. It was more that I needed to touch base, so to speak. Antaeus coming to earth so he might renew his strength.
> ROBERT A. CARTER *Written in Blood* 1992

Antigone In Greek myth, Antigone was the daughter of Oedipus and his mother, Jocasta. According to Sophocles' play *Antigone* (441 BC), when blind Oedipus left Thebes, Antigone accompanied him and they travelled eventually to Colonus, near Athens. In his absence, Antigone's brothers Polyneices and Eteocles killed each other in their fight over who would rule

a

Thebes. Jocasta's brother Creon decreed that Polyneices started the fight and ruled that he was not to be buried. Antigone defied his ruling and was herself ordered to be walled up alive in a tomb, whereupon she hanged herself.

> Is she pretty? More—beautiful. A subject for the pen of Nonnus, or the pencil of Zeuxis. Features of all loveliness, radiant with all virtue and intelligence. A face for Antigone. A form at once plump and symmetrical, that . . . would have been a model for Venus of Cnidos.
> THOMAS LOVE PEACOCK *Crotchet Castle* 1831

> 'Who is this Antigone who would stand before the walls of the city and risk public censure? No. Not the public. The public doesn't give a damn. Let us say she risks her place among her peers. Why does she do it?' Gail had to laugh. 'It isn't that dramatic. I'm a lawyer, I have a client and I believe in him.'
> BARBARA PARKER *Suspicion of Guilt* 1995

Antiphates' wife Antiphates was the chief of the Laestrygonians, a tribe of flesh-eating giants encountered by Odysseus and his companions on their journey back to Ithaca. According to Homer's account, his wife was repulsive-looking.

> Mandras' mother was one of those perplexing creatures as ugly as the mythical wife of Antiphates, of whom the poet wrote that she was 'a monstrous woman whose ill-aspect struck men with horror'.
> LOUIS DE BERNIÈRES *Captain Corelli's Mandolin* 1994

Antisthenes Antisthenes (*c.*445–*c.*365) was the founder of the Cynic school of philosophy, whose pupils included Diogenes. Antisthenes despised art and learning, and the luxuries and comforts of life, and taught that virtue consists in self-control and independence of worldly needs.

Antony and Cleopatra Mark Antony (*c.*83–30 BC), a Roman general and triumvir, met Cleopatra (69–30 BC), the queen of Egypt, and followed her to Egypt, where he stayed with her during the winter of 41–40. He was recalled to Italy, where he took control of the eastern part of the Roman Empire and married Octavia, sister of the emperor, Augustus. After three years he left his wife and rejoined Cleopatra. Augustus eventually declared war on Cleopatra and the couple fled back to Egypt after their defeat at the battle of Actium in 31 BC. Antony, after being erroneously informed of Cleopatra's suicide, fell on his sword. Cleopatra is said to have committed suicide by being bitten by an asp. Their love affair forms the basis of Shakespeare's play *Antony and Cleopatra* (1623). *See also* CLEOPATRA, SHAKESPEARE.

> Passion is destructive. It destroyed Antony and Cleopatra, Tristan and Isolde.
> W. SOMERSET MAUGHAM *The Razor's Edge* 1944

> Sex has left the body and entered the imagination now; that is why Arnauti suffered so much with Justine, because she preyed upon all that he might have kept separate—his artist-hood if you like. He is when all is said and done a sort

of minor Antony, and she a Cleo. You can read all about it in Shakespeare.
LAWRENCE DURRELL *Justine* 1957

'You could have telephoned.' 'I'm very sorry that I didn't.' As indeed he was,
and he knew he was going to go on being sorry. 'But you forgot me.' 'Not
exactly forgot, Stella. And I have apologized.' 'And I have accepted it,' Stella
said with dignity, with the air of one whom to do less would be beneath her. So
might Cleopatra have spoken to Antony.
GWENDOLINE BUTLER *The Coffin Tree* 1994

Anubis Anubis was the Egyptian god of the dead and the protector of tombs,
who conducted the souls of the dead to their judgement. Anubis was the son
of Osiris and is often represented with the head of a jackal.

Aphrodite In Greek mythology, Aphrodite was the goddess of beauty,
fertility, and sexual love, identified by the Romans with Venus. She is
supposed to have been born from the sea-foam on the shores of the island of
Cythera, and references to Aphrodite sometimes exploit this feature of the
myth. One of the names under which she was worshipped was Cytherea.

Ah, there is beauty! beauty in perfection. What a cloud of sable curls about the
face of a houri! What fascinating lips! What glorious black eyes! Your Byron
would have worshipped her, and you—you cold, frigid islander!—you played
the austere, the insensible in the presence of an Aphrodite so exquisite?
CHARLOTTE BRONTË *The Professor* 1857

And by one of those paradoxes in which love delights I found myself more
jealous of him in his dying than I had ever been during his life. These were
horrible thoughts for one who had been so long a patient and attentive student
of love, but I recognized once more in them the austere mindless primitive face
of Aphrodite.
LAWRENCE DURRELL *Justine* 1957

Eighteen he remembered her, and not too tall, with almost masculine features
below short chestnut hair: brown eyes, full cheeks and proportionate lips, like
Aphrodite his inward eye had commented time and time again, only a little
sweeter.
ALAN SILLITOE *The Loneliness of the Long Distance Runner* 1959

Who is this goddess who comes in a vision with uncovered breast cutting the
air? It is Aphrodite, but not smile-loving Aphrodite, patroness of pleasures: an
older figure, a figure of urgency, of cries in the dark, short and sharp, of blood
and earth, emerging for an instant, showing herself, passing.
J. M. COETZEE *Age of Iron* 1990

Apocalypse The Apocalypse is a name given to the book of Revelation, the
last book of the New Testament. The book recounts a divine revelation of the
future to St John, including the total destruction of the world: 'And, lo, there

was a great earthquake; and the sun became black as sackcloth of hair, and the moon became as blood' (Rev. 6: 12). Following this comes the last battle between the forces of good and evil, the final defeat of Satan, and the creation of a new heaven and earth. The four agents of destruction, personified in the Four Horsemen of the Apocalypse, are Pestilence, Famine, War, and Death. The word 'apocalypse' has now come to mean any event of great or total destruction, in more recent times especially a nuclear holocaust.

> The land about them was laid to waste in a small but extravagant apocalypse; bushes were uprooted and leafless, the ground was littered with little pieces of bridge.
> LOUIS DE BERNIÈRES *The War of Don Emmanuel's Nether Parts* 1990

> For a year I had lived with the possibility of Liam Brady's transfer to another club in the same way that, in the late fifties and early sixties, American teenagers had lived with the possibility of the impending Apocalypse.
> NICK HORNBY *Fever Pitch* 1993

Apollo In Greek mythology, Apollo was the son of Zeus and Leto and the twin brother of Artemis. He was born on the island of Delos, the site of his most important cult festival. The other main shrine for the worship of Apollo was the oracle at Delphi. While a boy he had travelled to Delphi, killed a huge snake called Python, and taken control of the oracle there. He came to be associated with the sun and was sometimes given the epithet Phoebus (the Bright One). Apollo later usurped Helios' place as the god of the sun who drove the sun's chariot across the sky each day. He had a wide range of other attributes such as music (his instrument was a seven-stringed lyre), medicine (he was the father of Aesculapius, or Asclepius, the god of medicine and healing), poetic inspiration, archery, prophecy, and pastoral life (he protected herdsmen). Apollo, representing order, reason, and self-discipline, is often contrasted with Dionysus, representing creativity, sensuality, and lack of inhibition. In art Apollo is represented as an ideal type of male beauty, for example in the famous statue the Apollo Belvedere, now in the Vatican. Apollo had numerous affairs with nymphs, mortal women, and also young men. Among his unsuccessful encounters were those with Daphne and Cassandra. *See also* AESCULAPIUS, CASSANDRA, DAPHNE, DELPHI, DIONYSUS.

> Your words have delineated very prettily a graceful Apollo; he is present to your imagination,—tall, fair, blue-eyed, and with a Grecian profile.
> CHARLOTTE BRONTË *Jane Eyre* 1847

> I do not admire the tones of the concertina, as a rule; but oh! how beautiful the music seemed to us both then—far, far more beautiful than the voice of Orpheus or the lute of Apollo.
> JEROME K. JEROME *Three Men in a Boat* 1889

> The little priest was not an interesting man to look at, having stubbly brown hair and a round and stolid face. But if he had been as splendid as Apollo no

one would have looked at him at that moment.
G. K. CHESTERTON 'The Hammer of God' in *The Innocence of Father Brown* 1911

He had only a nodding acquaintance with the Hippocratic oath, but was somehow aware that he was committed to Apollo the Healer to look upon his teacher in the art of medicine as one of his parents.
JOHN MORTIMER *Paradise Postponed* 1985

Apollyon Apollyon (meaning 'the Destroyer') is the 'angel of the bottomless pit' described in the book of Revelation (9: 11). In Christian thought he is often identified with the Devil. In Bunyan's *The Pilgrim's Progress*, Apollyon is the foul fiend, the personification of evil, who bars Christian's way but is ultimately defeated by the latter's virtue. *See also* ABADDON, PILGRIM'S PROGRESS.

He may be stern; he may be exacting: he may be ambitious yet; but his is the sternness of the warrior Greatheart, who guards his pilgrim convoy from the onslaught of Apollyon.
CHARLOTTE BRONTË *Jane Eyre* 1847

Feeling stronger than ever to meet and subdue her Apollyon, she pinned the note inside her frock, as a shield and a reminder.
LOUISA M. ALCOTT *Little Women* 1868

He anxiously descended the ladder, and started homewards at a run, trying not to think of giants, Herne the Hunter, Apollyon lying in wait for Christian.
THOMAS HARDY *Jude the Obscure* 1896

Apple of Discord The Apple of Discord was a golden apple marked with the words 'for the fairest' that Eris, the Greek goddess of discord, threw among the guests at the wedding of Peleus and Thetis, causing disagreement between three goddesses, Hera, Athene, and Aphrodite. The goddesses asked Paris to judge which of them was the fairest; Aphrodite won the contest by offering him Helen of Troy as a bribe. Paris' abduction of Helen led to the Trojan War. *See also* ERIS, HELEN, PARIS, TROJAN WAR.

Macedonia . . . became the apple of discord between the newly forming nation-states that were destined to replace the Ottoman Empire. *New York Review of Books* 1995

Johnny Appleseed Johnny Appleseed was the nickname of John Chapman (1774–1847) because he planted orchards for settlers in Pennsylvania, Ohio, Indiana, and Illinois. He was known for his woodcraft and the help that he gave to pioneer settlers.

What about the doctor down in Hillsborough? The one with the runaway daughter and the fistful of amphetamines he's scattering around like Johnny goddam Appleseed?
MAX BYRD *Finders Weepers* 1983

Apples of Sodom *See* DEAD SEA FRUIT.

Arabian Nights *The Arabian Nights* is a collection of exotic and fantastic stories written in Arabic, also called *Arabian Nights' Entertainments* or *The Thousand and One Nights*. The stories are set in the following framework: Shahriyar, the king of Samarkand, has executed all his wives following the wedding night until he marries Scheherazade, who saves her life by entertaining him with a story each night for 1 001 nights. The tales include the stories of Aladdin, Ali Baba, and Sinbad the Sailor. *See also* ALADDIN'S CAVE, ALI BABA, BARMECIDE'S FEAST, OLD MAN OF THE SEA, SCHEHERAZADE, SINBAD THE SAILOR.

> My father had brought me out of Scotland at the age of six, and I had never been home since; so England was a sort of Arabian Nights to me, and I counted on stopping there for the rest of my days.
> JOHN BUCHAN *The Thirty-Nine Steps* 1915

> A great tale of marvels. Real Arabian Nights stuff.
> ROBERTSON DAVIES *World of Wonders* 1975

> As I talked I was aware that it sounded like some horrible Arabian Nights fairy tale, and yet it was actually happening to us.
> ZANA MUHSEN *Sold* 1991

Arachne Arachne was a weaver who lived in Lydia in ancient Greece. She challenged the goddess Athene to a weaving contest and wove a piece of cloth representing the loves of the gods. When Athene could find no flaw in the cloth, she refused to admit that Arachne had won the contest, destroying the cloth and changing Arachne into a spider.

Aramis *See* THREE MUSKETEERS.

Arcadia A mountainous district in the Peloponnese of southern Greece, Arcadia (or Arcady) represents in classical poetic fantasy an idealized region of rural contentment and simplicity. It is also the setting of Philip Sidney's prose romance *Arcadia*, published posthumously in 1590. The tomb inscription 'Et in Arcadia ego', often depicted in classical paintings, is sometimes quoted as meaning 'I too once lived in Arcady', to express the idea of a perfect happiness now lost. This interpretation of the phrase is, however, disputed. The association of Arcadia with beautiful music may derive from the fact that Arcadia was the home of Pan, the god who frequented mountains, caves, and lonely places, and invented the pan pipes. *See also* PAN.

> It was as though the wood and the strings of the orchestra played Arcadian melodies and in the bass the drums, softly but with foreboding, beat a grim tattoo.
> W. SOMERSET MAUGHAM *The Painted Veil* 1925

What he wanted was an English bride of ancient lineage and Arcadian innocence.
EDITH WHARTON *The Buccaneers* 1938

I had not forgotten Sebastian. He was with me daily in Julia; or rather it was Julia I had known in him, in those distant Arcadian days.
EVELYN WAUGH *Brideshead Revisited* 1945

Their little valley in the mountains was densely wooded and well watered, and the guerrillas lived a life of Arcadian simplicity and leisure, only venturing forth when one of them had a good idea about what to blow up next.
LOUIS DE BERNIÈRES *The War of Don Emmanuel's Nether Parts* 1990

Archers *The Archers*, a radio soap opera described as 'an everyday story of country folk', was first broadcast in 1950 by the BBC in order to give agricultural advice to farmers. The programme portrays the inhabitants of a fictional Midlands village, Ambridge, and in particular a farming family, the Archers. *The Archers*, now broadcast on Radio 4, is the longest-running radio serial in the world.

Soon Davenport described the layout of the village. He spoke of Stonebury in almost reverential terms, characterising it as the epitome of a rural world that was vanishing. The sort of place where you'd half expect the Mayor of Casterbridge to bump into the cast of the Archers and have a chummy discussion about the price of turnips.
DEXTER DIAS *False Witness* 1995

Moira had made a point of introducing herself to all the neighbours: the 'locals', she called them. Most of them were no more local than she was—they were summer visitors, too, a motley multinational crew—but nevertheless she persisted in behaving like an incomer to Ambridge ingratiating herself with the Archers.
HILARY WHELAN *Frightening Strikes* 1995

Archimago Archimago is the evil enchanter in Edmund Spenser's *The Faerie Queene* (1590, 1596), who symbolizes hypocrisy and uses cunning disguises to trick and deceive people. *See also* SPENSER.

Archimedes Archimedes (*c.*287–212 BC) was a Greek mathematician and inventor, born in Syracuse in Sicily. There is a famous story relating to his discovery of the principle of fluid displacement. He had been given the task of finding a method for determining whether a crown was pure gold or alloyed with silver. He is supposed to have made the crucial discovery when taking a bath and seeing the water overflow. Archimedes ran naked through the streets shouting 'Eureka! Eureka!' ('I have found it! I have found it!').

I did not jump up and shout 'Eureka!' like Archimedes did.
BART KOSKO *Fuzzy Thinking* 1993

Arden The Forest of Arden is the name of a former forest region of north Warwickshire in the English Midlands, the setting of most of Shakespeare's *As You Like It* (1623). It is often used to represent the ideal of rural as opposed to urban or courtly life. The Forest of Arden can be used as an equivalent of the Garden of Eden, an earthly paradise.

Enoch Arden In Tennyson's poem of the same name (1864), Enoch Arden is shipwrecked with two companions. When his fellow survivors die, 'in those two deaths he read God's warning "wait" '. So Enoch patiently waits to be rescued and after ten years a ship finally does appear. When he returns home, he finds his wife, Annie, has remarried and resolves not to reveal his identity to her in order to preserve her new happiness.

> I knew I could outwait them. I could outwait Enoch Arden if I had to. But it would be nice if, when they finally got sick of waiting, I knew which way they'd exit.
> ROBERT B. PARKER *Walking Shadow* 1994

Ares In Greek mythology, Ares, the son of Zeus and Hera, was the god of war, corresponding to the Roman god Mars.

Argonauts In Greek mythology, the Argonauts were the group of heroes who accompanied Jason on board the ship *Argo* in the quest for the Golden Fleece. The Argonauts included Hercules, Orpheus, Theseus, Nestor, and Castor and Pollux. Among the dangers they faced on their perilous voyage were the Symplegades, or clashing cliffs, which clashed together and crushed ships as they passed between them. *See also* GOLDEN FLEECE, JASON AND THE ARGONAUTS.

> 'Come along, Captain Robinson,' he shouted, with a sort of bullying deference under the rim of the old man's hat; the Holy Terror gave a submissive little jump. The ghost of a steamer was waiting for them. Fortune on that fair isle! They made a curious pair of Argonauts. Chester strode on leisurely, well set up, portly, and of conquering mien; the other, long, wasted, drooping, and hooked to his arm, shuffled his withered shanks with desperate haste.
> JOSEPH CONRAD *Lord Jim* 1900

Argus
many-eyed giant In Greek mythology, Argus was a giant with 100 eyes, whom Hera made guardian of Io (transformed into a heifer by Zeus). Argus never slept with more than one pair of eyes at a time, so he was able to watch Io constantly. After Hermes had killed Argus on behalf of Zeus, Hera took the eyes to deck the peacock's tail. The term 'Argus-eyed' has come to mean vigilant or observant.

> Well, thought I, I hope still, Argus, to be too hard for thee. Now Argus, the poets say, had an hundred eyes, and was set to watch with them all, as she does, with her goggling ones.
> SAMUEL RICHARDSON *Pamela* 1741

Woe betide the six-foot hero who escorts Mrs Proudie to her pew in red plush breeches, if he slips away to the neighbouring beer shop, instead of falling into the back seat appropriated to his use. Mrs Proudie has the eyes of Argus for such offenders.

ANTHONY TROLLOPE *Barchester Towers* 1857

shipbuilder In Greek mythology, Argus was the craftsman who built the ship *Argo*, on which Jason and the Argonauts voyaged to recover the Golden Fleece.

Ariadne In Greek mythology, Ariadne was the daughter of King Minos of Crete and Pasiphae. She fell in love with Theseus and helped him escape from the labyrinth of the Minotaur by giving him a ball of thread, which he unravelled as he went in and followed back to find his way out again after killing the Minotaur. Such a ball of thread used to be called a clew, and it is from this idea of its being used to trace a path through a maze (and by extension being applied to anything that guides through perplexity, a difficult investigation, etc.) that we derive the modern word 'clue'. *See also* LABYRINTH.

Her body muffled in furs, her heart muffled like her steps, and the pain of living muffled as by the deepest rich carpets, while the thread of Ariadne which led everywhere, right and left, like scattered footsteps in the snow, tugged and pulled within her memory and she began to pull upon this thread . . . as one pulls upon a spool, and she heard the empty wooden spool knock against the floor of different houses.

ANAÏS NIN *Children of the Albatross* 1947

Ariel Ariel is a fairy or spirit in Shakespeare's *The Tempest* (1623), who has no physical form or substance and is therefore divorced from human emotions. *See also* SHAKESPEARE.

She had never shown any repugnance to his tenderness, but such response as it evoked was remote and Ariel-like.

EDITH WHARTON *The Custom of the Country* 1913

Aristeides the Just Aristeides (d. *c.*468 BC), whose name is sometimes spelled Aristides or Aristedes, was a Greek military commander and politician who became one of the rulers of Athens. After disagreements with another prominent politician, a vote was taken and he was banished temporarily from Athens. Plutarch relates how an illiterate citizen asked him to vote for his banishment, and when Aristeides asked what harm he had done the man, he replied that he didn't even know Aristeides but he was sick of always hearing him called 'the Just'. Aristeides returned from his banishment to take up again a prominent role in Athens' political and military life. He was famous for his patriotism, justice, and discretion.

Mr. Hale's over-praise had the usual effect of over-praise upon his auditors: they were a little inclined to rebel against Aristides being always called the Just.

ELIZABETH GASKELL *North and South* 1854–5

She's too good, too kind, too clever, too learned, too accomplished, too
everything. She's too complete, in a word. I confess to you that she acts on my
nerves and that I feel about her a good deal as that intensely human Athenian
felt about Aristedes the Just.
HENRY JAMES *Portrait of a Lady* 1881

'It's damned unfair,' the Commissioner said. 'I can do nothing more than I have
done, Scobie. You are a wonderful man for picking up enemies. Like Aristides
the Just.'
GRAHAM GREENE *The Heart of the Matter* 1948

Aristophanes Aristophanes (*c*.448–380 BC) was an Athenian comic
playwright whose plays include *The Clouds*, *The Wasps*, and *Lysistrata*. In all
there are eleven extant plays by Aristophanes. *See also* LYSISTRATA.

What might be tragedy if Sophocles got hold of it, is funny in the four or five
daily frames of the funnies. While the funnies live, Aristophanes is never quite
dead.
ROBERTSON DAVIES *The Cunning Man* 1994

Aristotle Aristotle (384–322 BC) was a Greek philospher and scientist. A
pupil of Plato and tutor to Alexander the Great, in 335 BC he founded the
Peripatetic school and library (the Lyceum) outside Athens. Aristotle
established the inductive method of reasoning, maintaining that systematic
logic, based upon syllogism, was the essential method of all rational inquiry
and hence the foundation of all knowledge. Aristotle's philosophy was to
become the basis of medieval Christian scholasticism. *See also* PERIPATETIC.

A boy's sheepishness is by no means a sign of overmastering reverence; and
while you are making encouraging advances to him under the idea that he is
overwhelmed by a sense of your age and wisdom, ten to one he is thinking you
extremely queer. The only consolation I can suggest to you is, that the Greek
boys probably thought the same of Aristotle.
GEORGE ELIOT *The Mill on the Floss* 1860

'I don't understand why you denigrate yourself so much,' Charlotte said in
mock desperation. 'You're a combination of Getty and Aristotle, compared to
most of the management this lot will have encountered.'
REBECCA TINSLEY *Settlement Day* 1994

Ark The book of Genesis relates how God warned Noah that he was going to
send a great flood to destroy the world and instructed him to build the Ark, a
huge ship, to save his family and a pair of every species of animal and bird.
References to Noah and expressions such as 'out of the Ark' can be used in
connection with something that is very antiquated or out of date. *See also*
NOAH.

Then he sat down near his brief-case on the far side of a scarred oak table that
came out of the Ark. Noah bought it second-hand.
RAYMOND CHANDLER *The Long Goodbye* 1953

And it would balance her table, thought Mair, although that was hardly likely to have been a consideration. She despised the Noah's Ark convention which decreed that a superfluous man, however unattractive or stupid, was acceptable; a superfluous woman, however witty and well-informed, a social embarrassment.
P D. JAMES *Devices and Desires* 1989

Ark of the Covenant The Ark of the Covenant was a box containing tablets giving the law as revealed to Moses by God. The Ark was carried by the Israelites on their wanderings, and when they settled was placed in the temple at Jerusalem. An extremely sacred object, it was lost when Jerusalem was captured in 586 BC.

I had in my pocket the fetish of the whole black world; I had their Ark of the Covenant, and soon Laputa would be on my trail.
JOHN BUCHAN *Prester John* 1910

He hummed as he filled the kettle, it was a good sign to use the big brown pot. They took the big pot round with them from job to job, it was their Ark of the Covenant almost.
GWENDOLINE BUTLER *A Dark Coffin* 1995

Armageddon According to the book of Revelation, Armageddon is the site of the last battle between the forces of good and evil before the Day of Judgement. The term is often used to describe a destructive conflict on a huge scale, latterly especially a nuclear war.

I had a long drink, and read the evening papers. They were full of the row in the Near East, and there was an article about Karolides, the Greek Premier. . . . I gathered that they hated him pretty blackly in Berlin and Vienna, but that we were going to stick by him, and one paper said that he was the only barrier between Europe and Armageddon.
JOHN BUCHAN *The Thirty-Nine Steps* 1915

He has read somewhere that eighty per cent of all aircraft accidents occur at either take-off or landing. . . . By taking the non-stop polar flight to London, in preference to the two stage journey via New York, Zapp reckons that he has reduced his chances of being caught in such an Armageddon by fifty per cent.
DAVID LODGE *Changing Places* 1975

We expect Armageddon; the Bible has trained us well. We assume either annihilation or salvation, perhaps both. Millenarian beliefs are as old as time; the apocalypse has always been at hand.
PENELOPE LIVELY *Moon Tiger* 1988

Benedict Arnold Benedict Arnold (1741–1801) was an American general in the American Revolution, chiefly remembered as a traitor who in 1780 plotted, with the British army major John André, to betray the American post at West Point to the British. When the plot was discovered, Arnold escaped and later fought on the side of the British.

He had carried Mark O'Meara's clubs in the 1997 matches before switching to the young Spaniard. On an alcoholic high after his country's win, a burly American fan no doubt saw him as a golfing Benedict Arnold. *The Guardian* 1999

I hold the glass for Beth, bending the straw to her lips. 'You were lucky Lyle was there. To explain.' 'That Benedict Arnold?' She takes a couple of sips. 'He told them. Betrayed my confidence.'
SUSAN SUSSMAN with SARAJANE AVIDON *Audition for Murder* 1999

Artemis In Greek mythology, Artemis was the twin sister of Apollo and the virgin goddess of chastity, the hunt, and the moon. She was believed to protect virgins and women in childbirth. A huntress, she was often depicted with a bow and arrows, and noted for her strength and speed. The Romans called her Diana. *See also* DIANA, HECATE.

The purity of his nature, his freedom from the grosser passions, his scrupulous delicacy, had never been fully understood by Grace till this strange self-sacrifice in lonely juxtaposition to her own person was revealed. The perception of it added something that was little short of reverence to the deep affection for him of a woman who, herself, had more of Artemis than of Aphrodite in her constitution.
THOMAS HARDY *The Woodlanders* 1887

Artful Dodger The Artful Dodger is the nickname of Jack Dawkins, a clever young pickpocket and a member of Fagin's gang of thieves in Dickens's *Oliver Twist* (1837–8). He is known for quick-wittedness and his ability to get himself out of trouble without ever being caught. *See also* DICKENSIAN.

Dozens of little Artful Dodgers hustling the white men who invaded their parents' country.
ARMISTEAD MAUPIN *Babycakes* 1984

In these supposedly rational times, the spectacle of someone repeatedly engaging in sexual behaviour which is dangerously risky, and, potentially, exceedingly self-destructive, provokes many people to resort to some psychopathological explanation. Many see President Clinton as an Artful Dodger who just got caught. *The Independent* 1998

King Arthur Arthur, historically perhaps a 5th- or 6th-century Romano-British chieftain or general, is in legend the king of Britain who presided over the knights of the Round Table at Camelot. King Arthur and his knights have been the focus of many romantic legends in various languages, recounted by authors such as Chrétien de Troyes and later Thomas Malory. According to one story, after being fatally wounded by his nephew Mordred, the dying king was borne away to the island of Avalon, where he was buried. In some versions of the legend it is said that Arthur is not dead but sleeping, ready to awaken and return in the hour of Britain's need. Arthurian literature is associated with the romantic notions of chivalry and courtly

love, in which the knight serves his lady and woos her honourably. *See also*
AVALON, EXCALIBUR, SIR GALAHAD, GUINEVERE, HOLY GRAIL, LADY OF THE LAKE,
LANCELOT, MERLIN, MORGAN LE FAY, NIMUE.

> They are drunk with the knightly love one reads about in the Arthurian
> legends—knight and rescued lady.
> LAWRENCE DURRELL *Clea* 1960

> Looka there!—is it a girl? Is it a, sorry, woman? No—It's the Phantom Nympho!
> And she's raring to go, as per! Like King Arthur, see, she wasn't really dead; just
> sleeping (around) till her people felt in need of her once more. And now she's
> back. Back!
> JULIE BURCHILL 'The Phantom Nympho Rides Again' in *Sex and Sensibility* 1989

Ascalaphus In Greek mythology, Ascalaphus, the son of Acheron, was an
inhabitant of the underworld. After Persephone had been abducted by Hades
to be his queen in the underworld, she was granted the opportunity to
return to the earth on condition that she had eaten nothing in the
underworld. However, she had eaten some pomegranate seeds from a tree,
and Ascalaphus revealed this. Persephone was ordered by Zeus to remain six
months with Hades and to spend the rest of the year on the earth with her
mother, Demeter. Persephone turned Ascalaphus into an owl for his act of
betrayal. *See also* DEMETER, PERSEPHONE.

Ashtoreth Ashtoreth (or Ashtaroth) is the name used in the Bible for the
Phoenician goddess Astarte. *See also* ASTARTE.

> The bailiff was pointed out to Gabriel, who, checking the palpitation with his
> breast at discovering that this Ashtoreth of strange report was only a
> modification of Venus, the well-known and admired, retired with him to talk
> over the necessary preliminaries of hiring.
> THOMAS HARDY *Far from the Madding Crowd* 1874

Aspasia Aspasia was a famous Greek courtesan, daughter of Axiochus of
Miletus. She came to Athens, where she acquired fame by her beauty,
culture, and wit. She so captivated Pericles that he made her his lifelong
companion.

> The Athenian virgins . . . grew up into wives who stayed at home . . . and
> looked after the husband's dinner. And what was the consequence of that, sir?
> that they were such very insipid persons that the husband would not go home
> to eat his dinner, but preferred the company of some Aspasia or Lais.
> THOMAS LOVE PEACOCK *Crotchet Castle* 1831

> Mr. Valera is merely describing what all men desire in a woman, an Aspasia, the
> captivating femme galante, indifferent to morality, who was the adoring
> mistress and adviser to Pericles of ancient Greece.
> ALFRED BESTER *Galatea Galante, the Perfect Popsy* 1980

Asphodel The Plain of Asphodel is described in Homer's *Odyssey* as the part of Hades where the ghosts of the dead lead a vague, unsubstantial life, a shadowy continuation of their former life where 'the soul hovers to and fro'. *See also* HADES.

> It was dreadful to be thus dissevered from his dryad, and sent howling back to a Barchester pandemonium just as the nectar and ambrosia were about to descend on the fields of asphodel.
> ANTHONY TROLLOPE *Barchester Towers* 1857

Assisi *See* ST FRANCIS OF ASSISI.

Fred Astaire Fred Astaire (1899–1987), who was born Frederick Austerlitz, was an American actor, singer, and dancer. His first partner was his sister Adele, who starred with him in Broadway shows such as *Lady Be Good* in the 1920s. When his sister married, he moved to Hollywood, where he paired up with Ginger Rogers. Together they made many successful film musicals including *Top Hat* (1935) and *Shall We Dance?* (1937). Astaire starred without Rogers in later films such as *Easter Parade* (1948) and *The Band Wagon* (1953).

> Lucifer sank his teeth into a woman's nose, anointed a teenaged boy's hair with brown slickum, and leaped from pew to pew like a demonic little version of Fred Astaire.
> ROBERT R. McCAMMON *Boy's Life* 1991

> He was taller than me and more graceful by far—had a Fred Astaire kind of elegance that my brother and I had totally missed out on.
> ANNE TYLER *A Patchwork Planet* 1998

Astarte Astarte was a Phoenician goddess of fertility and sexual love, corresponding to the Babylonian Ishtar, the Egyptian Isis, the Greek Aphrodite, and others. She is referred to in the Bible as Ashtoreth or Ashtaroth, and worship of her is linked with worship of Baal and similarly condemned: 'And the children of Israel did evil again in the sight of the Lord, and served Baalim, and Ashtaroth' (Judg. 10: 6).

Atalanta In Greek mythology, Atalanta was a huntress who was extremely fleet-footed. She had been warned against marriage by the Delphic oracle and so refused to marry any man unless he first defeated her in a race. If the runner lost, he was put to death. Many suitors tried to outrun her, but all failed until one, variously identified as Hippomenes or Melanion, asked Aphrodite for help and was given three golden apples by her. When he dropped these at intervals during the race, Atalanta was unable to resist the apples' beauty and stopped to pick them up. *See also* CALYDONIAN BOAR HUNT.

> Laurie reached the goal first and was quite satisfied with the success of his treatment, for his Atalanta came panting up with flying hair, bright eyes, ruddy

cheeks, and no signs of dissatisfaction in her face.
LOUISA M. ALCOTT *Little Women* 1868

Even in the early days when she had lived with her parents in a ragged outskirt of Apex, and hung on the fence with Indiana Frusk, the freckled daughter of the plumber 'across the way', she had cared little for dolls or skipping ropes, and still less for the riotous games in which the loud Indiana played Atalanta to all the boyhood of the quarter.
EDITH WHARTON *The Custom of the Country* 1913

Athene Athene (also called Pallas Athene) was the Greek goddess of wisdom, of war, and of handicrafts, especially spinning and weaving. She corresponds to the Roman goddess Minerva. Athene is said to have sprung fully grown and fully armed from the brain of her father, Zeus. She is usually represented in sculpture and paintings in armour. In classical times the owl was regularly associated with her. *See also* MINERVA.

It did not do to think, nor, for the matter of that, to feel. She gave up trying to understand herself, and joined the vast armies of the benighted, who follow neither the heart nor the brain, and march to their destiny by catchwords. . . . They have sinned against passion and truth, and vain will be their strife after virtue. . . . They have sinned against Eros and Pallas Athene, and not by any heavenly intervention, but by the ordinary course of nature, those allied deities will be avenged.
E. M. FORSTER *A Room with a View* 1908

Darwin was a passionate anti-saltationist, and this led him to stress, over and over again, the extreme gradualness of the evolutionary changes that he was proposing. The reason is that saltation, to him, meant what I have called the Boeing 747 macromutation. It meant the sudden calling into existence, like Pallas Athene from the head of Zeus, of brand-new complex organs at a single stroke of the genetic wand.
RICHARD DAWKINS *The Blind Watchmaker* 1986

And the old man replied that once he had freed himself from those underpants, he had only to slash the hide with his knife, and he would emerge like Minerva from Jove's head.
UMBERTO ECO *The Island of the Day Before* 1994

Athos *See* THREE MUSKETEERS.

Atlantis Atlantis was a legendary island continent in the ocean west of the Pillars of Hercules. According to Plato in the *Timaeus*, Atlantis was beautiful and prosperous and ruled part of Europe and Africa, but following volcanic eruptions it was swallowed up by the sea.

Under the clouds out there it's as still, and lost, as Atlantis.
THOMAS PYNCHON *Gravity's Rainbow* 1973

I made a serious attempt to be sensitive, culturally aware and all that. I

borrowed Sanchez from Ramparts Division to translate. We brought food, kept a low profile. I got nada. Hear no evil, speak no evil. I honestly don't think they knew much about Elena's life. To them West L.A.'s as distant as Atlantis. But even if they did they sure as hell weren't going to tell me.
JONATHAN KELLERMAN *When the Bough Breaks* 1992

In those days . . . the island of Britain was no island at all but part of the ancient kingdom of Atlantis, which, when it sank beneath the waves, left this western part to be our kingdom.
PETER ACKROYD *The House of Dr Dee* 1993

Atlas Atlas was one of the Titans in Greek mythology, punished for rebelling against Zeus by being made to support the heavens on his shoulders. The image of Atlas holding up the sky, or sometimes the earth itself, is a common one in art and literature. The name can be applied to anyone who is forced to bear a heavy burden.

I am like a spy who has signed a covenant of perpetual secrecy, I am like someone who is the only person in the world that knows the truth and yet is forbidden to utter it. And this truth weighs more than the universe, so that I am like Atlas bowed down forever beneath a burden that cracks the bones and solidifies the blood.
LOUIS DE BERNIÈRES *Captain Corelli's Mandolin* 1994

Charles Atlas Charles Atlas was the name adopted by the body-builder Angelo Siciliano (1894–1974), a '98-pound weakling' who became 'the world's strongest man'. The advertisements for his body-building course carried the famous slogan 'You too can have a body like mine'.

Atreus In Greek mythology, Atreus was the progenitor of a family known as the House of Atreus. His brother Thyestes laid a curse on it after Atreus had tricked him into eating the flesh of Thyestes' own sons at a feast. The family were subsequently involved in mutual murder and betrayal for several generations. One of Atreus' sons, Agamemnon, leader of the forces who besieged Troy, was murdered by his wife, Clytemnestra. The other son, Menelaus, was married to Helen of Troy, whose abduction by Paris led to the Trojan War. *See also* THYESTES, TROJAN WAR.

'I'm trying to protect my sister. That's all I'm concerned about. You're not helping.' 'You can't hide things for ever. The Mordifords should know that by now.' 'What's left of us. Beatrice would say it's a family curse, like the House of Atreus. A bit above our mercantile station, wouldn't you say?'
GILLIAN LINSCOTT *Widow's Peak* 1994

Attila the Hun Attila (406–453) was the king of the Huns in 434–453. Having attacked and devastated much of the Eastern Roman Empire in 445–450, Attila invaded the Western Empire but was defeated by the Romans and the Visigoths in 451. He and his army, noted for its savagery, were the terror of Europe during his lifetime, and Attila later came to be called the Scourge of

God. He is supposed to have died either by poison or from a massive nosebleed.

> In the grey-green light of the Embassy he listened thoughtfully to the latest evaluations of the new Attila, and a valuable summary of the measured predictions which for months past had blackened the marbled minute-papers of [the] German Department.
> LAWRENCE DURRELL *Mountolive* 1958

> 'Don't deliver your publicity lecture to me,' Lotty snapped. Her thick brows contracted to a solid black line across her forehead. 'As far as I am concerned he is a cretin with the hands of a Caliban and the personality of Attila.'
> SARA PARETSKY *V.I. for Short* 1995

> Colonel Gadaffi's metamorphosis from dictator to sensitive writer is as incongruous as Attila the Hun revealing a passion for Buddhist theology. *The Observer* 1996

Aucassin and Nicolette Aucassin and Nicolette were the subjects of a popular late 13th-century French romance composed in alternating prose and songs. Aucassin, son of the count of Beaucaire, falls in love with Nicolette, a Saracen captive. They endure a number of misfortunes and adventures but are eventually reunited and married.

> 'I repeat, madame, something has occurred.' 'Peter is away,' said Harriet. 'Is that what your gimlet eyes have discovered?' 'But you trust him, non? You expect him back, like the faithful Aucassin?' 'Well, yes,' said Harriet, 'I do.'
> DOROTHY L. SAYERS and JILL PATON *Thrones, Dominations* 1998

Augean stables In Greek mythology, the stables of the king of Augeas housed a very large herd of oxen and had never been cleaned out. Hercules undertook the task of cleaning them as one of his twelve labours. He achieved this task by diverting two rivers, the Alpheus and the Peneus, through the stables. The phrase 'cleaning the Augean stables' is often now used to mean not merely cleaning up a mess but putting right a corrupt or morally unacceptable situation. *See also* HERCULES.

> 'What are you doing here, Warshawski?' 'Cleaning the Augean stables, Todd. You can call me Hercules. Although I think he had some help. In a way I've outperformed him.'
> SARA PARETSKY *Guardian Angel* 1992

> I am convinced we need fundamental constitutional reform at all levels. We must cleanse the Augean stables at Westminster of the mess of patronage and special interests which do so much to discredit democracy.
> EMMA NICHOLSON *The Observer* 1995

St Augustine St Augustine (354–430) was one of the early Christian leaders and writers known as the Fathers of the Church. He became bishop of Hippo (in North Africa) in 396. His influence on both Roman Catholic and

Protestant theology was immense, and he is regarded as the patron saint of scholars. He is often remembered for praying in his *Confessions* (*c*.400) 'Give me chastity and continency, but not yet.'

> Helena, at that time suffering more from the irregularities of her relationship with Robert, more, because of its newness over which the protective skin of habit had not yet grown, had looked at the halcyon detachment and passionless benevolence of the Great-aunt and envied them. Though she recognised they were qualities attainable by her, at least, like St Augustin, not yet.
> ELIZABETH IRONSIDE *Death in the Garden* 1995

Aunt Chloe In Harriet Beecher Stowe's *Uncle Tom's Cabin* (1851), Uncle Tom, a Negro slave, is about to be sold to a slave trader and separated from his family. When his wife, Chloe, protests at how unfair this is, Uncle Tom urges her to look on the bright side: 'Let's think on our marcies!' Aunt Chloe then repeats this advice to their children. *See also* UNCLE TOM.

> We needed that lesson, and we won't forget it. If we do, you just say to us, as old Chloe did in Uncle Tom, 'Tink ob yer marcies, chillen! Tink ob yer marcies!'
> LOUISA M. ALCOTT *Little Women* 1868

Auschwitz Auschwitz was a concentration camp established by the Nazis in 1940 near the town of Oświęcim (Auschwitz) in German-occupied Poland in the Second World War. Initially, Poles were sent there, then gypsies and prisoners of war, and finally European Jews, many of whom were sent to the gas chambers. It is remembered as a place of horror. *See also* HOLOCAUST.

> His round face stayed angry, even after he restored the smile. 'But I understand. The cognitive dissonance must be painful for you. Coming here expecting Pleasure Island and getting Auschwitz.'
> JONATHAN KELLERMAN *The Web* 1995

Austerlitz The battle of Austerlitz took place in 1805 near the village of Austerlitz (now Slavkov in the Czech Republic). It was a victory for Napoleon but a serious defeat for the allied Austrians and Russians.

> That dinner at the King's Arms with his friends had been Henchard's Austerlitz: he had had his successes since, but his course had not been upward.
> THOMAS HARDY *The Mayor of Casterbridge* 1886

Autolycus In Greek mythology, Autolycus, the son of Chione, was a cunning thief who stole animals from the herds of Sisyphus. He had the power to change the appearance of whatever beasts he stole and so, although Sisyphus noticed that his own herds were growing smaller and those of Autolycus were growing larger, he was unable to make any accusations. Sisyphus finally caught Autolycus by marking the hooves of his cattle. Autolycus is also the name of a character in Shakespeare's *Winter's Tale*, a light-fingered rogue, 'a snapper-up of unconsidered trifles'.

Avalon In Arthurian legend, Avalon was the place to which Arthur was conveyed after his death, often portrayed as a paradise. *See also* KING ARTHUR.

Avenger of Blood In ancient Israel, a man who had the right to avenge the death of one of his kinsmen was called the Avenger of Blood or the Revenger of Blood. The practice is mentioned several times in the Bible, for example in Numbers (35: 19): 'The revenger of blood himself shall slay the murderer; when he meeteth him, he shall slay him.'

> [They] footed it as if the Avenger of Blood had been behind them.
> WALTER SCOTT *The Bride of Lammermoor* 1819

Avenging Angel The Angels of Vengeance, or Avenging Angels, were the first angels created by God. Traditionally there are twelve Avenging Angels, of whom six are known by name: Satanel, Michael, Gabriel, Uriel, Raphael, and Nathanael. They are sometimes associated with the role of punishing wrongdoers.

> He thought of himself as an heroic avenging angel of death, not as a wandering boy with a rifle that would bruise his shoulder every time he fired it.
> LOUIS DE BERNIÈRES *The War of Don Emmanuel's Nether Parts* 1990

Avernus Avernus is the name of a lake near Cumae and Naples. Close to the lake was the cave through which Aeneas descended to the underworld. The name means literally 'Without Birds', from the belief that its poisonous waters would cause any bird that attempted to fly over it to fall into the water.

Aveyron *See* WILD BOY OF AVEYRON.

Azrael In Jewish and Islamic mythology, Azrael (literally 'Help of God') was the angel who severed the soul from the body at death.

Baal Baal was the most important god in the pantheon of the Canaanites. He was the god of storms, associated with the rain that alleviated drought and brought agricultural fertility. After the long journey back from Egypt made by the Israelites under the leadership of Moses, the Canaanites were among those peoples whose land the Israelites believed to be given them by their god Yahweh. The first of the Ten Commandments given to the tribes of Israel was 'Thou shalt have none other god before me' and there is considerable opposition to the worship of Baal in successive books of the Old Testament, particularly from the prophets, such as Elijah and Jehu. In Christianity, Baal has been seen as a demon and a ruler in hell.

> There, down tubes which fed into the cellar, it was dropped into the sighing vent of an incinerator which sat like evil Baal in a dark corner.
> RAY BRADBURY *There Will Come Soft Rains* 1950

Baba Yaga Baba Yaga is a witch in Russian folklore who lives in a house that stands on chicken legs, flies about in a mortar using a pestle for an oar, and eats children.

Babel According to the book of Genesis, there was a time near the beginning of the world when all men lived in one place and all spoke the same language. They built a tall tower, the Tower of Babel, in an attempt to reach up to Heaven. On seeing the tower, God was concerned that man was becoming too powerful and so decided to thwart him by introducing different languages. He therefore went down to 'confound their language, that they may not understand one another's speech' (Gen. 11: 7). Once different languages were introduced and men no longer understood one another, the building of the tower stopped. The Tower of Babel has come to symbolize a noisy confusion of voices or a chaotic mixture of languages.

> Discipline prevailed: in five minutes the confused throng was resolved into order, and comparative silence quelled the Babel clamour of tongues.
> CHARLOTTE BRONTË *Jane Eyre* 1847

> Everyone seemed eager to talk at once, and the result was Babel.
> H. G. WELLS *The Invisible Man* 1897

> He woke to a babel the next morning, and when he went down to the hall

found the sisters getting their children ready for school.
V. S. NAIPAUL *A House for Mr Biswas* 1961

The crew's mess on board the *Kronos* is a Tower of Babel of English, French, Filipino, Danish, and German.
PETER HØEG *Miss Smilla's Feeling for Snow* 1992

Babes in the Wood Originally 'The Children in the Wood', an old ballad written in 1595, 'The Babes in the Wood' is the story of two infants, brother and sister, abandoned in a wood by their uncle, who wants their property. The children die and a robin covers them with leaves. The wicked uncle loses his own sons and his property, and dies in gaol. A reference to the Babes in the Wood usually signifies innocent suffering or unsophisticated innocence.

Everything looked strange and different in the darkness. We began to understand the sufferings of the Babes in the Wood.
JEROME K. JEROME *Three Men in a Boat* 1889

He could not deplore . . . that he had not a blank page to offer his bride in exchange for the unblemished one she was to give to him. He could not get away from the fact that if he had been brought up as she had they would have been no more fit to find their way about than the Babes in the Wood.
EDITH WHARTON *The Age of Innocence* 1920

Babylon Babylon was an ancient city in Mesopotamia which lay on the Euphrates and was first settled around 3000 BC. Hammurabi made Babylon the capital of the Babylonian Empire and it became renowned for its grandeur and decadence. The Jews were exiled there from 597 to about 538 BC. The name of the city is now often applied to a place or group that is considered to be materialistic, corrupt, and associated with the pursuit of sensual pleasure. *See also* HANGING GARDENS OF BABYLON, RIVERS OF BABYLON, WHORE OF BABYLON.

Imagine! Him! The budding star of the McCoy case—and no place—no place at all!—in the very Babylon of the twentieth century!—to take a lovely willing girl with brown lipstick.
TOM WOLFE *The Bonfire of the Vanities* 1987

Tell me why is Nunes here? Why does he beat old women? Why does he lock up someone who has done no wrong? What have we done, what horrible sin lies buried in this village that these poor people must be made to live in such mortal terror? It is enough to make me stop believing. Here is no Sodom, no Gomorrah, no Babylon. This is an ordinary village with ordinary people.
MIKE NICOL *The Powers That Be* 1989

Bacchanalia The Bacchanalia was the name given to the annual feast and celebrations in honour of the Greek god Dionysus, also called Bacchus. The celebrations were characterized by wild orgies and drunkenness. The corresponding adjective 'Bacchanalian' can refer to drunkenness or to wild or drunken partying. *See also* DIONYSUS.

> The learned profession of the law was certainly not behind any other learned profession in its Bacchanalian propensities.
> CHARLES DICKENS *A Tale of Two Cities* 1859

> That was what she might well do, he feared, to teach him not to venture out of the familiar, safe dustbin of their world into the perilous world of night-time bacchanalia, revelry and melodrama.
> ANITA DESAI *In Custody* 1984

> Jagger runs and cycles; Aerosmith singer Steve Tylor has banned sugar, salt, wheat, yeast, fat, red meat and alcohol from his band's menus. Even the Grateful Dead while publicly burning the Bacchanalian flame at both ends, were secretly calorie watching. *The Independent* 1997

Bacchante In Greek mythology, the Bacchantes or Maenads were the female devotees of the cult of Dionysus, also known as Bacchus. They took part in frenzied, orgiastic, and ecstatic celebrations at the festivals of Dionysus. *See also* DIONYSUS.

> The praise of folly, as he went on, soared into a philosophy, and Philosophy herself became young, and catching the mad music of Pleasure, wearing, one might fancy, her wine-stained robe and wreath of ivy, danced like a Bacchante over the hills of life, and mocked the slow Silenus for being sober. Facts fled before her like frightened forest things. Her white feet trod the huge press at which wise Omar sits, till the seething grape-juice rose round her bare limbs in waves of purple bubbles.
> OSCAR WILDE *The Picture of Dorian Gray* 1891

> She drank, and she loved, and she danced. But she never again became the Bacchante, the beloved, the high priestess of her Art.
> DOROTHY PARKER *Constant Reader* 1928

Bacchus Bacchus is another name for the Greek god Dionysus, the son of Zeus and Semele. Originally a god of the fertility of nature, associated with wild and ecstatic religious rites, in later traditions he is a god of wine who loosens inhibitions and inspires creativity in music and poetry. The adjective 'Bacchic' usually describes orgiastic or drunken revelry. *See also* DIONYSUS.

> She was shaken by a Bacchic and bawdy mood.
> GRAHAM GREENE *Brighton Rock* 1938

> Now Eastman enters Atkins's tea-room, that holy of holies, shrine—one supposes—of the anti-Bacchus.
> TIMOTHY MO *An Insular Possession* 1986

Bach Johann Sebastian Bach (1685–1750) was a German composer and organist, the outstanding representative of German baroque music. Bach was a master of counterpoint and developed the fugue form (in which a succession of parts or voices are interwoven) to a high art.

The music of our Lord's skin sliding over His flesh!—more exact than the fugues of Bach.
NATHANAEL WEST *The Dream Life of Balso Snell* 1931

Francis Bacon Francis Bacon (1561–1626) was a philosopher and essayist, best known as the author of *The Advancement of Learning* (1605) and many essays. He is sometimes mentioned as an exemplar of a beautiful, often epigrammatic, English writing style.

For his orations convulsed his hearers and his contributions were excellent, being patriotic, classical, comical, or dramatic, but never sentimental. Jo regarded them as worthy of Bacon, Milton, or Shakespeare.
LOUISA M. ALCOTT *Little Women* 1868

Bilbo Baggins Bilbo Baggins is the main character in *The Hobbit* (1937) by J. R. R. Tolkien. He is a hobbit, a member of an imaginary race of small, hairy-footed, burrow-dwelling people. Accompanied by a party of dwarves and the wizard Gandalf, Bilbo travels a great distance and experiences many adventures before finally winning his share of the dwarves' lost treasure. He is a somewhat reluctant adventurer, often wishing himself back in his nice, warm hobbit-hole. During his adventures he acquires a magic ring that confers invisibility on the wearer. This ring, 'so powerful that in the end it would utterly overcome anyone of the mortal race who possessed it', is central to the plot of Tolkien's later work *The Lord of the Rings* (1954–5). *See also* FRODO, HOBBIT.

'I'll call myself Mary,' Alison said, loudly enough to be sure of his hearing. 'That sounds nice and innocuous.' 'No one would suspect a meek, mild Mary of any skullduggery,' . . . It would be like wearing a cloak of invisibility or Bilbo Baggins' stolen magic ring.
SUSAN KELLY *Hope Will Answer* 1992

Baiae Baiae was a small town on the Bay of Naples with warm springs containing minerals which became a fashionable resort for the ancient Romans.

That Royal port and watering-place, if truly mirrored in the minds of the health-folk, must have combined, in a charming and indescribable manner, a Carthaginian bustle of building with Tarentine luxuriousness and a Baian health and beauty.
THOMAS HARDY *The Return of the Native* 1880

Balaam's ass Balaam was a prophet who was approached by emissaries from the land of Moab, alarmed by the invasion of the Israelites from Egypt. The Moabites begged him to curse the Israelites but God told him that the Israelites were blessed and must not be cursed (Num. 22). Eventually, Balaam set off with his donkey to accompany the Moabites. On the journey, an angel stood in the path of the donkey, which, on seeing him, moved aside from the path. Balaam beat the donkey and forced it back on the path. The angel again stood in the donkey's path, which turned aside and was again beaten. The third time the angel stood in front of the donkey it lay down and Balaam again beat it. 'And the Lord opened the mouth of the ass, and she said unto Balaam, What have I done unto thee, that thou hast smitten me these three times?' (Num. 22: 28). Balaam replied that the donkey had mocked him, whereupon the donkey pleaded that it had never done anything like this before. 'Then the Lord opened the eyes of Balaam, and he saw the angel of the Lord standing in the way, and his sword drawn in his hand: and he bowed down his head, and fell flat on his face' (Num. 22: 31). Balaam completed his journey to Moab, where he persistently blessed the Israelites until the Moabites sent him home.

> This fellow said: 'I am a free-born sovereign, sir, an American, sir, and I want everybody to know it!' He did not mention that he was a lineal descendant of Balaam's ass; but everybody knew that without his telling it.
> MARK TWAIN *The Innocents Abroad* 1869

> With one accord, aghast, they turned and stared at her. They felt as Balaam must have felt when his ass broke into speech.
> SOMERSET MAUGHAM *The World Over* 1951

Balboa Vasco Núñez de Balboa (1475–1519) was a Spanish explorer who joined an expedition to Darien (in Panama), initially as a stowaway, later as commander. During one of his further expeditions he became the first European to sight the Pacific Ocean, in 1513.

> At last he reached the summit, and a wide and novel prospect burst upon him with an effect almost like that of the Pacific upon Balboa's gaze.
> THOMAS HARDY *Far from the Madding Crowd* 1874

> And the man named Dick kept standing up in the car as if he were Cortez or Balboa, looking over that grey fleecy undulation.
> F SCOTT FITZGERALD *The Last Tycoon* 1941

Balder In Scandinavian mythology, Balder was the son of Odin. Beautiful and popular, he was the god of light. When Balder had a dream that he would die, his mother, Frigga, exacted a promise from all things that they would not harm him, but she overlooked the mistletoe. Loki tricked the blind god Hodur into throwing a branch of mistletoe at Balder, and this killed him. *See also* ODIN.

Bambi *Bambi* is the title of the Walt Disney animated film, first released in 1942 and rereleased in 1947, about a young deer growing up in the forest whose mother is shot by a hunter. He makes friends (including Thumper, the rabbit) and learns the lessons and dangers of growing up in the wild. In a memorable scene, he learns how to stand on the ice of a pond in wintertime. Eventually he falls in love with another fawn, Faline. The film was based on a story by Felix Salten (1923).

It is fifteen minutes more before he can stand. And even then he's like Bambi on the ice.
PETER HØEG *Miss Smilla's Feeling for Snow* 1992

That was one of the nastiest pieces of work I'd come across in a long time. He made David Stronge look like Bambi.
LAUREN HENDERSON *The Black Rubber Dress* 1997

Banquo's ghost In Shakespeare's *Macbeth* (1623), the victorious Scottish generals Macbeth and Banquo meet three witches who prophesy that Macbeth will be king and that Banquo's heirs will sit on the throne. Macbeth murders the king and takes his crown and then, in an attempt to defeat the prophecy, hires three murderers to kill Banquo and his son. At the start of a banquet held by the Macbeths, the first murderer arrives to inform Macbeth that they have killed Banquo but that his son Fleance has escaped. On returning to the banqueting table Macbeth finds his place taken by Banquo's ghost. None of the guests present can see the ghost, but Macbeth is so distressed that Lady Macbeth brings the banquet to a hasty close.

One night, however, during one of our orgies—one of our high festivals, I mean—he glided in, like the ghost in Macbeth, and seated himself, as usual, a little back from the table, in the chair we always placed for 'the spectre', whether it chose to fill it or not.
ANNE BRONTË *The Tenant of Wildfell Hall* 1848

I was closeted with our Head of Chambers who rose, on my arrival, with the air of a somewhat more heroic Macbeth who is forcing himself to invite Banquo's ghost to take a seat, and would he care for a cigarette.
JOHN MORTIMER *Rumpole's Return* 1980

Hovering like Banquo's ghost around the conference will be the former Chancellor Kenneth Clarke. *The Observer* 1997

Barbie ® Barbie is the name of a doll made by Mattell Inc. in the form of a conventionally attractive American young woman, popular with young girls. Many fashion items and accessories are available for clothing Barbie. A companion male doll is called Ken.

'It's very nice to see you . . . again,' she replied feebly in her honeyed drawl. With her smooth, peachy makeup, she looked remarkably like a Barbie doll.
SPARKLE HAYTER *What's a Girl Gotta Do?* 1994

Opposite him, across the sweeping curve of the presentation console, were two Ken-and-Barbie-style presenters of indeterminate age.
BEN ELTON *Popcorn* 1996

I was hailed by one of the Barbie dolls at the check-in desk, a pretty child with the charm button switched to FULL.
MICHÈLE BAILEY *Haycastle's Cricket* 1996

Bardolph In Shakespeare's *Henry IV* and *Henry V*, Bardolph is one of Falstaff's companions. His bright red nose inspires Falstaff to say to him: 'Thou art our admiral, thou bearest the lantern in the poop, but 'tis in the nose of thee; thou art the Knight of the Burning Lamp' (*Henry IV*, Part 1).

> If beauty is a matter of fashion, how is it that wrinkled skin, grey hair, hairy backs and Bardolph-like noses have never been 'in fashion'? *Frontiers: Penguin Popular Science* 1994

Brigitte Bardot Brigitte Bardot (b. Camille Javal, 1934) is a French actress whose appearance in the film *And God Created Woman* (1956) established her reputation as an international sex symbol. After retiring from acting she became an active supporter of animal welfare and of the cause of endangered animal species.

> As one might have guessed from the mountains of dogs and cats they destroy every year (and sometimes exhibit in Benetton-style adverts), the RSPCA is no Brigitte Bardot. No mushy rescuing of cats from burning Malibu beach houses here.*The Independent* 1993

Barmecide's Feast In *The Arabian Nights*, a prince of Baghdad named Barmecide invites Schacabac, a poor beggar, to dine with him. The table is set with ornate plates and dishes, but all are empty. When, to test Schacabac's humour, Barmecide asks his guest how he finds the food, and offers him illusory wine, Schacabac declines, pretending to be already drunk, and knocks Barmecide down. Relenting, Barmecide gives Schacabac a proper meal. Barmecide's name is used to describe something, especially food or hospitality, that is in fact illusory or unreal. *See also* ARABIAN NIGHTS.

> That night, on going to bed, I forgot to prepare in imagination the Barmecide supper of hot roast potatoes, or white bread and new milk, with which I was wont to amuse my inward cravings.
> CHARLOTTE BRONTË *Jane Eyre* 1847

> Your lighter boxes of family papers went up-stairs into a Barmecide room that always had a great dining-table in it and never had a dinner.
> CHARLES DICKENS *A Tale of Two Cities* 1859

> It was a curious sort of a feast, I reflected, in appearance indeed, an entertainment of the Barmecide stamp, for there was absolutely nothing to eat.
> RIDER HAGGARD *She* 1887

St Bartholomew St Bartholomew was an Apostle who is said to have been martyred in Armenia by being flayed alive, and is hence regarded as the patron saint of tanners.

> If they knew how old I am they would flay me with their terrible brushes—flay me like St Bartholomew.
> ROBERTSON DAVIES *Fifth Business* 1970

> The last of them, excoriated like a Saint Bartholomew, held up in his right hand his still-bleeding skin limp as an unused cape.
> UMBERTO ECO *The Island of the Day Before* 1994

Bartleby 'Bartleby the Scrivener' (1856) is a short story by Herman Melville. The story is narrated by a New York lawyer who tells of Bartleby, one of his scriveners, or copyists, who when asked to do more than simply copying says 'I would prefer not to'. Eventually, he even stops copying and eating and gradually wastes away.

> When he put down his glass and saw Tess, holding out her card, he sighed. 'I don't wanna,' he said. 'What do you mean?' 'Whatever it is you want, I don't wanna talk about it. I'm off, okay? This is my time, my dinner.' 'I'll buy you dinner.' 'I don't wanna.' 'And give you some cash for your time.' 'I don't wanna,' repeated this modern-day Bartleby.
> LAURA LIPPMAN *The Last Place* 2002

Dick Barton Dick Barton, Special Agent, was the hero of a radio series broadcast between 1946 and 1951, in which he courageously pursued and defeated arch-criminals.

basilisk The basilisk was a legendary monster, the king of serpents, which could reputedly strike someone dead with its stare. A 'basilisk stare' is thus a cold stare.

> Gloucester: Thine eyes, sweet lady, have infected mine.
> Anne: Would they were basilisks, to strike thee dead!
> WILLIAM SHAKESPEARE *Richard III* 1597

> Without softening very much the basilisk nature of his stare, he said, impassively: 'We are coming to that part of my investigation, sir.'
> JOSEPH CONRAD *The Secret Agent* 1907

Bastille The Bastille was a fortress in Paris, built as a royal castle by Charles V, and completed in 1383. Used as a prison in the 17th and 18th centuries, it became a symbol of repression. It was stormed and sacked by the Parisian mob in 1789 on 14 July, now commemorated as Bastille Day, marking the beginning of the French Revolution.

> I would fain unite the duties of existence and have my mother at home with me, but alas, fate has arranged it otherwise, and here we are imprisoned as completely as if we were in the Bastille.
> CELIA THAXTER *Letters* 1873

Norman Bates *See* PSYCHO.

Bathsheba In the Bible, Bathsheba was the beautiful wife of Uriah the Hittite (2 Sam. 11) whom King David took as his mistress after he had seen her bathing from the roof of the palace. David sent for her, slept with her, and she became pregnant. David then arranged for Uriah to be sent into the front line of the battle in which the Israelites were besieging Rabbah, and he was killed. After Bathsheba's period of mourning, David married her (2 Sam. 11). Bathsheba became the mother of Solomon. *See also* DAVID, URIAH.

Batman and Robin The crime-fighting superheroes Batman and Robin made their first appearance in 1939 in an American comic strip, and have since appeared both on television and in films. In normal life the two are the wealthy Bruce Wayne and his young ward Dick Grayson, but as Batman and Robin, with the aid of clever gadgets and their speedy Batmobile, they fight against cunning super-criminals such as the Joker and the Penguin in order to protect Gotham City.

Batmobile The Batmobile is the fast and futuristic car driven by Batman and Robin. In the television series *Batman* (1966–8), the Batmobile was a converted Lincoln Continental. *See also* BATMAN AND ROBIN.

> I mean, he's married, which is a scary thing, and he's got the sort of car keys that you jangle confidently, so he's obviously got, like, a BMW or a Batmobile or something flash.
> NICK HORNBY *High Fidelity* 1995

> I gazed longingly at his car. 'Nice Mercedes.' 'Transportation,' Ranger said. 'Nothing fancy.' Compared to what? The Batmobile?
> JANET EVANOVICH *High Five* 1999

Battus In Greek mythology, Battus was a shepherd of Arcadia, who saw the god Hermes steal the flocks of Admetus. He was bribed by the god not to tell, and pointing to a stone declared: 'Sooner will that stone tell of your theft than I.' When he was tricked into breaking his promise, Hermes turned him into a stone.

Beardsley Aubrey Beardsley (1872–98) was an English artist and illustrator who worked in the Art Nouveau style. He is chiefly known for his stylized black-and-white illustrations for such works as Oscar Wilde's *Salome* (1894) and Pope's *The Rape of the Lock* (1896) and for the periodical *The Yellow Book*, of which he became artistic director in 1894. Beardsley's work, often dealing with grotesque or erotic subjects, epitomized the 'decadence' of the 1890s.

> He kept a bevy of boys himself, over whom he ruled with great severity, jealous and terrible as a Beardsleyan queen.
> JOHN BANVILLE *The Book of Evidence* 1989

Beatrice *See* DANTE.

Beatrice and Benedick Beatrice and Benedick are the two chief characters in Shakespeare's romantic comedy *Much Ado about Nothing* (1600). At the start of the play Benedick is determined to remain a bachelor, and the characters engage in mutual barbed teasing. When their friends and relatives trick each of them into believing that the other is in love, each does, in fact, fall for the other. At the end of the play, still teasing each other, they agree to marry.

Beau Geste *Beau Geste* (1924) by P. C. Wren is an adventure story dealing with the exploits of the French Foreign Legion. It contains a famous scene in which, with hardly any soldiers left alive to defend a fort, the corpses of the dead are arranged on the fort's battlements to give the illusion of a strongly armed presence.

Caz got back to John Street for half past two. There were a couple of voices in the back office behind the front desk, but other than that, the place was still a cheap version of Beau Geste meets the Marie Celeste.
ALEX KEEGAN *Kingfisher* 1995

Beauty and the Beast *Beauty and the Beast* is the title of a fairy tale in which a beautiful young woman, Beauty, is forced to live with the Beast, an ugly monster, in order to save her father's life. Having come to pity and love the Beast, she finally consents to marry him. Her love frees the Beast from the enchantment he is under and he is restored to the form of a handsome prince. Any couple of widely contrasting physical attractiveness can be described as Beauty and the Beast.

When he was about fifteen they used to call him Beauty about the College, and me they nicknamed the Beast.
H. RIDER HAGGARD *She* 1887

Attorney Callender handed the writ of habeas corpus to the Lieutenant and Fats said, 'Come on, Katy,' and took the tall mini-skirted, naked-looking, hot-skinned, cold sex-pot by the elbow and marched her toward the door. They looked like Beauty and the Beast.
CHESTER HIMES *Blind Man with a Pistol* 1969

They were looking at each other, not touching, looking long and quiet at each other. The girl entirely wrapped in furs, so it was hard to tell where her own glossy hair began and ended, and the poor beast, with his rough and yellow hide—Beauty and her Beast, in this guise, but Beauty was so close to her Beast now, wrapped in beast's clothing, as sharp and wary as a beast, surviving as one.
DORIS LESSING *The Memoirs of a Survivor* 1974

Beavis and Butthead Beavis and Butthead are two dim-witted, dirty-minded cartoon teenagers who torture animals, chortle at words they think rude or suggestive, and like extremely loud rock music. They were created by Mike Judge, and the television series of the same name in which they featured was broadcast on MTV from 1993 to 1997.

Luc Claudel was the nameless unfortunate newly partnered with Quickwater. Great. Now I'd have to work with Beavis and Butthead.
KATHY REICHS *Deadly Decisions* 2000

Samuel Beckett The plays of the Irish writer and playwright Samuel Beckett (1906–89), such as *Waiting for Godot* (1955), *Krapp's Last Tape* (1958, pub 1959), and *Play* (1964), express the author's bleak view of the vanity and futility of human endeavour in the face of man's inevitable death and oblivion.

It is a joy sufficiently muted to accord with prevailing moods that range from Chekhovian-autumnal to Beckettian-wintry. *New York Review of Books* 1997

Bedlam Bedlam was the popular name of the Hospital of St Mary of Bethlehem, founded as a priory in 1247 at Bishopsgate, London, and by the 14th century a mental hospital. In 1675 a new hospital was built in Moorfields and this in turn was replaced by a building in the Lambeth Road in 1815 (now the Imperial War Museum) and transferred to Beckenham in Kent in 1931. 'Bedlam' is an archaic word for a mental hospital or an asylum. The word now denotes a state of wild disorder or noisy uproar. The name Tom o' Bedlam used to be applied to a person who was mentally ill.

> I'm sure the child's half an idiot i' some things; for if I send her up-stairs to fetch anything, she forgets what she's gone for, an' perhaps 'ull sit down on the floor i' the sunshine an' plait her hair an' sing to herself like a Bedlam creatur', all the while I'm waiting for her down-stairs.
> GEORGE ELIOT *The Mill on the Floss* 1860

> There was a muleteer to every donkey and a dozen volunteers beside, and they banged the donkeys with their goad-sticks, and pricked them with their spikes, and shouted something that sounded like 'Sekki-yah!' and kept up a din and a racket that was worse than Bedlam itself.
> MARK TWAIN *The Innocents Abroad* 1869

> Their usual scene of operations, Meridian's billiard-room, is tonight rowdy beyond all previous nights, and it has been a Bedlam in the past.
> TIMOTHY MO *An Insular Possession* 1986

Mrs Bedonebyasyoudid In Charles Kingsley's children's story *The Water-Babies* (1863), Mrs Bedonebyasyoudid is a character encountered by Tom after he becomes a water-baby. She rewards good behaviour and punishes bad, illustrating the moral lesson that you reap what you sow.

> Any qualms I might have had about deceiving Anita, disappeared completely on her wedding day. She had turned into Mrs Be-Done-By-As-You-Did.
> FAY WELDON *Life Force* 1992

Beelzebub In the Old Testament, Beelzebub (literally 'the Lord of the Flies') is the god of the Philistine city Ekron (2 Kgs. 1). He is mentioned in several of the Gospels, where he is called 'the prince of demons'. Beelzebub is often identified with the Devil. In *Paradise Lost*, however, Milton gives the name to one of the fallen angels, next to Satan in power.

> She 'spaed fortunes', read dreams, composed philtres, discovered stolen goods, and made and dissolved matches as successfully as if, according to the belief of the whole neighbourhood, she had been aided in those arts by Beelzebub himself.
> WALTER SCOTT *The Bride of Lammermoor* 1819

> Winterborne was standing in front of the brick oven in his shirt-sleeves, tossing in thorn-sprays, and stirring about the blazing mass with a long-handled, three-pronged Beelzebub kind of fork.
> THOMAS HARDY *The Woodlanders* 1887

Beersheba *See* DAN TO BEERSHEBA.

Beethoven Ludwig van Beethoven (1770–1827) was a German composer, born in Bonn. His music is often said to have bridged the classical and Romantic traditions. Although he began to be afflicted with deafness in 1802, an affliction which became total by 1817, his musical output was prodigious.

> I soon found out why Old Chong had retired from teaching piano. He was deaf. 'Like Beethoven!' he shouted to me. 'We're both listening only in our head!'
> AMY TAN *Two Kinds* 1989

Sir Toby Belch Sir Toby Belch is the uncle of Olivia in Shakespeare's *Twelfth Night* (1623), known for his love of good food and drink, for 'cakes and ale'. *See also* SHAKESPEARE.

> At present I share Balliol with one . . . man . . . who rather repels me at meals by his . . . habit of showing satisfaction with the food: Sir Toby Belch was not in it.
> ALDOUS HUXLEY *The Letters of Aldous Huxley* 1915

Belle Dame Sans Merci *La Belle Dame Sans Merci* is the title of a ballad by Keats, published in 1820. It tells the story of a knight who becomes enthralled by the charms of a fairy woman who pretends to love him and care for him, as a result of which his strength fails him and he is seen 'alone and palely loitering'. The name in fact pre-dates Keats, and *La Belle Dame sans mercy* was the title of a French poem of 1424 by Alain Chartier.

> I imagine she was one of the few women who ever turned you down. That rankled; and having one's advances received with howls of mirth must have hurt. If she'd remained here in Pine Grove, married, turned into an ordinary aging housewife, you'd have forgotten her. But the mystery and the romance of her life, added to her rejection, transformed her into the unattainable ideal woman. La Belle Dame sans Merci.
> ELIZABETH PETERS *Naked Once More* 1989

Bellerophon In Greek myth, Bellerophon was the son of Glaucus and the grandson of Sisyphus. While staying with King Proteus of Argos, the king's wife, Anteia, fell in love with him. When he rejected her, she told her husband that Bellerophon had tried to seduce her. Proteus was unwilling to kill Bellerophon to avenge her, as he was a guest, and so sent him to his father-in-law, King Iobates of Lydia, with a sealed letter asking Iobates to kill him. Iobates set Bellerophon many dangerous and difficult tasks, but with the aid of Pegasus, the winged horse, Bellerophon always managed to complete the task. Eventually, he tried to ride Pegasus to heaven, which made the gods angry and Pegasus threw him. At the end of his life he was alone and an outcast. *See also* PEGASUS.

> Henchard was stung into bitterness; like Bellerophon, he wandered away from the crowd, cankered in soul.
> THOMAS HARDY *The Mayor of Casterbridge* 1886

Belphoebe In Edmund Spenser's *Faerie Queene* (1590, 1596), Belphoebe is a daughter of the nymph Chrysogone and is a chaste huntress. *See also* SPENSER.

> She had a look, he thought fancifully, of a modern Belphoebe in those garments, sunny hair and the accoutrements of a huntress.
> A. S. BYATT *The Virgin in the Garden* 1978

Belsen Bergen-Belsen was a Nazi concentration camp near the city of Celle in north-west Germany. Many thousands of prisoners died there from starvation or disease while others were shot. *See also* HOLOCAUST.

> Or else take the contemporarily untenable position that evil, undiluted by any hint of childhood trauma, does exist in the world, exists for its own precise sake, the pustular bequest from the beast, as inexplicable as Belsen.
> JOHN D. MACDONALD *The Deep Blue Goodbye* 1964

Belshazzar Belshazzar, king of Babylon, gave a great banquet for 1 000 of his lords (Dan. 5: 1–28). During the banquet they drank from goblets taken from the temple and praised the gods of gold, silver, bronze, iron, wood, and stone. Suddenly the fingers of a human hand appeared and wrote on the wall the words 'Mene, Mene, Tekel, Upharsin'. Daniel translated the words, explaining to Belshazzar that his reign was over, that he had been weighed in the balance and found wanting, and that his kingdom would be divided and given to the Medes and the Persians. The writing on the wall is thus a herald of doom. *See also* DANIEL.

> A sideboard was set out . . . on which was a display of plate that might have vied . . . with Belshazzar's parade of the vessels of the temple.
> WASHINGTON IRVING *The Sketch-Book of Geoffrey Crayon, Gent.* 1820

> This inexplicable incident, this reversal of my previous experience, seemed, like the Babylonian finger on the wall, to be spelling out the letters of my judgment.
> ROBERT LOUIS STEVENSON *The Strange Case of Dr Jekyll and Mr Hyde* 1886

> 'I always like this room,' said Spandrell as they entered. 'It's like a scene for Belshazzar's feast.'
> ALDOUS HUXLEY *Point Counter Point* 1928

> And there at the centre of his desk was a large buff envelope with his name printed on it in a hand which was unmistakably Dalziel's. Why did the name Belshazzar suddenly flit into his mind?
> REGINALD HILL *Child's Play* 1987

Benedick *See* BEATRICE AND BENEDICK.

Ben Hur Ben Hur is the hero of Lew Wallace's novel *Ben-Hur, a Tale of the Christ* (1880). Set in Rome at the time of Christ, the novel tells the story of Ben Hur, a Jew who converts to Christianity. The story was popularized by two Hollywood epics, a 1925 silent film and a 1959 remake starring Charlton Heston. Both films featured memorably exciting scenes of a chariot race.

Leslie Beck's Life Force is the energy not so much of sexual desire as of sexual discontent: the urge to find someone better out there, and thereby something better in the self, the one energy working against the other, creating a fine and animating friction: or else racing along side by side, like the Chariots in Ben Hur, wheels colliding, touching, hell-bent, sparking off happiness and unhappiness.
FAY WELDON *Life Force* 1992

Mrs Bennet In Jane Austen's *Pride and Prejudice* (1813), the vulgar, gossipy Mrs Bennet is preoccupied with finding wealthy husbands for her five unmarried daughters.

So, by some mysterious transference, the children's birthday party has turned into a battleground of social ambitions, ripe for the attention of a contemporary Jane Austen. No one considers the embarrassment of the mother who can't afford to keep up, or the danger of turning our children into spoilt little brats. Or is it merely a harmless indulgence in parental pride? After all, today's Mrs Bennets aren't trying to marry off their five-year-olds, they just want the fun of dressing them up and clucking over them. *The Independent* 1996

Beowulf Beowulf was a legendary Scandinavian hero celebrated in the Old English epic poem *Beowulf*. The poem describes Beowulf's killing first of the monster Grendel in King Hrothgar's hall, then of Grendel's mother in an underwater cave, and finally Beowulf's own death in combat with a dragon. The poem is set in the Scandinavia of the 5th and 6th centuries, but the poem itself is believed to have been composed in the 8th century.

We were on a beach, and someone . . . suggested we engrave our names in big letters upon the sand, then one of us would mount the promenade and photograph inscription plus inscriber. A cliché in Beowulf's time, I know, but you can't keep coming up with new games.
JULIAN BARNES *Talking It Over* 1991

Cyrano de Bergerac Cyrano de Bergerac (1619–55) was a French soldier, duellist, and writer of comedies and satires. He is supposed to have had a prodigiously long nose. He is celebrated in the play by Edmond Rostand that bears his name (1897).

Derek Griffiths is a young coloured comedian with a face like crushed rubber . . . and a hooter to rival Cyrano de Bergerac. *The Times* 1972

Berlin Wall In 1961 a wall was built between East and West Berlin in order to curb the numbers of East Germans fleeing to the West. Originally, it was a low barbed-wire barricade but it was rebuilt several times, each time bigger and stronger until eventually it was a heavily guarded concrete barrier with an average height of 3.6 metres (11.8 feet) with fortifications. For many years, anyone caught escaping over the wall was shot. On 9 November 1989, following the collapse of the communist regime in East Germany, the wall was opened up. It was subsequently dismantled.

After three days of his model performance, Judy had given up the daybed in

the dressing room and come back to the bedroom. True, the Berlin Wall now ran down the center of the bed, and she wouldn't give him an inch of small talk. But she was always civil to him when Campbell was around.
TOM WOLFE *The Bonfire of the Vanities* 1987

Rows of police cars are parked along Eastman Avenue, one of the most formidable ethnic 'Berlin Walls' in all America. *The Observer* 1996

The aim is to break down the 'Berlin walls' which separate health and community care, in Secretary of State for Health Frank Dobson's phrase. *The Independent* 1997

Bermuda Triangle The Bermuda Triangle is an area of the western Atlantic bounded by Bermuda, Florida, and Puerto Rico which is supposedly associated with an unusually high number of unexplained disappearances of ships and aircraft.

I'd entered what Renée's mother calls the Bermuda Triangle of Health, which is pretty terrifying.
SIMON GRAY *Gray's Anatomy* 1993

Bethesda In the Bible, Bethesda was a pool in Jerusalem that was supposed to have healing powers. It was there that Jesus healed a paralytic 'who had been ill for thirty-eight years'. Knowing that the man had been lying by the pool for some time, Jesus asked whether he wanted to be healed. The sick man answered: 'I have no man to put me into the pool when the water is troubled, and while I am going another steps down before me' (John 5: 7).

She has sent her here to be healed, even as the Jews of old sent their diseased to the troubled pool of Bethesda.
CHARLOTTE BRONTË *Jane Eyre* 1847

The new-comer stepped forward like the quicker cripple at Bethesda, and entered in her stead.
THOMAS HARDY *The Mayor of Casterbridge* 1886

Beulah Beulah (Hebrew, literally 'Married Woman') is the land of Israel: 'thou shalt be called Hephzibah, and thy land Beulah: for the Lord delighteth in thee, and thy land shall be married' (Isa. 62: 4). In Bunyan's *The Pilgrim's Progress*, Beulah lies beyond the Valley of the Shadow of Death and also out of the reach of Giant Despair: 'Yea, here they heard continually the singing of birds, and saw every day the flowers appear in the earth . . . in this country the sun shineth night and day.' *See also* PILGRIM'S PROGRESS.

I thought sometimes I saw beyond its wild waters a shore, sweet as the hills of Beulah.
CHARLOTTE BRONTË *Jane Eyre* 1847

Big Bad Wolf In the folk tale *The Three Little Pigs*, three pigs each make a house, one of straw, one of twigs, and one of bricks. A wolf arrives and asks to be let into the house of straw. The pig refuses and the wolf says 'I'll huff and I'll puff and I'll blow the house down', which he does, eating the pig. He then does the same to the next pig and the house made of twigs. He is unable, however, to blow down the house made of bricks. Thwarted, he announces that he will come down the chimney. The pig makes a fire and hangs a cauldron over it and the wolf comes down the chimney into the boiling cauldron and is cooked and eaten by the pig. The story was made into a successful cartoon by Disney in 1933 featuring the song 'Who's afraid of the Big, Bad Wolf?' written by Frank Churchill.

> He shows me a rusty knife which he claims he used to slash off the hair of a cousin who came home with a perm. Does he get paid for this community service? He would not say but instead broke into another deeply-felt speech on the poisonous spittle of the big, bad, Western wolf. *The Independent* 1998

Big Brother Big Brother is a character in George Orwell's novel *Nineteen Eighty-Four* (1949). He is the head of the totalitarian Party and dictator of the state in which Winston Smith lives. His portrait, with the caption 'Big Brother is watching you', is ubiquitous. *See also* ORWELL.

> It's a world I don't know. The world of the computer and the microwave oven. . . . Younger people growing up will find it easier to contend with, but I doubt it. They'll conform because it's the only way to go. Big Brother is there. I think they will become digits. I don't see myself as a digit, but I know I'm becoming one. It's necessary for me to have my Social Security number available or my driver's licence, because I don't have credit cards. It's un-American. Anywhere I gotta pay cash. You see, I'm not a digit yet.
> STUDS TERKEL *American Dreams: Lost and Found* 1980

> He censored our reading, selected our playmates—we weren't allowed many—and watched us like Big Brother.
> BARBARA MICHAELS *Search the Shadows* 1988

> Labour's Shadow Social Security Secretary rules it out as a Big Brother scheme. Jack Straw reiterated Labour's long-standing objection to compulsory ID cards, but supports a voluntary scheme. *The Independent* 1996

Big-Endians and Little-Endians In Jonathan Swift's *Gulliver's Travels* (1726) the Big-Endians are a group of people in Lilliput who believe that eggs should be broken at the big end rather than at the little end, as commanded by the Emperor of Lilliput. The Big-Endians have taken refuge in the neighbouring land of Blefuscu, and as a result of this disagreement Lilliput and Blefuscu have 'been engaged in a most obstinate war for six and thirty moons past'. *See also* GULLIVER.

Biggles Biggles is a fictional British pilot. The hero of many adventures in two world wars, created by Captain W. E. Johns and first appearing in books in the 1930s, his name is associated with British stiff-upper-lip courage and patriotism.

Bighorn See LITTLE BIGHORN.

Billy Goat Gruff In the fairy tale, three billy goats named Gruff are journeying up the hillside in search of fodder when they come to a bridge guarded by a troll. The first Billy Goat Gruff starts to cross the bridge when the troll roars 'Who's tripping across my bridge?' and claims he will eat the goat. The first Billy Goat Gruff, who is the youngest, protests in a small voice that he is small and that a bigger, more tempting Billy Goat Gruff will come after him. The troll lets him go. The second Billy Goat Gruff starts to cross the bridge with the same response and, in a somewhat less small voice, persuades the troll to let him go because a bigger Billy Goat Gruff will follow him. The third Billy Goat Gruff, on being challenged and told he is to be eaten, replies in a hoarse, ugly voice:
'Well, come along! I've got two spears,
And I'll poke your eyeballs out at your ears;
I've got besides two curling-stones,
And I'll crush you to bits, body and bones.'
He carries out his threat and throws the troll's body into the river before following the others up the hill.

> 'Well, get it ready, get it ready,' Billy Grenaby said, a little cross because he hadn't scared either of them. Billy loved to play at being a Billygoat Gruff, to watch people wince and turn pale when he growled at them.
> CHARLOTTE LAMB *In the Still of the Night* 1995

Billy Liar Keith Waterhouse's 1959 novel *Billy Liar* tells the story of Billy Fisher, a compulsive daydreamer who dreams of a better and more glamorous life. A Billy Liar is therefore a daydreamer who lives in a fantasy world.

Billy the Kid William H. Bonney (1859–81), known as Billy the Kid, was an American bandit and bank robber, involved in the Lincoln County cattle war in New Mexico. He allegedly committed his first murder at the age of 12. He was finally shot by sheriff Pat Garrett.

> He did not look like a jailbird. Billy the Kid and Crippen did not look like Murderers.
> FRANK PARRISH *Voices from the Dark* 1993

Birnam Wood In Shakespeare's *Macbeth* (1623), the witches assure Macbeth that he will not be defeated until Birnam Wood comes to Dunsinane Castle. Later, when the army of Malcolm and Macduff passes through Birnam Wood, Malcolm instructs every man to cut a branch, and under the camouflage of this 'leafy screen' the army marches on Dunsinane, giving the impression that the wood is indeed moving. *See also* MACBETH, SHAKESPEARE.

> When the curtain call came, some of the girls who had been serving as ushers

rushed to the footlights like Birnam Wood moving to Dunsinane, loaded with bouquets.
ROBERTSON DAVIES *The Manticore* 1972

Bismarck Karl Otto Eduard Leopold von Bismarck (1815–98) was a Prussian-German politician and statesman. He entered the Prussian parliament in the 1840s and became a member of the German diet in 1851. He was made a count, then a prince, and in 1871 became chancellor of Germany, later known as the Iron Chancellor. He presided over the reorganization and unification of Germany.

Clark . . . called Kaishu the 'Bismarck of Japan' for his role in unifying the Japanese nation in the dangerous aftermath of the fall of the Tokugawa.
JADE DRAGON *Online* 2003

Black Beauty Anna Sewell's novel *Black Beauty* (1877) gives an account of the life and adventures of a horse who has many different owners and experiences. The book became an enduring children's classic.

Black Death The Black Death is the name commonly given to the great epidemic of bubonic plague that killed between a third and a half of the population of Europe in the mid-14th century. The plague originated in central Asia and China and spread rapidly through Europe, transmitted by the fleas of black rats.

'What we need is a cataclysm,' Fish was saying. . . . 'A cataclysm. Another Black Death, a vast explosion, millions wiped from the face of the earth, civilization as we know it all but obliterated, then Birth would be essential again.'
MARGARET ATWOOD *The Edible Woman* 1969

Black Hander The name Black Hand has been used by a number of secret societies, most notably a group of terrorists and blackmailers composed mainly of Sicilians active in the United States in the late 19th and early 20th centuries. The name was also used for a secret society which aimed at the unification of the southern Slavs at the beginning of the 20th century.

He became the Black Hander once more. He looked this way and he looked that. He peeped hither and peered thither. Then he lowered his voice to such a whisper that I couldn't hear a damn word.
P G. WODEHOUSE *Laughing Gas* 1936

Black Hole of Calcutta The Black Hole of Calcutta was a dungeon in Fort William, Calcutta. Following the capture of Calcutta by Siraj-ud-Dawlah, nawab of Bengal, 146 English prisoners were said to have been confined there in a narrow cell, 20 feet square, for the night of 20 June 1756. Only 23 people survived to the morning, all the others suffocating. A severely overcrowded place, especially one in which people are trapped, can be described as a Black Hole of Calcutta.

As I passed Erskine-Brown's open door I could see his room was bursting at the

seams, and, as I hung up my hat and coat in the hallway, I heard the voice of Erskine-Brown say he supposed they'd have to hang on in that Black Hole of Calcutta a little longer.
JOHN MORTIMER *Rumpole of the Bailey* 1978

Black Lagoon *See* CREATURE FROM THE BLACK LAGOON.

Modesty Blaise Modesty Blaise is the heroine of a strip cartoon created by Peter O'Donnell and first published in the London *Evening Standard* in 1963. A retired gangster, she fights against crime and wrongdoing showing great courage and resourcefulness.

Blake William Blake (1757–1827) was an English artist and poet. His intensely imaginative and visionary watercolours and engravings include illustrations for *The Book of Job* (1826), for works by Dante and Shakespeare, and for his own *Prophetic Books* (1783–1804). His figures are usually heavily muscled and the colours in pale pastel tones. Blake's writings and visual work were largely ignored during his lifetime.

And the people in the streets, it seemed to him, whether milling along Oxford Street or sauntering from lion to lion in Trafalgar Square, formed another golden host, beautiful in the antique cold-faced way of Blake's pastel throngs.
JOHN UPDIKE *Bech: A Book* 1970

Blefuscudian navy In Jonathan Swift's *Gullivers Travels* (1726), Gulliver finds himself in the land of Lilliput, where the people are only 6 inches tall. They have a continuing historic war with the people of the neighbouring land of Blefuscu. During Gulliver's stay, Blefuscu has amassed a navy and is preparing to launch it over the sea between the islands, a channel 800 yards wide and at its deepest, 6 feet. Gulliver conceives a plan to assist the Lilliputians in which he wades and swims over to Blefuscu, terrifying the sailors, who flee back to land. He ties the boats together and then pulls them back across the channel. *See also* BIG-ENDIANS AND LITTLE-ENDIANS, GULLIVER, LILLIPUTIAN.

On achieving the bar, Pascoe was gratified to be received like a Butcher of Broadway. 'Pete, honey!' cried Chung, heading towards him with lesser beings bobbing in her wake like the Blefuscudian navy behind Gulliver.
REGINALD HILL *Child's Play* 1987

Captain Bligh William Bligh (1754–1817) was a British naval officer. In 1787 he was chosen as captain of HMS *Bounty* on a voyage to Tahiti and the West Indies. In 1789 part of the crew, under the first mate, Fletcher Christian, mutinied, setting Bligh and eighteen crew adrift in an open boat with few supplies and no charts. They succeeded in sailing to Timor, a journey of nearly 4 000 miles. Two films about this event, both entitled *The Mutiny on the Bounty* (1935, 1962), have depicted Bligh as a domineering tyrant.

According to Peasemarch, his butler, with whom I correspond, his manner

towards her is still reminiscent of that of Captain Bligh of the Bounty displeased
with the behaviour of one of the personnel.
P G. WODEHOUSE *Cocktail Time* 1958

Colonel Blimp Colonel Blimp is the name of a pompous, obese, elderly
character invented by the cartoonist David Low during the Second World
War. His name has come to represent anyone with reactionary Establishment
opinions, inflexible in his opposition to anything new.

'Well, he's a damn sight more interesting than Colonel Blimp,' Miriam said.
'He's a sensible generous warm-hearted man. Not a stuffed shirt trying to find
something to do to fill in his retirement.'
PHILIPPA GREGORY *Perfectly Correct* 1997

Blind Pew In R. L. Stevenson's *Treasure Island* (1883), Blind Pew is the sinister
blind pirate, the 'horrible, soft-spoken, eyeless creature', whose approach is
signalled by the tapping of his stick along the road. It is Pew who delivers the
dreaded 'Black Spot' to the old captain at the Admiral Benbow inn, and who
leads the pirates' attack on the inn. He is abandoned by his companions,
however, and is trampled to death by a horse.

Blondel According to tradition, Blondel de Nesle, a French poet, was the
friend of Richard I of England, known as Richard Cœur de Lion. Blondel set
out to find the king after Richard, returning from the Holy Land in 1192, was
imprisoned by the duke of Austria. Sitting under the castle window, Blondel
sang a song in French that he and the king had composed together. Half-way
through, Richard took the song up himself to reveal his whereabouts.

Two ground-floor windows, three upstairs, all shuttered. . . . I felt like Blondel
beneath Richard Cœur-de-Lion's window; but not even able to pass messages
by song.
JOHN FOWLES *The Magus* 1977

Bloody Tower The Bloody Tower is a nickname for a part of the Tower of
London, built in 1377–99. It derived its name from the belief that it was the
place where the Princes in the Tower were murdered. It also housed famous
prisoners such as Sir Walter Ralegh.

Leopold Bloom James Joyce's novel *Ulysses* (1922) charts the wanderings of
Leopold Bloom, a Jewish advertisement canvasser, and Stephen Dedalus, a
young poet, around Dublin on 16 June 1904. The various chapters roughly
correspond to the episodes of Homer's *Odyssey*, with Bloom representing
Odysseus and Stephen, Telemachus. In the course of the story, a public bath,
a cemetery, a newspaper office, a library, public houses, a maternity hospital,
and a brothel are visited.

As a youth, he worked variously as a bricklayer, coffin-polisher and artist's
model at the local college of art. The milk round, however, was special; it

offered him a daily, Bloom-like odyssey of Edinburgh and he grew to know its streets so well that even when he had left it far behind, he would be able to trace its contours in his head. *The Guardian* 1998

Bluebeard Bluebeard is a character in a tale by Charles Perrault in the collection *Histoires et contes du temps passé* (1697). In the story, Bluebeard has a reputation for marrying women who subsequently disappear. He leaves his most recent wife, Fatima, in charge of their house while he is away, instructing her not to open a locked room in the house, although he leaves her the key. Overcome with curiosity, she opens the room, only to discover the bodies of his previous wives. Any murderous husband can be described as a Bluebeard. Bluebeard's Castle is referred to as a place of danger, where grisly deeds are performed.

I lingered in the long passage to which this led, separating the front and back rooms of the third story: narrow, low, and dim, with only one little window at the far end, and looking, with its two rows of small black doors all shut, like a corridor in some Bluebeard's castle.
CHARLOTTE BRONTË *Jane Eyre* 1847

'It'll be his wife,' said the woman, peering at the Doctor in awe and horror. 'Murdered his wife! You Bluebeard!'
HUGH LOFTING *Dr Dolittle's Circus* 1924

This is one of the strangest cases this court may ever have heard. The case of a Bluebeard who kept his wife a virtual prisoner in their flat in Muswell Hill.
JOHN MORTIMER *Rumpole of the Bailey* 1978

It slides easily into the serrated slit of the lock, and I cannot suppress the light thrill that runs down my spine. It is like entering a story, something by Grimm, Bluebeard's Castle.
ANDRÉ BRINK *Imaginings of Sand* 1996

Bluebottle Bluebottle was a character in *The Goon Show*, an extremely popular BBC radio comedy series which ran from 1952 to 1960. Bluebottle, played by Peter Sellers, spoke in a comical high-pitched, whiny voice.

Enid Blyton Enid Blyton (1897–1968) was a prolific author of children's books, including the Noddy books, series such as the Famous Five and the Secret Seven, and school stories such as the Malory Towers series. The majority of her books were published in the 1940s and 1950s, and they can now be alluded to as depicting an era of idealized childhood innocence.

Boadicea *See* BOUDICCA.

Boeotian Boeotia was a district of ancient Greece known for the stupidity of its inhabitants. Hence a Boeotian can mean a stupid person.

An opportunity . . . which I should have been a Bœotian indeed had I neglected.
JOHN GIBSON LOCKHART *Valerius* 1821

Bohemia Bohemia was formerly a central European kingdom, now forming the western part of the Czech Republic. The name is often applied to any district frequented by artists, writers, and other socially unconventional people.

This, in the social order, is the diversion, the permitted diversion, that your original race has devised: a kind of superior Bohemia, where one may be respectable without being bored.
EDITH WHARTON *The Custom of the Country* 1913

Napoleon Bonaparte Napoleon Bonaparte (1769–1821) was born in Ajaccio, Corsica, and commissioned in the French army in 1785, where he quickly rose in seniority, being made commander of the army of Italy in 1796. He became involved in a *coup d'état* against the Directorate, the French political regime, and in the new regime became first consul of the three ruling consuls, later being elected first consul for life, and finally assuming the title of emperor in 1804. He conquered and ruled much of Europe until his final defeat at the battle of Waterloo in 1815. Napoleon can be alluded to as someone who wields great power.

With his expertise, energy and international contacts, he could really put Rummidge on the map, and that would be kind of fun. Morris began to project a Napoleonic future for himself at Rummidge.
DAVID LODGE *Changing Places* 1975

Gaëtan has very thickly fringed eyes with light-grey irises; into which, because of his height, one looks down. I always find being taller than him disconcerting. He knows it and uses it for his greater success, for he imposes himself, Napoleonically, on his surroundings.
ELIZABETH IRONSIDE *Death in the Garden* 1995

Another, Orlando Figes, has accused him of being a man of 'Bonapartist ambitions'. *The Independent* 1997

James Bond James Bond is the secret agent 007 in the novels by Ian Fleming and a series of highly successful films. His 'double-0' code number indicates that he is licensed to kill. Bond is a suave and resourceful hero, with a taste for fast cars and beautiful women, who likes his vodka dry martini to be 'shaken and not stirred'. Many of the films based on Fleming's novels feature sophisticated gadgets and include a scene in the villain's vast, often subterranean, high-tech headquarters or control room.

He was still lightheaded, and grew more so as he sipped his Bintang. Then he realised, he said, that she had managed to put something in his beer: some

drug. I laughed at this. Too much James Bond, I suggested.
CHRISTOPHER J. KOCH *The Year of Living Dangerously* 1978

In the far distance stand large buildings where, presumably, workers in white space suits wander around in rooms that look like something out of a James Bond film.
BILL BRYSON *The Lost Continent* 1989

But forget flashy cars with ejector seats, or fountain pens packed with explosives. The real-life 007s in Robin Cook's 'refocused' SIS may find a bottle of mosquito repellent more useful in their new mission: to combat Asia's ruthless drug traffickers. *The Independent* 1997

This is particularly true following the manager's decision to make a playing comeback at the age of 40. There are already signs it could produce a Coventry rescue act of which any James Bond would be proud. *The Observer* 1997

Brom Bones In Washington Irving's story 'The Legend of Sleepy Hollow' (1820), Brom Bones impersonates a ghostly headless horseman, using a pumpkin and a hat for the head that he is supposedly carrying, to scare off his rival suitor, Ichabod Crane. *See also* SLEEPY HOLLOW.

Bonnie and Clyde Bonnie Parker (1911–34) and Clyde Barrow (1909–34) were the leaders of a gang in the United States who conducted a series of robberies and murders. They were shot dead in their car by police in Louisiana in 1934. A film presenting a rather glamorized version of their lives, *Bonnie and Clyde* (1967), ends with a memorable slow-motion sequence depicting their bodies jerking and falling in a barrage of gunfire.

Determined to defend her honour, the couple are soon on the run pursued by all and sundry— a modern day Bonnie and Clyde. *Film Focus* 1994

These wackos are attention-seekers. Serial show-offs. I mean, for Christ's sake, making out against a Slurpy Pup in front of a bunch of bullet-riddled shoppers! They think they're some kind of twenty-first-century Bonnie and Clyde.
BEN ELTON *Popcorn* 1996

Bonnie Prince Charlie Charles Edward Stuart (1720–88), known as the Young Pretender or Bonnie Prince Charlie, was the son of James Stuart and pretender to the British throne. After spending some time in exile in France, he returned to Scotland and led the Jacobite uprising of 1745–6, invading England and advancing as far as Derby. However, he was driven back to Scotland and defeated at the battle of Culloden. He again escaped to France and died later in exile in Rome. Bonnie Prince Charlie became the subject of much romantic literature, and his supporters always hoped that he would one day return and defeat the English.

But they would never find a leader. If there was some exiled prince of Chaka's blood, who came back like Prince Charlie to free his people, there might be danger; but their royalties are fat men with top hats and old frock coats, who live in dirty locations.

JOHN BUCHAN *Prester John* 1910

Book of Kells The Book of Kells is an illuminated manuscript of the Gospels kept at Trinity College, Dublin. It is thought to have been made on the island of Iona by Irish monks in the 8th or 9th century. Lavishly decorated with full-page illustrations, it is considered the most distinguished of the manuscripts of its type still extant.

Fogarty picked up the folder and opened it and looked at it for a moment as if he were studying the Book of Kells.

ROBERT B. PARKER *Thin Air* 1995

Daniel Boone Daniel Boone (1735–1820) was an American explorer, hunter, and frontiersman. He was born in Pennsylvania, then moved with his family to North Carolina. From there he travelled west, establishing a settlement in Boonesborough, and explored much of the state of Kentucky. Later, he moved to Missouri, claiming that Kentucky was 'too crowded'. The publication of *The Adventures of Daniel Boone* in 1784 established him as an American folk hero.

He watched his ma looking around for him. She didn't call any more, trying to slip up on him. Old chicken came in the door and looked at him. 'Goway, you old tattle tale,' he thought, but he was scared to move, scared to breathe. His ma went on off, 'round the house; he saw her going down the picket fence by Miss Mittybelle's sun flowers, going on to the store herself. He got up and peeped out the door, looking around. He felt like old Daniel Boone. Wasn't nobody in sight.

CHESTER HIMES *Mama's Missionary Money* 1949

Betty Boop Betty Boop was a glamorous, sexy, animated cartoon figure featuring in movies produced by Fleischer Studios in the 1930s. She has enormous eyes, long eyelashes, a rosebud mouth, and a short curly bob of hair. Dressed in a short, backless dress, she has adventures and sings musical numbers.

Her bangs are arranged in tiny spit curls around her face; an aging Betty Boop, down to the spidery eyelashes.

LISA SCOTTOLINE *Final Appeal* 1994

Lizzie Borden Lizzie Borden (1860–1927) was an American woman acquitted in 1893 of the charge of murdering her father and stepmother the previous year. Nevertheless, many believed that she had killed them, giving rise to a popular rhyme:
'Lizzie Borden took an axe
And gave her mother forty whacks;
When she saw what she had done

She gave her father forty-one!'

'I gather she's a fairly nice girl from a fairly nice family. Maybe not a happy girl,
her father said, but a girl you can depend on.' 'That's what Lizzie Borden's
father used to say about her.'
R. MCDONALD *The Underground Man* 1971

Boreas In ancient Greek literature, Boreas was a god, the personification of
the north wind.

The dusty drops of the Widow's chandelier were laced with gossamer cobwebs
and chimed and tinkled in the fierce draughts that gusted through Arden, as if
Boreas and Eurus were holding a competition somewhere in the vicinity of the
front hall or the great eagle Hraesvelg was flying up and down just to annoy
them.
KATE ATKINSON *Human Croquet* 1997

Borgias The Borgias were a Neapolitan family with Spanish origins. Alfonso
de Borgia (1378–1458) became pope as Calixtus III in 1455, and his nephew
Rodrigo succeeded him as Alexander VI in 1492. Cesare Borgia (1476–1507)
and Lucrezia (or Lucretia) Borgia (1480–1519) were two of Alexander's
children, born before he became pope. Cesare was a ruthless political and
military leader, and was said to be the model for the ruler in Machiavelli's
The Prince. His father made him a cardinal in 1493 and subsequently the duke
of Romagna. His name is popularly associated with ruthless plotting and the
use of poison to dispatch his enemies. Lucrezia, for her part, is alleged to
have committed incest with both her father and her brother. Although her
court became a centre for Renaissance artists, poets, and scientists, she has
acquired, probably unfairly, her brother's reputation for intrigue and
poisoning.

I'm not talking hot air, my friend. I happen to know every detail of the hellish
contrivance, and I can tell you it will be the most finished piece of
blackguardism since the Borgias.
JOHN BUCHAN *The Thirty-Nine Steps* 1915

She makes that helpless gesture and has that goddamned headache and you
would like to slug her except that you are glad you found out about the
headache before you invested too much time and money and hope in her.
Because the headache will always be there, a weapon that never wears out and
is as deadly as the bravo's rapier or Lucrezia's poison vial.
RAYMOND CHANDLER *The Long Goodbye* 1953

I watched her recoiling from that poulet en casserole, as if it had been
something dished up by the Borgias.
P G. WODEHOUSE *Cocktail Time* 1958

All cabinets are riddled with frictions, but this lot seem to be consumed with
more feuds than the Borgias, and to have a similar penchant for poisoning as
the preferred method of bumping off rivals. *The Observer* 1997

Borodino The French army invaded Russia in 1812, during the Napoleonic Wars, and the Russians chose Borodino, 120 kilometres (74 miles) from Moscow, to challenge them. Napoleon threw his entire army at the Russians with initial success, but in time the Russians, unlike the French, were able to add reserves. The French eventually won through to continue their march to Moscow but took 33 000 casualties. The Russians withdrew with 44 000 casualties.

> Lisa carries in her spirit matters she knows not of. I find that interesting. I find that enthralling, indeed. I look at Lisa and wolves howl across the steppe, the blood flows at Borodino, Irina sighs for Moscow. All derivative, all in the mind—the confection of fact and fantasy that is how we know the world. Nevertheless, Lisa had a Russian grandfather, and that signifies.
> PENELOPE LIVELY *Moon Tiger* 1988

George Borrow George Borrow (1803–81) was an English writer and traveller. His travels in England, Europe, Russia, and the Far East provided material for his narrative of gypsy life, *Lavengro* (1851), and its sequel, *The Romany Rye* (1857). These works present a partly factual, partly fictional account of his travels.

> Staggering along the path like some lost shepherd, doubtless living out his own private dreams as Dr Johnson or George Borrow or somebody, came Councillor Duxbury himself, dabbing his streaming eyes and clutching his gnarled old stick.
> KEITH WATERHOUSE *Billy Liar* 1959

Borrowers *The Borrowers* (1952) by Mary Norton is the story of Pod, Homily, and Arrietty, a family of tiny people living beneath the floors of an old country mansion. They 'borrow' everything they need from the household of the 'human beans' above them.

Hieronymus Bosch Hieronymus Bosch (*c.*1450–1516) was a Flemish painter whose allegorical works are filled with grotesque creatures, horribly ugly people, and macabre images, often set in strange hell-like landscapes. Bosch's caricature-like faces are typically deformed, bloated, cadaverous, or disease-ridden.

> He still wasn't entirely happy about Goodenough's sexual inclinations. 'If you'd seen that gay bar,' he told Vera. 'I mean I don't care what people do but it was like a vision of Hell by Hieronymus Bosch.'
> TOM SHARPE *Grantchester Grind* 1995

> Hardcastle fixed me with her reptilian eyes. If Hieronymus Bosch had turned his talents to gargoyles, Hilary Hardcastle would have been one of his most treasured creations.
> DEXTER DIAS *False Witness* 1995

Boston Tea Party The Boston Tea Party is the name given to a violent demonstration by American colonists in 1773, prior to the War of American

Independence. As a protest against the imposition of a tax on tea by the British parliament, in which they had no representation, the colonists dressed as American Indians, boarded three British ships moored in the harbour of Boston, Massachusetts, and threw overboard their cargo of tea.

Botticelli Sandro Botticelli (1445–1510), born Alessandro di Mariano Filipepi, was a Florentine painter of religious and mythological subjects, whose work includes such paintings as *Primavera* ('Springtime', *c.*1478) and *Birth of Venus* (*c.*1480). Botticelli is known for the delicate beauty of his Madonnas and goddesses and for his gracefulness of line. His women usually have pale skin and long, wavy, fair hair.

As Miriam sang her mouth seemed hopeless. She sang like a nun singing to heaven. It reminded him so much of the mouth and eyes of one who sings beside a Botticelli Madonna, so spiritual.
D. H. LAWRENCE *Sons and Lovers* 1913

With great gentleness he moved towards the hospitable regions of her being, towards the peaceful fields of her interior landscape, where white flowers placed themselves against green backgrounds as in Botticelli paintings of spring.
ANAÏS NIN *Children of the Albatross* 1947

She had, yes, I suppose a Botticelli beauty, long fair hair, grey violet eyes.
JOHN FOWLES *The Magus* 1966

Anthea had a face like a Botticelli Venus, a Beauty Queen's body, and a dignified manner.
A. S. BYATT *The Virgin in the Garden* 1978

Boudicca Boudicca or Boadicea (d. AD 62) was queen of the Iceni tribe of Britons living in East Anglia. After her husband, Prasutagus, died in AD 60, the Romans broke the treaty he had made, annexing Iceni land. Boudicca led a revolt against the Romans, succeeding in sacking Colchester (Camulodonum) and London (Londinium), and razing St Albans (Verulamium) to the ground. The Iceni were defeated by the Roman governor of Britain, Suetonius Paulinus, and two legions. An enduring popular image of Boudicca is that of her standing, in armour, driving a chariot.

'And I had a poker. Don't think I wouldn't have used it.' I had an explosive mental picture of her thrashing out like an elderly Boudicca.
SARAH LACEY *File under: Deceased* 1992

'I told that last woman I'd have her if I saw anything in the papers,' he said. 'Sue her for libel.' 'Which last woman?' 'That one came down from London. Boadicea type, waving banners and papers at me.'
SUSAN MOODY *Grand Slam* 1994

The only textbooks for private eyes are on the fiction shelves, and I don't remember ever reading one that told me how to interrogate an eight-year-old without feeling like I was auditioning for the Gestapo. It didn't help that Alexis

was standing in the doorway like a Scouse Boadicea, arms folded, a frown on her face, ready to step in as soon as I stepped out of line.
VAL MCDERMID *Crack Down* 1994

Lady Bountiful Lady Bountiful is a wealthy character in George Farquhar's comedy *The Beaux' Stratagem* (1707). Her name can be used to describe a woman whose generosity is coupled with a certain degree of condescension.

Approaching, he heard her say in her kindly Lady Bountiful manner, 'You must come and have dinner with us one day. I've got a lot of books that might interest you.'
GRAHAM GREENE *The Heart of the Matter* 1948

Lindsay arrived back with refreshments for everyone—Lord Bountiful dispensing alms to the poor, Fizz thought ungratefully—and whistled in the rest of the Am Bealach contingent to partake.
JOYCE HELM *Foreign Body* 1997

Bounty The *Bounty* was a British navy ship which, in 1789, was bound from Tahiti to the Cape of Good Hope and the West Indies under the command of Captain Bligh. Some members of the crew, led by Fletcher Christian, mutinied and set the captain and eighteen companions adrift in an open boat. The mutineers returned to Tahiti and from there some of them went on to Pitcairn Island, where they formed a colony. Bligh and his companions managed to reach Timor in the East Indies, nearly 4 000 miles away. The episode was popularized by two films, made in 1935 and 1962, both called *The Mutiny on the Bounty. See also* CAPTAIN BLIGH.

Emma Bovary Emma Bovary, in Flaubert's novel *Madame Bovary* (1857), is married to a country doctor in provincial Normandy. Aspiring to a more romantic and sophisticated life, she is drawn into first one affair and then a second. When the second affair ends because her lover, Léon, has tired of her, she kills herself with arsenic.

Bowery Boys A series of comic B movies produced between 1946 and 1958 featured the Bowery Boys, a group of layabouts from Brooklyn. The 'boys' were played by Leo Gorcey, Huntz Hall, Gabriel Dell, Bobby Jordan, David Gorcey, Bernard Gorcey, Billy Benedict, and Benny Bartlet. The earlier films, in the 1940s, were gangster melodramas. Later, they descended into slapstick.

Casey was not impressed with Hookshot's office, either. The midtown news kiosk was shabby and festooned with cheesy tabloids. It looked its age. 'Oh, brother,' Casey muttered as they got out of the cab. 'I've never seen a news stand that beat up.' 'Relax, will you?' R.J. told her. 'It looks like a Bowery Boys set.'
STEPHEN BOGART *Play it Again* 1994

Boy's Own The *Boy's Own Paper* was a popular boys' magazine sold in the late 19th and early 20th century. Founded by W. H. G. Kingston and published from 1879 until 1967, the magazine contained exciting adventure stories with titles such as 'From Powder Monkey to Admiral' and 'How I Swam the Channel'.

> But Jack Keane had always been the stuff of *Boy's Own Paper*; fearless, handsome, acclaimed for defending the rights of ordinary people against the big battalions of the rich and powerful.
> MICHAEL MALLOY *Cat's Paw* 1993

> Pointless his journey may have been, but it is still an exhilarating *Boys' Own* adventure story.
> SEBASTIAN SHAKESPEARE *Literary Review* 1994

Lady Bracknell In Oscar Wilde's comedy *The Importance of Being Earnest* (1895), Lady Bracknell is Gwendolen Fairfax's mother. In a famous scene Gwendolen's suitor, Jack Worthing, explains that he was discovered as a baby in a handbag, to which Lady Bracknell responds 'A handbag?' The incredulous, withering delivery of this line by Edith Evans in the 1952 film of Wilde's play is well known and often imitated.

> 'Why are you walking around with it in your handbag?' he demanded, giving Lady Bracknell a run for her money.
> VAL MCDERMID *Clean Break* 1995

> 'The reason I came to tell you about it tonight was to warn you that you will almost certainly be woken at dawn by drumming.' 'Drumming?' bellowed the dean, giving the word an emphasis and inflexion reminiscent of Lady Bracknell and the handbag.
> RUTH DUDLEY EDWARDS *Murder in a Cathedral* 1996

> 'I am not of the habit,' she snapped, 'of keeping staff and doing the cooking myself.' A touch of the Lady Bracknells; a strictly amateur production there, I thought.
> RAYMOND FLYNN *Busy Body* 1998

Brady Bunch The *Brady Bunch* was an American television series about the family of a second marriage between a widow and widower. The wife, Carol, had three daughters while the husband, Mike, had three sons. The family lived in suburbia, where the parents presided over good-natured tussles between the children, all accompanied by cheerful shiny-white-toothed smiles. The series was shown between 1969 and 1974 in the United States and on ITV from 1970 to 1973. It was succeeded by several sequels.

> She was a pharmacist's daughter who grew up in the Kmart/Long John Silver/ Brady Bunch culture of suburban Americana.
> SHARYN MCCRUMB *The Hangman's Beautiful Daughter* 1996

> Mrs Morley gave Mai the nod and she swayed her non-existent hips into Jack's office. The door shut firmly behind her and the entire office ceased operations,

their ears stretched off the sides of their heads as they hoped, longed, yearned for a row. But seconds later Jack and Mai emerged, smugly holding hands. Watched by a hungry-eyed throng they made their Brady-Bunch way to the exit, and then they were gone.
MARIAN KEYES *Sushi for Beginners* 2000

Marlon Brando Marlon Brando (1924–2004) was an American actor whose films include *A Streetcar Named Desire* (1951), *On the Waterfront* (1954), and *The Godfather* (1972). A leading exponent of method acting, he was particularly associated with the mumbling delivery of his lines.

Colin the Englishman is distrusted because he talks not too much but too well. Real painters grunt, like Marlon Brando.
MARGARET ATWOOD *Cat's Eye* 1988

Bray *See* VICAR OF BRAY.

St Brendan St Brendan (484–577) was an Irish abbot. The *Navigatio Brendani* (The Navigation of St Brendan, *c.*1050) recounts the story of a voyage made by St Brendan and a band of monks to a land of saints far to the north and west of Ireland, possibly Orkney or the Hebrides.

Brer Rabbit Brer Rabbit is the trickster hero of many of the tales told by Uncle Remus in Joel Chandler Harris's various volumes of folklore tales published between 1881 and 1910. He can be alluded to as someone who is used to enduring hardships and deprivation and will use their wits to survive. *See also* TAR BABY.

Dusty ride, isn't it? I don't mind it myself; I'm used to it. Born and bred in de briar patch, like Br'er Rabbit.
WILLA CATHER *A Death in the Desert* 1905

Brigadoon Brigadoon is a Broadway musical by Lerner and Loewe set in Scotland, where a village, Brigadoon, lies under an enchantment that makes it invisible to the rest of the world except for one day every hundred years. Two American visitors, Tommy Albright and Jeff Douglas, arrive on the appropriate day and discover the village. Tommy falls in love with local girl Fiona, but if she leaves with him, Brigadoon will be lost for ever; if he stays, he will be cut off for ever from his family, friends, and normal life. The show takes place in a grotesquely stereotypical version of Scotland featuring kilts, bagpipes, and Highland flings. A film of the musical starring Gene Kelly was made in 1954.

Isle Royale was like a place out of time, out of the ordinary run of lives. No one but the wild creatures really lived there. The human population appeared for six months out of each year, a full-blown society with the cops and robbers, houses and boats, shovels and Hershey bars, pumping gas and drinking vodka, making love and money. Then, October 19, humanity closed up shop and left the island to heal itself under the winter snows. A government-issue Brigadoon.

And what is known of the people of Brigadoon?
NEVADA BARR *A Superior Death* 1994

Kincaid left the motorway and soon reached the outskirts of Grantchester. The streets seemed eerily empty, with only the curls of smoke rising from the occasional chimney giving evidence that the village hadn't succumbed to some Brigadoon-like enchantment.
DEBORAH CROMBIE *Dreaming of the Bones* 1996

'For how long? The whole pattern is changing—who lives here and what they do. Out go the barns and in come the two-car garages and the shopping malls.' 'What do you want? Brigadoon? Christ, the towns along the river are half dead anyway. You been up the valley? Been to Hudson?'
NORA KELLY *Old Wounds* 1998

Britomart In the third book of Edmund Spenser's *The Faerie Queene* (1590, 1596) Britomart searches the world for Artegall, the knight of Justice. She is disguised as a knight wearing a helmet and armour. *See also* SPENSER.

If she was Belphoebe, Frederica, in a kind of brief knitted corselet of dark grey wool with a glitter in it, and boots with a metallic sheen, was Britomart, her hair itself cut into a kind of bronze helmet, more space-age, maybe, than Renaissance.
A. S. BYATT *The Virgin in the Garden* 1978

Brobdingnagian Brobdingnag is the land inhabited by giants in book II of Swift's *Gulliver's Travels* (1726). 'Brobdingnagian' can be used to describe anything that is gigantic in size or scale. *See also* GULLIVER, LILLIPUTIAN.

I felt a wish to quit the high road, which I had hitherto followed, and get in among those tilled grounds—fertile as the beds of a Brobdingnagian kitchen-garden—spreading far and wide even to the boundaries of the horizon.
CHARLOTTE BRONTË *The Professor* 1857

It was a pleasure, except that eating among these Brobdingnags, I felt for quite a while as though four inches had been clipped from my shoulders, three inches from my height, and for good measure, someone had removed my ribs and my chest had settled meekly in towards my back.
PHILIP ROTH *Goodbye, Columbus* 1959

Mighty Welsh muscleman Gary Taylor defends his title against 15 girthful Brobdingnagians in the soaring temperatures of an extinct South African volcano. *The Guardian* 1994

Miss Jean Brodie Muriel Spark's novel *The Prime of Miss Jean Brodie*, first published in 1961, tells the story of Miss Jean Brodie, an Edinburgh schoolmistress during the 1930s. She is a spinster with firm views on the education of young women, remembered for saying: 'I am putting old heads on your young shoulders . . . all my pupils are the crème de la crème.' She speaks in a distinctive polite, precise, and authoritative voice.

He left his post long enough to walk me to the gate. 'Sarge!' he yelled. One of the men by the door looked up. 'This is the Thayer girl's governess!' he called, cupping his hands. 'Thank you, Officer,' I said, imitating Miss Jean Brodie's manner.
SARA PARETSKY *Indemnity Only* 1982

Kevin would exclaim, 'Yoghurt! Steamed vegetables! Lots of fruit!—this is Miss Jean Brodie warning you!' Gabe would just smile feebly, sleep sand in his eyes.
EDMUND WHITE *Farewell Symphony* 1997

Brontë The Brontë sisters, Charlotte (1816–55), Emily (1818–48), and Anne (1820–49), together with their brother Branwell (1817–48), grew up in Haworth, Yorkshire, the children of an Irish curate. Their mother died in 1825, and they were then cared for by an aunt, Elizabeth Branwell. During their childhood, the siblings created imaginary worlds and wrote poetry, articles, and stories. The novels written by the sisters as adults (*Jane Eyre*, 1847, *Shirley*, 1849, and *Villette*, 1853, by Charlotte; *Agnes Gray*, 1847, and *The Tenant of Wildfell Hall*, 1848, by Anne; and *Wuthering Heights*, 1847, by Emily) address the emotional lives of their characters, who are capable of stong passions, in some cases associated with some violence. They combine romance with realism. Emily's work in particular, evokes the landscape of the moors to which she was deeply attached. *See also* HEATHCLIFF, JANE EYRE AND MR ROCHESTER, MRS ROCHESTER.

'You imagine that social precedence makes all that difference in women?' 'Yes, I do. The daughter of a county family is a finer being than any girl who can spring from the nomad orders.' 'Even supposing your nomads produce a Rachel or a Charlotte Brontë?' 'We are not talking of genius,' Peak replied.
GEORGE GISSING *Born in Exile* 1892

'In love?' The word implies a totality which was missing in my mistress, who resembled one of those ancient goddesses in that her attributes proliferated through her life and were not condensed about a single quality of heart which one could love or unlove. 'Possession' is on the other hand too strong: we were human beings not Brontë cartoons. But English lacks the distinctions which might give us (as Modern Greek does) a word for passion-love.
LAWRENCE DURRELL *Justine* 1957

If you lived up here, you supposed landscape was of the essence, you had a Brontësque sense of using it to think and perceive with but at the same time it was in the way.
A. S. BYATT *The Virgin in the Garden* 1978

Buster Brown Buster Brown was a US comic strip created by R. F. Outcault and published in the Sunday newspapers from 1902 until the 1920s. Buster Brown was a naughty little rich kid. His clothes inspired the 'Buster suit', which became a popular garment for young boys in the early years of the 20th century. This was a smock-like suit with a broad white collar.

He was about eight years old, with a pale, peaked face and a large, troubled

forehead. . . . Except for his Buster Brown collar, he was dressed like a man, in long trousers, vest and jacket.
NATHANIEL WEST *The Day of the Locust* 1939

John Brown John Brown (1800–59) was an American abolitionist who sought to free slaves by force. He was captured in 1859 after raiding a government arsenal at Harpers Ferry in Virginia in an attempt to arm runaway slaves and start an uprising. Brown was tried and executed, and became a martyr for abolitionists. He is remembered in the song 'John Brown's Body', which was popular in the North during the American Civil War.

Bruegel Pieter Bruegel (*c.*1525–69), known as Pieter Bruegel the Elder and nicknamed Peasant Bruegel, was a Flemish artist. Bruegel produced landscapes, religious allegories, and satirical paintings of peasant life, such as *Peasant Wedding Feast* (1566). His work displays a real interest in village customs combined with a satirical view of folly, vice, and the sins of the flesh. His name is sometimes spelt Brueghel or Breughel.

Daniel was without his uniform, in the fisherman's sweater and a vast shapeless black duffel coat, hooded and toggled, that he had bought at an army surplus store. It made him look, the enormous man, something like a Brueghel peasant.
A. S. BYATT 'The Human Element' in *The Virgin in the Garden* 1978

Brutus Marcus Junius Brutus (85–42 BC) was a Roman senator who, with Cassius, was a leader of the conspirators who assassinated Julius Caesar in AD 44. Caesar's dying words as he was stabbed by his friend Brutus are supposed to have been 'Et tu, Brute?' ('You too, Brutus?'). Brutus subsequently committed suicide after being defeated by Antony and Octavian at Philippi.

I rose to my feet with some of the emotions of a man who has just taken the Cornish Express in the small of the back. She was standing looking at me with her hands on her hips, grinding her teeth quietly, and I gazed back with reproach and amazement, like Julius Caesar at Brutus.
P G. WODEHOUSE *Laughing Gas* 1936

I heard the woman yell, 'Gaston! Get out here!' and then a man appeared and engulfed them both with bearlike arms. I had a sinking feeling as I watched them, like Brutus might've felt just before he stabbed Caesar.
JOHN DUNNING *The Bookman's Wake* 1995

Brynhild In Scandinavian mythology, Brynhild was a Valkyrie whom Sigurd won by penetrating the wall of fire behind which she lay in an enchanted sleep, from which he revived her. She corresponds in the *Nibelungenlied* to Brunhild, the wife of Gunther, who instigated the murder of Siegfried. As Brunnhilde she is one of the main characters in Wagner's operatic cycle *The Ring of the Nibelungs. See also* WAGNER.

Yul Brynner Yul Brynner (1915–85) was a US film star whose films include *The King and I* (1956) and *The Magnificent Seven* (1960), but he is probably remembered chiefly for his shaved head.

> A tall, cheerful man with a Yul Brynner hairstyle (he jokes of being 'follicly challenged'), a keen intellect and a penchant for icon-smashing, Mr. Braiden has become the guru of a back-to-basics movement that advocates turning conventional police culture and organization on its head. *Globe & Mail* 1994

John Buchan John Buchan (1875–1940) was a Scottish novelist chiefly remembered for his adventure stories, often featuring elaborate cross-country chases. Of these, the five thrillers featuring his hero Richard Hannay are perhaps the most popular, particularly *The Thirty-Nine Steps* (1915).

> At other times, Mary would have enjoyed the circumstances of their departure: they had elements of romantic adventure, as if lifted from a novel by John Buchan or Dornford Yates.
> ANDREW TAYLOR *Mortal Sickness* 1995

> In the old days it was Salt Lake Flats, Utah, now it's the Nevada desert. If you are British, and in the John Buchan tradition, you have to go abroad to enjoy the true spirit of speedy adventure. *The Observer* 1997

Buckingham Palace Buckingham Palace is the official residence of the British sovereign in Westminster, London. It was originally built as a town house for the first duke of Buckingham in 1703 and was purchased by King George III in 1762. It was substantially rebuilt in 1826 and became the official residence in 1837, when Queen Victoria came to the throne. It was expanded in 1847 and now has 19 state rooms, 52 principal bedrooms, 188 staff bedrooms, 92 offices, and 78 bathrooms. It can be alluded to as the height of aristocratic opulence and for its size.

> She and Lisa were on the sofa. Alice sat upright as though doing afternoon tea at Buckingham Palace, both feet squarely on the carpet, cup and saucer squarely in her lap. Lisa sat with her long legs tucked beneath herself, one long feline arm stretched out along the sofa's back.
> WALTER SATTERTHWAITE *At Ease with the Dead* 1993

> She had been enchanted by her night in the hotel: when you're young and poor and the best thing you've ever slept in was a $20 room by the railroad tracks, the Hilton must seem like Buckingham Palace.
> JOHN DUNNING *The Bookman's Wake* 1995

> You gotta be kidding. If I kept sign-in sheets from every audition I ever held, I'd have to move into Buckingham Palace just to stack them up.
> LINDSAY MARACOTTA *Playing Dead* 1999

Buddha The Buddha, born Siddhartha Gautama (*c*.563-*c*.480 BC), was an Indian religious teacher and the founder of Buddhism. Statues or pictures represent him in a state of tranquil meditation.

> The gorilla . . . sat like a hairy mystified Buddha on the shallow ledge.
> ALICE WALKER *Entertaining God* 1994

> Now his face was as serene as a Buddha.
> BARBARA PARKER *Suspicion of Guilt* 1995

> Dalziel nipped into a spot ahead of an old lady who scanned his screen furiously
> for a resident's disc, found none, started to get out of her car to remonstrate,
> glimpsed that huge face regarding her with a Buddha's benevolence, felt her
> road rage evaporate and drove on.
> REGINALD HILL *On Beulah Height* 1998

Bugs Bunny Bugs Bunny is a cartoon rabbit who first appeared in 1938 in a Warner Brothers animated cartoon and was more fully developed in 1940 in the film *A Wild Hare*. He has two prominent front teeth, wide white cheeks, and tall vertical ears. He successfully resolves his feuds with other characters using wit and resourcefulness and his trademark line is 'Eh. What's up, Doc?'

> It had sounded too loud and too careless to be any kind of lizard, and my
> immediate thought had been one of J.T.'s gophers coming up for air. I had a
> vision of a wide-eyed cartoon-type rodent with Bugs Bunny teeth and a 'What's
> up Doc?' kind of mischief.
> SARAH DUNANT *Snow Storms in a Hot Climate* 1988

John Bull *See under* JOHN.

Bulldog Drummond Bulldog Drummond is the hero of a series of stories by 'Sapper', published from 1920 onwards. Drummond is an ex-army officer who fights against the master criminal Carl Peterson.

Bull Run During the American Civil War, two battles were fought between the Union and Confederate armies at Manassas Junction in Virginia, near a stream named Bull Run. In the first battle in 1861 General Jackson's Confederate Army held off Union troops until relieved by reinforcements, in the process earning for Jackson the nickname Stonewall. In the second battle, General Robert E. Lee defeated the Union army, driving them from the battleground and forcing them to retreat to Washington, DC.

Mr Bumble Mr Bumble is the beadle of the parish in Dickens's *Oliver Twist* (1837–8) who makes the orphan Oliver's life a misery. He is a fat, pompous, petty tyrant. *See also* DICKENSIAN, OLIVER TWIST.

> He had fought in the open, like a man, against stupidity, and Bumbledom, and
> mediocrity, and he knew the world well enough to expect a bitter return.
> ROBERTSON DAVIES *Leaven of Malice* 1954

Bunbury Bunbury is the fictitious character invented by Algy Moncrieff in Wilde's *The Importance of Being Earnest* (1895) whose sickly disposition requiring visits from Algy provide a refuge for him when he wishes to avoid engagements in town, in particular to avoid his aunt, Lady Bracknell.

> 'I rather get the impression he'll be over to see you as soon as he gets a moment. Oh, and your sister phoned. One or the other of them—they hardly ever say—I told her you were in Norfolk. Norfolk's getting to be your Bunbury, isn't it?' Troy had need of a Bunbury. If there was one thing his life lacked it was a good, irrefutable Bunbury.
> JOHN LAWTON *Black Out* 1995

Archie Bunker Archie Bunker is the main character in the US television sitcom *All in the Family* shown on CBS from 1971 to 1991. The series derived from the British series *Till Death Us Do Part* and has approximately the same situation, that of a bigoted working-class man fighting with his daughter and son-in-law. Archie, a dock foreman, also rails at his downtrodden wife and his ethnic neighbours. It was succeeded by a sequel and two spin-offs. *See also* ALF GARNETT.

> I see guys getting tired of being put down as economic apes, as Archie Bunkers.
> STUDS TERKEL *American Dreams: Lost and Found* 1980

Bunker Hill Bunker Hill in Boston was the site of the first pitched battle of the American Revolution in 1775, where the American colonists were forced to retreat by superior British weaponry. Although the victory was British, the colonists' tenacity and the losses they inflicted on the British boosted the Americans' morale.

Billy Bunter Billy Bunter is the rotund schoolboy hero of a series of stories by Frank Richards set in a boys' public school called Greyfriars. The stories first appeared in the *Magnet* comic in 1908. Known as 'the Fat Owl of the Remove' on account of his large, round spectacles, Bunter has an obsessive love of 'tuck' and is willing to do anything, even steal from his friends, in order to obtain it.

> I took after my mother, and already at that age was inclined towards flab. (Yes, m'lud, you see before you a middling man inside whom there is a fattie trying not to come out. For he was let slip once, was Bunter, just once, and look what happened.)
> JOHN BANVILLE *The Book of Evidence* 1989

> She has turned my Romeo into a sad-eyed Billy Bunter who blinks his passions quietly when no one's looking. Oh, that his too, too solid flesh should melt.
> MINETTE WALTERS *The Scold's Bridle* 1994

> In 1953, the Tory government of Mr Churchill lifted the wartime rationing on sweets. That day I was violently sick. But not before consuming a quantity of toffee, chocolate, sherbet and gobstoppers with a Bunter-like passion.
> TRISTAN GAREL-JONES *The Observer* 1996

Paul Bunyan Paul Bunyan is an American folk hero, a giant lumberjack of tremendous strength, who was accompanied on his travels by Babe, a gigantic blue ox.

> The total aroma profile of the full malolactic wine . . . is huge. This is no wimp wine. It's Paul Bunyan, overalls and all. *Wine and Spirits* 1991

Buridan's ass Buridan, a French scholastic philosopher at the end of the 12th century, is credited with the following sophism: if a hungry ass were placed exactly between two haystacks in every respect equal, it would starve to death, because there would be no motive why it should go to one rather than to the other. 'Like Buridan's ass between two bundles of hay' is said of a person who cannot decide between two courses of action and who adopts neither.

> So she continued to brood and suffer, standing flat as Buridan's Ass between equal bundles of hay . . .
> ALEXANDER THEROUX *Adultery* 1987

Burne-Jones Edward Burne-Jones (1833–98) was an English painter and designer whose work was largely inspired by medieval legends and other literary themes. His paintings, in subdued tones and peopled by pale knights and damsels, evoke a romantic mythical dreamworld. He also produced many tapestry and stained-glass designs for William Morris's firm.

> A silly woman would say he looked romantic. He reminded you of one of the knights of Burne-Jones though he was on a larger scale and there was no suggestion that he suffered from the chronic colitis that afflicted those unfortunate creatures.
> W. SOMERSET MAUGHAM 'The Human Element' in *The World Over* 1951

burning bush According to the story in the Bible, God appeared to Moses in the form of a burning bush: 'And the angel of the Lord appeared to him in a flame of fire out of the midst of a bush; and he looked, and lo, the bush was burning, yet it was not consumed' (Exod. 3: 2).

> 'She has revelations. All this stuff about Darcy's Utopia is dictated to her, she claims, by a kind of shining cloud.' I laughed. I couldn't help it. 'Like God appearing to Moses in a burning bush, or the Archangel Gabriel to Mohammed as a shining pillar?' I asked.
> FAY WELDON *Darcy's Utopia* 1990

Butch Cassidy Butch Cassidy, whose real name was Robert Leroy Parker (1866–1937?), formed a gang called the Wild Bunch, which was responsible for numerous train and bank robberies and murders in the United States. Cassidy and his partner, the Sundance Kid, went to South America and it is not known what then happened to them or how they died. The film *Butch Cassidy and the Sundance Kid* (1969), starring Paul Newman and Robert

Redford, romanticized their lives and showed them dying by running from a hiding place into a hail of bullets.

Rhett Butler The dashing and charming Rhett Butler is the hero of Margaret Mitchell's novel *Gone with the Wind* (1936). The book was made into an immensely popular Hollywood film in 1939, with the role of Butler played by Clark Gable. Set at the time of the American Civil War, the book tells the story of Butler's romance with southern belle Scarlett O'Hara, and he has come to represent an archetype of the romantic hero. *See also* GONE WITH THE WIND, SCARLETT O'HARA.

Byron George Gordon, Lord Byron (1788–1824), was an English Romantic poet, famous for his passionate love affairs as much as for his poetry. His major works include *Childe Harold's Pilgrimage* (1812–18) and *Don Juan* (1819–24). He travelled widely in Europe, and left England permanently following a series of scandals, most notably the suggestion of incest with his sister, and problems with debts. In 1824 he joined the fight for Greek independence, but died of a fever before he saw any real fighting. Byron is often alluded to as one who led an unconventional, romantically adventurous life. One of the best-known portraits of the poet, by Richard Westall, shows Byron in profile with thick, curly, slightly tousled black hair. His name gives rise to the terms 'Byronic' and 'Byronism', which can suggest both passionate romanticism and libertinism.

He's got a streak of his father's Byronism. Why, look at the way he threw up his chances when he left my office; going off like that for six months with a knapsack, and all for what?—to study foreign architecture—foreign!
JOHN GALSWORTHY *The Man of Property* 1906

Head on, his widow's peak and the longish wavy blond hair that flowed back from it still looked . . . well, Byronic . . . rather than a bit lonely on the dome of his skull.
TOM WOLFE *The Bonfire of the Vanities* 1987

Mark Underhill looked Byronic in his oversized white shirt, his dark hair curling about the collar.
SHARYN MCCRUMB *The Hangman's Beautiful Daughter* 1996

Anyway, there I am on my own and who should turn up but, yes! Carl Phipps, all brooding and Byronic looking in a big coat.
BEN ELTON *Inconceivable* 1999

Byzantine The Byzantine Empire between the 4th and 15th centuries was characterized by highly ritualized politics and complex bureaucratic structures. The word 'Byzantine' has therefore come to be used to mean extremely convoluted and devious.

Now they saw each other a dozen times a month, if that. Their schedules

created Byzantine complications of timing.
BARBARA PARKER *Suspicion of Guilt* 1995

[They are] trying to cut 'bureaucracy' and claw power away from the Byzantine layers of local education administration. *The Observer* 1997

Caesar Caesar was the title given to Roman emperors from Augustus (63 BC–AD 14) to Hadrian (AD 76–138). The title is usually taken to refer to Julius Caesar (100–44 BC), who established the First Triumvirate in ancient Rome with Pompey and Crassus and became consul in 59. He commanded large parts of Gaul, extending Roman rule to the west, and invaded Britain in 55–54. Against Roman law, he brought his army back to Rome (49–48), successfully fought Pompey and the Senate, and was made dictator of the Roman Empire. *See also* RUBICON.

> I remember that my head was full of a text from the Psalms about not putting one's trust in horses. I prayed that this one horse might be an exception, for he carried more than Caesar and his fortunes.
> JOHN BUCHAN *Prester John* 1910

> He surveyed their business, unsmiling, like a stout imperious Caesar.
> P D. JAMES *Devices and Desires* 1989

> 'I thought your piece on corruption in the health service was first class,' said the figure at the bar. 'Praise from Caesar,' smiled the younger man beside him.
> KEN MCCLURE *Requiem* 1992

Caesar's wife When it was suggested that Pompeia, wife of Julius Caesar, was having an extramarital affair, Caesar divorced her saying that, although he knew nothing of the affair, 'Caesar's wife must be above suspicion.' Caesar's wife may be invoked in the context of a person being required to behave in such a way that no suspicion of guilt can ever fall on them.

> Bradley, your conduct has given rise to rumours—and I hope for your sake they are no more than that—so unspeakably distasteful that . . . I mean Caesar's wife . . . hrump . . . that is, the Department must be above suspicion . . . certainly above such suspicions as you have seemingly aroused.
> WILLIAM BURROUGHS *The Naked Lunch* 1959

> 'You're forgetting Caesar's wife, Crosby.' Crosby double-declutched to give himself time to think. 'Who sir?' 'Caesar's wife. She was above suspicion.'
> CATHERINE AIRD *The Religious Body* 1966

Cagliostro Count Alessandro Cagliostro (1743–95), whose real name was Giuseppe Balsamo, was a charlatan and adventurer born in Palermo. He claimed to be able to grant everlasting youth to anyone who would pay him for his secret. Cagliostro was imprisoned for life by the Inquisition on the grounds of his association with freemasonry.

> Marat has a family? I mean a mother and a father and the usual things? The ordinary arrangement, the cook said. Odd, really, I never thought of Marat having a beginning. I thought he was thousands and thousands of years old, like Cagliostro. Can I see him?
> HILARY MANTEL *A Place of Greater Safety* 1992

James Cagney James Cagney (1899–1986) was an American film star. He was a talented and versatile actor although he is usually remembered chiefly for his roles as a tough gangster in films such as *The Public Enemy* (1931) and *White Heat* (1949). He won an academy award for his role as the vaudeville dancer George M. Cohan in *Yankee Doodle Dandy* (1942).

> Surely this mother must have taught him the difference between right and wrong and instilled into his infant bosom at least the rudiments of chivalry. . . . I know, if I was a mother, the very first thing I would do would be to put the offspring straight about the homage and deference which the male owes to the more delicate sex and give him the low-down on the iniquity of pulling this James Cagney stuff.
> P G. WODEHOUSE *Laughing Gas* 1936

> 'O.K. Where the hell do you think you're going babe?' 'That is pure Cagney.'
> REGINALD HILL *On Beulah Height* 1998

Cain In the book of Genesis, Cain was the first-born son of Adam and Eve who murdered his younger brother Abel. Cain was a tiller of the ground and Abel a keeper of sheep. When they brought their offerings to God, Abel's lamb was accepted but Cain's offering from his harvest was not. In jealous anger Cain killed his brother. God demanded an explanation for Abel's absence, to which Cain responded 'Am I my brother's keeper?' Once his crime was revealed, Cain was cursed by God for ever. He was cast out from his homeland and forced to live a life of vagrancy as an outcast for the rest of his life. God branded him with a mark, to indicate that no one should kill him and shorten his nomadic punishment. The phrase 'mark of Cain' has come to stand for the sign of a murderer.

> In this manner, Hester Prynne came to have a part to perform in the world. With her native energy of character and rare capacity, it could not entirely cast her off, although it had set a mark upon her, more intolerable to a woman's heart than that which branded the brow of Cain.
> NATHANIEL HAWTHORNE *The Scarlet Letter* 1850

> He never even seemed to come to his work on purpose, but would slouch in as if by mere accident; and when he went to the Jolly Bargemen to eat his dinner, or went away at night, he would slouch out, like Cain or the Wandering Jew, as if he had no idea where he was going and no intention of ever coming back.
> CHARLES DICKENS *Great Expectations* 1861

> 'If I had only got her with me—if I only had!' he said. 'Hard work would be

nothing to me then! But that was not to be. I—Cain—go alone as I deserve—an outcast and a vagabond.'
THOMAS HARDY *The Mayor of Casterbridge* 1886

Marks may not even have been his real name, she said; it should have been Mark, for the Mark of Cain, as he had a murderous look about him.
MARGARET ATWOOD *Alias Grace* 1996

Calamity Jane Calamity Jane was a nickname given to Martha Jane Burke (*c.*1852–1903), the famous American frontierswoman, because she is said to have warned that 'calamity' would come to any man who tried to court her. Often dressing in men's clothes, she was renowned for her skill at riding and shooting. Her name can be applied to any female prophet of disaster.

It wasn't hard to picture her in mud and trees and other uncivilized accoutrements. He'd never seen her anywhere else and wondered if he'd be disappointed should she ever turn up in Chicago in pantyhose, pumps and perfume; if the Calamity Jane aspect of the woman piqued a palate that had become slightly jaded.
NEVADA BARR *Firestorm* 1996

'It's dark back here,' Morelli said to Mary Lou. 'And you've just been contaminated by Calamity Jane. You're not getting out of sight until you're safely locked in your car.'
JANET EVANOVICH *High Five* 1999

Calchas In Greek mythology, Calchas was the wisest of the Greek soothsayers at the time of the Trojan War. He is supposed to have died of grief and disappointment after another soothsayer, Mopsus, was shown to be better than him at prophecy.

Caliban Caliban is a character in Shakespeare's *The Tempest* (1623). A brutish and misshapen monster, Caliban is the son of the witch Sycorax, and was the sole inhabitant of the island before Prospero's arrival. His name can be applied to a man of savage and bestial nature, or to the brutish side of human nature in general. *See also* SHAKESPEARE, SYCORAX.

He escorted them to their box with a sort of pompous humility, waving his fat jewelled hands, and talking at the top of his voice. Dorian Gray loathed him more than ever. He felt as if he had come to look for Miranda and had been met by Caliban.
OSCAR WILDE *The Picture of Dorian Gray* 1891

I was wrestling with my unconscious, an immense dark brother who seeped around me when I was awake, flowed over me when I slept . . . a force with a baby's features, greedy orifices, a madman's cunning and an animal's endurance, a Caliban as quicksilver as Ariel.
EDMUND WHITE *A Boy's Own Story* 1982

Caligula Gaius Caesar Germanicus (AD 12–41) was a Roman emperor, the son of Germanicus Caesar and Agrippina. His nickname, Caligula, came from the miniature military boots (*caligulae*) that he wore as a small child. He became emperor at a young age after the death of Tiberius in 37, and his brief reign was notorious for its cruelty and tyrannical excesses. Caligula was famously supposed to have given a consulship to his horse Incitatus.

> To my mind, his most serious competition [for BBC Sports Personality of the Year] comes from a couple of horses—Best Mate and Persian Punch—and keen as the British are on animals, I don't think they are ready to go the full Caligula and promote a nag to such a prestigious position. *The Observer* 2003

Calliope Calliope was one of the nine Muses in Greek mythology, associated especially with epic poetry. *See also* MUSES.

Calpurnia Calpurnia was the wife of Julius Caesar. In Shakespeare's play *Julius Caesar* (1623), Calpurnia begs Caesar not to go out because many strange or horrible portents have occurred and she believes he is in danger. She has dreamed of his statue,
'Which, like a fountain with an hundred spouts,
Did run pure blood.'
Caesar refuses to heed her warning and is assassinated.

Calvary Calvary, also known as Golgotha (both of which come from words, in Latin and Aramaic respectively, meaning the Place of the Skull), was the hill just outside Jerusalem where Jesus Christ was crucified. The word can be applied to any experience of intense mental suffering.

> In a very special, very private sense DeQuincey is your Cross and your marriage is your Calvary.
> EDMUND WHITE *A Boy's Own Story* 1982

> Of course, the FA Cup could still prove United's Calvary this season, as it nearly did in the third round against Sunderland, who led at Old Trafford and Roker Park. *The Guardian* 1996

John Calvin John Calvin (1509–64) was a French Protestant theologian and reformer, a leader of the Protestant Reformation in France and Switzerland. His name has come to be closely identified with strict puritanism and a rigid moral code.

> 'When did you get to be such a little Calvinist, anyway?' 'I'm not talking about sex; I'm talking about lying.'
> ARMISTEAD MAUPIN *Sure of You* 1990

> 'I never agreed with all that entertainment for the tourists,' the old man added. 'At least the gambling and whoring. I'm no Calvinist, but to me that's just dirty money.'
> PAUL JOHNSTON *Body Politic* 1997

> Hell and damnation: he knew about the very unofficial tapes. And Teddy with a

puritan conscience that made Messrs Knox and Calvin look flexible, even soft. Not the moment to be precipitate myself. Not the occasion for the full and frank admission.
RAYMOND FLYNN *Busy Body* 1998

Calydonian boar hunt In Greek mythology, when Artemis sent a huge boar to devastate the land of Calydon, its ruler, Meleager, assembled a band of heroes, including Castor and Pollux, Theseus, and Jason, to hunt the boar in what became known as the Calydonian boar hunt. Meleager himself killed the boar and gave the head to Atalanta, who had first wounded it. *See also* ATALANTA.

Calypso In Greek myth, Calypso was a nymph who lived on the island of Ogygia. When Odysseus was shipwrecked on the island, Calypso took him for her lover, offering him immortality if he would become her husband. She kept him on her island for seven years until Zeus intervened and ordered her to release him. Like the Sirens, Calypso can represent a woman who is dangerously attractive to men. *See also* ODYSSEUS.

Perhaps he had too fixed an idea of what a siren looked like and the circumstances in which she appeared—long tresses, a chaste alabaster nudity, a mermaid's tail, matched by an Odysseus with a face acceptable in the best clubs. There were no Doric temples in the Undercliff; but here was a Calypso.
JOHN FOWLES *The French Lieutenant's Woman* 1969

Camilla Camilla was a Volscian princess, dedicated when young to the service of Diana. A huntress and warrior, Camilla was so fast a runner she could run over a field of corn without crushing it, and over the surface of the sea without her feet getting wet.

Not so, when swift Camilla scours the Plain,
Flies o'er th'unbending Corn, and skims along the Main.
ALEXANDER POPE *An Essay on Criticism* 1711

Margaret ran, swift as Camilla, down to the window.
ELIZABETH GASKELL *North and South* 1854–5

Camille *Camille* is the title of several films based on the novel and play by Alexandre Dumas (*fils*) *La Dame aux camélias* (1852). The version starring Greta Garbo in 1936 followed six previous silent films. The story is that of the beautiful tubercular courtesan Marguerite Gautier who has a doomed love affair with the innocent young Armand Duval. Their romance cannot be sanctioned by society and his father persuades Marguerite to give up Armand for his own benefit. She dies of her disease (in the Garbo film, dying in Armand's arms). The story is also the basis for Verdi's *La Traviata*.

As she started to speak she coughed slightly, then, laughing, said, in a low, rich

voice, a trifle husky: 'You see I make the traditional Camille entrance—with the cough.'
WILLA CATHER *A Death in the Desert* 1905

'Look, most of what I know about Lily are things Beth told me.' 'Like?' 'Like Lily's weak heart. Like some great tragedy in Lily's life.' 'What?' 'Beth never said. That's one of the great things about Beth. When you confide a secret, it stays a secret. Personally, I always thought Lily laid the Camille routine on a bit thick. Especially around Beth who is much too trusting.'
SUSAN SUSSMAN with SARAJANE AVIDON *Audition for Murder* 1999

Canaan Canaan was the land, later known as Ancient Palestine, which the Israelites gradually conquered and occupied during the latter part of the second millennium BC. In the Bible, it was the land promised by God to Abraham and his descendants (Gen. 12: 7). By extension, the name Canaan can be applied to any promised land or to heaven.

Fresh green of the river bank; faded terra-cotta of the dining-room wallpaper, colours of distant Canaan, of deserted Eden.
EVELYN WAUGH *Scoop* 1938

Up there at the top of the hill, 161st Street and the Grand Concourse had been the summit of the Jewish dream, of the new Canaan, the new Jewish borough of New York, the Bronx!
TOM WOLFE *The Bonfire of the Vanities* 1987

Candaules King Candaules of Lydia (d. *c.*685 BC) continually praised his wife's beauty to his favourite officer, Gyges. Eventually, he insisted that Gyges should see the queen naked, in order to prove how beautiful she was. Though Gyges was to remain hidden, the queen realized what had happened and sent for Gyges, offering him the alternatives of killing the king and ruling with her as his wife or dying immediately. He opted for life and killed the king. *See also* GYGES.

'You are mistaken. What do you mean?' The reddleman had decided to play the card of truth. 'I was at the meeting by Rainbarrow last night and heard every word,' he said. 'The woman that stands between Wildeve and Thomasin is yourself.' It was a disconcerting lift of the curtain, and the mortification of Candaules's wife glowed in her.
THOMAS HARDY *The Return of the Native* 1880

'My observation has been that we get the women we deserve, King Candaules,' I said, 'And those who eat jam before breakfast are cloyed before bedtime.'
ROBERTSON DAVIES *The Deptford Trilogy* 1970

Candide Candide is the naive young hero of Voltaire's satire *Candide*, published in 1759. Accompanied by his tutor, Pangloss, who assures him repeatedly that 'all is for the best in the best of all possible worlds', Candide has many adventures and suffers many mishaps, often as a result of his ingenuous and trusting nature. Candide has become synonymous with youthful innocence and naivety. *See also* PANGLOSS.

> He plunged into the heart of Mayfair. The mist thickened, not so much to obscure all but sufficiently to give what he passed a slightly dreamlike quality; as if he was a visitor from another world, a Candide who could see nothing but obvious explanations.
> JOHN FOWLES *The French Lieutenant's Woman* 1969

Canute Canute (d. 1035) was a Danish-born king of England, Denmark, and Norway. According to the famous story, Canute reproved his flattering courtiers by demonstrating that, although he was king, he did not have the power to stop the incoming tide. He is traditionally remembered, however, as foolishly and obstinately attempting to command the advancing waves to stay back and failing. He has come to stand for an attempt to prevent change, particularly a futile attempt.

> 'Louise,' he called, 'Louise.' There was no reason to call: if she wasn't in the living-room there was nowhere else for her to be but the bedroom . . . yet it was his habit to cry her name, a habit he had formed in the days of anxiety and love. The less he needed Louise the more conscious he became of his responsibility for her happiness. When he called her name he was crying like Canute against a tide—the tide of her melancholy and disappointment.
> GRAHAM GREENE *The Heart of the Matter* 1948

> Fifty is OK if it looks like 36 in full camera make-up—step forward, Joan Collins, Goldie Hawn—but even the most imaginative and prestigious photographers find it hard to offer us any variety of woman at that age. Following the American model, you spend a great deal of your time, money and energy attempting, Canute-like, to hold back the tide of age. *The Independent* 1997

> The words are all so similar, so utterly useless really, that after a while they merge into a blur. It is not their fault; no one can say anything. Even the promise of a cross-border security summit, announced last night, sounds like King Canute's courtiers raging at the waves.
> JONATHAN FREEDLAND *The Guardian* 1998

Cape Horn Cape Horn is the extreme tip of South America. Bad weather and dangerous sea currents mean that it is very difficult to navigate safely round the cape.

> 'Did the sugar on the raspberry tarts you ate in your mouth taste the worse for being sweetened with the tear of slavery—for it should have tasted salt, but it did not. Did you think of the nigger who cut the cane? You did not. Merely to exist is to be involved in the system others have created to tend your daily needs.' 'Monstrous, Walter, monstrous.' 'There is a Cape Horn of the mind, too, which is as difficult to double as the real. Monstrous? Yes, I would allow that its waves are monstrous.'
> TIMOTHY MO *An Insular Possession* 1986

Al Capone Al (Alphonse) Capone (1899–1947) was notorious for his involvement in organized crime in Chicago in the 1920s. Though it was never possible to find sufficient evidence to convict him of his crimes, he was eventually imprisoned in 1931 for tax evasion. Capone died in prison.

> The Greek's muscles were dough-colored. You wouldn't have wanted him to take a headlock on you. That's the kind of man the Organization hired. The Capone people were now in charge.
> SAUL BELLOW *Something to Remember Me By* 1991

> 'There's no shortage of smart operators like Heriot 07 who get what they can from the city. They cover their arses. If they're spotted, they pay people off. Or arrange a good kicking.' 'Sounds like Chicago under Al Capone.'
> PAUL JOHNSTON *Body Politic* 1997

Frank Capra Frank Capra (1897–1991) was an Italian-born US film director. Many of his films, such as *Mr Deeds Goes to Town* (1936), *Mr Smith Goes to Washington* (1939), and *It's a Wonderful Life* (1946), celebrate the idea of the humble common man whose idealism, honesty, and goodness always triumph over materialism, deceit, and selfishness. Such a rose-tinted view of the world is sometimes referred to as 'Capraesque'.

> But all the activity went on without raised voices, and even the cars that circled the square did it quietly. There wasn't a loud muffler to be heard anywhere. The town was a Norman Rockwell painting come to life; a Frank Capra movie in 3-D and color.
> JOHN MADDOX ROBERTS *A Typical American Town* 1995

Capulet In Shakespeare's *Romeo and Juliet* (1599), Capulet is Juliet's quick-tempered father. He flies into a rage when his daughter refuses to marry Count Paris, violently berating her for her disobedience and threatening to drag her to the church if necessary. *See also* SHAKESPEARE.

Caravaggio Michelangelo Merisi da Caravaggio (*c.*1571–1610) was an Italian painter whose paintings are distinctive in their dramatic use of light and shade (chiaroscuro), often showing figures against a very dark background with light shining from one side or from below onto their faces.

> [The table] was lit by one tall lamp with a dark shade; the light flowed downwards, concentrated on the white cloth, and was then reflected up, lighting our faces strangely, Caravaggio fashion, against the surrounding darkness.
> JOHN FOWLES *The Magus* 1966

Carry On films The *Carry On* films were a series of British films, the first of which, *Carry On Sergeant*, was made in 1958 and the last in 1974. Starring comedians such as Sid James, Kenneth Williams, Barbara Windsor, and Hattie Jacques, the films were characterized by a combination of bawdy humour, bad puns, and slapstick comedy.

Barbara Cartland Barbara Cartland (1901–2000) was an English writer of light romantic fiction, which she produced prolifically over many years. Her popular romances include *Bride to a Brigand* (1983) and *A Secret Passage to Love* (1992).

Sidney Carton Sidney Carton is a lazy English barrister in Dickens's *A Tale of Two Cities* (1859) who loves Lucie Manette and strongly resembles Charles Darnay, whom she falls in love with and marries. When Darnay is imprisoned in Paris, about to face the guillotine, Carton sacrifices himself by taking Darnay's place in prison. On the scaffold, he utters the famous last words of the novel: 'It is a far, far better thing I do, than I have ever done; it is a far, far better rest that I go to, than I have ever known.' *See also* DICKENSIAN.

> Charles Courts' case came immediately after the one for selling clockwork parrots without a street trading licence. The tattered hawker went down from the dock and up came an almost equally tattered Charles. He was unshaven, his jacket minus several buttons and his shirt was held together by a safety pin. When the clerk of the court asked his name he gave it with the air of Sidney Carton at the guillotine, only gloomier.
> GILLIAN LINSCOTT *Stage Fright* 1994

Casanova Giovanni Jacopo Casanova de Seingalt (1725–98) was an Italian adventurer, spy, gambler, and librarian who, according to his *Memoirs*, engaged in a prodigious number of promiscuous love affairs.

> Everybody looked like a broken-down movie extra, a withered starlet; disenchanted stunt-men, midget auto-racers, poignant California characters with their end-of-the-continent sadness, handsome, decadent, Casanova-ish men, puffy-eyed motel blondes, hustlers, pimps, whores, masseurs, bellhops—a lemon lot, and how's a man going to make a living with a gang like that?
> JACK KEROUAC *On the Road* 1957

> She had satisfied herself that there was no Lady Chatterley situation in progress and that was all that interested her. She would have been quite staggered if the reverse had proved to be the case since, not only did Alistair have very little going for him in the Casanova department, but Rowena would need major surgery to uncross her legs.
> JOYCE HELM *Foreign Body* 1997

Casey Casey is the eponymous hero of the late 19th-century ballad 'Casey at the Bat' by Ernest L. Thayer. Casey was confidently expected to save the day in a baseball game but, having not even tried to hit the first two balls, he struck out on the third: 'There is no joy in Mudville—Mighty Casey has struck out.' The name can be used to refer to failure when success was confidently expected.

Cassandra In Greek mythology, Cassandra was a daughter of Priam, king of Troy. Apollo loved her and gave her the gift of prophecy. When she resisted his advances, he turned the gift into a curse by ensuring that, although her prophecies were true, they would not be believed. Cassandra foretold the fall of Troy and the death of Agamemnon, fulfilled when his wife, Clytemnestra, murdered him. The name Cassandra can be used to describe anyone whose warnings go unheeded.

> But Cassandra was not believed, and even the wisdom of *The Jupiter* sometimes falls on deaf ears.
> ANTHONY TROLLOPE *Barchester Towers* 1857

> Times of change, disruption, and revolution are naturally times of hope also, and not seldom the hopes of something better to come are the first tokens that tell people that revolution is at hand, though commonly such tokens are no more believed than Cassandra's prophecies.
> WILLIAM MORRIS *News from Nowhere and Other Writings* 1886

> 'I suppose my day wasn't as bad as yours,' Laurie said. 'But I'm beginning to understand how Cassandra felt when Apollo made sure that she was not to be heeded.'
> ROBIN COOK *Blindsight* 1993

Cassidy *See* BUTCH CASSIDY.

Cassius Gaius Cassius Longinus (d. 42 BC) was a praetor in ancient Rome who allied himself with the aristocrats who opposed Julius Caesar. He managed to enlist Marcus Brutus to be a part of a conspiracy, of which they were joint leaders, to assassinate Caesar in AD 44. After Caesar's death, he had to flee Rome and, defeated with Brutus at Philippi by Antony and Octavian, he ordered his freeman to kill him.

> Maxwell could be as conspiratorial as Cassius when he had a mind.
> M. J. TROW *Maxwell's Movie* 1998

Castalia In Greek mythology, the Castalian spring was a spring on Mount Parnassus that was sacred to Apollo and to the Muses, and its waters were said to have the power of inspiring the gift of poetry in those who drank of them. *See also* MUSES.

> A stream of prophecy, which rivalled the truth and reputation of the Delphic oracle, flowed from the Castalian fountain of Daphne.
> EDWARD GIBBON *History of the Decline and Fall of the Roman Empire* 1781

Castor and Pollux In Greek and Roman mythology, Castor and Pollux (or Polydeuces) were the twin sons (also known as the Dioscuri, *Dios kouroi*, 'sons of Zeus') born to Leda, wife of Tyndareus, after her seduction by Zeus. They were believed to have hatched from a single egg. Castor was the son of Tyndareus and was mortal; Pollux was the son of Zeus and was immortal. When Castor was killed, Pollux offered to share his immortality between them, spending half their time below the earth with Hades and the other half on Olympus. They were eventually transformed by Zeus into the constellation Gemini so that they would not be separated.

> They operated in perfect, entwined counterpoint—a diplomatic Castor and Pollux.
> ED VULLIAMY *The Observer* 1997

Catch-22 Joseph Heller's 1961 novel *Catch-22* deals with the dilemma of an American airforce bombardier who wishes to avoid combat duty. In order to do so, he has to be adjudged insane, but since anyone wishing to avoid combat duty is obviously sane, he must therefore be fit for duty. A Catch-22 is therefore any situation or dilemma from which there is no escape because of two mutually incompatible conditions.

> 'Our particular problem is that until we can find some witnesses, we can't prove it was murder and not suicide, and we can't get the manpower to do the sort of investigation we need to find witnesses until we can show that it was murder.' 'Catch twenty-two,' Mackay said triumphantly.
> CYNTHIA HARROD-EAGLES *Blood Lines* 1996

> Some say debt relief undermines a country's credit worthiness. This is a classic Catch 22 because we know that while countries remain heavily indebted they find it hard to attract investment. *The Observer* 1997

Cato Marcus Porcius Cato (234–149 BC), known as Cato the Elder or Cato the Censor, was a Roman statesman, orator, and writer. As censor in 184 BC he was vigorously opposed to luxury and decadence and tried to restore simplicity to Roman life. He became convinced that Rome would never be safe until Carthage was destroyed, ending all his speeches in the Senate with the words 'Delenda est Carthago' ('Carthage must be destroyed'). His name is associated with severity and austerity in matters of morality.

> Seduced by an ageing libertine, Mr Quarles's mistresses were surprised to find themselves dining with a Hebrew prophet, and taking their amusements with a disciple of Cato or of Calvin.
> ALDOUS HUXLEY *Point Counter Point* 1928

> Other editors, who were disguised neither as preachers nor as farmers, donned newsprint togas and appeared as modern Catos, ready to shed the last drop of their ink in defence of those virtues which they believed to be the exclusive property of the party not in power.
> ROBERTSON DAVIES *Leaven of Malice* 1954

Holden Caulfield Holden Caulfield is the adolescent hero of J. D. Salinger's novel *The Catcher in the Rye*, published in 1951. He is an archetypal adolescent rebel, full of angst and disaffection and rebelling against all that is 'phoney', 'corny', and 'old bull'. After being expelled from an expensive private school, Caulfield goes to New York, but after a series of unsuccessful adventures, including an encounter with a prostitute and an abortive reunion with an old girlfriend, he is forced to go back home and is sent by his parents for psychiatric treatment.

cavalry In many old American Western films, the US cavalry arrives just in time to save the heroes from certain death. Someone who arrives to help out in the nick of time can be described as being like the cavalry.

> 'If you don't have a way to lock your door, I can bring some tools and maybe scare up a new lock and—' 'That's okay,' I said. 'Thanks anyhow, but there's a padlock and a hasp I can still use.' 'You're sure now?' 'I'm positive,' I said firmly. Kidd had blatantly eavesdropped on the whole conversation and he was smiling broadly. 'More cavalry to the rescue, Ms Judge?'
> MARGARET MARON *Shooting at Loons* 1994

> Put a roadblock at the other end of the lane. If I don't contact you within five minutes, send in the cavalry.
> PAUL JOHNSTON *Body Politic* 1997

St Cecilia St Cecilia (2nd or 3rd century) was a Roman martyr. According to legend, she took a vow of celibacy but was forced to marry a Roman. She converted her husband to Christianity, and both were martyred. She is frequently pictured playing the organ and is the patron saint of church music.

> They have combined their voices, such as they are, even if they could be supposed to be 'parlor voices', 'thin voices', 'poor voices' or any other kind of voice than St. Cecilia's own. *Harper's Monthly* 1880

Celestial City In John Bunyan's religious allegory *The Pilgrim's Progress* (1678, 1684), Christian undertakes a pilgrimage to the Celestial City, encountering on the way such adversaries as Giant Despair and Apollyon, the foul fiend. When he finally arrives at the Celestial City, set on a hill, and the gates are opened, he sees that 'it was builded of pearls and precious stones, also the street thereof was paved with gold'. *See also* PILGRIM'S PROGRESS.

> Gold and purple clouds lay on the hilltops, and rising high into the ruddy light were silvery white peaks that shone like the airy spires of some Celestial City.
> LOUISA M. ALCOTT *Little Women* 1868

centaur In Greek mythology, a centaur is one of a race of creatures who has the upper body, arms, and head of a man and the body and legs of a horse.

> But as he straightened and pressed ahead, care caught up with him again. Turning half-beast and half-divine, divining himself like a heathen Centaur, he had escaped his death once more.
> EUDORA WELTY 'A Still Moment' in *The Collected Stories of Eudora Welty* 1943

Cephalus In Greek mythology, Cephalus, husband of Procris, was heard to speak sweet words of love to a gentle breeze that was cooling him. His wife, on hearing of this, and believing him to have a lover, crept into some nearby

bushes to listen. Cephalus heard movement in the bushes and, thinking it
was some wild beast, threw his spear and killed his wife.

Cerberus Cerberus was the three-headed dog that guarded the entrance to
Hades in Greek mythology. Cerberus could be appeased with a cake, as by
Aeneas, or lulled to sleep, as by Orpheus, with lyre music. One of the twelve
labours of Hercules was to bring him up from the underworld. Someone who
guards the entrance to a place can be described as a Cerberus. *See also* HADES.

> She longed to mention that Claridges were looking for a doorman. He'd be
> perfect in the role, now he was so well-groomed and barking like Cerberus.
> ALICE THOMAS ELLIS *The 27th Kingdom* 1982

> A call to his office got me as far as his secretary, Veronica, who watched over
> his working day like Cerberus in human form. After diligent cross-examination
> she allowed me to talk to her master, who was as affable as his secretary was
> chilly.
> MALCOLM HAMMER *Shadows on the Green* 1994

> As we got out of the car I warned Vico not to talk in the stairwell. 'We don't
> want the dogs to hear me and wake Mr. Contreras.' 'He is a malevolent
> neighbor? You need me perhaps to guard you?' 'He's the best-natured
> neighbor in the world. Unfortunately, he sees his role in my life as Cerberus,
> with a whiff of Othello thrown in.'
> SARA PARETSKY *V.I. for Short* 1995

Cesare Borgia *See* BORGIAS.

Chagall Marc Chagall (1887–1985), a great 20th-century painter and stained-
glass artist, was born a Russian Jew but in 1922 moved to France, where he
lived for most of the rest of his life. His paintings mix reality with surrealistic
fantasy in rich colours, often depicting scenes from Russian Jewish village
life, Jewish and biblical themes, and Russian folklore. He also created twelve
stained-glass windows for the Hadassah University Hospital in Jerusalem.

> Mrs Coppett's make-up was so lurid, particularly the green eyelids, and so
> clumsily applied that in the half-light she looked like something Chagall had
> painted in a particularly inspired mood.
> TOM SHARPE *Ancestral Vices* 1980

Professor Challenger Professor George Edward Challenger is the
distinguished zoologist and anthropologist who leads the expedition to the
land of dinosaurs in Arthur Conan Doyle's *The Lost World* (1912). He also
appears in other books by Conan Doyle and is a somewhat irascible and
unconventional scientist, given to developing his own individual and rather
unlikely theories.

> If you took a living body and cut it up into ever smaller pieces, you would
> eventually come down to specks of pure protoplasm. At one time in the last
> century, a real-life counterpart of Arthur Conan Doyle's Professor Challenger

thought that the 'globigerina ooze' at the bottom of the sea was pure protoplasm. When I was a schoolboy, elderly textbook authors still wrote about protoplasm although, by then, they really should have known better.
RICHARD DAWKINS *The Blind Watchmaker* 1986

Neville Chamberlain Neville Chamberlain (1869–1940) was a British Conservative statesman and prime minister in 1937–40. In 1938 he signed the Munich Agreement ceding the Sudetenland (then in Czechoslovakia) to Germany, and returned to Britain triumphantly waving a copy of the agreement, which he claimed would bring 'peace in our time'.

'I was never one for rows and trouble, you know that. Peace is more my line.' She made a joke at which we both laughed. 'Like that bloke Chamberlain!'
ALAN SILLITOE *The Loneliness of the Long Distance Runner* 1959

Chamber of Horrors The Chamber of Horrors is a section of the Madame Tussaud's waxworks in London that contains a macabre series of tableaux of notorious murderers at their work and of scenes of torture.

Flora was trying to decide just what the kitchen looked like, and came to the conclusion it was the Chamber of Horrors at Madame Tussaud's.
STELLA GIBBONS *Cold Comfort Farm* 1932

Charlie Chan Charlie Chan is the ace Chinese detective appearing in over 40 films from 1925 to 1945. The films are loosely based on six novels by Earl Derr Biggers. Charlie Chan is witty and has an endless supply of aphorisms. He is a family man with fourteen children and usually has assistance from his impulsive number one son or number two son in solving murder mysteries.

I cruised on autopilot, my thoughts sliding from Uncle Fred to Joe Morelli to Charlie Chan. Life was good for Charlie Chan. He knew freaking everything.
JANET EVANOVICH *High Five* 1999

Lon Chaney Lon Chaney, born Leonidas Frank Chaney (1883–1930), was an American film actor who starred in mainly silent films. He was known as 'the man of a thousand faces' because of his talents at make-up and miming. In *The Phantom of the Opera* (1925), a horror film based on a novel by Gaston Leroux, he played the phantom, a mysterious masked figure who threatens a famous singer, Carlotta, at the Paris Opera.

Two white doves coo in a cage hanging from the ceiling. Their soft song is totally wrong. This scene begs for Lon Chaney, the mad 'Phantom of the Opera', wildly attacking the organ.
SUSAN SUSSMAN with SARAJANE AVIDON *Cruising for Murder* 2000

Chang and Eng Chang and Eng (1811–74) were the original Siamese twins, born in Siam and joined by a fleshy band in the region of the waist. They married sisters and each fathered several children. Their names, or the term

'Siamese twins', can be used to describe any two people or things that are always together or very closely associated.

> Now envy and antipathy, passions irreconcilable in reason, nevertheless in fact may spring conjoined like Chang and Eng in one birth.
> HERMAN MELVILLE *Billy Budd* 1924

Charlie Chaplin Charlie Chaplin (1889–1977) was an English film actor and director. In many of his silent comedies, such as *The Kid* (1921) and *The Gold Rush* (1925), he portrayed a little tramp who wore a bowler hat and baggy trousers, twirled a cane, and had a comical wide-legged, tottering walk.

> There was a soldier who crossed his eyes and folded down his lower lip, another who pouted and blew her a kiss, another who converted his marching into a Charlie Chaplin walk.
> LOUIS DE BERNIÈRES *Captain Corelli's Mandolin* 1994

Chappaquiddick On 8 July 1968 Edward Kennedy, at that time a likely US presidential candidate, drove off a bridge in Chappaquiddick, Massachusetts. His passenger, Mary Jo Kopechne, drowned, and Kennedy himself was found guilty of leaving the scene of an accident. It is widely thought that this event blighted his chance of becoming president. Chappaquiddick can be used to allude to a serious error of judgement that subsequently dogs someone's career.

> Resettled in Soweto, the vast black metropolis outside Johannesburg, she set up her own office, built her own following, spoke her own mind and organised the now infamous Mandela United Football Club. Ostensibly a soccer team intended to keep youngsters out of trouble, it became a band of thugs who terrorised the township. By 1991, four members of the club had been convicted of murder. The most notorious case, that of the 14-year-old resistance hero, Stompie Mocketsi Seipei, became Mrs Mandela's Chappaquiddick.
> *The Independent* 1995

Charlemagne Charlemagne (742–814) was the king of the Franks in 768–814. He defeated and Christianized the Lombards, Saxons, and Avars and created the Holy Roman Empire, which he ruled from 800 to 814. As well as encouraging commerce and agriculture, he promoted the arts and education.

> 'And wherever ye go and show that button, the friends of Alan Breck will come around you.' He said this as if he had been Charlemagne and commanded armies.
> ROBERT LOUIS STEVENSON *Kidnapped* 1886

Nick and Nora Charles Nick Charles is the retired detective hero of Dashiell Hammett's *The Thin Man* (1932). Nora Charles is his wealthy wife. Together the pair investigate and solve the murder of an eccentric inventor. A film starring William Powell and Myrna Loy was released in 1934.

'Pull him in,' was Superintendent Malcolm's order over the car phone. 'Pull both of them in. If they're going to play Nick and Nora Charles all over the place, they must expect to have their collars felt. You've got their address?'
M. J. TROW *Maxwell's Flame* 1995

Charley's Aunt In Brandon Thomas's farce *Charley's Aunt*, which opened in London in 1892, Lord Fancourt Babberly is persuaded by two friends to assist them in their amorous endeavours by impersonating his rich aunt. He introduces himself with the famous line 'I'm Charley's aunt from Brazil—where the nuts come from', but runs into difficulties when the real aunt appears.

Charlie *See* BONNIE PRINCE CHARLIE.

Charon In Greek mythology, Charon was the ferryman who ferried the souls of the dead across the rivers Styx and Acheron to Hades. He was described as an old but vigorous man, with a hideous countenance, long white beard, and piercing eyes. His clothes were tattered and filthy. *See also* HADES.

Then when he was a little older the undergraduates found fresh names for us. They called me Charon, and Leo the Greek God!
H. RIDER HAGGARD *She* 1887

So there I was at Bush Hill, where Rush had assigned me with my brother, to bury the flow of dead that did not ebb just because the Charon who was their familiar could no longer attend them.
JOHN EDGAR WIDEMAN *Fever* 1989

Charybdis *See* SCYLLA AND CHARYBDIS.

Chateau d'If The Chateau d'If is a castle on a small rocky island named If off the coast of Marseille in the Mediterranean Sea. It was built in 1524 and was later used as a state prison. The castle features in Alexandre Dumas's novel *The Count of Monte Cristo* (1844), being the site of incarceration for Dumas's hero, Edmund Dantès, for a period of fourteen years until he escapes. *See also* COUNT OF MONTE CRISTO.

'Thank you for this, Max,' Rachel said, pouring for them both. 'Wait till you've tasted it first,' Maxwell advised. 'They've been a little over-zealous, I think, with the cinnamon.' 'No, I mean, taking me out of Carnforth. It was beginning to resemble the Chateau d'If.'
M. J. TROW *Maxwell's Flame* 1995

He intended to go into Chicago and demand that the police hold his sister without bail, without trial, send her to the Château d'If for the rest of her life, which he prayed would be short.
SARA PARETSKY *Ghost Country* 1998

Lady Chatterley The story of Lady Chatterley is told in D. H. Lawrence's *Lady Chatterley's Lover*, first published privately in Florence in 1928, published in full by Grove Press in the United States in 1959 and by Penguin in 1960. Constance Chatterley is married to Sir Clifford Chatterley, who after being injured in the First World War is confined to a wheelchair. After an unsuccessful affair, she falls in love with Oliver Mellors, a gamekeeper and ex-Indian army officer and they have a passionate affair.

> Help, help. Lucas Simmonds is stark raving mad in the Bilge pond and Alexander's up there and he's threatening him with a knife. And when I say stark, I mean stark. Help. Covered with flowers and things, like King Lear or Lady Chatterley's lover.
> A. S. BYATT *The Virgin in the Garden* 1978

> Fizz felt she was unlikely to say anything to anybody about the sort of petty tiff that was all too common in Am Bealach, where people fell out and in again with each other all the time. she had satisfied herself that there was no Lady Chatterley situation in progress and that was all that interested her.
> JOYCE HELM *Foreign Body* 1997

Chaucer The poet Geoffrey Chaucer (*c.*1343–1400) is best known for his *Canterbury Tales* (*c.*1387), in which 29 pilgrims who have met at the Tabard Inn in Southwark agree to each tell a story to pass the time. The collection's reputation for coarse or ribald humour is based on some of the better-known stories, such as 'The Miller's Tale'. *See also* WIFE OF BATH.

> He could also break wind at will, with a prolonged whining note of complaint, and when he did so in class and then looked around with an angry face, whispering, 'Who done that?' our mirth was Chaucerian, and the teacher was reduced to making a refined face, as if she were too good for a world in which such things were possible.
> ROBERTSON DAVIES *Fifth Business* 1970

Cheeryble brothers Charles and Edwin Cheeryble are the elderly wealthy twins who employ Nicholas Nickleby in Dickens's novel of the same name (1838–9). They are cheerful and benevolent and help Nicholas, his mother and sister, and Madeleine Bray, with whom Nicholas has fallen in love. *See also* DICKENSIAN.

> I recently attended the Second European Theatre Forum in St Etienne where some 60 or so critics, directors, writers and actors debated the state of the art in apocalyptic tones that made Cassandra look like the Cheeryble Brothers. With a few striking exceptions, everyone seemed to agree that European theatre was in extreme crisis.
> MICHAEL BILLINGTON *The Guardian* 1997

Cheshire Cat In Lewis Carroll's *Alice's Adventures in Wonderland* (1865), Alice encounters a large cat grinning from ear to ear. When she asks the Duchess the reason for this, the Duchess replies, 'It's a Cheshire Cat, and that's why.' Later Alice watches the Cheshire Cat vanish, 'beginning with the end of the tail, and ending with the grin, which remained some time after the rest of it had gone'. The expression 'to grin like a Cheshire cat', meaning to grin fixedly and broadly, pre-dates Carroll's story. *See also* ALICE IN WONDERLAND.

'Affairs of greater moment' would occupy more and more of his attention, until gradually, like the Cheshire cat, he had faded altogether out of the world of the schoolroom and the nursery into higher and more comfortable spheres. The boys settled down again to happiness.
ALDOUS HUXLEY *Point Counter Point* 1928

He nodded and was gone. The unnatural brightness of his smile seemed to linger in the air after the door closed, like the smile of a Cheshire cat.
RAYMOND CHANDLER *The High Window* 1943

He seated himself, dodged a lump of sugar which a friendly hand had thrown from a neighbouring table, and beamed on his friends like a Cheshire cat.
P G. WODEHOUSE *Cocktail Time* 1958

'Where's the elevator?' I called out. 'Don't work.' He disappeared, leaving a cackle hanging in the air behind him like the Cheshire cat's grin.
MIKE PHILLIPS *Point of Darkness* 1994

Labour policies are like the Cheshire cat: look twice and they have disappeared, leaving only Mr Blair's enduring smile. *Independent on Sunday* 1996

Chewbacca Chewbacca is the large Wookiee, covered with long fur, who accompanies Hans Solo in the original *Star Wars* trilogy of films (*Star Wars*, 1977; *The Empire Strikes Back*, 1980; and *Return of the Jedi*, 1983). Played by Peter Mayhew, Chewbacca is an expert starship pilot and frequently tinkers with the pair's beloved starship freighter, the *Millennium Falcon*, in efforts to improve its performance. *See also* STAR WARS.

One was young, straggly haired and skeletal, the waistband of his sweatpants barely clinging to his starved hips. The other was older and had his face buried in a huge beard and insane hair, as if wild cats had been Sellotaped all around the border of his face. . . . Feeling slightly embarrassed, Ashling shook hands with both of them. What if Clodagh saw her now—she'd have a fit! Chewbacca in particular looked filthy and when his crusty hand clasped Ashling's she fought back the urge to shudder.
MARIAN KEYES *Sushi for Beginners* 2000

Chicken-Licken In the fairy story, Chicken-Licken is walking in the wood and she thinks that the sky has fallen and that she must tell the king. She warns each of her friends Hen-Len, Cock-Lock, Duck-Luck, Goose-Loose, Gander-Lander, and Turkey-Lurkey that the sky has fallen and that they must inform the king. On the way to do this they meet Fox-Lox, who says he will show them the way to the king, but takes them back to his foxhole, where he and his cubs eat them. So 'they never saw the king to tell him that the sky had fallen'.

Clinton has a line which gets the old folk slapping their Zimmer frames with glee. 'Everybody is going around like Chicken Licken and saying "Oh, the sky is falling". We have problems in Medicare because everybody is living. Because people are staying alive.' Long pause. A meaningful look around the crowd. 'That's a problem?' Prolonged and tumultuous applause. *The Observer* 1996

Chillon *See* PRISONER OF CHILLON.

Chingachgook Chingachgook is the old Indian chief in *The Last of the Mohicans* (1826) and other novels by James Fenimore Cooper. Chingachgook, with his son Uncas, the last of the Mohican aristocracy, accompanies the scout Hawkeye (or Natty Bumppo) in his adventures.

She scanned the ground at the edge of the hardstanding in hope of seeing something to show that someone had headed down the slope. Rapidly she realized it was not a very profitable way of spending her time. She was no Chingachgook to read in bent and heather who had passed this way and when.
REGINALD HILL *On Beulah Height* 1998

Mr Chips In James Hilton's *Goodbye, Mr Chips* (1935), Mr Chipping is a classics teacher at Brookfield School. Known to his pupils as Mr Chips, he devotes himself to teaching generations of boys at the school until his retirement. He is the archetype of the dedicated schoolmaster.

Opposite Bruce sat Professor Chambers, a sad-looking, dusty old Mr Chips whom the students had asked to chair the occasion.
BEN ELTON *Popcorn* 1996

Chiron In Greek mythology, Chiron was a learned centaur who acted as tutor to many heroes in their youth, including Jason, Hercules, and Achilles.

Something less unpleasingly oracular he tried to extract; but the old sea Chiron, thinking perhaps that for the nonce he had sufficiently instructed his young Achilles, pursed his lips, gathered all his wrinkles together, and would commit himself to nothing further.
HERMAN MELVILLE *Billy Budd* 1924

Chloe *See* AUNT CHLOE, DAPHNIS AND CHLOE.

Christ *See* JESUS.

Christian Christian is the central character of Bunyan's religious allegory *The Pilgrim's Progress* (1678, 1684) who undertakes a pilgrimage to the Celestial City, encountering on the way such adversaries as Giant Despair and Apollyon, the foul fiend. *See also* PILGRIM'S PROGRESS.

Christie John Reginald Halliday Christie (1898–1953) was an English murderer who killed his wife, for which he was hanged, and confessed to strangling five other women. It is also possible that he killed the wife and daughter of Timothy Evans, who were living in his house, for which Mr Evans was hanged in 1950.

He's guilty and he still gets me to find him an out. Nothing is ever totally certain in this business. Sow a seed of doubt and you might end up believing Crippen was innocent. Or Christie.
PETER LOVESEY *The Summons* 1995

Agatha Christie Agatha Christie (1890–1976) was an English writer of detective fiction, in particular 'whodunnits'. Many of her novels feature one or other of her two most famous creations, the Belgian Hercule Poirot and Miss Jane Marple.

Gripping stuff from the Parisian software developer. An Agatha Christie-style murder mystery using the fantastic Cinematique system. *CU Amiga* 1992

Winston Churchill Winston Churchill (1874–1965) was a British politician and prime minister who led the coalition government during the Second World War. He was a gifted orator whose wartime speeches, broadcast over the radio in his deep, slightly rasping voice, included many famous passages such as 'We shall fight on the beaches, we shall fight on the landing grounds, we shall fight in the fields and in the streets, we shall fight in the hills; we shall never surrender'.

The last phrase he pronounced in the strange (man-sawing-wood) delivery of Churchill.
LAWRENCE DURRELL *Clea* 1960

'Yes. The truth is the last repository of youth. And while a man is prepared to look truth in the face and see the mirror of his defects, let no man call him old.' And having delivered himself of this phrase so redolent of Churchill, Beaverbrook and possibly even Baldwin at his most meaningless, Lord Petrefact blew a smoke ring from his cigar with great expertise.
TOM SHARPE *Ancestral Vices* 1980

Cicero Marcus Tullius Cicero (106–43 BC) was a Roman orator, statesman, and writer. Cicero's name and the adjective 'Ciceronian' are sometimes mentioned to suggest eloquence or oratory.

You'd scarce expect one of my age
To speak in public on the stage;
And if I chance to fall below
Demosthenes or Cicero,
Don't view me with a critic's eye,
But pass my imperfections by.
Large streams from little fountains flow,
Tall oaks from little acorns grow.
DAVID EVERETT *Lines Written for a School Declamation* 1776

'Except,' said Dalziel. And paused. There was something splendidly Ciceronian about Dalziel's 'except'. A single word left hanging, ungrammatically, in the air. And amidst the serried ranks of senators a small sough of intaken breath, then

utter silence as they concentrated all their attention on the next eloquent weighty sentence to emerge from that eloquent weighty figure, statuesque at the centre of the tessellated floor. 'Except it's all balls,' said Dalziel.
REGINALD HILL *A Pinch of Snuff* 1978

Cimmerian In Greek mythology, the Cimmerians were people who lived in a land on the edge of the world that was perpetually covered with mist and cloud and where the sun never shone. In Homer's *Odyssey* the land of the Cimmerians is the place nearest to Hades, the land of the dead. It contains Persephone's grove, to which Odysseus goes to make contact with the spirits of the dead.

A kind of landscape and weather which leads travellers from the South to describe our island as Homer's Cimmerian land, was not, on the face of it, friendly to women.
THOMAS HARDY *The Return of the Native* 1880

Cinderella In the fairy story, Cinderella's life is made miserable after her father's remarriage by her stepmother and stepsisters. She is kept in poverty, dressed in rags, and forced to do menial tasks. When her stepsisters go off to a royal ball leaving Cinderella behind, she is found weeping by her fairy godmother, who waves her wand, turning a pumpkin into a coach, six mice into horses to pull it, and a rat into a coachman. Cinderella's rags are turned into beautiful clothes and glass slippers appear on her feet. She is instructed by her fairy godmother to leave the ball by midnight, before her beautiful clothes and coach and horses revert to their normal forms. At the ball she meets the prince. Rushing away at the stroke of midnight, she leaves behind a glass slipper. The prince announces that he will marry whoever can wear the slipper, and he eventually discovers that it fits only Cinderella. The name Cinderella can be used to describe a transformation from poverty or plainness to prosperity or glamour, or refer to an undervalued service that nobody will provide for, while the fairy godmother can represent the agent of transformation. Cinderella is also mentioned in the context of an instruction that must be followed precisely, or more specifically when referring to a late-night deadline that must be adhered to. The name Cinderella is sometimes shortened to Cinders, and the prince in the fairy story has come to be known as Prince Charming.

'Suppose I try,' said Mr. Hale. 'Everybody else has had their turn at this great difficulty. Now let me try. I may be the Cinderella to put on the slipper after all.'
ELIZABETH GASKELL *North and South* 1854

She had acquired such wonderful arts, that the woman and girl who formed the staff of domestics regarded her as quite a Sorceress, or Cinderella's Godmother: who would send out for a fowl, a rabbit, a vegetable or two from the garden, and change them into anything she pleased.
CHARLES DICKENS *A Tale of Two Cities* 1859

Quarter of an hour to midnight. Poor Cinderella. I must get my father home

before the clock strikes or he'll lose his beauty-sleep.
LAWRENCE DURRELL *Balthazar* 1958

The story of how she was cast is a delightful one, and adds to the Cinders quality of her tale. Her fairy godmother was the director Joel Schumacher, who happened to walk past her in a corridor at Universal. He says he saw 'this incredible-looking girl coming towards me like a young Arabian racehorse. I told my assistant to follow her and find out if she was an actress.' *The Observer* 1997

Stephen Spiro, professor of respiratory medicine at University College London Hospital, believes lung cancer has long been perceived as a Cinderella disease. 'It is seen as a disease of the working classes. Everyone knows the cause. It has connotations of guilt so patients are not demanding enough.' *The Independent* 1998

Circe In Greek mythology, Circe was a sorceress who lived on the island of Aeaea. She detained Odysseus on Aeaea for a year on his return from the Trojan War. Although she turned his men into swine, Odysseus managed to protect himself from this fate using the mythical herb moly, and he was able to make her restore his men to their human form. Allusions to Circe are usually in the context of a bewitching, dangerously attractive woman or place. *See also* ODYSSEUS.

None of the books I had read explained this sinister-fascinating, this Circe-like quality of Greece; the quality that makes it unique.
JOHN FOWLES *The Magus* 1977

From the mountains comes the wind, bringing clear weather and falling temperatures. As a tribute to its dubious transforming powers it is called the Circe. *The Oldie* 1992

Being pretty is no great matter. Any young lady with bright eyes and passable teeth can claim that much. Better to be clever, quick, and intrepid—to charm with your mind and enchant with your wit—in short, to be the one radiant Circe in a season of dreary Helens.
KATE ROSS *Cut to the Quick* 1993

Claude Claude Lorraine (1600–82), originally named Claude Gellée, was a French landscape painter celebrated for his subtle and poetic treatment of light. His paintings lead the eye into the expansive panoramas through variations of colour: dark greenish-brown in the foreground, light green in the middle distance, and blue in the far distance.

The sea and the mountains floated in the steady evening sunshine. It was all peace, elements and void, golden air and mute blue distances, like a Claude.
JOHN FOWLES *The Magus* 1977

Cassius Clay *See* MUHAMMAD ALI.

June and Ward Cleaver June Cleaver and her husband, Ward, were the parents of Beaver in the television series *Leave it to Beaver*, which was broadcast in the United States by CBS between 1957 and 1963. June (played by Barbara Billingsley) was a quintessential American 1950s-style Mom, a homemaker who kept her house spotless and brought up her two children, Beaver and Wally. Ward, who was played by Hugh Beaumont, was her responsible businessman husband.

> She wasn't promiscuous; she paid her bills on time; she didn't do drugs even on a recreational basis; she didn't smoke, she didn't drink. There wasn't a swag of beads anywhere in her apartment, and she was a regular June Cleaver in her personal life.
> LINDA HOWARD *Now You See Her* 1998

> So keep your eye on her. You're the ones trying to decide if you're going to be long-suffering, star-crossed lovers, or Ward and June Cleaver.
> NORA ROBERTS *Dance Upon the Air* 2001

> Quick knows if it all comes out, he's in big trouble with his family, not to mention the law. So he cuts out and leaves Sheila to fend for herself. This is not Ward Cleaver.
> JONATHAN KELLERMAN *Therapy* 2004

Cleopatra Cleopatra (69–30 BC) was the queen of Egypt in 47–30 BC. She is usually remembered for her beauty, for her affairs with Julius Caesar and Mark Antony, and for committing suicide by allowing herself to be bitten by an asp. Her relationship with Antony is the subject of Shakespeare's *Antony and Cleopatra* (1623) and Dryden's *All for Love* (1678), while her relationship with Caesar is the subject of Shaw's *Caesar and Cleopatra* (1907). The name Cleopatra can be used to typify a woman of exotic beauty and allure. *See also* ANTONY AND CLEOPATRA, SHAKESPEARE.

> In a word, all Cleopatra—fierce, voluptuous, passionate, tender . . . and full of . . . rapturous enchantment.
> NATHANIEL HAWTHORNE *The Marble Faun* 1860

Clio Clio was one of the nine Muses in Greek mythology, associated especially with history. *See also* MUSES.

Cloud Cuckoo Land Cloud Cuckoo Land (a translation of the Greek Nephelokokkygia) is the imaginary city built in the air by birds in Aristophanes' play *The Birds*. Hence any fanciful realm can be described as Cloud Cuckoo Land, a world or state of mind that exists only in a person's imagination, distanced from reality.

> The government is in cloud-cuckoo-land if it thinks privatising prisons will solve the mess. *The Observer* 2004

Clouseau Inspector Clouseau was a character played by Peter Sellers in the comedy film *The Pink Panther* (1963) and its sequels. He was a stupid, bungling, accident-prone police detective.

Clytemnestra In Greek mythology, Clytemnestra was the wife of Agamemnon, king of Mycenae. During her husband's absence at the Trojan War she had taken a lover, Aegisthus. On Agamemnon's triumphant return from the war, she and Aegisthus laid a trap for him, murdering him in his bath.

> She held herself beautifully erect, walked with a measured tread dominated by a statuelike passivity. To me, she seemed like a figure in a Greek tragedy—all parts played, all oracles read, all actions come full circle. Clytemnestra, having dealt the inevitable blow, waiting, waiting.
> LINDA BARNES *Cold Case* 1997

Cockaigne The Land of Cockaigne (or Cockayne; from the Old French *pais de cocaigne*, 'fool's paradise') was in medieval legend an imaginary land of luxury and idleness, where good food and drink were plentiful.

> She watched the car drive away. It was going to Cloud Cuckoo Land; it was going to the Kingdom of Cockaigne; it was going to Hollywood.
> STELLA GIBBONS *Cold Comfort Farm* 1932

Colditz Colditz is a medieval castle near Leipzig in eastern Germany. It was used as a top-security prison camp during the Second World War, particularly for prisoners who were known as likely escapees, and became famous as a camp from which escape was considered almost impossible.

> Former residents described Bryn Estyn as the 'Colditz of residential care'. *The Observer* 1996

Wilkie Collins Wilkie Collins (1824–89) was an English novelist chiefly remembered as the writer of the first full-length detective stories in English, notably *The Woman in White* (1860) and *The Moonstone* (1868). *See also* WOMAN IN WHITE.

> Suppose the servant really killed the master, or suppose the master isn't really dead, or suppose the master is dressed up as the servant, or suppose the servant is buried for the master; invent what Wilkie Collins's tragedy you like, and you still have not explained a candle without a candlestick, or why an elderly gentleman of good family should habitually spill snuff on the piano.
> G. K. CHESTERTON *The Honour of Israel Gow* 1911

Colossus The Colossus of Rhodes, one of the seven ancient wonders of the world, was a huge bronze statue of the sun-god Helios standing beside the harbour entrance at Rhodes. According to Pliny the Elder it stood 30.5 metres (100 feet) high. The Colossus was built *c.*292–280 BC and was destroyed in an earthquake in 224 BC. The familiar image of a statue so vast that its legs were either side of the harbour, used by Cassius in Julius Caesar, is not historically accurate. Colossus was Greek for 'gigantic statue'.

> Why, man, he doth bestride the narrow world
> Like a Colossus; and we petty men
> Walk under his huge legs, and peep about
> To find ourselves dishonourable graves.
> WILLIAM SHAKESPEARE *Julius Caesar* 1623

> Richter has been called an intellectual Colossus.
> THOMAS CARLYLE *Tales by Musaeus, Tieck, Richter* 1827

> I found the wall—it was only a foot or two beyond my reach. With a heave I had my foot on the spike, and turning, I had both hands on the opposite wall. There I stood, straddling like a Colossus over a waste of white waters, with the cave floor far below me in the gloom.
> JOHN BUCHAN *Prester John* 1910

Columbo Lt. Philip Columbo, memorably played by Peter Falk in the TV series *Columbo* (US 1971–77, 1991–; UK 1972–), was a police detective from the Los Angeles Police Department. Working alone to solve his murder cases, he wears a shabby raincoat and affects an air of naive puzzlement as he questions his suspects, often catching them off guard with one last question just as he is apparently taking his leave. The viewers know who the murderer is from the start, and wall-eyed, cigar-smoking Columbo guesses who he or she is early on and then tries to puzzle out how the crime was committed and obtain the necessary evidence to prove it.

> 'I'm trying to refresh my memory of the case,' Diamond told him as if the facts had all deserted him. For once he was being as amiable as the television detective Columbo, whose style of questioning he aspired to, but only rarely approached. 'You're the obvious man to ask about Britt.'
> PETER LOVESEY *The Summons* 1995

Columbus Christopher Columbus (1451–1506) was an Italian explorer who, sponsored by the rulers of Spain, Ferdinand and Isabella, set out across the Atlantic Ocean in 1492 with the intention of reaching Asia and proving that the world was round. In fact, he discovered the New World, reaching the Bahamas, Cuba, and Hispaniola (now the Dominican Republic and Haiti). He made three further journeys, during which he also discovered the South American mainland.

> The disturbance was as the first floating weed to Columbus—the contemptibly little suggesting possibilities of the infinitely great.
> THOMAS HARDY *Far from the Madding Crowd* 1874

> So, Flora mused, must Columbus have felt when the poor Indian fixed his solemn, unwavering gaze upon the great sailor's face. For the first time a Starkadder looked upon a civilized being.
> STELLA GIBBONS *Cold Comfort Farm* 1932

Comus *Comus* is a masque, or pastoral drama, written by Milton and presented to the earl of Bridgewater at Ludlow Castle in 1634. Comus is an imaginary Greek god who has the power to turn the faces of travellers into those of wild animals. Into his clutches comes the Lady (a part taken at Ludlow by Milton's daughter Alice), who has become separated from her brothers (played by her two brothers). She finds herself in 'a stately Palace', in an enchanted chair, with Comus and his crew of enchanted travellers. Her brothers, who have had the assistance of a spirit, Thyrsis, in the form of a protective herb root, arrive and disperse Comus and the crew of travellers and eventually the Lady is freed from her chair.

> Effigies, donkey, lanterns, band all had disappeared like the crew of Comus.
> THOMAS HARDY *The Mayor of Casterbridge* 1886

Conan the Barbarian Conan the Barbarian was a 1981 movie starring Arnold Schwarzenegger as Conan. The film was based on the sword-and-sorcery adventure stories by Robert E. Howard about Conan of Cimmeria which appeared in *Weird Tales* in the 1930s. Conan, a Dark Ages barbarian warrior (garbed in rather sketchy leather armour and boots), freed from slavery, seeks to avenge the murder of his parents by a warlord.

> 'He was a cop,' I said. 'And a particular kind of cop. He was used to scaring people. He was a big tough guy. He was used to getting things done by slapping people around.' 'Maybe so,' Healy said. 'But I don't see why he comes on like Conan the Barbarian.'
> ROBERT B. PARKER *Small Vices* 1997

Concordia Concordia was the Roman goddess of peace and harmony.

Confucius Confucius (551–479 BC) was a Chinese philosopher and teacher of ethics. He spent much of his life as the moral teacher of a group of disciples, expounding his ideas about the importance of practical codes of personal morality, etiquette, and statesmanship which formed the basis of the philosophy of Confucianism. His teachings and sayings were collected by his pupils after his death.

> You would be better off at the present time to imagine yourself as one of the great shots of the day, or even a competent one, rather than as Confucius.
> TIMOTHY MO *An Insular Possession* 1986

Connecticut Yankee In Mark Twain's satirical fantasy *A Connecticut Yankee in King Arthur's Court* (1889), Hank Morgan is a Connecticut mechanic who is knocked unconscious in a fight and awakens to find himself transported back to 6th-century Camelot. Using his 19th-century knowledge of technology and history, he determines to introduce to Arthur's kingdom the supposed benefits of advanced civilization.

Constance In Shakespeare's *King John* (1623), Constance of Brittany is the mother of Arthur, the king's young nephew, and a claimant to the throne.

Her son's death draws from her a passionate expression of grief:
'Grief fills the room up of my absent child,
Lies in his bed, walks up and down with me,
Puts on his pretty looks, repeats his words.'

> Few of us wish to disturb the mother of a litter of puppies when mouthing a bone in the midst of her young family. Medea and her children are familiar to us, and so is the grief of Constance.
> ANTHONY TROLLOPE *Barchester Towers* 1857

Captain Cook Captain James Cook (1728–79), English navigator and explorer, led expeditions to the Pacific in the *Endeavour*, to the Antarctic in the *Resolution*, and finally to try to discover a passage round the north coast of America from the Pacific. He was forced to turn back from his last voyage and, reaching Hawaii, was killed by the islanders.

> You wave an airy adieu to the boys on shore, light your biggest pipe, and swagger about the deck as if you were Captain Cook, Sir Francis Drake, and Christopher Columbus all rolled into one.
> JEROME K. JEROME *Three Men in a Boat* 1889

Cook's tour Thomas Cook (1808–92) was an English travel agent who founded the travel firm named after him in 1841 and originated the guided tour. A Cook's tour is a tour or journey in which many places are visited, often briefly.

> The cars and petrol will be requisitioned by the army and the trains'll be packed with troops. I doubt if anyone'll get away, but if you do, you'll go empty-handed, and it won't be no Cook's tour.
> OLIVIA MANNING *The Great Fortune* 1960

Gary Cooper The American film actor Gary Cooper (1901–61) is often associated with his role as the small-town marshal Will Kane in the film *High Noon* (1952). In an iconic scene at the climax of the film, Cooper walks alone down the street to confront several outlaws single-handedly. *See also* HIGH NOON.

> As I passed along the bar the men on the stools eyed me narrowly, then fidgeted uneasily in their seats. I felt like Gary Cooper making that solitary walk down Main Street.
> SARA PARETSKY *Tunnel Vision* 1994

King Cophetua King Cophetua was a legendary African king who was unmarried and had come to disdain women. One day when he was out riding he saw a beggar-maid 'clad all in gray', fell in love with her and proposed marriage. Their marriage was happy and successful. The story is told in the ballad 'King Cophetua and the Beggar-Maid' in Thomas Percy's *Reliques of Ancient English Poetry* (1765).

Miriam seemed as in some dreamy tale, a maiden in bondage, her spirit dreaming in a land far away and magical. And her discoloured, old blue frock and her broken boots seemed only like the romantic rags of King Cophetua's beggar-maid.

D. H. LAWRENCE *Sons and Lovers* 1913

'He'll come and see you,' said Sylvia. 'No, he won't,' said Eiluned. 'Why not?' said Harriet. 'I like that young man,' said Eiluned. 'You needn't grin. I do like him. He's not going to do the King Cophetua stunt, and I take off my hat to him. If you want him, you'll have to send for him.'

DOROTHY SAYERS *Strong Poison* 1930

Captain Corcoran Captain Corcoran is the captain of HMS *Pinafore* in Gilbert and Sullivan's opera of the same name (1878). He sings a song in which he proudly tells his crew of the things that he 'never, never' does. When challenged, he concedes that this is not quite true:

'What, never?'

'No, never.'

'What, never?'

'Well—hardly ever.'

Nature is so wondrously complex and varied that almost anything possible does happen. Captain Corcoran's 'hardly ever' is the strongest statement that a natural historian can make.

STEPHEN JAY GOULD *Ever Since Darwin* 1978

Cordelia When in Shakespeare's play *King Lear* (1623) the king asks his three daughters which of them loves him the best, the two older sisters, Goneril and Regan, flatter their father with extravagant declarations of their love. The youngest daughter, Cordelia, is the only one to speak truthfully, acknowledging that she loves her father according to her duty, but refusing to say that she will always love only him, for when she marries she must also love her husband. Lear furiously denounces what he believes to be her lack of love for him: 'So young and so untender?' Cordelia replies: 'So young, my lord, and true.' Later, however, when the king has lost his sanity, it is Cordelia, rather than either of her sisters, who takes him in and cares for him. Cordelia thus represents the ideal of a daughter's love for her father. *See also* KING LEAR, SHAKESPEARE.

Mrs. Whittaker was Cordelia-like to her father during his declining years. She came to see him several times a month, bringing him jelly or potted hyacinths. Sometimes she sent her car and chauffeur for him, so that he might take an easy drive through the town, and Mrs. Bain might be afforded a chance to drop her cooking and accompany him.

DOROTHY PARKER *The Wonderful Old Gentleman* 1944

Coriolanus Coriolanus is the main character in Shakespeare's play of the same name (1623). He is a proud, courageous soldier who shows in an arrogant outburst in the forum his contempt for the Roman rabble and resentment at having to solicit their votes. *See also* SHAKESPEARE.

> There was just a hint of Coriolanus going before the plebs as Lord Irvine defended his choice of wallpaper to the select committee. *BBC Radio 4* 1998

Cornucopia In Greek mythology, Amalthea was a she-goat or goat-nymph, whose milk Zeus drank when he was first born. In gratitude, Zeus placed Amalthea's image among the stars as the constellation Capricorn. Zeus also took one of Amalthea's horns and endowed it with the magical property of refilling itself endlessly with whatever food or drink was desired. The horn of plenty was later stylized as the Cornucopia (from the Latin *cornu copiae*, literally 'horn of plenty'), pictured as a goat's horn spilling over with fruit, flowers, and stalks of corn. The name is used to allude to an unending and bountiful supply of food.

> There was a cornucopia of food and drink almost forbidding in its plentitude.
> FRED CHAPPELL *Farewell, I'm Bound to Leave You* 1997

Correggio Antonio Allegri da Correggio (*c.*1494–1534) was an Italian painter of the High Renaissance. His best-known works are a series of frescos in the Camera di San Paolo and other Parma churches, painted in a sensual style, with a soft play of light and colour and striking use of foreshortening. These frescos often depict frolicking *putti* (cherubs) with an exuberance that captures the vitality and joyfulness of children.

> The rush of conflicting feelings was too great for Maggie to say much when Lucy, with a face breathing playful joy, like one of Correggio's cherubs, poured forth her triumphant revelation.
> GEORGE ELIOT *The Mill on the Floss* 1860

Cortés Hernando Cortés (or Hernán Cortez; 1485–1547) was a Spanish adventurer who conquered Mexico, then known as New Spain. Darien, mentioned in Keats's poem below, was the name for the isthmus of Panama.

> Then felt I like some watcher of the skies
> When a new planet swims into his ken;
> Or like stout Cortez, when with eagle eyes
> He stared at the Pacific—and all his men
> Looked at each other with a wild surmise—
> Silent, upon a peak in Darien.
> JOHN KEATS *On First Looking into Chapman's Homer* 1816

> This was the first sign of humanity she had encountered among the Starkadders, and she was moved by it. She felt like stout Cortez or Sir James Jeans on spotting yet another white dwarf.
> STELLA GIBBONS *Cold Comfort Farm* 1932

country mouse *See* TOWN MOUSE AND COUNTRY MOUSE.

Cowardly Lion The Cowardly Lion is one of the companions of Dorothy in her journey to find Oz in the children's story *The Wizard of Oz* by L. Frank

Baum (1900). The lion roars very loudly to frighten other creatures away and to disguise the fact that he is scared of them himself. He hopes that the Wizard of Oz will give him courage, although, in fact, he acts bravely to protect his companions throughout their travels. *See also* WIZARD OF OZ.

> Mr. Perot transformed a tale about fistfights during a union-certification campaign (which the union won) into the 20th-century equivalent of the Haymarket riot. This small-minded appeal to jingoism not only batters facts, it also makes the U.S. look like the Cowardly Lion of world politics. *New York Times* 1993

Cox and Box In the operetta *Cox and Box* by Burnand and Sullivan (1867), Cox and Box are two lodgers whose occupations allow their landlady to let the same room out to each of them, one using it by day and one using it by night. They discover their landlady's duplicity when Cox, who sleeps in the room at night, is given a holiday. The operetta was based on a play entitled *Box and Cox* by J. M. Morton, published in 1847.

Hart Crane Harold Hart Crane (1899–1932) was an American poet born in Ohio. In 1932, after a period in Mexico, where he failed to write an epic poem on Montezuma, and believing he had betrayed the woman he loved, he committed suicide by leaping from the deck of SS *Orizaba* in the Caribbean off the coast of Florida.

> He said he almost jumped off the ship like Hart Crane on the way back. JACK KEROUAC *On the Road* 1957

Ichabod Crane In Washington Irving's short story 'The Legend of Sleepy Hollow' (1820), Ichabod Crane is the village schoolmaster, suitor to the local girl Katrina Van Tass. He is skinny and gangly, with a nose 'like a snipe'. His rival suitor, Brom Bones, disguises himself as a ghostly headless horseman and scares the timid Ichabod out of the village. *See also* SLEEPY HOLLOW.

> 'Tall chap with exophthalmic eyes, prominent nose. Walks with a stoop,' Ecco said out of the blue, remembering. Cordelia blushed. The bluntness of the description—which was deadly accurate—took her by surprise. Among undergraduates back home, Wain was known affectionately behind his back as Ichabod. JOHN SPENCER HILL *The Last Castrato* 1995

> He had an Ichabod Crane body and a wild thatch of Einstein-like white hair. His sunken, permanently sad eyes and big, expressive hands had held many a courtroom spellbound as he'd pled for the rights of underdogs of all shapes, colors and sizes through the years in a booming evangelistic voice. DEANNIE MILLS FRANCIS *Trap Door* 1995

> They follow a lanky man with a prodigious Adam's apple—Ichabod Crane incarnate. SUSAN SUSSMAN with SARAJANE AVIDON *Cruising for Murder* 2000

Bob Cratchit Bob Cratchit is Ebenezer Scrooge's clerk in Dickens's *A Christmas Carol* (1843). He is poorly paid (15 shillings a week), and the father of five living in a small four-roomed house in Camden Town. His youngest son, Tiny Tim, is weak and crippled. Despite his poverty, Cratchit is a devoted husband and father. *See also* DICKENSIAN.

Creation The Creation is the name given to the account in the book of Genesis of God's creating of the universe and the first people, Adam and Eve.

> This has been a key principle of taxation since the Creation. *The Observer* 1997

Creature from the Black Lagoon *The Creature from the Black Lagoon* is a 1954 film in which a party of scientists in the Amazon in search of fossils discover a mysterious fanged creature which is half-man and half-fish. He is a prehistoric 'Gill man' who comes from the legendary Black Lagoon.

> For years we had had our differences, and it didn't take much to push these nettling grievances to the surface. Although it had to have pained him to do so, Buck once summed up our problems with comic incisiveness. 'Show you what a crock of shit both heredity and environment are. Here we had the same parents, same schools, same boyhood experiences. We crawled out of the same gene pool. But you became Prince Valiant and I mutated into the Creature from the Black Lagoon.
> MICHAEL MEWSHAW *True Crime* 1991

Admirable Crichton The Admirable Crichton was James Crichton (1560–85), a Scottish scholar, poet, and linguist who travelled in France and Italy, served in the French army, and died in a brawl in Mantua. His career was described by Sir Thomas Urquhart in his writings in praise of the Scots nation *The Discoverie of a Most Exquisite Jewel* (1652) and the Admirable Crichton developed a reputation as a perfect man with many varied talents. J. M. Barrie adopted the phrase as the title of his play *The Admirable Crichton* about a perfect butler cast on a desert island with his employers.

> 'Wow!' he said quietly. 'I thought the man there sounded surly when Mrs Tinsley rang through about accommodation.' 'So watch out for yourself.' 'The eye of the storm, isn't that it? Couldn't be anywhere safer. Anyway, I'd best scarper now and get my head down. It's heavy work being the Admirable Crichton.'
> CLARE CURZON *Cold Hands* 1999

Dr Crippen Hawley Harvey Crippen (1862–1910), known as Dr Crippen, was an American-born British murderer. Crippen poisoned his wife, burying her remains in the cellar of their London home, for which crime he was later hanged. He nearly escaped, boarding an Atlantic liner with his secretary, but the suspicious captain of the ship contacted the police by radiotelegraphy, the first use of this medium in a criminal investigation, and he was apprehended.

Gary's client, the Dr Crippen of fund management, was delirious with joy.
REBECCA TINSLEY *Settlement Day* 1994

Betty Crocker Betty Crocker ® is the name given to a range of American food products such as cake and other food mixes. The name was invented by the milling company the Washburn Crosby Company of Minneapolis (later part of General Mills), which received many requests for information about baking in the 1910s and early 1920s and wished to make the replies sound more personal. A female employee supplied a signature. In 1924 a radio cookery show was broadcast with actresses playing the part. In 1936 an official portrait was made of Betty Crocker (which changes periodically) and many Americans believed that Betty Crocker was a real woman.

I made two peanut butter sandwiches and brought them into the living room. Morelli looked at his sandwich. 'What are these lumps?' 'Olives.' He opened the sandwich and looked inside. 'Where's the jelly?' 'No jelly.' 'I think I need another beer.' 'Just eat it!' I yelled. 'What do I look like, Betty Crocker? I didn't have a great day, either, you know. Not that anybody asked me about my day!'
JANET EVANOVICH *Four to Score* 1998

Croesus Croesus (6th c. BC) was the last king of Lydia, a country on the east coast of the Aegean Sea in what is now Turkey. He was famed for his great wealth. The phrase 'as rich as Croesus' has become proverbial.

'This girl's father,' said William, 'is as rich as Croesus. He owns property without end.'
D. H. LAWRENCE *Sons and Lovers* 1913

It did not seem quite fair to Marion, but Marion was as rich as Croesus, everyone knew, and Marion had sold Leslie Beck's baby and perhaps didn't deserve too much.
FAY WELDON *Life Force* 1992

Here is a man barely into his forties who has already amassed riches beyond Croesus (he owns 141 million shares in Microsoft, currently trading at $83.37 apiece). Last year the rise in the value of his stock meant that he earned about $30 million a day. *The Observer* 1997

Lara Croft Lara Croft is the heroine of the video game *Tomb Raider* ®. She is an animated archaeologist who hunts down artefacts from ancient ruins often in circumstances of extreme danger. She is well armed and combat-trained while wearing skin-tight clothing and high heels and she has a bust of considerable dimensions. Two films have been made of her adventures starring Angelina Jolie as Croft: *Lara Croft Tomb Raider* (2001) and *Lara Croft Tomb Raider: The Cradle of Life* (2003).

'Don't be ridiculous. It's a lovely house and they offer accommodation. It'll be like a camping holiday.' 'When did you last go on a camping trip? Your idea of an expedition to the Lost World is a visit to Brent Cross Shopping Centre.' 'Look

who's talking. I never had you pegged for Indiana Jones.' 'And you're no Lara Croft.'
MIKE RIPLEY *Angel Underground* 2002

Oliver Cromwell Oliver Cromwell (1599–1658) was the English general who led the parliamentary forces, or Roundheads, against Charles I in the English Civil War. After the Roundhead victory, Cromwell helped to arrange the trial and execution of Charles I and set up a republican government, becoming in 1653, as lord protector, the ruler of Scotland, Ireland, and England and Wales. He is sometimes alluded to as an anti-royalist revolutionary.

> A number of varied fellow-creatures, some happy, many serene, a few depressed, one here and there bright even to genius, some stupid, others wanton, others austere; some mutely Miltonic, some potentially Cromwellian.
> THOMAS HARDY *Tess of the D'Urbervilles* 1891

> The pity of it is, I hear such stuff from my peers. Elegant ideas for a social re-ordering. Pleasing plans for a community of reason. And Louis is weak. Let him give an inch, and some Cromwell will appear. It'll end in revolution. And that'll be no tea party.
> HILARY MANTEL *A Place of Greater Safety* 1992

Cronus In Greek mythology, Cronus (or Cronos) was one of the Titans and the father of Zeus. Cronus married his sister Rhea, and because he knew that he would one day be supplanted by one of the new gods, he swallowed all his children at birth. Rhea hid Zeus and gave Cronus a stone to swallow instead. As an adult, Zeus forced Cronus to bring up the stone and all the other children. Cronus and the Titans fought the new Olympian gods but lost to them.

> 'He's an impulsive young lad,' said Dalziel. 'But good-hearted. I'll have a fatherly word with him.' He gave her a savage smile suggesting the father he had in mind was Cronos.
> REGINALD HILL *On Beulah Height* 1998

Cruella de Vil Cruella de Vil is the rich, evil, screeching villainess in Dodie Smith's *One Hundred and One Dalmatians* (1956), who steals 99 Dalmatian puppies in order to make a spotted fur coat from their skins. Two Disney film versions have been made, an animated one in 1961 and a live-action remake in 1996.

> Something terrible had happened to the toughest office manager in Manchester. Imagine Cruella De Vil transformed into one of those cuddly Dalmatian puppies, only more so. It was like watching Ben Nevis grovel. 'And could you sign one, "for Ted"?' she begged.
> VAL MCDERMID *Star Struck* 1988

Robinson Crusoe The eponymous hero of Daniel Defoe's novel *Robinson Crusoe* (1719) survives a shipwreck and lives on an uninhabited island for 24 years, at first alone and later joined by Man Friday. Crusoe's adventures are based on those of Alexander Selkirk (1676–1721), a sailor who, at his own request, was put ashore on an island in the Pacific and survived there for over four years. One of the most memorable episodes in the novel is Crusoe's horrified discovery of a footprint on the beach. *See also* MAN FRIDAY.

> Once, like another Crusoe, by the edge of the river he came upon a track—the faint tracery of a snowshoe rabbit on the delicate snow-crust. It was a revelation. There was life in the Northland.
> JACK LONDON *In a Far Country* 1900

> With more staff and more machinery the place would take shape as a sound economic unit, and the present hand-to-mouth arrangements, which were nerve-rending although they had a certain Robinson Crusoe charm, would come to an end.
> IRIS MURDOCH *The Bell* 1958

> He must have found the recipe in the pages of Postlethwaite's *Vade Mecum For Travellers in Foreign Lands*, a book which he kept under lock and key in his trunk and by which he absolutely swore. It contained, he said, everything that a man in Robinson Crusoe's position ought to know—even how to make a fire by rubbing sticks together; it was a mine of marvellous information.
> LAWRENCE DURRELL *Clea* 1960

Cumaean Sibyl The Cumaean Sibyl was the prophetess (or Sibyl) of the Temple of Apollo at Cumae in south Italy who guided Aeneas through the underworld in the *Aeneid*. It was said that in her youth Apollo had been enamoured of her and had offered to give her whatever she wished. She took a handful of sand and asked to live as many years as there were grains of sand in her hand, but she forgot to ask for health and youth as well. So she grew old and decrepit and had already lived 700 years by the time Aeneas encountered her. To equal the number of sand grains she still had another three centuries to live. *See also* SIBYL.

Cupid In Roman mythology, Cupid was the god of love, corresponding to the Greek god Eros. He is often pictured as a beautiful naked boy with wings, carrying a bow and arrows, with which he wounds his victims and makes them fall in love. According to the story, Cupid fell in love with the beautiful Psyche. He visited her only at night in the dark, insisting that she did not see what he looked like. When Psyche succumbed to curiosity and lit a lamp while he slept, a few drops of hot oil fell on him and woke him. He left her, and she wandered across the earth looking for him and accomplishing various tasks set for her by Venus. Eventually Psyche was reunited with Cupid and married him in heaven. *See also* EROS.

> And off I started, cursorily glancing sideways as I passed the toilet-table, surmounted by a looking-glass: a thin irregular face I saw, with sunk, dark eyes under a large, square forehead, complexion destitute of bloom or attraction;

something young, but not youthful, no object to win a lady's love, no butt for
the shafts of Cupid.
CHARLOTTE BRONTË *The Professor* 1857

Ah, he doesn't know in the least what he is saying. This is not what he meant
to say. His arm is stealing round the waist again, it is tightening its clasp; he is
bending his face nearer and nearer to the round cheek, his lips are meeting
those pouting child-lips, and for a long moment time has vanished. He may be
a shepherd in Arcadia for aught he knows, he may be the first youth kissing the
first maiden, he may be Eros himself, sipping the lips of Psyche—it is all one.
GEORGE ELIOT *Adam Bede* 1859

Playing Cupid, I should have you know, isn't just a matter of flying around
Arcadia and feeling your tiny winkle throb when the lovers finally kiss. It's to do
with timetables and street maps, cinema times and menus, money and
organisation.
JULIAN BARNES *Talking It Over* 1991

Currier and Ives Currier and Ives was a New York City lithography shop run
by Nathaniel Currier and Jim Ives that sold coloured prints between 1834
and 1907. They described themselves as 'publishers of cheap and popular
pictures', and their prints depicted the history of America in the second half
of the 19th century in pictorial form.

Where I live looks exactly like the MGM back-lot idea of a small New England
town. There's no pressure in Connecticut, it's all okay. Nobody is working much,
there aren't many jobs, a lot of businesses are failing. But it looks so sweet. It
looks endearing. During the blizzard, you would have thought that Currier and
Ives came in there.
STUDS TERKEL *American Dreams: Lost and Found* 1980

I drove past farms out of Currier and Ives. They looked like there should be
bearded guys in straw hats working them with horses, but this wasn't Amish
country.
JOHN MADDOX ROBERTS *A Typical American Town* 1995

Horns blared. Brakes screeched. Startled, I slipped off my branch as a speeding
caravan of Range Rovers forced Hopkins Septic's tanker off the road. Arrogant
DPL-plated sons of bitches from Henry King's Morris Mountain estate. I hung
for my life like a three-toed sloth. 'Don't drop her,' screamed Alison, and the
Nikon's motor drive began whining eagerly. Upside down, from elm height,
Newbury looked like a Currier and Ives New England miniature enamelled on
Grandma's brooch: clapboard churches clustered around the tallest flagpole in
Connecticut; snug Colonials; snow-white mansions; barn-red General Store; a
sturdy bank; and Town Hall. All crisp in the piercing March sunlight.
JUSTIN SCOTT *Frostline* 1997

Custer's last stand George Armstrong Custer (1839–76) was an American
cavalry general who was sent to Dakota to protect goldminers and railway
surveyors against the Sioux after gold had been found in what had been

Sioux tribal lands. In 1876, while scouting, his regiment, the 7th cavalry, came upon a large encampment of Sioux and Cheyenne in the Little Bighorn valley in southern Montana. Custer and his men were surrounded and killed by the Sioux under their leader, Sitting Bull, in a battle subsequently known as Custer's last stand.

'If I sneak out of here before the debt is paid off, I won't be worth a goddamned thing to myself.' 'Custer's last stand.' 'That's it. The old put-up-or-shut-up routine.'
PAUL AUSTER *Music of Chance* 1990

When we got out of the car I made a last-ditch stand to prevent him following me down the basement steps. Custer had better luck.
ANN GRANGER *Keeping Bad Company* 1997

Cyclops In Greek mythology, the Cyclops (or Cyclopes) were a race of savage one-eyed giants who were said to have lived as shepherds or to have made thunderbolts for Zeus. The building of massive prehistoric structures was supposed to have been the work of the Cyclops. The related adjective is 'Cyclopean'.

To birds on the wing its glassy surface, reflecting the light sky, must have been visible for miles around as a glistening Cyclops' eye in a green face.
THOMAS HARDY *Far from the Madding Crowd* 1874

A Canadian washing machine, with a round window in its middle, spied on them with this Cyclops eye.
ROBERTSON DAVIES *A Mixture of Frailties* 1951

He stopped, squinting at me with Cyclopean irritation.
RALPH ELLISON *Invisible Man* 1952

From time to time he came upon the great smooth stones, remains of the ancient wall, which had once separated two kingdoms, and touching their smooth surfaces with his hands he could not help thinking that there was something eerie about them. They seemed left over from some forgotten Cyclopean age.
LAWRENCE DURRELL *White Eagles over Serbia* 1957

Dachau Dachau was a Nazi concentration camp just outside the town of Dachau in Bavaria from 1933 to 1945. It was used to imprison 'enemies of the state' including communists, Social Democrats, trade union leaders, resistance fighters, Catholic priests, criminals, gypsies, and homosexuals. Jewish prisoners started being taken there from November 1938. Hundreds of prisoners died in medical experiments to find a cure for malaria, and a gas chamber was built in 1942. *See also* HOLOCAUST.

> He was living by himself on that farm of his free as a bird, eating the bread of freedom, yet he arrived here looking like a skeleton. He looked like someone out of Dachau.
> J. M. COETZEE *Life and Times of Michael K* 1983

Dada Dada was an early 20th-century artistic and literary movement which rejected traditional moral and aesthetic values and emphasized the illogical and absurd. The movement was started in Zurich in 1916 by the poet Tristan Tzara and others, and soon spread to New York, Paris, and Cologne. Artists associated with Dada included Jean Arp, André Breton, Max Ernst, Man Ray, and Marcel Duchamp. One of the most famous works produced was Duchamp's version of the *Mona Lisa* decorated with a moustache and an obscene caption.

> Nevertheless, his dreams continue, and are, if anything, more varied, more vivid, more Dadaist in their narration, and more persistent in their reaching after odd tossed chunks of history.
> CAROL SHIELDS *Mary Swan* 1990

Daddy Warbucks Daddy Warbucks is a rich businessman in the American comic strip *Little Orphan Annie*, who takes care of Annie. As his name suggests, he was originally a munitions manufacturer. *See also* ORPHAN ANNIE.

Daedalus In Greek mythology, Daedalus was an Athenian craftsman. He fled from Athens to Crete after jealously killing his pupil Talos, whose skills threatened to outdo his own. In the service of King Minos of Crete, Daedalus designed and built the labyrinth in which the Minotaur was kept. When Minos later refused to allow him to leave Crete, he escaped by making wings for himself and his son Icarus. Although Daedalus escaped and flew to safety, Icarus flew too high and the sun melted the wax holding his wings together, so that he plunged to his death. Daedalus can be alluded to as a clever craftsman or maker of clever or complicated devices. *See also* ICARUS.

> It was a dirty reeking room into which we entered, with men and women idling upon stools and cushions—I know not if Daedalus would have made a labyrinth for such monsters.
> PETER ACKROYD *The House of Dr Dee* 1993

Dalek The Daleks are an enemy life form in the long-running BBC television science fiction series *Doctor Who* (from 1963). The ferocious Daleks are the Doctor's most persistent enemy. Round with domed tops, they are approximately 5 feet high, and have various sink-plunger-style appendages. They are inclined to utter the syllables 'Ex-ter-min-ate' or, in response to such an instruction, 'I o-bey', in robotic voices. *See also* DOCTOR WHO.

> He reached out and opened the door of the airing cupboard. The vacuum cleaner lay coiled there, like an alien pet belonging to the Dalek of the boiler.
> MARTIN AMIS *The Information* 1995

> The people and the places will have to wait, Rosetti. His master commands and we must obey, just like the Daleks.
> MEL STEIN *White Lines* 1997

Arthur Daley Arthur Daley was a character in the ITV series *Minder* (1979–94), a shady wheeler-dealer always full of schemes to make money quickly, usually involving selling goods of dubious origin. Daley always managed to avoid being arrested, but never actually made any money from his schemes.

> Burglars are being encouraged by the public's 'Arthur Daley' mentality to crime and willingness to turn a blind eye to stolen goods, one of Britain's most senior police officers said yesterday. *The Independent* 1994

Salvador Dalí Salvador Dalí (1904–89) was a Spanish painter and prominent member of the Surrealist movement, who was greatly influenced by Sigmund Freud's writings on dreams and the unconscious. Many of his paintings depict fantastic dream images painted with almost photographically realist detail and set in arid Catalan landscapes. *The Persistence of Memory* (1931) features the famous image of limp, melting watches.

> I am a breast. A phenomenon . . . took place within my body between midnight and 4 am on February 18, 1971, and converted me into a mammary gland disconnected from any human form, a mammary gland such as could only appear, one would have thought, in a dream or a Dali painting.
> PHILIP ROTH *The Breast* 1972

> He pulled himself up into a sitting position and the movement made his interior world slide and melt like a Dali painting.
> MICHAEL CONNELLY *The Last Coyote* 1995

Damascus According to the Bible, the road to Damascus was the site of the sudden and dramatic conversion to Christianity undergone by Saul of Tarsus. With a reputation as a committed persecutor of Christians, he had set out planning to take prisoner any Christians he found in Damascus. On the way he suddenly found himself the centre of a blinding light and, falling to the ground, heard God's voice crying 'Saul, Saul, why persecutest thou me?' (Acts 9: 4). Saul, later known as Paul, became a powerful and influential Christian. References to the road to Damascus are usually in the context of a sudden realization, particularly a sudden conversion to a belief, opinion, or cause.

d

> Richard underwent some sort of religious conversion—the full road-to-Damascus number, so I heard. When he came out of gaol, he couldn't cope with the real world. He didn't have any support, I suppose that was the problem: no job to go back to, no family— he wasn't married and in all the years I knew him I never heard him mention any relatives. Jesus was probably all he had.
> HILARY WHELAN *Frightening Strikes* 1995

> There was no Damascus experience for me, no great leap for mankind (or womankind for that matter), only a series of small shifts, each insignificant in its own right, but each making possible the next.
> ANDRÉ BRINK *Imaginings of Sand* 1996

> Mum had been to church and suddenly realized in a St Paul-on-road-to-Damascus-type blinding flash that the vicar is gay.
> HELEN FIELDING *Bridget Jones's Diary* 1996

Damocles *See* SWORD OF DAMOCLES.

Damon and Pythias Damon and Pythias (also called Phintias) were legendary friends of the 4th century BC. The tyrant Dionysius I of Syracuse had sentenced Pythias to death. When Pythias went home to settle his affairs, Damon stood surety with his life for Pythias' return to certain execution. Pythias did return in time to redeem his pledge and was then reprieved. Damon and Pythias are synonymous with faithful friendship.

> Papa, I am really longing to see the Pythias to your Damon. You know, I never saw him but once, and then we were so puzzled to know what to say to each other that we did not get on particularly well.
> ELIZABETH GASKELL *North and South* 1854–5

> 'I thought you had a bond of common interest.' 'We had,' was the reply. 'But it is more than ten years since Henry Jekyll became too fanciful for me . . . Such unscientific balderdash,' added the doctor, flushing suddenly purple, 'would have estranged Damon and Pythias.'
> ROBERT LOUIS STEVENSON *The Strange Case of Dr Jekyll and Mr Hyde* 1886

> Of course she thinks, since I'm Fontclair's groomsman, he and I must have been Damon and Pythias for years.
> KATE ROSS *Cut to the Quick* 1993

Dan Dare Dan Dare was a comic-strip cartoon hero who appeared in the *Eagle* comic between 1950 and 1967. A commander of the Space Fleet, Dan Dare battled against his arch-enemy from Venus, the Mekon.

> The Middle East, with all its complexities and dangers and religious tension—yes, and its evils—is being turned into a comic strip in which Dan Dare will launch his space-age high-tech at the Mekon of Baghdad. *The Independent* 1998

Daniel According to the book of Daniel, Daniel was a devout Jew who spent his life as one of those taken into exile in Babylon. He had a gift for interpreting visions and dreams. He was able to explain the meaning of a strange dream that Nebuchadnezzar, the king of Babylon, had had, for which he was made the king's chief adviser. Later, Daniel interpreted a second dream of Nebuchadnezzar to foretell his insanity, which immediately came to pass.

When, after a successful career, he was appointed sole administrator over all the other officials and princes, they plotted to bring about Daniel's downfall. They asked King Darius to establish a decree saying that for thirty days no one should pray to any God or man except the king. Daniel ignored this command. As a result of this disobedience, he was cast into the lions' den and left for the night. In the morning he was discovered by the king, unscathed. Daniel explained, 'My God hath sent his angel, and hath shut the lions' mouths, that they have not hurt me' (Dan. 6: 22). Daniel has thus come to represent the courage of someone who faces great danger alone without any material protection.

In the apocryphal book of Susanna, Daniel is portrayed as a wise judge, proving the falsely accused Susanna to be innocent. In Shakespeare's *The Merchant of Venice*, Shylock praises Portia, who is disguised as a lawyer, with the words:
'A Daniel come to judgment! Yea, a Daniel!
O wise young judge, how I do honour thee!'
See also BELSHAZZAR, NEBUCHADNEZZAR, SHADRACH, MESACH AND ABEDNEGO, SUSANNA, WRITING ON THE WALL.

> Weigh me the two, you Daniel, going to judgement, when your day shall come!
> CHARLES DICKENS *The Chimes* 1844

> You nearly caught me, Major Scobie, that time. It was a matter of import duties, you remember. You could have caught me if you had told your policeman to say something a little different. I was quite overcome with astonishment, Major Scobie, to sit in a police court and hear true facts from the mouths of policemen. . . . I said to myself, Yusef, a Daniel has come to the Colonial Police.
> GRAHAM GREENE *The Heart of the Matter* 1948

> Don't you feel like Daniel setting off for the lion's den, going back there? If you

really think one of the Fontclairs is a murderer, how can you sit down to dinner with them, sleep under their roof?
KATE ROSS *Cut to the Quick* 1993

Older than the crew, in their thirties. They were two lost little lamb-i-kins who had wandered into the lions' den.
CHARLES HIGSON *Full Whack* 1995

Dante Dante Alighieri (1265–1321) was an Italian poet whose epic *The Divine Comedy* (c.1309–20) relates the poet's imagined visit to Hell, Purgatory, and Paradise. References to Dante are often in the context of a hideous or horrific sight, suggestive of the horrors of Hell depicted by the poet. Dante's first book, *La Vita Nuova* (c.1290–4), details, in poetry and prose, his adoration for Beatrice Portinari (1265–90). He was platonically devoted to her all his life, although she did not apparently return his love and both were married to others.

I gazed on him while unfinished; he was ugly then; but when those muscles and joints were rendered capable of motion, it became a thing such as even Dante could not have conceived.
MARY SHELLEY *Frankenstein* 1831

It was the purest, most selfless romantic devotion. It was Dante and Beatrice in a suburban key.
DAVID LODGE *Therapy* 1995

Beijing became a Dantean pit of underworld activity in the years following the country's economic expansion.
PAUL JOHNSTON *Body Politic* 1997

Dante's Inferno The term 'Dante's Inferno' refers to the part of Dante's epic poem *The Divine Comedy* (c.1309–20) that depicts the poet's journey through Hell. Any hell-like vision or scene can be described as being like Dante's Inferno.

Bored, she stepped outside, on to a steel gallery overlooking the factory floor. She surveyed the scene, feeling more than ever like Dante in the Inferno. All was noise, smoke, fumes and flames.
DAVID LODGE *Nice Work* 1988

Dan to Beersheba Dan was a town in the north of Canaan, the Promised Land to which Moses led the people of Israel in the Bible. It marked the northern limit of the ancient kingdom of Israel. Beersheba, which still exists, was the town which marked the southern limit of the kingdom. According to the book of Judges, the people of Israel were 'gathered together as one man, from Dan even to Beersheba' (Judg. 20: 1). Something that happens from Dan to Beersheba therefore happens everywhere.

What profits it to have a covenanted State and a purified Kirk if a mailed

Amalekite can hunt our sodgers from Dan to Beersheba?
JOHN BUCHAN *Witch Woods* 1927

Daphne In Greek mythology, Daphne was a nymph, daughter of Peneus, with whom the god Apollo fell in love. In attempting to escape his pursuit, Daphne called upon the gods for help and was turned into a laurel tree. She is often depicted in art, literally rooted to the spot as she undergoes her transformation, for example in Bernini's marble sculpture *Apollo and Daphne* (1622–5).

> A spasm passed through Grace. A Daphnean instinct, exceptionally strong in her as a girl, had been revived by her widowed seclusion; and it was not lessened by her affronted sentiments towards the comer, and her regard for another man.
> THOMAS HARDY *The Woodlanders* 1887

> Alexander slid into the seat beside her, Alexander's Old Spice smell brushed her nostrils, Alexander's soft-modulated voice murmured no, surely not muscle-bound, but with her nerves chained up in alabaster and she a statue, or as Daphne was, root-bound, that fled Apollo.
> A. S. BYATT *The Virgin in the Garden* 1978

Daphnis and Chloe Daphnis and Chloe are the subjects of an ancient Greek pastoral romance, *Daphnis and Chloe*, by Longus (AD 2–3). The story relates how the two young people meet, fall in love, and discover sexual desire, eventually marrying.

Darby and Joan Darby and Joan are alluded to as personifying an elderly but happily married couple. They were originally described in a poem in the *Gentleman's Magazine* (1735):
'Old Darby, with Joan by his side,
You've often regarded with wonder:
He's dropsical, she is sore-eyed,
Yet they're never happy asunder.'

> I can assure you I don't want any procession at all. I should be quite contented to go down with Alexandrina, arm in arm, like Darby and Joan, and let the clerk give her away.
> ANTHONY TROLLOPE *The Small House at Allington* 1862

Mr Darcy Fitzwilliam Darcy is the hero of Jane Austen's novel *Pride and Prejudice* (1796), who courts and finally wins Elizabeth Bennet. Wealthy and extremely handsome, with a proud and rather aloof manner, he has come to represent a certain type of romantic hero.

> She was busy running her tresses through her manicured fingers and flapping her blue-mascaraed eyelashes at James Rattray-Potter, who was propped against the desk in a suave, man-of-the-world pose, ankles crossed. He was a generic Mills and Boon hero to Dominic Planchet's Mr Darcy, but I could see

that his brand of florid good looks would appeal to secretaries and girls who lacked confidence.
LAUREN HENDERSON *The Black Rubber Dress* 1997

Dark Ages The term 'the Dark Ages' has sometimes been used to designate the period in the West between the fall of the Roman Empire and the high Middle Ages (that is, from about the 5th to the 11th century), so called because it used to be regarded as a time of relative unenlightenment and obscurity. In other contexts the term can suggest any unenlightened or ignorant period or, when used humorously, any little-regarded period before the present. To 'live in the Dark Ages' is to be old-fashioned or prejudiced in one's behaviour and attitudes.

> Jim's brow darkened. 'Look, old son. The law's no place for Luddites. We're in business, remember? We need to compete, to provide a decent service.' 'I haven't heard Kevin or Jeannie Walters complaining.' 'You've done a superb job, I'm the first to say so. But we must move with the times. We can't keep living in the Dark Ages.'
> MARTIN EDWARDS *Yesterday's Papers* 1994

Darkest Africa Before Africa had been fully explored by Europeans it was known to them as the Dark Continent. Darkest Africa was therefore an unexplored land far away from modern European life and full of potential dangers. The term may have originated from titles of works by the explorer Henry Morton Stanley, *Through the Dark Continent* (1878) and *Through Darkest Africa* (1890).

Grace Darling Grace Darling (1815–42), the daughter of a lighthouse keeper on the Farne Islands off the coast of Northumberland, became a national heroine when in September 1838 she and her father rowed through a storm to rescue the survivors of the wrecked *Forfarshire*.

> When she was seventeen, she had been somewhere between Queen Elizabeth I and Grace Darling, with a will of tungsten and the biddability of a mobile howitzer.
> SAM LLEWELLYN *Maelstrom* 1995

D'Artagnan *See* THREE MUSKETEERS.

Darth Vader Darth Vader ® is the villain in the film *Star Wars* (1977) and its sequels. Formerly Anakin Skywalker, a Jedi knight who has been corrupted to 'the dark side', Darth Vader is always dressed in black and wears a helmet. *See also* STAR WARS.

> Markby looked towards the large studio portrait of the late Jack glowering handsomely from a sidetable. A dark-haired, thick-browed, lantern-jawed thug.

Women often found that type attractive. Glyn didn't resemble him particularly. Perhaps he rode around on the motorbike, dressed up like Darth Vader, to compensate.

ANN GRANGER *Candle for a Corpse* 1995

Dartmoor Dartmoor is a high-security prison on Dartmoor, a moorland district in Devon, originally built to hold French prisoners of war during the Napoleonic Wars.

Darwin Charles Darwin (1809–82) was an English naturalist and geologist who formulated the theory of evolution by natural selection to explain the origin of animal and plant species. His work *On the Origin of Species* was published in 1859 and *The Descent of Man* in 1871.

David Allusions to David relate to various episodes in his long life as described in the Bible, in particular his defeat of Goliath. The youngest son of Jesse, David was noted as a musician and is traditionally regarded as the author of the Psalms. The young David relieved King Saul's melancholy by playing the lyre: 'And whenever the evil spirit from God was upon Saul, David took the lyre and played it with his hand; so Saul was refreshed, and was well, and the evil spirit departed from him' (1 Sam. 16: 23).

When still a shepherd boy, David accepted the challenge from the Philistine champion Goliath to single combat. Although Goliath was over 9 feet tall and wore full armour including a brass helmet, David went to fight him armed only with a sling and five pebbles. Using the sling, he struck Goliath on the forehead and killed him.

David's success was greeted by the women coming out to meet Saul and singing: 'Saul hath slain his thousands, and David his ten thousands.' From this time on Saul became jealous of David's popularity and on a number of occasions tried to kill him. David and Saul's son Jonathan had become bosom friends and had sworn a compact of love and mutual protection, Jonathan repeatedly trying to intercede on David's behalf with his father.

On Saul's death David was made king of Judah and later he was chosen as ruler of the whole of Israel. He made Jerusalem his capital and reigned there for 33 years. David's later years were darkened by the rebellion and death of his favourite son, Absalom.

In an episode not long before his death, the elderly King David chastely shared his bed with a young woman called Abishag in order that she could warm his body with hers: 'So they . . . found Abishag the Shunammite, and brought her to the king. The damsel was very fair and cherished the king; but the king knew her not' (1 Kgs. 1: 1–4). Modern allusions to David and Goliath often take the form of an individual or small, relatively powerless, group defeating a powerful or global organization. *See also* ABSALOM, BATHSHEBA, DAVID AND JONATHAN, GOLIATH, URIAH.

That night when Beth played to Mr. Laurence in the twilight, Laurie, standing in

the shadow of the curtain, listened to the little David, whose simple music always quieted his moody spirit.
LOUISA M. ALCOTT *Little Women* 1868

Poor man, he's so sad. His wife dead. I only stayed to comfort him, and he couldn't anyway. He said he was like King David, and could I just warm him all night.
FAY WELDON *Life Force* 1992

Every day we hear of more Italian armies driven back or defeated, and we feel the jubilation of David with Goliath dead at his feet.
LOUIS DE BERNIÈRES *Captain Corelli's Mandolin* 1994

On this public relations battlefront the odds against a Greenpeace victory shorten dramatically. A master of global communications, the environmental group recently played David against Shell's Goliath over the Brent Spar and won. *The Observer* 1995

David and Jonathan In the Old Testament (1 Sam. 18: 1–3, 20: 17), Jonathan, the son of Saul, and David, Saul's appointed successor as king of Israel, swore a compact of love and mutual protection: 'the love of Jonathan was knit with the soul of David, and Jonathan loved him as his own soul'. When Saul grew jealous of David's popularity and sought to bring about his death, Jonathan repeatedly tried to intercede on David's behalf with his father.

Among the members of his church there was one young man, a little older than himself, with whom he had long lived in such close friendship that it was the custom of their Lantern Yard brethren to call them David and Jonathan.
GEORGE ELIOT *Silas Marner* 1861

Why should you not make friends with your neighbour at the theatre or in the train, when you know and he knows that feminine criticism and feminine insight and feminine prejudice will never come between you! Though you become as David and Jonathan, you need never enter his home, nor he yours.
E. M. FORSTER *Where Angels Fear to Tread* 1905

After that there's an undignified struggle for possession of the gun, which Archie wins, followed by a lot of weeping, mostly by the husband, then they sit down and talk and by the time they get back to the house they're like David and Jonathan.
BARRY NORMAN *The Mickey Mouse Affair* 1995

Doris Day The US actress and singer Doris Day (b. Doris Kappelhoff, 1924) played the cheerful, freckle-faced girl-next-door in numerous musicals and comedies in the late 1940s and early 1950s. In the late 1950s and early 1960s she appeared in a series of innocent sex comedies such as *Pillow Talk* (1959), in which she habitually played the virginal heroine. Groucho Marx claimed to have 'been around so long I can remember Doris Day before she was a virgin'.

What feminism does not need . . . is an endless recycling of Doris Day Fifties clichés about noble womanhood.
CAMILLE PAGLIA *'Big Udder: Suzanne Gordon's "Prisoners of Men's Dreams" '* in *Sex, Art, & American Culture* 1991

Maybe because I wanted to lend the moment that sort of corny Doris Day romance, make it more memorable than it otherwise would have been.
NICK HORNBY *High Fidelity* 1995

There was a rap on the door and my sister bounced in, looking Doris Day–Meg Ryan perky. Probably perfect for California, but we don't do perky in Jersey.
JANET EVANOVICH *Seven Up* 2001

Dead Sea Fruit The Dead Sea Fruit, also known as Apples of Sodom, were fruits reputed to grow at Sodom, near the Dead Sea. They were beautiful to look at but bitter to the taste or full of ashes, and the expression is now used of anything that promises pleasure but brings only disappointment.

Like Dead Sea fruits, that tempt the eye,
But turn to ashes on the lips!
THOMAS MORE *Lalla Rookh* 1817

Your poor mother's fond wish, gratified at last in the mocking way in which over-fond wishes are too often fulfilled—Sodom apples as they are—has brought on this crisis.
ELIZABETH GASKELL *North and South* 1854–5

He had looked for rapturous joy in loving this lovely creature, and he already found that he met with little but disappointment and self-rebuke. He had come across the fruit of the Dead Sea, so sweet and delicious to the eye, so bitter and nauseous to the taste.
ANTHONY TROLLOPE *Barchester Towers* 1857

James Dean James Dean (1931–55) was an American actor best remembered for his role in the 1955 film *Rebel Without a Cause*. The film opened just weeks after Dean's death in a car crash, and he became strongly associated with the character he played in the film, a confused, rebellious, and self-destructive adolescent.

Over her shoulder, the trailer door opened. Lonnie stood there in a pair of worn jeans and a white T-shirt. He could do James Dean with the best of them, I thought.
STEVEN WOMACK *Dead Folks' Blues* 1992

The one riding shotgun had the James Dean look, dark, wavy hair over a fuck-you pout. They thought they were badasses and I was an old fart. That made two surprises they had coming.
JOHN DUNNING *The Bookman's Wake* 1995

Death Death was one of the Four Horsemen of the Apocalypse: 'And I looked, and behold, a pale horse, and his name that sat on him was Death'

(Rev. 6: 8). The other horsemen were Pestilence, War, and Famine.

> Not knowing whether to expect friend or foe, prudence suggested that he
> should cease his whistling and retreat among the trees till the horse and his
> rider had gone by, a course to which he was still more inclined when he found
> how noiselessly they approached, and saw that the horse looked pale, and
> remembered what he had read about Death in the Revelation.
> THOMAS HARDY *The Woodlanders* 1887

Degas (Hilaire Germain) Edgar Degas (1834–1917) was a French painter and
sculptor associated with Impressionism. He is best known for his drawings,
paintings, and pastels of ballet dancers, cabaret artistes, and women dressing
and bathing.

> She was a big, sexy brunette—as Garcia said, 'Something straight out of
> Degas.'
> JACK KEROUAC *On the Road* 1957

Deianira In Greek mythology, Deianira was the wife of Hercules. When on
one occasion the centaur Nessus tried to abduct her, Hercules shot him
through the breast with an arrow. Nessus told Deianira to take some of his
blood and use it as a love potion by smearing it onto a garment of Hercules if
ever she suspected that he was being unfaithful. Some time later, Deianira
became jealous of her husband's attraction towards Iole, a princess whom he
had captured while away from home and was intending to bring home with
him. Hercules had asked Deianira to send him some ceremonial robes and
she used the opportunity to test the supposed love potion, by smearing some
of the blood of Nessus onto one of the robes in an attempt to win back his
love. The blood was in fact a poison, Nessus' revenge, and caused the death
of Hercules. When she realized what she had done, Deianira took her own
life. *See also* HERCULES, NESSUS.

Deimos In Greek mythology, Deimos was one of the sons of Aphrodite and
Ares. He is sometimes seen as a personification of fear.

Deirdre In Irish legend, Deirdre was the beautiful daughter of the harper to
King Conchobar of Ulster. According to a prophecy her beauty would bring
death and ruin to the men of Ulster. Although she was the intended bride of
Conchobar, she fell in love and eloped with Naoise. When Naoise was
treacherously slain by Conchobar, Deirdre took her own life, ending her
misery.

Del Boy Del Boy (Derek Trotter) is the lead character in the television sitcom
Only Fools and Horses (1981–96). In pursuit of easy wealth, and with the
assistance of his naive younger brother Rodney, he runs Trotter's
Independent Trading Company, selling dodgy products, which he stores in
their council flat. Memorably played by David Jason, Del Boy is a classic wide
boy.

That is, the businessmen, financiers, entrepreneurs and Del Boys who have been happy to skirt the limelight so sought after by our elected representatives and provided by our startstruck media.
SHEENA MCDONALD *The Guardian* 1988

Delectable Mountains In Bunyan's *Pilgrim's Progress*, the summit of the Delectable Mountains, Emmanuel's Land, is within sight of the Celestial City. *See also* PILGRIM'S PROGRESS.

We call this hill the Delectable Mountain, for we can look far away and see the country where we hope to live some time.
LOUISA M. ALCOTT *Little Women* 1868

Delilah According to the Old Testament book of Judges, Delilah used her guile to extract from Samson the secret of his prodigious strength so that she could betray him to the Philistines in return for money. She repeatedly asked Samson the secret of his strength and when he had given her three false answers said: 'How canst thou say, I love thee, when thine heart is not with me? Thou hast mocked me these three times, and hast not told me wherein thy great strength lieth' (Judg. 16: 15). Samson finally relented and told her that his great strength lay in his long hair and that if it were cut short he would 'become weak, and be like any other man'. Delilah had his hair shaved while he slept, after which she delivered him up to the Philistines. Any treacherous woman can be described as a Delilah. *See also* SAMSON.

Ay, and I fancy I've baited the hook right. Our little Delilah will bring our Samson.
ANTHONY HOPE *The Prisoner of Zenda* 1894

'Lassiter!' Jane whispered, as she gazed from him to the black, cold guns. Without them he appeared shorn of strength, defenseless, a smaller man. Was she Delilah? Swiftly, conscious of only one motive—refusal to see this man called craven by his enemies—she rose, and with blundering fingers buckled the belt round his waist where it belonged.
ZANE GREY *Riders of the Purple Sage* 1912

Delphi Delphi was the site of the Delphic oracle on the slopes of Mount Parnassus in ancient Greece, which was consulted on a wide range of religious, political, and moral questions. The pronouncements of the Oracle were made by the priestess of Apollo, Pythia. They were often ambiguous and riddle-like and had to be interpreted. A Delphic prediction or warning is one that is enigmatic or difficult to interpret. *See also* APOLLO.

She could utter oracles of Delphian ambiguity when she did not choose to be direct.
THOMAS HARDY *The Return of the Native* 1880

She had a turn for improvising and phrasing ambiguous but startling messages

that would have done credit to the Oracle at Delphi.
ROBERTSON DAVIES *Fifth Business* 1970

This really is very pleasant—to escape. I'm not sure why it is, but I find that a roomful of 'scholars' tends to bring on an attack of mental indigestion. That Delphic tone they love to take. And something chilly and unhelpful about them too.
CAROL SHIELDS *Mary Swann* 1990

As for the second prediction, it's not quite so Delphic, but perhaps I can permit myself to claim as foretelling the use of just such enclosures in places like present-day leisure park complexes. *New Scientist* 1994

Demeter In Greek mythology, Demeter was the goddess of cornfields and fecundity, whose symbol is an ear of corn. She was the mother of Persephone, and when Persephone was abducted by Hades and taken to the underworld, Demeter wandered around looking for her daughter and swore that the earth would remain barren until Persephone was restored to her. A compromise was finally reached whereby Persephone would spend six months of each year with her mother, the time when plants grow and produce fruit, and six months of each year with Hades in the underworld, the time when the earth is cold and barren. *See also* HADES, PERSEPHONE.

Demodocus Demodocus was a blind bard at the Phaeacian court of Alcinous who, according to Homer's *Odyssey*, entertained Odysseus with his songs telling of the adulterous love of Ares and Aphrodite and of the famous story of the Wooden Horse of Troy.

It was quite impossible—recounting tales in the presence of people who knew them already. She wondered how Taliesin, Demodocus and all the other storytellers had coped.
ALICE THOMAS ELLIS *The 27th Kingdom* 1982

Demosthenes Demosthenes (384–322 BC) was an Athenian orator and statesman famous for a series of orations attacking the rising power of Philip of Macedon.

The explorer waxes eloquent as Antony, Demosthenes and the Speaker of the House all rolled into one.
T. CORAGHESSAN BOYLE *Water Music* 1981

Dennis the Menace Dennis the Menace is a trouble-making boy who first appeared in the British comic *The Beano* in 1951. Dennis has a shock of thick black hair, wears a red and black striped jumper, and has a dog called Gnasher. A character of the same name has appeared in US comic strips also since 1951, though he is blond and younger than the British Dennis.

Depression *See* GREAT DEPRESSION.

Desdemona In Shakespeare's play *Othello* (1622), Desdemona is the daughter of a Venetian senator who falls in love with and marries the Moorish general Othello. The treacherous Iago, Othello's ensign, convinces Othello that Desdemona is being unfaithful to him and, although she is completely innocent, Othello murders her in jealous rage.

Norma Desmond Norma Desmond is the ageing retired silent-screen star in the film *Sunset Boulevard* (1950), played by Gloria Swanson. An impecunious Hollywood scriptwriter, Joe Gillis, stumbles upon her mansion when on the run from men who are trying to repossess his car. She persuades him to stay to write a script for her 'comeback movie'. Sublimely narcissistic, she is delusional about her current celebrity status and becomes increasingly possessive of Joe. The film famously starts with Joe floating face down in the swimming pool and then covers the incidents of the previous six months which eventually leads to Joe being shot by Norma. By the time the cameras finally come for her, she is sufficiently deluded to believe they are celebrating her, rather than filming the news story of Joe's murder.

> 'You know what's so tragic?' she said. 'After all I've done, all I've been through, I'm still alone.' I didn't say anything. There wasn't anything to say. I just looked at her vapid, empty, uncomprehending face, bottomless in its self-absorption, a monster's face. 'Get your stuff together,' I said to Jocelyn. 'We're going.' . . . 'So we be going up to Port City again,' Hawk said. 'Yeah.' 'What are we going to do with Norma Desmond?' Hawk said. 'We'll bring her along. Maybe she'll be useful.' 'Sure,' Hawk said. 'There's a first time for everything.'
> ROBERT B. PARKER *Walking Shadow* 1994

> The ill-assorted, mostly Victorian, buildings of Kensington Church Street blurred to beauty like Norma Desmond through a skilful cameraman's soft filter.
> ANABEL DONAL *Destroy Unopened* 1999

Deucalion In Greek mythology, Deucalion was the son of Prometheus. When Zeus, angered by the crimes of men, decided to destroy them by a great flood, Prometheus warned Deucalion, who built a boat for himself and his wife, Pyrrha, in which they floated until the waters subsided and they safely came to land on Mount Parnassus. *See also* FLOOD.

Devil In Christian and Jewish belief, the Devil is the supreme spirit of evil. He is the enemy of God and the tempter of humankind. In theological tradition he was regarded as the chief of the fallen angels, cast out of Heaven for rebellion against God. He presided over those condemned to eternal fire. Popularly, the Devil is often represented as a man with horns, a forked tail, and cloven hooves, an image derived from figures of Greek and Roman mythology such as Pan and the satyrs. The Devil is known by numerous names, especially Satan and Lucifer. Other names include 'the Evil One', 'Old Harry', 'Old Nick', and 'the Prince of Darkness'. *See also* LUCIFER, SATAN.

> I am very sure I had no manner of design in my head, when I went out; I neither knew, nor considered where to go, or on what business; but as the devil carried

me out, and laid his bait for me, so he brought me to be sure to the place, for I knew not whither I was going, or what I did.
DANIEL DEFOE *Moll Flanders* 1722

But it was only a thought, put into my head by the Devil, no doubt.
MARGARET ATWOOD *Alias Grace* 1996

Devil's Island Devil's Island is a small island off the coast of French Guiana. It was used as a convict settlement, initially for prisoners with contagious diseases but later for political prisoners. Its most famous prisoner was Albert Dreyfus (1859–1935), the French army officer of Jewish descent who was falsely accused of passing secrets to the Germans. His trial, imprisonment, and eventual release caused a major political crisis in France. *See also* DREYFUS.

Each of these transgressions isolated the club and its devotees further and further from the lip-pursing, right-thinking, Arsenal-hating mainland; Highbury became a Devil's Island in the middle of north London, the home of no-goods and miscreants.
NICK HORNBY *Fever Pitch* 1993

Diana In Roman mythology, Diana was identified with the Greek goddess Artemis and was associated with hunting, virginity, and, in later literature and art, with the moon. She was the personification of feminine grace and vigour.

There have been plenty of young heroes, of middle stature and feeble beards, who have felt quite sure they could never love anything more insignificant than a Diana, and yet have found themselves in middle life happily settled with a wife who waddles.
GEORGE ELIOT *Adam Bede* 1859

In her dress of white and silver, with a wreath of silver blossoms in her hair, the tall girl looked like a Diana just alighting from the chase.
EDITH WHARTON *The Age of Innocence* 1920

Princess Diana Diana, Princess of Wales (1961–97) was born Lady Diana Frances Spencer. She married the prince of Wales in 1981 in a ceremony in St Paul's Cathedral, London, and had two sons, Prince William and Prince Henry (Harry). She and the prince of Wales later divorced. She died on 31 August 1997, following a car crash in Paris. Diana devoted much time to charitable work, concentrating particularly on helping children, homeless people, and AIDS sufferers, and at the time of her death she had also become known for her work for a campaign to ban landmines.

It is really a caring multinational in a special post-Diana way. *The Observer* 1998

As we get to know him we discover Ernesto (pre Che, at this point known as 'Fuser') isn't quite the lecherous med-student on Spring Break we were led to believe: quite the sensitive young thing . . . he has a Diana-like compassion for the sick, poor and helpless (no rubber gloves for him when he meets the lepers, thank you very much!).

OLLY BUXTON *Amazon.com* 2004

Dickensian The novels of Charles Dickens (1812–70) are notable for their satirical humour and treatment of contemporary social problems, including the plight of the urban poor. The term 'Dickensian' is used to suggest a number of distinct characteristics. Given the vivid portrayal of some of the novelist's more eccentric or physically grotesque characters, the term can suggest a person's almost caricature-like oddness in behaviour, mannerisms, or appearance. The novels are filled with slums, workhouses, debtors' prisons, and other examples of social deprivation, and 'Dickensian' can thus be used to suggest conditions of poverty, squalor, and hardship. It can likewise denote a corrupt and brutal educational regime like that at Dotheboys Hall in Dickens's *Nicholas Nickleby*. Finally, the term may describe one of the writer's young heroines, whose kind, sweet, open nature contrasts with the harshness and wickedness of the world around them. *See also* ARTFUL DODGER, MR BUMBLE, SIDNEY CARTON, CHEERYBLE BROTHERS, BOB CRATCHIT, FAGIN, MRS GAMP, GRADGRIND, MISS HAVISHAM, URIAH HEEP, LITTLE NELL, MARLEY'S GHOST, MR MICAWBER, PECKSNIFF, MR PICKWICK, PODSNAP, SCROOGE, WACKFORD SQUEERS, OLIVER TWIST, DOLLY VARDEN.

Hilda kept up all the appearance of Dickensian young-girlishness, but contrived at the same time to make all the advances, create all the opportunites and lead the conversation into all the properly amorous channels.

ALDOUS HUXLEY *Point Counter Point* 1928

I wanted to go back and leer at my strange Dickensian mother in the hash joint.

JACK KEROUAC *On the Road* 1957

I can't help describing him as if he were some sort of Dickensian freak.

ROBERTSON DAVIES *The Manticore* 1972

So Eddie and his older brother, Mark, were suddenly dispatched to boarding school when they were six and eight respectively—unfortunately, a Dickensian school which rang to the thwack of the cane. *The Observer* 1997

Dido and Aeneas Dido was the queen of Carthage, and the story of her love affair with Aeneas is recounted in Virgil's *Aeneid* (29–19 BC). Aeneas, on his way home from Troy, is shipwrecked off the coast of Carthage, where Dido falls in love with him. The affair is consummated when, during a storm while out hunting, they take shelter in the same cave. Aeneas, however, is commanded by Jupiter to sail to Italy. Seeing the ships preparing to leave, Dido pleads with Aeneas, begging him to stay. When he has departed, she kills herself by building a pyre and throwing herself on it. *See also* AENEAS.

In such a night
Stood Dido with a willow in her hand
Upon the wild sea-banks, and waft her love

To come again to Carthage.
WILLIAM SHAKESPEARE *The Merchant of Venice* 1600

Of all the ladies of my acquaintance I think Lady Dido was the most absurd. Why did she not do as Cleopatra did? Why did she not take out her ships and insist on going with him? She could not bear to lose the land she had got by swindle; and then she could not bear the loss of her lover. So she fell between two stools. Whatever you do, my friend, do not mingle love and business. Either stick to your treasure and your city of wealth, or else follow your love like a true man. But never attempt both. If you do, you'll have to die with a broken heart as did poor Dido.
ANTHONY TROLLOPE *Barchester Towers* 1857

Peter, on the other hand, though not blind to its flaws, felt himself duty driven to work from within. A right pious little Aeneas, *Italiam non sponte sequor* and all that crap. Which made her . . . Odysseus? Fat, earthy, cunning old Odysseus? Hardly! That was much more Andy Dalziel. Then Dido? Come on! See her chucking herself on a pyre 'cos she'd been jilted. Helen? Ellie looked at herself in the mirror. Not today.
REGINALD HILL *On Beulah Height* 1998

John Dillinger John Dillinger (1903–34) was an armed bank robber based in Indiana, named the FBI's 'public enemy number one' in 1933. He was shot dead by FBI agents in Chicago acting on information given by his girlfriend, now popularly known as the Lady in Red.

'You always wanted it that way, Jess. You changing your mind?' 'No. It's just . . .' He sighed. 'Spring'. 'Don't feel bad. It turns even the best of us to mush.' 'Leave it to Tark—more Diogenes than Dillinger these days—to understand that.'
MEG O'BRIEN *Eagles Die Too* 1993

Arthur Dimmesdale The Reverend Arthur Dimmesdale is a character in Nathaniel Hawthorne's *The Scarlet Letter* (1850). A young and much-respected church minister, he keeps secret the fact that he is the father of Hester Prynne's illegitimate baby while she is ostracized by the community and condemned to wear a scarlet 'A', for 'adulteress', on her bosom. Hester's husband, under the assumed name of Roger Chillingworth, discovers his secret and tortures him mentally with it until he finally confesses publicly and dies in Hester's arms. *See also* HESTER PRYNNE, SCARLET LETTER.

In all, the doctor he reminded me of most was Dr. Roger Chillingworth in Hawthorne's *Scarlet Letter*. Appropriate enough, because I sat facing him as full of shameful secrets as the Reverend Arthur Dimmesdale.
PHILIP ROTH *My Life as a Man* 1970

Diogenes Diogenes (*c*.400–*c*.325 BC) was a Greek philosopher, the most famous of the Cynics. He promoted self-sufficiency and the denial of physical pleasure and rejected social conventions. According to legend he lived in a barrel, to demonstrate his belief that the virtuous life was the simple life. One story told of him is that he carried a lantern out in daylight, saying that he was seeking an honest man.

> The significance of the name will not escape you. Lantern—it is the lantern of Diogenes, searching for the honest, the true, and the good.
> ROBERTSON DAVIES *A Mixture of Frailties* 1951

> I was filled with a sour scorn that I now know was nothing but envy, but then mistook it for philosophy. I didn't really want the clothes, I didn't really want the girl or the booze, but it scalded me to see him enjoying them, and I hobbled away grumbling to myself like Diogenes.
> ROBERTSON DAVIES *Fifth Business* 1970

> He immediately built himself a grass hut, Indian style, thatched it with palm, and to the wonder of the locals began to live like Diogenes and labour like Sisyphus, except with better results.
> LOUIS DE BERNIÈRES *The War of Don Emmanuel's Nether Parts* 1990

Dionysus In Greek mythology, Dionysus (also called Bacchus) was the son of Zeus and the mortal Semele. Zeus had taken Semele as a lover and when she asked Zeus to reveal himself to her in all the splendour of a god, he acceded to this rash request. The fire of the thunderbolts that flashed about him incinerated Semele, but Zeus just had time to snatch the unborn child from her womb. He sewed it up immediately inside his own thigh for protection, from where a few months later the baby Dionysus emerged. This is why Dionysus was sometimes known as 'the twice-born god'.

Originally a god of the fertility of nature, in later traditions Dionysus is a god of wine who loosens inhibitions and inspires creativity in music and poetry. His cult was celebrated at various festivals throughout the year, some of which included orgies and ecstatic rites. His female devotees were called the Bacchantes, or maenads. Dionysus, representing creativity, sensuality, and lack of inhibition, is often contrasted with Apollo, representing order, reason, and self-discipline. The adjectives 'Dionysian' and 'Dionysiac' usually describe frenzied and unrestrained abandon or ecstasy.

Dionysus was said to have made an expedition to eastern lands including India, spreading his cult and teaching mankind the elements of civilization and the use of wine. On his travels Dionysus is frequently represented drawn in a chariot by tigers and accompanied by Pan, Silenus, and a rowdy retinue of satyrs and maenads.

> Someone dimmed the lights and turned up the sitar music. They swayed and pressed and wriggled against each other in the twanging, orange, smoky twilight, it was a kind of dance, they were all dancing, he was dancing—at last: the free, improvised, Dionysian dancing he'd hankered after.
> DAVID LODGE *Changing Places* 1975

Wilkie told Marina Yeo that he would create a true Apollonian order from a Dionysiac cacophony.
A. S. BYATT *The Virgin in the Garden* 1978

Oh, how Sir Gerald . . . would love to be able to wallow in that filth with such Dionysian abandon!
TOM WOLFE *The Bonfire of the Vanities* 1987

Dirty Harry Harry Callaghan, nicknamed Dirty Harry, is a tough San Francisco police inspector played by Clint Eastwood in several films including *Dirty Harry* (1971) and *Magnum Force* (1973). When violent criminals escape justice through lack of evidence, Callaghan resorts to his own brutal vigilante methods of law enforcement.

The 2,000 or so people who earn their living chasing bail jumpers are essentially unscreened, untrained, unlicensed and unregulated. They operate outside the laws that apply to everyone else, even laws that impose restrictions on the police, and it's a line of work that tends to appeal to those who have Dirty Harry fantasies and macho, self-dramatising visions of hunting down 'skippers' and returning them to justice in the boots of their cars. *The Observer* 1997

Agreeing to the *People* interview was one of my worst mistakes; the reporter had made me sound more macho than Dirty Harry and in the accompanying photograph I looked like someone Harry himself wouldn't want to meet in a dark alley.
MARCIA MULLER *While Other People Sleep* 1998

Walt Disney Walt Disney (1901–66), the creator of Donald Duck and Mickey Mouse, is sometimes associated with the 'cute' portrayal of animals, both in such full-length animated cartoons as *Snow White* and *Bambi* and in his nature documentaries.

There are a lot of animals slaughtered in his books. He isn't Walt Disney, no. He was interested in cruelty, I agree.
JULIAN BARNES *Flaubert's Parrot* 1984

Dives Dives (from the Latin for 'rich') is the name traditionally given to the rich man in the parable of the rich man and Lazarus (Luke 16: 19–31). The rich man lived in great luxury while Lazarus was a beggar at his gate, covered with sores and longing even for the crumbs from the rich man's table. When both died, Dives found himself in Hell and, looking up, saw Lazarus being taken up to Heaven by Abraham. Abraham explained to him that he had already had good things in his lifetime whereas Lazarus had not. Consequently, Lazarus received comfort in the afterlife while the rich man endured agony. *See also* ABRAHAM'S BOSOM, LAZARUS.

Remember, we are bid to work while it is day—warned that 'the night cometh when no man shall work'. Remember the fate of Dives, who had his good

things in this life. God give you strength to choose that better part which shall not be taken from you!
CHARLOTTE BRONTË *Jane Eyre* 1847

Mrs Doasyouwouldbedoneby In Charles Kingsley's children's story *The Water-Babies* (1863), Mrs Doasyouwouldbedoneby is a benevolent character encountered by Tom after he became a water-baby. She teaches that you should behave towards others in the way that you would want them to behave to you.

Doctor Dolittle In Hugh Lofting's books (1920–52), Doctor John Dolittle is an animal-loving doctor whose human patients desert his practice because his house resembles a menagerie. Dolittle decides that he would much prefer to treat animals instead, and his parrot Polynesia helps him to learn all the animal languages, starting with the ABC of birds.

Doctor Foster According to the nursery rhyme,
'Doctor Foster went to Gloucester
In a shower of rain.
He stepped in a puddle right up to his middle,
And never went there again.'
Doctor Foster can be alluded to in the context of refusing or being reluctant to return to a place.

Doctor Who Doctor Who, in the long-running science-fiction television series of the same name, is a 720- (or 900-)year-old Time Lord from the planet Gallifrey who travels through space-time in his time machine, the *Tardis*. The periodic need for Time-Lords to 'regenerate' has allowed several different actors to play the part of the Doctor, all with different personalities and styles. The quotation below refers to the cheerfully witty Doctor played by Tom Baker who habitually wore a very long scarf. *See also* DALEK, TARDIS.

> She looked up and down the road. Thank God there was no one about yet to see the freak that stood before her front door, in scarf and cycle clips, like some sort of deranged Doctor Who.
> M. J. TROW *Maxwell's Movie* 1998

Dodge City Dodge City, in Kansas, United States, had a reputation as a rowdy frontier town until Wyatt Earp became chief deputy marshal in 1876 and introduced order. Dodge City can be alluded to as a place characterized by lawless or unregulated conflict, particularly involving gunfights.

> An 'off-duty' gun. It was the first thing they all did twenty-two years ago, those slick-sleeved, scrubbed, and hard-muscled rookies with their big eyes and crewcuts and bags full of hope. They ran out and bought 'off-duty' guns. Dodge City. The John Wayne syndrome.
> JOSEPH WAMBAUGH *The Glitter Dome* 1981

Sometimes I don't feel like a very nice person anymore. We grow up with these

little, safe notions about the lives we want to lead, the people we want to love, the work we want to do, and how we'll be rewarded for our hard work. Then we get out there in twentieth century urban America and it's Dodge City all over again. The spoils go to the ones with the best aim, the quickest draw, the biggest guns.
STEVEN WOMACK *Dead Folks' Blues* 1992

Sally handed me the translation of the coded message and looked around. 'I thought there'd be wanted posters on the walls and gun racks filled with shotguns.' 'This isn't Dodge City,' Lula said. 'We got some class here. We keep the guns in the back room with the pervert.'
JANET EVANOVICH *Four to Score* 1998

Donald Duck Donald Duck is a cartoon character created by Walt Disney who has a distinctive high-pitched, quacking voice.

Besides, he was kind of a sweet kid and had a voice like Donald Duck.
JOSEPH WAMBAUGH *The Glitter Dome* 1981

Don Juan Don Juan Tenorio was a legendary Spanish nobleman famous for his seductions. The character appears in various works of literature and music, such as Mozart's opera *Don Giovanni*, Byron's poem *Don Juan*, and the 'Don Juan in Hell' section of Shaw's play *Man and Superman*. The term 'Don Juan' is now often used to describe a man with a reputation for seducing women.

It was a highly original, rather overwritten piece of sustained description concerned with a Don Juan of the New York slums.
F SCOTT FITZGERALD *The Beautiful and the Damned* 1922

'Marigold's taken up choral singing. They're doing the Saint Matthew Passion.' 'Oh yes. And what passion are you doing, Featherstone?' Miss Trant looked at her host with some suspicion. Featherstone, thinking he was being treated like a dangerous Don Juan, was flattered.
JOHN MORTIMER *Rumpole's Return* 1980

Don Quixote Don Quixote is the ageing hero of a romance, *Don Quixote de la Mancha* (1605–15) by Miguel de Cervantes. He is devoted to tales of chivalry and romance, becoming so obsessed with these stories that 'the moisture of his brain was exhausted to that degree, that at last he lost the use of his reason'. Unable to distinguish the fanciful from the real, he determines to turn knight errant himself and sets out in search of adventures. Tall, lean, and thin-faced, he dons rusty armour and is accompanied by his scrawny old horse Rosinante and a short, fat squire, Sancho Panza. In a famous episode he attacks a group of windmills in the belief that they are giants. In Don Quixote's confused mind, a good-looking village girl, whom he names Dulcinea del Toboso, is elevated to the ideal of womanly beauty and virtue. His determination to keep to what he perceives to be a life of chivalry only ends when one of his friends disguises himself as another knight, defeats

Don Quixote, and makes him end his exploits. As the quotations below illustrate, allusions to Don Quixote can pick up on various attributes of the character, including his insanity, his idealism, and his thinness. A Don Quixote is a foolish, mistaken idealist or someone who naively believes that they can set the world to rights single-handedly. The character can also represent someone who fights against illusory evils or who fails to see things as they really are. To tilt at windmills is to attack imaginary or impossible targets. *See also* DULCINEA, ROSINANTE.

> We are most of us like Don Quixote, to whom a windmill was a giant, and Dulcinea a magnificent princess: all more or less the dupes of our own imagination.
> THOMAS LOVE PEACOCK *Nightmare Abbey* 1818

> A tall, thin, Don Quixote-looking old man came into the shop for some woollen gloves.
> ELIZABETH GASKELL *Cranford* 1851–3

> No one in his senses would dream of following her. To idealize so repulsive a Dulcinea one would have to be madder than Don Quixote himself.
> ALDOUS HUXLEY *Point Counter Point* 1928

> Without a win in five matches, the Cup represents the chance for Newcastle to bring tangible reward for a once refreshing approach, just as next Sunday's home match against Manchester United appears a last tilt at the Championship windmill. *Independent on Sunday* 1995

Eliza Doolittle In Bernard Shaw's play *Pygmalion* (1913), Eliza Doolittle is the cockney flower-seller who is coached by the phonetician Professor Henry Higgins to acquire a standard accent and to fit into upper-class society. *See also* HENRY HIGGINS, PYGMALION.

> 'That's sort of what I'd like to discuss with you . . . business. You know how you've kind of been my mentor with this bounty hunting stuff?' 'Eliza Doolittle and Henry Higgins Do Trenton.'
> JANET EVANOVICH *High Five* 1999

Dudley Do-Right Dudley Do-Right is a character in a segment of Jay Ward's animated television series *The Rocky and Bullwinkle Show* (1961–4). He is a dedicated but not very bright Canadian Mountie who is always trying to catch his deadly foe Snidely Whiplash.

> 'Seems like any other place. Scotty showed me around last night.' 'Dudley, you mean.' He laughed. 'Dudley Do-right. Goes to church every Sunday, coaches the hockey team. Wouldn't say shit if he had a mouthful.'
> TED WOODS *On the Inside* 1990

> I am not, I trust, a craven coward, but neither do I claim to be Dudley Doright.
> LAWRENCE SANDERS *McNally's Risk* 1993

> 'You wanted to see me, Lieutenant?' Reggie, all square-jawed and hair-gelled,

enters in dress whites. Dudley Doright at Sea.
SUSAN SUSSMAN with SARAJANE AVIDON *Cruising for Murder* 2000

Dormouse The Dormouse is one of the characters that Alice meets at the Mad Hatter's tea party in Lewis Carroll's *Alice's Adventures in Wonderland* (1865). The Dormouse snoozes all through the tea party, despite attempts to wake it by pinching it. *See also* ALICE IN WONDERLAND.

Dotheboys Hall *See* WACKFORD SQUEERS.

Doubting Thomas Thomas, known also as Thomas Didymus, meaning 'twin' in Aramaic, was one of the twelve Apostles in the New Testament. After the Crucifixion, when Jesus appeared before the disciples to show them that he had risen from the dead, Thomas was not present. When the other disciples told Thomas that they had seen Jesus, he said he would not believe that it was true 'except I shall see in his hands the print of the nails, and put my finger into the print of the nails, and thrust my hand into his side' (John 20: 25). The expression 'doubting Thomas' is now used to mean an incredulous or sceptical person.

> Since he became news, he's been at pains to let the figures speak for themselves. 'The lab data's there in black and white.' It's also in the Vanderbilt computer system which means others can review it. When doubting Thomases from the press or the medical world come to speak to him, 'I print out the lab sheets, boom, boom, boom.' *The Observer* 1997

dove *See* NOAH.

Arthur Conan Doyle Arthur Conan Doyle (1859–1930) was a Scottish novelist remembered for his exciting adventure stories such as *The Lost World*, and for his creation of the character of Sherlock Holmes. *See also* SHERLOCK HOLMES.

> I told the story well . . . I described an attack on my life on the voyage home, and I made a really horrid affair of the Portland Place murder. 'You're looking for adventure,' I cried; 'well, you've found it here. The devils are after me, and the police are after them. It's a race that I mean to win.' 'By God!' he whispered, drawing his breath in sharply, 'it is all pure Rider Haggard and Conan Doyle.'
> JOHN BUCHAN *The Thirty-Nine Steps* 1915

Draco Draco (7th c. BC) was an Athenian legislator. The notorious severity of his codification of Athenian law has given rise to the English adjective 'draconian'.

> Since time immemorial the forces of Draco have massed in such stillness, and they were massing again behind the door.
> MIKE NICOL *The Powers That Be* 1989

> The CBI has condemned the measures as 'Draconian'. But Beckett is convinced

that tough action is needed. *The Observer* 1997

Dracula The famous Count Dracula, created by Bram Stoker in his 1879 novel *Dracula*, is a vampire, one of the Undead, who lies in his coffin by day and comes out at night to suck blood from the necks of his victims. He can only be destroyed by having a stake driven through his heart while he is resting.

> I knew I'd gone as white as a piece of chalk since coming in as if I'd been got at by a Dracula-vampire.
> ALAN SILLITOE *The Loneliness of the Long Distance Runner* 1959

> 'I know some people believed that, coming from a family as old as ours, he should have chosen a British girl. I've never been of that narrow way of thinking. We should always be ready to welcome new blood of the right kind.' I just stopped myself saying Count Dracula would agree with her.
> GILLIAN LINSCOTT *Stage Fright* 1994

Sir Francis Drake Sir Francis Drake (*c.*1540–96), English explorer and privateer, was the first Englishman to see the Pacific and the first to sail round the globe. He harried the Spanish, both in Spain and in South America, and took a leading part in foiling the Spanish Armada in 1588. Despite Spanish protests, he was knighted in 1581 by Queen Elizabeth I.

Dresden Dresden is a city in eastern Germany, on the river Elbe. It was one of Germany's most beautiful cities until it was almost totally destroyed by heavy Allied bombing on the night of 13 February 1945. Dresden has been extensively rebuilt since 1945.

Nancy Drew Nancy Drew is the name of an American teenage detective created in the 1930s by Edward Stratemeyer and the heroine of a series of novels for children written by a variety of writers under the name Carolyn Greene.

> He shook his head. 'What happened?' 'I fell into a yucca plant.' 'Ouch!' He flinched in sympathy. 'Just jumped up and bit you, huh?' 'What I get for playing Nancy Drew,' I said, and told him about chasing the burglar who'd broken into Andy Bynum's house.
> MARGARET MARON *Shooting at Loons* 1994

Dreyfus Alfred Dreyfus (1859–1935) was a French army officer of Jewish descent who in 1894 was falsely accused of passing military secrets to the Germans. His trial, imprisonment on Devil's Island, and eventual release caused a major political crisis in France. Dreyfus can be alluded to as an innocent person falsely accused or punished. *See also* DEVIL'S ISLAND.

> As things stood we had an offender, a detected crime, and no demands for a second PM. The coroner had therefore released the body for burial. Not the wisest move: Klondike Bill was beginning to look about as guilty as Captain

Dreyfus, and I sincerely hoped that the hierarchy had given HM Coroner an explanation, together with the lawyers' version of a frank and sincere smile.
RAYMOND FLYNN *A Public Body* 1996

Bulldog Drummond *See under* BULLDOG.

Duessa In Spenser's allegory *The Faerie Queene* (1590, 1596), Duessa, representing Falsehood, assumes the appearance of a beautiful girl, Fidessa, but is later revealed to be in reality a hideous hag. *See also* SPENSER.

Dufy Raoul Dufy (1877–1953) was a French painter and textile designer, whose chief subjects were racecourses, boating scenes, and society life. Dufy's style is characterized by bright colours and lively calligraphic draughtsmanship.

There was a bright wind, it was a Dufy day, all bustle, movement, animated colour.
JOHN FOWLES *The Magus* 1977

Dulcinea Dulcinea is the name of Don Quixote's love in Cervantes' picaresque romance *Don Quixote de la Mancha*, published in 1605–15. Her real name is Aldonza Lorenzo, but Don Quixote, who naively idealizes her, gives her the name Dulcinea del Toboso and finds in her inspirations for his many deeds of misplaced heroism. *See also* DON QUIXOTE.

No one in his senses would dream of following her. To idealize so repulsive a Dulcinea one would have to be madder than Don Quixote himself.
ALDOUS HUXLEY *Point Counter Point* 1928

Isadora Duncan The American dancer Isadora Duncan (1878–1927) developed a new style of fluid barefoot dancing derived from classical Greek art. She travelled widely in Europe, and founded several dancing schools there. She was strangled accidentally when her trailing scarf became entangled in the wheel of a car.

The girl, on her knees, arms thrown back, was a dancer. She was effecting some kind of Isadora Duncan, swan-raped, Noh swoon: demonstrating both her 'inner stillness' and the power she exercised over her body.
IAIN SINCLAIR *Downriver* 1991

Dunkirk Dunkirk (Dunkerque) is a port on the north French coast from where over 335 000 Allied soldiers were evacuated under German fire during the Second World War by a mixture of naval and ordinary civilian vessels. Although from a military point of view this represented a defeat, the soldiers having been forced to retreat to the shore, Dunkirk is remembered by the British as something of a triumph, and the 'Dunkirk spirit' has come to refer to a stubborn refusal to admit defeat no matter how dangerous or difficult the circumstances.

Technical lighting and electronic glitches reduced Glyndebourne's new smash hit to a concert performance, in costume, against plain black drapes, relying on music, text and everybody's Dunkirk spirit. *Oxford Times* 1994

The Metro was crowded but a Dunkirk spirit reigned. On personal observation, passengers were unusually polite to one another and almost chatty. *The Independent* 1997

Jimmy Durante Jimmy Durante (1893–1980) was a US pianist–comedian who had a long career in vaudeville, nightclubs, and films. He referred to his splendid nose as his 'schnozzola'.

Even Jimmy Durante's famous schnozzola, which Keith had had a chance to see up close . . . was a peanut compared to Sperry's.
VINCE STANTON *Keith Partridge Master Spy* 1971

Little Dutch Boy The tale of the Little Dutch Boy is recounted as a story entitled 'The Hero of Haarlem' in Mary Mapes Dodge's children's classic *Hans Brinker; or, The Silver Skates* (1865). The boy is returning from a visit when he hears the sound of trickling water and sees a small hole in the dyke. He climbs up the dyke and plugs the hole with his finger in order to stop it becoming enlarged and leading to flooding. The boy undergoes a terrible ordeal alone all night and unable to move before being rescued and relieved at daybreak the following morning.

'Watch. Call me if you see anybody. Don't let them wander by, Howard. Don't let them get lost.' The crew boss made it sound as if he was addressing Horatio on the bridge or the little boy with his finger in the dike.
NEVADA BARR *Firestorm* 1996

But now that president sometimes looks rather like the boy with his hand in the dyke, behind which the water is building up pressure. *The Observer* 1997

Dying Swan *See* PAVLOVA.

Amelia Earhart Amelia Earhart (1898–1937) was an American aviator, the first woman to fly the Atlantic in 1928, and the first woman to do so solo in 1932, completing the journey from Newfoundland to Londonderry in a time of 13¼ hours. The aircraft carrying Earhart and her navigator, Frederick J. Noonan, disappeared over the Pacific Ocean during a subsequent round-the-world flight in 1937.

Eccles Eccles was a character in *The Goon Show*, an extremely popular BBC radio comedy series which ran from 1952 to 1960. Eccles, played by Spike Milligan, spoke in a slow, foolish-sounding voice. *See also* BLUEBOTTLE.

Echo In Greek myth, Echo was a nymph who kept Hera talking when she wanted to spy on the infidelities of Zeus, her husband, with the other nymphs. Hera punished Echo by depriving her of speech except for a repetition of the last words spoken to her. Echo fell in love with Narcissus but was rejected by him and gradually wasted away until there was nothing left but her voice. *See also* NARCISSUS.

> What a sheer waste of herself to be dressed thus while another was shining to advantage! . . . The power of her face all lost, the charm of her emotions all disguised, the fascinations of her coquetry denied existence, nothing but a voice left to her: she had a sense of the doom of Echo.
> THOMAS HARDY *The Return of the Native* 1880

Eden Eden (meaning 'Delight'), or the Garden of Eden, was the home of Adam and Eve in the biblical account of the Creation, from which they were banished by God for their disobedience in eating the forbidden fruit of the Tree of Knowledge. It is imagined as a place of lush beauty, in which grows 'every tree that is pleasant to the sight and good for food' (Gen. 2: 9). The name can be used to refer to a place or state of supreme happiness, innocence, and concord. *See also* ADAM AND EVE.

> His eyes rested happily on the spreading green of the bread-fruit trees. 'By George, it's like the garden of Eden.'
> W. SOMERSET MAUGHAM 'Mackintosh' in *The World Over* 1951

> Yet this was—the way she relayed it—a redeemed forest and an Eden.
> THOMAS KENEALLY *The Playmaker* 1987

> For the first seven thousand feet it is the Garden of Eden, a luxuriance of

orchids, humming-birds, and tiny streams of delicious water that run by miracle alongside every path.
LOUIS DE BERNIÈRES *The War of Don Emmanuel's Nether Parts* 1990

Flowers, shrubs, saplings had been brought here with their roots and earth, and set in baskets and makeshift cases. But many of the containers had rotted; the earth had spilled out to create, from one container to the next, a layer of damp humus, where the shoots of some plants were already taking root. It was like being in an Eden sprouting from the very planks of the *Daphne*.
UMBERTO ECO *The Island of the Day Before* 1994

Edsel The Edsel was a car launched by the Ford Motor Company in 1957 as part of a $250 million investment in an attempt to compete with General Motors and in particular with their Oldsmobile. The car was a complete flop.

When Petra told him she was pregnant, he looked at her as if she were an Edsel.
JONATHAN KELLERMAN *Billy Straight* 1998

Eeyore Eeyore is the gloomy old grey donkey in A. A. Milne's books about Winnie the Pooh. *See also* WINNIE THE POOH.

Eeyore of the Year was, as usual, a toss-up between Peter Owen ('If anything, it is getting worse') and Tom Rosenthal ('Among those books which sold less badly'). *The Bookseller* 1995

Everyone had warned me rather gloomily about interviewing Glenda Jackson. I was told by journalists who knew her that she was 'very prickly' and 'hates talking about her acting career'. One of these Eeyores added: 'The problem is to stop her banging on about Labour transport policy and get her to talk about Hollywood.' *Independent on Sunday* 1997

Einstein Albert Einstein (1879–1955) was a German-born American mathematician and theoretical physicist who formulated the theory of relativity. He was awarded the Nobel Prize for physics in 1921. He is often regarded as the greatest scientist of the 20th century and is frequently mentioned as the archetype of the extremely intelligent person. The phrase 'no Einstein' is commonly used to mean 'unintelligent'.

Bech, rather short for his age, yet with a big nose and big feet that promised future growth, was recognized from the first by his classmates as an only son, a mother's son more than a father's, pampered and bright though not a prodigy (his voice had no pitch, his mathematical aptitude was no Einstein's); naturally he was teased.
JOHN UPDIKE *Bech: A Book* 1970

You didn't have to be Einstein to get the number, but it would have taken more than one step, because Roz had herself listed in the phone book as Rosie

O'Grady, having tired of the hate calls that her father's last name sometimes attracted.
MARGARET ATWOOD *The Robber Bride* 1993

He walked her to the door. They made an odd couple: he, short, slightly rumpled, inclined to corpulence; she, tall, slender elegant. Einstein and Aphrodite.
JOHN SPENCER HILL *The Last Castrato* 1995

El Dorado El Dorado (literally 'the Gilded One') was the fabled city or country of gold sought in the 16th century by the Spanish conquistadores, who believed it existed somewhere in the area of the Orinoco and Amazon rivers. Hence, any place of fabulous wealth can be described as an El Dorado.

Thousands of mushroom pickers . . . stomp through British Columbia forests every fall looking for the mushroom picker's El Dorado: a bed of Canadian matsutake, or pine mushrooms—massive white mushrooms for which Japanese buyers are willing to pay $55 a pound.*Equinox* 1989

They would regain the ship and sail under his orders, asking no questions. Their recompense: a share of a treasure as vast as a dozen Eldorados.
UMBERTO ECO *The Island of the Day Before* 1994

One should have thought a transfer to a continental club would have made more sense, even though Italian fooball is no longer the El Dorado it used to be.*Sunday Telegraph* 1995

El Greco El Greco (1541–1614) was a Spanish painter, born in Crete as Domenikos Theotokopoulos. His portraits and religious works are characterized by elongated and distorted figures, solemn facial expressions, and vibrant use of colour (blues, lemons, livid pinks). Among his famous works are the altarpiece *The Assumption of the Virgin* (1577–9) and the painting *The Burial of Count Orgaz* (1586).

They're like the hands in El Greco's portraits.
W. SOMERSET MAUGHAM *The Razor's Edge* 1944

Mrs Overend had recently got rid of her black-and-orange striped divans, cushions and sofas. In their place were curiously cut slabs, polygons, and three-legged manifestations of Daisy Overend's personality, done in El Greco's colours.
MURIEL SPARK *The Collected Stories* 1958

His face was as gloomy as an El Greco; insufferably bored, decades of boredom, and probably, I decided, insufferably boring.
JOHN FOWLES *The Magus* 1977

Senor Aguirre joined his El Greco hands and looked at me over the spire of his fingertips.
JOHN BANVILLE *The Book of Evidence* 1989

Electra In Greek mythology, Electra was the daughter of Agamemnon and Clytemnestra. She persuaded her brother Orestes to kill Clytemnestra and her lover, Aegisthus, in revenge for the murder of Agamemnon. In psychoanalytical theory, an Electra complex is a daughter's subconscious sexual attraction to her father and hostility towards her mother, corresponding to the Oedipus complex in a son.

> 'Do all fathers think their daughters are so beautiful?' It's a line that Arthur quotes approvingly to his beloved, thus snaring the movie in an Electra complex.*New Yorker* 1995

Elephant Man Joseph Merrick (1862–90) was born with severe facial deformities caused by a rare disease, now thought to be Proteus syndrome. As an adult he was exhibited as a fairground freak, the Elephant Man, until he was rescued by the surgeon Sir Frederick Treves and given sanctuary in the London Hospital.

> If either party . . . does not wish to continue the relationship, they must clearly and considerately state this in a manner that reassures the other party that they are not the Elephant Man/Woman without being patronising.
> HELEN FIELDING *Bridget Jones's Diary* 1999

Elephant's Child *The Elephant's Child* is one of Kipling's *Just-So Stories* (1902) and relates how the elephant got his trunk. The elephant's child is full of 'satiable curtiosity' and constantly asks questions of his animal relatives. Eventually he comes up with 'What does the crocodile eat for dinner?' and is directed by the Kolokolo Bird to 'the banks of the great grey-green, greasy Limpopo River, all set about with fever-trees' to find out. When he finds the crocodile, he asks this question, to which the crocodile, catching hold of the Elephant's Child's short snout, replies 'I think, today, I will begin with you.' The crocodile tries to pull the Elephant's Child into the water while the Elephant's Child resists, and during this tug-of-war the Elephant's Child's nose is elongated into a trunk. With the help of a snake, the Elephant's Child pulls free and is eventually reconciled to his new nose. *See also* KIPLING.

> I was torn between calling Caroline to tell her the deal was off and the elephant child's 'satiable curiosity' to find out what had rattled Chigwell so badly.
> SARA PARETSKY *Toxic Shock* 1990

> I'm only telling you because I know how hard it is to stop you when you've got your teeth in a problem, so I know you'll be worse trouble and probably uncover more stuff if I don't give you a little now. But I'd hate to have to explain to the Council that I couldn't head off a sixteen-year-old's 'satiable curiosity,' so just keep it to yourself, will you, Elephant's Child?
> ANNE MCCAFFREY and MARGARET BALL *Acorna's Quest* 1998

Eleusinian mysteries The Eleusinian mysteries were the most famous of the 'mysteries', or religious ceremonies, of ancient Greece, held at the city of Eleusis near Athens. They were dedicated to the corn goddess Demeter and her daughter Persephone, and were thought to celebrate the annual cycle of death and rebirth in nature. Such mysteries or mystery religions were secret forms of worship, and were available only to people who had been specially initiated.

> Been playing golf? I thought so. Wonderful game, so fascinating, such a challenge, as much intellectual as physical, I understand. I wish I had time for it myself. One feels so much at sea when talk turns to mashie-niblicks, cleeks, and mid-irons. Quite an Eleusinian mystery.
> LOUIS DE BERNIÈRES *Captain Corelli's Mandolin* 1994

Elijah Elijah (9th c. BC) was a Hebrew prophet who maintained the worship of Jehovah against that of Baal and other pagan gods. According to the Bible, he was carried to heaven in a chariot of fire: 'And as they still went on and talked, behold, a chariot of fire and horses of fire separated the two of them. And Elijah went up by a whirlwind into heaven' (2 Kgs. 2: 11–13).

Elisha Elisha (9th c. BC) was a Hebrew prophet, disciple and successor of Elijah, whose mantle he received: 'And [Elisha] took up the mantle of Elijah that had fallen from him, and went back and stood on the bank of the Jordan' (2 Kgs. 2: 13). *See also* ELIJAH.

> But like the prophet in the chariot disappearing in heaven and dropping his mantle to Elisha, the withdrawing night transferred its pale robe to the breaking day.
> HERMAN MELVILLE *Billy Budd* 1924

Elli In a story from Scandinavian mythology, Elli is the personification of old age who in the form of Utgard, Loki's foster-mother, a toothless old crone, wrestles the mighty Thor to the ground. The episode illustrates the point that no one, not even the strongest, can withstand old age.

Elm Street *See* NIGHTMARE ON ELM STREET.

Elysium In Greek mythology, Elysium, or the Elysian Fields, was the name of the fields at the end of the earth to which certain favoured heroes were conveyed by the gods to enjoy a life after death. The name can be used to refer to a place of perfect happiness or bliss.

> Antoine and Françoise with their children, but without ever knowing why, joined the refugees for the sake of their vision of elysium and because of Don Emmanuel's enthusiasm.
> LOUIS DE BERNIÈRES *The War of Don Emmanuel's Nether Parts* 1990

emperor's new clothes Hans Christian Andersen's story *The Emperor's New Clothes*, first published in 1836, tells the story of an emperor obsessed with beautiful clothes. He is visited by two swindlers who promise to make him the most beautiful clothes ever seen. Using an empty loom, they pretend to weave the cloth and stitch the clothes, telling the Emperor that the cloth they are using is invisible to anyone who is unfit for his office or stupid.

Although no one, including the Emperor, can see the clothes, all collude in the deception for fear of appearing foolish or incompetent. The Emperor parades naked through the streets of the town, with all the people cheering except for one small boy who cries, 'But the Emperor has nothing on at all!' 'The emperor's new clothes' can describe something that is promised or believed in but does not in fact exist.

> Common sense is a very poor guide to scientific insight for it represents cultural prejudice more often than it reflects the native honesty of a small boy before the naked emperor.
> STEPHEN JAY GOULD *Ever Since Darwin* 1978

end of the rainbow According to legend, there is a pot of gold buried at the spot where a rainbow comes down and touches the earth. The end of the rainbow is therefore a distant place where dreams come true. The idea was popularized by the song 'Over the Rainbow' which features in the 1939 film *The Wizard of Oz*, and begins with the words:
'Somewhere over the rainbow
Way up high,
There's a land that I heard of
Once in a lullaby.'
See also WIZARD OF OZ.

> The Japanese stock market was the last-but-one in a long line of Wall Street Loreleis. Like Xerox, conglomerates, and convertible debentures, it had been the legendary pot of gold at the end of some local rainbows. Those happy few blessed with foresight got more than sordid, material gain. They got brief immortality. Going into Japan at the right time was like predicting exactly when Dow-Jones would reach five- or fifteen-hundred.
> EMMA LATHEN *Sweet and Low* 1978

Witch of Endor In the book of Samuel, the Witch of Endor was the woman consulted by Saul when he was threatened by the Philistine army. At his request she summoned up the ghost of the prophet Samuel, who prophesied the death of Saul and the destruction of his army by the Philistines (1 Sam. 28). Rudyard Kipling associates Endor with spiritualism in his poem 'The Road to Endor':
'Oh, the road to Endor is the oldest road
And the craziest road of all!
Straight it runs to the Witch's abode
As it did in the days of Saul.'

> I merely lit that fire because I was dull, and thought I would get a little excitement by calling you up and triumphing over you as the Witch of Endor called up Samuel. I determined you should come; and you have come!
> THOMAS HARDY *The Return of the Native* 1880

Endymion Endymion was a beautiful young man in Greek mythology who was loved by the moon goddess Selene. According to one version of his story,

Zeus caused him to sleep for ever so that he would remain eternally young and handsome. This story is the basis of Keats's poem *Endymion* (1818).

> But your Endymion, your smooth, Smock-fac'd Boy . . . shall a Beauteous Dame enjoy.
> JOHN DRYDEN *Juvenal Satires* x 1693

Enterprise *See* STARSHIP ENTERPRISE.

Epeius In Greek mythology, Epeius, a skilled craftsman, built the Trojan Horse with the help of Athene. *See also* TROJAN WAR.

Epicurus The Greek philosopher Epicurus (341–271 BC) founded a school of philosophy that espoused hedonism, described by Epicurus in one of his letters thus: 'We say that pleasure is the beginning and end of living happily.' In his philosophy, happiness is achieved by becoming free from pain and anxiety by, among other things, freeing oneself from fear of the supernatural and death. A hedonistic or supremely happy state can be described as Epicurean.

> Ten o'clock was the hour fixed for this meeting, and Wimsey was lingering lovingly over his bacon and eggs, so as to leave no restless and unfilled moment in his morning. By which it may be seen that his lordship had reached that time of life when a man can extract an Epicurean enjoyment even from his own passions—the halcyon period between the self-tormenting exuberance of youth and the fretful *carpe diem* of approaching senility.
> DOROTHY SAYERS *Have his Carcass* 1932

Erato Erato was one of the nine Muses in Greek mythology, associated especially with the lyre and lyric love. *See also* MUSES.

> Now, Erato, thy poet's mind inspire,
> And fill his soul with thy celestial fire.
> VIRGIL *Aeneid* VII *trans.* JOHN DRYDEN 1697

Erebus In Greek mythology, Erebus was the primeval god of darkness, born from Chaos right at the beginning of the world. The name was later identified with Hades, and is used with this meaning in the *Iliad* and the *Odyssey. See also* HADES.

Erinyes In Greek mythology, the Erinyes, better known as the Furies, were the avenging spirits of punishment. *See* FURIES.

Eris Eris was the Greek goddess of discord. *See also* APPLE OF DISCORD.

Eros In Greek mythology, Eros (called Cupid by the Romans) was the god of love, usually represented as a winged boy with a bow and arrows. Eros is now generally used to represent the idea of sexual love or the libido.

Introduced as lymph on the dart of Eros, it eventually permeated and coloured her whole constitution.
THOMAS HARDY *Far from the Madding Crowd* 1874

The family system will disappear; society, sapped at its very base, will have to find new foundations; and Eros, beautifully and irresponsibly free, will flit like a gay butterfly from flower to flower through a sunlit world.
ALDOUS HUXLEY *Crome Yellow* 1921

The dark tides of Eros, which demand full secrecy if they are to overflow the human soul, burst out during carnival like something long dammed up.
LAWRENCE DURRELL *Balthazar* 1958

She had loved Private Dukes and spawned a false oath to save him—affronting solider deities for the sake of honeyed, treacherous Eros.
THOMAS KENEALLY *The Playmaker* 1987

Esau In the Bible, Esau and Jacob were the twin sons of Isaac and Rebecca, Esau being the first-born. He is described as a red, hairy man (Gen. 25: 25). When faint with hunger one day, Esau begged his brother for some of the food he was preparing, a 'mess of pottage' (lentil stew). Jacob would only give Esau the food if he swore to sell Jacob his birthright as the elder of the twins. Esau is therefore alluded to as someone who chooses to accept material comfort in exchange for something more valuable.

The book of Genesis also relates how Jacob, with his mother, Rebecca's, help, dressed as his elder brother Esau in order to obtain the blessing of their father, Isaac. When Esau found out what Jacob had done, he hated him and swore to kill him: 'And Esau hated Jacob because of the blessing wherewith his father blessed him: and Esau said in his heart, The days of mourning for my father are at hand; then will I slay my brother Jacob' (Gen. 27: 41). Esau can also be alluded to as someone filled with anger and hatred. *See also* JACOB.

He's of a rash, warm-hearted nature, like Esau, for whom I have always felt great pity.
GEORGE ELIOT *Adam Bede* 1859

As for those benighted creatures who are disgracefully happy with their chains, they must be prevented from bartering their birthrights, like female Esaus, for a mess of pottage in the guise of a bribe to stay at home. *Glasgow Herald* 1998

Escher M. C. Escher (1902–72) was a Dutch graphic artist, whose prints often exploit puzzling visual paradoxes and illusions. Many of his works play with perspective to create examples of impossible architecture. One of his most famous images is the lithograph *Ascending and Descending* (1960), in which hooded figures endlessly walk up (or down) a staircase.

The house was taking on the appearance of an Escher drawing—lots of steps leading nowhere.
FAYE KELLERMAN *Sanctuary* 1994

Esther In the Old Testament book that bears her name, Esther was a woman who was chosen on account of her beauty by King Ahasuerus of Persia to be his queen in place of the deposed queen Vashti. Esther used her influence with him to save the Israelites in captivity from persecution. She is one of the most popular Jewish heroines. *See also* AHASUERUS, VASHTI.

> Presently my mother went to my father. I know I thought of Queen Esther and King Ahasuerus; for my mother was very pretty and delicate-looking, and my father looked as terrible as King Ahasuerus.
> ELIZABETH GASKELL *Cranford* 1851–3

Estragon In Samuel Beckett's play *Waiting for Godot* (1952), Estragon is one of the two tramps who discuss philosophical issues while they await the arrival of the mysterious character Godot. His name can now evoke someone who waits patiently. *See also* GODOT.

> I approached the Audi and passed it. Fielding was reading a paper and seemed to be waiting. They were great lads for waiting. They could have out-waited Estragon.
> RICHARD HALEY *Thoroughfare of Stones* 1995

E.T. In the 1982 Steven Spielberg film *E.T.—The Extraterrestrial*, an alien being accidentally left behind by a mission to Earth befriends a lonely suburban boy. The boy helps him to build a makeshift radio transmitter after E.T. has expressed his desire to make contact with his home planet with the phrase 'E.T. phone home'. At the end of the film a spaceship comes to take E.T. back home.

Etty William Etty (1787–1849) was an English artist best known for his sensual paintings of the nude.

> She was his passive victim, her head resting on his shoulder, marble made warmth, an Etty nude, the Pygmalion myth brought to a happy end.
> JOHN FOWLES *The French Lieutenant's Woman* 1969

Eumenides In Greek mythology, Eumenides was an alternative name for the Furies. It was considered unwise to mention the Furies, or Erinyes, by name and so they were often referred to euphemistically as the Eumenides, meaning 'Kindly Ones'. *See also* FURIES.

Euphrosyne In Greek mythology, Euphrosyne was one of the three Graces, three beautiful goddesses, daughters of Zeus, who personified charm, grace, and beauty. *See also* GRACES.

Euros In ancient Greek literature, Euros was a god, the personification of the east wind.

Euterpe Euterpe was one of the nine Muses in Greek mythology, associated especially with lyric poetry and flute-playing. *See also* MUSES.

He offended her by refusing to go into a dance-hall on the grounds that the music was so bad that it was a sacrilege against St Cecilia and Euterpe and Terpsichore, when she just wanted to go in and lose her unhappiness in dancing.
LOUIS DE BERNIÈRES *Señor Vivo and the Coca Lord* 1991

Eve According to the book of Genesis, Eve was the first woman, wife of Adam, who lived in innocence with Adam in the Garden of Eden. Tempted by the serpent, Eve ate the forbidden fruit from the Tree of Knowledge. Having eaten, and committed the first sin, she then persuaded Adam to do the same: 'And the eyes of them both were opened, and they knew that they were naked.' As a punishment for disobeying God's command, they were banished from the Garden of Eden. Because Eve had eaten first and then tempted Adam, God told her that as a punishment women would henceforth always suffer in childbirth: 'I will greatly multiply thy sorrow and thy conception; in sorrow thou shalt bring forth children.' *See also* ADAM AND EVE, FORBIDDEN FRUIT, SERPENT.

There she stood before us as Eve might have stood before Adam, clad in nothing but her abundant locks.
H. RIDER HAGGARD *She* 1887

I was firm as a man could be till I saw those eyes and that mouth again—surely there never was such a maddening mouth since Eve's!
THOMAS HARDY *Tess of the D'Urbervilles* 1891

'Why can't these American women stay in their own country? They are always telling us that it is the Paradise for women.' 'It is. That is why, like Eve, they are so excessively anxious to get out of it.'
OSCAR WILDE *The Picture of Dorian Gray* 1891

We were the only humans on the river, Eve and her mother in a grotesque mockery of Eden.
SARA PARETSKY *Toxic Shock* 1990

Evil One The Evil One is another name for the Devil or Satan, the arch-tempter in the Bible. *See also* SATAN.

Where, to what distance apart, had her father wandered, led by doubts which were to her temptations of the Evil One?
ELIZABETH GASKELL *North and South* 1854–5

Sophia wandered about, a prey ripe for the Evil One.
ARNOLD BENNETT *The Old Wives' Tale* 1908

Excalibur In Arthurian legend, Excalibur was King Arthur's sword. It had been embedded in a stone and Arthur was able to draw it out when no one else could move it, thus proving himself the rightful king of England. *See also* KING ARTHUR.

The wall had a surprising grip on it. It was like the whole structure of that wall

had settled down around this useless, forgotten piece of iron. I said to
Valentina: 'This is like trying to extract the sword Excalibur from the stone!'
ROSE TREMAIN *The Way I Found Her* 1998

Exodus Exodus is the second book of the Bible, relating the departure of the
Israelites under the leadership of Moses from their slavery in Egypt and their
journey towards the promised land of Canaan. This journey is ascribed by
scholars to various dates within the limits *c.*1580–*c.*1200 BC. The word
'exodus' can now be applied to any mass departure of people, especially
emigrants. *See also* CANAAN, MOSES, PROMISED LAND.

> The English Department had changed its quarters since his arrival at Rummidge.
> . . . The changeover had taken place in the Easter vacation amid much wailing
> and gnashing of teeth. Oy, oy, Exodus was nothing in comparison.
> DAVID LODGE *Changing Places* 1975

Jane Eyre and Mr Rochester Jane Eyre is the heroine of Charlotte Brontë's
novel of the same name (1847). Jane, an orphan, grows up to be an
independent woman who earns her living first as a teacher then as a
governess. In the latter occupation she meets Mr Rochester, father to her
illegitimate pupil Adèle. The couple fall in love and, although Jane is initially
resistant to the idea, they eventually agree to marry. The ceremony is
disrupted, however, and it is revealed that Mr Rochester is already married to
an insane Creole woman, Bertha, who has been kept in an upstairs room in
Mr Rochester's house. Jane flees and nearly marries another man, but is
eventually reunited with Mr Rochester after his house has burned down, his
wife has been killed in the fire, and he himself has been badly burned and
injured. They are alluded to as devoted lovers. *See also* BRONTËS, MR ROCHESTER.

Mr Facing-Both-Ways Mr Facing-Both-Ways is one of several characters who are relatives of Mr By-Ends in the first part of Bunyan's *The Pilgrim's Progress* (1678). Someone who changes their behaviour or opinions to please different people can be called a Mr Facing-Both-Ways. *See also* PILGRIM'S PROGRESS.

> There is a serious danger that Britain's national interests will be betrayed if the Government try to assure the United States that we are four-square behind NATO and, at the same time, seek to assure our EU partners that we are at the heart of Europe. However, that is the typical stance of Mr. Facing Both Ways, our Prime Minister.
> GERALD HOWARTH in the House of Commons, 2003

Fagin In Charles Dickens's novel *Oliver Twist* (1838), Fagin is the leader of the gang of child pickpockets into whose hands the runaway Oliver falls. *See also* DICKENSIAN, OLIVER TWIST.

> Of course this is true. All good writers, if they are honest, will acknowledge that when they come across a good thing in someone else's work, either consciously or unconsciously they store it away for the day when inspiration fails. And if writers are pickpockets, then Shakespeare is our Fagin, always on the look out for a shiny new phrase. *The Observer* 1999

> In their search for company they may be lucky enough to find a kindly outreach worker from a charity, or join a gang of other street children, but too often the overtly friendly offer of help turns out to come from a modern Fagin, or drug dealer, or pimp or paedophile. *Amnesty International Magazine* 1999

fairy godmother In the fairy story of Cinderella, the fairy godmother finds Cinderella weeping because she cannot go to the royal ball. The fairy godmother transforms a pumpkin into a coach, mice into horses, and Cinderella's rags into beautiful clothes so that she is able to attend the ball. A fairy godmother is therefore someone who can magically grant someone's wishes. *See also* CINDERELLA.

Falernian Falernian was a particularly good-quality wine made in Roman times from the grapes of the Falernian territory in Campania and praised by both Horace and Virgil.

> 'If I am to take more of the severe falernian,' said he, laying his hand on the

decanter of port, 'I must know the lady's name.'
ANTHONY TROLLOPE *The Small House at Allington* 1862

the Fall The Fall, or the fall of Man, is the time in Jewish and Christian
theology when humankind fell from a state of innocence into a state of sin.
This is taken to be the act of disobedience by Adam and Eve in the Garden of
Eden in eating from the Tree of Knowledge of good and evil. *See also* ADAM
AND EVE.

But as in Regensburg DP camp, between Eden and the Fall lay only the briefest
interval.
THOMAS KENEALLY *A Family Madness* 1985

Falstaff Sir John Falstaff is the fat, witty, good-humoured old knight in
Shakespeare's *Henry IV* and *The Merry Wives of Windsor*. Falstaff's enormous
paunch prompts the young Prince Hal to ask: 'How long is't ago, Jack, since
thou sawest thine own knee?' Observing Falstaff fleeing an ambush, Hal
remarks:
'Falstaff sweats to death
And lards the lean earth as he walks along.'

It was all so fine, so precise, and it was a wonder that this miracle was wrought
by a whiskered Falstaff with a fat belly and a grubby singlet showing through
the layers of wet, sour hessian.
PETER CAREY *Oscar and Lucinda* 1988

The professor was a big, jovial man of Falstaffian appearance.
MARJORIE ECCLES *A Species of Revenge* 1996

Fat Controller In the Revd W. Awdry's series of books about Thomas the
Tank Engine (first appearing in 1946), the accurately named Fat Controller
presides over the Big Station with self-important and bureaucratic
officiousness.

Fate Fate is the name given to a goddess who controls people's destinies,
especially one of the Fates or one of the Norns. *See also* FATES, NORNS.

Not only is the hand of Fate discernible in this affair; Fate has been leaving
fingerprints all around the place ever since Higgins got his bright idea.
ROBERTSON DAVIES *Leaven of Malice* 1954

In many subtle ways, but mainly by her silence, she showed that Mr Biswas,
however grotesque, was hers and that she had to make do with what Fate had
granted her.
V. S. NAIPAUL *A House for Mr. Biswas* 1961

Kenneth Cracknell, Esq. . . . was the learned judge whom Fate had selected to
preside over the trial of the unhappy Revenue official.
JOHN MORTIMER *Rumpole's Return* 1980

Fates In Greek and Roman mythology, the Fates were three sisters,
daughters of Night, who presided over the birth, life, and death of every

mortal individual. They were represented as three women spinning: Clotho, who held the distaff and spun the thread of a person's life, Lachesis, who drew off the thread and determined the luck that a person would have, and Atropos, who cut short the thread and so determined when a person's life would end. They were also called, by the Greeks, the Moirae and, by the Romans, the Parcae. *See also* PARCAE SISTERS.

> The Fates had unexpectedly (and perhaps just a little officiously) removed an obstacle from his path.
> SAKI 'Cross-Currents' in *Reginald in Russia* 1910

Father Christmas *See* SANTA CLAUS.

Father Time Father Time is the personification of time, usually depicted as an old bearded man with a scythe and hourglass.

> Little Father Time is what they always called me. It is a nickname; because I look so aged, they say.
> THOMAS HARDY *Jude the Obscure* 1895

> The American portion of our community 'saw in' the greatest day of their national calendar in a fittingly splendid style and circumstances today a fortnight previous. As our issue of that very date proceeded to the press some days earlier, not possessing mastery of Old Father Time and his scythe, we were unavoidably prevented from commenting on those happy rites.
> TIMOTHY MO *An Insular Possession* 1986

Father William In Lewis Carroll's *Alice's Adventures in Wonderland* (1865), the Caterpillar instructs Alice to recite the poem 'You are old, Father William'. She begins:
' "You are old, Father William," the young man said,
"And your hair has become very white;
And yet you incessantly stand on your head—
Do you think, at your age, it is right?" '
Father William is also sprightly enough to turn back-somersaults and balance an eel on the end of his nose. He is alluded to as someone who is extremely old. *See also* ALICE IN WONDERLAND.

> He had gone partly bald, which made him look like a youthful Father William.
> SARA PARETSKY *Toxic Shock* 1990

fatted calf In the parable of the Prodigal Son told by Jesus in the Bible (Luke 15: 11–32), the father welcomed his spendthrift son home and ordered the servants to 'bring hither the fatted calf, and kill it; and let us eat and be merry'. *See also* PRODIGAL SON.

Faust Faust is the subject of a medieval legend and subsequently of dramas by Marlowe (*Dr Faustus*, 1604) and Goethe (*Faust*, 1808, 1832). In the Marlowe version, Faustus, greedy for earthly power, sells his soul to Mephistopheles in exchange for 24 years during which Mephistopheles will provide anything he wants. For much of the time, however, he is despondent and dissatisfied, and he experiences the agony of utter despair as his contract with Mephistopheles ends and his life and soul are forfeit.

The character of Faust can be alluded to either as someone ambitious for earthly power and riches, or as someone who experiences deep despair. To enter a Faustian pact is to sacrifice one's spiritual or moral values for material gains. *See also* GRETCHEN, MEPHISTOPHELES.

> Farfrae's character was just the reverse of Henchard's, who might not inaptly be described as Faust has been described—as a vehement gloomy being who had quitted the ways of vulgar men, without light to guide him on a better way.
> THOMAS HARDY *The Mayor of Casterbridge* 1886

> The object of the exercise . . . was not to enhance others' enjoyment and understanding of Jane Austen, still less to honour the novelist herself, but to put a definitive stop to the production of any further garbage on the subject. . . . The thought gave him deep satisfaction. In Faustian moments he dreamed of going on, after fixing Jane Austen, to do the same job on the other major English novelists, then the poets and dramatists.
> DAVID LODGE *Changing Places* 1975

> [If] I had been offered the chance to play for Liverpool as a child . . . on condition that I agreed to die on my 30th birthday. I would have signed this Faustian contract in a twinkling. *Radio Times* 1997

> The story of how Hazar, 31, became involved with what is reputed to be one of the deadliest terrorist organisations in the world has elements of the classic Faustian bargain. *The Observer* 1997

Guy Fawkes Guy Fawkes (1570–1606) was a Catholic extremist who, with a small group of colleagues, was involved in the Gunpowder Plot, a conspiracy to blow up James I and his parliament on 5 November 1605. After being discovered in the cellar of the House of Lords with barrels of gunpowder, Fawkes, together with seven of his co-conspirators, was tried and executed. Guy Fawkes is alluded to as a clever schemer or secret conspirator, and the Gunpowder Plot as an unsuccessful attempt to remove someone from power.

> Missis was, she dared say, glad enough to get rid of such a tiresome, ill-conditioned child, who always looked as if she were watching everybody, and scheming plots underhand. Abbot, I think, gave me credit for being a sort of infantile Guy Fawkes.
> CHARLOTTE BRONTË *Jane Eyre* 1847

> He went forward, tiptoeing down the stairs more conspiratorially than ever—Guy Fawkes discovered, but yet irrationally hoping that he might escape notice by acting as though the Gunpowder Plot were still unrolling itself according to plan.
> ALDOUS HUXLEY *Point Counter Point* 1928

> He'd have called in the Dean, the Treasurer, the Seneschal and these other

fellows in the Cathedral, and they'd have put the Box in the Cathedral treasure vaults. And you know what kind of vaults those are: Guy Fawkes and his powder wouldn't get through those, as we know from bitter experience.
JOHN MASEFIELD *The Box of Delights* 1935

Basil Fawlty Basil Fawlty is the highly irascible hotelier played by John Cleese in the BBC television comedy series *Fawlty Towers*, which ran from 1975 until 1979. He is temperamental, rude to the guests, and loses his temper uncontrollably with the slightest provocation.

How Not to Become a Basil Fawlty. Resist the temptation to explode at work—it might feel better out than in, but invariably you will end up directing your anger at the innocent, either at home or in the office. *The Independent* 1998

Dr Fell Dr John Fell (1625–86) was an Anglican divine and Dean of Christ Church, Oxford. One of his students was Thomas Brown, who later became a well-known satirist. Dr Fell asked Brown to translate one of the epigrams of Martial:
'Non amo te, Sabidi, nec possum dicere quare;
Hoc tantum possum dicere, non amo te.'
('I do not love you, Sabidius, and I cannot say why;
All I can say is this, that I do not love you.')
Thomas Brown's famous translation read:
'I do not love thee, Dr Fell,
The reason why I cannot tell;
But this I know, and know full well,
I do not love thee, Dr Fell.'
Dr Fell is alluded to as a person whom one dislikes for no particular reason.

There is something more, if I could find a name for it. God bless me, the man seems hardly human! Something troglodytic, shall we say? or can it be the old story of Dr. Fell? or is it the mere radiance of a foul soul that thus transpires through, and transfigures, its clay continent?
ROBERT LOUIS STEVENSON *The Strange Case of Dr Jekyll and Mr Hyde* 1886

Look, I don't really care for Franklin much more than you do, John, but it's a perfectly irrational dislike. He's done nothing to me at all—or to you, for that matter. It's a pure case of Dr Fell.
SUSAN HILL *Strange Meeting* 1971

Fenris-wolf In Norse mythology, the Fenris-wolf (real name Fenrir) was the offspring of Loki, god of mischief, and a giantess. The gods brought him to Asgard, where he grew huge, powerful, and fierce. Eventually, only the god Tyr, who had played with him as a cub, would go near the wolf. The gods feared him, so they tricked him into being fettered. He broke the fetters. So they had a light soft fetter made which would be impossible to break. With this he was securely held until Ragnarok, the destruction of the world, but he bit off Tyr's hand by way of revenge. *See also* LOKI, RAGNAROK.

The telegraph is a limp band that will hold the Fenris-wolf of war. For now, that a telegraph line runs through France and Europe, from London, every message it transmits makes stronger by one thread, the band which war will have to cut.
RALPH WALDO EMERSON *English Traits* 1856

Fermat's last theorem Pierre de Fermat (1601–65) was a French mathematician, a founder of probability theory and number theory. In 1640 he formulated the proposition 'There do not exist positive integers x, y, z, n such that $xn + yn = zn$ when n is greater than 2.' Intriguingly, Fermat noted that he had 'a truly wonderful proof of this proposition but it does not fit into the margin of this page'. For the next 350 years mathematicians tried to furnish a proof for what became known as Fermat's last theorem (or Fermat's theorem), until Andrew Wiles finally succeeded in 1995.

You know this infallible system I have for becoming very rich by judicially investing in the velocity and stamina of horses with legal names? Ascot was going to provide the ultimate proof of its validity, a sort of Fermat's Last Theorem for racing.
MARCEL BERLINS *The Guardian* 1997

fiddle while Rome burns *See* NERO.

Huckleberry Finn Huckleberry Finn is the main character in *The Adventures of Huckleberry Finn* (1884) by Mark Twain. He is a spirited, self-reliant, and unconventional boy who fakes his own death in order to escape from his drunken, brutal father and he has many adventures.

Flash Gordon Flash Gordon is the spaceman hero created by the American cartoonist Alex Raymond in 1934. He has many adventures in space, notably on the planet Mongo, where he combats the evil Ming the Merciless.

Flood In the biblical story related in Genesis, God brought a great flood upon the earth in the time of Noah because of the wickedness of the human race. Apart from Noah, his family, and the animals he was instructed to shelter on the ark, all inhabitants of the earth perished in the Flood, which lasted for 40 days and 40 nights. There are similar flood myths in other traditions, such as in the epic of Gilgamesh and in the Greek legend of Deucalion. References to a time before the Flood are intended to suggest the very distant past. *See also* DEUCALION, NOAH.

Putting an arm around his sopping half-sleeve shirt, I say, 'I bet if you set your mind to it you could go back before the Flood.'
PHILIP ROTH *The Professor of Desire* 1978

But at last we came upon the shore, and were tumbled out upon the dry land. What a restoration that was; I felt like a giant who had survived the Flood.
PETER ACKROYD *The House of Dr Dee* 1993

Flora In Roman mythology, Flora was the goddess of flowers and spring, depicted in Sandro Botticelli's celebrated painting *Primavera*. Anyone carrying flowers can be described by invoking her name.

> I rang the door-bell, holding my flowers spread across both outstretched forearms. I did not want to appear like a delivery man. Rather I was a simple, a frangible petitioner, assisted only by the goddess Flora.
> JULIAN BARNES *Talking It Over* 1991

Flying Dutchman The *Flying Dutchman* was a legendary ghost ship supposed to be seen in the region of the Cape of Good Hope and presaging disaster. It was said to haunt the seas eternally as a result of a murder that had been committed on board. The term is sometimes applied to the ship's captain. In Wagner's opera of the same name (1843), Captain Vanderdecken is freed from a curse when he finds a woman willing to sacrifice herself for him. *See also* WAGNER.

Errol Flynn Errol Flynn (1909–59) was an Australian-born American actor who became famous for his swashbuckling roles in such costume adventure films as *Captain Blood* (1935) and *The Adventures of Robin Hood* (1938).

> I gave him a smile. *Dawn Patrol.* Errol Flynn courageous in the face of certain doom.
> ROBERT CRAIS *Lullaby Town* 1992

Phileas Fogg In Jules Verne's novel *Around the World in Eighty Days* (1873), the Englishman Phileas Fogg wagers other members of his London club that he can travel around the world in 80 days. He just manages it, travelling with his French valet Passepartout by many forms of transport including train, boat, sledge, and elephant.

> Decker thumbed through Yalom's passport—pages of stamped entries back into the States, Yalom's residing country. Then there were many other pages of foreign ink—Canada, Mexico, countries of Western and Eastern Europe including Russia, entries from the Far East, Latin America, and Africa. Lots from Africa—Egypt, South Africa, Kenya, Namibia, Liberia, Angola, Sudan, Ethiopia, Zaire, plus a host of other countries Decker didn't know existed. . . . Marge said, 'Yalom was quite the Phileas Fogg.'
> FAYE KELLERMAN *Sanctuary* 1994

Jane Fonda Jane Fonda (b. 1937) is a US film actress who won an Oscar for her performance in *Klute* (1971). She has abundant tawny hair and is known not only for her films but also for her successful fitness videos.

> At that time she assumed a long-legged, supple, Jane Fonda look; hair plentiful and curly about the head.
> FAY WELDON *Darcy's Utopia* 1990

Margot Fonteyn Margot Fonteyn was the stage name of the English classical ballet dancer Margaret Hookham. She danced for the company that became the Royal Ballet and was trained by Ninette de Valois. She started her partnership with Rudolph Nureyev in 1962 and created many roles with notable choreographers such as Frederick Ashton and Kenneth MacMillan. Fonteyn was named 'prima ballerina assoluta' in 1979, a title that has only been awarded three times. *See also* RUDOLPH NUREYEV.

> 'That's Bella on the terrace of our hotel.' Featherstone had produced his wallet, from which he proudly drew a number of creased and faded snaps from the space between his credit cards and his cheque book. 'What's she doing?' said Miss Trant, giving a cursory look, 'The Dying Swan?' 'Oh, yes,' said Featherstone proudly. 'Quite a little Margot Fonteyn, isn't she?'
> JOHN MORTIMER *Rumpole's Return* 1980

forbidden fruit According to the account in the book of Genesis, God commanded Adam and Eve not to eat the fruit of the Tree of Knowledge but, tempted by the Serpent, Eve disobeyed him and then persuaded Adam to do the same: 'So when the woman saw that the tree was good for food, and that it was a delight to the eyes, and that the tree was to be desired to make one wise, she took of its fruit and ate; and she also gave some to her husband, and he ate' (Gen. 3: 6). The phrase 'forbidden fruit' can be used to describe something that is desired or enjoyed all the more because it is not allowed, especially illicit sexual pleasure. *See also* ADAM AND EVE, EVE.

> Later, we had to sneak. I'd hired on at Rent-a-Back by then, and she would ride along on my jobs—spend the day with me while her parents thought she was swimming at their club. 'Oh forbidden fruit! No wonder you two were attracted,' Sophia said.
> ANNE TYLER *A Patchwork Planet* 1998

Forth Bridge The Forth Bridge is a cantilevered railway bridge built in 1890 across the Firth of Forth, linking Fife and Lothian on the east coast of Scotland. The bridge requires constant maintenance and the expression 'painting the Forth Bridge' alludes to the idea that as soon as workers have finished painting the bridge, they immediately have to start repainting it.

> So a treaty that took ten years to negotiate is out of date before it even comes into force. What you might call the Forth Bridge theory of arms control. *BBC Radio 4* 1995

Fort Knox Fort Knox is a building in north Kentucky, part of a military reservation, which houses the US gold reserves in the form of bullion. It is alluded to as a place that is extremely secure and well guarded.

> It's important to chip away at Ford's defences here because they seem to be protecting the Fort Knox of his imagination. *The Observer* 1997

Fortuna In Roman mythology, Fortuna was the goddess of fortune. She is often represented turning a wheel, as a symbol of random luck or change.

> Fortuna's wheel had turned on humanity, crushing its collarbone, smashing its

skull, twisting its torso, puncturing its pelvis, sorrowing its soul.
JOHN KENNEDY TOOLE *A Confederacy of Dunces* 1980

Fortunate Isles The Fortunate Isles, better known as the Islands of the Blest, were the place to which people in classical times believed the souls of heroes and the good were conveyed to a life of bliss. They were also known as the Happy Islands. The term Fortunate Isles can be applied to heaven or paradise.

Fountain of Youth The Fountain of Youth was a legendary spring which was supposed to have the power of rejuvenation and in which Alexander the Great and his army were said to have bathed. In the early 16th century it was sought by the Spanish explorer Juan Ponce de León.

Four Horsemen of the Apocalypse *See* APOCALYPSE.

St Francis of Assisi St Francis (*c.*1181–1226), born Giovanni di Bernardone, was an Italian monk who founded the Franciscan order of friars, an order devoted to chastity, poverty, and obedience. St Francis exemplifies humility, simple faith, and in particular a great love for, and empathy with, birds and animals. He is often depicted in art preaching to birds or holding wild animals.

I shall get a job in an arts and crafts shop in Horsham and do barbola work in my spare time. I shall be all right . . . and later on I can go to Italy and perhaps learn to be a little like St Francis of Assisi.
STELLA GIBBONS *Cold Comfort Farm* 1932

You can always tell that the crash is coming when I start getting tender about Our Dumb Friends. Three highballs, and I think I'm St. Francis of Assisi.
DOROTHY PARKER *Just a Little One* 1944

Sure he could get under your skin but so would St Francis of Assisi on a job like this. He'd have spent all his time looking at the bloody birds in the Jungle instead of reading his cue-cards.
JULIAN BARNES *A History of the World in 10½ Chapters* 1989

Anne Frank Anne Frank (1929–45) was born in Frankfurt am Main and fled with her Jewish family from the Nazis in 1933. After the Nazi occupation of the Netherlands, where the family were living, she hid with her own family and four others in a sealed-off upper room (usually referred to as an attic) in Amsterdam. During this period of incarceration, she wrote a diary, which was published in 1947. The fugitives were betrayed in 1944 and Anne died in Belsen concentration camp.

Her smile, when it came, was the smile of someone who, like Anne Frank, persists against the odds in believing that people are really good at heart.
MICHELLE SPRING *Running for Shelter* 1994

At least I now knew how to get round client confidentiality. Forget the thumbscrews and the cigarette burns. Give her a cup of Horlicks and a new pair

of tights and she'd tell you Anne Frank was in the attic.
MIKE RIPLEY *Angel Confidential* 1995

Frankenstein Mary Shelley's gothic novel *Frankenstein* (1818) relates the
exploits of Victor Frankenstein, a Genevan student of natural philosophy,
who builds a grotesque manlike creature out of corpses and brings it to life.
The creature, or monster, superhuman in size and strength and terrible in
appearance, inspires horror in all who see it, but is miserably lonely and
longs to be loved. When Frankenstein refuses to create a mate for his
creature, it turns on him and murders both his bride and his brother.
Frankenstein decides that he must destroy his own creation, but is himself
killed by his monster, which then goes away to end its own life, distraught at
the death of its creator.

Senator McDull contended that the government could not carry such a debt
and remain a democratic nation, so he campaigned tirelessly and zealously
against it. 'It will destroy the very foundations of the government which we are
fighting to preserve,' he argued. 'Like a Frankenstein monster it would turn
upon us and destroy us.'
CHESTER HIMES *A Modern Fable* 1939

If Brocky had a fault, as a friend, it was just the tiniest assumption that he had
created me out of some unlikely assemblage of oddments, as the young
Frankenstein had created his Monster.
ROBERTSON DAVIES *The Cunning Man* 1994

There are some things they don't share, however. Charles, for instance, is
human (despite what he likes to think to the contrary) but Richard is possibly
not. Possibly an extra-terrestrial experiment gone wrong in fact—an alien's idea
of what a human is like, put together from spare parts, the creation of a
Martian Frankenstein.
KATE ATKINSON *Human Croquet* 1997

Freudian Sigmund Freud (1856–1939) was an Austrian neurologist and
psychotherapist who was the first to draw particular attention to the role of
the subconscious mind in human behaviour. He also emphasized the
importance of sex as a prime motive force in human behaviour. A Freudian
slip or accident is a remark, gesture, or action, apparently accidental, that in
fact reveals subconscious desires or fears, especially sexual ones.

The loss of the manuscript, I thought, was a Freudian accident.
I. B. SINGER *The Lecture* 1968

His service has been all on that most commonplace of battlefields, the domestic
front; and he has the baggy eyes and saddened heart to prove it. He has known
the Freudian hungers, received, at the age of twenty, a sound education in
complicated misery from a bouncy-breasted Swedish girl friend, which still
haunts his middle life, felt the desire for change and complication, but never
satisfied it.
MALCOLM BRADBURY *Rates of Exchange* 1983

Freyja In Norse mythology, Freyja was the goddess of love and also of fertility, fecundity, peace, and plenty.

Friday See MAN FRIDAY.

Frodo Frodo Baggins is one of the central characters of *The Lord of the Rings* (1954–5) by J. R. R. Tolkien. He is a hobbit, a small hairy-footed creature who lives in a burrow. Frodo ultimately succeeds in his quest to destroy the One Ring. *See also* BILBO BAGGINS, HOBBIT.

> The England captain could lead his players there to stare at the empty space. Youngsters could be taken there and be inspired by the Frodo-like challenge of bringing them [the Ashes] home. *The Guardian* 1997

frog prince In the fairy story *The Frog Prince*, a princess, playing with a golden ball, inadvertently drops it into a fountain. A frog, who is really a handsome prince placed under an enchantment, offers to retrieve the ball if she will, in return, love him and let him be her companion. The princess agrees, but when the frog demands to sleep in her bed, she throws it against the wall. As the frog falls, he turns back into a handsome prince. In some versions, the frog is transformed back into a prince after being kissed by a princess.

> The princess had started to kiss the frog, and chickened out. The transformation was only half complete. The man's wide, lipless mouth was Batrachian, and so were his eyes—small and protuberant, set back in a sloping forehead. His sleek shining black hair looked like a satin skullcap. His figure was upright but frog-shaped; even the skillful tailoring of his navy blazer and gray slacks could not conceal a barrel-shaped torso and short, stubby limbs.
> ELIZABETH PETERS *Naked Once More* 1989

> I don't mean I've done a sudden transformation. I'm not a frog that's been kissed by a princess or whatever the fairy tale is.
> JULIAN BARNES *Talking It Over* 1991

Elmer Fudd Elmer Fudd is an animated cartoon character in a series of Warner Brothers films. He is a short, dimwitted hunter who goes after, but is generally outwitted by, Bugs Bunny. He is known for saying 'Be vewy, vewy quiet. I'm hunting wabbits.' Underneath his tall, red stovepipe hat he is bald. *See also* BUGS BUNNY.

> His thumb resembled a lightly cooked sausage, wrinkled, as if it had been grilled and left in the fridge for a couple of days. There was a small ridge of nibbled nail above the cuticle and a huge expanse of gnawed skin above it forming a dome, like the pate of Elmer Fudd's cartoon head.
> DENISE DANKS *Better Off Dead* 1991

Fu Manchu Dr Fu Manchu was a moustached Chinese master-criminal created by the British writer Sax Rohmer (1883?–1959), first appearing in the novel *Dr Fu Manchu* (1913) and subsequently in several films. He is the archetype of the sinister 'oriental' villain.

> Maxwell looked at the Chief Inspector. If he read the man aright, here was one who gave nothing away, let nothing slip; whose face was a mask of inscrutability for the world. Miles Warren made Fu Manchu look like an *ingénue*.
> M. J. TROW *Maxwell's Flame* 1995

> I'd been met at the gate by a Fu Manchu-bearded production assistant hoisting a placard with my name, Lucy Freers, except Lucy was spelled Loosy, as in Loosy-Goosy.
> LINDSAY MARACOTTA *The Dead Celeb* 1997

Furies In Greek mythology, the Furies (also known as the Erinyes) were the avenging spirits of punishment, often represented as three winged goddesses with snakes twisted in their hair. Their names were Alecto, Megaera, and Tisiphone, and they relentlessly pursued and punished wrongdoers who had otherwise escaped punishment, often when there was no human avenger left alive. Among the crimes they were particularly concerned with were the killing by one member of a family of another, blasphemy against the gods, and treachery to a host or guest. They were sometimes called the Eumenides, 'the kindly ones', a euphemism intended to placate them. *See also* ORESTES.

> The Vengeance, uttering terrific shrieks, and flinging her arms about her head like all the forty Furies at once, was tearing from house to house, rousing the women.
> CHARLES DICKENS *A Tale of Two Cities* 1859

> He eyed them with distaste, resenting this universal calm at a time when he himself was feeling like a character in a Greek tragedy pursued by the Furies.
> P G. WODEHOUSE *Cocktail Time* 1958

Gabriel In the Bible, Gabriel is one of the archangels closest to God and the one used by God to deliver revelations to men and women. Gabriel revealed to Zacharias that his wife, Elisabeth, would bear a son to be called John, who grew up to be John the Baptist (Luke 1: 8–20). He also appeared to the Virgin Mary to tell her that she would bear a son to be called Jesus (Luke 1: 26–38). In Christian tradition, he is thought to be the archangel who will blow the trumpet to announce the general resurrection: 'For the Lord himself shall descend from heaven with a shout, with the voice of the archangel, and with the trump of God: and the dead in Christ shall rise first' (1 Thess. 4: 16). In Islam, Gabriel appeared to Muhammad and revealed the Koran to him.

> Blowing harder than Gabriel's trumpet, it is, and enough snow already down to bury a whale.
> JOAN AIKEN *The Whispering Mountain* 1968

> 'She has revelations. All this stuff about Darcy's Utopia is dictated to her, she claims, by a kind of shining cloud.' I laughed. I couldn't help it. 'Like God appearing to Moses in a burning bush, or the Archangel Gabriel to Mohammed as a shining pillar?' I asked.
> FAY WELDON *Darcy's Utopia* 1990

> There may be no winning the next election for the Tories, even if they could draft a new leader combining the purity of the Archangel Gabriel, the cunning of Machiavelli and the strength of Hercules.
> ANDREW RAWNSLEY *The Observer* 1995

Gadarene swine The Gadarene swine were the herd of pigs into which Jesus, preaching in the territory of the Gadarenes, cast the demons that had possessed a madman (Matt. 8: 28–32). As a result the pigs ran down a steep cliff into the Sea of Galilee and were drowned. 'Gadarene' means involving or engaged in a headlong or potentially disastrous rush to do something.

> With a sense almost of shock, he recalled his father talking of the English as the Gadarene swine, almost fifty years before.
> JON THURLEY *The Enigma Variations* 1988

Sir Galahad In Arthurian legend, Sir Galahad was one of the knights of the Round Table, the son of Sir Lancelot and Elaine. Galahad's immaculate purity and virtue predestines him to succeed in the quest for the Holy Grail. His name is a byword for chivalrous heroism, and the image of him riding up on his charger to rescue a maiden in distress is a common one. *See also* KING ARTHUR.

> 'I have to go out,' I said. 'I have to go over there and see what has happened. And she can't stay here alone. And no man, not even a doctor, is going to put her to bed. Get a nurse. I'll sleep somewhere else.' 'Phil Marlowe,' he said. 'The shop-soiled Galahad. Okay. I'll stick around until the nurse comes.'
> RAYMOND CHANDLER *The High Window* 1943

> The usher called her again. I dropped the remnants of the small cigar on the marble floor of the Shire Hall and ground it underfoot. The lance was in the rest, Sir Galahad Rumpole was about to do battle for the damsel in distress, or words to that effect.
> JOHN MORTIMER *Rumpole of the Bailey* 1978

> 'I guess it shocked me,' he said. 'There I was, the naïve romantic, thinking of myself as Sir Galahad saving the damsel from the dragon, and I find out the damsel is out partying with the dragon.'
> TONY HILLERMAN *The Fallen Man* 1997

Galatea In Greek mythology, Galatea was the name given to the ivory statue of a woman carved by the sculptor Pygmalion. Revolted by the imperfections of living women, Pygmalion had resolved never to marry, but he fell in love with his own creation. When Aphrodite brought the beautiful statue to life, he married her. *See also* PYGMALION.

> And with a sudden motion she shook her gauzy covering from her, and stood forth in her low kirtle and her snaky zone, in her glorious radiant beauty and her imperial grace, rising from her wrappings, as it were, like Venus from the wave, or Galatea from her marble.
> H. RIDER HAGGARD *She* 1887

> She hated Spielvogel for what Spielvogel had written about the Peter who was to *her* so inspirational and instructive, the man she had come to adore for the changes he was helping to bring about in her life. Spielvogel had demythologized her Pygmalion—of course Galatea was furious.
> PHILIP ROTH *My Life as a Man* 1970

> Your motive was as strong as Hattie's—stronger, because your feelings for Valentine are as violent and perverse as Laurie's were. You've fallen in love with your Galatea, the image you and Hattie created to assume the role of Valerie Valentine, and if the truth came out you'd lose her.
> ELIZABETH PETERS *Die for Love* 1984

Galileo Galileo Galilei (1564–1642) was an Italian astronomer and physicist. Under torture he publicly recanted his view that the sun was the centre of the universe and the earth moved around the sun, but is later reported as declaring 'Eppur si muove' ('But it does move'). His name is now associated with the defiant upholding of scientific truth and integrity.

Remember Galilyo. Always stick up for yourself!
V. S. NAIPAUL *A House for Mr Biswas* 1969

But a man does not attain the status of Galileo merely because he is
persecuted; he must also be right.
STEPHEN JAY GOULD *Ever Since Darwin* 1977

Mrs Gamp Sarah Gamp in Dickens's *Martin Chuzzlewit* (1844) is a gin-
drinking and somewhat disreputable nurse who carries a large cotton
umbrella. She continually refers to an imaginary Mrs Harris to validate her
opinions. 'Gamp' is a dated British term for an umbrella, especially a large,
unwieldy one. *See also* DICKENSIAN.

In *Oswald's Tale*, Mailer concludes his re-perusal of JFK's assassination with a
modest, grateful tribute to the assassin's mother. Marguerite Oswald, he
remarks, does the novelist's work for him; she is one of those outrageous,
hyperbolic American facts which intimidate fiction . . . During her interrogation,
she railed at the slight to her dignity when she wasn't permitted to leave the
room to urinate; a guard presented her with a paper-lined rubbish bin for the
purpose. Mailer calls Marguerite a worthy colleague for Micawber and Uriah
Heep. I'd say she was Mrs Gamp transmogrified to Texas.
PETER CONRAD *The Observer* 1995

Gandalf Gandalf is the white wizard in J. R. R. Tolkien's fantasy adventures
The Hobbit (1937) and *The Lord of the Rings* (1954–5). At the start of the latter he
is described as an old man wearing a tall pointed hat and a long grey cloak,
with 'a long white beard and bushy eyebrows that stuck out beyond the brim
of his hat'. He is renowned for his spectacular firework displays.

Gandhi Mohandas Karamchand Gandhi (1869–1948), usually called
Mahatma ('Great Soul') Gandhi, was an Indian nationalist and spiritual
leader who pursued a policy of passive resistance and non-violent civil
disobedience in opposition to British rule. He was influential in the Indian
National Congress and was regarded as the country's supreme political and
spiritual leader and the principal force in achieving India's independence. He
was assassinated by a Hindu nationalist following his agreement to the
creation of the state of Pakistan. Gandhi is sometimes referred to as the
epitome of a pacifist.

Anna was attempting a Zen-like state and failing miserably. The heat, the
boredom, and Rick were a combination that would have gotten Gandhi's
loincloth in a bundle.
NEVADA BARR *Endangered Species* 1997

Ganesh In Hinduism, Ganesh (or Ganesha), the son of Siva and Parvati, is
the elephant-headed god of wisdom and prudence. He is worshipped as the
remover of obstacles and the patron of learning.

Ganymede In Greek mythology, Ganymede (or Ganymedes) was a Trojan youth who was so beautiful that he was carried off by an eagle to be Zeus' cup-bearer. He is the archetype of a youth of extraordinary beauty and desirability.

> What little child ever refused to be comforted by that glorious sense of being seized strongly and swung upwards? I don't believe Ganymede cried when the eagle carried him away, and perhaps deposited him on Jove's shoulder at the end.
> GEORGE ELIOT *Adam Bede* 1859

> Her chair being a far more comfortable one than his she still slept on inside his great-coat, looking warm as a new bun and boyish as Ganymedes.
> THOMAS HARDY *Jude the Obscure* 1895

> He was always on the look-out for promising young men who could be advanced in his service. . . . I do not suggest that Boy ever recognized these young men as anything but business associates; but they were business associates with an overtone of Jove's cup-bearer that I, at least, could not ignore. Corporation Ganymedes, they did not know their role and were thus disappointments.
> ROBERTSON DAVIES *Fifth Business* 1970

> Now listen: were it by any chance the case that Oliver's radiant sexuality occasionally put aside the workaday, and were his heliotropic gaze to turn towards Stoke Newington's unlikely Ganymede, then, to enlist a vernacular which my accuser herself will be able to grasp, *I wouldn't have any trouble there, mate.*
> JULIAN BARNES *Talking It Over* 1991

Greta Garbo Greta Garbo (1905–90) was a fair-haired Swedish-born US actress, born Greta Gustafsson. She had a haunting beauty and a compelling screen presence. Her films include *Queen Christina* (1933), *Anna Karenina* (1935), and *Ninotchka* (1939). She gave up her film career in 1941 and remained a recluse from then until her death. The phrase 'I want to be alone', used by Garbo in the 1932 film *Grand Hotel*, became closely identified with her.

> 'How long will it take it to grow long?' 'Really long?' 'No, I mean to thy shoulders. It is thus I would have thee wear it.' 'As Garbo in the cinema?' 'Yes,' he said thickly.
> ERNEST HEMINGWAY *For Whom the Bell Tolls* 1941

> Fischer withdrew completely from professional chess and entered a Garboesque seclusion, freezing in perpetuity the popular image of himself as the intense young man from Brooklyn who had triumphed so spectacularly at Reykjavik.
> *The Independent* 1992

Garden of Eden *See* EDEN.

Gargantua Gargantua (whose name means 'gullet') is a prince of gigantic proportions and prodigious appetite in Rabelais's satire *Gargantua* (1534), from whom we drive the word 'gargantuan'. He is the father of Pantagruel.

> Then the baking would begin, and in a few days there would be a party, consisting chiefly of a Gargantuan feed, with Mrs. Gall the heart and soul of it.
> ROBERTSON DAVIES *A Mixture of Frailties* 1951

> She . . . saw the two giant connecting rods churning round and round, a nightmare from Gargantua.
> PETER CAREY *Oscar and Lucinda* 1988

> Broadway followed, and marriage the same year, at the age of 19. The birth of a daughter in this first, as in his two subsequent marriages, in no way slowed down his gargantuan promiscuity.
> BRENDA MADDOX *The Observer* 1996

Garibaldi Giuseppe Garibaldi (1807–82) was the hero of the movement for Italian independence and unification, leading a volunteer force, the Red Shirts, to victory in Sicily and Naples.

> Slowly Russo began to shake his head from side to side: this was no Capone, this was a Garibaldi!
> PHILIP ROTH *You Can't Tell a Man by the Song he Sings* 1959

Garm Garm is the dog that guards the gates of hell in Norse mythology, a Norse equivalent of Cerberus.

Alf Garnett Alf Garnett, played by Warren Mitchell, was the central character of the BBC TV series *Till Death Us Do Part* (1964–74). A working-class bigot from the East End of London, Alf Garnett is best remembered for haranguing his family every week with his right-wing, xenophobic, sexist, and racist views.

> He's a fat, foul-mouthed slob. and he has struck a raw nerve. The arrival of the testicle-scratching Friedhelm Motzki on German television caused a wave of indignation throughout the country yesterday. . . . Motzki is an Alf Garnett-style figure, who rants incessantly against all east Germans—including his sister-in-law. *The Independent* 1993

David Garrick David Garrick (1717–79) was regarded as the foremost Shakespearean actor of 18th-century England and manager of Drury Lane Theatre for nearly 30 years (1747–76). According to Oliver Goldsmith he was 'an abridgement of all that was pleasant in man'.

> 'Is the play up to viewing, Mr Garrick?' one or other of the gentlemen would periodically ask Ralph, and Ralph was ecstatic for this merely whimsical comparison of himself to the great actor–manager.
> THOMAS KENEALLY *The Playmaker* 1987

Bill Gates Bill Gates (b. 1955) is the US computer entrepreneur who co-founded the Microsoft ® computer company in 1975. By the end of the 1980s Gates had become the youngest multi-billionaire in American history. The year 2004 was the eleventh in a row that Gates headed *Forbes* magazine's list of the wealthiest people in the United States. References to Bill Gates tend to relate to his enormous wealth or his computing expertise.

> '. . . I wanted this meet to tell you that young Elizabeth has been swindled.' I led him through the sequence of events very gently, but I could see that he was having difficulty in following. He was the least computer-literate person I had ever met and compared to him I was Bill Gates in person.
> GERALD HAMMOND *Illegal Tender* 2000

GCHQ The Government Communications Headquarters (or GCHQ) is the UK government department responsible for monitoring communications intelligence, which since 1953 has been based in Cheltenham, Gloucestershire. References to GCHQ are often in the context of electronic surveillance.

> The woman's eyes opened very wide. 'Yet he hasn't been out for the last twenty-four hours. I would have known.' Harry did not doubt it. Living next door to GCHQ would have carried less risk of surveillance.
> MARTIN EDWARDS *Yesterday's Papers* 1994

Gehenna Gehenna is the Hebrew name for the Valley of Hinnom, a valley to the south of Jerusalem. Hinnom was known as the Valley of Slaughter (Jer. 7: 31–2), and was used for idolatrous worship, with children being burnt alive as sacrifices to the idol Moloch. The name came to be associated with the fires of Hell.

> Down to Gehenna or up to the Throne,
> He travels fastest who travels alone.
> RUDYARD KIPLING *The Story of the Gadsbys* 1890

Gordon Gekko Gordon Gekko is the predatory and ruthless company trader played by Michael Douglas in the 1987 film *Wall Street*. His catchphrases include 'Lunch is for wimps' and 'Greed is good'.

> But you know, the six months I spent there [working on Wall Street] really exploded some myths. For instance, the men who power-dressed, and shuttled about in limousines talking into two mobile phones at once, were not always worthy of the Gordon Gecko image.
> REBECCA TINSLEY *Settlement Day* 1994

Genghis Khan Genghis Khan (1162–1227) was a military leader and founder of the Mongol Empire, which at his death stretched from the Pacific to the Black Sea. Though a brilliant military leader and administrator, he acquired a reputation for horrific cruelty. Modern-day people holding fanatically right-wing views are sometimes humorously described as being 'to the right of Genghis Khan'.

Atkinson came slowly into the room. As so often, especially in the mornings, his demeanour seemed to imply that he was unacquainted with the other two and had, at the moment, no intention of striking up any sort of relation with them. This morning he looked more than ever like Genghis Khan meditating a purge of his captains.
KINGSLEY AMIS *Lucky Jim* 1953

He seems to assume I'm about as liberal-minded as Genghis Khan and the annoying thing is, when he talks to me, I start sounding like the worst sort of reactionary. He provokes it. I take up points of view I don't actually support strongly and start defending them to the hilt.
ANN GRANGER *A Season for Murder* 1991

What he is and what he says he is—two different things. I think the guy's a hard-nosed reactionary. To the right of Genghis Khan.
JANE STANTON HITCHCOCK *The Witches' Hammer* 1995

George III George III (1738–1820) reigned as king of Great Britain and Ireland from 1760 to 1820. The American colonies were lost during his reign. His political influence declined from 1788 after repeated bouts of insanity. In 1811 it became clear that the king's mental health made him unfit to rule and his son was made regent. It is now believed that the king suffered from porphyria, a rare hereditary disease.

Even we hacks live with the unspoken dread that, quite suddenly, we could become as cuckoo as King George III and be offered jobs as *Daily Mail* leader writers. *The Guardian* 1997

St George St George is the patron saint of England, and is popularly portrayed as the archetypal dragon-slayer and rescuer of fair maidens.

Geppetto Geppetto is the carpenter who makes Pinocchio, the wooden puppet that comes to life in the story *Le Avventure di Pinocchio* (1883) by G. Lorenzini, who wrote under the name of Carlo Collodi. *See also* PINOCCHIO.

Next to the shoe store was the jewelry store that had always had a clever clockwork display that fascinated me as a child. The display changed every few months and it was like something out of Gepetto's workshop, with little human and animal figures going in and out of miniature buildings, dancing, playing instruments.
JOHN MADDOX ROBERTS *A Typical American Town* 1995

Gestapo The Gestapo were the secret police in Germany under the Nazis. They were founded by Goering in 1933 and were feared for their ruthlessness and cruelty, especially in their methods of interrogation.

Harlan Potter is a cold-hearted son of a bitch. All Victorian dignity on the outside. Inside he's as ruthless as a Gestapo thug.
RAYMOND CHANDLER *The Long Goodbye* 1953

There would have been a place in the Gestapo for the lady; she had a way of

interrogation that could reduce the sturdiest girls to tears in the first five minutes.
JOHN FOWLES *The French Lieutenant's Woman* 1981

Given what she had learned from Liz, Lolly's so-called strength of character was beginning to degenerate into Gestapo-like cruelty. She appeared to have ditched a husband, kept two daughters entirely ignorant of their background and family ties, lied over and over again.
SUSAN MOODY *Sacrifice Bid* 1997

Gethsemane Gethsemane was a garden lying in the valley between Jerusalem and the Mount of Olives, where Jesus went with his disciples to pray on the night before his Crucifixion and which was the scene of his agony and betrayal by Judas (Matt. 26: 36–46). The name Gethsemane is sometimes used to typify a scene of mental or spiritual anguish, as is the phrase 'agony in the garden'. *See also* JESUS.

It was a night which led the traveller's thoughts instinctively to dwell on nocturnal scenes of disaster in the chronicles of the world, on all that is terrible and dark in history and legend—the last plague of Egypt, the destruction of Sennacherib's host, the agony in Gethsemane.
THOMAS HARDY *The Return of the Native* 1878

Jean Paul Getty Jean Paul Getty (1892–1976) was an American oil billionaire who was widely described as the world's richest man. As well as being alluded to for his wealth, he was also renowned for his miserliness, allegedly keeping a public payphone for the use of his guests.

Alberto Giacometti Alberto Giacometti was a Swiss sculptor (1901–66) noted for the exaggerated length and thinness of his figures.

Their Giacometti-like thinness is a withering by pitiless experience.
CAMILLE PAGLIA *Sexual Personae* 1990

Giant Despair Giant Despair is a character in *The Pilgrim's Progress* by John Bunyan (1678, 1684). The giant finds Christian and his companion Hopeful sleeping in the grounds of his castle, Doubting Castle, and puts them in the castle dungeon, where 'they lay from Wednesday morning till Saturday night, without one bit of bread, or drop of drink, or light, or any to ask how they did'. Giant Despair beats them and advises them to kill themselves. Eventually, they escape using 'the key called Promise' which opens all the locks in the castle. *See also* PILGRIM'S PROGRESS.

Edward Gibbon Edward Gibbon (1737–94) was an English historian and author of *The History of the Decline and Fall of the Roman Empire* (1776–88), generally regarded as a monumental work of literature as well as historical analysis. Ranging from the 2nd century AD to the fall of Constantinople in 1453, Gibbon's work covers the founding of Christianity, the movement and settlement of the Teutonic tribes, the conquests of the Muslims, and the

Crusades. The famous remark 'Another damned, thick, square book! Always scribble, scribble, scribble! Eh! Mr Gibbon?' is usually attributed to the duke of Gloucester.

It is my ambition to out-Gibbon Mr Gibbon.
WILLIAM GOLDING *Rites of Passage* 1980

Gibson Girl Charles Dana Gibson (1867–1944) was an American artist and illustrator whose drawings popularized the fashionable ideal of American womanhood in the 1890s and early 1900s: well-built, wasp-waisted, and dressed in tailored Edwardian style.

The young girl in the picture had a massed pile of light hair, and a sharp waist, and that plump-softness of skin and slightly heavy Gibson-girl handsomeness of feature that the age so much admired.
JOHN FOWLES *The Magus* 1966

Gilderoy's kite Gilderoy was a famous Scottish highwayman said to have been hanged higher than other criminals because of the wickedness of his crimes. To be hanged higher than Gilderoy's kite is to be punished more severely than the very worst criminal.

Gilead In the book of Jeremiah, the prophet laments the fact that there seems no remedy for the Jews' distress with the words 'Is there no balm in Gilead? Is there no physician there?' (Jer. 8: 22). The phrase 'balm in Gilead' has come to mean 'comfort in distress, succour'.

There was a long pause and Junior stood sucking on an eyetooth and studying deep on something, and then he said, What you about to learn is they ain't no balm in Gilead.
CHARLES FRAZIER *Cold Mountain* 1997

Gin Lane *Gin Lane* (1751), depicting a scene of drunkenness and squalor, is one of the most famous prints by William Hogarth, the English painter, engraver, and satirist. Gin-drinking was widespread at the time, and regarded by many as a cause of crime and other social problems. *See also* HOGARTH.

In his intrepid trip down the stairs he encountered every sort of vice: fornication, crack smoking, heroin injecting, dice games and three-card monte, and more fornication. . . . 'It's bloody Hogarth,' said Steiner. 'Gin Lane. Except that it's vertical.'
TOM WOLFE *The Bonfire of the Vanities* 1987

Ginnungagap In Scandinavian mythology, Ginnungagap (also spelt Ginnung-Gap) was the Great Void, the dark space between Niflheim, the land of the dead, and Muspelheim, the region of intense heat. It had no beginning or end and no night and day.

She wrapped round her a long red woollen cravat and opened the door. The

night in all its fulness met her flatly on the threshold, like the very brink of an absolute void, or the antemundane Ginnung-Gap believed in by her Teuton forefathers. For her eyes were fresh from the blaze, and here there was no street lamp or lantern to form a kindly transition between the inner glare and the outer dark.
THOMAS HARDY *The Woodlanders* 1887

Gioconda *See* MONA LISA.

Giotto Giotto di Bondone (*c.*1267–1337) was an Italian painter generally recognized as the founder of Florentine painting and the initiator of a more naturalistic and dramatic style in contrast to the rather stiff, two-dimensional design of Byzantine art. According to the story in Vasari's *Lives of the Artists* (1550), when the Pope sent for an example of Giotto's work before commissioning him to paint in St Peter's, he drew a perfect circle with one turn of his hand.

To keep his heart high and yet out of his throat, he made a song . . .
Full Ringing Round
As the Belly of Silenus
Giotto Painter of Perfect Circles
NATHANAEL WEST *The Dream Life of Balso Snell* 1931

Gloucester In Shakespeare's *King Lear* (1623), the Earl of Gloucester, whose pity for Lear has led him to assist the old king's escape to Dover, has his eyes put out by the Duke of Cornwall. The blinding of Gloucester is one of the most gruesome scenes in Shakespeare. *See also* SHAKESPEARE.

God *See* JEHOVAH.

Godfather 'The Godfather' is the term used to denote the head of a Mafia family, popularized by Mario Puzo in his novel *The Godfather* (1968) and by the 1972 film which, together with two sequels, was based on it. The original Godfather, Don Corleone (played by Marlon Brando in the film), is succeeded by his son Michael Corleone (played by Al Pacino). The book and films document the power struggles and vendettas between Mafia families. The name can now be applied to any ruthless head of a criminal dynasty.

Lady Godiva Lady Godiva (d. 1080) was an English noblewoman, wife of Leofric, earl of Mercia. According to a 13th-century legend, she rode naked through the marketplace of Coventry, clothed only in her long, golden hair, to persuade her husband to reduce the heavy taxes he had imposed on the people. All the townspeople stayed indoors and shut up their windows, except for Tom the Tailor, who looked at her through a window as she rode past and was thereafter known as Peeping Tom. He was struck blind as a consequence of his action. *See also* PEEPING TOM.

To say I was cold would be like saying Lady Godiva was underdressed.
KATHY REICHS *Death du Jour* 1999

Godot In Samuel Beckett's play *Waiting for Godot* (1952), two tramps, Estragon and Vladimir, discuss philosophical issues while they await the arrival of the mysterious character Godot. Godot never appears, despite the promises of a young boy who comes on at the end of each act claiming to be his emissary. A long wait can be described as like waiting for Godot. *See also* ESTRAGON.

Godzilla Godzilla is a huge fictitious dinosaur-like monster who was aroused from the sea-bed by an atomic explosion and threatened to destroy Tokyo. He first appeared in a 1955 film, and later in several sequels.

I should have realised something unusual was up when my cat Hortense shot in from the garden with a tail like a flue-brush and disappeared into the cupboard in the upstairs loo. This was uncharacteristic of a cat who is second cousin to Godzilla.
MICHÈLE BAILEY *Haycastle's Cricket* 1996

Joseph Goebbels Joseph Goebbels (1897–1945) became Hitler's minister of propaganda in 1933. He had control of the press and radio, and used these in order to control the flow of information to the German public and thus further the Nazi cause. He is sometimes mentioned as an archetypal propagandist.

Bhutto has rejected all these charges as politically motivated, saying that they were 'hatched up by the Goebbels of the Pakistani government'. *The Observer* 1997

I mean, let's face it, the propaganda that the car industry puts out would give Goebbels and Stalin a run for their money in terms of pure Utopian disinformation.
BEN ELTON *Inconceivable* 1999

Rube Goldberg Reuben Goldberg (1883–1970) was a US comic-strip artist known for his drawings of ludicrously complex machinery designed to perform simple everyday tasks. His name has become a byword for any unnecessarily complicated and inefficient machine, structure, or system.

Orchids are Rube Goldberg machines; a perfect engineer would certainly have come up with something better.
STEPHEN JAY GOULD *Ever Since Darwin* 1978

Golden Fleece In Greek mythology, the Golden Fleece was the fleece of pure gold taken from the ram that carried Phrixus through the air to Colchis on the Black Sea. Phrixus sacrificed the ram to Zeus and offered its fleece to Aeetes, king of Colchis, who hung it from an oak tree guarded by a dragon that never slept. Jason set out with the Argonauts to find and recover the

Golden Fleece, which he did with the help of Medea. The Golden Fleece can be alluded to as something of great value, especially something that is difficult to obtain. *See also* JASON AND THE ARGONAUTS.

> All along, the company's engineers pursued TV's Golden Fleece, the elusive 'passive' audience meter, a device capable of recognizing each TV viewer and recording even his briefest exit, without his having to lift a finger. *Atlantic* 1992

Goldilocks Goldilocks is the name of a little girl in a traditional fairy story, *Goldilocks and the Three Bears*, and the name can be applied to any person with light blonde hair. In the story, Goldilocks visits the bears' house, eats the little bear's porridge, and is eventually found by the bears asleep in his bed.

> You just potter about . . . while I repair to the kitchen with young Goldilocks here and show him how to cook a sausage.
> P G. WODEHOUSE *Laughing Gas* 1936

> 'Fish,' he said to the beard, 'this is Goldilocks.' I smiled rigidly. I am not a blonde.
> MARGARET ATWOOD *The Edible Woman* 1969

Golgotha Golgotha, also known as Calvary (both of which come from words, in Aramaic and Latin respectively, meaning 'the Place of the Skull'), was the hill, just outside Jerusalem, where Jesus was crucified. The word can be applied to any experience of intense mental suffering. *See also* JESUS.

> Billy dozed, awakened in the prison hospital again. The sun was high. Outside were Golgotha sounds of strong men digging holes for upright timbers in hard, hard ground. Englishmen were building themselves a new latrine.
> KURT VONNEGUT *Slaughterhouse-Five* 1969

> Gladiators, Wellingtons and Blenheims began to appear in the sky over our heads, and so the British added their strength to the Greek daggers twisting in our wounds. General Soddu inspected us and compared us to granite. 'Does granite bleed,' asked Francesco, 'on Golgotha?'
> LOUIS DE BERNIÈRES *Captain Corelli's Mandolin* 1994

Goliath Goliath was the Philistine giant in the Bible who issued a challenge to single combat to any opponent from the Israelite army. The challenge was accepted by the young David, who slew the over nine-foot tall Goliath with a stone from a sling (1 Sam. 17). A large or powerful person or organization can be described as a Goliath, especially if they are being challenged by someone small and weak. *See also* DAVID.

> Silas was impressed with the melancholy truth of this last remark; but his force of mind failed before the only two penal methods open to him, not only because it was painful to him to hurt Eppie, but because he trembled at a moment's contention with her, lest she should love him the less for it. Let even an affectionate Goliath get himself tied to a small tender thing, dreading to

hurt it by pulling, and dreading still more to snap the cord, and which of the two, pray, will be master?
GEORGE ELIOT *Silas Marner* 1861

You call him small? He's a regular Goliath compared with the shortest man in the Bible.
ROBERTSON DAVIES *World of Wonders* 1975

They were unable to bar the door to those diabolic bestioles which crawl through the smallest hole even as David found the chink in Goliath's armour.
JULIAN BARNES *A History of the World in 10½ Chapters* 1989

Fischer was a maximalist, a killer, and he slew the Goliath of Soviet chess. *The Independent* 1992

Gollum In J. R. R. Tolkien's *The Hobbit* (1937) and *The Lord of the Rings* (1954–5), Gollum is a former hobbit named Smeagol who has been transformed by the power of the One Ring (his 'precious') he once possessed into a repulsive but pitiful creature. Gollum accompanies Frodo on part of his quest to destroy the ring but, consumed by a desire to regain possession of it, is a furtive and untrustworthy guide. *See also* FRODO.

I see styles as the Gollum of desktop editing. They are extremely useful, malleable and sometimes deceptive. *Newsletter of the Society of Editors* 2001

Gomorrah *See* SODOM AND GOMORRAH.

Gone with the Wind Margaret Mitchell's novel *Gone with the Wind* (1936), made into a film in 1939 starring Clark Gable and Vivien Leigh, is set during the American Civil War. At its centre is the romance between Scarlett O'Hara and the dangerously dashing Rhett Butler. *Gone with the Wind* can be alluded to as an example of glamorous or overblown romanticism.

Robin Goodfellow Robin Goodfellow is another name for Puck. *See also* PUCK.

Good Samaritan One of Jesus's parables tells of a Samaritan who stopped to help a victim of thieves left wounded by the roadside and already ignored by a priest and a Levite, both of whom passed by on the other side (Luke 10: 30–7). The Samaritan, by contrast, 'had compassion, and went to him and bound up his wounds, pouring on oil and wine; then he set him on his own beast and brought him to an inn, and took care of him'. Inhabitants of Samaria would have been regarded by the Jews as enemies and outcasts, having split from mainstream Judaism, recognizing only the Pentateuch (the first five books of the Bible). The term 'Good Samaritan' is now used to describe a person who is helpful and compassionate, especially to those in adversity.

I told her that I had had a fall—I didn't say how—and she saw by my looks that I was pretty sick. Like a true Samaritan she asked no questions, but gave me a

bowl of milk with a dash of whisky in it, and let me sit for a little by her kitchen fire.
JOHN BUCHAN *The Thirty-Nine Steps* 1915

'Can I do anything for you?' 'We have been stranded a half hour,' Yusef said. 'The cars have gone by, and I have thought—when will a Good Samaritan appear?'
GRAHAM GREENE *The Heart of the Matter* 1948

That Brian Cassidy from the hotel, he was going to let her die right there, but a Good Samaritan in the garage, he sometimes feeds her on the sly when Mr Cassidy isn't watching, he called for an ambulance.
SARA PARETSKY *Ghost Country* 1998

Goody Two-Shoes Little Goody Two-Shoes is the heroine of a 1765 children's book by John Newbery, published under the full title *The History of Little Goody Two-Shoes; Otherwise called, Mrs Margery Two-Shoes. With the Means by which she acquired her Learning and Wisdom, and in consequence thereof her Estate*. An orphan who is delighted with a pair of new shoes (from which she gets her nickname), Margery becomes educated and ultimately wealthy through her own virtue and industry. Her name has now come to be used for a smugly virtuous person.

Do you have to swear every other word?' 'Do you have to be such a stuck-up goody two shoes?' We carried on in silence.
SHYAMA PERERA *Haven't Stopped Dancing Yet* 1999

Goons *The Goon Show* was an extremely popular BBC radio comedy series which ran from 1952 to 1960. The Goons were originally Peter Sellers, Harry Secombe, Spike Milligan, and Michael Bentine, and the off-beat humour was expressed through a set of regular characters, including Eccles and Bluebottle, who spoke in silly voices and were involved in absurd plots.

Gordian knot Gordius was a peasant who was chosen king of Phrygia, whereupon he tied the pole of his wagon to the yoke with an intricate knot. An oracle prophesied that whoever undid it would become the ruler of all Asia. Alexander the Great is said to have simply cut through the knot with his sword. Hence a Gordian knot is a complex problem or task, and 'to cut the Gordian knot' is to solve a seemingly inextricable problem by force or by evading the conditions that caused the problem in the first place.

The book rang with the courage alike of conviction and of the entire absence of conviction; it appeared to be the work of men who had a rule-of-thumb way of steering between iconoclasm on the one hand and credulity on the other; who cut Gordian knots as a matter of course when it suited their convenience.
SAMUEL BUTLER *The Way of All Flesh* 1903

One can only guess at the purposes of our Creator, in fashioning of Humanity such a complex and Gordian knot.
MARGARET ATWOOD *Alias Grace* 1996

Gorgon In Greek mythology, the Gorgons were three sisters, Stheno, Euryale, and Medusa (the only mortal one), who had snakes for hair and the power to turn anyone who looked at them to stone. A gorgon is a frightening or repulsive woman. *See also* MEDUSA.

> She was an unnatural-looking being—so young, fresh, blooming, yet so Gorgon-like. Suspicion, sullen ill-temper were on her forehead, vicious propensities in her eye, envy and panther-like deceit about her mouth.
> CHARLOTTE BRONTË *The Professor* 1857

> She was wearing something very like a man's evening suit, made in dark velvet, and looked remarkably elegant. I was beginning not to notice her Gorgon face.
> ROBERTSON DAVIES *The Manticore* 1972

Goshen Goshen was the fertile region in Egypt allotted to Jacob and the Israelites, where there was light during the plague of darkness: 'there was thick darkness in all the land of Egypt three days . . . but all the people of Israel had light where they dwelt' (Exod. 10: 23). The name Goshen can be applied to a place of plenty and comfort, or a place of light.

> It's a bleak and barren country there, not like this land of Goshen you've been used to.
> GEORGE ELIOT *Adam Bede* 1859

> 'As to my clothes—simply I will not have any,' replies Belinda, with a look of imperative decision. 'I should have thought them the one Goshen in your desert,' says Sarah, with an annoyed laugh; 'them and the presents.'
> RHODA BROUGHTON *Belinda* 1883

Gotham *See* WISE MEN OF GOTHAM.

Goths The Goths were one of the Germanic peoples who, along with the Vandals, Visigoths, Huns, etc., overran part of Roman Europe in the 4th and 5th centuries AD. Although it is the Vandals whose name is most closely associated with the idea of ravaging invasion, the name of the Goths can also be used in this way. *See also* VANDAL.

> The glittering dresses on the blank-faced or headless mannequins are no longer what they seemed, the incarnation of desire. Instead they look like party trash. Crumpled paper napkins, the rubble left by rowdy crowds or looting armies. Although nobody saw them or could say for certain who they were, the Goths and the Vandals have been through.
> MARGARET ATWOOD *The Robber Bride* 1993

Götterdämmerung In Germanic mythology, Götterdämmerung was the Twilight of the Gods, their destruction and that of the world in a final battle with the forces of evil. This is the title of the last opera in Wagner's *Ring Cycle*. The term can be used to refer to the cataclysmic downfall of a powerful organization or regime. *See also* RAGNAROK, WAGNER.

> That same night at the national stadium, England faced their gotterdammerung

against the All Blacks. *Scottish Rugby* 1991

'There was certainly a huge dust-up about it,' she said. 'I mean, we're talking
mega here, right? Apparently it had been going on for the best part of a year
and Myra was the last to know. When she did find out it was like
Götterdämmerung. I believe Myra brandished a knife at Lara and told her to be
on the next stagecoach out of town and, according to local legend, she had
Simon's balls bronzed and still wears them round her neck on a chain.'
JOYCE HELM *Foreign Body* 1997

Jay Gould Jay Gould (1836–92) was a US railroad financier and speculator.
His efforts to corner the gold market are said to have caused the financial
panic of Black Friday, on 24 September 1869. Gould's name became
synonymous with financial predatoriness.

'They home,' a woman screamed through the shutters of the house next door,
an architect's vision of Jay Gould domestic.
JOHN KENNEDY TOOLE *A Confederacy of Dunces* 1980

But you can't make Milton K. Rogers rich, any more than you can fat a hide-
bound colt. It ain't *in* him. He'd run through Vanderbilt, Jay Gould, and Tom
Scott rolled into one, in less than six months, give him a chance, and come out
and want to borrow money of you.
W. D. HOWELLS *The Rise of Silas Lapham* 1885

Goya Francisco José de Goya y Lucientes (1746–1828) was a Spanish painter
and etcher. He became official portrait-painter to the Spanish court,
producing portraits of extraordinary, sometimes brutally frank, realism.
Goya also painted society portraits, many of women dressed in the style of a
maja, in traditional black Spanish dress with black lace mantilla. His set of 65
etchings *The Disasters of War* (1810–14) depict the French occupation of Spain
and express the cruelty and horror of war through scenes of death,
execution, pillage, and famine. One such engraving, called *Great Exploits with
Dead Men*, depicts mutilated corpses hanging from a tree. The name of Goya
can evoke either the idea of a beautiful woman, or a picture of death,
mutilation, and the horror of war.

Gladys de Grey is a black-haired beauty straight off a Goya canvas, all passion
and fire.
PETER LOVESEY *Bertie and the Tinman* 1987

Three bodies hung from the branches, pale in the shadow, as monstrous as
Goya etchings.
JOHN FOWLES *The Magus* 1966

The wounded bicycle stood in the dim light from the stable, like a victim in a
Goya engraving of a casualty of war.
FRANK PARRISH *Voices from the Dark* 1993

Betty Grable Betty Grable (1916–73) was a US film actress and dancer whose
'million-dollar legs' made her the most popular pin-up of the Second World

War. She was a curly-haired blonde with a peaches-and-cream appeal.

> She wore her usual Betty Grable hairdo.
> MARGARET ATWOOD *The Edible Woman* 1969

Graces In Greek mythology, the Graces were three beautiful goddesses, Aglaia, Thalia, and Euphrosyne, daughters of Zeus, who personified charm, grace, and beauty, which they bestowed upon the world as physical, intellectual, artistic, and moral qualities.

> How incongruous it seemed to be telephoning a woman like that. The Graces assembling seemed to have joined hands in meadows of asphodel to compose that face.
> VIRGINIA WOOLF *To the Lighthouse* 1927

Gradgrind Thomas Gradgrind is the chief character in Dickens's *Hard Times* (1854). He believes in 'facts and calculations', thinking he is following the precepts of utilitarianism. He brings these principles to the task of raising his five children, ruling out their imagination and creativity. A Gradgrind is thus someone who adheres too strictly to a set of rules or principles. *See also* DICKENSIAN.

> Obviously the ideal of education for its own sake, which is at the heart of every civilised society, will suffer as businesses demand a utilitarian curriculum. No business believes poets are more important than accountants. The loss would matter less if the new Gradgrinds were providing Britain with coherent and demanding vocational education to replace the widely ridiculed NVQs. *The Observer* 1997

> Women and children—especially in one-parent families—haven't had a lot to cheer about since the Government began its Gradgrind benefits review. *Big Issue* 1998

Sir Charles Grandison Sir Charles Grandison is the hero of Samuel Richardson's novel *The History of Sir Charles Grandison* (1753–4). He was intended to represent the author's ideal of a perfect English gentleman, a model of formal courtesy and chivalric magnanimity. The term 'Grandisonian' used to be applied to a manner or deportment thought to reflect such qualities.

> Maggie actually forgot that she had any special cause of sadness this morning, as she stood on a chair to look at a remarkable series of pictures representing the Prodigal Son, in the costume of Sir Charles Grandison, except that, as might have been expected from his defective moral character, he had not, like that accomplished hero, the taste and strength of mind to dispense with a wig.
> GEORGE ELIOT *Mill on the Floss* 1860

Grandma Moses Grandma Moses was Anna Mary Robertson Moses (1860–1961), a self-taught US painter who did not begin to paint until she was nearly 70, going on to produce more than a thousand paintings in naive style, mostly of rural life in New England.

> The creamy ribbon of beach undulates for miles before curving out of sight. Occasional chaises and umbrellas dot the distant landscape like miniature objects in a Grandma Moses painting.
> SUSAN SUSSMAN with SARAJANE AVIDON *Cruising for Murder* 2000

Dorian Gray In Oscar Wilde's novel *The Picture of Dorian Gray* (1890), Dorian is an extraordinarily handsome young man who remains youthful-looking while the portrait he has had painted ages on his behalf and reflects Dorian's inner moral corruption. A person who is described as a Dorian Gray or who is said to have a portrait in the attic is someone who looks unnaturally young, especially if in addition they are suspected of having a somewhat dissipated lifestyle.

> Attenborough has grown from a young man into an old one on television. At the same time, the natural history programme—a genre which he helped invent—has done a Dorian Gray. Infra-red, slo-mo, 'Starlight' cameras: with every year, the genre is fresher, more agile and has a bigger stash of tricks up its sleeve. *The Observer* 1998

Great Depression The Great Depression was a prolonged period of economic depression in the United States, Europe, and elsewhere during the 1930s following the Wall Street stock market crash in 1929.

Great Divide The Great Divide or Continental Divide is another name for the Rocky Mountains, a range of mountains in North America that extends from the US–Mexico border to the Yukon territory in northern Canada. It was once thought of as the epitome of a faraway place.

> Albert had then crossed the Great Divide and gone to work as a solicitor's clerk in a grey and wind-blasted town called Grimble, in the north of England.
> JOHN MORTIMER *Rumpole's Return* 1980

Greatheart Greatheart, a character in Part 2 of *The Pilgrim's Progress* by John Bunyan (1684), escorts and guards Christiana and her children on their pilgrimage. He slays Giant Despair and overcomes various other monsters. *See also* PILGRIM'S PROGRESS.

> He may be stern; he may be exacting; he may be ambitious yet; but his is the sternness of the warrior Greatheart, who guards his pilgrim convoy from the onslaught of Apollyon.
> CHARLOTTE BRONTË *Jane Eyre* 1847

Great Wall of China The Great Wall of China is a fortified wall in northern China, extending 2 400 kilometres (1 500 miles) from Kansu province to the Yellow Sea north of Beijing. It was first built in the 3rd century BC, as a protection against Turkish and Mongol invaders. Most of the present wall dates from the Ming dynasty.

What is striking, however, is how un-French, and how American, these murders seem. They are suburban, youthful and disjointed, and redolent of sex, random violence and the cinema. For all the French talk of erecting a cultural Great Wall of China against Americanism, the closest you can come in Europe to New Jersey or northern Virginia is the sprawl of dormer-bungalows, malls, fast-food joints and broken marriages that surrounds large French cities—just the kind of background from which both girls came. *The Independent* 1998

Greeks bearing gifts The phrase 'Beware Greeks bearing gifts' alludes to Laocoön's words of warning to the Trojans not to admit the large wooden horse, supposedly an offering to Athene, into the walls of Troy: 'Timeo Danaos et dona ferentes' ('I fear the Greeks even when they bring gifts'). A 'Greek gift' is a gift or peace offering given with a suspected intention of doing harm. *See also* LAOCOÖN, TROJAN HORSE, TROJAN WAR.

. . . the children appeared highly suspicious of a non-Greek woman bearing gifts.
ANDRÉ BRINK *Imaginings of Sand* 1996

Grendel The Old English poem *Beowulf* tells of the adventures of the Geatish hero Beowulf, and how he fights and destroys the ferocious monster Grendel, who has been terrorizing the court of the Danish king Hrothgar, and then Grendel's mother, who comes after him to avenge her son's death.

The nest was like Grendel's lair: a bed of penguin feathers, broken eggshells, dried egg membranes, tufts of moss, decaying food, a few bones, excrement.
D. G. CAMPBELL *Crystal Desert* 1992

Gretchen Gretchen is the name of the simple, innocent girl seduced and then abandoned by Faust in Goethe's *Faust* (1808). In extended usage the name can be applied to a girl thought to resemble her, a typically German girl or woman. *See also* FAUST.

The dead have committed some portion of the evil of the night; sleep and love, the other. For what is not the sleeper responsible? What converse does he hold, and with whom? He lies down with his Nelly and drops off into the arms of his Gretchen. Thousands unbidden come to his bed. Yet how can one tell truth when it's never in the company? Girls that the dreamer has not fashioned himself to want, scatter their legs about him to the blows of Morpheus.
DJUNA BARNES *Nightwood* 1936

She is, and will most likely remain, the last woman I made love to. Love? Can I call it that? What else can I call it. She trusted me. She smelled the blood and the horror and did not recoil, but opened herself like a flower and let me rest in her for a moment, my heart shaking, as we exchanged our wordless secret. Yes, I remember her. I was falling, and she caught me, my Gretchen.
JOHN BANVILLE *The Book of Evidence* 1989

Gretna Gretna Green is a village in the Dumfries and Galloway region of Scotland just north of the English border. It was formerly a popular place for couples eloping from England to be married according to Scots law, without the parental consent required in England for those who were under age.

> 'Do not ask me, sir,' Remington says coldly. 'I am not here to give you the directions to Gretna. You will not from this moment see my niece nor are you to attempt to open any communication with her, open or clandestine.'
> TIMOTHY MO *An Insular Possession* 1986

Grim Reaper The Grim Reaper, a cloaked figure wielding a scythe, is a traditional personification of death.

> Virginia is the No 1 source-state for handguns on the East Coast . . . We must stop the trafficking or become known as the Grim Reaper State. *The Independent* 1993

Grimm The brothers Jacob (1785–1863) and Wilhelm (1786–1859) Grimm published their collection of traditional fairy tales between 1812 and 1822. Many of the tales, such as *Hansel and Gretel*, deal with such primitive childlike fears as being deserted by parents or being attacked by wild animals.

> It slides easily into the serrated slit of the lock, and I cannot suppress the light thrill that runs down my spine. It is like entering a story, something by Grimm.
> ANDRÉ BRINK *Imaginings of Sand* 1996

Grinch In the US children's story *How the Grinch Stole Christmas* (1957) by Dr Seuss, the Grinch is a mean-spirited creature whose heart is 'two sizes too small' and who hates the idea of Christmas. He tries to spoil Christmas for the people of Whoville by stealing their presents, food, decorations, and Christmas trees, but finds on Christmas morning that everyone is singing and celebrating despite his efforts.

Griselda Griselda is the heroine of the last tale of Boccaccio's *Decameron* (1353), used by Chaucer for 'The Clerk's Tale' (*c.*1387) in *The Canterbury Tales*. Her husband, the Marquis Walter, subjects her to various cruelties to test her love and patience, including making her believe that her children have been murdered and that he intends to divorce her and remarry. Griselda bears his cruelty to the end, when her children are restored to her and her husband accepts her again as his wife. Griselda represents the ideal of patience and wifely obedience.

> Monica made no reply. She had made several resolutions as she worked, and one of them was that she would never draw attention to anything she did for him, or seem to seek praise. Patient Griselda was only one of the parts she meant to play in the life of Giles Revelstoke and it was certainly not the principal one.
> ROBERTSON DAVIES *A Mixture of Frailties* 1951

> Clifford didn't look happy but he went. I waited, hands folded in my lap like patient Griselda.
> SARAH LACEY *File under: Deceased* 1992

Groundhog Day In the United States, Groundhog Day is 2 February, the day when the groundhog is said to come out of its burrow at the end of hibernation. According to tradition, if the weather is sunny enough for the groundhog to see its own shadow, then this is supposed to portend six more weeks of winter weather. In the 1993 film *Groundhog Day*, a TV weather presenter finds himself reliving the same day over and over again. If something is 'like Groundhog Day', an experience is being repeated again and again.

Everybody here was having the same perfectly Groundhog Day experience: You woke up only to repeat the day before, and no matter what you did or said or thought, you were helpless to effect a change in the next day. So everybody asked the same questions about Basra and the supply lines and the whereabouts of the WMDs and Saddam, and got the same answers. OUP *Incomings* 2003

'It seems like the same song every day,' said Brenly, whose team has lost four in a row. 'We don't throw strikes. We don't get big hits when we need them. It's like Groundhog Day.' *Washington Post* 2003

Mrs Grundy Mrs Grundy is an off-stage character from Thomas Morton's play *Speed the Plough* (1798), whose name is repeatedly invoked with the words 'What will Mrs Grundy say?' In the play she represents conventional propriety and prudery. 'Grundyism' is the narrow-minded condemnation of unconventional behaviour.

Fastidious men do not live in pigsties, nor can they long remain in politics or business. There are nature's Greeks and nature's Mrs Grundies. ALDOUS HUXLEY *Point Counter Point* 1928

Perhaps it would turn out to be a fortuitous early warning, making Dalziel step back before he got in too deep. Shit, thought Wield with sudden self-disgust. How mealy-minded could you get! A few months of what felt like a stable partnership had turned him into Mrs Grundy! REGINALD HILL *The Wood Beyond* 1996

Grünewald Mathias Grünewald (*c*.1460–1528) was a German painter whose most famous work, the nine-panel *Isenheim Altar*, contains scenes of figures suffering, with twisted limbs and contorted postures. The central panel of the altar depicts the crucifixion of Christ, with Christ's body distorted by the torture of the Cross and covered with festering wounds. His name is associated with the idea of grotesque horror.

'The neighbours don't care. The children love you. Come live with us and see in the spring. You're dying of carbon monoxide down here.' 'I'd drown in flesh up there. You pin me down and the others play pile-on.' 'Only Donald. And aren't you funny about that? Rodney and I absolutely agreed, a child shouldn't be excluded from anything physical. We thought nothing of being nude in front of them.' 'Spare me the picture, it's like a Grünewald.' JOHN UPDIKE *Bech: A Book* 1970

Guantanamo Bay Guantanamo Bay is the US naval base in Cuba. Since 2002 part of the base has been used as a high-security detention centre for suspected al-Qaida and Taliban prisoners captured in Afghanistan and elsewhere.

> Asylum seekers and advocates said detention centers like the tan brick former warehouse in Queens are a little like local Guantanamos, in the sense that the asylum detainees have no way to know how long they will be locked up. *OUP Incomings* 2004

Martin Guerre Martin Guerre was a 16th-century Gascon peasant who disappeared from his village for nine years. Subsequently a certain Arnaud du Thil, bearing a close resemblance to Guerre, presented himself as the missing man and was accepted by Guerre's wife as her husband. He was later revealed as an impostor by the true Martin Guerre. The story is the subject of the film *Le Retour de Martin Guerre* (1982).

Guinevere In Arthurian legend, Guinevere is the wife of King Arthur and the lover of Lancelot. Her adulterous affair with Lancelot is seen as contributing to the destruction of the Round Table and ultimately to Arthur's death. *See also* KING ARTHUR, LANCELOT.

> Her beauty was timeless. Guinevere, Maid Marian, Botticelli's Venus, Mucha's model for his painting of autumn: Rhiannon could have been any of them or all of them.
> PAUL BENNETT *False Profits* 1998

Gulag Archipelago The Gulag Archipelago is the name of the system of forced-labour camps in the Soviet Union, specifically in the period 1930–55, in which hundreds of thousands, perhaps millions, died. The term can now be used in a more general sense.

> Much has been made by commentators about Delia's celebrated dullness. We are told repeatedly that she was once exiled to the TV equivalent of the Gulag Archipelago because she wasn't 'sexy enough'. *The Guardian* 1995

Gulliver Lemuel Gulliver is the hero of Jonathan Swift's satire *Gulliver's Travels* (1726). In the first part of the book, Gulliver is shipwrecked on the island of Lilliput, a land inhabited by tiny people only 6 inches tall. The Lilliputians, Gulliver soon discovers, are as small-minded as they are small-bodied, being petty, pretentious, and factious. In his next adventure, Gulliver visits Brobdingnag, a land inhabited by giants who are as tall as steeples. This time it is Gulliver himself who is perceived to be a moral pygmy. Gulliver can thus be alluded to either as a giant dwarfing those around him, or as a small person among giants. In one famous episode, Gulliver wakes on the shore of Lilliput and finds himself unable to move: 'I found my arms and legs were strongly fastened on each side to the ground; and my hair, which was long and thick, tied down in the same manner. I likewise felt several slender ligatures across my body, from my armpits to my thighs.' This image is used to evoke the idea of being restricted, especially by petty constraints.

In the course of the book Gulliver visits many other strange lands, and encounters a range of strange people and creatures, many of whose names have also come into the language as allusions. *See also* BIG-ENDIANS AND LITTLE-ENDIANS, BLEFUSCUDIAN NAVY, BROBDINGNAGIAN, HOUYHNHNM, LILLIPUTIAN, STRULDBRUG, YAHOO.

> Hypotheses pinned me down, as Gulliver was pinned by the countless threads of the Lilliputians.
> JOHN FOWLES *The Magus* 1966

> He found it ridiculously easy; the slight Javanese bodies he was dealing with were dwarfed by his own. A clumsy, foolish Gulliver, he looked around for fresh attackers.
> CHRISTOPHER J. KOCH *The Year of Living Dangerously* 1978

> Having stabbed one leader in the back, he felt he could not do it again. Besides, he owed Margaret Thatcher no loyalty—and he feels genuine loyalty to Major. Bound by Lilliputian cords, the great Gulliver could do nothing but hope. *The Observer* 1995

> The smaller university presses such as Edinburgh and Manchester are but Lilliputians to Oxford's Gulliver. *Daily Telegraph* 1995

Worzel Gummidge Worzel Gummidge is the talking scarecrow with straw hair who is the central character of a series of children's books by Barbara Euphan Todd, later televised. His name may be applied to anyone with a scarecrow-like appearance.

> She wished she looked less like Worzel Gummidge with protruding unbendable arms and legs.
> A. S. BYATT *The Virgin in the Garden* 1978

Gunga Din Rudyard Kipling's poem 'Gunga Din' (1892) tells of an Indian water-carrier who is killed bringing water to a wounded English soldier in the battlefield. The poem ends with the famous lines:
'Tho' I've belted you an' flayed you,
By the livin' Gawd that made you,
You're a better man than I am, Gunga Din!'
See also KIPLING.

Ben Gunn Ben Gunn is the marooned pirate in Robert Louis Stevenson's adventure story *Treasure Island* (1883). Abandoned on the island by his shipmates, he has spent three years alone, living on 'goats and berries and oysters', and dreaming of toasted cheese. *See also* LONG JOHN SILVER.

> 'Well, here I am, marooned,' Kay said to himself; keeping well under cover lest they should send another cannon ball. 'Now I am like poor Ben Gunn in *Treasure Island*: unless I am able to run down the goats, if there are any, I am not likely to get much dinner.'
> JOHN MASEFIELD *The Box of Delights* 1935

Gunpowder Plot *See* GUY FAWKES.

Gurth In the opening chapter of Walter Scott's novel *Ivanhoe* (1819), the swineherd Gurth is described wearing a brass collar welded round his neck and engraved with the words 'Gurth, the son of Beowulph, is the born thrall of Cedric of Rotherwood'. *See also* WALTER SCOTT.

> Between them [the bull's nostrils], through the gristle of his nose, was a stout copper ring, welded on, and irremovable as Gurth's collar of brass.
> THOMAS HARDY *The Mayor of Casterbridge* 1886

Gyges Gyges (*c*.685–*c*.657 BC) was a Lydian shepherd who, according to the story told by Plato, descended into a chasm, where he found a horse made of brass. He opened its side and found inside it the body of a man of great size. Gyges removed from the man's finger a brazen ring which, when he wore it, made him invisible. He subsequently used this ring to make himself known to the queen, marry her, and usurp the crown of Lydia's king Candaules.

> What is the practical meaning of this silvery appearance which is generally absent in fishes that live in very deep and dark waters? The probable answer has been suggested several times—that the silveriness gives its possessors a Gyges' ring, a power of becoming invisible.
> J. ARTHUR THOMSON *Biology for Everyman* 1934

Hades In Greek mythology, Hades, also known as Pluto, was the brother of Zeus and Poseidon and the lord of the underworld, the land of the dead. Those who died were said to have gone to the house of Hades. The name Hades later came to refer to the place itself, a place of perpetual darkness and gloom. Hades contained the Plain of Asphodel, where the ghosts of the dead led a vague, unsubstantial life, a shadowy continuation of their former life where 'the soul hovers to and fro' (*Odyssey*). Those who had been virtuous went on to Elysium, a happy land of perpetual day. Those who had been enemies of the gods were taken to the punishment fields of Tartarus for eternal punishment, the most famous of these being Tantalus, Ixion, and Sisyphus. The land of the dead was separated from the land of the living by one of the rivers of Hades, the Styx or the Acheron. The dead were ferried across the river Styx by Charon. At the entrance to the underworld stood the watchdog Cerberus, who prevented any of the living from entering and any of the dead from leaving. Three other rivers intersected the underworld, Phlegethon (or Pyriphlegethon), Cocytus, and Lethe. The lord of the underworld was known as Hades or Pluto. His wife was Persephone, whom he captured and took down to live with him in the underworld. *See also* ACHERON, CERBERUS, CHARON, IXION, LETHE, PERSEPHONE, PHLEGETHON, PLUTO, SISYPHUS, STYX, TANTALUS, TARTARUS.

> He stood motionless, undecided, glaring with his eyes, thinking of the pains and penalties of Hades.
> ANTHONY TROLLOPE *Barchester Towers* 1857

> On we went for many minutes in absolute awed silence, like lost souls in the depths of Hades.
> H. RIDER HAGGARD *She* 1887

Hagar In the Bible, Hagar was the Egyptian maid of Abraham's wife, Sarah. Hagar bore Abraham a son, Ishmael (Gen. 16: 21). She and Ishmael were driven away as outcasts after Sarah gave birth to Isaac.

> Beside the milk-bush sat the Kaffir woman still—like Hagar, he thought, thrust out by her mistress in the wilderness to die.
> OLIVE SCHREINER *The Story of an African Farm* 1883

Rider Haggard Henry Rider Haggard (1856–1925) was an English writer of thrilling adventure novels. Many of his novels are set in Africa, drawing on the time he spent in South Africa in the 1870s. His best-known novels are *King Solomon's Mines* (1885) and *She* (1889). *See also* SHE.

There is something of the contemporary 'boys book'—or say of the spirit of Rider Haggard.
HENRY JAMES *America Writers* 1865–1912

'You're looking for adventure,' I cried; 'Well, you've found it here. The devils are after me, and the police are after them. It's a race that I mean to win.' 'By God,' he whispered, drawing his breath in sharply, 'it is all pure Rider Haggard and Conan Doyle.'
JOHN BUCHAN *The Thirty-Nine Steps* 1915

Ham In the Bible, Ham was one of Noah's sons. According to the book of Genesis, he disrespectfully mocked his father when he saw him drunk and naked. In return Noah cursed Ham's son Canaan, prophesying that he would be 'the lowest of slaves'. This episode was sometimes used in the 19th century as a biblical justification of African slavery, black people being referred to as 'children of Ham' or 'sons of Ham'. *See also* NOAH.

. . . he turned his nose full upon a small Kaffir of two years old. That small, naked son of Ham became instantly so terrified that he fled to his mother's blanket for protection . . .
OLIVE SHREINER *The Story of an African Farm* 1883

He has the heart of a poet and a king, and it is God's curse that he has been born among the children of Ham.
JOHN BUCHAN *Prester John* 1910

Hamadryad Hamadryads were nymphs in Greek and Roman mythology, beautiful maidens who lived in trees and died when the tree died.

'I shall be sitting for my second portrait then,' she said, smiling. 'Will it be larger than the other?' 'Oh, yes, much larger. It is an oil-painting. You will look like a tall Hamadryad, dark and strong and noble, just issued from one of the fir-trees, when the stems are casting their afternoon shadows on the grass.'
GEORGE ELIOT *The Mill on the Floss* 1860

Perhaps, too, she had at last recognized herself in the Hamadryad of the popular sapling; the slim Hamadryad whose movements were like the swaying of a young tree in the wind. 'The Woman who was a Tree' was what he had called the poem.
ALDOUS HUXLEY *Crome Yellow* 1921

Hamlet Hamlet, a legendary prince of Denmark, is the hero of Shakespeare's play of the same name (1604). Hamlet is a tormented character, devastated by the death of his father and remarriage of his mother, and uncertain as to what action to take. He is obsessively introspective and delivers long soliloquies expressing his mental anguish, most famously his contemplation of suicide in the speech beginning 'To be, or not to be: that is the question.' Hamlet can be alluded to as someone who talks at length, expressing anxieties, doubts, or unhappiness. *See also* SHAKESPEARE.

> To what extent was he, Gloster Ridley, justified in imposing his taste upon the newspaper's subscribers? Still, was it not for doing so that he drew his excellent salary and his annual bonus, reckoned upon the profits? What about the barber's chair; might there not be a few buttocks for Shillito? But he could go on in this Hamlet-like strain all day.
> ROBERTSON DAVIES *Leaven of Malice* 1954

> I said I wanted to be best man, I said I wanted a church wedding. I went on about it. I started shouting. I came the Hamlets a bit. I was drunk at the time, if you must know.
> JULIAN BARNES *Talking It Over* 1991

h

Hanging Gardens of Babylon The Hanging Gardens of Babylon, one of the Seven Wonders of the World, were said to have been built by Nebuchadnezzar (*c.*600 BC) for his wife, Amytis, who longed to be reminded of the mountains and greenery of her native Media. Built in a series of terraces, the gardens were irrigated by a hydraulic system, using water from the Euphrates. *See also* BABYLON.

> The room was arranged to provide a setting that would awe most visitors. Its high windows, draped in gold swags and festoons, opened onto a terrace so thickly planted with shrubs and flowers that it looked like a descendant of one of the Hanging Gardens.
> ELIZABETH PETERS *Street of the Five Moons* 1978

Hannibal Hannibal (247–182 BC) was the Carthaginian general who precipitated the second Punic War by attacking the town of Saguntum in Spain, an ally of Rome. He crossed the Alps in 218 with an army of about 30 000 and 40 elephants. In Italy Hannibal inflicted a series of defeats on the Romans over a period of sixteen years but failed to take Rome itself. After being recalled to Africa to defend Carthage he was defeated at Zama by Scipio Africanus in 202. Hannibal has subsequently enjoyed a reputation as one of history's great military geniuses.

> He is not the Caesar, but the Hannibal of French politics. *Century Magazine* 1883

Hansel and Gretel Hansel and Gretel are a brother and sister who appear in a traditional fairy story first published by the Brothers Grimm. Abandoned in a forest by their parents, the terrified children come across a house made of bread, cakes, and sweets. The house in fact belongs to a witch, who imprisons the children and plans to eat them. Hansel and Gretel succeed in killing the witch by pushing her into her own oven, and escape back to their parents, taking with them jewels they have found in the witch's house. *See also* GRIMM.

Entering the tunnel's blackness, leaving behind the brightly lit world of sleepy readers, a tiny rush of adrenaline, like MSG after a Chinese dinner, coursed through my blood-stream. Part of it was pure reversion to childhood's fears. Hansel and Gretel. Snow White. Lost in dark woods, with enemies all around.
CAROLYN WHEAT *Ghost Station* 1991

Happy Hooligan The Happy Hooligan was an American comic-strip character who appeared from 1900 to 1932, an Irish tramp with a red nose and a tin can for a hat. He was an innocent and an unconquerable optimist despite the fact that his attempts to help himself and others often ended with his falling into the hands of the law.

Never tol' you 'bout him. Looked like Happy Hooligan. Harmless kinda fella. Always was gonna make a break. Fellas all called him Hooligan.
JOHN STEINBECK *The Grapes of Wrath* 1939

Happy Islands The Happy Islands, better known as the Islands of the Blest, were the place to which people in classical times believed the souls of heroes and the good were conveyed to a life of bliss. They were also known as the Fortunate Isles. The term Happy Islands can be applied to heaven or paradise.

Andy Hardy The Hardy family appeared in a series of Hollywood films between 1937 and 1947. They were portrayed as a typical all-American family who embodied homely small-town values. In 1942 the films were accorded a special Academy Award 'for representing the American Way of Life'. The clean-living teenager Andy Hardy was played by Mickey Rooney.

It is difficult now to say why the book was so 'sensational', but we can make a guess: the town—Peyton Place, that is—is exactly like the Carvel of the Andy Hardy picture, a prim and proper little apple-pie town whose major occasions are the senior prom, graduation and the Labor Day picnic. *The Independent* 1992

Harpagan In Molière's comedy *L'Avare* (The Miser), Harpagon is a miser who, when forced to choose between the casket containing his treasure and the woman he loves, chooses the treasure.

In old-fashioned times, an 'independence' was hardly ever made without a little miserliness as a condition, and you would have found that quality in every provincial district, combined with characters as various as the fruits from which we can extract acid. The true Harpagons were always marked and exceptional characters.
GEORGE ELIOT *The Mill on the Floss* 1860

harpy In Greek and Roman mythology, harpies (originally from the Greek *harpuiae*, meaning 'snatchers') were fierce monsters with the heads and bodies of women and wings and claws of vultures. The word 'harpy' has now become part of the language, meaning a cruel or grasping, unscrupulous woman.

And all the time, as we were pitching it in red hot, we were keeping the women off him as best we could, for they were as wild as harpies.
ROBERT LOUIS STEVENSON *The Strange Case of Dr Jekyll and Mr Hyde* 1886

Harvey Harvey is a six-foot-tall rabbit created by Mary C. Chase in her 1944 comic play *Harvey* and popularized in a 1950 film of the same name. Harvey is invisible to everyone except the drunken Elwood P. Dowd.

Kaspar Hauser Kaspar (or Caspar) Hauser (1812–33) was a German foundling who mysteriously appeared in Nuremberg in 1828, aged 16, dressed in peasant clothes, and behaving like an infant. He later claimed to have been reared in isolation, spending most of his life confined in a small underground cell. Speculation about his true origins included the theory that he was the rightful heir to the Grand Duchy of Baden.

To any stray inheritor of these primitive qualities found, like Caspar Hauser, wandering dazed in any Christian capital of our time, the good-natured poet's famous invocation, near two thousand years ago, of the good rustic out of his latitude in the Rome of the Caesars, still appropriately holds.
HERMAN MELVILLE *Billy Budd* 1924

Miss Havisham Miss Havisham is a character in Dickens's *Great Expectations* (1861) who was jilted by her bridegroom on her wedding day and spent years afterwards sitting in her room alone, wearing her wedding dress. *See also* DICKENSIAN.

She'd also suffered the tragic history of having been jilted by the same man on two different wedding days, a condition that prompted Dr. Lowji Daruwalla to privately refer to her as 'the Miss Havisham of Bombay—times two'.
JOHN IRVING *A Son of the Circus* 1994

I love Magda and Jeremy. Sometimes I stay at their house, admiring the crisp sheets and many storage jars full of different kinds of pasta, imagining that they are my parents. But when they are together with their married friends I feel as if I have turned into Miss Havisham.
HELEN FIELDING *Bridget Jones's Diary* 1996

Stephen Hawking Stephen Hawking (b. 1942) is an English theoretical physicist whose main work has been on quantum gravity and black holes. Confined to a wheelchair because of a progressive disabling neuromuscular disease, he performs his complex mathematical calculations mentally. He is the author of *A Brief History of Time* (1988).

On Tuesday Van Gaal issued a memo to English football: think more about the game (he has been saying that for years). English football took him up on it. In front of an ecstatic but still disbelieving crowd Newcastle out-played, out-fought and, most of all, out-thought their visitors, whose coach is supposed to be the game's Stephen Hawking, and who carry a spaniel-like sheen that speaks of endless grooming and refining. *The Guardian* 1997

Rita Hayworth Rita Hayworth (1918–87), born Margaret Carmen Cansino, was an American film actress, star of such films as *Gilda* (1946) and *The Lady from Shanghai* (1948). A cousin of Ginger Rogers, she was an accomplished dancer.

> Brenda, who'd been drinking champagne like her Uncle Leo, did a Rita Hayworth tango with herself.
> PHILIP ROTH *Goodbye, Columbus* 1959

Heathcliff Heathcliff is the passionate gipsy hero of Emily Brontë's romantic novel *Wuthering Heights* (1847). He has long dark hair and a rugged, wild attractiveness. *See also* BRONTËS.

> She had grown agreeably used to breakfast with Ken Cracknell, who looked this morning, with his dark hair and smouldering eyes, like a young Heathcliff of the legal aid system.
> JOHN MORTIMER *Rumpole's Return* 1980

> Dominic, as always, had positioned himself slightly back from the family group, his black suit and darkly brooding eyes giving him a touch of Heathcliff.
> LAUREN HENDERSON *The Black Rubber Dress* 1997

> He seemed much younger than her, had Heathcliff-type hair and wore jeans.
> *The Independent* 1997

Heath Robinson William Heath Robinson (1872–1944) was an English cartoonist who drew humorous cartoons of absurdly ingenious and complicated machines which performed simple everyday tasks. Like that of Rube Goldberg, his name has become synonymous with any device or system that seems unnecessarily complicated.

> You remember that kid's game, Mousetrap? That ludicrous Heath Robinson machine you had to build, where silver balls went down chutes, and little men went up ladders, and one thing knocked into another to set off something else, until in the end the cage fell on to the mouse and trapped it?
> NICK HORNBY *High Fidelity* 1995

Hebe In Greek mythology, Hebe, the daughter of Zeus and Hera, was the goddess of youth. She had the power of restoring the aged to youth and beauty. Hebe attended on Hera and was the cup-bearer of the gods, in which role she was later succeeded by Ganymede. Her Roman name was Juventus.

> Olivia, now about eighteen, had that luxuriancy of beauty with which painters generally draw Hebe; open, sprightly, and commanding.
> OLIVER GOLDSMITH *The Vicar of Wakefield* 1766

> Girlhood just ripening into womanhood . . . Upon my word—a very Hebe!'
> ANNE BRONTË *The Tenant of Wildfell Hall* 1848

> I went to look at the pretty butter-maker, Hetty Sorrel. She's a perfect Hebe; and if I were an artist, I would paint her. It's amazing what pretty girls one sees

among the farmer's daughters, when the men are such clowns.
GEORGE ELIOT *Adam Bede* 1859

Hecate In some Greek myths, Hecate was one of the forms of the triple-formed goddess Artemis: Selene in the sky, Artemis on the earth, and Hecate in the underworld. Later Hecate was regarded as the goddess of dark places, often associated with ghosts and sorcery and worshipped with offerings at crossroads. In statues Hecate was often represented in triple form, with three heads or three bodies standing back to back. She appears with the three witches in Shakespeare's *Macbeth*. *See also* ARTEMIS.

> I have a great abomination of this learned friend; as author, lawyer, and politician, he is triformis, like Hecate.
> THOMAS LOVE PEACOCK *Crotchet Castle* 1831

Hector In Greek mythology, Hector, eldest son of Priam and Hecuba, was the leading Trojan hero in the Trojan War. He was killed in single combat by Achilles, in revenge for the death of Patroclus. Achilles then dragged his body behind the wheels of his chariot three times round the walls of Troy. Homer's *Iliad* ends with the funeral of Hector.

> So it has been since the days of Hecuba, and of Hector, tamer of horses: inside the gates, the women with streaming hair and uplifted hands offering prayers, watching the world's combat from afar, filling their long, empty days with memories and fears: outside, the men, in fierce struggle with things divine and human, quenching memory in the stronger light of purpose, losing the sense of dread and even of wounds in the hurrying ardour of action.
> GEORGE ELIOT *The Mill on the Floss* 1860

> He sped like Hector flying the noblest of the Greeks.
> SOMERSET MAUGHAM *Cakes and Ale* 1930

> Mind you, Olivier and St. Clare were both heroes—the old thing, and no mistake; it was like the fight between Hector and Achilles.
> G. K. CHESTERTON *Father Brown Stories* 1931

Hecuba Hecuba was the wife of King Priam of Troy and mother of numerous children, including Hector, Paris, Cassandra, and Troilus. Homer's *Iliad* tells of her suffering and grief during the Trojan War as she witnesses the deaths of many of her sons at the hands of the Greeks, in particular the slaying of her eldest son, Hector, by Achilles and the desecration of his body. Her name has come to represent terrible grief, especially as the result of the death of one's children. *See also* TROJAN WAR.

Uriah Heep Uriah Heep is the shrewd, deceitful clerk of the lawyer Mr Wickfield in Dickens's *David Copperfield* (1850). Feigning humility, he describes himself as 'so very 'umble', while repeatedly wringing his hands. He insinuates his way into Mr Wickfield's confidence and becomes one of his partners. Heep uses this position to defraud people of money, until he is exposed, sent to prison, and condemned to transportation for life. His name is a byword for obsequiousness and false humility, and his often repeated gesture of rubbing his hands together as he speaks is sometimes alluded to in this context. *See also* DICKENSIAN.

> He began to wonder if there wasn't something of a Uriah Heep beginning to erupt on the surface of Sam's personality; a certain duplicity.
> JOHN FOWLES *The French Lieutenant's Woman* 1969

> Under Asbery's urbane expression you could imagine a secret grimace of pleasure at Margot's confusion, at my shock. Uriah Heep's servility had disguised a lot of hate.
> MAX BYRD *Finders Weepers* 1983

> He has these annoying mannerisms—he wrings his hands, just like Uriah Heep!
> KATE CHARLES *A Dead Man Out of Mind* 1994

Hugh Hefner Hugh Hefner (b. 1926) founded *Playboy*, an erotic magazine for men, in 1953 and later set up the Playboy chain of nightclubs, whose 'bunny girl' hostesses wore skimpy costumes which incorporated a rabbit's ears and tail. Hefner's name is associated with sexual permissiveness and a hedonistic lifestyle.

> Young people are put off because they think it is a hotel for the older generation . . . and the family crowd is frightened away because the fellow to whom my father sold out . . . was nothing but a 'two-bit Hugh Hefner' who tried to build a clientele out of 'riffraff, and worse.'
> PHILIP ROTH *Chez Claire* 1977

Heidi Johanna Spyri's novel *Heidi* (1881) tells the story of an orphaned Swiss girl who from the age of 5 is brought up in idyllic alpine surroundings. When she is 8, Heidi is taken to a more prosperous city life in Frankfurt but she pines until returned to the mountains. References to Heidi are usually in the context of Swiss girls and alpine scenery.

> Sherman stared at the plaited vines. They looked like something dropped by Gretel or little Heidi of Switzerland at a feast of Lucullus.
> TOM WOLFE *The Bonfire of the Vanities* 1987

> In a tight Tyrolean tunic and skirt, embroidered with forget-me-nots, she looked a bit like Heidi.
> CHRISTOPHER HOPE *Darkest England* 1996

Helen In Greek mythology, Helen was the daughter of Zeus and Leda who grew into the most beautiful woman in the world. She married Menelaus, and her abduction by the Trojan prince Paris led to the Trojan War.
   Doctor Faustus, in Marlowe's play of that title (1604), calls up the spirit of Helen of Troy and addresses her with these well-known lines:
'Was this the face that launch'd a thousand ships
And burnt the topless towers of Ilium?'

See also TROJAN WAR.

> I, whose loveliness is more than the loveliness of that Grecian Helen, of whom they used to sing, and whose wisdom is wider, ay, far more wide and deep than the wisdom of Solomon the Wise.
> H. RIDER HAGGARD *She* 1887

> Who's love is given over-well
> Shall look on Helen's face in hell,
> Whilst they whose love is thin and wise
> May view John Knox in paradise.
> DOROTHY PARKER 'Partial Comfort' in *Sunset Gun* 1928

Helicon In Greek mythology, Helicon was the largest mountain of Boeotia and was associated with the Muses. The spring of Aganippe and fountain of Hippocrene, believed to give inspiration to those who drank of their waters, were on its slopes. *See also* MUSES.

Helios Helios was the Greek sun god, represented as a charioteer who each day drove the chariot of the sun pulled by four white horses across the sky from east to west. Helios was later supplanted by Apollo.

Hell According to Christian, Jewish, and Islamic tradition, Hell is the place of punishment where the souls of the damned are condemned after death. It is described in the Bible as 'everlasting fire, prepared for the devil and his angels' (Matt. 26: 41) and 'a lake of fire, burning with brimstone' (Rev. 19: 20).

Héloïse *See* ABELARD AND HÉLOÏSE.

Ernest Hemingway Ernest Hemingway (1899–1961) was a US novelist, short-story writer, and journalist, whose works include *For Whom the Bell Tolls* (1940) and *The Old Man and the Sea* (1952). He had a reputation for machismo and for celebrating such tough masculine pursuits as big-game hunting, bull-fighting, and deep-sea fishing.

> Cameron is what used to be quaintly called a man's man. For pleasure, he likes to race cars and shoot guns in the desert. But nothing, he'll tell you, is as 'hard, as physically demanding' as making films. Play sceptical and suggest, for mischief, that messing with images is hardly a proper manly pursuit and he'll turn into Hemingway with a lens. *The Observer* 1998

Patrick Henry Patrick Henry (1736–99) was an American political leader and patriot. A few weeks before the beginning of the War of American Independence he made a famous speech urging the American colonies to revolt against English rule. The speech contained the famous words 'I know not what course others may take, but as for me, give me liberty or give me death!'

> She was very angry. Give her nails, she'd chew them up and spit tacks. 'I have a

hard time respecting my parents. I have nothing but contempt for th—
were. I won't do that.' Her voice rang out. Echoes, shades of Patrick He.
Admirable, no question.
KAREN KIJEWSKI *Wild Kat* 1994

Hephaestus *See* VULCAN.

Hera In Greek mythology, Hera was the wife and sister of Zeus. She was worshipped as the queen of heaven and as a marriage goddess, associated with fertility and childbirth. In many stories she is depicted as jealously enraged by the philanderings of her husband, Zeus. Her Roman equivalent is Juno. *See also* JUNO.

Heraclitus Heraclitus (*c.*500 BC) was an early Greek philosopher who maintained that all things in the universe are in a state of constant change and that the mind derives a false idea of permanence of the external world from the passing impressions of experience. His gloomy view of the fleeting character of life led to him being called 'the weeping philosopher'.

> He laments, like Heraclitus the Maudlin Philosopher, at other Men's Mirth.
> SAMUEL BUTLER *Remains* 1759

Hercules In Greek and Roman mythology, Hercules (called Heracles by the Greeks) was a hero of superhuman strength and courage, usually depicted with a lion-skin, club, and bow. He was the son of Zeus by Alcmene, wife of Amphitryon. He performed twelve immense tasks, or 'labours', imposed on him by Eurystheus, king of Argos. The labours were as follows:

1. The killing of the lion of Nemea, which Hercules strangled with his bare hands, and whose skin he cut off with its own claws and afterwards wore.
2. The killing of the Lernaean Hydra, a water-serpent with many heads, each of which when cut off gave place to two new ones. With the help of his companion Iolaus, Hercules seared each neck with a burning torch as he cut off the head.
3. The capture of an incredibly swift stag, the Cerynean Hind, sacred to Artemis. Hercules had to capture it unharmed, which he did by pursuing it for a year and finally ensnaring it.
4. The capture of a destructive wild boar that lived on Mount Erymanthus. Hercules drove the boar from its lair, then chased it through the snow until it became exhausted.
5. The cleansing of the stables of Augeas, which had never been cleaned out. Hercules accomplished the task by diverting the two rivers Alpheus and Peneus so that they flowed through the stables and washed away the piles of dung.
6. The killing of the carnivorous birds near Lake Stymphalus. He drove them out of the trees by clashing bronze castanets and then shot them down with his bow.
7. The capture of the Cretan wild bull, which Hercules succeeded in bringing back alive to Eurystheus.

8. The capture of the mares of Diomedes, which fed on human flesh. In so doing Hecules fed Diomedes to his own mares.
9. The obtaining of the girdle of Hippolyta, the queen of the Amazons.
10. The capture of the oxen of the three-bodied monster Geryon.
11. The obtaining of the golden apples from the garden of the nymphs of the Hesperides. Hercules achieved this with the help of Atlas, the giant who bore the world on his shoulders.
12. The removal from Hades of the three-headed dog, Cerberus, which guarded the entrance to the underworld.

After his death he was granted immortality among the gods. Any exceptionally strong or muscular man can be described as a Hercules, or by the adjective 'Herculean'. A Herculean task is one that is formidably difficult. *See also* AUGEAN STABLES, CERBERUS, DEIANIRA, HYDRA, NESSUS, PILLARS OF HERCULES.

A man entered who could hardly have been less than six feet in height, with the chest and limbs of a Hercules.
ARTHUR CONAN DOYLE *A Scandal in Bohemia* 1892

He had already been at work on it for more than seven years and as yet, he would say to anyone who asked him about the progress of the book . . . 'It's a labour of Hercules.'
ALDOUS HUXLEY *Point Counter Point* 1928

He was strong and sturdy and this appealed to me, for one of my ambitions was to become a kind of Hercules.
L. P HARTLEY *The Go-Between* 1953

These cases, and thousands more in scores of other countries, are detailed in *Index on Censorship*, the bimonthly magazine which has just celebrated (though that hardly seems an appropriate word) its 25th anniversary. The magazine has a Lilliputian circulation and a Herculean task: winning for the people of the world one of the most basic of human rights, the freedom of expression. *The Guardian* 1997

Hermes In Greek mythology, Hermes was the messenger of the gods, identified with the Roman god Mercury. *See also* MERCURY.

Herne the Hunter In English legend, Herne the Hunter was a ghostly hunter with stag's antlers who haunted Windsor Forest. Herne was said to have been in medieval times a keeper in the forest who hanged himself from a tree known as Herne's (or later Falstaff's) oak. According to Shakespeare's *Merry Wives of Windsor* (IV, iv), he
'doth all the winter-time, at still midnight,
Walk round about an oak, with great ragg'd horns;
And there he blasts the tree, and takes the cattle,
And makes milch-kine yield blood, and shakes the chain
In a most hideous and dreadful manner.'

He anxiously descended the ladder, and started homewards at a run, trying not

to think of giants, Herne the Hunter, Apollyon lying in wait for Christian.
THOMAS HARDY *Jude the Obscure* 1895

Hero and Leander In the ancient Greek legend or folk tale, Hero lived on
one side of the Hellespont (now named the Dardanelles) and her lover,
Leander, lived on the other. Every night he would swim across to her, guided
by a torch that she held for him. One night there was a storm, the torch went
out, and Leander drowned. His body was washed up on the shore the next
morning and Hero threw herself into the sea. The story was told in a poem
by Musaeus (AD 5–6), and provides the subject matter for poems by Marlowe
and Hood. They can be alluded to in a similar way to Romeo and Juliet, as
tragic lovers.

Herod Herod the Great (*c.*74–4 BC) was the Roman king of Judaea who,
according to Matthew's Gospel, ordered the Massacre of the Innocents,
hoping that by killing all male children under two he would ensure the
death of the infant Jesus. Allusions to Herod are often in the context of the
killing of children on a large scale.

> 'I think of the A4,' sez he, 'as a baby Jesus, with endless committees of Herods
> out to destroy it in its infancy.'
> THOMAS PYNCHON *Gravity's Rainbow* 1973

> The infant Udin is dead. I mourn him as though he had been my own. I say
> Sukarno killed him, as surely as though he were a Herod.
> CHRISTOPHER J. KOCH *The Year of Living Dangerously* 1978

> All babies start off looking like the last tomato in the fridge, but 'cute',
> 'gorgeous' and 'adorable', which were the adjectives Lucy was throwing about
> the place with gay abandon, struck me as the ravings of an insane and blind
> woman. Quite frankly, I began to see King Herod in a wholly different light.
> BEN ELTON *Inconceivable* 1999

Herod and Salome Salome was the daughter of Herodias, wife of King
Herod Antipas. She danced for her stepfather, the king, 'whereupon he
promised with an oath to give her whatsoever she would ask'. Salome was
instructed by her mother to demand the head of John the Baptist, as a
punishment for John's condemning her marriage. 'And the king was sorry:
nevertheless for the oath's sake, and them which sat with him at meat, he
commanded it to be given her' (Matt. 14: 6–9).

> I remembered that he considered all this to be pleasure, as Herod thought
> Salome's dance was fun until he heard what she wanted as a reward.
> EDMUND WHITE *A Boy's Own Story* 1982

James Herriot James Herriot, the pseudonym of James Alfred Wight
(1916–95), used his experiences working as a veterinary surgeon in north
Yorkshire as the source for a series of short stories, collected in *If Only They
Could Talk* (1970), *All Creatures Great and Small* (1972), and *The Lord God Made*

Them All (1981). His amusing and extremely popular stories were made into a British television series as well as a number of films, and his name has come to represent an archetypal lover of animals.

Hesperus *See* WRECK OF THE HESPERUS.

Henry Higgins In George Bernard Shaw's play *Pygmalion* (1913), Henry Higgins, a professor of phonetics, embarks on a six-month experiment to teach the cockney flower girl Eliza Doolittle how to speak properly so that he can pass her off in polite society as a duchess. Professor Higgins has an irascible, bullying manner with his pupil. *See also* PYGMALION.

> 'Is there something wrong with cleverness?' Tess asked sharply, uncomfortable with Crow's attitude. He was supposed to be her Sancho, servile and worshipful, not a hectoring Henry Higgins.
> LAURA LIPPMAN *Baltimore Blues* 1997

High Noon *High Noon* is the title of a classic 1952 western starring Gary Cooper. He plays a small-town marshal who, deserted by the rest of the townspeople, has to confront alone a gang of four outlaws who are due to arrive in town on the noon train. The phrase 'high noon' is often invoked when someone is facing a potentially fatal confrontation.

> We don't want to go to High Noon over this. *The World at One, BBC Radio 4* 1998

Hinnom The Valley of Hinnom to the south of Jerusalem was known as the Valley of Slaughter (Jer. 7: 31–2). According to the Bible, it was used for idolatrous worship, with children being burnt alive as sacrifices to the idol Moloch, and there is a strong association between the name and the fires of Hell.

> The lightning had struck the tree. A sulphurous smell filled the air; then all was silent, and black as a cave in Hinnom.
> THOMAS HARDY *Far from the Madding Crowd* 1874

Hippocrates Hippocrates (*c.*460–377 BC) is probably the most famous of all physicians, but in fact almost nothing is known about him. His name was attached to a body of ancient Greek medical writings which contained diverse opinions on the nature of illness and treatment. The Hippocratic oath, named after him, is an oath stating the duties of physicians, formerly taken by those taking up medical practice.

> The renowned British Hippocrates of the Pestle and Mortar.
> RICHARD STEELE *The Spectator* 1711

Hippocrene In Greek mythology, Hippocrene was a fountain sacred to the Muses on Mount Helicon, created for them by the winged horse Pegasus, who stamped his moon-shaped hoof. It was believed to give the power of poetic inspiration to those who drank of it. It is alluded to in John Keats's poem 'Ode to a Nightingale'. In the Huxley quotation below, the writer quotes directly from Keats. *See also* MUSES.

> O for a beaker full of the warm South,
> Full of the true, the blushful Hippocrene.
> JOHN KEATS *Ode to a Nightingale* 1820

> 'Warbling your native woodnotes wild!' said Willie. 'May I help myself to some of that noble brandy? The blushful Hippocrene.'
> ALDOUS HUXLEY *Point Counter Point* 1928

Hippolyta In Greek mythology, Hippolyta, also known as Antiope, was the queen of the Amazons, a race of fierce fighting women warriors. Her name can invoke a strong or fierce woman.

> No one . . . could any longer doubt the speaker to be the British Hippolyta of her epoch, and so the earliest progenitress of Parliament's petticoated invaders.
> *Chambers Journal* 1909

Hiroshima Hiroshima is a city and port on the south coast of the island of Honshu, western Japan. It was the first city to be the target of an atomic bomb, dropped by the United States on 6 August 1945, which resulted in the deaths of more than a third of the city's population of 300 000. Its name can suggest destruction on a huge scale.

> There was every likelihood that they would freeze on Friday, or fry, or vanish in pure energy with nothing left of them but shadows like the men of Hiroshima after the lightburst.
> A. S. BYATT *The Virgin in the Garden* 1978

Alfred Hitchcock Alfred Hitchcock (1899–1980) was an English film director chiefly associated with suspenseful thrillers such as *Psycho* (1960) and *The Birds* (1963), in which huge flocks of birds turn on people and attack them. *See also* PSYCHO.

> As I bend over to resume my pyrotechnics there is a whirring sound, as if in response to the peacock's shriek, and when I look up I see a great multicoloured cloud descending. It's the birds, even more of them than I have seen before, covering the sky . . . I hunch down to protect myself. This is pure Hitchcock.
> ANDRÉ BRINK *Imaginings of Sand* 1996

Hitler Adolf Hitler (1889–1945) was the Austrian-born founder of the National Socialist German Workers' Party (Nazi Party) and Chancellor of the Third Reich in 1933–45. Following his appointment as Chancellor of Germany in 1933, he established a totalitarian regime, the Third Reich, proclaiming himself Führer ('Leader'). His territorial aggression led to the Second World War, and his anti-semitic policies to the Holocaust. His name can be applied to anyone tyrannical or despotic, and his face, with the little black moustache, is a familiar image in 20th-century iconography. *See also* HOLOCAUST, MUSSOLINI.

> Dr Carl Moss was a big burly Jew with a Hitler moustache, pop eyes and the calmness of a glacier.
> RAYMOND CHANDLER *The High Window* 1943

> Little Hitlers, every one, Diamond thought. How does anything ever get decided these days? Maybe on the orders of a bigger Hitler, like me.
> PETER LOVESEY *The Summons* 1995

> And within a few weeks, Saddam—and yes, he *is* a venal, cruel, wicked, evil man—was being transformed into the Hitler of Iraq, just as the Israelis had called Yasser Arafat the Hitler of Beirut in 1982, and just as Eden had called Nasser the Mussolini of the Nile in 1956. *The Independent* 1998

Hobbit Hobbits are an imaginary race similar to humans, of small size and with hairy feet, in the stories of J. R. R. Tolkien. They live in burrows and their name was said by Tolkien to mean 'hole-dweller'. *See also* BILBO BAGGINS, FRODO.

> Valerie Jane lived in a Hansel and Gretel storybook cottage on Crescent Heights, complete with a mock thatched roof and a Hobbit-sized red door that she no doubt needed to duck to enter.
> LINDSAY MARACOTTA *Playing Dead* 1999

Jimmy Hoffa Jimmy Hoffa (1913–*c.*1975) was a US labour leader, president of the Teamsters' Union (transport workers) from 1957. He disappeared mysteriously in 1975 and is believed to have been murdered.

> Finding first-rate outfield arms today is like searching river bottoms for Jimmy Hoffa. *Show* 1990

Hogarth William Hogarth (1697–1764) was an English painter, engraver, and satirist. His series of engravings on 'modern moral subjects', such as *A Rake's Progress* (1735) and *Marriage à la Mode* (1743–5), satirized the vices of both high and low life in 18th-century England. *Gin Lane* (1751), depicting a scene of drunkenness and squalor, is one of Hogarth's most famous prints. *See also* GIN LANE.

> That evening Lord Marchmain was in good spirits; the room had a Hogarthian aspect, with the dinner-table set for the four of us by the grotesque, *chinoiserie* chimney-piece, and the old man propped among his pillows sipping champagne, tasting, praising, and failing to eat, the succession of dishes which had been prepared for his homecoming.
> EVELYN WAUGH *Brideshead Revisited* 1945

> In his intrepid trip down the stairs he encountered every sort of vice: fornication, crack smoking, heroin injection, dice games and three-card monte,

and more fornication . . . 'It's bloody Hogarth,' said Steiner. 'Gin Lane. Except that it's vertical.'
TOM WOLFE *The Bonfire of the Vanities* 1987

Sherlock Holmes Sherlock Holmes is an extremely perceptive private detective in a series of stories by Arthur Conan Doyle. Holmes's exceptional powers of observation and deductive reasoning enable him to solve the seemingly impenetrable mysteries that are brought to him by troubled clients. Probably the most famous fictional detective of all, Holmes plays the violin, smokes a pipe, has an opium habit, and wears a deerstalker. He is a master of disguise. Holmes is assisted by his stalwart associate Dr Watson, with whom he shares rooms at 221B Baker Street, London. His arch-enemy is the criminal mastermind Professor Moriarty.

They were curious. Something was fishy. They tried some amateur Sherlocking by asking the same questions twice, expecting us to make a slip.
JACK KEROUAC *On the Road* 1957

At once I took up my pipe, violin and deerstalker like a veritable Sherlock. I have always been an X-marks-the-spot man. 'Let us go and revisit it,' I said briskly.
LAWRENCE DURRELL *Clea* 1960

This is the 'inorganic mineral' theory of the Glasgow chemist Graham Cairns-Smith, first proposed 20 years ago and since developed and elaborated in three books, the latest of which, *Seven Clues to the Origin of Life*, treats the origin of life as a mystery needing a Sherlock Holmes solution.
RICHARD DAWKINS *The Blind Watchmaker* 1986

You were all right as a jockey. You should give up this pretence of being Sherlock Holmes.
DICK FRANCIS *Come to Grief* 1995

Holocaust The Holocaust is the name given to the mass murder of Jews and other persecuted groups under the German Nazi regime. In the period 1941–5 more than 6 million European Jews were killed in concentration camps such as Auschwitz, Dachau, and Treblinka as part of Adolf Eichmann's 'final solution', the Nazi policy of exterminating Jews.

Baroness Thatcher stepped up the political pressure for a military crackdown on the Serbs last night—with a call for air strikes, a suggestion that Western inaction had 'given comfort' to the aggressor and a warning of a 'second Holocaust'. *The Independent* 1992

Holofernes In the Apocrypha, Holofernes was the Assyrian general of Nebuchadnezzar's forces, who was beheaded by Judith. *See also* JUDITH.

As I passed, Herr Stroh shuffled out to his front door, rather drunk. He did not see me. He was looking at the clock where it hung in the sunset, he looked up at it as did the quaking enemies of the Lord upon the head of Holofernes.
MURIEL SPARK *The Collected Stories* 1958

Holy Grail The Holy Grail was an object of quest in medieval legend. It was supposed to be the dish or cup used by Christ at the Last Supper and in which Joseph of Arimathea had caught some of the blood of the crucified Christ. By the early 13th century it was closely associated with the Arthurian cycle of legends as a symbol of perfection sought by the knights of the Round Table. The term 'Holy Grail' is often applied to the object of a long and difficult quest. *See also* KING ARTHUR.

> How many months he will be away we don't know yet, but he is setting out with all the air of a knight in search of the holy Grail.
> LAWRENCE DURRELL *Mountolive* 1958

> I've won the America's Cup. It's considered the Holy Grail of yachting.
> STUDS TERKEL *American Dreams: Lost and Found* 1980

> There was a widening picture of me looking young and in racing colours: a piece of old film taken years ago of me weighing-in after winning the Grand National. I was holding my saddle in two hands and my eyes were full of the mystical wonder of having been presented with the equivalent of the Holy Grail.
> DICK FRANCIS *Come to Grief* 1995

Holy of Holies The Holy of Holies was a sacred inner chamber in the temple in Jerusalem in which the Ark of the Covenant was kept before it was lost. It can be used to refer to a place that is considered to be extremely important or sacred. *See also* ARK OF THE COVENANT.

> They never spoke of such things again, as it happened; but this one conversation made them peculiar people to each other; knit them together, in a way which no loose, indiscriminate talking about sacred things can ever accomplish. When all are admitted, how can there be a Holy of Holies?
> ELIZABETH GASKELL *North and South* 1854–5

> She discerned that Mrs Wilcox, though a loving wife and mother, had only one passion in life—her house—and that the moment was solemn when she invited a friend to share this passion with her. To answer 'another day' was to answer as a fool. 'Another day' will do for brick and mortar, but not for the Holy of Holies into which Howards End had been transfigured.
> E. M. FORSTER *Howards End* 1910

Homer Homer (8th c. BC) was a Greek epic poet to whom the *Odyssey* and the *Iliad* are traditionally attributed, though it is probable that these were based on much older stories which had been passed down orally. Homer is traditionally supposed to have been blind, sometimes referred to as the Blind Bard. The adjective 'Homeric' can be used to describe an epic journey or voyage, especially one that is hazardous. It is also used to denote actions and events that happen on a grand, superhuman scale or people who perform such actions.

> *Songdogs* by Colum McCann . . . Sublimely written Homeric story traces the

nomadic narrator's search across Mexico, the USA and Ireland for his missing mother. *Big Issue* 1995

The papers in South Africa eulogised them [the Springboks rugby team] in Homeric terms. *Daily Telegraph* 1995

The story of the yachtsman's rescue—with its primal Homeric resonances of shipwreck and mythic rebirth—delighted the world. *The Guardian* 1997

Hood *See* ROBIN HOOD.

Hooverville A Hooverville was a shanty town built by impoverished unemployed people in the United States during the Great Depression. The shanty towns were named after the president of the time, Herbert C. Hoover.

And now in my mind I stood upon the walk looking out across the hole past a Hooverville shanty of packing cases and bent tin signs, to a railroad yard that lay beyond.
RALPH ELLISON *Invisible Man* 1952

Hopper Edward Hopper (1882–1967) was an American realist painter. Works such as *Early Sunday Morning* (1930) and *Nighthawks* (1942) depict scenes from everyday American city life in which static figures appear in bleak settings such as motel rooms and diners, conveying an atmosphere of loneliness and isolation.

Childcott's balding head gleamed briefly as he turned his head to stare out of the window at the Edward-Hopper-type starkness of suburban London after the shops have closed.
SUSAN MOODY *Grand Slam* 1994

Horatius Horatius Cocles (530–500 BC) was a Roman hero who volunteered to be one of the last three defenders of a bridge over the river Tiber against an Etruscan army under Lars Porsena intent on invading Rome. Initially, he and two others, Herminius and Lartius, fought on the bank while the Roman army crossed back to Rome and prepared to destroy the bridge. His companions darted across to Rome just before the bridge fell, but Horatius swam back across the Tiber in full armour. The story of Horatius' defence of the bridge is retold in the poem 'Horatius at the Bridge' in *Lays of Ancient Rome* (1842) by Macaulay.

To the abuse in front and the coaxing behind she was equally indifferent. How long she would have stood like a glorified Horatius, keeping the staircase at both ends, was never to be known. For the young lady whose sleep they were disturbing awoke, and opened her bedroom door, and came out onto the landing.
E. M. FORSTER *Where Angels Fear to Tread* 1905

Perhaps I would have taken the easy way. I am only a man, but Carlo was like one of those heroes in our old stories, like Horatius Cocles, or whoever it was

who held the bridge of Porsenna [*sic*] against a whole army.
LOUIS DE BERNIÈRES *Captain Corelli's Mandolin* 1994

But who will be the brave Horatio in the House of Commons and move the Bill and seek the support and withstand the hounding that could well come from the press, and the scolding that might proceed from Their Lordships and Their Ladyships and the full gale force 10 of the Brits in a high puff of morality? *The Independent* 1996

Horn of Plenty *See* CORNUCOPIA.

Horsemen of the Apocalypse *See* APOCALYPSE.

Hotspur 'Hotspur', or 'Harry Hotspur', was a name given to Sir Henry Percy (1364–1403), son of the first earl of Northumberland. He is a character in Shakespeare's *Henry IV*, Part 1 (1598). Known for his fiery, uncontrolled temper and impetuousness, he is described in the play as a 'wasp-stung and impatient fool'.

I must say anger becomes you; you would make a charming Hotspur.
THOMAS LOVE PEACOCK *Crotchet Castle* 1831

Houdini Harry Houdini (b. Erik Weisz; 1874–1926) was a Hungarian-born American magician and escape artist. Famous for his escapes from chains, handcuffs, padlocks, straitjackets, and numerous locked containers, his name has become associated with the idea of being able to escape from any situation, however dangerous or difficult.

'I kept wondering if maybe he hadn't been there all along, hiding out somewhere on the balcony, listening to our conversation.' 'Houdini he may be, God he isn't,' I said lightly, but she didn't seem to hear.
SARAH DUNANT *Snow Storms in a Hot Climate* 1991

Her wrists and ankles had been cuffed to a solid wooden chair that was bolted to the stone-flagged floor. 'How's she going to make a break?' I asked. 'Unless she happens to be related to Houdini, of course.'
PAUL JOHNSTON *Body Politic* 1997

Hound of the Baskervilles *The Hound of the Baskervilles* (1902) is the title of a novel by Arthur Conan Doyle featuring the detective Sherlock Holmes. In the story, set mainly on Dartmoor, a monstrous and supposedly demonic hound is believed to haunt, and hunt to their deaths, the Baskerville family, in revenge for their ancestor Hugo Baskerville's crimes. *See also* SHERLOCK HOLMES.

But the red-eye did what the red-eye does. Oh, my Jesus, I look like the Hound of the Baskervilles.
MARTIN AMIS *London Fields* 1989

House of Usher 'The Fall of the House of Usher' (1839) is the title of one of Edgar Allan Poe's *Tales of Mystery and Imagination*, set in an eerie mansion in the vault of which Roderick Usher has buried his sister alive. The name now evokes mystery and supernatural happenings.

> She motioned frantically to him not to make a noise. . . . 'My dear, why all this Fall-of-the-House-of-Usher stuff?'
> STELLA GIBBONS *Cold Comfort Farm* 1932

> My hair is hanging along my cheeks, my skirt is swaddling about me. I can feel the cold damp of my brow. I must look like something out of 'The Fall of the House of Usher.'
> DOROTHY PARKER *The Waltz* 1944

Houyhnhnm In Jonathan Swift's *Gulliver's Travels* (1726), the Houyhnhnms are a race of intelligent talking horses, who have 'a general disposition to all virtues', have no conception of evil, and try always to 'cultivate reason, and to be wholly governed by it'. They live alongside the barbaric Yahoos, who resemble human beings but have no intelligence or reason and live entirely according to their animal instincts. *See also* GULLIVER.

hubris In Greek tragedy, hubris was excessive pride or defiance of the gods, which led to total failure or destruction, brought about by the avenging goddess Nemesis. *See also* NEMESIS.

> In both Japan and the West, the fall of the tiger economies has been read as a simple tale of hubris and nemesis. *The Observer* 1997

Howard Hughes Howard Hughes (1905–76) was an American millionaire businessman and film producer who is remembered as being a recluse for the last 25 years of his life.

> But as Olazabal was producing his pyrotechnics, David Gilford was slipping surreptitiously around in 67. This excellent Staffordshire player is as determinedly anonymous as Howard Hughes and despite the presence of microphones in the press interview area, it was still difficult to make out what he was saying. *The Guardian* 1995

Hulk The Incredible Hulk is a US comic-book character. The scientist Bruce Banner is exposed to gamma ray radiation which causes him to be transformed periodically into the Hulk, a huge, green-skinned, manlike monster of extraordinary strength. A man of seemingly superhuman strength or proportions can be described as a Hulk.

Sir Humphrey Sir Humphrey Appleby is the senior civil servant in the television series *Yes, Minister* (1980–2) and *Yes, Prime Minister* (1986–8). While appearing to defer to his minister and later prime minister Jim Hacker, Sir Humphrey in fact aims to run things behind the scenes as Whitehall deems appropriate.

> It is good to know that Sir Humphrey survived the fallout on 1 May and that

policy is still in the same old safe pair of hands. *The Observer* 1997

Humpty Dumpty Humpty Dumpty is a nursery rhyme character whose name is taken to refer to an egg:
'Humpty Dumpty sat on a wall,
Humpty Dumpty had a great fall.
All the king's horses, and all the king's men
Couldn't put Humpty together again.'
The name can be applied to anything fragile, especially something that, once damaged, cannot be restored.

> It would be hundreds of years before any emergent Amazons would ever grasp the fact that a man is vulnerable only in his pride, but delicate as Humpty-Dumpty once that is meddled with.
> F SCOTT FITZGERALD *Tender Is the Night* 1934

> It is, we would remind our readers . . . impossible to make an omelette without first breaking eggs. We . . . cannot wait to see the great Chinese Humpty Dumpty given a forceful shove off his wall of secrecy and deceit and broke all to pieces. Not all the Emperor's men shall put him together again.
> TIMOTHY MO *An Insular Possession* 1986

> We should not bang on about Gascoigne throwing it away because in our hearts we always knew that this was a footballer as fragile as Humpty Dumpty with a bout of vertigo.
> PAUL WEAVER *The Guardian* 1998

Hunchback of Notre Dame The Hunchback of Notre Dame is another name for Quasimodo, the ugly, deaf, hunchbacked bell-ringer of the Cathedral of Notre Dame in Victor Hugo's novel *Notre-Dame de Paris*, usually translated as *The Hunchback of Notre Dame* (1831). The popular image of the character has been largely formed by Charles Laughton's 1939 film portrayal, in which a hauntingly pitiful hunchback finds comfort and solace in the bell tower of the cathedral with his beloved bells.

Huns The Huns were a warlike nomadic people who originated in north-central Asia and overran Europe in the 4th–5th centuries. Led by Attila, they inflicted devastation on the Eastern Roman Empire, invaded Gaul, and threatened Rome. They can be alluded to in the context of a large number of people moving across an area and causing destruction.

> Various veterans had told him tales. Some talked of gray, bewhiskered hordes who were advancing with relentless curses and chewing tobacco with unspeakable valor; tremendous bodies of fierce soldiery who were sweeping along like the Huns.
> STEPHEN CRANE *The Red Badge of Courage* 1895

Mr Hyde In Robert Louis Stevenson's *The Strange Case of Dr Jekyll and Mr Hyde* (1886), Mr Hyde is the separate, purely evil, personality that the physician Dr

Jekyll is able to assume by means of a drug he discovers. A person who reveals an unsuspected evil side to their character can be said to be changing into Mr Hyde. *See also* JEKYLL AND HYDE.

> Now we are getting to know Mr Hyde. Only he isn't Dr Jekyll's gaudy monster, who trampled a child; he is just a proud little boy who hurt some humble people, and knew it and enjoyed it.
> ROBERTSON DAVIES *The Manticore* 1972

> 'Domestic violence,' said Boehlinger. 'More P.C. crap. All we do is rename things. It's wife-beating! I've been married thirty-four years, never laid a finger on my wife! First he woos her like Prince Charming then it all goes to hell in a handbasket and he's Mr Hyde—she was *frightened* of him, Miss Connor. Scared clean out of her mind. That's why she left him.'
> JONATHAN KELLERMAN *Billy Straight* 1998

Hydra In Greek mythology, the Hydra was a many-headed snake of the marshes of Lerna in the Peloponnese, whose heads grew again as they were cut off. As one of his labours, Hercules had to kill the Hydra. With the help of his companion Iolaus, he did this by searing each neck with a burning torch as he cut off the head. The hydra can be alluded to when talking about something that seems to be never-ending or indestructible because new parts keep developing. *See also* HERCULES.

> His letters were usually all common form and padding, for . . . if he wrote about anything that really interested him, his mother always wanted to know more and more about it—every fresh answer being as the lopping off of a hydra's head and giving birth to half a dozen or more new questions.
> SAMUEL BUTLER *The Way of All Flesh* 1903

> The footnotes engulfed and swallowed the text. They were ugly and ungainly, but necessary, Blackadder thought, as they sprang up like the heads of the Hydra, two to solve in the place of one solved.
> A. S. BYATT *Possession* 1990

> Yet, it had no real effect. The supplies of cocaine from Colombia remained constant, and as one of the Hydra's heads was cut off, another dozen sprang up to replace it.
> MEL STEIN *White Lines* 1997

Hygiea Hygiea was the Greek goddess of health, the daughter of Aesculapius.

Hymen The son of Dionysus and Aphrodite, Hymen was the Greek god of marriage, usually represented as a handsome young man crowned with flowers and carrying a torch.

> To such lengths, indeed, does an intemperate love of pleasure carry some prudent men, or worn out libertines, who marry to have a safe bedfellow, that

they seduce their own wives. Hymen banishes modesty, and chaste love takes
its flight.
MARY WOLLSTONECRAFT *A Vindication of the Rights of Women* 1792

I myself sincerely hope that Captain Anderson, gloomiest of Hymens, will marry
them aboard so that we may have a complete collection of all the ceremonies
that accompany the forked creature from the cradle to the grave.
WILLIAM GOLDING *Rites of Passage* 1980

Hypatia Hypatia (*c.*370–415) was a Greek philosopher, astronomer, and
mathematician. She was head of the Neoplatonist school at Alexandria and
wrote several learned treatises. She was murdered by Christian fanatics
opposed to her Neoplatonist philosophy.

'A little bit of a bore sometimes,' Molly went on. 'But mind you, a most
charming creature. I've known her since we were children together. Charming,
but not exactly a Hypatia.'
ALDOUS HUXLEY *Point Counter Point* 1928

Hyperboreans In Greek mythology, the Hyperboreans were a fabled race
worshipping Apollo and living in a land of perpetual sunshine and happiness
in a distant northerly land 'beyond the north wind'. Although the
Hyperboreans can be alluded to as people enjoying perpetual happiness,
because of the location of the fabled land the adjective 'Hyperborean' has
come to denote cold northern climes.

It's the unnatural combat of the four primal elements.—It's a blasted
heath.—It's a Hyperborean winter scene.—It's the breaking-up of the ice-bound
stream of Time.
HERMAN MELVILLE *Moby Dick* 1851

Hypnos Hypnos was the Greek god of sleep, son of Nyx (night).

Hyrcania Hyrcania was an ancient mountainous region bordering the
Caspian Sea noted for its rough wooded terrain full of serpents and wild
beasts. It can denote a wild or inhospitable place.

Iago Iago is the villainous ensign in Shakespeare's *Othello* (1622). Partly out of anger at being passed over for promotion and partly out of a general, bitter envy of Othello, Iago brings about an end to Othello's success and happiness by tricking him into believing that his wife, Desdemona, has been unfaithful to him. As a result of this, Othello kills first Desdemona and later himself. Although Iago is secretly plotting the downfall of Othello, the latter believes Iago to be completely loyal and honest, 'for I know thou'rt full of love and honesty'. Othello addresses Iago repeatedly as 'honest Iago'. Iago's name has become a byword for scheming duplicity. *See also* SHAKESPEARE.

> 'And you say Mathilda was evil-minded?' Furiously, she ground into gear.
> 'Compared with you she was a novice. Juliet to your Iago.'
> MINETTE WALTERS *The Scold's Bridle* 1994

> Politicians who peddle their sincerity between whiles become transparent liars.
> Men who trade on integrity turn Iagos.
> PETER PRESTON *The Guardian* 1995

> She was like some Iago. Or some evil guardian angel.
> CONNIE WILLIS *Bellwether* 1996

Icarus In Greek mythology, Icarus was the son of Daedalus. Daedalus constructed wings which he and Icarus used to fly to freedom from Crete. However, the wings were attached by wax, and when Icarus flew too close to the sun, the wax melted and he fell to his death in the Aegean Sea. Icarus can be alluded to as someone who fails because of excessive ambition.

> Of outside influences, Marian's favour had been the Jacob's ladder of my ascent; had the balance of my feelings for her been disturbed by a harsh look, I should have fallen, like Icarus.
> L. P HARTLEY *The Go-Between* 1953

> To fly into the air on flapping wings is the goal of two North American engineers. They have already flown a radio-controlled model ornithopter on a flight lasting almost three minutes, and they believe that within three years they could create an ornithopter that would carry a person into the skies—hopefully with more success than Icarus. *New Scientist* 1992

> The spyglass allowed him to see spindles, feathery bullets, black shudders or other shudders of indistinct hue, who flung themselves from a taller tree aiming

at the ground with the insanity of an Icarus eager to hasten his own destruction.
UMBERTO ECO *The Island of the Day Before* 1994

Incredible Hulk *See* HULK.

Ingres Jean Auguste Dominique Ingres (1780–1867) was a French painter whose elegant portraits and sensuous female nudes, including *La Grande Baigneuse* (1808), demonstrate his brilliant draughtsmanship.

But when I see her in dreams . . . it is not with that terrible aspect she wore the last time I saw her, when her face could hardly be called a face at all, but with the look of a portrait by Ingres or Goya, a full pale face, with dark, lustrous eyes, a fixed, unchanging regard, and two or three black curls, or crescents of curls, stealing down over her forehead.
L. P HARTLEY *The Go-Between* 1953

inquisitor An inquisitor was an officer of the Inquisition, a court set up by the Catholic Church, originally in the 13th century, to determine whether individuals were heretics. The inquisitors of both the original Inquisition and the later Spanish Inquisition were known for their ruthlessness and use of torture.

'The wearing of dark glasses,' she said, 'is a modern psychological phenomenon. It signifies the trend towards impersonalization, the weapon of the modern Inquisitor.'
MURIEL SPARK 'The Dark Glasses' in *The Collected Stories* 1961

Invisible Man *The Invisible Man* is the title of a novel by H. G. Wells, published in 1897, in which a scientist by the name of Griffin discovers a means of making himself invisible. Although he himself is completely invisible, his clothes remain visible, as do his footprints. The story was filmed in 1933 with Claude Rains as the scientist, and there have been numerous other film and television versions.

Between the arrogant, stretched legs of that colossus ran a stringy pattern of grey footprints stamped upon the white snow. 'God!' cried Angus involuntarily; 'the Invisible Man!'
G. K. CHESTERTON 'The Invisible Man' in *The Innocence of Father Brown* 1911

Black faces now melted into blackness; one saw apparently empty garments walking about, as in *The Invisible Man*.
LAWRENCE DURRELL *Mountolive* 1958

Io In Greek mythology, Io was a mortal woman and priestess of Hera with whom Zeus fell in love. In order to protect Io from the jealousy of his wife, Hera, Zeus turned her into a heifer. Hera was not deceived, and sent a stinging insect to goad the heifer, which fled to Egypt, where Zeus returned her to human form. *See also* HERA.

Irene Irene was the Greek goddess of peace and conciliation.

Iris In Greek mythology, Iris was the goddess of the rainbow, who acted as a messenger of the gods.

Isaac In the Old Testament, God commanded Abraham to take his son Isaac and offer him as a burnt offering. Abraham did as he was bid: he built an altar, laid wood on it, bound his son, and laid him on the altar. Abraham took a knife and was just about to slay Isaac when the angel of the Lord appeared and said 'Lay not thine hand upon the lad, neither do any thing unto him' (Gen. 22: 12). When Abraham looked up, there was a ram caught in a thicket nearby, which Abraham took and used instead of his son for the burnt offering. Isaac can be alluded to as someone who escapes death or danger at the last moment. *See also* SARAH.

Isaiah Isaiah was an Old Testament prophet whose prophecies are contained in the book of Isaiah. He warned the Israelites that they had adopted foreign or unacceptable religious practices and that they should return to their former religious rites. Isaiah predicted the fall of Jerusalem and of Judah.

Iseult *See* TRISTRAM AND ISEULT.

Ishmael The biblical Ishmael was the son of Abraham by Hagar, the maid of Abraham's wife, Sarah. Ishmael was cast out when Sarah gave birth to Isaac. The name of Ishmael, like that of his mother, Hagar, is used allusively for an outcast. The name is used for the narrator of Herman Melville's *Moby Dick*, the opening words of which are 'Call me Ishmael'. *See also* HAGAR.

> I always did hate those people . . . and they always have hated and always will hate me. I am an Ishmael by instinct as much as by accident of circumstances, but if I keep out of society I shall be less vulnerable than Ishmaels generally are.
> SAMUEL BUTLER *The Way of All Flesh* 1903

> They were a jumble of people wearing about every tinge of skin there is. Inman guessed them to be as outlaw and Ishmaelite as himself. Show folk, outliers, a tribe of Irish gypsy horse traders all thrown in together.
> CHARLES FRAZIER *Cold Mountain* 1997

Ishtar Ishtar was the Babylonian and Assyrian goddess of sexual love, fertility, and war.

Isis and Osiris Isis was an ancient Egyptian goddess married to her brother, the god Osiris, who was king of Egypt. Together with their son Horus, they formed a trinity. Isis and Osiris can be alluded to as devoted lovers. *See also* VEIL OF ISIS.

> They met once and then Michael began to write her letters as soon as he returned to college. In these letters he appointed her Isis and Arethusa, Iseult and the Seven Muses. Djuna became the woman with the face of all women.

With strange omissions: he was neither Osiris nor Tristram, nor any of the
mates or pursuers.
ANAÏS NIN *Children of the Albatross* 1947

Islands of the Blest The Islands of the Blest, often located near where the
sun sets in the west, were the place to which people in classical times
believed the souls of heroes and the good were conveyed to a life of bliss.
They were also known as the Fortunate Isles or the Happy Islands. Like
Elysium or the Elysian Fields, the term Islands of the Blest can be applied to
heaven or paradise. Tennyson's 'Ulysses' (1842) includes the lines:
'It may be we shall touch the Happy Isles,
And see the great Achilles, whom we knew.'

There were no lands of sunshine, heavy with the perfume of flowers. Such
things were only old dreams of paradise. The sunlands of the West and the
spicelands of the East, the smiling Arcadias and blissful Islands of the
Blest—ha! ha!
JACK LONDON *In a Far Country* 1900

Isolde *See* TRISTRAM AND ISEULT.

Israelites The Israelites were the Hebrew people who were living in slavery
in Egypt at some period during the second millennium BC. They were
rescued from their plight by Moses, who led them to the land of Canaan, the
biblical name for an area of ancient Palestine west of the river Jordan, which
had been promised to the descendants of Abraham by God. They can be
alluded to as people enslaved and in poverty, or liberated from this plight.
See also MOSES.

'If I go furze-cutting we shall be fairly well off.' 'In comparison with slaves, and
the Israelites in Egypt, and such people!'
THOMAS HARDY *The Return of the Native* 1880

Ithuriel In Milton's *Paradise Lost* (1667), Ithuriel is one of the cherubim, 'a
strong and subtle spirit', who is sent by Gabriel to search for Satan in the
Garden of Eden. Touched by Ithuriel's spear, which 'no falsehood can
endure', Satan starts up in his own shape and is ejected. The touch of
Ithuriel's spear can be invoked when describing any touch to a person which
provokes a strong reaction.

Rainbarrow had again become blended with night when Wildeve ascended the
long acclivity at its base. On his reaching the top a shape grew up from the
earth immediately behind him. It was that of Eustacia's emissary. He slapped
Wildeve on the shoulder. The feverish young innkeeper and engineer started
like Satan at the touch of Ithuriel's spear.
THOMAS HARDY *The Return of the Native* 1880

Ivan the Terrible Ivan IV, born Ivan Vasilyevich (1530–84), was the grand
duke of Muscovy in 1533–47 and proclaimed himself the first tsar of Russia

in 1547. As he grew increasingly paranoid and tyrannical, he conducted a reign of terror against the Boyars (the old Russian aristocracy), executing thousands of people. He consequently acquired the nickname 'the Terrible'.

Ixion In Greek mythology, Ixion was a Thessalian king who tried to seduce Hera, for which he was punished by being bound to a fiery wheel that revolved unceasingly through the underworld. The phrase 'Ixionian wheel' can be used to mean endless torment. *See also* HADES.

> So, floating on the margin of the ensuing scene, and in full sight of it, when the half-spent suction of the sunk ship reached me, I was then, but slowly, drawn towards the closing vortex. . . . Round and round, then, and ever contracting towards the button-like black bubble at the axis of that slowly wheeling circle, like another Ixion I did revolve.
> HERMAN MELVILLE *Moby Dick* 1851

Jack and the beanstalk In the children's fairy story of Jack and the beanstalk, Jack exchanges his mother's cow for some magic beans from which an enormous beanstalk grows up into the clouds. Jack climbs up and steals treasure from the giant's castle, eventually cutting down the beanstalk and killing the giant.

> The next morning, when Thomasin withdrew the curtains of her bedroom window, there stood the Maypole in the middle of the green, its top cutting into the sky. It had sprung up in the night, or rather early morning, like Jack's bean-stalk.
> THOMAS HARDY *The Return of the Native* 1880

Jack the Giant-Killer *Jack the Giant-Killer* is the title of an old nursery tale about Jack, the son of a Cornish farmer in the time of King Arthur. After killing his first giant by trapping him in a pit, Jack acquires a coat that makes him invisible, shoes that give him great speed in running, and a magic sword, and with the help of these he rids the land of giants.

> If her father would but come by in the gig and take her up! Or even if Jack the Giantkiller, or Mr. Greatheart, or St. George who slew the dragon on the halfpennies, would happen to pass that way!
> GEORGE ELIOT *Mill on the Floss* 1860

Jack the Ripper Jack the Ripper is the name given to an unidentified English 19th-century murderer. From August to November 1888 at least six prostitutes were found brutally murdered, their bodies mutilated. The crimes were never solved, but the authorities received taunting notes from a person calling himself Jack the Ripper, who claimed to be the murderer.

Jacob In the Old Testament, Jacob was the son of Isaac and Rebecca and twin brother of Esau, Esau being the first-born. Several stories relating to Jacob are commonly alluded to.

Jacob fell in love with Rachel, the daughter of his uncle Laban. He offered to work for seven years in return for Rachel's hand in marriage. 'And Jacob served seven years for Rachel; and they seemed unto him but a few days, for the love he had to her' (Gen. 29: 20). At the end of the seven years Jacob was tricked into marrying Leah, Rachel's older sister. He was given Rachel a week later, after promising to work for a further seven years. Jacob and Rachel can be alluded to as patient lovers.

The story of the mess of pottage tells how one day Esau, returning from the countryside, found Jacob cooking 'red pottage of lentils', or lentil stew. He was extremely hungry and asked for some of the stew. Jacob would only give Esau the food if he swore to sell Jacob his birthright as the elder of the twins. Esau sold his birthright to Jacob and had the stew (Gen. 25: 29–34). Jacob's pottage is therefore something pleasant and immediately satisfying for which one gives up something far more valuable.

In another story, Jacob, with his mother, Rebecca's, help, dressed as his elder brother Esau in order to obtain the blessing of their father, Isaac, who was old and unable to see well. He put on Esau's clothes and his mother put the skins of young goats on his hands and neck so that they would feel hairy like Esau's. Despite recognizing Jacob's voice, Isaac was fooled: 'The voice is Jacob's voice, but the hands are the hands of Esau' (Gen. 27: 22). He therefore gave Jacob the blessing of the first-born, which should have belonged to Esau. Jacob can be alluded to as someone who tricks or deceives others to gain what he wants.

Jacob's great success is also related in the Bible in the account of how, having worked for his uncle Laban, he married his daughters Leah and Rachel and fathered twelve sons, who became the founders of the twelve tribes of ancient Israel. Eventually Jacob wished to stop working for his uncle and set up his own flock. In lieu of wages, he agreed with Laban to take from his uncle's flocks any sheep, lambs, or goats that were dark-coloured, spotted, or speckled. Gradually, Jacob built up his own flocks from these animals until he was 'prosperous with large flocks, servants, camels, and asses' (Gen. 27: 28–30, 43).

According to another story, one night Jacob wrestled with a man until the break of day, refusing to release him until he blessed Jacob. The man eventually revealed himself to be an angel, who then changed Jacob's name: 'Your name shall no more be called Jacob, but Israel, for you have striven with God and with men, and have prevailed' (Gen. 32: 28). *See also* ESAU.

'Croft's going to marry Bell!' exclaimed Eames, thinking almost with dismay of the doctor's luck in thus getting himself accepted all at once, while he had been suing with the constancy almost of a Jacob.
ANTHONY TROLLOPE *The Small House at Allington* 1862

The fact remained that whatever he touched he prospered in. Like Jacob in Padan-Aram, he would no sooner humbly limit himself to the ringstraked-and-spotted exceptions of trade than the ringstraked-and-spotted would multiply and prevail.
THOMAS HARDY *The Mayor of Casterbridge* 1886

New Deliverance was borderline charismatic and not the sort of church I felt comfortable attending; but at lunch the day before, Nadine had caught me off guard—a fudge delight cookie has the power to cloud minds—and laid on the guilt. 'Isabel says you went to her and Haywood's church last Sunday and to

Seth and Minnie's Sunday before last, but you haven't been to ours in almost two years.' With Jacob's pottage rich and chocolaty on my tongue, I had no quick words with which to resist.
MARGARET MARON *Southern Discomfort* 1993

But finally it is impossible to escape those monsters that devour from the inner depths, and the only ways to vanquish them are either to wrestle with them like Jacob with his angel or Hercules with his serpents, or else ignore them until they give up and disappear.
LOUIS DE BERNIÈRES *Captain Corelli's Mandolin* 1994

Jacob's ladder In the Bible, Jacob was a Hebrew patriarch, the son of Isaac and Rebecca. At a place that he named Bethel he had a dream: 'And he dreamed that there was a ladder set up on the earth, and the top of it reached to heaven; and behold, the angels of God were ascending and descending on it!' (Gen. 28: 12).

In our dreams we sometimes struggle from the oceans of desire up Jacob's ladder to that orderly place. Then human voices wake us and we drown.
JEANETTE WINTERSON *The Passion* 1987

Jain Jainism is a non-theistic religion founded in India in the 6th century BC by the Jina Vardhamana Mahavira. One of its central doctrines is non-injury to any living creatures.

The total abstainer from all forms of animal product enjoys a clear, Jain-like conscience to parade before the rest of us. He or she can claim that his presence on earth hurts no other creature.
JEREMY PAXMAN *The Observer* 1995

Jesse James Jesse Woodson James (1874–82) was a US bank and train robber who formed a gang of outlaws with his brother Frank. In 1882 a member of the gang shot Jesse in order to claim the reward on his head. Jesse James is seen as an archetypal adventurous and heroic outlaw.

But that night he hadn't pitied himself, he had been imbued with all the self-complacency of the man behind the gun. He had thought condescendingly of Jesse James—such a cheap, two-bit chiseler compared with himself.
CHESTER HIMES *Prison Mass* 1933

Janus Janus was one of the earliest Roman gods, generally represented as Janus Bifrons ('With Two Faces') by a head with two faces looking in opposite directions, one facing forwards and the other facing backwards. He was thus a god of wisdom and knowledge, as he had knowledge of the past and was able to see the future. He was also the god of doorways, and of beginnings and endings.

A friend is Janus-faced: he looks to the past and the future. He is the child of all

my foregoing hours, the prophet of those to come.
RALPH WALDO EMERSON 'Friendship' in *Essays* 1841

Marian sat on one side of him, his good side: I soon came to think of him as
two-sided, like Janus. Together, they looked like Beauty and the Beast.
L. P HARTLEY *The Go-Between* 1953

It is, of course, its essentially schizophrenic outlook on society that makes the
middle class such a peculiar mixture of yeast and dough. . . . Now this Janus-like
quality derives from the class's one saving virtue, which is this: that alone of the
three great castes of society it sincerely and habitually despises itself.
JOHN FOWLES *The French Lieutenant's Woman* 1969

Jared According to the book of Genesis, Jared was one of the patriarchs and
is supposed to have lived to be 962 years old (Gen. 5: 20). He was the
grandfather of Methuselah (who lived seven years longer).

It was one of those faces which convey less the idea of so many years as its age
than of so much experience as its store. The number of their years may have
adequately summed up Jared, Mahalaleel, and the rest of the antediluvians, but
the age of a modern man is to be measured by the intensity of his history.
THOMAS HARDY *The Return of the Native* 1880

Jason and the Argonauts In Greek mythology, Jason was the son of Aeson.
Jason's uncle Pelias usurped the throne of Thessaly that was rightfully
Jason's. Pelias promised that he would surrender it when his nephew
brought him the Golden Fleece from Colchis at the furthest end of the Black
Sea. This fleece of pure gold hung from an oak tree in a sacred grove and was
guarded by an unsleeping dragon. Pelias in fact hoped that Jason would
never return.

Jason accepted this challenge. First he asked the shipwright Argus to
construct him a ship, which was named the *Argo* after its builder. Then he
assembled a crew, the Argonauts, who included such heroes as Hercules,
Orpheus, Theseus, Nestor, and Castor and Pollux. Jason set out with the
Argonauts to find and recover the Golden Fleece. Among the dangers they
faced on their perilous voyage were the Symplegades, or clashing cliffs,
which clashed together and crushed ships as they passed between them.

At Colchis, King Aeetes agreed to give Jason the fleece provided he
accomplished various tasks the king set him. Jason was challenged to yoke
the two fire-breathing bulls of Hephaestus, the god of fire and craftsmen. He
was helped by the king's daughter Medea, who was a sorceress. She gave
Jason a magic ointment to spread on his body to protect him from the bulls'
fiery breath. Then Jason was required to plough and sow a field with
dragon's teeth. Medea warned him that armed men would spring up from
the dragon's teeth, telling him to throw a stone in their midst, at which they
would ignore him and turn on one another. Having succeeded in ploughing
the field, sowing the dragon's teeth, and overcoming the armed warriors,
Jason seized the fleece after Medea had charmed the dragon guarding it. The

Argonauts fled Colchis with Aeetes in pursuit. In order to delay her father, Medea killed her younger brother Apsyrtus and dismembered his body, throwing pieces of his corpse over the side of the ship. She knew this would slow Aeetes down as he tried to recover the pieces of his son.

Jason married Medea but later abandoned her for Glauce, the daughter of Creon, king of Corinth. Medea was so enraged that she took revenge by murdering their two children as well as Jason's young bride, sending Glauce a poisoned gown which burnt her to death. Jason himself finally met his death when a timber broke off the *Argo* and struck his head, killing him. *See also* ARGONAUTS, ARGUS, GOLDEN FLEECE, MEDEA, SYMPLEGADES.

Jeeves Jeeves is the resourceful and unflappable valet of Bertie Wooster in a series of novels by P. G. Wodehouse. According to Bertie, Jeeves 'shimmers' into a room: 'There was Jeeves, standing behind me, full of zeal. In this matter of shimmering into rooms the chappie is rummy to a degree. You're sitting in the old armchair, thinking of this and that, and then suddenly you look up, and there he is' (*My Man Jeeves*, 1919). *See also* BERTIE WOOSTER.

> Knebworth opened the door and was there with champagne and the tall glasses. Grizel had said to Bone before this that Knebworth had Jeeves' trick of shimmering in. One became aware of him manifesting rather than entering.
> STAYNES AND STOREY *Bone Idle* 1993

> The man had already made it clear that he was a stickler for protocol and inclined to be pompous, a Jeeves in police uniform.
> PETER LOVESEY *The Vault* 1999

Judge Jeffreys George Jeffreys (*c*.1645–1689) was a Welsh judge who took part in the Popish Plot prosecutions and from 1683 was chief justice of the King's Bench. Judge Jeffreys became popularly known as the Hanging Judge because of his brutal sentencing at the Bloody Assizes of 1685, when he condemned to the gallows 300 or so supporters of the duke of Monmouth's rebellion.

> Frightfully sorry to keep you waiting, Mater, but I had to say a word to Biggy. He's having a rotten time, and that old Jeffreys of a judge looks as though he was getting measured for a black cap.
> DOROTHY L. SAYERS *Strong Poison* 1930

> 'Sir Frederick Foxgrove was known and respected as a wise judge and just sentencer. His behaviour in Court was always a model of dignity.' In other words, old Foxy was Judge Jeffries without the laughs.
> JOHN MORTIMER *Rumpole's Return* 1980

Jehoshabeath According to the Bible, Ahaziah was a king of Judah who followed Ahab in his worship of Baal instead of God. He was killed by Jehu, and after his death his mother 'arose and destroyed all the seed royal of the house of Judah' (2 Chr. 22: 10). However, her daughter Jehoshabeath took one of the sons, Joash, and hid him in a bedchamber to keep him safe. Jehoshabeath can be alluded to as someone who saves or protects another person.

Jehovah Jehovah is an Old Testament name for God used by Christians. The name is sometimes used in the context of the severity of divine retribution. The voice of Jehovah, imagined to be loud and booming, can also be used allusively.

> Standing as she stood in Grammer Oliver's shoes, he was simply a remorseless Jehovah of the sciences, who would not have mercy, and would have sacrifice; a man whom save for this, she would have preferred to avoid knowing.
> THOMAS HARDY *The Woodlanders* 1887

> The thousand voices burst out with that almost supernatural sound which choral singing always has. Enormous, like the voice of Jehovah.
> ALDOUS HUXLEY *Point Counter Point* 1928

> You placate him like Jehovah. That's no good.
> A. S. BYATT *The Virgin in the Garden* 1978

Jehu Jehu, a king of Israel (841–815 BC), was known for driving his chariot very fast and recklessly. According to the Old Testament book of Kings: 'he driveth furiously' (2 Kgs. 9: 20).

> And at last away he drove, Jehu-like, as they say, out of the court-yard.
> SAMUEL RICHARDSON *Pamela* 1740

> A drunken postilion . . . who frightened her by driving like Jehu the son of Nimshi, and shouting hilarious remarks at her.
> GEORGE ELIOT *Adam Bede* 1859

> Those who only ever saw him behind a desk supposed the Mercedes was a status symbol. But Sale learnt his trade before mobile phones, when the ability to drive like Jehu could mean the difference between hold-the-front and a page-two filler, and when the need arose he could still burn rubber like a Hollywood stuntman.
> JO BANNISTER *The Primrose Switchback* 1999

Jekyll and Hyde In Robert Louis Stevenson's *The Strange Case of Dr Jekyll and Mr Hyde* (1886), Dr Jekyll discovers a drug that allows him to create a separate personality, Mr Hyde, through which he can express the evil side of his character. Periodically, he changes from the worthy physician into the evil Hyde, and eventually Hyde gains the upper hand over Jekyll. The term 'Jekyll and Hyde' can thus be used to refer to someone whose personality appears to undergo an abrupt transformation, particularly from gentleness to aggressiveness or violence. A person who reveals an unsuspected evil side to their character can be said to be changing into Mr Hyde.

I just said a double thing. I said I would rob a bank. And then I said I hate corruption. Hmmm. Jekyll and Hyde.
STUDS TERKEL *American Dreams: Lost and Found* 1980

I told her that she had had a lucky escape from my father, but she defended him, saying, 'He is another person when he is on his own with me. He is so sweet and kind.' Yes, and so was Dr Jekyll.
SUE TOWNSEND *The Growing Pains of Adrian Mole Aged 13¾* 1984

Under normal circumstances Bruce was a happy drinker, not one of those sad Jekyll and Hyde characters who turn into social psychopaths with their third glass.
BEN ELTON *Popcorn* 1996

Jephthah's daughter In the Bible, Jephthah was a judge of Israel who sacrificed his daughter to fulfil a rash vow he had made that if victorious in battle he would sacrifice the first living thing that he met on his return home. He consented to her request to go into the mountains to bewail the fact that she was dying a virgin. At the end of two months, 'she returned to her father, who did with her according to his vow which he had vowed: and she knew no man' (Judg. 11: 39).

'Well,' said he, 'I will not be too urgent; but the sooner you fix, the more obliging I shall think you. Mr Andrews, we must leave something to these Jeptha's daughters, in these cases. I suppose, the little bashful folly, which, in the happiest circumstances, may give a kind of regret to a thoughtful mind, on quitting the maiden state, is a reason with Pamela; and so she shall name her day.'
SAMUEL RICHARDSON *Pamela* 1740

Jeremiah Jeremiah was an Old Testament prophet whose prophecies are contained in the book of Jeremiah. These concern the unhappy fate that awaits the Israelites because they have rebelled against God. The book of Lamentations, foretelling the destruction of Jerusalem, is traditionally attributed to him. Jeremiah's name can be applied to someone who predicts doom or disaster.

His was a soft world, fuzzy with private indecisions masked by the utterance of public verities which gave him the appearance of a lenient Jeremiah.
TOM SHARPE *Porterhouse Blue* 1974

Test win knocks Jeremiahs for six. *The Guardian* 1995

Since we have so far emerged comparatively unscathed from all these predicted plagues and catastrophes, it is hard to take too seriously the latest Jeremiah-like pronouncements of Lacey and his colleagues about beef. *The Observer* 1996

Jericho Jericho is a town in Palestine, one of the world's oldest settlements and believed to have been occupied from at least 9000 BC. According to the Bible, Jericho was a Canaanite city destroyed by the Israelites after they crossed the Jordan into the Promised Land, led by Joshua. Its walls were flattened by the shout of the army and the blast of the trumpets. 'So the people shouted when the priests blew with the trumpets: and it came to pass, when the people heard the sound of the trumpet, the people shouted with a great shout, and the wall fell down flat . . . and they took the city' (Josh. 6: 20).

> At that period English society was still a closed body and it was not easy for a Jew to force its barriers, but to Ferdy they fell like the walls of Jericho.
> W. SOMERSET MAUGHAM *The Alien Corn* 1951

> As Jenny Long drove to the hospital the next morning she sang softly to herself. She was quite confident that it wouldn't be long before Harry gave in and said it was time they got married. After all, even Jericho fell in the end.
> MAX MARQUIS *Written in Blood* 1995

Jeroboam In the Bible, Jeroboam rebelled against Solomon and, after Solomon's death, encouraged the Israelites to rebel against Solomon's successor, Rehoboam. Jeroboam incited the Israelites to commit the sin of idolatry, encouraging them to worship two golden calves as gods. He also established a priesthood and, even though warned against it, continued to appoint priests. In punishment God decreed that Jeroboam's entire family be destroyed. 'Therefore, behold, I will bring evil upon the house of Jeroboam . . . And will take away the remnant of the house of Jeroboam, as a man taketh away dung, till it be all gone' (1 Kgs. 14: 10).

> 'How horrid that story was last night! It spoiled my thoughts of today. It makes me feel as if a tragic doom overhung our family, as it did the house of Atreus.'
> 'Or the house of Jeroboam,' said the quondam theologian.
> THOMAS HARDY *Jude the Obscure* 1894

Jesuit A Jesuit is a member of the Society of Jesus, a Roman Catholic order of priests founded in 1534 by St Ignatius Loyola, Francis Xavier, and others to do missionary work throughout the world. The Jesuits have also been noted as educators and theologians. The term 'Jesuitical' has acquired a pejorative use to describe a person who uses over-subtle, hair-splitting arguments.

> He was as diligent as any Jesuit at arranging the arguments in every case under *Pro* and *Contra* and examining them thoroughly.
> ROBERTSON DAVIES *Tempest-Tost* 1951

Jesus Jesus Christ is the central figure of the Christian religion, a Jewish religious leader worshipped by Christians as the Son of God and the saviour of mankind. The main sources of his life are the four Gospels of Matthew, Mark, Luke, and John.

According to these accounts, Jesus was born in Bethlehem to Mary, the wife of Joseph, a carpenter of Nazareth, having been miraculously conceived. At the age of 30 Jesus was baptized by John the Baptist in the river Jordan. He spent 40 days fasting in the wilderness, where he was challenged by Satan with a series of temptations. Jesus came out of the wilderness to begin his ministry and for the next three years taught and preached in Galilee. His message was the coming of the kingdom of God. He chose a group of twelve disciples to accompany him. Jesus told parables (such as those of the Good Samaritan and the Prodigal Son), healed the sick, and performed miracles, including turning water into wine and raising Lazarus from the dead. In his Sermon on the Mount he preached love, humility, and charity. His teachings aroused the hostility of the Pharisees and the governing Romans.

In the third year of his mission, Jesus was betrayed to the authorities in Jerusalem by Judas Iscariot, one of his disciples. After sharing the Last Supper with his disciples, he went to pray in the garden of Gethsemane, where he was arrested. He was taken before the high priest, and then turned over to the Romans as a blasphemer and political agitator. Following a hurried trial and despite the misgivings of the Roman procurator, Pontius Pilate, Jesus was condemned to be crucified at Calvary, outside Jerusalem. On the third day after his death his tomb was found to be empty. According to the New Testament, he rose from the dead and ascended into heaven. Various aspects of the character, life, and death of Jesus are referred to allusively.

The Bible portrays Jesus Christ as coming from a humble background and preaching a message of humility and meekness. He described himself as 'meek and lowly in heart' (Matt. 11: 29) and in the Sermon on the Mount he stated, 'Blessed are the meek: for they shall inherit the earth' (Matt. 5: 5). He can therefore be alluded to as someone who is genuinely humble and meek.

His 40 days' fast in the wilderness as related in the New Testament (Matt. 4: 1–11) can be invoked to suggest a long period of solitude and contemplation. His temptation by Satan is referred to when describing someone who successfully resists temptations.

When Jesus was crucified, the Bible relates how he spoke to God from the Cross saying, 'Father, forgive them; for they know not what they do' (Luke 23: 34). This is sometimes cited as the greatest possible act of forgiveness. *See also* CALVARY, GETHSEMANE, GOLGOTHA, JUDAS, LAZARUS, PONTIUS PILATE, SATAN, SERMON ON THE MOUNT.

> 'I been thinkin', he said. 'I been in the hills thinkin', almost you might say like Jesus went into the wilderness to think His way out of a mess of troubles.'
> JOHN STEINBECK *The Grapes of Wrath* 1939

> And Daniel—to his cousin a sort of Christ between thieves—was hurried past the privileged loafers in the corridor, and down the broad steps.
> ARNOLD BENNETT *The Old Wives' Tale* 1908

> Well, he looks awfully nice. Of course you never really know someone till you've been married to them for a while and discover some of their scruffier habits. I remember how upset I was when I realized for the first time that after all Joe wasn't Jesus Christ. I don't know what it was, probably some silly thing like finding out he's crazy about Audrey Hepburn. Or that he's a secret philatelist.
> MARGARET ATWOOD *The Edible Woman* 1969

Jezebel Jezebel was a Phoenician princess of the 9th century BC, the wife of Ahab, king of Israel. She was denounced by Elijah for promoting the worship of the Phoenician god Baal, and trying to destroy the prophets of Israel. Her idolatry and her use of cosmetics led to the use of her name to represent female depravity, shamelessness, and wickedness. At the command of Jehu she was thrown out of a window and killed. Her carcass was eaten by dogs, so that when they went to bury her, 'they found no more of her than the skull, and the feet, and the palms of her hands'. It was decreed that 'in the portion of Jezreel shall dogs eat the flesh of Jezebel: And the carcase of Jezebel shall be dung upon the face of the field in the portion of Jezreel; so that they shalt not say This is Jezebel' (2 Kgs. 9: 32–7).

> I have been a Jezebel, a London prostitute, and what not.
> SAMUEL RICHARDSON *Pamela* 1740

> 'Mr Slope,' said Mrs Proudie, catching the delinquent at the door, 'I am surprised that you should leave my company to attend on such a painted Jezebel as that.'
> ANTHONY TROLLOPE *Barchester Towers* 1857

> Red flames will lick round their feet like the dogs lickin' Jezebel's blood in the Good Book.
> STELLA GIBBONS *Cold Comfort Farm* 1932

> Certainly, she had not seduced him; had not vamped him like some wicked Jezebel.
> RANDALL KENAN *Let the Dead Bury their Dead* 1992

Jim In Mark Twain's novel *Huckleberry Finn* (1884), Jim is a runaway slave who meets up with Huck and travels with him down the Mississippi on a raft. During the course of the book Jim is sold back into slavery and then rescued again by Huck and Tom Sawyer.

> I was trying to tell you that I know many things about you—not you personally, but fellows like you . . . With us it's still Jim and Huck Finn. A number of my friends are jazz musicians, and I've been around. I know the conditions under which you live—why go back, fellow? There is so much you could do here where there is more freedom.
> RALPH ELLISON *Invisible Man* 1952

Joan of Arc St Joan of Arc (*c.*1412–1431), also known as the Maid of Orléans, was the daughter of peasants and became a French heroine and martyr. As a teenager she heard voices she believed to be the voices of saints urging her to fight for the Dauphin against the English in the Hundred Years War. She led the French army to relieve the English siege of Orléans and then led the Dauphin through occupied territory to Reims, where he was crowned Charles VII. Unable to persuade the king to support further attacks on the English, Joan was captured by the Burgundians, who sold her to the English in 1430. The English tried her as a heretic and burnt her at the stake. She was canonized in 1920. Both her heroism and her martyrdom can be alluded to.

So, slipping and sliding, with Jane now circling helplessly around them and now leading the way, like a big-arsed Joan of Arc, they reached Jane's pad.
JAMES BALDWIN *Another Country* 1963

Her cheeks were flushed, her eyes sparkling, her question a battle cry. She had the simple, single-minded, passionate fervor of a Joan of Arc: This is right. It must be done. I must do it, whatever the cost.
KAREN KIJEWSKI *Wild Kat* 1994

Joash *See* JEHOSHABEATH.

Job The Old Testament book of Job tells the story of Job, a prosperous man whose patience and piety God tries, first by taking away his wealth and then by heaping other misfortunes upon him, including 'loathsome sores from the sole of his foot to the crown of his head' (Job 2: 7). In spite of all his suffering, he remains humble and accepting: 'the Lord gave, and the Lord hath taken away; blessed be the name of the Lord' (Job 1: 21). He does not lose his confidence in the goodness and justice of God, and his patience is finally rewarded with wealth and long life. He is alluded to primarily as the epitome of forbearance. In the United States, extreme poverty can also be described by mention of 'Job's house cat' or 'Job's turkey'. If Job is poor, how much worse off, presumably, must be an animal in his care.

'That's splendid. One feels a certain pang of pity for whoever it is he's starting to work for, but that's splendid. The family were worried about him.' 'I don't wonder. I can't imagine anybody more capable of worrying a family than Eggy. Just suppose if Job had had him as well as boils!'
P G. WODEHOUSE *Laughing Gas* 1936

'And I suppose you're Job himself.' 'I'd have to be. To put up with you.'
JOHN MORTIMER *Rumpole of the Bailey* 1978

Amiable as the old man was, prolonged exposure to him would test anyone's patience. But Dolly Harris would have made Job seem like a chain-smoking neurotic.
MARTIN EDWARDS *Yesterday's Papers* 1994

'But stop nets do stop fish,' I said, enjoying the novelty of his position enough to play devil's advocate. 'Well, of course they do. But if they stopped *all* the fish, crews on the east would be richer'n Midas and those working the westermost part of Bogue Banks would be poorer'n Job's house cat.'
MARGARET MARON *Shooting at Loons* 1994

Job's comforter A Job's comforter is someone whose attempts to give sympathy and comfort have the opposite effect. The term derives from an episode in the story of Job in which his three friends Eliphaz, Bildad, and Zophar come to comfort him but only increase his distress by telling him that his misfortunes are the result of his sinfulness. Job responds to this with the words 'Miserable comforters are ye all' (Job 16: 2). *See also* JOB.

'Of course,' she added in true Job's-comforter style, 'I needn't take them all today.'
RAYMOND FLYNN *A Public Body* 1996

John Bull John Bull is the personification of England or of an Englishman, first appearing in the satire *Life is a Bottomless Pit; or, The History of John Bull* by John Arbuthnot (1712). He has often appeared in cartoons in the 19th and 20th centuries and is usually depicted as a stout country squire in tailcoat, breeches, a top hat, and boots.

'Don't you think the English nation perfect in every respect?' asked Sallie. 'I should be ashamed of myself if I didn't.' 'He's a true John Bull.'
LOUISA M. ALCOTT *Little Women* 1868

In 1799, when Napoleon was still vying for power, General Hoche, a schoolboys' hero and onetime lover of Madame Bonaparte, had landed in Ireland and almost succeeded in defeating John Bull outright.
JEANETTE WINTERSON *The Passion* 1987

John O'Groats to Land's End John O'Groats is a village at the extreme north-eastern point of the Scottish mainland. Land's End is a rocky promontory in south-west Cornwall, which forms the westernmost point of England. John O'Groats and Land's End are considered to be the two extreme ends of the British mainland.

The sexual antics of public figures—Cecil Parkinson, Bill Clinton, Paddy Ashdown, Frank Bough, Alan Clark—never fail to send the same old-maidish frisson reverberating from John O'Groats to Land's End. *The Guardian* 1993

John the Baptist John the Baptist was a Jewish preacher and prophet, who preached at the time of Jesus, demanding that his hearers repent of their sins and be baptized.

He was a John the Baptist who took ennoblement rather than repentance for his text.
THOMAS HARDY *The Return of the Native* 1880

Dr Johnson Samuel Johnson (1709–84), often referred to as Dr Johnson, was an English lexicographer, writer, critic, and celebrated conversationalist. In 1773 he undertook a journey with James Boswell to the Scottish Highlands and Hebrides, recorded in his *A Journey to the Western Islands of Scotland* (1775) and in Boswell's *Journal of a Tour to the Hebrides* (1785). The image of Johnson striding purposefully along while engaged in witty conversation is an enduring one.

Even Dr Johnson could not have carried on a conversation when he was walking down Fleet Street at the speed of an express train.
W. SOMERSET MAUGHAM *Cakes and Ale* 1930

Jolly Green Giant The Jolly Green Giant is the trademark of the Green Giant food company, producers of sweetcorn and other tinned and frozen vegetables. He is a friendly, cheerful, green-skinned giant who booms, 'Ho, ho, ho!'

> My father sits at the head of the table, beaming like the Jolly Green Giant.
> MARGARET ATWOOD *Cat's Eye* 1988

Jolly Miller Isaac Bickerstaffe's comic opera *Love in a Village* (1762) contains a song about the jolly miller, in which the miller declares, 'I care for nobody, not I, If no one cares for me'.

> And then sometimes, very disquietingly for poor Susan, he would suddenly interrupt his emotions with an oddly cynical little laugh and would become for a while somebody entirely different, somebody like the Jolly Miller in the song. 'I care for nobody, no, not I, and nobody cares for me.'
> ALDOUS HUXLEY *Point Counter Point* 1928

Jonah In the Bible, Jonah was a Hebrew minor prophet, who was commanded by God to 'go to Nineveh, that great city, and cry against it; for their wickedness is come up before me' (Jonah 1: 2). However, Jonah refused to obey God's command and, instead, he embarked on a ship bound for Tarshish. God sent a storm as punishment and, to save the ship, the other sailors cast Jonah into the water as a bringer of bad luck, whereupon the storm abated. Jonah was then swallowed by a huge fish (traditionally a whale), and spent three days and three nights in its belly, in which time he repented and prayed to God to save him. After three days 'the Lord spake unto the fish, and it vomited out Jonah upon the dry land' (Jonah 2: 10).

Although Jonah lived to comply with God's instructions, his disobedience had endangered the unwitting sailors with whom he had sailed and his name has subsequently stood for a bringer of ill luck. He can also be alluded to as someone who survives a very difficult or dangerous situation.

> His presence was a perpetual reminder of bad luck, and soon he was suffering the cold shoulder that had been my lot when Happy Hannah first decided I was a Jonah.
> ROBERTSON DAVIES *World of Wonders* 1975

> I am back: again and again I am back, from the belly of the whale disgorged.
> J. M. COETZEE *Age of Iron* 1990

Jonathan *See* DAVID AND JONATHAN.

Indiana Jones Indiana Jones is the whip-cracking archaeologist–explorer hero of the film *Raiders of the Lost Ark* (1981) and its sequels. The films are set in the 1930s and all feature hair-raising chase sequences. The first film was promoted with the slogan 'The hero is back'.

Foreign correspondents were a revered, much romanticized group—the Indiana Joneses of journalism. *New Yorker* 1995

'What about you?' I said crossly. 'If you hadn't been behaving like some sexagenarian Indiana Jones, we wouldn't have got into this mess in the first place.'
MICHÈLE BAILEY *Haycastle's Cricket* 1996

Joseph Joseph was the son of Jacob and Rachel. In his boyhood, he was his father's favourite son, and when his father gave him a coat of many colours his brothers became jealous, and 'hated him, and could not speak peaceably unto him' (Gen 37: 4). They also hated him for his prophetic dreams. They attacked him, stripped him of his coat, and threw him into a pit. Then they sold him into slavery to the Ishmaelites, who brought him to Egypt. Taking his coat, Joseph's brothers dipped it in the blood of a kid they had killed and took it to their father to convince him that Joseph was dead.

In Egypt, Joseph was bought by Potiphar, an Egyptian officer, in whose house he was soon made overseer. Potiphar's wife tried to seduce him but Joseph repeatedly refused her advances because of his loyalty to his master. Potiphar's wife subsequently made a false accusation that he had attempted to rape her and as a result Joseph was put in prison. There he interpreted the dreams of Pharaoh's butler and baker. Two years later Pharaoh was troubled by dreams that he could not understand and, hearing of Joseph's gift from his butler, sent for him. Joseph interpreted Pharaoh's dream as predicting seven years of plenty followed by seven years of famine, advising Pharaoh to store grain in preparation for the long famine ahead. Joseph became adviser to Pharaoh and rose to high office, eventually becoming governor of Egypt.

During the famine years, Jacob sent his sons to Egypt to try to buy corn. When Joseph's brothers came to him for help, Joseph at first treated them roughly but, when his brothers revealed how their father had suffered since his disappearance, he eventually revealed to them who he was. He was reconciled with his family and helped them during a famine in Canaan, showing particular compassion for his father and his youngest brother, Benjamin.

Various aspects of Joseph's character and life can be alluded to. He is the best known interpreter of dreams, and he is also often alluded to as the archetype of a powerful person who acts with kindness and loyalty to his own people. Because he resisted the advances of Potiphar's wife, he can also be described as a man who remains chaste. *See also* PHARAOH, POTIPHAR'S WIFE.

The honour and love you bear him is nothing but meet, for God has given him great gifts, and he uses them as the patriarch Joseph did, who, when he was exalted to a place of power and trust, yet yearned with tenderness towards his parent, and his younger brother.
GEORGE ELIOT *Adam Bede* 1859

I don't believe you ever knew what a sore touch it was with Boy that you were such a Joseph about women. He felt it put him in the wrong. He always felt

that the best possible favour you could do a woman was to push her into bed.
ROBERTSON DAVIES *The Manticore* 1972

Joshua Joshua, Moses' successor as leader of Israel, led the Israelites in their
return to the land of Canaan. The book of Joshua includes an account of the
Israelites' victory over the Amorites, during which Joshua prayed to God:
' "Sun, stand thou still at Gibeon, and thou Moon in the valley of Aijalon."
And the sun stood still, and the moon stayed, until the nation took
vengeance on their enemies' (Josh. 10: 12–13).

We were gaining about twenty minutes every day, because we were going east
so fast—we gained just about enough every day to keep along with the moon.
It was becoming an old moon to the friends we had left behind us, but to us
Joshuas it stood still.
MARK TWAIN *The Innocents Abroad* 1869

Jotun In Scandinavian mythology, the Jotuns were a race of frost giants who
fought against the gods for possession of the world. While the gods lived in
Asgard, the home of the Jotuns was Jotunheim.

The Amphitheatre was a huge circular enclosure, with a notch at opposite
extremities of its diameter north and south. From its sloping internal form it
might have been called the spittoon of the Jotuns.
THOMAS HARDY *The Mayor of Casterbridge* 1886

Judas Judas Iscariot was the disciple who, in return for thirty pieces of
silver, betrayed Jesus to the Jewish authorities with a kiss of identification:
'Now the betrayer had given them a sign, saying, "The one I shall kiss is the
man; seize him." And he came up to Jesus at once and said, "Hail, Master!"
And he kissed him. Jesus said to him, "Friend, why are you here?" Then they
came up and laid hands on Jesus and seized him' (Matt. 26: 48–50). When he
learned that Jesus had been condemned to death, he realized the enormity of
his betrayal and repented, returned the money to the priests who had paid
him, and then hanged himself (Matt. 27: 3–5). The term 'Judas' can be used to
refer to a person who treacherously betrays a friend, and a 'Judas kiss' is an
act of betrayal. Judas' subsequent feelings of guilt and repentance are also
alluded to. His appearance can be invoked when describing someone with
red hair, as Judas is traditionally depicted in art as red-headed. *See also* JESUS.

Eustacia was always anxious to avoid the sight of her husband in such a state as
this, which had become as dreadful to her as the trial scene was to Judas
Iscariot. It brought before her eyes the spectre of a worn-out woman knocking
at a door which she would not open; and she shrank from contemplating it.
THOMAS HARDY *The Return of the Native* 1880

Everybody, when he spoke, listened attentively to him as if he was addressing
them in church. He wondered where the inevitable Judas was sitting now, but
he wasn't aware of Judas as he had been in the forest hut.
GRAHAM GREENE *The Power and the Glory* 1940

Are we to watch our words and stick out our necks to the knives of potential traitors here in this place where we meet to put our minds and hearts in the struggle . . . are we to sit with Judas in our midst?
NADINE GORDIMER *My Son's Story* 1990

St Jude St Jude, also known as Judas and traditionally identified with Thaddaeus, was one of the apostles. St Jude is regarded as the patron saint of hopeless causes.

With an LLB from Baltimore University, he introduced himself as a graduate of Agnew U. and boasted that Spiro had been his professor of Legal Ethics. A fierce defender of hopeless cases, he dubbed himself 'the St. Jude of the judicial system' and startled prosecutors and juries with his audacious courtroom antics.
MATTHEW MEWSHAW *True Crime* 1991

Judgement Day In Christian tradition, the Day of Judgement is the day when God will judge all the living and the dead and reward or punish them accordingly. The quotation below refers to the sound of all the people gathered together to be judged by God.

At that there was a great outcry in the courtroom, like the uprush of voices at the Judgement Day; and I knew I was doomed.
MARGARET ATWOOD *Alias Grace* 1996

Judith In the apocryphal book of Judith, Judith was a rich and beautiful Jewish widow who saved the town of Bethulia from a siege by the Babylonian army. She entered the enemy camp and, having promised to sleep with the Babylonian general Holofernes, was left alone with him in his tent. When Holofernes fell into a drunken sleep, she cut off his head with his own sword.

There certainly was some beauty about her. Her eyes were large and bright, and her shoulders were well turned. She might have done as an artist's model for a Judith, but I doubt whether any man, looking well into her face, could think that she would do well as a wife.
ANTHONY TROLLOPE *The Small House at Allington* 1862

For he had thought that if anyone might darkly store up a vengeance it was Nancy. Perhaps she intended, like Judith with Holofernes, to bed down with him and decapitate him in his sleep.
THOMAS KENEALLY *The Playmaker* 1987

Juggernaut In Hindu mythology, Juggernaut, or Jagannath (meaning Lord of the World), is the name of an image of Krishna annually carried in procession on an enormous cart. Devotees of the god are said to have thrown themselves under its wheels to be crushed in the hope of going straight to paradise. The word can be used to denote a huge destructive force that crushes whatever is in its path.

That human Juggernaut trod the child down and passed on regardless of her screams.

ROBERT LOUIS STEVENSON *The Strange Case of Dr Jekyll and Mr Hyde* 1886

And now, young Pongo, stand out of my way, or I'll roll over you like a Juggernaut.

P G. WODEHOUSE *Cocktail Time* 1958

The horse was terrified already by the noise and the proximity of the horse box, but horses don't altogether understand about the necessity of removing themselves pronto from under the wheels of thundering juggernauts. Frightened horses, on the whole, are more apt to run *into* the paths of vehicles, than away.

DICK FRANCIS *Trial Run* 1978

Juliet *See* ROMEO AND JULIET.

Juno In Roman mythology, Juno was the wife and sister of Jupiter, and queen of Heaven, equivalent to the Greek Hera. In many stories she is depicted as jealously enraged by the philanderings of her husband. The Trollope quotation below refers to the wrath of Juno, or Hera, at being slighted by Paris when he chose Aphrodite instead of her as the fairest of three goddesses. *See also* APHRODITE, HERA.

Not allowed to dispose of money, or call any thing their own, they learn to turn the market penny; or, should a husband offend, by staying from home, or give rise to some emotions of jealousy—a new gown, or any pretty bawble [*sic*], smooths Juno's angry brow.

MARY WOLLSTONECRAFT *A Vindication of the Rights of Women* 1792

We know what was the wrath of Juno when her beauty was despised. We know too what storms of passion even celestial minds can yield. As Juno may have looked at Paris on Mount Ida, so did Mrs Proudie look on Ethelbert Stanhope when he pushed the leg of the sofa into her lace train.

ANTHONY TROLLOPE *Barchester Towers* 1857

Jurassic In geology, the Jurassic period lasted from about 213 to 144 million years ago. Dinosaurs were abundant and attained their maximum size. Popularized by Steven Spielberg's blockbuster dinosaur film *Jurassic Park* (1993), the term is sometimes used informally to mean 'extremely out of date or antiquated'.

Call me Jurassic, but I couldn't care less about authenticity and immediacy when I'm engrossed in a good story. *The Observer* 1997

Jurassic Park *Jurassic Park* is the title of a film (1993) based on a book of the same name by Michael Crichton (1991). The plot features a theme park inhabited by dinosaurs which have been created from DNA taken from ancient mosquitoes preserved in amber. The dinosaurs are not supposed to be able to breed, but it is discovered that one particularly dangerous species, the carnivorous velociraptor, is able to reproduce. At the end of the film the velociraptors are moving out of the confines of the park.

> For prison is like Jurassic Park, but infinitely more dangerous: a single-sex society where some specimens, through a freak of genes, can mutate to the opposite sex. And others, through an excess of libido, willingly lose the ability to differentiate.
> PAUL BENNETT *False Profits* 1998

Just William William Brown is the unruly, usually grubby-faced, schoolboy created by Richmal Crompton and featuring in a series of books (1922–70). Though well-intentioned, William has the knack of unwittingly producing chaos. He is the leader of a gang of friends known as the Outlaws.

> Detective Superintendent Honeyman was a small, tidy man with a pale face and a repressed expression, which always made Slider think of Richmal Crompton's William scrubbed clean and pressed into his Eton suit for a party he didn't want to go to.
> CYNTHIA HARROD-EAGLES *Blood Lines* 1996

j

Kafka The novels of Franz Kafka (1883–1924), a Czech novelist who wrote in German, portray the individual's isolation, bewilderment, and anxiety in a nightmarish, impenetrably oppressive world. In *The Trial* (1925), Joseph K. is arrested and subjected to a baffling ordeal by sinister figures of authority. The corresponding adjective is 'Kafkaesque'.

> When she brought them in, he understood her apprehensiveness at once. He could see that they were men of tremendous authority. He had never read Kafka, but if he had he would have recognized them. They wore black suits, and did not smile when they greeted him, or offer to shake hands.
> ALAN PATON *Ah, But Your Land Is Beautiful* 1981

> Toiling up the slope from Falmer railway station, you had the Kafkaesque sensation of walking into an endlessly deep stage set where apparently three-dimensional objects turned out to be painted flats, and reality receded as fast as you pursued it.
> DAVID LODGE *Nice Work* 1988

> When I asked why, the spokesman, a decent man just trying to earn a crust like the rest of us, tried his best to explain the Government's Kafkaesque logic. *The Observer* 1997

Anna Karenina In Tolstoy's novel *Anna Karenina* (1873–7), Anna is married to a government official, Karenin. Anna has a love affair with Count Vronsky, and when she becomes pregnant she confesses her adultery to her husband, who insists she choose between himself and her lover. She chooses Vronsky but, unable to tolerate the social isolation that this leads to, eventually kills herself by throwing herself under a train. She can be alluded to as the archetypal adulteress.

> It was one thing reading Tolstoy in class, another playing Anna and Vronsky with the professor.
> PHILIP ROTH *My Life as a Man* 1970

Boris Karloff Boris Karloff (1887–1969), born William Henry Pratt, was a British-born American actor. His gaunt looks made him particularly well suited to roles in horror films, and his most memorable performance was as the monster in *Frankenstein* (1931).

The people protecting you have morticians who could make Boris Karloff look like Marilyn Monroe.
TOM SHARPE *Grantchester Grind* 1995

Karma In Buddhist philosophy, Karma is the doctrine that the sum total of a person's actions and experiences in all their incarnations determines the fate of their next incarnation.

Karnac Karnac is a village in Egypt, on the Nile near Luxor. It is the site of ancient Thebes, whose ruins, including the great temple of Amun, still survive there. Its name can invoke an empty or deserted place.

Half-past ten in the morning was about her hour for seeking this spot—a time when the town avenues were deserted as the avenues of Karnac.
THOMAS HARDY *The Mayor of Casterbridge* 1886

Ned Kelly Ned Kelly (1855–80) was an Australian outlaw whose father had been transported from Ireland. Kelly headed a four-man gang of bandits, notorious for killing three policemen in 1878. After an attempted train ambush, Kelly tried to escape in a homemade suit of armour, but was apprehended and hanged.

And you're game, Monny. Game as Ned Kelly, and you'll get on your feet again.
ROBERTSON DAVIES *A Mixture of Frailties* 1951

Clark Kent Clark Kent appears to be a shy bespectacled reporter for the *Daily Planet* newspaper. However, when trouble threatens he transforms himself into Superman, a superhero from the planet Krypton who is able to fly and has superhuman strength. Originally a US comic-book character, Superman has also appeared in a series of successful films. Clark Kent's instant transformation takes place out of sight and typically in a telephone box, from which he emerges fully garbed in cape and tights as Superman. *See also* SUPERMAN.

'Fire away,' he said, all business. We might just have met. I was impressed by this Clark Kent-like transformation: from admirer to news hound in half a minute, and no need to pop into a telephone booth.
LAUREN HENDERSON *The Black Rubber Dress* 1997

Keystone Kops The Keystone Kops were a troupe of film comedians led by Ford Sterling who, between 1912 and 1920, made a number of silent comedies at the Keystone Studios in Hollywood. Dressed in oversized police uniforms, the bumbling Keystone Kops took part in chaotic chase scenes involving daring comic stunts.

Once the Keystone Kops-like operation was in the air, another failing of the Canadian device was noted: it did not adjust well to altitude-induced air pressure differences.
LAURIE GARRETT *Coming Plague* 1995

Martin Luther King Martin Luther King (1929–68) was a US Baptist minister and civil rights leader who opposed discrimination against blacks by organizing non-violent resistance and peaceful mass demonstrations. He was awarded the 1964 Nobel Peace Prize. A brilliant and inspiring orator, his most famous speech reiterates the words 'I have a dream'. King was assassinated in Memphis, Tennessee, in 1968.

> Many seem to believe that you are destined to be to the unborn what Martin Luther King was to the black people of America, and the late Robert F. Charisma to the disadvantaged Chicanos and Puerto Ricans of the country.
> PHILIP ROTH *Our Gang* 1971

King Kong Kong, or King Kong, is a gigantic, monstrous ape featured in the film *King Kong* (1933). Kong is discovered on a remote Pacific island, captured, and brought to New York to be exhibited. He escapes and runs amok in the city, climbing the Empire State Building with the heroine (played in the film by Fay Wray) in his grasp before fighter planes shoot him down. The scene in which King Kong clings to the top of the Empire State Building while swatting away a swarm of biplanes is an iconic moment of cinema.

> We stock our zoos with elephants, hippopotamuses, giraffes, and gorillas; who among you was not rooting for King Kong in his various battles atop tall buildings?
> STEPHEN JAY GOULD *Ever Since Darwin* 1977

> She kept bumping into her own furniture. Then she put on her glasses. Like bottle tops. When I asked her, she said she wasn't wearing them when she went into the house. If King Kong had been in the corridor she wouldn't have seen him.
> MAX MARQUIS *Written in Blood* 1995

Kipling Born in India, Rudyard Kipling (1865–1936) was an English novelist, short-story writer, and poet. Poems such as 'The White Man's Burden', 'If', and 'Gunga Din' came to be regarded as epitomizing British colonial and imperialistic attitudes. His other works include stories such as *The Jungle Book* (1894) and the *Just So Stories* (1902) and novels such as *Kim* (1901). Kipling received the Nobel Prize for literature in 1907. *See also* ELEPHANT'S CHILD, GUNGA DIN.

> The trumpets had sounded a fanfare and the thousand had sung the four verses of Everard's rather Kiplingesque 'Song of the Freemen'.
> ALDOUS HUXLEY *Point Counter Point* 1928

> Rather the Kipling type, you know. Very keen on his work. Hearty. Empire-builder and all that sort of thing.
> SOMERSET MAUGHAM *The World Over* 1952

Lord Kitchener The face of the first Earl Kitchener of Khartoum (1850–1916), known as Lord Kitchener, is well known from a famous recruiting poster during the First World War that carried his large-moustached face and pointing finger above the slogan 'Your country needs you!' This iconic image, or more specifically Kitchener's extravagant moustache, are often alluded to.

> They stood next to each other, like pieces opposing each other on a chess board, oblivious of the interest of the ageing porter with the Lord Kitchener moustache.
> PETER CAREY *Illywhacker* 1985

Klimt Gustav Klimt (1862–1918) was an Austrian painter and designer, the greatest of Art Nouveau painters. He achieved a jewelled effect in his work similar to mosaics, combining stylized human forms with decorative and ornate clothing or backgrounds in elaborate patterns, often using gold leaf. One of his most famous paintings is *The Kiss* (1909).

> She was pale, and looked tired and distracted. I noticed for the first time how she had aged. The woman I knew fifteen years ago was still there, but fixed inside a coarser outline, like one of Klimt's gem-encrusted lovers.
> JOHN BANVILLE *The Book of Evidence* 1989

John Knox John Knox (*c.*1505–1572) was a Scottish Protestant reformer, the founder of the Presbyterian Church of Scotland. Like those of other famous Protestant figures, his name is sometimes used in the context of stern moral uprightness or puritanical disapproval.

> The handsome sergeant's features were during this speech as rigid and stern as John Knox's in addressing his gay young queen.
> THOMAS HARDY *Far from the Madding Crowd* 1874

> 'Camille has been famous for a whole year now,' she said dejectedly, 'and we're no nearer getting married. I thought it would be neat if I got pregnant, it would hurry things up. But—there you are—can't get him into bed. You've no idea what Camille's like when he's got one of his fits of rectitude. John Knox was merely a beginner.'
> HILARY MANTEL *A Place of Greater Safety* 1992

> Hell and damnation: he knew about the very unofficial tapes. And Teddy with a puritan conscience that made Messrs Knox and Calvin look flexible, even soft. Not the moment to be precipitate myself. Not the occasion for the full and frank admission.
> RAYMOND FLYNN *Busy Body* 1998

Kojak Kojak was the bald-headed police detective played by Telly Savalas in the American television series *Kojak* (1973–7). His catchphrase was 'Who loves ya, baby?'

> Many of the sallies were aimed at his lack of hair. He was called Kojak at first, but this was a gross slander; Farmer's hair receded at the temples and was less than luxuriant on the crown, that was all.
> MAX MARQUIS *Written in Blood* 1995

Kong *See* KING KONG.

Kon-Tiki The *Kon-Tiki* is the name of the raft made of balsa logs in which, in 1947, the Norwegian anthropologist Thor Heyerdahl sailed from Peru to the islands of Polynesia in order to prove that ancient people could have migrated in this way. The *Kon-Tiki* expedition is alluded to in the context of a long, difficult journey.

Krakatoa Krakatoa is a small volcanic island in Indonesia. An eruption in 1883 destroyed most of the island.

> He took the lectern to a Krakatoa of applause.
> MARTIN AMIS *The Information* 1995

Kraken The Kraken was an enormous mythical sea-monster said to appear off the coast of Norway and attack ships. It looked like a gigantic squid and, according to the earliest stories dating from the 12th century, was the size of an island. A poem by Tennyson (1830) describes the Kraken waking from 'his ancient, dreamless, uninvaded sleep' and a science fiction novel by John Wyndham has the title *The Kraken Wakes* (1953).

> The last night. Tomorrow she need not lie in darkness, confined with the hobgoblins of night. Tonight, her mind was stirring, like the Kraken, dislodging from fathomless trenches the ugliness she had buried there.
> ALINE TEMPLETON *Last Act of All* 1995

> What I am talking about are those lapses that first begin to awaken the Kraken of irritation in the reader's mind. *The Observer* 2001

Freddy Krueger Freddy Krueger is the scarred killer with knives for fingernails who brutally murders teenagers in their dreams in the horror film *Nightmare on Elm Street* (1984) and its sequels. *See also* NIGHTMARE ON ELM STREET.

> How lucky fate wasn't running a dating agency, I thought bitterly. It would probably pair up Mother Theresa with Freddie Kruger.
> LIZ EVANS *Who Killed Marilyn Monroe?* 1997

Kryptonite Kryptonite is a fictional green rock, the alien mineral that can weaken the powers of the US comic-book superhero Superman and ultimately kill him if he were to be exposed to it for long enough. Individual pieces of kryptonite are fragments of Superman's home planet, Krypton. *See also* SUPERMAN.

> Rick was not to be borne. To hear him tell it, he was the only one capable, trained, qualified, and spiritually prepared to make a major drug bust. Leaving him behind was tantamount to shackling Superman with kryptonite just as the busload of schoolchildren plummeted off the cliff.
> NEVADA BARR *Endangered Species* 1997

> 'It's easy for you,' he said. 'You're not married, you don't have kids.' 'Nope,' she

said. 'Tried that. Failed before making it to the kid part. Now it's too late. Kids would be like kryptonite to my career.'

RICHARD DOOLEY *Brainstorm* 1998

Kublai Khan Kublai Khan (1214–94) was a Mongol emperor of China and founder of the Yuan dynasty. The grandson of Genghis Khan, by 1259 he had completed his family's conquest of China and established his capital on the site of the modern Beijing. He had his residence, described in Coleridge's poem 'Kubla Khan' (1816) as 'a stately pleasure-dome', in Xanadu, an ancient city in south-east Mongolia. *See also* XANADU.

'Turn off and drive round the ring road,' he said suddenly to Abigail as the Kubla Khan glass domes of the new shopping centre at the top of the town came into view.

MARJORIE ECCLES *A Species of Revenge* 1996

I told myself I was curious for a peek at King's estate, rumoured to rival Kublai Khan's.

JUSTIN SCOTT *Frostline* 1997

k

Labyrinth In Greek legend, the Labyrinth was a huge maze constructed by Daedalus at Knossos (also Cnossos or Cnossus) in Crete for King Minos. It was designed as a home for the Minotaur, a creature with a man's body and a bull's head. The Labyrinth was such a complex network of passages and chambers that it was thought no one could escape from it. The term can be applied to any intricate or complicated arrangement. *See also* ARIADNE, MINOS, MINOTAUR, THESEUS.

> Such an elaborately developed, perplexing, exciting dream was certainly never dreamed by a girl in Eustacia's situation before. It had as many ramifications as the Cretan labyrinth, as many fluctuations as the Northern Lights, as much colour as a parterre in June, and was as crowded with figures as a coronation.
> THOMAS HARDY *The Return of the Native* 1880

> The pattern of His veins!—more intricate than the Maze at Cnossos.
> NATHANAEL WEST *The Dream Life of Balso Snell* 1931

> She remembered the sadness she had earlier noticed in his eyes. He was a man who had known both good and evil. She was sure of it now. His mind was a dark labyrinth, intricate and convoluted, with a Minotaur of some kind crouching at the core. There was something frightening as well as fascinating about him.
> JOHN SPENCER HILL *The Last Castrato* 1995

Lady in Red The mysterious Lady in Red was the mistress of the bank robber and murderer John Dillinger (named the FBI's 'public enemy number one' in 1933). She betrayed Dillinger's whereabouts to the FBI, whose agents shot him dead in Chicago in 1934, and is alluded to as an archetypal betrayer.

> 'But what about the money?' she asked. China hooted. 'She's makin' like she's the Lady in Red that told on Dillinger. Dillinger wouldn't have come near you lessen he was going hunting in Africa and shoot you for a hippo.'
> TONI MORRISON *The Bluest Eye* 1970

Lady of the Lake In Arthurian legend, the Lady of the Lake was the sorceress who gave the sword Excalibur to Arthur and regained it when he died. She stole the infant Lancelot from his parents, raised him in her lake, and presented him to King Arthur when he had grown to manhood. In many versions of the legend, she is identified with Nimue (or Vivien), the mistress of Merlin. *See also* KING ARTHUR, LANCELOT, NIMUE.

Laelaps In Greek mythology, Laelaps was a hound so swift it always caught its quarry.

Lais Lais was a celebrated Greek courtesan, a Sicilian, carried to Corinth at the time of the Athenian expedition to Sicily. Popular with philosophers like Demosthenes, Xenocrates, and Diogenes, she was killed by the townswomen, who were jealous of her beauty.

Veronica Lake Veronica Lake (1919–73) was a petite US film actress who often played slinky femmes fatales in 1940s thrillers. She had a distinctive peek-a-boo hairstyle, her long blonde hair draped over one eye, a style much imitated by filmgoers of the time.

> I noticed that, when he remembered to, he clipped his words; he's learned that from Ronald Colman, I thought, and felt a little less impressed—it puts him on the same level as the millhand with the Alan Ladd deadpan and the millgirl with the Veronica Lake hair style.
> JOHN BRAINE *Room at the Top* 1957

Lamb of God The lamb is a biblical symbol of innocence and meekness, and the Lamb of God is a name sometimes given to Jesus, famously in the quotation from the Bible: 'The next day John seeth Jesus coming unto him, and saith, Behold the Lamb of God, which taketh away the sin of the world' (John 1: 29). The Lamb of God is the epitome of innocence and goodness.

> 'Why, I wonder, is he so suspicious of poor Guy?' 'Him!' Inchcape snorted in amused contempt. 'He'd be suspicious of the Lamb of God.'
> OLIVIA MANNING *The Spoilt City* 1962

Lancelot According to Arthurian legend, Lancelot, or Launcelot, was the most famous of King Arthur's knights of the Round Table. Unfortunately, he fell in love with Guinevere, Arthur's wife. When Arthur was informed about their affair, the lovers fled to Lancelot's castle. Arthur laid siege to the castle and Guinevere returned to him while Lancelot went back to Brittany. He returned to fight alongside Arthur in his battle with Mordred but was too late to save the king and, finding that Guinevere had taken the veil, became a priest. As well as being mentioned in the context of his love affair, his name has become a byword for chivalrous heroism, especially as a rescuer of fair damsels in distress. *See also* KING ARTHUR, GUINEVERE.

> Marutha's hero was a Circassian warrior, a sort of Eastern Sir Lancelot, and every home she subsequently made with Moshe retained an Oriental flavour.
> T. PALMER *Menuhin* 1991

> 'You must have fainted. You slid forward off the lounger and nearly fell in the pool. *He*,' Kat made up by emphasis for not knowing his name, 'came along

just at the right moment and got you out. Sir Lancelot'.
STAYNES AND STOREY *Dead Serious* 1995

land of milk and honey In the Bible, God promised Moses to deliver the Israelites from slavery in Egypt to a land of plenty: 'And I am come down to deliver them out of the hand of the Egyptians, and to bring them up out of that land unto a good land and a large, unto a land flowing with milk and honey' (Exod. 3: 8). The term is now applied to any imagined land of plenty and happiness.

Land of Nod In the Bible, the Land of Nod was the land east of Eden to which Cain was banished after he had slain his brother Abel (Gen. 4: 16). Although 'Nod' probably meant 'Wandering', the phrase, inviting a pun on 'nod', 'to fall asleep', has now come to refer to a mythical land of sleep.

At last I slid off into a light doze, and had pretty nearly made a good offing towards the land of Nod, when I heard a heavy footfall in the passage, and saw a glimmer of light come into the room from under the door.
HERMAN MELVILLE *Moby Dick* 1851

Land of Promise *See* PROMISED LAND.

Laocoön In Greek mythology, Laocoön was a Trojan priest who warned the Trojans not to let the Wooden Horse into Troy: 'Do not trust the horse, Trojans. Whatever it is, I fear the Greeks even when they bring gifts.' As a punishment from the gods for this attempted intervention, he and both his sons were crushed to death by two enormous sea-serpents. A classical marble sculpture (*c.*50 BC) of the death-struggle of Laocoön and his sons, with the serpents coiled around their limbs, was rediscovered in the Renaissance and is now in the Vatican Museum. It is, in fact, this sculpture rather than the story that is often alluded to. *See also* GREEKS BEARING GIFTS, TROJAN HORSE.

If he had been a woman he must have screamed under the nervous tension which he was now undergoing. But that relief being denied to his virility, he clenched his teeth in misery, bringing lines about his mouth like those in the Laocoön, and corrugations between his brows.
THOMAS HARDY *Jude the Obscure* 1895

'And seeing it's you, I'll give you a hint: the way the string's tied, you can get loose at once if he lies down flat and you crawl right up over his head; then the string drops off without untying the knots. Bye now.' And she was off to encourage other strugglers, who lay in Laocoon groups about the floor.
ROBERTSON DAVIES *Leaven of Malice* 1954

Laodicean The Laodiceans in the Bible were a group of Christians who were indifferent to religion, being 'lukewarm, and neither cold nor hot' (Rev. 3: 16). A Laodicean is thus someone who is or seems indifferent, showing no strong feeling.

He felt himself to occupy morally that vast middle space of Laodicean neutrality which lay between the Communion people of the parish and the drunken section.

THOMAS HARDY *Far from the Madding Crowd* 1874

Laon and Cythna Laon and Cythna are a brother and sister in Shelley's epic poem *The Revolt of Islam* (1818). The pair attempt to organize a revolution along the lines of Shelley's idea of the French Revolution, and consummate their success sexually. However, their success is short-lived.

'Their supreme desire is to be together—to share each other's emotions, and fancies, and dreams.' 'Platonic!' 'Well no. Shelleyan would be nearer to it. They remind me of—what are their names—Laon and Cythna. Also of Paul and Virginia a little . . .'

THOMAS HARDY *Jude the Obscure* 1896

Laura Laura is the Italian Renaissance poet Petrarch's name for the woman in praise of whom his sonnet sequence is written. Her identity is not known. *See also* PETRARCH AND LAURA.

. . . you were always my Beatrice. My Laura. I thought, who wants second best?

LOUIS DE BERNIÈRES *Captain Corelli's Mandolin* 1994

Laurel and Hardy Arthur Stanley Jefferson (1890–1965), known as Stan Laurel, and Norvell Hardy Junior (1892–1957), known as Oliver Hardy, became one of the most famous comic film duos of all time. The thin Stan, often looking confused, scratching his head, and bursting into tears, and the fat, blustering, bossy Ollie appeared in many films together from the 1920s until the 1940s, and their simple slapstick humour and disaster-prone adventures have enjoyed enduring popularity.

Lautrec *See* TOULOUSE-LAUTREC.

St Lawrence St Lawrence (d. 258) was a Roman martyr and deacon of Rome. According to tradition, Lawrence was ordered by the prefect of Rome to hand over the Church's treasure, in response to which he assembled the poor people of the city and presented them to the prefect. For this he was put to death by being roasted on a gridiron.

It is very easy to talk of repentance, but a man has to walk over hot ploughshares before he can complete it; to be skinned alive as was St Bartholomew; to be stuck full of arrows as was St Sebastian; to lie broiling on a gridiron like St Lorenzo!

ANTHONY TROLLOPE *Barchester Towers* 1857

Lawrence of Arabia T. E. Lawrence (1888–1935), known as Lawrence of Arabia, was a British soldier and writer who, from 1916 onwards, helped to organize and lead the Arab revolt against Turkey. His book *The Seven Pillars of Wisdom* (1926) was an account of the events of this period. He is sometimes alluded to as a brave, romantic adventurer.

My Texan got back into the coach again, stowing his photographic equipment away, having preserved for posterity some *mafioso* on camel-back who brandished a Lawrence of Arabia rifle in one hand and a string of plastic lapis lazuli beads in the other.

PENELOPE LIVELY *Moon Tiger* 1988

Lazarus

poor man In the Bible, Lazarus was the name of the ailing beggar who sat at the gate of the rich man (traditionally named Dives) in the parable of the rich man and Lazarus (Luke 16: 19–31). Lazarus was covered with sores and begged for crumbs from the rich man's table. He was rewarded for his misfortunes in life by being taken to Heaven by Abraham after death.

Others toil and moil all their lives long—and the very dogs are pitiful in our days, as they were in the days of Lazarus.

ELIZABETH GASKELL *North and South* 1854–5

The earl living down at Guetwick did not understand that the Income-tax Office in the City, and the General Committee Office at Whitehall, were as far apart as Dives and Lazarus, and separated by as impassable a gulf.

ANTHONY TROLLOPE *The Small House at Allington* 1862

man raised from the dead Lazarus, the brother of Mary and Martha, was a friend of Jesus who was raised from the dead by Jesus in a miracle described in the New Testament. Lazarus had already been dead for four days when Jesus arrived at the tomb: 'He cried with a loud voice, Lazarus, come forth. And he that was dead came forth, bound hand and foot with graveclothes: and his face was bound about with a napkin' (John 11: 43–4). Lazarus is alluded to in the context of a literal or metaphorical resurrection. *See also* MARTHA.

If her absence was a cause of well exercised tongues, then her Lazarus-like resurrection must have created much oral fatigue.

MIKE NICOL *The Powers That Be* 1989

He placed himself protectively by his mother. He was a lanky lad, as tall as she was, with bright blue eyes and a crest of reddish hair. Otherwise they were not alike, and he prided himself on taking after his dead father. If he was dead, he cherished the idea that what Alfreda had told him of the death in an accident was a lie, and that Dad would turn up, rich and famous. He had to be both or need not bother acting Lazarus.

GWENDOLINE BUTLER *A Dark Coffin* 1995

King Lear Lear, a legendary early king of Britain, is the central figure in Shakespeare's tragedy *King Lear* (1623). In the play, the foolish and petulant old king divides his kingdom between his two older daughters, Goneril and Regan, but is subsequently driven mad by his outrage at the grudging hospitality and ill treatment he feels he receives at their hands. His 'mad scenes' take place on a heath in a violent storm. Before his wits leave him, Lear speaks of his fear of becoming deranged:

'O let me not be mad, not mad, sweet heaven!
Keep me in temper; I would not be mad!'

It was, Ralph thought in a remote and detached way, better to labour for a sane king than mad Lear.
THOMAS KENEALLY *The Playmaker* 1987

We are all scared of it, be honest. Madness. Don't tell me, as you flick through these pages in that rather airy way of yours, that you have never considered the dark, almost subliminal fear that you might awake one morning as barking as Lear, for I know better. *The Guardian* 1997

Hannibal Lecter Hannibal Lecter is the brilliant psychiatrist turned psychopathic serial killer in *The Silence of the Lambs* (1988) and other books by Thomas Harris, later made into films. Dr Lecter eats his victims after killing them, hence his nickname Hannibal the Cannibal. He has maroon eyes and six fingers on his left hand. In *The Silence of the Lambs*, Clarice Starling, a young female trainee FBI agent, interviews Lecter in his high-security cell in a hospital for the criminally insane.

'I was just saying, aren't you just longing to be pregnant too?' 'Christ, no!' It came out more explosively than Cassie had intended. Despite the occasional weakness, at the moment the idea had all the charm of an invitation to share a cell with Hannibal Lecter.
SUSAN MOODY *King of Hearts* 1995

Christopher Lee The prolific English actor Christopher Lee (b. 1922) is chiefly associated with the roles he played in horror films made by the British film company Hammer, most notably *Dracula* (1958). More recently, he has also played the wizard Saruman in the *Lord of the Rings* films. Lee has a commanding physical presence and a rich deep voice.

'And the lemon sponge,' Atherton's voice descended to a tomb of horror, 'was made with synthetic flavouring.' 'Dear God! Hollis responded like a poor man's Christopher Lee. 'I can't believe it!'
CYNTHIA HARROD-EAGLES *Shallow Grave* 1998

Simon Legree Simon Legree is the cruel cotton plantation owner in Harriet Beecher Stowe's *Uncle Tom's Cabin* (1851–2) to whom Tom is sold and who beats Tom to death. *See also* UNCLE TOM.

I don't mind him. He's a pretty good sort of old stiff. It's his sister Beulah. She was the one who put him up to it. She's the heavy in the sequence. As tough as they come. Ever hear of Simon Legree?
P G. WODEHOUSE *Laughing Gas* 1936

Leonardo Leonardo da Vinci (1452–1519) was an Italian painter, sculptor, scientist, and engineer, generally celebrated as the supreme example of the

Renaissance genius. He painted two versions of *The Virgin of the Rocks*, one (1483–5) now in the Louvre, Paris, and the other (*c.*1508) now in the National Gallery, London. Both depict the Virgin Mary with the infant St John adoring the infant Christ, grouped in front of a background of strange rocks. The subject of the *Mona Lisa* (1504–5) is also positioned above a landscape of rocks and a winding stream. These paintings demonstrate Leonardo's careful use of *sfumato*, the technique of achieving a transition from light to shadow by gradually shading one into the other. *See also* MONA LISA.

> She reminded him of a Leonardo more than ever; her sunburnt features were shadowed by fantastic rocks; at his words she had turned and stood between him and the light with immeasurable plains behind her.
> E. M. FORSTER *A Room with a View* 1908

Leontes Leontes is the king of Sicily in Shakespeare's play *The Winter's Tale* (1623). Leontes mistakenly believes that his wife, Hermione, has been unfaithful to him with his childhood friend, Polixenes. In his jealousy he attempts unsuccessfully to have Polixenes poisoned, throws Hermione into prison, and orders that his own baby daughter Perdita be left on a desert shore to die. *See also* SHAKESPEARE.

Leporello In Mozart's opera *Don Giovanni* (1787), Leporello is the servant of Don Giovanni, the legendary Spanish seducer of women. In a famous scene, Leporello recites the catalogue he has compiled of his master's sexual conquests, categorized by nationality and type. *See also* DON JUAN.

> I'll spare you a catalogue of his conquests—we should be here all night. I do think it's rather hard, seeing that I'm the master and he's the servant, that I should have to play Leporello to his Don Giovanni.
> KATE ROSS *A Broken Vessel* 1994

Lesbos Lesbos is a Greek island in the eastern Aegean. Its artistic golden age of the late 7th and early 6th centuries BC produced the poet Sappho, whose love poems express her passionate friendships with women. This explains the association of the island with female homosexuality and the derivation of the words 'lesbian' and 'Sapphic'. *See also* SAPPHO.

> Most of the men I know are defective. Most of them are vain. My good friend and mentor Peggy O'Reggis lives in a universe in which men are only marginally visible. Ditto my lawyer, Virginia Goodchild, a committed citizen of Lesbos.
> CAROL SHIELDS *Mary Swann* 1990

Lethe In Greek mythology, Lethe was one of the rivers of the underworld Hades, whose water caused those who drank it to lose all memory of their past life on earth. Lethe thus represents oblivion or forgetfulness and, occasionally, death. *See also* HADES.

Minds that have been unhinged from their old faith and love, have perhaps sought this Lethean influence of exile, in which the past becomes dreamy because its symbols have all vanished, and the present too is dreamy because it is linked with no memories.
GEORGE ELIOT *Silas Marner* 1861

Abused river! You bear upon your face wares as deadly and soporiferous as the very waters of Styx or Lethe.
TIMOTHY MO *An Insular Possession* 1986

In his seven-year voyage on the waters of Lethe (the north island of New Zealand actually), Gordon forgot all about Eliza (not to mention us) and came back with a different wife altogether.
KATE ATKINSON *Human Croquet* 1997

Leviathan A number of passages in the Bible (e.g. Job 41; Ps. 74: 14) allude to God's victory over a sea-monster called Leviathan, identified by biblical scholars as a whale or crocodile. Hobbes's title *Leviathan* refers to sovereign power in his treatise on political philosophy, published in 1651. The word can be used to describe anything immense or powerful, but especially a whale.

Listening . . . from the upper rooms of the empty house only gigantic chaos streaked with lightning could have been heard tumbling and tossing, as the winds and waves disported themselves like the amorphous bulks of leviathans whose brows are pierced by no light of reason, and mounted one on top of another, and lunged and plunged in the darkness or the daylight.
VIRGINIA WOOLF *To the Lighthouse* 1927

Captain Anderson had left the quarterdeck to Summers, who still stared forward with a tense face as if he expected the appearance of the enemy or Leviathan or the sea serpent.
WILLIAM GOLDING *Rites of Passage* 1980

Now South America, as we have seen, was isolated during the period in which horses and cattle were evolving in other parts of the world. But South America has its own great grasslands, and it evolved its own separate groups of large herbivores to exploit the resource. There were massive rhino-like Leviathans that had no connection with true rhinos.
RICHARD DAWKINS *The Blind Watchmaker* 1986

Liar *See* BILLY LIAR.

Lilliputian In book 1 of Jonathan Swift's *Gulliver's Travels* (1726), Gulliver finds himself shipwrecked on the island of Lilliput. The tiny Lilliputians are only 6 inches tall and, as Gulliver discovers, are as small-minded as they are small-bodied, being petty, pretentious, and factious. *See also* GULLIVER.

The children fill the house with the Lilliputian din of drums, trumpets, and penny-whistles.
WASHINGTON IRVING *The Sketch-Book* 1819–20

A Lilliputian chest-of-drawers no doubt containing sea-shells and locks of children's hair.
KINGSLEY AMIS *Lucky Jim* 1953

The engines were laid out sort of like a giant car engine, with every piece exposed so it could be cared for quickly. If you were a Lilliputian you would climb up and down a car engine just this way.
SARA PARETSKY *Deadlock* 1984

Abraham Lincoln Abraham Lincoln (1809–65) was an American Republican statesman and the sixteenth president of the United States from 1861 to 1865. He is sometimes referred to as Honest Abe or the Great Emancipator on account of his involvement in the abolition of slavery. He was noted for oratory and his eloquent speeches, including his speech of 1863 during the American Civil War at the dedication of the cemetery of those killed in the battle of Gettysburg, known as the Gettysburg Address. As well as his oratory and political achievements, Lincoln is also remembered for his physical appearance. He was a tall man, standing over 6 feet, and had a gaunt face with sunken, wrinkled cheeks.

What a technique that guy had. What he'd do was, he'd start snowing his date in this very quiet, *sincere* voice—like as if he wasn't only a very handsome guy but a nice, *sincere* guy, too. I damn near puked, listening to him. His date kept saying, 'No—*please*. Please, don't. *Please*'. But old Stradlater kept snowing on her in this Abraham Lincoln, sincere voice, and finally there'd be this terrific silence in the back of the car.
J. D. SALINGER *The Catcher in the Rye* 1951

I looked at him, at the long, bony, almost Lincolnesque face.
RALPH ELLISON *Invisible Man* 1952

Inside was the church pew, as straight and spare as Abe Lincoln lying down.
ALICE WALKER *Advancing Luna—and Ida B. Wells* 1980

Linus blanket Linus is a character in the *Peanuts* cartoon strip, created in 1950 by Charles M. Schulz. The cartoons feature a group of children, including Charlie Brown with his dog, Snoopy. Linus is always shown carrying a piece of old blanket as a comforter, and the term 'Linus blanket' has come to represent anything that provides reassurance and a feeling of security.

Roy went to the closet for a jacket. He gave it to his brother who laid his bible down and put on the coat, then picked up the bible again. It was his Linus blanket, I figured. He never went anywhere without it.
TED WOOD *A Clean Kill* 1995

lions' den *See* DANIEL.

Little Bighorn The battle of Little Bighorn, also referred to as Custer's last stand, was a defeat for George Custer and his troops at the hands of Sioux warriors. The battle took place in the valley of the Little Bighorn river in what is now Montana.

Little Engine that Could *The Little Engine that Could* is the title of a children's picture-book by Watty Piper (1945), illustrated by Lois Lenski. It tells the story of a small railway engine that pants encouragingly as it struggles up a slope: 'I think I can—I think I can—I think I can.'

> The plane rolled away from the terminal and taxied out onto the runway. There was a pause, and then the plane began to surge forward, picking up speed with much earnest intent. We rumbled and bumbled like the little engine that could. The plane lifted off into the night sky, the lighted buildings below becoming rapidly smaller until only a hapless grid of lights remained.
> SUE GRAFTON *L Is for Lawless* 1995

Little Match Girl The Little Match Girl is the character in a story of the same name by Hans Christian Andersen (1848). She is so poor that she tries to warm herself by lighting the matches that she was intending to sell. Her body is found the next morning, frozen to death in the snow.

> I tripped through the sleet like the little match girl. *The Observer* 1996

Little Nell Nell Trent, known as Little Nell, is the child heroine of Charles Dickens's novel *The Old Curiosity Shop* (1841). Exhausted by her attempts to protect her grandfather from the clutches of the evil moneylender Daniel Quilp, she eventually dies. Her prolonged deathbed scenes, full of pathos, epitomized Victorian sentimentality for later readers but were immensely popular at the time. The novel was originally serialized in instalments and the story goes that crowds of American readers would rush to the New York docks for news of the heroine's fate from ships arriving from England, asking 'Is Little Nell dead?' *See also* DICKENSIAN.

> The ideal has many names and beauty is but one of them. I wonder if . . . their passion for beauty, the Little Nell of this shamefaced day, is anything more than sentimentality.
> SOMERSET MAUGHAM *Cakes and Ale* 1930

Little Orphan Annie *See* ORPHAN ANNIE.

Little Red Riding Hood *See* RED RIDING HOOD.

Dr Livingstone David Livingstone (1813–73) was a Scottish missionary and explorer, who began his missionary career in Bechuanaland in 1841. On extensive travels, he discovered the Zambezi river in 1851 and the Victoria Falls in 1855. In 1866 he went in search of the source of the Nile, and was found in poor health by Henry Morton Stanley in 1871. Stanley is said to have greeted him with the famous words 'Dr Livingstone, I presume?' *See also* STANLEY.

My exchanges with Marcus, which had been as urgent and much more expansive than those of Dr Livingstone and Stanley, grew more desultory.
L. P HARTLEY *The Go-Between* 1953

Lochinvar Lochinvar, the hero of Sir Walter Scott's ballad *Marmion* (1808), is a young Highlander who goes to the wedding of the woman he loves, abducts her, and rides away with her. Young Lochinvar is the archetypal romantic hero:
'So faithful in love, and so dauntless in war,
There never was knight like the young Lochinvar'.
See also WALTER SCOTT.

He had been quite shocked to learn that at the present point in time she was the only resident of the place, except for Tom away down at the stables and too far away to hear any cries for help—although Tom could get there fairly rapidly if summoned by phone. On the other hand, given Tom's reputation as the local rural Don Juan, perhaps the idea of Tom galloping up to Rose Cottage on a foaming steed looking like young Lochinvar was not exactly the sort of protection he, Markby, fancied for her.
ANN GRANGER *A Season for Murder* 1991

Lohengrin According to medieval Germanic legend, Lohengrin was the son of Perceval (Parsifal) and a knight of the Holy Grail. He was summoned from the temple of the Holy Grail and taken in a swan-drawn boat to Antwerp, where he rescued Elsa, the princess of Brabant, from a forced marriage. He consented to marry her himself, on condition that she did not ask who he was, because as a knight of the Grail he was obliged not to disclose his identity. Elsa broke this condition on their wedding night and Lohengrin was carried away in the swan-boat back to the Grail castle. The story of Lohengrin, sometimes called the Swan Knight, is the subject of an opera by Wagner (1850). *See also* WAGNER.

'*Wedded*' he shouted again, seizing the towel with a magnificent operatic gesture, and went on singing while he rubbed as though he had been Lohengrin tipped out by an unwary Swan and drying himself in the greatest haste before the tiresome Elsa came along.
KATHERINE MANSFIELD *Mr Reginald Peacock's Day* 1920–4

Loki In Scandinavian mythology, Loki was the god of mischief and discord. He was instrumental in the death of Balder. Loki discovered that mistletoe was the only substance that had not been asked by Balder's mother, Frigga, to swear that it would not harm her son and so was the only thing to which Balder was vulnerable. Loki shaped a dart from the wood and tricked the blind god Hod into throwing it at Balder, who immediately fell dead to the ground. For this Loki was punished by the gods by being bound to a rock.

On one flank Singer is a trickster, a prankster, a Loki, a Puck.
CYNTHIA OZICK *Art & Ardour* 1984

Lolita Vladimir Nabokov's novel *Lolita* (1958) concerns the obsession of the middle-aged Humbert Humbert with his 12-year-old stepdaughter Lolita, whom Humbert describes as a 'nymphet'. The word Lolita can be used to describe any sexually precocious young girl.

> My present wife. I didn't 'seduce' her, she didn't do a Lolita act on me. We met (out of school as it happens), and bang, that was that.
> JULIAN BARNES *Talking It Over* 1991

> One thing's for sure, if anyone would have been immune to the charms of a Liverpudlian Lolita, Benny's the man. Now if you'd been talking about a pretty schoolboy, things would have been different.
> MARTIN EDWARDS *Yesterday's Papers* 1994

Willy Loman Willy Loman is the main character in Arthur Miller's play *Death of a Salesman* (1949), a travelling salesman for a lingerie company. He comes to realize that his life has been a complete failure, and finally commits suicide in order to help his son get a new start in life with the insurance money.

Lone Ranger The Lone Ranger is a masked law-enforcer in the American West, created in 1933 by George W. Trendle and Fran Striker for a radio series and popularized in a later television series (1956–62). His true identity remains concealed and he is known only as the 'masked man' or 'masked rider'. In the stories he is sometimes accompanied by an American Indian called Tonto. The Lone Ranger's name, though, is generally applied to an individual who acts alone in undertaking a rescue mission of some kind. *See also* TONTO.

> 'I don't think of myself as an opera director,' insists Jonathan Miller, 'I can't read music and I don't even go to the opera very much.' But for 25 years Dr Miller has been the Lone Ranger of the international opera world, the outsider whose productions strip away the cliches and hammy performances imposed by tradition. *Daily Telegraph* 1997

Long John Silver Long John Silver is the one-legged ship's cook who is the leader of the mutinous pirates among the crew of the *Hispaniola* in R. L. Stevenson's *Treasure Island* (1883). *See also* BEN GUNN.

> But I do play a bit of tennis still, wearing a kind of brace on the knee which keeps it more or less rigid. I have to sort of drag the right leg like Long John Silver when I hop around the court, but it's better than nothing.
> DAVID LODGE *Therapy* 1995

Pippi Longstocking Pippi Longstocking is the main character in a series of children's books (1945–59) by the Swedish writer Astrid Lindgren. She is a 9-year-old girl with red hair, long mismatched stockings, and superhuman strength. Pippi lives alone in an old house, with a monkey and a horse but entirely unsupervised by adults.

> It was just a tad annoying to a grownup like me to be friends with people who could sleep until the afternoon and get away with it, especially at a time when I had been working very hard to get and stay in touch with my inner grownup. Nigh thirty, and Tamayo still lives like Pippi Longstocking.
> SPARKLE HAYTER *Revenge of the Cootie Girls* 1997

Lorelei In Germanic folklore, Lorelei is the name of a rock at the edge of the Rhine, held to be the home of a siren with long blonde hair whose song lures boatmen to destruction. The name can also be applied to the siren herself. A Lorelei is a dangerously fascinating woman, a siren.

> My parents lived deep in the burg in a narrow duplex that on a cold day like this would smell like chocolate pudding cooking on the stove. The effect was similar to Lorelei, singing to all those sailors, sucking them in so they'd crash on the rocks.
> JANET EVANOVICH *Three to Get Deadly* 1997

Lothario Lothario is a character from Nicholas Rowe's play *The Fair Penitent* (1703), 'that haughty, gallant, gay Lothario'. As with those of Casanova and Don Juan, his name is now a byword for libertinism.

> And yet Eleanor understood him as thoroughly as though he had declared his passion with all the elegant fluency of a practised Lothario.
> ANTHONY TROLLOPE *Barchester Towers* 1857

> But what of the men they choose to live out their fantasies with? All too often men who work in tourist resorts are condemned as lecherous Lotharios interested only in sex. *The Independent* 1997

> The difference is, when you see somebody here going from hotel room to hotel room at 3 am, they're not Lotharios out for a couple of shags—they're doing business deals. *The Observer* 1997

Lot The book of Genesis (19: 24) relates how Lot, the nephew of Abraham and an inhabitant of the town of Sodom, was seen by God to be a righteous man. He was allowed to escape from the town before God destroyed it by fire and brimstone in order to punish the depravity and wickedness of its inhabitants.

> We thought a bolt had fallen in the middle of us, and Joseph swung onto his knees, beseeching the Lord to remember the Patriarchs Noah and Lot; and, as in former times, spare the righteous, though he smote the ungodly.
> EMILY BRONTË *Wuthering Heights* 1847

> What the deuce is the hurry? Just so must Lot have left Sodom, when he expected fire to pour down upon it out of burning brass clouds.
> CHARLOTTE BRONTË *The Professor* 1857

Lot's wife According to the book of Genesis (19: 24), God destroyed the towns of Sodom and Gomorrah by fire and brimstone as a punishment for the depravity and wickedness of their inhabitants. Lot, the nephew of Abraham, was allowed to escape from the destruction of Sodom with his family. His wife disobeyed God's order not to look back at the burning city and she was turned into a pillar of salt.

> Don't ever look back, kid. . . . You turn into some old cow's salt lick.
> WILLIAM BURROUGHS *The Naked Lunch* 1959

> Pokler, billeted at a fisherman's cottage, came in from his evening walks behind a fine mask of salt. Lot's wife. What disaster had he dared to look back on?
> THOMAS PYNCHON *Gravity's Rainbow* 1973

> I tell you, if you look back, you will get turned, like Lot's wife, to a pillar of salt; Lot's wife, nostalgic for the past.
> FAY WELDON *Darcy's Utopia* 1990

Lotus-Eaters The Lotus-Eaters, as described in Homer's *Odyssey*, are a people who live in a far-off land and eat the fruit of the lotus. When some of Odysseus' men taste the fruit they lose their desire to return home and 'their only wish was to linger there with the Lotus-Eaters, to feed on the fruit and put aside all thought of a voyage home'. *See also* ODYSSEUS.

> Her presence brought memories of such things as Bourbon roses, rubies, and tropical midnights; her moods recalled lotus-eaters and the march in 'Athalie'; her motions, the ebb and flow of the sea; her voice, the viola.
> THOMAS HARDY *The Return of the Native* 1880

> The summons to this lotus-eating existence had come from my son, Nick . . . who had crowned his academic career by becoming Head of the Department of Social Studies in the University of Miami. He had also acquired a sizeable house with a swimming bath in the garden.
> JOHN MORTIMER *Rumpole's Return* 1980

Louis XIV Louis XIV (1638–1715), also known as the Sun King, was 5 years old when he succeeded to the throne. He appointed himself to be his own chief minister, and kept tight control over government and policy. He is said to have coined the phrase 'L'état c'est moi' ('I am the state'). His reign was a period of magnificence in terms of art and literature and represented a time of great power for the French in Europe. *See also* SUN KING.

> Dixon was not unconscious of this awed reverence which was given to her; nor did she dislike it; it flattered her much as Louis the Fourteenth was flattered by his courtiers shading their eyes from the dazzling light of his presence.
> ELIZABETH GASKELL *North and South* 1854–5

> Michael came in soaked to the skin—his taxi had broken down and he'd walked the rest of the way—but still behaving as if he was Louis XIV making a grand entrance at a court ball.
> PETER DICKINSON *The Yellow Room Conspiracy* 1995

Lovelace In Samuel Richardson's *Clarissa* (1747–8), Robert Lovelace is the dashing but unscrupulous womanizer who attempts to seduce the virtuous Clarissa.

> Mr Dagonet's notion of the case was almost as remote from reality. All he asked was that his grandson should 'thrash' somebody, and he could not be made to understand that the modern drama of divorce is sometimes cast without a Lovelace.
> EDITH WHARTON *The Custom of the Country* 1913

Lowry L. S. Lowry (1887–1976) was an English painter who spent most of his life in Salford, near Manchester. He is best known for his paintings of northern industrial townscapes peopled by small matchstick figures.

> She had perhaps been unprepared for such tedium as she had identified in the Lowry-like setting. Looking back on it—and the details were still astonishingly clear—she gave more prominence to the factory chimneys in the background.
> ANITA BROOKNER *Visitors* 1997

Lord Lucan Lord Lucan (b. 1934) was a British aristocrat who mysteriously disappeared in 1974 on the night that his wife was attacked and his children's nanny was murdered. He has never been found.

> He stood beside her car. 'You're that sure he's coming back?' she said, getting in. He extended his hand. 'Bet,' he said. 'How much?' 'Why so sure?' she pressed. 'Who wants to do a Lucan? The guy's got . . . What's her name? The girlfriend? Sarah?'
> DAVID ARMSTRONG *Thought for the Day* 1997

Lucifer Lucifer (literally 'Bearer of Light') is another name for the Devil or Satan, particularly when regarded as the leader of the angels who rebelled against God and as a punishment were hurled from Heaven down to Hell: 'How art thou fallen from heaven, O Lucifer, son of the morning! how art thou cut down to the ground, which didst weaken the nations!' (Isa. 14: 12). Lucifer is also another name for the Morning Star, the planet Venus. As well as being associated with wickedness, Lucifer is evoked in the context of excessive pride that leads to one's own destruction, as it was his pride that led him to rebel against God. His name is also closely identified with the idea of falling or failure. *See also* DEVIL, SATAN.

> I had no exultation of triumph, still less any fear of my own fate. I stood silent, the half-remorseful spectator of a fall like the fall of Lucifer.
> JOHN BUCHAN *Prester John* 1910

> But the Fontclairs are an old Norman family, and proud as Lucifer.
> KATE ROSS *Cut to the Quick* 1993

> She knows now what it was. It was Pride, deadliest of the Seven Deadlies; the sin of Lucifer, the wellspring of all the others.
> MARGARET ATWOOD *The Robber Bride* 1993

That was what had happened to Derek, too. He had been treated by the public and the press as a big name because of his part in the series, but Derek had actually been a man obsessed with failure, a star that had fallen, Lucifer-like, from a great height, after playing the major Shakespearian roles in his youth.
CHARLOTTE LAMB *In the Still of the Night* 1995

Lucretia In Roman legend, Lucretia (or Lucrece) was a woman who was raped by Sextus, a son of Tarquinus Superbus, king of Rome, and took her own life. According to tradition, this incident led to the expulsion of the Tarquins from Rome by a rebellion under Brutus, and the introduction of republican government. The story is told in Shakespeare's poem *The Rape of Lucrece* (1594). *See also* TARQUIN.

He then, though I struggled against him, kissed me and said, 'Who ever blamed Lucretia? The shame lay on the ravisher only.'
SAMUEL RICHARDSON *Pamela* 1740

Lucrezia Borgia *See* BORGIAS.

Lucullus Lucius Licinius Lucullus (*c.*110–56 BC) was a wealthy Roman general who led a luxurious life and was famed for hosting spectacularly lavish feasts.

There had been placed in the middle of each table . . . a basket woven from hardened vines in a highly rustic Appalachian Handicrafts manner. . . . Sherman stared at the plaited vines. They looked like something dropped by Gretel or little Heidi of Switzerland at a feast of Lucullus.
TOM WOLFE *The Bonfire of the Vanities* 1987

Luddites The Luddites were groups of early 19th-century English textile workers who believed that the introduction of new machinery was threatening their jobs. They responded by breaking up the machines. The name derives from a workman called Ned Ludd, nicknamed King Ludd, who is thought to have destroyed two stocking frames. Anybody who opposes change, especially in the form of new technology, can be referred to as a Luddite.

Now this is most inconvenient. It is to throw a spanner into the very works of the machine—much as the Luddites at home.
TIMOTHY MO *An Insular Possession* 1986

The whole apparatus of structuralist and post-structuralist thought is founded in fraudulence, speciousness, hopelessly ill-digested scientism, witting obfuscation and the hubris of a quasi-hieratic caste to whom compatriots meekly submit, lest they be reckoned intellectually Luddite. *The Observer* 1997

St Luke St Luke was an evangelist who is traditionally believed to be the author of the third Gospel and the Acts of the Apostles. He was a physician, thought to be the person referred to in Colossians as 'Luke, the beloved physician' (Col. 4: 14).

Lysistrata Lysistrata is the heroine of a comic play of the same name by Aristophanes, first produced in 411 BC. The play was both written and set during the Peloponnesian War between Athens and her empire and Sparta and the Peloponnesian states. Lysistrata decides that the men are not serious about negotiating for peace, so she assembles women from both sides of the conflict and persuades them to refuse to have sex with their husbands until there is peace. The play ends with Lysistrata and the women triumphant and a banquet for both sides in the Acropolis. *See also* ARISTOPHANES.

> Although she declined an offer to live in a glass coffin in a shark-filled pool, she made regular headlines by stunts such as offering sex to striking car workers whose wives had adopted Lysistrata tactics to get them back to work. *The Guardian* 1998

Macavity In T. S. Eliot's collection of poems *Old Possum's Book of Practical Cats* (1939), Macavity the Mystery Cat is the criminal mastermind, the 'fiend in feline shape', who always has an alibi and always manages to elude Scotland Yard and the Flying Squad: 'For when they reach the scene of crime—Macavity's not there!'

Macbeth In Shakespeare's play *Macbeth* (1623), Macbeth, spurred on by his wife, Lady Macbeth, kills King Duncan so that he can assume the throne in Duncan's place. After this murder, and the subsequent murder of Banquo, which Macbeth and his wife also order, they are both troubled by guilt for what they have done. Macbeth becomes distracted and suffers nightmares and visions as a result of his feelings of guilt. *See also* LADY MACBETH, SHAKESPEARE, WITCHES.

> Mrs Todd rocked gently for a time, and seemed to be lost, though not poorly, like Macbeth, in her thoughts.
> SARAH ORNE JEWETT *A Dunnet Shepherdess* 1899

Lady Macbeth In Shakespeare's play *Macbeth* (1623), Lady Macbeth, ambitious for her husband's advancement, spurs him on, despite his hesitation and reluctance, to murder King Duncan so that Macbeth will seize the throne. The first murder is followed by others and eventually Lady Macbeth loses her wits and is observed sleepwalking and rubbing her hands in an attempt to remove the spots of blood that she imagines to be on them. She finally goes mad and commits suicide. As well as being alluded to as an ambitious, cold-blooded, and scheming woman, Lady Macbeth is mentioned in the context of sleepwalking, extreme feelings of guilt, and the gesture of rubbing one's hands together. *See also* MACBETH, SHAKESPEARE, WITCHES.

> Ellen is just too ruthless for comfort. Ellen and Lady Macbeth? Nothing in it!
> FAY WELDON *Darcy's Utopia* 1990

> 'Why don't you get her to play in the shop? A personal appearance? You've never done one of those before. . . . And you'd probably sell a few of her tapes, and probably a couple of extra things besides. And you could get it put into the *Time Out* gigs list.' 'Ooer, Lady Macbeth. Calm down and listen to the music.'
> NICK HORNBY *High Fidelity* 1995

> Now he was rubbing his hands like Lady Macbeth on speed.
> PAUL JOHNSTON *Body Politic* 1996

> Maria . . . took to interviewing Mandalari's clients during his absence, gradually

becoming the Lady Macbeth of Palermo's money launderers, yet all the while protesting her ignorance of the Mafia's wider operators. *The Observer* 1997

Senator McCarthy Joseph Raymond McCarthy (1909–57) was an American Republican senator. He became chairman of the Permanent Subcommittee on Investigations in 1953 and carried out a campaign against supposed communists, which resulted in many citizens who were suspected of being members of the Communist Party being blacklisted and facing discrimination. His name is now evoked in the context of a witch-hunt, especially a political one.

Machiavelli Niccolò di Bernardo dei Machiavelli (1469–1527) was an Italian statesman and political philosopher. His best-known work is *The Prince* (1532), in which he argues that rulers may have to resort to methods that are not in themselves desirable in order to rule effectively. His name has come to represent the use of deceit and cunning in the pursuit of personal power, and the adjective 'Machiavellian' has entered the language meaning 'elaborately cunning and scheming'.

> Sidney talked for the same reason as the hunted sepia squirts ink, to conceal his movements. Behind the ink-cloud of the Ancient Indians he hoped to go jaunting up to town unobserved. Poor Sidney! He thought himself so Machiavellian. But his ink was transparent, his cunning like a child's.
> ALDOUS HUXLEY *Point Counter Point* 1928

> Beware of that Machiavel of a policeman. If he gets wind of the plot, we're lost.
> JOHN KENNEDY TOOLE *A Confederacy of Dunces* 1980

> 'Who was Iago?' Jack grinned. 'You didn't come here to ask me that.' 'You're quite right, but I'd still like to know.' 'He's a character from *Othello*. A Machiavelli who manipulated people's emotions in order to destroy them.'
> MINETTE WALTERS *The Scold's Bridle* 1994

McLuhan Marshall McLuhan (1911–80) was a Canadian writer and thinker who was particularly interested in the ways in which different communication media affect societies. He claimed that electronic forms of communication had turned the world into a 'global village'. McLuhanite openness is thus complete openness and good communication.

Mad Hatter In Lewis Carroll's *Alice's Adventures in Wonderland* (1865), Alice attends a bizarre tea party in the company of the Hatter, the March Hare, and the Dormouse. The Hatter's conversation consists mainly of non sequiturs and strange riddles like 'Why is a raven like a writing-desk?' To be 'as mad as a hatter' is to be wildly eccentric, a phrase that derives from the effects of mercury poisoning that was formerly a common disease suffered by hatters. *See also* ALICE IN WONDERLAND.

> So for a while, like two mad hatters, we hunted them by torch light, topping each other's scores.
> MAVIS NICHOLSON *Martha Jane and Me* 1992

Mad Hatter's tea party The Mad Hatter is a character in Lewis Carroll's *Alice's Adventures in Wonderland* (1865) and one of the participants at a strange tea party where the Hatter and the March Hare talk nonsense and the Dormouse falls asleep. *See also* ALICE IN WONDERLAND.

Staff meetings at Rummidge had been bad enough under Master's whimsically despotic regime. Since his departure they made the Mad Hatter's Tea Party seem like a paradigm of positive decision-making.
DAVID LODGE *Changing Places* 1975

Madonna The Madonna (literally 'My Lady') is a name for the Virgin Mary, the mother of Jesus Christ, used especially when she is represented in a painting or sculpture. The name can be applied to a woman of serene and saintly beauty, or one of perfect virtue and purity.

The expression of the countenance was in the last degree gentle, soft, timid, and feminine, and seemed rather to shrink from the most casual look of a stranger, rather than to court his admiration. Something there was of the Madonna cast, perhaps the result of delicate health, fiercer, more active, and energetic, than her own.
WALTER SCOTT *The Bride of Lammermoor* 1819

Wynonna was pretty because she was twenty-something, but Naomi was something out of a Renaissance painting, a mountain Madonna.
SHARYN MCCRUMB *The Hangman's Beautiful Daughter* 1996

As she stitches away at her sewing, outwardly calm as a marble Madonna, she is all the while exerting her passive stubborn strength against him.
MARGARET ATWOOD *Alias Grace* 1996

Maecenas Gaius Cilnius Maecenas (d. 8 BC) was a wealthy Roman statesman and patron of Virgil, Horace, and other poets.

When Mrs Felpham asked him to tea, Rampion wanted to refuse the invitation—but to refuse it without being boorish or offensive. After all, she meant well enough, poor woman. She was only rather ludicrous. The village Maecenas, in petticoats, patronizing art to the extent of two cups of tea and a slice of plum cake.
ALDOUS HUXLEY *Point Counter Point* 1928

But let's just say for the moment that Saatchi was a Maecenas to an important generation of British artists, and that even if he never buys another painting, or mounts another show, we should be grateful to him for giving us Sensation.
LYNN BARBER *The Observer* 2000

maenad In Greek mythology, maenads were female participants in the orgiastic rites of Dionysus. They were also known as Bacchae. *See also* BACCHANTE.

I do not think I shall ever forget the impression she made on me at the party at which I first saw her. She was like a maenad. She danced with an abandon that made you laugh, so obvious was her intense enjoyment of the music and the movement of her young limbs.

W. SOMERSET MAUGHAM *The Human Element* 1951

Mafeking Mafeking (now Mafikeng) is a town in South Africa that was attacked by Boers at the start of the Boer War. It was defended by British troops during a seven-month siege before they were relieved by the British army. The success of the defence was a boost to national morale at a time when the course of the war was turning against the British.

Mafia The Mafia is a secret society of organized criminals, which originated in Sicily in the 13th century and now operates internationally, especially in the United States, where it developed among Italian immigrants under the name of Cosa Nostra. Mafia families are known for sticking together and ruthlessly avenging wrongs done to any member of the family.

Lucas bought me a penknife. He is trying to bribe me into liking him again. Hard luck, Lucas! Us Moles never forget. We are just like the Mafia, once you cross us we bear a grudge all our lives.

SUE TOWNSEND *The Secret Diary of Adrian Mole Aged 13¾* 1982

Magdalene *See* MARY MAGDALENE.

Magi The Magi were the 'three wise men from the East' (Matt. 2: 1) who travelled to Bethlehem to pay homage to the infant Jesus and bring him gifts of gold, frankincense, and myrrh. Later tradition identified them as kings and named them Caspar, Melchior, and Balthazar.

Mr Magoo Mr Magoo is a US cartoon character whose first appearance was in 1949. Bald-headed, crotchety, and severely myopic, Quincy Magoo blunders around from one mishap to the next, forever mistaking one object for another.

Richard Conway was the complete opposite, small, wiry, totally dependent upon thick glasses which some of his camera crew delighted in hiding to give them the chance to watch him stagger around like Mr Magoo in vain search of them.

MEL STEIN *White Lines* 1997

René Magritte René Magritte (1898–1967) was a Belgian Surrealist painter. His paintings have a dreamlike quality, juxtaposing the ordinary, the strange, and the erotic, all depicted with meticulous realism.

Mahalalel According to the book of Genesis, Mahalalel was one of the patriarchs and lived to the age of 895 (Gen. 5: 17). He was the great-grandfather of Methuselah.

Mrs Malaprop In Sheridan's *The Rivals* (1775), Mrs Malaprop is the aunt and guardian of Lydia Languish. She is noted for her aptitude for misusing long words, responsible for such remarks as 'Illiterate him, I say, quite from your memory' and 'She's as headstrong as an allegory on the banks of the Nile'. Solecisms of this kind are now of course known as malapropisms.

Malvolio In Shakespeare's *Twelfth Night* (1623), Malvolio is Olivia's arrogant, pompous and puritanical steward, 'the best persuaded of himself, so cramm'd, as he thinks, with excellencies that it is his grounds of faith that all that look on him love him'. *See also* SHAKESPEARE.

> He smiled on me in quite a superior sort of way—such a smile as would have become the face of Malvolio.
> BRAM STOKER *Dracula* 1897

Mambrino's helmet In Ariosto's poem *Orlando Furioso* (1532), Mambrino is a pagan king whose golden helmet makes the wearer invisible. In Cervantes' *Don Quixote* (1605), Quixote sees a barber riding with his brass basin upon his head and, mistaking this for Mambrino's helmet, gets possession of it.

Mammon Deriving from the Aramaic word for 'riches', mammon is sometimes used in the Bible to mean wealth when considered as an idol whose worship is in opposition to that of God. The most familiar reference is probably Jesus' teaching that 'No man can serve two masters: for either he will hate the one and love the other; or else he will hold to the one, and despise the other. Ye cannot serve God and mammon' (Matt. 6: 24). Mammon was taken by medieval writers as the proper name of the devil of covetousness, and this use was revived by Milton in *Paradise Lost*. The name is now used as the personification of wealth, seen as greedy and selfish materialism.

> I know poetry is not dead, nor genius lost; nor has Mammon gained power over either, to bind or slay: they will both assert their existence, their presence, their liberty and strength again one day.
> CHARLOTTE BRONTË *Jane Eyre* 1847

> Carling is so closely identified with the increasing commercialisation of rugby union it's as if he personally got hold of the compass and swung the game in the direction of Mammon. He didn't. *The Guardian* 1995

> Hucknall, it transpires, is no fan of out-of-town shopping: 'invariably a planning error.' He fears for the future of the city-centre mall—where he has interests in a bar and a hotel. 'A city centre is about the buzz of people and great buildings; the Trafford Centre is about the supremacy of Mammon and bad taste,' he said. *The Independent* 1998

Man Friday In Daniel Defoe's novel *Robinson Crusoe* (1719), Man Friday is the name given by Crusoe to the man that he meets on his island (on a Friday) after spending many years there alone following a shipwreck. The two become close friends and constant companions.

> You're the one everybody envies, in that journalist crowd—you're not really

aware of that, and you take it for granted that Billy should be your Man Friday.
CHRISTOPHER J. KOCH *The Year of Living Dangerously* 1978

Manichaean Manichaeism was a dualistic religious philosophy founded in Persia in the 3rd century by the prophet Manes (*c*.216–*c*.276). Combining elements of Christian, Gnostic, and Zoroastrian thought, the philosophy was based on a supposed primeval conflict between light and darkness and between the opposing powers of good and evil. It spread widely in the Roman Empire and in Asia, and survived in Chinese Turkestan until the 13th century. To describe a situation as Manichaean is to suggest that it involves a dualistic conflict between the forces of good and evil.

For Blair to throw his weight publicly behind Woodhead, whose powerful attacks on destructive education ideologies have left both the Government and Labour scrambling feebly to follow suit, sends a powerful signal to those educationists, teacher unions and sympathisers for whom Woodhead has become a hate figure of Manichean proportions. *The Observer* 1997

On one side, there are duty, decency, self-sacrifice, and on the other, personal joy. And in that good old Manichaean tradition of ours, never the twain shall meet. *The Observer* 1997

Man in the Iron Mask During the reign of Louis XIV (1643–1715), 'the Man in the Iron Mask' was the name given to a mysterious state prisoner held for over 40 years in various prisons until he died in the Bastille in November 1703. Whenever he travelled between different prisons he wore a black mask, made not in fact of iron, but of velvet. Although his identity was never revealed, he was buried under the name of 'M. de Marchiel'. It has been suggested that he was an illegitimate son or an illegitimate elder brother of Louis XIV.

At all times the privileged prisoner's cell was in semi-darkness. . . . The other prisoners nicknamed him 'The Man in the Iron Mask' . . . No one knew his real name.
ALEXANDER SOLZHENITSYN *The First Circle* trans. M. GUYBON 1968

manna Manna was the 'bread' provided by God for the Israelites when they were crossing the desert during their flight from Egypt (Exod. 16). The manna appeared as small white flakes like frost on the desert floor and would not keep overnight except on the sixth day, when enough was provided to keep for the seventh day also, the sabbath, on which the travellers were to rest. It was white like coriander seed and tasted like wafers made with honey, and it sustained the Israelites until they arrived at the border of Canaan.

The word is not prepared beforehand; it falls on me mind like the manna fell from heaven into the bellies of the starving Israelites.
STELLA GIBBONS *Cold Comfort Farm* 1932

Man of Uz The Old Testament book of Job begins with the words 'There was a man in the land of Uz, whose name was Job.' Job is therefore sometimes known as the Man of Uz. *See also* JOB.

Manson Charles Manson (b. 1934) is the US cult leader who in the 1960s founded a hippy commune outside Los Angeles, called the Family. The quasi-religious lifestyle of its members was based on free love, experimentation with drugs, and complete subordination to Manson. In 1969 members of the Family carried out a series of brutal murders, including that of the US actress Sharon Tate, for which Charles Manson and some of his followers received the death sentence, later commuted to life imprisonment.

> And television shots of the cops made it hard to tell the players without a program, since Just Plain Bill looked like Pat Boone and the narcs looked like Manson Family rejects.
> JOSEPH WAMBAUGH *The Glitter Dome* 1981

> 'I thought the whole thing had the ring of Greek tragedy to it,' he charged on. 'Two brothers, one girl. Brother meets girl, gets engaged to girl, girl goes off with other brother. Classic recipe for a family feud.' 'Only if the family is called Addams, Father, or maybe Manson.'
> MIKE RIPLEY *Family of Angels* 1996

Marat Jean-Paul Marat (1743–93) was a French revolutionary politician and journalist. He founded a radical newspaper which supported the French Revolution and criticized the moderate Girondists, contributing to their overthrow. Earlier forced into hiding, he had hidden in the Paris sewers, where he contracted a skin disease which meant he spent much of his later life sitting in his bath. It was here that he was stabbed to death by the Girondist Charlotte Corday. There is a famous painting called *The Death of Marat* by Jacques-Louis David.

> On moving my hand above the surface of the water, I experienced the greatest fright I ever received in the whole course of my life; for imagine my horror on discovering my hand, as I thought, full of blood. My first thought was that I had ruptured an artery, and was bleeding to death, and should be discovered, later on, looking like a second Marat, as I remember seeing him in Madame Tussaud's.
> GEORGE and WEEDON GROSSMITH *The Diary of a Nobody* 1892

Marcel Marceau Marcel Marceau (b. 1923) is a French mime artist. He is most closely associated with his white-faced clown character Bip, developed by Marceau from the French Pierrot character.

> 'Someone softshoes up behind him and banjoes him, yes?' 'I doubt it. He'd have to be very quiet about it . . . even if the guy had come up behind him like Marcel Marceau, he'd have been hit a downwards blow to the top of the head . . .'
> QUINTIN JARDINE *Skinner's Round* 1995

March Hare The March Hare is a character in Lewis Carroll's *Alice's Adventures in Wonderland* (1865), who is present at the Mad Hatter's tea party: 'The March Hare took the watch and looked at it gloomily: then he dipped it into his cup of tea, and looked at it again.' The term 'as mad as a March hare' comes from the leaping and boxing and other excitable behaviour characteristic of hares in the breeding season in March. *See also* ALICE IN WONDERLAND.

> Then, mad as a bunch of March hares, yelling and hooting at the top of our voices, we rushed as fast as our legs would carry us, through the wood to home.
> WINIFRED FOLEY *Child in the Forest Trilogy* 1974

Marie-Antoinette Marie-Antoinette (1755–93) was the wife of Louis XVI and queen of France. Her extravagant lifestyle, combined with a much-quoted response 'Qu'ils mangent de la brioche' (traditionally translated as 'Let them eat cake'), supposedly made on being told that the poor people of Paris were unable to afford bread, have led to her being regarded as a figure of arrogance, indifferent to the plight of the poor. She was beheaded during the French Revolution. Marie-Antoinette is said to have had an idealized view of peasant life. At the Petit Trianon, a small country house in the grounds of the Palace of Versailles, she enjoyed living her version of the simple life of a poor country woman.

> It was not merely tramping that Mary liked. She got almost as much enjoyment out of the more prosaic settled life they led when they returned to England. 'Marie-Antoinette at the Trianon' was what Rampion called her, when he saw her cooking the dinner; she did it with such child-like enthusiasm.
> ALDOUS HUXLEY *Point Counter Point* 1928

> You sang your folksongs like a cheap Marie Antoinette pretending to be a shepherdess.
> ROBERTSON DAVIES *A Mixture of Frailties* 1951

> 'He's forgotten the Marhaen,' he said. 'He's forgotten them, as people. They're nothing but an extension of himself, to make speeches to. He said it himself: when he speaks to the people, it's a dialogue with his alter-ego.' His voice rose above the drunken conversation. 'What a disgusting admission, while the people starve,' he said. 'The Bung's a Marie Antoinette, but *he* says, "Let them eat rats." '
> CHRISTOPHER J. KOCH *The Year of Living Dangerously* 1978

> 'And they have such long holidays! Why can't they do two jobs, if they're short of money?' 'Let them eat cake,' murmured Freddie. 'I never understood why poor Marie Antoinette got such stick for saying that,' said Eleanor. 'It seems a perfectly good suggestion to me, though cake's not very good for you.'
> FAY WELDON *Darcy's Utopia* 1990

Marius Gaius Marius (157–86 BC), the great Roman general, was overcome by his rival Sulla, and fled to Africa, landing at Carthage. When the Roman governor there sent word that he had to leave the country, Marius' reply was: 'Tell the praetor you have seen Gaius Marius a fugitive sitting among the ruins of Carthage.'

> And here Bartleby makes his home; sole spectator of a solitude which he has seen all populous—a sort of innocent and transformed Marius brooding among the ruins of Carthage!
> HERMAN MELVILLE *Bartleby* 1856

Marley's ghost In Charles Dickens's *A Christmas Carol* (1843), Jacob Marley is Ebenezer Scrooge's late business partner, whose chained ghost appears to the miserly Scrooge on the night of Christmas Eve and warns him to change his ways. The long chain Marley has wound round him is made 'of cash-boxes, keys, padlocks, ledgers, deeds, and heavy purses wrought in steel'. *See also* DICKENSIAN, SCROOGE.

> He says he's been weighted down with worldly possessions all his life, like Marley's Ghost. Getting rid of some of the stuff makes him feel young again.
> A. J. ORDE *A Long Time Dead* 1994

Philip Marlowe Philip Marlowe is the hard-boiled private detective in such novels as *The Big Sleep* (1939) and *Farewell, My Lovely* (1940) by the US writer Raymond Chandler. Tough, cynical, yet honourable, the Marlowe character is well known from the films of Chandler's novels, notably as embodied by Humphrey Bogart and Robert Mitchum.

> 'I'm following my own leads.' She looked at Robin. 'Philip Marlowe here?' Robin gave her a helpless look. 'Is this dangerous, Alex?' 'No. I just want to look into a few things.'
> JONATHAN KELLERMAN *When the Bough Breaks* 1992

Silas Marner In George Eliot's novel *Silas Marner* (1861), Silas is a bitter, antisocial linen-weaver whose only consolation is the growing pile of gold coins he has accumulated. Only after his gold is stolen does he find new meaning to his life when he adopts, and comes to love, an abandoned village girl called Eppie. He is alluded to as an archetypal miser.

> To answer this question, we must examine the intricate tapestry of meteorological dreariness, Silas Marnerian stinginess, Uriah Heepian creepiness and Ron Woodian slovenliness that coalesce to make Great Britain. *Spy* 1993

Miss Marple Jane Marple is the elderly detective created by the crime writer Agatha Christie. She lives in the village of St Mary Mead, indulging in her hobbies of knitting and gardening. Her disarming appearance as a mildly gossipy old spinster hides a shrewdness and acuteness of observation that she uses to solve murders.

> I tried Ralph again. This time he answered on the fourth ring. 'What's up, Miss

Marple?' he asked. 'I thought you were out after Professor Moriarty until tomorrow.'
SARA PARETSKY *Indemnity Only* 1982

Would you kindly stop shining that light in my eyes? Your Miss Marple act is less polished if I may say so, than your . . . letters.
CAROL SHIELDS *Mary Swann* 1990

Mars In Roman mythology, Mars was the god of war, corresponding to the Greek god Ares.

'Ha, ha!—you must have your joke; well, I'll think o' that. And so they expect Buonaparty to choose this very part of the coast for his landing, hey? And that yeomanry be to stand in front as the forlorn hope?' 'Who says so?' asked the florid son of Mars, losing a little redness.
THOMAS HARDY *The Trumpet Major* 1880

I have already said that I am not much of an actor, but I gave a powerful, if crude impersonation of the hero who is tremendous on the field of Mars but slighted in the courts of Venus.
ROBERTSON DAVIES *Fifth Business* 1970

Marsyas In Greek mythology, Marsyas was a satyr who was a skilful flute-player. He challenged Apollo to a musical contest and was flayed alive for his presumption when he lost.

'His present indigence is a sufficient punishment for former folly; and I have heard my pappa himself say, that we should never strike our unnecessary blow at a victim over whom providence holds the scourge of its resentment.'—'You are right, Sophy,' cried my son Moses, 'and one of the ancients finely represents so malicious a conduct, by the attempts of a rustic to flay Marsyas, whose skin, the fable tells us, had been wholly stript off by another.'
OLIVER GOLDSMITH *The Vicar of Wakefield* 1766

Martha In the New Testament, Martha is the sister of Mary and Lazarus and a friend of Jesus. When Jesus visits their house, Mary sits and listens to Jesus while Martha fusses about with meal preparations and other household chores (Luke 10). Martha's name is used allusively for a woman who is constantly busying herself with domestic affairs. *See also* LAZARUS.

Her cousins began a tiresome dispute about clearing the table and doing the washing-up, each one trying to outdo the others in laying up for themselves treasure in heaven . . . 'How about a turn round the garden, Uncle Sam?' she said, while the twins threw bilious glances at her, grudging Marthas to her unlikely Mary.
SUSAN MOODY *King of Hearts* 1995

Captain Marvel Captain Marvel was an American comic-book hero from the 1940s, who used his superhuman powers to defeat evil villains. He transformed himself into his costumed form by uttering the magic word 'Shazam!'

Marvin Marvin, referred to as the Paranoid Android, is a gloomy and depressed robot in Douglas Adams's book *The Hitch-Hiker's Guide to the Galaxy* (1979, first radio broadcast 1978) and its sequels. He takes a universally pessimistic view about everything and is prone to complain that he has a pain down all the diodes on his left side.

Groucho Marx Groucho Marx (Julius Henry Marx, 1890–1977) was one of the US comedy team the Marx Brothers. His urgent, crouching walk was as distinctive as his wisecracking one-liners and his facial appearance, complete with painted black moustache, glasses, and cigar.

> He rushed out of the car like Groucho Marx to get cigarettes—that furious, ground-hugging walk with the coattails flying.
> JACK KEROUAC *On the Road* 1957

Harpo Marx Adolph Arthur Marx (1888–1964), known as Harpo, was one of the Marx Brothers, a family of American comedians who made comic films in the 1930s. In the films, Harpo is always mute, communicating by means of an old-fashioned car horn.

> 'How did you know about us?' 'Her mother mentioned it. Talkative woman.' 'Her mother? She's about as talkative as Harpo Marx.'
> MAX MARQUIS *Written in Blood* 1995

Marx Brothers The Marx Brothers were a family of American film comedians consisting of the brothers Chico (Leonard, 1886–1961), Harpo (Adolph, 1888–1964), Groucho (Julius Henry, 1890–1977), and Zeppo (Herbert, 1901–79). Their films are characterized by an anarchic humour and madcap zaniness, and include *Duck Soup* (1933) and *A Night at the Opera* (1935).

Mary Celeste The *Mary Celeste* (often erroneously referred to as the *Marie Celeste*) was an American brig that set sail from New York for Genoa and was found drifting in the north Atlantic in December 1872, in perfect condition but abandoned, and with evidence of very recent occupation. The fate of the crew was never discovered, and the abandonment of the ship remains one of the great mysteries of the sea.

> She boarded the lift, stuffing the booklet back into the folder. By the tenth and final floor, she was alone in the lift, and she emerged into a corridor that seemed about as lively as the deck of the Marie Celeste.
> VAL MCDERMID *Union Jack* 1993

> And, anyway, it won't always be like this, with all her things around. She'll clear it out soon, and the Marie Celestial air about the place—the half-read Julian

Barnes paperback on the bedside table and the knickers in the dirty clothes basket—will vanish.

NICK HORNBY *High Fidelity* 1995

A quick scoping of the kitchen didn't tell me much. There were no half-eaten meals on the table, no coffee bubbling on the hotplate. This wasn't a Marie Celeste situation, this looked like somebody who'd gone on holiday in a slight rush.

MIKE RIPLEY *Family of Angels* 1996

Mary Magdalene In the New Testament, Mary Magdalene was one of the followers of Jesus. She is often identified with the woman, a sinner ashamed of her sins, who came to Jesus in the Pharisee's house, washed his feet with her tears, dried them with her hair, and anointed them with ointment (Luke 7: 38). She can therefore typify the reformed prostitute. In art, she is often portrayed weeping repentant tears, and the word 'maudlin' is derived from her name.

'Trying to help women who've come to grief.' Old Jolyon did not quite understand. 'To grief?' he repeated; then realised with a shock that she meant exactly what he would have meant himself if he had used that expression. Assisting the Magdalenes of London! What a weird and terrifying interest!

JOHN GALSWORTHY *A Man of Property* 1906

m

Perry Mason Perry Mason is the fictional defence lawyer in a series of novels by Erle Stanley Gardner and in a US television series of the 1960s. The stories frequently end with a dramatic courtroom scene in which Mason proves his client innocent of the crime.

How like Denn to choose a place like this for a rendezvous. He knew perfectly well he should turn himself in to Sheriff Bo Poole and try to hire himself a Perry Mason.

MARGARET MARON *Bootlegger's Daughter* 1992

'Given that Scotty, for whatever reason, decided to murder his wife,' she began, trying a new tack, 'doesn't it seem odd that with access to a boat and hundreds of square miles of deep water, he would choose to dispose of the body by eating it?' 'Not if he was the reincarnation of Charlie Mott,' Damien said triumphantly. He and Tinker looked at her expectantly, twin Perry Masons having delivered the coup de grace.

NEVADA BARR *A Superior Death* 1994

Mata Hari Mata Hari (1876–1917), born Margaretha Geertruida Zelle, was a Dutch dancer, courtesan, and spy. She became a professional 'oriental' dancer in Paris in 1905 and probably worked for both French and German intelligence services during the First World War, obtaining military secrets from high-ranking Allied officers. She was executed by the French for espionage in 1917. The term 'Mata Hari' can be applied to any beautiful, seductive woman.

I had a bad time at the hands of male journalists during Julian's trial and in the period leading up to it: some residual paranoia sticks. They look for a *femme fatale*, a Mata Hari of world finance, a seductress. If a woman is to be taken seriously she must either be past the menopause or very plain, preferably both.
FAY WELDON *Darcy's Utopia* 1990

A junior partner promoted by their lover can be seen as a Mata Hari. *The Observer* 1997

Match Girl *See* LITTLE MATCH GIRL.

Matilda Hilaire Belloc's *Cautionary Tales* (1939) contains the story of 'Matilda, Who Told Lies and Was Burned to Death'. Matilda, a young girl who 'told such Dreadful Lies', had called out the fire brigade as a joke, only to find herself a few weeks later at home when a real fire broke out. Despite her screams for help, no one would believe that there really was a fire:
'For every time She shouted "Fire!"
They only answered "Little Liar!" '
Matilda and the house were both burned.

Mecca Mecca (in Arabic, Makkah) is a city in western Saudi Arabia, an oasis town in the Red Sea region of Hejaz, east of Jiddah. It was the birthplace in AD 570 of the prophet Muhammad. Mecca is held to be the holiest city of the Islamic world and is the destination for Muslims undertaking the haj (pilgrimage). In general usage, a Mecca is hence any place that attracts many visitors or the enthusiasts of a particular activity.

'But here we are at the Mecca of English cricket,' said Lord Ickenham, suspending his remarks as the cab drew up at the entrance of Lord's.
P G. WODEHOUSE *Cocktail Time* 1958

Where 125th Street crossed Seventh Avenue is the Mecca of Harlem. To get established there, an ordinary Harlem citizen has reached the promised land.
CHESTER HIMES *Blind Man with a Pistol* 1969

Meddlesome Matty Meddlesome Matty appears in *Original Poems, for Infant Minds by Several Young Persons*, a collection of poems for children by Ann and Jane Taylor and others, published in two volumes in 1804 and 1805. Matilda, 'though a pleasant child' in other respects, is a compulsive meddler.

His passion for playing the literary Meddlesome Mattie was aroused.
ROBERTSON DAVIES *The Deptford Trilogy* 1975

Medea In Greek mythology, Medea, princess of Colchis, was a sorceress who fell in love with Jason and helped him to obtain the golden fleece. When Jason later abandoned her to marry the daughter of Creon, king of Corinth, she was so enraged that she took revenge by murdering their two children as well as Jason's young bride. *See also* JASON AND THE ARGONAUTS.

Few of us wish to disturb the mother of a litter of puppies when mouthing a bone in the midst of her young family. Medea and her children are familiar to us, and so is the grief of Constance.

ANTHONY TROLLOPE *Barchester Towers* 1857

Medes and Persians In the book of Daniel, King Darius signed a decree saying that for 30 days no one should pray to any God or man except the king. The king's officials called for him to 'establish the decree, and sign the writing, that it be not changed, according to the law of the Medes and Persians, which altereth not' (Dan. 6: 8). Hence a law of the Medes and Persians is one that cannot be altered. It was as a punishment for ignoring Darius' command that Daniel was cast into the lion's den.

I know what my aim is, and what my motives are; and at this moment I pass a law, unalterable, as that of the Medes and Persians, that both are right.

CHARLOTTE BRONTË *Jane Eyre* 1847

Medusa In Greek mythology, Medusa was one of the Gorgons who, like her sisters, had snakes for hair and the power to turn anyone who looked at her to stone. Medusa, the only mortal one of the sisters, was killed by Perseus, who cut off her head. *See also* GORGON, PEGASUS, PERSEUS.

He saw her—the marble whiteness of the sea-goddess' face, hair combed back upon her shoulders, staring out across the park where the dead autumn leaves and branches flared and smoked; a Medusa among the snows, dressed in her old tartan shawl.

LAWRENCE DURRELL *Mountolive* 1958

The wind had picked up considerably, invading Anna's hair to create a sort of Medusa effect.

ARMISTEAD MAUPIN *Sure of You* 1990

Mekon The Mekon is Dan Dare's arch-enemy in the comic strip by Frank Hampson which appeared in the *Eagle* comic between 1950 and 1967. He originates from the planet Venus, is green-skinned, and has a small body and an enormous bald head. A person with a large domelike head can sometimes be referred to as a Mekon.

Crash bade farewell to another student, a rich teenage boy with the good build and space-ranger short-back-and-sides and Mekon cranium of the future.

MARTIN AMIS *The Information* 1995

Victor Meldrew Victor Meldrew is the prematurely retired curmudgeon played by Richard Wilson in the British television comedy series *One Foot in the Grave* (1990–2000). He continually expresses his irritation with the petty annoyances and indignities of life with the incredulous exclamation 'I don't believe it!'

I was too old, wasn't I? Too old for all the chanting and Mexican waves and silly wigs and obscene language. OK, cricket's only a game, and a carnival atmosphere never comes amiss. But it all seemed so contrived: young men

coming to drink and yell, not to watch the game. I sat among other Victor and
Victoria Meldrews, some of them younger than I, to be fair, lamenting the
incursions of the loud, vulgar, drunken yob element.
JUDITH CUTLER *Dying to Score* 1999

Melpomene Melpomene was the Muse of tragedy in Greek mythology. *See
also* MUSES.

His face is like the tragic mask of Melpomene.
THOMAS HARDY *Jude the Obscure* 1895

Adolph Menjou Adolph Menjou (1890–1963) was a dapper French
American film actor who was always elegantly dressed and had a curly
moustache, turned up at the ends.

We took a Hungarian Airlines plane from East Berlin. The pilot had a handlebar
mustache. He looked like Adolph Menjou. He smoked a Cuban cigar while the
plane was being fueled. When we took off, there was no talk of fastening seat
belts.
KURT VONNEGUT *Slaughterhouse-Five* 1969

Mephistopheles Mephistopheles is the evil spirit to whom Faust in
German legend sold his soul, especially as represented in Marlowe's *Doctor
Faustus* (*c.*1590) and Goethe's *Faust* (1808–32). Mephistopheles entraps Faust
with wit, charm, and rationality. His name, and the adjective
'Mephistophelean', are often used to describe a fiendish but urbane tempter.
See also FAUST.

When it was over he pulled my head round so that he could see my face and
said, 'You O.K. kid?' I can remember the tone now. He was obviously happy
and the Mephistophelian smile had given place to an expression that was
almost boyish.
ROBERTSON DAVIES *World of Wonders* 1975

[The show's] core [is] the Faustean pact between a young college teacher and
the Mephistopheles of NBC television desperate for a hero with whom they
believed the viewers could identify. *The Guardian* 1995

Mercury In Roman mythology, Mercury was the messenger of the gods,
identified with the Greek Hermes. He is pictured as a herald wearing winged
sandals which enable him to travel very swiftly.

The affair of the carriage was arranged by Mr Harding, who acted as Mercury
between the two ladies.
ANTHONY TROLLOPE *Barchester Towers* 1857

Viscount Trimingham said I was like Mercury—I run errands.
L. P HARTLEY *The Go-Between* 1953

I know the height of your ambition and your unrest, but it is given to you to
encompass all your ends. Remember that no moss may stick to the stone of

Sisyphus, no, nor grass hang upon the heels of Mercury.
PETER ACKROYD *The House of Dr Dee* 1993

Merlin In Arthurian legend, Merlin was the wizard who counselled and guided King Arthur and his father, Uther, before him. Late in his life he fell in love with Nimue. She tricked him into giving her the secrets of his magic and then imprisoned him in the forest of Brocéliande, near Brittany. According to the legend, he never escaped and lies there still. As well as being an archetypal magician, his name can be used to typify a wise counsellor. *See also* KING ARTHUR, NIMUE.

And you know you were never much of a lover, Magnus. What does that matter? You were a great magician, and has any great magician ever been a great lover? Look at Merlin: his only false step was when he fell in love and ended up imprisoned in a tree for his pains. Look at Klingsor: he could create gardens full of desirable women, but he had been castrated with a magic spear.
ROBERTSON DAVIES *The Deptford Trilogy* 1975

The Blair government is well aware of this, which is why it has embarked on a wholesale overhaul of our constitutional arrangements. In this light, the plan for a London mayor is distinct from the soccer and drugs appointments. We need a new democratic framework that can engage an active citizenry who can then dispense, for the most part, with the ministrations of modern Merlins. *The Observer* 1997

Meshach *See* SHADRACH, MESHACH, *and* ABEDNEGO.

Mesmer Franz Anton Mesmer (1734–1815) was an Austrian physician who had a successful practice in Vienna, where he used a number of novel treatments. He is chiefly remembered for the introduction of hypnotism, known as mesmerism, as a therapeutic technique.

Like some magical Mesmer, he has persuaded his people to feel well about themselves. *The Observer* 1997

Messiah The Messiah (from Hebrew *Masiah*, meaning 'anointed') is the promised deliverer of the Jewish nation prophesied in the Hebrew Bible. In Christianity, the term is applied to Jesus Christ, and it is used allusively to refer to any person who saves or delivers others.

'Why did you say in the letter that you threw up all the time?' 'I was really talking about Mickey there. I was talking *for* him. He would never write, sergeant, though I pleaded with him. He'll waste away to nothing if I don't help, sergeant . . .' 'You're a regular Messiah, aren't you?'
PHILIP ROTH *Defender of the Faith* 1959

In the gallery of the old photographs she was always the same, staring out, while everyone else seemed disgracefully protean, kaftaned Messiahs, sideburned Zapatas.
MARTIN AMIS *The Information* 1995

mess of pottage *See* JACOB.

Methuselah In the Bible, Methuselah was the oldest of the patriarchs, grandfather of Noah. He is supposed to have lived 969 years (Gen. 5: 27). His name is now proverbial for longevity.

> I would rather travel with an excursion party of Methuselahs than have to be changing ships and comrades constantly, as people do who travel in the ordinary way.
> MARK TWAIN *An Innocent Abroad* 1869

> The throne, being lowered, was placed before the altar as it has been every year since the oldest Methuselah in the habitation can remember.
> JULIAN BARNES *A History of the World in 10½ Chapters* 1989

> So around Richard were arrayed a few tattoo-bespattered warthogs and authentic thirty-year-old Methuselahs fingering their earrings as they applied themselves to their tabloids.
> MARTIN AMIS *The Information* 1995

Mr Micawber Mr Wilkins Micawber, in Dickens's novel *David Copperfield* (1850), dreams up elaborate schemes for making money which never materialize. Ever-impecunious, he famously encapsulates the principle of balancing income and expenditure as follows: 'Annual income twenty pounds, annual expenditure nineteen nineteen six, result happiness. Annual income twenty pounds, annual expenditure twenty pounds nought and six, result misery.' Despite his lack of success, he remains undaunted and optimistic, never losing his belief that something will 'turn up'. *See also* DICKENSIAN.

> No good news yet, but I have a Micawber-faith that something will turn up.
> GEORGE ELIOT *Letters* 1852

> 'Christ, no!' said Lomas angrily. 'All that crap about running his car off the road because his company was collapsing was just gutter press garbage. He beat Micawber for optimism!'
> REGINALD HILL *Child's Play* 1987

> If a government can pilot its way to a budget surplus, the economic and political results are very happy, especially for the Left. Our highly political Chancellor has noted and learned; financial Micawberism brings substantial rewards.
> WILL HUTTON *The Observer* 1999

Michelangelo Michelangelo Buonarroti (1475–1564) was an Italian sculptor, painter, architect, and poet. A leading figure during the high Renaissance, he established his reputation in Rome with sculptures such as the *Pietà* (*c.*1497–1500) and then in Florence with his marble *David* (1501–4). In his portrayal of the nude, Michelangelo depicted the beauty and strength of the human body. He is probably best known for painting the ceiling of the

Sistine Chapel in Rome (1508–12). Many of Michelangelo's works depict heroically muscular male nudes, so his name can evoke male beauty.

> Primitive yet complex, elephantine but delicate; as full of subtle curves and volumes as a Henry Moore or a Michelangelo.
> JOHN FOWLES *The French Lieutenant's Woman* 1969

> I have seldom seen a more splendid young fellow. He was naked to the waist and of a build that one day might be over-corpulent. But now he could stand as a model to Michelangelo!
> WILLIAM GOLDING *Rites of Passage* 1980

> At twenty, he had the body of Michelangelo's David, now he resembles an entire family group by Henry Moore.
> MINETTE WALTERS *The Scold's Bridle* 1994

Mickey Mouse Mickey Mouse is a Walt Disney cartoon character, first appearing in 1928. His name can now be used to describe something insignificant or trivial, and he can also be alluded to for his distinctive squeaky, high-pitched voice.

> I began to repeat this sentence in a variety of tones, stresses and dialects, ranging from a rapid Mickey Mouse squeak to a bass drawl.
> KEITH WATERHOUSE *Billy Liar* 1959

> We got a Mickey Mouse educational system that doesn't teach us how things work, how the government works, who runs it.
> STUDS TERKEL *American Dreams: Lost and Found* 1980

> 'This whole case could blow up on us,' Vince said. 'We don't have a body, number one.' 'We don't have a body *yet*,' I said. 'And the two prior cases on Calvert weren't just mine, they were IAD's as well. If we failed, we both failed. And anyway, those cases were Mickey Mouse compared to the gravity of the current allegation.'
> LINDA CHASE and JOYCE ST GEORGE *Perfect Cover* 1995

Midas Midas was a legendary king of Phrygia, a country in what is now part of Turkey. In Greek legend, Midas was granted his wish that everything he touched should be turned to gold. However, when the food in his mouth and, according to some versions, even his beloved daughter, turned to gold, he begged to be released from his gift, and was allowed to do so by bathing in the river Pactolus. The name of Midas is thus used for someone very rich, and the Midas touch is a gift for making money, seemingly without effort. He is also sometimes mentioned as someone who suffers on account of his greed for money.

According to another story, Midas was one day asked to judge a musical contest between Apollo and Pan. He unwisely chose Pan, whereupon Apollo punished him by giving him ass's ears to show his stupidity. Midas concealed his appearance from all but his barber who, unable to keep the secret but afraid to reveal it publicly, told it to a hole in the ground, which he then filled in. Reeds grew over the hole and whispered 'Midas has ass's ears' when the wind blew.

> 'All I saw was the money. I just didn't want to look down that road. If I had . . . It's like some story I heard once. Some guy, Greek I think, was so greedy he begged the gods to give him a gift—everything he touched would turn to gold. Only thing is, these gods, they zap you: they always give you what you ask for but it turns out not to be what you want. Well, this guy was like me: he had a daughter that he loved more than life. But he forgot to look down the road. And when he touched her, she turned to gold, too. That's what I've done, haven't I?' 'King Midas,' I said.
> SARA PARETSKY *Indemnity Only* 1982

> Custom dictates that carolers be asked in and offered a cookie . . . and so must any person who comes to your door, otherwise the spirit of Christmas will leave your house, and even if you be as rich as Midas, your holiday will be sad and mean.
> GARRISON KEILLOR *Lake Wobegon Days* 1985

> Ferguson's inspired signing of Cantona, and other purchases of his, have shown him to have a bit of a transfer Midas touch. Once he has ventured money on a player, the Manchester United manager usually manages to get the best out of him. *Sunday Telegraph* 1995

hosts of Midian The Midianites were a tribal group portrayed in the Bible as nomadic shepherds and traders. The book of Judges relates the story of a battle led by Gideon against the Midianites in which he defeated the 'host of Midian'. The host of Midian can be alluded to as any unfriendly or hostile group.

> I shouldn't be surprised if Tommy and his little friend weren't still lurking in the shadows somewhere. They're like the hosts of Midian. They prowl and prowl around.
> P G. WODEHOUSE *Laughing Gas* 1936

> I knew which side I was on; yet the traitor within my gates felt the issue differently, he backed the individual against the side, even my own side, and wanted to see Ted Burgess pull it off. But I could not voice such thoughts to the hosts of Midian prowling round me under the shade of the pavilion verandah.
> L. P HARTLEY *The Go-Between* 1953

Daisy Miller Daisy Miller is the heroine of a short novel with the same name by Henry James, published in 1879. She is a naive young American woman who is touring Europe with her mother and brother and finds herself in compromising situations because of her trusting nature and ignorance of social conventions. When she is found viewing the Colosseum one evening with a young Italian and no chaperone, she is criticized for her lack of social decorum. She returns hurt to her hotel, where she contracts malaria and is dead within a week.

Millet Jean-François Millet (1814–75) was a French painter, etcher, and draughtsman, known especially for his scenes of peasants at work such as *The Gleaners* (1857) and *The Angelus* (1858–9). Such paintings express the artist's immense sympathy for the simplicity of the rural life.

> I found myself possessed of a surprising interest in the shepherdess, who stood far away in the hill pasture with her great flock, like a figure of Millet's, high against the sky.
> SARAH ORNE JEWETT *A Dunnet Shepherdess* 1899

Mills and Boon Mills and Boon is the name of a publishing partnership formed by Gerald Mills (d. 1927) and Charles Boon (1877–1943), which specializes in publishing popular romantic fiction.

> In some respects this is a Mills & Boonish story, with moments of cloying sentimentality and throbbing musical crescendoes. *The Independent* 1995

> Ralph stopped himself abruptly. He hadn't come in here to sniff Jem's clothes and form elaborate Mills and Boon-style fantasies about her.
> LISA JEWELL *Ralph's Party* 1999

Caspar Milquetoast Caspar Milquetoast was a timid comic-strip character created by the American cartoonist H. T. Webster in 1924. A Milquetoast is thus any meek, submissive, or timid person.

> And UN Secretary General Kofi Annan, momentarily abandoning his customary Caspar Milquetoast approach, actually has gone to NATO and said a credible threat of force was 'essential' to make diplomacy effective. *Chicago Tribune* 1999

Milton John Milton (1608–74) was a major English poet of the 17th century whose works include *Lycidas* (1638), *Paradise Lost* (1667), *Paradise Regained* (1671), and *Samson Agonistes* (1671). His name can represent a great or poetic writer.

Mimir In Scandinavian mythology, Mimir was a giant who guarded the well of wisdom near the roots of the great ash tree Yggdrasil.

> Allfadir did not get a drink of Mimir's spring.
> RALPH WALDO EMERSON *The Conduct of Life* 1860

Mindanao Trench The Mindanao Trench (also known as the Philippine Deep) is a submarine trench in the floor of the Philippine Sea bordering the east coast of the island of Mindanao. This abyss is one of the deepest places on earth, its deepest point being 10 850 metres below sea level.

> 'If she had visited my daughter, she would have said so. Frances is incapable of lying. She hasn't the wit,' he said, his voice cold and dark as the Mindanao Trench.
> CYNTHIA HARROD-EAGLES *Shallow Grave* 1998

Minerva In Roman mythology, Minerva was the goddess of handicrafts, wisdom, and also of war, identified with the Greek Athene. She was also believed to have invented the flute. While she was playing the flute before Juno and Venus, the goddesses laughed at the distorted face she made while blowing the instrument, which caused Minerva to throw it indignantly away. *See also* ATHENE.

> She started the pen in an elephantine march across the sheet. It was a splendid round, bold hand of her own conception, a style that would have stamped a woman as Minerva's own in more recent days.
> THOMAS HARDY *The Mayor of Casterbridge* 1886

> 'Thank you very much,' said Oak, in the modest tone good manners demanded, thinking, however, that he would never let Bathsheba see him playing the flute; in this resolve showing a discretion equal to that related of its sagacious inventress, the divine Minerva herself.
> THOMAS HARDY *Far from the Madding Crowd* 1874

> There was, as I have said, a Minerva fully armed.
> MARILYNNE ROBINSON *Mother Country* 1989

Ministry of Silly Walks The Ministry of Silly Walks appears in a well-known sketch from *Monty Python's Flying Circus*, a popular British television comedy series of the 1970s. A spoof government department, the Ministry employs bowler-hatted civil servants, each of whom has an outlandish style of walking. *See also* MONTY PYTHON.

Minos In Greek mythology, Minos was a legendary king of Crete, son of Zeus and Europa. His wife, Pasiphae, gave birth to the Minotaur, which was kept in the Labyrinth constructed by Daedalus. Minos demanded an annual tribute from Athens of seven youths and seven girls to be fed to the Minotaur, though it was eventually killed by Theseus. After his death, Minos became the judge of the dead in the underworld. Minos can be alluded to in the context of a labyrinth-like arrangement of rooms and passages and also to denote one stern in judgement. *See also* LABYRINTH, MINOTAUR, PASIPHAE.

> But it is an ancient, rambling pile, and would require another Minos to trace its regions, with its bedchambers and byrooms and passages and parlours and other rooms severally partitioned.
> PETER ACKROYD *The House of Doctor Dee* 1993

> 'Because you missed a filing deadline,' hissed the judge, his face swelling and purpling with rage, 'and now you're seeking leave to file a late answer. Over there!' he bellowed with the authority of Minos sending a damned soul down to the lowest rung of Hell.
> RICHARD DOOLEY *Brainstorm* 1998

Minotaur In Greek mythology, the Minotaur was the creature with a bull's head and a man's body that was the offspring of Pasiphae (wife of King Minos of Crete) and a bull with which she fell in love. The Minotaur, confined in the

Labyrinth built by Daedalus, devoured human flesh. Seven youths and seven girls from Athens were sacrificed to the Minotaur annually, until it was eventually killed by Theseus, with the aid of Ariadne. *See also* ARIADNE, LABYRINTH, MINOS, THESEUS.

> They sat opposite each other, on either side of the fire—the monumental matron . . . and the young, slim girl, so fresh, so virginal, so ignorant, with all the pathos of an unsuspecting victim about to be sacrificed to the minotaur of Time.
>
> ARNOLD BENNETT *The Old Wives' Tale* 1908

> She remembered the sadness she had earlier noticed in his eyes. He was a man who had known both good and evil. She was sure of it now. His mind was a dark labyrinth, intricate and convoluted, with a Minotaur of some kind crouching at the core. There was something frightening as well as fascinating about him.
>
> JOHN SPENCER HILL *The Last Castrato* 1995

Miranda Miranda is the beautiful and innocent daughter of Prospero in Shakespeare's play *The Tempest* (1623). Brought up on a deserted island with only her father for company, Miranda has never seen the deceit, wickedness, and corruption of the world, and on becoming acquainted with men who have been shipwrecked on the island she utters the famous lines:
'How beauteous mankind is! O brave new world,
That has such people in't!'
   Ironically, the people she is speaking of are the very ones who deposed and exiled Prospero many years before. Miranda's name can suggest a young innocent unaware of the darker side of human nature and full of wonder and joy at the world and human society. *See also* PROSPERO, SHAKESPEARE.

> She found herself standing, in the character of hostess, face to face with a man she had never seen before—moreover, looking at him with a Miranda-like curiosity and interest that she had never yet bestowed on a mortal.
>
> THOMAS HARDY *A Pair of Blue Eyes* 1873

> He escorted them to their box with a sort of pompous humility, waving his fat jewelled hands, and talking at the top of his voice. Dorian Gray loathed him more than ever. He felt as if he had come to look for Miranda and had been met by Caliban.
>
> OSCAR WILDE *The Picture of Dorian Gray* 1891

Miriam In the Bible, Miriam was the sister of Aaron, who went with Moses when he led his people across the Red Sea and out of Egypt. When they had crossed the Red Sea safely, Miriam 'took up a timbrel in her hand' and said 'Sing ye to the Lord, for he hath triumphed gloriously' (Exod. 15: 20–1). This is sometimes referred to as the Song of Miriam. Miriam can therefore be alluded to as someone who sings, especially for joy. (The reference to hiding her little brother in the Forster quotation depends upon the assumption that it was Miriam who was the sister who watched the infant Moses in his basket in the bulrushes in Exod. 2: 4.) *See also* MOSES.

> A new little brother is a valuable sentimental asset to a schoolgirl, and her school was then passing through an acute phase of baby-worship. Happy the girl who had her quiver full of them, who kissed them when she left home in the morning, who had the right to extricate them from mail-carts in the interval, who dangled them at tea ere they retired to rest! That one might sing the unwritten song of Miriam, blessed above all schoolgirls, who was allowed to hide her baby brother in a squashy place, where none but herself could find him!
> E. M. FORSTER *Where Angels Fear to Tread* 1905

Mithras Mithras was a Persian god of light and truth who was also adopted as a god by the Romans, especially in the military world. He was usually represented in the act of sacrificing a bull.

Walter Mitty James Thurber's short story 'The Secret Life of Walter Mitty' (1939) relates how a henpecked husband escapes his wife's nagging by retreating into his own world of daydreams in which he is the hero of many adventures. A Walter Mitty is someone who lives in a fantasy world, especially someone who has lost touch with reality.

> A chauffeur described as a Walter Mitty character was jailed for a year yesterday for dishonestly trying to claim a share of the National Lottery's first jackpot of nearly 6m. Knightsbridge Crown Court in central London was told that James Madel had walked into the organiser Camelot's London offices on 21 November last year, amid a blaze of publicity, and handed officials a ticket he claimed had been ripped up by his dog but which nevertheless entitled him to £839 254. *The Independent* 1995

> Compulsive shoppers can ring for help when they have the urge to buy something expensive; former sufferer Lawrence Michaels will try to talk them out of it. 'A lot are Walter Mittys who need to face reality,' says Michaels, who chairs self-help group Walletwatch. *The Observer* 1997

Mnemosyne Mnemosyne was the mother of the Muses and goddess of memory in Greek mythology. *See also* MUSES.

> But the sight of old Mr Woodford standing in the entrance archway snapped his line of thought before Mnemosyne could come to his aid.
> CHESTER HIMES *Headwaiter* 1937

Moab Moab was an ancient region east of the Dead Sea, the inhabitants of which, the Moabites, were said to be incestuously descended from Moab, son of Lot and Lot's daughter. Adultery between Israelites and 'the daughters of Moab' is fiercely condemned in the Old Testament: 'And Israel abode in Shittim, and the people began to commit whoredom with the daughters of Moab' (Num. 25: 1). Allusions to Moab tend to be in the context of an interracial union.

This resembled, in the divine's opinion, the union of a Moabitish stranger with a daughter of Zion.
WALTER SCOTT *The Bride of Lammermoor* 1819

Their faces were contorted by hatred, their voices were uncontrolled and raucous, they brandished knobthorn sticks, they cried out in outraged protest against the supreme apostasy, and who could wonder at it, for were they not witnessing the abomination of abominations, the sight of Afrikaners who conspire with men and women of other races and colours to challenge all those things that are held most dear in Afrikanerdom, who in the words of Holy Writ have committed whoredom with the daughters of Moab?
ALAN PATON *Ah, But Your Land Is Beautiful* 1981

Moby Dick In Herman Melville's *Moby Dick* (1851), the great white whale of that name is the object of Captain Ahab's passionate and obsessional quest, driven by revenge for the loss of his leg in a previous encounter with the whale.

Amedeo Modigliani Amedeo Modigliani (1884–1920) was an Italian painter and sculptor. Influenced by African sculpture, his portraits and nudes have boldly simplified features and distinctively elongated forms.

She was . . . waiting like a longbodied emaciated Modigliani surrealist woman in a serious room.
JACK KEROUAC *On the Road* 1957

It was enough, however, for Mayo to see everything that needed to be seen: a longer shadow depending from one of the newel posts, a Modigliani figure, grotesquely elongated, its own shadow dancing alongside as it gently swung, a heavy, carved-oak upright chair kicked away and lying on its back.
MARJORIE ECCLES *A Species of Revenge* 1996

Moloch Moloch was a Canaanite deity referred to in several books of the Old Testament to whom worshippers sacrificed their children. The Israelites, moving into the land of Canaan, were expressly forbidden to worship Moloch (Lev. 18: 21). Anything that has great power and demands a terrible sacrifice can be described as a Moloch.

Indeed . . . the national education of women is of the utmost consequence, for what a number of human sacrifices are made to that Moloch prejudice!
MARY WOLLSTONECRAFT *A Vindication of the Rights of Women* 1792

The reduction of the Premier League to 20 teams will help by easing the fixture list but certain dates should still be declared no-go areas for that insatiable Moloch, television. *The Guardian* 1994

Mona Lisa *Mona Lisa* is the title of a painting by Leonardo da Vinci, perhaps the most famous painting in the world. The painting is also known as *La Gioconda* because the sitter was the wife of Francesco di Bartolommeo del Giocondo di Zandi. Her enigmatic smile has become one of the most famous images in Western art. *See also* LEONARDO.

> She declined to express an opinion, answering only with a Mona Lisa smile.
> A. S. BYATT *Possession* 1990

> She grinned a smile of pure gold; it was like seeing Mona Lisa break into a laugh.
> CHESTER HIMES *Blind Man with a Pistol* 1969

> Billy's smile as he came out of the shrubbery was at least as peculiar as Mona Lisa's.
> KURT VONNEGUT *Slaughterhouse-Five* 1969

Marilyn Monroe The American film actress Marilyn Monroe (b. Norma Jean Mortenson, later Baker, 1926) became the definitive Hollywood sex symbol, a breathy-voiced blonde who combined sex appeal with innocence and vulnerability. She starred in such films as *Gentlemen Prefer Blondes* (1953) and *Some Like It Hot* (1959) before her death from an overdose of sleeping pills in 1962.

> A small, curvaceous woman with platinum blonde hair sashayed towards us across the newsroom like some latter-day Marilyn Monroe.
> ANNIE ROSS *Moving Image* 1995

> The people protecting you have morticians who made Boris Karloff look like Marilyn Monroe.
> TOM SHARPE *Grantchester Grind* 1995

Montagues and Capulets The Montagues and the Capulets are warring Veronese families in Shakespeare's *Romeo and Juliet* (1599). As the first lines of the play explain:
'Two households, both alike in dignity,
In fair Verona, where we lay our scene,
From ancient grudge break to new mutiny,
Where civil blood makes civil hands unclean.'
Juliet is a Capulet and Romeo a Montague, and their love and secret marriage are doomed when Romeo reluctantly becomes embroiled in the bitter hatred and fighting between the families. *See also* ROMEO AND JULIET, SHAKESPEARE.

> The Molloys and the Timsons are like the Montagues and the Capulets.
> JOHN MORTIMER *Rumpole of the Bailey* 1978

> There were soon two factions facing off like Montagues and Capulets. *BBC Radio 4* 1997

> I told them I liked it when things were vast and made of iron. And I described a courtyard I went into where there was an iron girder strung between two houses. It seemed to be holding the two buildings apart, as if one was the Capulet house and the other was the house of the Montagues.
> ROSE TREMAIN *The Way I Found Her* 1998

Count of Monte Cristo The Count of Monte Cristo is the hero of a novel of the same name by Alexandre Dumas published in 1844. The novel relates how Edmond Dantès is betrayed by enemies and incarcerated in the Chateau d'If. After fourteen years he finally manages to escape, having been told by a fellow prisoner of buried treasure on the island of Monte Cristo. Dantès finds the treasure, assumes the title of Count of Monte Cristo, and sets about taking revenge on those who had brought about his imprisonment.

> Digween held his breath, suddenly fearful that his world might be about to dissolve beneath his feet. But what Wield had said was, 'He's not going back there. He escaped.' Hiding his relief, Digween exclaimed, 'He . . . it . . . is a monkey, not the Count of bloody Monte Cristo. All right, we can't send him . . . it . . . back to that place, but the proper place for him . . . it . . . is a zoo.'
> REGINALD HILL *On Beulah Height* 1998

Monty Python *Monty Python's Flying Circus* was a British television comedy series which was first broadcast between 1969 and 1974 and is remembered for its combination of satire, bad taste, and surrealist sense of the absurd. The word 'Pythonesque' is used to describe humour of a similarly bizarre or zany kind. *See also* MINISTRY OF SILLY WALKS.

> She had only, after all, meant the thing as a sort of English—as a sort of *Monty Python*-esque—joke.
> REBECCA GOLDSTEIN *Strange Attractors* 1993

> At Brize Norton, at least, someone seemed to be making attempts to set up a kind of rapport between the local and the military presences. There were notices advertising a camp car boot sale and a summer fete, besides the one cheerfully alerting the villagers to the dangers of 'RAF police dogs on patrol'. A sort of surreal, Monty-Pythonish charm hangs over these juxtapositions. *The Observer* 1997

John Pierpoint Morgan John Pierpoint Morgan (1837–1913) was an American banker whose wealth was sufficient to enable him to stabilize the American economy in 1895.

> I bought a dozen volumes on banking and credit and investment securities and they stood on my shelf in red and gold like new money from the mint, promising to unfold the shining secrets that only Midas and Morgan and Maecenas knew.
> E SCOTT FITZGERALD *The Great Gatsby* 1925

Morgan le Fay In Arthurian legend, Morgan le Fay was the half-sister of King Arthur. A former pupil of Merlin, she was an enchantress, possessed of magical powers. After Arthur's final battle, Morgan le Fay transported him to Avalon. In some versions of the legend, she was hostile to Arthur and endeavoured to kill him. *See also* KING ARTHUR.

> The largest mirage ever recorded was sighted in the Arctic . . . It included hills, valleys, and snow-capped peaks extending through at least 120 degrees of the

horizon. It was the type of mirage known as the 'Fata Morgana,' so called because such visions were formerly believed to be the nasty work of Morgan le Fay, King Arthur's evil fairy half-sister. *Queen's Quarterly* 1994

Moriarty In Arthur Conan Doyle's Sherlock Holmes stories, the fiendish Professor Moriarty is the detective's greatest enemy, 'the Napoleon of crime'. *See also* SHERLOCK HOLMES.

She no longer paled or trembled at the idea of sudden death. The renowned John Goss, with all the cool skill, clever thinking and iron fists of detectives in novels, would get her safely past every Moriarty going. She finished the last of her sandwich with obvious pleasure.
RICHARD HALEY *Thoroughfare of Stones* 1995

Morpheus In Roman mythology, Morpheus was the god of dreams, son of Somnus, the god of sleep. To fall into the arms of Morpheus is thus to fall asleep.

Just begin a story with a phrase such as 'I remember Disraeli—poor old Dizzy!—once saying to me, in answer to my poke in the eye,' and you will find me and Morpheus off in a corner, necking.
DOROTHY PARKER *Book Reviews* 1927–33

After coffee I announced myself eager for the fleecy crook of Morpheus' shoulder, and they buggered off.
JULIAN BARNES *Talking It Over* 1991

Keith, even more irritable than Cooper to be dragged from the arms of Morpheus far away in London, perked up a little to hear that Jack was under arrest.
MINETTE WALTERS *The Scold's Bridle* 1994

Moses Moses (*c.*14th–13th *c.* BC) was a Hebrew prophet and lawgiver. According to the Bible, he was born at a time when Pharaoh had decreed that all male Hebrew children were to be killed at birth. His mother hid him for three months and then, when she could hide him no longer, made him a small basket out of bulrushes and placed him in the basket amid the reeds of the Nile. Moses was discovered by Pharaoh's daughter, who took pity on him and decided to raise him as her own child, using the child's own mother for a nurse. So Moses was brought up at the court of Pharaoh.

When a grown man, he killed an Egyptian overseer whom he had seen beating a Hebrew, and was forced to flee to the land of Midian. Here Moses lived as a shepherd in the desert, until after 40 years he was called by God, who appeared in the form of a bush that was in flames but was not consumed by them. God told him to return to Egypt and demand that Pharaoh set his people free.

Moses was accompanied by his brother Aaron, who acted as his spokesman. Together they confronted Pharaoh with God's demand 'Let my people go'. When Pharaoh persisted in refusing to allow Moses to lead the

Israelites out of Egypt, God sent ten plagues to afflict the Egyptians. Pharaoh finally freed the Israelites from bondage and Moses led them out of Egypt. Changing his mind, Pharaoh sent his army in pursuit. The Israelites passed through the Red Sea, which God caused to part for them, but the pursuing Egyptians were drowned when the waters closed on them.

After three months the Israelites reached Mount Sinai. They camped at the foot of the mountain and it was at the top that God gave Moses the Ten Commandments. Led by Moses, the Israelites wandered through the Sinai desert for another 40 years until they finally reached the borders of Canaan. Moses did not enter the Promised Land himself, but was allowed a glimpse of it from Mount Pisgah before he died, at the age of 120. *See also* BURNING BUSH, CANAAN, EXODUS, ISRAELITES, LAND OF MILK AND HONEY, MANNA, PHARAOH, PLAGUES OF EGYPT, PROMISED LAND, RED SEA.

'And now our Prophet has arrived,' he said with his eyes popping expressively. 'Our latterday Moses, who shall lead us out of the wilderness.'
CHESTER HIMES *Blind Man with a Pistol* 1969

But going back to what's fundamental, Vic, it seems to me you guard everything you do like you were protecting baby Moses from the Pharaoh.
SARA PARETSKY *Tunnel Vision* 1994

Mother Hubbard In the nursery rhyme, Old Mother Hubbard
'went to the cupboard,
To fetch her poor dog a bone.
But when she got there
The cupboard was bare,
And so the poor dog had none.'

I stepped over an' looked down the other rows. They were bare as Mama Hubbard's cubbard.
CHESTER HIMES 'Let Me at the Enemy—an' George Brown' (1944) in *The Collected Stories of Chester Himes* 1990

I drove back home, changed into leggings and a baggy white T-shirt and took a look in the fridge. Mother Hubbard would have been right at home there. I dumped out a slice of ham that had curled up to die and settled for a meal of pasta and pesto.
SARAH LACEY *File under: Arson* 1995

Mother Teresa *See* TERESA.

Mozart Wolfgang Amadeus Mozart (1756–91) was an Austrian composer, one of the most gifted and prolific in the history of music. A child prodigy, he was composing by the age of 5. His vast output of works includes more than 40 symphonies, nearly 30 piano concertos, over 20 string quartets, and operas including *The Marriage of Figaro* (1786), *Don Giovanni* (1787), and *The Magic Flute* (1791). Mozart came to epitomize classical music in its purity of form and melody. His name is sometimes mentioned as the archetypal creative genius or child prodigy.

> Each step was like multiplying 235 by 9 478 in your head while we walked and slid down a desert mountain in a snowstorm. Mozart would have had no problem with it but we struggled.
> BART KOSKO *Fuzzy Thinking* 1993

Muhammad According to legend, Muhammad (sometimes called Mahomet) summoned Mount Safa to come to him after being challenged to demonstrate his miraculous powers. When it failed to do so, he attributed this to the mercy of Allah, for if it had come it would have crushed him and the bystanders. If the mountain would not come to him, said Muhammad, then he would go to the mountain. This phrase can be used in any context when a person or thing that you want is unwilling or unable to come to you, as a result of which you must make an effort to go yourself.

> The child scrambled up to the top of the wall and called again and again; but finding this of no avail, apparently made up his mind, like Mahomet, to go to the mountain, since the mountain would not come to him.
> ANNE BRONTË *The Tenant of Wildfell Hall* 1848

Munch Edvard Munch (1863–1944) was a Norwegian painter and engraver. Many of his works portray intense emotional states to express his themes of fear, death, and anxiety. In his most famous painting, *The Scream* (1893), a figure covers his ears, his eyes and mouth wide open, below a swirling red and yellow sky.

> The street door opened and a woman's head inserted itself into the space. Her body didn't follow through. Her mouth was frozen Munch-like, locked in a scream without sound.
> GILLIAN SLOVO *Close Call* 1995

Baron Munchausen Baron Munchausen (sometimes spelled Münchhausen) is the hero of a book by Rudolf Erich Raspe entitled *Baron Munchausen's Narrative of his Marvellous Travels and Campaigns in Russia* (1785). The book recounts stories of the Baron's travels and adventures, which always emphasize the intelligence and prowess of the hero, and are far-fetched in the extreme. The original Baron Munchausen, believed to have lived in 1720–97, is said to have served in the Russian army against the Turks and related wildly extravagant tales of his adventures.

> And when in after days I lost my awe of Mr. Peter enough to question him myself, he laughed at my curiosity, and told me stories that sounded so very

much like Baron Münchausen's, that I was sure he was making fun of me.
ELIZABETH GASKELL *Cranford* 1851–3

From that moment Blenkinthrope was tacitly accepted as the Münchausen of
the party. No effort was spared to draw him out from day to day in the exercise
of testing their powers of credulity, and Blenkinthrope, in the false security of
an assured and receptive audience, waxed industrious and ingenious in
supplying the demand for marvels.
SAKI 'The Seventh Pullet' in *Beasts and Super-Beasts* 1914

Munchkin In L. Frank Baum's children's story *The Wizard of Oz* (1900), the
Munchkins are little people who live in the land of Oz. *See also* WIZARD OF OZ.

Unfortunately, the chairs at Momo are of the children's bedroom variety and if
you hang your jacket on the back, it dusts the floor. Meanwhile, waiters loom
over you in their designer Momo T-shirts . . . and in this unnecessarily authentic
and uncomfortable Munchkin world, even for a regular-sized woman like me,
scrunched-up Madam looked—and apparently felt—like the Wicked Witch of
the West. *The Observer* 1997

Muses In Greek mythology, the nine Muses were the daughters of Zeus and
Mnemosyne, the goddess of memory. They were the patron goddesses of
intellectual and creative ability, literature, music, and dance, providing
inspiration to mortals. Later, each individual Muse became associated with
one particular art:
Calliope: epic poetry
Clio: history
Erato: the lyre and lyric love poetry
Euterpe: lyric poetry and flute playing
Melpomene: tragedy
Polyhymnia: songs to the gods
Terpsichore: dancing and the singing that accompanies it
Thalia: comedy and bucolic poetry
Urania: astronomy
Various places were associated with the worship of the Muses and were
therefore considered to be places of inspiration, notably Pieria on Mount
Olympus, Mount Helicon in Boeotia, and Mount Parnassus. Aganippe,
Castalia, Hippocrene, and the Pierian spring were all waters that were
associated with the Muses and supposed to give poetic inspiration to those
who drank of them. Poets, writers, and musicians call on the Muses for
inspiration, or refer to their inspiration as their Muse. The Muses are usually
alluded to collectively, though sometimes by their individual names.

Dinah, who required large intervals of reflection and repose, and was studious
of ease in all her arrangements, was seated on the kitchen floor, smoking a
short stumpy pipe, to which she was much addicted, and which she always
kindled up, as a sort of censer, whenever she felt the need of an inspiration in

her arrangements. It was Dinah's mode of invoking the domestic Muses.
HARRIET BEECHER STOWE *Uncle Tom's Cabin* 1852

The tribute to Irving had been specially written by that favoured child of the Muses, Urban Frawley.
ROBERTSON DAVIES *World of Wonders* 1975

If I am silent, it is but the tribute genius pays to art. The painter may daub to commission, but his Muse does not.
TIMOTHY MO *An Insular Possession* 1986

Mussolini Benito Mussolini (1883–1945), the founder and leader of the Italian Fascists, was born in Predappio in north-east Italy, the son of a blacksmith. Initially socialist, he founded the Italian Fascist Party after the First World War, becoming known as Il Duce ('the Leader'). He organized a march on Rome by his blackshirts in 1922 and was made prime minister. Mussolini established himself as a dictator and allied Italy with Germany during the Second World War. He was executed by Italian communist partisans shortly before the end of the war. *See also* HITLER.

'If you've finished being funny,' said Everard, 'I'll take my leave.' Tinpot Mussolini, Illidge was thinking.
ALDOUS HUXLEY *Point Counter Point* 1928

Herod wasn't just a tyrant and a unifier of his country, he was also a patron of the arts—perhaps we should think of him as a sort of Mussolini with good taste.
JULIAN BARNES *A History of the World in 10½ Chapters* 1989

Mutt and Jeff Mutt and Jeff were two characters in a US comic strip dating from 1907 and drawn by Bud Fisher. Mutt was tall and lanky, Jeff was short, bald, and wore a top hat. The phrase 'Mutt and Jeff' was subsequently used to describe a pair of people of greatly disparate heights.

'Wasn't the Old Man too mar-vellously funny?' Polly Logan had found a friend. 'And the little carroty man with him.' 'Like Mutt and Jeff.' 'I thought I should die of laughter,' said Nora.
ALDOUS HUXLEY *Point Counter Point* 1928

A ghost in a white sheet had left the procession long enough to stop and stare in stupefaction at one of the white-habited sisters. From this angle, the child and the nun looked like a pair of Mutt-and-jeff Klansmen.
ARMISTEAD MAUPIN *Sure of You* 1990

Myrmidons The Myrmidons were a warlike and brutal Thessalian people who were said to have devotedly followed Achilles to the siege of Troy. Their name means 'Ant People', and, according to legend, they were originally ants turned into human beings by Zeus. In extended usage, a myrmidon is a loyal follower, especially a subordinate or henchman who carries out orders ruthlessly and without scruple.

Roberto, no novice to the rites of delousing, discovered however its beauty for the first time, and he imagined being able to plunge his hands into those silken waves, to kiss those furrows, being himself the destroyer of those bands of infesting myrmidons.

UMBERTO ECO *The Island of the Day Before* 1994

Myron Myron (*c.*480–440 BC) was a Greek sculptor who produced very lifelike sculptures of people, most famously the *Discobolus*, a figure of a man throwing a discus.

Naboth's vineyard The Old Testament book of Kings (1 Kgs. 21) relates how Ahab, king of Samaria, coveted the vineyard of Naboth, a Jezreelite, because it was close to his palace. He asked Naboth to give it to him, offering him either another vineyard or money in return. When Naboth refused, saying that the Lord had forbidden him to give away his father's inheritance, Ahab's wife, Jezebel, plotted Naboth's death so that her husband could take over the vineyard. Ahab and Jezebel were both punished by God for their greed. Allusions to Naboth's Vineyard are usually in the context of a possession that is coveted and obtained by dishonest means.

Canada, where Biblical references are still understood by quite a few people, sees itself suddenly as Naboth's Vineyard.
ROBERTSON DAVIES *Merry Heart* 1998

naiad In Greek and Roman mythology, a naiad was a water-nymph, a beautiful long-haired maiden associated with lakes, rivers, and fountains.

She remained always as Michael had first seen her: a woman who talked with her Naiad hair, her winged eyelashes, her tilted head, her fluent waist and rhetorical feet.
ANAÏS NIN *Children of the Albatross* 1947

Nanook of the North *Nanook of the North* is the title of a silent documentary film made in 1922 by Robert Flaherty. The film chronicles the struggles of an Inuit and his family to survive in Arctic Canada.

He had added several sweaters beneath his overcoat and looked half a stone heavier. I went outside. 'Do I just call you Nanook of the North?'
LUCILLA ANDREWS *Marsh Blood* 1993

Napoleon *See under* BONAPARTE.

Narcissus In Greek mythology, Narcissus was a youth of extraordinary beauty who cruelly spurned many admirers, including the nymph Echo. On bending down to a pool one day to drink, he fell in love with his own reflection. There are various versions of the fate that subsequently befell Narcissus. According to one version, he fell into the pool as he tried to embrace his own reflection and drowned. Another version relates how, having tried to kiss and embrace his reflection and failed, Narcissus simply pined away and died. After his death, the gods turned his body into the white flower that bears his name. Narcissus is the epitome of excessive vanity, and his name has given us the word 'narcissism'. *See also* ECHO.

> A feeling of pain crept over him as he thought of the desecration that was in store for the fair face on the canvas. Once, in boyish mockery of Narcissus, he had kissed, or feigned to kiss, those painted lips that now smiled so cruelly at him.
>
> OSCAR WILDE *The Picture of Dorian Gray* 1891

> There were gilt cherubs in the bathroom holding white towels through rings in their mouths, and the walls and ceiling were made of looking-glass. Narcissus could lie in his nacreous bath and, gazing upward, see all of himself reflected.
>
> ALICE THOMAS ELLIS *The 27th Kingdom* 1982

Narnia Narnia is the name of the imaginary land in which C. S. Lewis set his children's allegorical fantasy *The Lion, the Witch and the Wardrobe* (1950) and six subsequent stories. Narnia's inhabitants include talking beasts (notably the lion Aslan), giants, centaurs, and witches.

> The first chapter of *Amelior Regained* consisted of a discussion between one of the men and one of the women, in a forest, about social justice. In other words, here was some Narnian waterbaby or other and some titless Hobbit or other, with her foot on a log, talking freedom.
>
> MARTIN AMIS *The Information* 1995

Nautilus Jules Verne's adventure classic *Twenty Thousand Leagues Under the Sea* (1869) describes the adventures on board the *Nautilus*, a giant submarine commanded by the mysterious Captain Nemo. The ship contains a library, drawing room, and dining room, all elegantly furnished, and the captain's room, in which hang all manner of instruments for navigating the ship, including thermometers, barometers, hygrometers, chronometers, and manometers.

> Gwyn stepped into his study. . . . Here the two cultures, Gwyn believed, were attractively reconciled: the bright flame of human inquiry, plus lots of gadgets. Give Gwyn a palatinate smoking-jacket, as opposed to a pair of tailored jeans and a lumberjack shirt, and he could be Captain Nemo, taking his seat at the futuristic bridge of the sumptuous Nautilus.
>
> MARTIN AMIS *The Information* 1995

Nazirite A Nazirite was an Israelite specially consecrated to the service of God, whose vows included letting his hair grow. 'All the days of his vow of separation no razor shall come upon his head; until the time is completed for which he separates himself to the Lord, he shall be holy; he shall let the locks of hair of his head grow long' (Num. 6: 1–5). The prophets Samuel and Samson were Nazirites. In the quotation below it is almost certainly Nazirite rather than Nazarene (a native of Nazareth) that is meant.

> His head was utterly concealed beneath a cascade of matted hair that seemed

to have no form or colour. In places it stuck out in twisted corkscrews, and in others it lay in congealed pads like felt; it was the hair of a Nazarene or of a hermit demented by the glory and solitude of God.
LOUIS DE BERNIÈRES *Captain Corelli's Mandolin* 1994

Nebuchadnezzar Nebuchadnezzar (*c*.630–562 BC) was king of Babylon in 605–562 BC, and built the massive fortification walls of Babylon and the Hanging Gardens. He conquered and destroyed Jerusalem in 586 BC and exiled the Israelites to Babylon. The prophet Daniel had a gift for interpreting visions and dreams. He was able to explain the meaning of a strange dream of Nebuchadnezzar's, for which he was made the king's chief adviser. Later, Daniel interpreted a second dream of Nebuchadnezzar's to foretell his insanity, which immediately came to pass. 'The same hour was the thing fulfilled upon Nebuchadnezzar; and he was driven from men, and did eat the grass as oxen, and his body was wet with the dew of heaven, till his hairs were grown like eagles' feathers, and his nails like birds' claws' (Dan. 4: 29–33). There is a famous drawing by William Blake depicting the king in this condition. *See also* DANIEL.

> You have a 'faux air' of Nebuchadnezzar in the fields about you, that is certain: your hair reminds me of eagles' feathers; whether your nails are grown like birds' claws or not, I have not yet noticed.
> CHARLOTTE BRONTË *Jane Eyre* 1847

nectar Nectar was the drink of the Greek gods. *See also* AMBROSIA.

> Then I say, I thank you from the bottom of my heart, Sir, this radish was like the nectar of the Gods.
> MARGARET ATWOOD *Alias Grace* 1996

Nefertiti Nefertiti (14th c. BC) was an Egyptian queen, the wife of Akhenaten. She is best known from the painted limestone portrait bust of her, now in Berlin, that depicts her as a woman of slender regal beauty.

> She had a beautiful neck; the throat of a Nefertiti.
> JOHN FOWLES *The Magus* 1966

> They stayed very late, all except Mrs Max, who left directly dinner was over. I watched as she was driven away, sitting up very straight in the back of one of the black limousines, a ravaged Nefertiti.
> JOHN BANVILLE *The Book of Evidence* 1989

Nelson Admiral Horatio Nelson (1758–1805), lost his right eye at Calvi in Corsica in 1794. According to tradition, at the battle of Copenhagen in 1801 Nelson put his telescope to his blind eye to look at the approaching Danish fleet, and, with the words 'I see no ships', ignored the order to withdraw the English navy. To 'turn the eye of Nelson' to something is the same as to 'turn a blind eye' to it, in other words to pretend not to notice. *See also* TRAFALGAR.

> No longer will a cumshaw ensure that the captains of the revenue cruisers turn

the blind eye of Lord Nelson to the nefarious trade.
TIMOTHY MO *An Insular Possession* 1986

'Yes. It was the coroner's opinion that, if she had been found and prompt action taken, her life could've been saved. And the beak went on to say that anyone living with a drug user should take that elementary precaution of checking that they're OK before retiring for the night.' 'Was there an implication that Slater did a Nelson?' 'Yes. I can just imagine the selfish sod leaving the poor girl to die while he went off to bed.'
MALCOLM HAMMER *Shadows on the Green* 1994

Nemesis In Greek mythology, Nemesis was the goddess responsible for retribution, either for a person who had transgressed the moral code or for a person who had taken too much pride in their success or luck (hubris). Nemesis can now be used to refer to a person's doom or terrible but unavoidable fate, or as a personification of punishment or retribution for wrongdoing or excessive pride. *See also* HUBRIS.

A Nemesis attends the woman who plays the game of elusiveness too often, in the utter contempt for her that, sooner or later, her old admirers feel.
THOMAS HARDY *Jude the Obscure* 1895

She refused to put so much as a piece of thread into a needle in anticipation of her confinement and would have been absolutely unprepared, if her neighbours had not been better judges of her condition than she was, and got things ready without telling her anything about it. Perhaps she feared Nemesis, though assuredly she knew not who or what Nemesis was.
SAMUEL BUTLER *The Way of All Flesh* 1903

'I've never seen anyone jump on a horse like you did,' Stephen said, as we set off to the Intourist. 'One second on the ground, the next, galloping.' 'You never know what you can do until Nemesis breathes down your neck.'
DICK FRANCIS *Trial Run* 1978

It was six a.m. and Bruce's appointment with nemesis was well under way. His old life was already over. Even if he survived his ordeal, nothing would ever be the same again.
BEN ELTON *Popcorn* 1996

Nepenthe Nepenthe was an Egyptian drug believed to make people forget their sorrows. In the *Odyssey* it is used by Helen and described as 'a drug that dispelled all grief and anger and banished remembrance of every trouble'.

'I know not Lethe nor Nepenthe,' remarked he; 'but I have learned many new secrets in the wilderness, and here is one of them . . .'
NATHANIEL HAWTHORNE *The Scarlet Letter* 1850

Neptune In Roman mythology, Neptune was the god of the sea, identified with the Greek god Poseidon. *See also* POSEIDON.

Flying fish. These extraordinary creatures, actually scaly denizens of the deep

and subjects of Neptune, are possessors, like the members of the feathered tribe, of wings.
TIMOTHY MO *An Insular Possession* 1986

He was not an athlete, but he was at the water's hissing edge when his father emerged, like a matted red-lipped Neptune, blue-nosed, encased in dripping wet wool and shining burnt toast.
PETER CAREY *Oscar and Lucinda* 1988

Nereid The Nereids were sea-nymphs in Greek mythology, daughters of Nereus. They include Galatea and Thetis, the mother of Achilles.

Mandras was too young to be a Poseidon, too much without malice. Was he a male sea-nymph, then? Was there such a thing as a male Nereid or Potamid?
LOUIS DE BERNIÈRES *Captain Corelli's Mandolin* 1994

Nereus In Greek mythology, Nereus was an old god of the sea and a son of Gaia. He and his wife, Doris, had 50 daughters, the Nereids.

And finally the storme impetuous
Sunke up these riches, second unto none,
Within the gulfe of greedie Nereus.
EDMUND SPENSER *Complaints* 1591

Nero Nero (AD 37–68) was a Roman emperor in 54–68, notorious for his tyranny and cruelty. He ordered the murder of his mother, Agrippina, in 59, and his reign was marked by the persecution of Christians and the executions of leading Romans who had plotted against him. Nero was alleged to have started the fire that destroyed half of Rome in 64. As the city burned, Nero allegedly played his fiddle and simply watched. To 'fiddle while Rome burns' is to stand by and watch while disaster occurs.

'Wicked and cruel boy!' I said. 'You are like a murderer—you are like a slave-driver—you are like the Roman Emperors!' I had read Goldsmith's *History of Rome*, and had formed my opinion of Nero, Caligula, etc.
CHARLOTTE BRONTË *Jane Eyre* 1847

'I have to denounce the vacillation of the government in the strongest terms,' he said. 'They fiddle while Ishmaelia burns.'
EVELYN WAUGH *Scoop* 1938

When we raise our eyes, we will see that He, having become for us a Nero, not in injustice but in severity, will not console us or succor us or sympathize with us, but, rather, he will laugh with inconceivable delight!
UMBERTO ECO *The Island of the Day Before* 1994

The horny young things of *And The Beat Goes On* are now the ruling elite—smug, decadent Neros who fiddle with themselves while the younger generation burns with resentment. *The Observer* 1996

Nessus In Greek mythology, Nessus was a centaur killed by Hercules, who shot him with his bow for trying to rape Hercules' wife, Deianira. As he lay dying, Nessus told Deianira that if ever she suspected that her husband was being unfaithful, she should smear a garment belonging to Hercules with Nessus' blood and this would act as a love potion. Deianira followed this advice when she feared that Hercules had fallen in love with the princess Iole, but the centaur's blood was a corrosive poison that caused Hercules to die in unendurable agony. The phrase 'shirt of Nessus' is sometimes used to denote a destructive force from which escape is impossible. *See also* DEIANIRA, HERCULES.

> Once, temporarily envious of Boy, I bought a silk shirt and paid nine dollars for it. It burned me like the shirt of Nessus, but I wore it to rags, to get my money out of it, garment of guilty luxury that it was.
> ROBERTSON DAVIES *The Deptford Trilogy* 1970

> I established the fact that Nancy had been in the habit of selling her employer's cast-off garments to the servants, with or without her master's permission; so McDermott could have come by his shirt of Nessus honestly enough. Unfortunately, Kinnear's corpse had churlishly slipped on one of McDermott's shirts, which was a stumbling block indeed.
> MARGARET ATWOOD *Alias Grace* 1996

Nestor In Greek mythology, Nestor was a king of Pylos. He lived to a great age and was one of the oldest and wisest of the Greek heroes in the Trojan War, which he survived, returning to Pylos. Nestor's name can be used to typify a wise old man or mentor. *See also* TROJAN WAR.

> Another attempt to refute atheistic pluralism, which carried more weight than this statement by an educated amateur, was that made by the Nestor of English science and cofounder of the theory of evolution, Alfred Russel Wallace.
> KARL GUTHKE *The Last Frontier* trans. H. ATKINS 1983

Never-Never Land Never-Never Land is the magical country to which Peter Pan escorts Wendy, John, and Michael Darling in J. M. Barrie's play *Peter Pan* (first performed 1904). The land is populated by staple characters from children's stories, such as mermaids and pirates, including the murderous pirate Captain Hook. Never-Never Land can be alluded to as an ideal place far from the problems encountered in the real world. *See also* PETER PAN.

> 'Of course,' he added with a flash of his normal style, 'I suppose she could have had a date or something.' The photographer chuckled. 'Yeah,' he said, 'maybe her prince came and took her to Never Never Land.'
> MOLLY MCKITTERICK *The Medium Is Murder* 1991

Newgate Newgate is London's famous historic prison. Originally the gatehouse of one of the city gates, Newgate was first used as a prison in the early Middle Ages, and the last prison on the site was closed in 1880 and demolished in 1902. The prison housed many notorious criminals as well as debtors, and became notorious in the 18th century for the wretched conditions in which the inmates lived.

> The Royal Palace . . . resembles Newgate whitewashed and standing on a sort of mangy desert.
> WILLIAM MAKEPEACE THACKERAY *Punch* 1844

New Jerusalem In Christian theology, the New Jerusalem is the abode of the blessed in Heaven. The term can be used to refer to an ideal place or situation.

> You think Victoria is like the New Jerusalem.
> G. K. CHESTERTON *The Man Who Was Thursday* 1908

> If their zeal for their salvation, he thought, began to equal their zeal for minding his business, the New Jerusalem would quickly be at hand.
> ROBERTSON DAVIES *Leaven of Malice* 1954

> There was talk of a coming election when the New Jerusalem might again be on offer.
> JOHN MORTIMER *Paradise Postponed* 1985

> It had to come from Cape Town, a place Samuel had never seen in her life but which in her reckoning ranked with the new Jerusalem.
> ANDRÉ BRINK *Imaginings of Sand* 1996

Isaac Newton Isaac Newton (1642–1727), the English mathematician and physicist, was the greatest single influence on theoretical physics until Einstein. In his work *Principia Mathematica* (1687), Newton gave a mathematical description of the laws and mechanics of gravitation. According to a famous story, first told by Voltaire, in 1665 or 1666 Newton watched an apple fall from a tree in a garden and this inspired his insights into gravity.

Nibelung In Germanic mythology, Nibelung was the king of a race of Scandinavian dwarves, also called the Nibelung, who owned a hoard of treasure and gold. In the 13th-century epic German poem the *Nibelungenlied*, the treasure is guarded by the dwarf Alberich and later taken by Siegfried, the hero of the poem. *See also* ALBERICH'S CLOAK, SIEGRIED.

Nietzsche Friedrich Wilhelm Nietzsche (1844–1900) was a German philosopher whose works include *Also Sprach Zarathustra* ('Thus Spoke Zarathustra', 1883–5) and *Jenseits von Gut and Böse* ('Beyond Good and Evil', 1886). Themes in his writings include contempt for Christian ethics and for democracy and admiration of the 'will to power', the *Übermensch* (superman), and the 'master class', the small group of superior people who dominate the mass of inferior people, the 'herd'. Nietzsche's *Übermensch* was an ideal being whose superior physical and mental qualities represent the goal of human evolution.

Because she was brave, because she was 'spoiled', because of her outrageous

and commendable independence of judgment, and finally because of her arrogant consciousness that she had never seen a girl as beautiful as herself, Gloria had developed into a consistent, practising Nietzschean.
F SCOTT FITZGERALD *The Beautiful and the Damned* 1922

'I should like some coffee,' she announced, with what she hoped was Nietzschean directness.
ANITA BROOKNER *Hotel du Lac* 1984

Niflheim In Scandinavian mythology, Niflheim was the underworld, a place of eternal cold, darkness, and mist. While those who died in battle were believed to go to Valhalla and feast with Odin, those who died of old age or illness were believed to go to Niflheim. *See also* VALHALLA.

But he continued motionless and silent in that gloomy Niflheim or fogland which involved him, and she proceeded on her way.
THOMAS HARDY *The Woodlanders* 1887

Florence Nightingale An English nurse and medical reformer, Florence Nightingale (1820–1910) became famous during the Crimean War for improving sanitation and medical procedures, achieving a dramatic reduction in the mortality rate. She became known as the Lady of the Lamp because of her nightly rounds of the wards carrying a lamp.

'Besides, there is sure to be a lot of material I can collect for my novel; and perhaps one or two of the relations will have messes or miseries in their domestic circle which I can clear up.' 'You have the most revolting Florence Nightingale complex,' said Mrs Smiling.
STELLA GIBBONS *Cold Comfort Farm* 1932

Every woman loves an invalid. I bring out the Florence Nightingale in them.
MARGARET ATWOOD *The Edible Woman* 1969

Every woman I've had turned to hate. First they cool the fires, all lovey-dovey, real little Florence Nightingales, darling this, darling that, then, when you think it's gone out for good, whoosh they've stoked up a blaze that would melt steel.
MIKE NICOL *The Powers That Be* 1989

Oh and why did she give up wanting to be a social worker? Was she too fucking sensitive to the pain of the world? Wrong way round: if you ask me, the pain of the world wasn't sensitive enough to *her*. All those damaged people and fucked-up families didn't appreciate the astonishing privilege they were being granted of having their troubles treated by Miss Florence Nightingale herself.
JULIAN BARNES *Talking It Over* 1991

Nightmare on Elm Street *Nightmare on Elm Street* is the title of a gory horror film made in 1984 in which a killer called Freddy Krueger, who has knives for fingernails, brutally murders teenagers in their dreams. The film was followed by several sequels. *See also* FREDDY KRUEGER.

If health professionals and writers took the middle line between Never-Never Land and Nightmare on Maternity Street perhaps *Life After Babies* wouldn't be quite such a rude awakening. *The Independent* 1994

Nijinsky Vaslav Nijinsky (1890–1950), the legendary Russian dancer, trained at the Imperial Ballet School in St Petersburg and became one of the leading dancers in Diaghilev's Ballet Russe. He appeared in the first performance of Stravinsky's *Petrouchka* (1911) and danced in Fokine's ballets as well as in the classical repertoire. His own choreography included *L'Après-midi d'un faune* (1912) and *Le Sacre du Printemps* (1913). His career ended when he was diagnosed as having paranoid schizophrenia in 1917.

It is said of the same puppets . . . that they are *antigrav,* that they can rise and leap, like Nijinsky, as if no such thing as gravity existed for them.
PAUL DE MAN *Rhetoric of Romanticism* 1983

Nike Nike was the Greek goddess of victory, usually represented as a winged figure. Statues of Nike are often referred to as 'Winged Victories', such as the Nike of Samothrace (*c.*200 BC), preserved in the Louvre in Paris.

She's a Nike . . . on the prow of a Greek ship.
ANNA DOUGLAS SEDGWICK *The Little French Girl* 1924

Nimrod In the Old Testament, Nimrod is named as the founder of the Babylonian dynasty and is described as 'a mighty hunter' (Gen. 10: 8–9). Thus any great or skilful hunter or sportsman can be described as a Nimrod.

It was not so positively stated, but the consensus seemed to be that Bertha Shanklin had shown poor taste in dying so soon and thus embarrassing the local Nimrod.
ROBERTSON DAVIES *Fifth Business* 1970

Nimue In Arthurian legend, Nimue (also known as Vivien) was the Lady of the Lake. The wily mistress of the wizard Merlin, Nimue extracted from him the secrets of his craft, which she used against him to imprison him in an oak tree for eternity. *See also* KING ARTHUR, LADY OF THE LAKE, MERLIN.

Nineveh Nineveh was an ancient city located on the east bank of the Tigris, opposite the modern city of Mosul, Iraq. It was the oldest city of the ancient Assyrian Empire and its capital during the reign of Sennacherib until it was destroyed by the Medes and the Babylonians in 612 BC. Its destruction is forecast by the Old Testament prophet Nahum. Elsewhere in the Bible, the prophet Jonah is called by God to preach to the people of Nineveh and warn them of the destruction of their city unless they reform their wicked behaviour. In the opening lines of John Masefield's poem *Cargoes* (1903), Nineveh and Ophir are presented as places of far-away exoticism:
'Quinquireme of Nineveh from distant Ophir
Rowing home to haven in sunny Palestine.'
See also JONAH, OPHIR.

I've been to Europe and the States but never to Nineveh and Distant Ophir.
JULIAN BARNES *Talking It Over* 1991

He had as much of a vested interest in the damnation of the trekkers as Jonah had had in the annihilation of Nineveh.
ANDRÉ BRINK *Imaginings of Sand* 1996

Ninth Plague of Egypt In the book of Exodus in the Old Testament the ninth plague of Egypt was 'a thick darkness in all the land of Egypt three days' (Exod. 10: 22). The Israelites in Goshen were spared this darkness. *See also* GOSHEN, MOSES, PLAGUES OF EGYPT.

By reason of the density of the interwoven foliage overhead, it was gloomy there at cloudless noontide, twilight in the evening, dark as midnight at dusk, and black as the ninth plague of Egypt at midnight.
THOMAS HARDY *Far from the Madding Crowd* 1874

Niobe In Greek mythology, Niobe was the daughter of Tantalus and the mother of numerous offspring. She boasted that her large family made her superior to the goddess Leto, who only had two children, Apollo and Artemis. Angered by this, Apollo slew all Niobe's sons, and Artemis her daughters. Niobe herself was turned into a stone, and her tears into streams that eternally trickled from it. She has become a symbol of inconsolable grief. In Shakespeare's *Hamlet*, Hamlet describes his mother at his father's funeral as 'Like Niobe, all tears'.

The Niobe of nations! there she stands,
Childless and crownless, in her voiceless woe.
LORD BYRON *Childe Harold* 1818

Nirvana Nirvana is the final goal of Buddhism, a transcendent state in which there is neither suffering, desire, nor sense of self.

He began to feel a drowsy attachment for this South—a South, it seemed, more of Algiers than of Italy, with faded aspirations pointing back over innumerable generations to some warm, primitive Nirvana, without hope or care.
F SCOTT FITZGERALD *The Beautiful and the Damned* 1922

'Then why didn't you just live there happily ever after?' 'Because there's a snake in every paradise, even if it is Valhalla, or Nirvana.'
ANDRÉ BRINK *Imaginings of Sand* 1996

Noah The book of Genesis (6–9) relates how God, seeing that 'the wickedness of man was great in the earth', decided to send a great flood to destroy the whole of mankind. Only Noah 'found grace in the eyes of the Lord' and so God warned him of the coming flood and instructed him to build an ark (a large boat about 133 metres long) in which to save himself and his family and also two of every species of creature on the earth. Apart from those in the Ark, all inhabitants of the earth drowned in the Flood, which lasted for 40 days and 40 nights. The floodwaters rose high with the Ark on their surface, and after the rain stopped gradually receded. The Ark came to rest on Mount Ararat. Noah sent out birds from the Ark in the hope they would bring back evidence of dry land. First he sent out a raven, and then a dove. After a week the dove returned with an olive leaf, so Noah knew the waters had completely receded. When Noah and his family were able to walk again on land, God blessed them, saying: 'Be fruitful, and multiply, and replenish the earth.' God promised Noah that he would never again send a flood to destroy all living things, and produced a rainbow as 'a token of a covenant between me and the earth'. Noah lived to the age of 950 and his sons, Ham, Shem, and Japhet, became the ancestors of many nations. *See also* ARK, FLOOD, HAM.

> The Nantucketer, he alone resides and riots on the sea; he alone, in Bible language, goes down to it in ships; to and fro ploughing it as his own special plantation. There is his home; there lies his business, which a Noah's flood would not interrupt, though it overwhelmed all the millions in China.
> HERMAN MELVILLE *Moby Dick* 1851

> The world had been destroyed and only the lamp-post, like Noah, preserved from the universal cataclysm.
> ALDOUS HUXLEY *Point Counter Point* 1928

> He had research assistants, in fluctuating numbers, whom he despatched like Noah's doves and ravens into the libraries of the world, clutching numbered slips of paper, like cloakroom tickets or luncheon vouchers, each containing a query, a half-line of possible quotation, a proper name to be located.
> A. S. BYATT *Possession* 1990

Noah's Ark *See* ARK.

noble savage The concept of the 'noble savage' was that of Jean-Jacques Rousseau (1712–78), the French philosopher and writer. His descriptions of the noble savage, an idealized man living a natural life free from the influences of civilization, reflect his belief in the fundamental goodness of human nature and the corrupting influence of modern society. *See also* ROUSSEAU.

> She was all loving to me at first, but then she got sarcastic and said she couldn't stand the sight of me. 'Here comes the noble savage,' she called out when I came home, and used longer words I didn't know the meaning of when I asked her where my tea was.
> ALAN SILLITOE *The Loneliness of the Long Distance Runner* 1959

Nod *See* LAND OF NOD.

Noddy Noddy is a character in children's stories by Enid Blyton, a boy whose head nods as he speaks. His name can be used to refer to anything childlike, over-simplistic, or trivial.

Norns In Nordic mythology, the Norns were three goddesses who spun the fate of both people and the gods. They were named Urd (the past), Verdandi (the present), and Skuld (the future), and gathered under the ash tree Yggdrasil.

> Yonder float the white swans—an Icelandic story-teller would say they are Norns, presiders over destiny.
> E METCALFE *Oxonian in Iceland* 1861

Nostradamus Nostradamus is the Latinized name by which Michel de Nostredame (1503–66) is generally known. He was a French astrologer and physician and the author of *Centuries* (1555), a collection of prophecies written in rhyming quatrains. Although cryptic and obscure, Nostradamus' verses have been interpreted as foretelling prominent global events over a span of more than 400 years.

> I spoke last week to the science fiction writer Arthur C. Clarke, the Nostradamus of space, whose predictions, among other things, have included the development of the communication satellite. *The Observer* 1997

Notre Dame *See* HUNCHBACK OF NOTRE DAME.

Rudolph Nureyev Rudolph Nureyev (1939–93) was a Russian ballet dancer who defected to the West while in Paris in 1961. His partnership with Margot Fonteyn, dancing for the Royal Ballet, was inspired. In addition to his wide range of roles in classical and modern ballet, he choreographed *La Bayadère* (1963) and other ballets, performed in films such as *Don Quixote* (1975), and was artistic director of the Paris Opera Ballet in 1983–9. *See also* MARGOT FONTEYN.

> So I Nureyeved the front steps and flowed through the door in a single motion of Yale and Chubb.
> JULIAN BARNES *Talking It Over* 1991

Nymph Nymphs were mythological semi-divine spirits represented as beautiful maidens and associated with aspects of nature, especially with rivers and woods. The corresponding adjective is 'Nymphean'.

> Without throwing a Nymphean tissue over a milkmaid, let it be said that here criticism checked itself as out of place, and looked at her proportions with a long consciousness of pleasure.
> THOMAS HARDY *Far from the Madding Crowd* 1874

> Nymph? Goddess? Vampire? Yes, she was all of these and none of them. She was, like every woman, everything that the mind of a man . . . wished to imagine.
> LAWRENCE DURRELL *Clea* 1960

Annie Oakley Annie Oakley (1860–1926) was an American markswoman. In 1885 she joined Buffalo Bill's Wild West Show, of which she became a star attraction for the next seventeen years. She was nicknamed Little Sure-Shot by the Sioux Indian chief Sitting Bull.

> It is many years since I owned a catapault and was generally referred to in the sporting world as England's answer to Annie Oakley . . .
> P G. WODEHOUSE *Cocktail Time* 1958

> 'Look'—she stood there, awkwardly, one hand on her waist, the other on her holster. A pint-sized Annie Oakley—'I'm working the next two days. If you still need help after, how about I give you a hand? I'm not talking about pay duty. This is to help.'
> TED WOOD *A Clean Kill* 1995

Captain Oates Captain Lawrence Oates (1880–1912) was an English explorer on Scott's expedition to the South Pole. Believing that his severe frostbite would jeopardize his companions' survival, he deliberately went out into a blizzard to sacrifice his own life. His famous last words were 'I am just going outside and may be some time.' His epitaph reads: 'Hereabouts died a very gallant gentleman, Captain L. E. G. Oates of the Inniskilling Dragoons. In March 1912, returning from the Pole, he walked willingly to his death in a blizzard, to try and save his comrades, beset by hardship. This note is left by the Relief Expedition 1912.'

> He didn't believe her. But he said, 'I suppose I'm a bit of a burden on you, Dora, these days. Perhaps I ought to go off and die.' Like Oates at the south Pole.
> MURIEL SPARK 'The Father's Daughters' in *The Collected Stories* 1961

> 'Will he have to stay?' 'Of course. This may take some time.' What had I committed Nick to? His last statement had a sinisterly permanent, Oates-stepping-out-into-the-Arctic-waste flavour.
> ANABEL DONAL *The Glass Ceiling* 1994

Odin In Scandinavian mythology, Odin (corresponding to the Germanic god Woden or Wotan) was the supreme god and creator, the husband of Frigga and the father of Thor and Balder. He was worshipped as the god of wisdom, war, poetry, and the dead. Odin obtained his wisdom by drinking from Mimir's well but had to sacrifice an eye to do so, and is consequently usually represented as one-eyed, often attended by two black ravens, Hugin (thought) and Munin (memory).

> But God, thank goodness, includes both Loki and Odin, the comedian and the scholar, the jester and the saint. God did not fashion a very regular universe after all. And we poor sods of his image are therefore condemned to struggle with calendrical questions till the cows come home, and Christ comes round.
> STEPHEN JAY GOULD *Questioning the Millennium* 1997

Odysseus In Greek mythology, Odysseus, known to the Romans as Ulysses, was the king of Ithaca, son of Laertes. As one of the suitors of Helen of Troy, Odysseus proposed that when she married, she and whoever she finally chose to be her husband would be defended by all the other suitors. She chose Menelaus, and when she was abducted by Paris, the Greeks, including Odysseus, mounted an expedition to bring her back from Troy.

Homer's epic poem the *Odyssey* is an account of Odysseus' ten-year journey home to Ithaca after the fall of Troy. His adventures included encounters with:

the Lotus-Eaters, whose lotus fruits when eaten made Odysseus' crew lose all memory of past events and their homes and made them wish never to leave;

the one-eyed giant Polyphemus, one of the Cyclopes, who was eventually blinded by Odysseus and his men;

the Laestrygones, a tribe of cannibalistic giants;

Circe, a beautiful enchantress who lived on the island of Aeaea. After she turned half his men into swine, Odysseus protected himself with the mythical herb moly and forced her to break the spell and restore his men to human form. Odysseus was detained on Circe's island for a year;

the Sirens, whose singing had the power to lure sailors to their death on dangerous rocks. Odysseus had himself tied to the mast of his ship in order to hear their song safely, having first ordered his crew to plug their ears with wax;

the nymph Calypso, who detained him on her island for seven years. He refused her offer to make him immortal.

When Odysseus finally reached Ithaca after an absence of 20 years, he found his wife, Penelope, waiting patiently and faithfully for her husband to return home and besieged by suitors. Athene disguised Odysseus as an old beggar so that he could arrive secretly at his palace. Assisted by his son Telemachus and two faithful retainers, he slew all the suitors and was finally reunited with Penelope. Because of the numerous obstacles and dangers that Odysseus had to overcome in returning from Troy, he can be associated with a long period of bad luck. He can also stand for a wanderer far from home.

See also CALYPSO, CIRCE, LOTUS-EATERS, ODYSSEY, PENELOPE, SIRENS, TROJAN WAR.

> Woeps was on the phone. Cook heard him say, 'Is it bad?' and he suspected his friend was talking to his wife about yet another domestic calamity. Woeps' only serious fault—and it could hardly be called a fault—was his Odyssean attraction for bad luck.
> DAVID CARKEET *Double Negative* 1980

It had been demoralising to wander like Odysseus from place to place, far from home, improvising a resistance that never seemed to amount to anything.
LOUIS DE BERNIÈRES *Captain Corelli's Mandolin* 1994

'What came after Shakespeare, then?' 'Television. A short stint in Hollywood. Back to the West End. Believe me, an actor's journey from obscurity to fame is as classic as that of Odysseus returning to his homeland, or indeed of those latter-day heroes, Stephen Dedalus and Leopold Bloom, on their progression through Dublin that summer's day in June 1904.'
SUSAN MOODY *Sacrifice Bid* 1997

Odyssey In Greek mythology, Odysseus was the son of Laertes, king of Ithaca, and central figure of the *Odyssey*. He was known to the Romans as Ulysses. Homer's epic poem the *Odyssey* recounts the ten-year voyage of Odysseus during his years of wandering after the fall of Troy, and of his eventual return home to Ithaca and his killing of the suitors of his faithful wife, Penelope. His adventures include encounters with the Cyclops, Circe, the Lotus-Eaters, and the Sirens. Any long series of wanderings or long, adventurous journey can be described as an odyssey. *See also* ODYSSEUS.

I took a walk down by the Mississippi River and watched the logs that came floating from Montana in the north—grand Odyssean logs of our continental dream.
JACK KEROUAC *On the Road* 1957

The roundabout could go on faster, judging by shouts and squeals from the girls. Colin's movements were clumsy, and he envied the attendant's dexterity a few yards in front, and admired Bert who had made this same circular Odyssey with so much aplomb.
ALAN SILLITOE *The Loneliness of the Long Distance Runner* 1959

This great American terminal was the starting point for his odyssey into homelessness, addiction and back to his new life as a writer. *The Independent* 1998

Oedipus In Greek mythology, Oedipus was the son of Jocasta and of Laius, king of Thebes. The infant Oedipus was left to die on a mountainside by Laius, who had been warned by an oracle that his own son would kill him. Found by a shepherd, Oedipus was subsequently adopted by the king of Corinth and his wife, whom he believed to be his parents. When an adult, Oedipus heard the oracle's prophecy and fled to Thebes, where he unwittingly killed his real father, Laius, and married Jocasta, by whom he had four children. When they discovered the truth, Odysseus blinded himself in a fit of madness and left Thebes as an outcast, while Jocasta hanged herself. In psychoanalytical theory, the Oedipus complex is a son's subconscious sexual attraction to his mother and hostility towards his father. Oedipus is thus alluded to especially in the context of the incestuous love of a son for his mother. He can also stand for someone who is predestined to act

in a particular way and is powerless to act otherwise and as an image of
blindness or being blinded.

> Mr. Tulliver's prompt procedure entailed on him further promptitude in finding
> the convenient person who was desirous of lending five hundred pounds on
> bond. 'It must be no client of Wakem's,' he said to himself; and yet at the end
> of a fortnight it turned out to the contrary; not because Mr. Tulliver's will was
> feeble, but because external fact was stronger. Wakem's client was the only
> convenient person to be found. Mr. Tulliver had a destiny as well as Oedipus,
> and in this case he might plead, like Oedipus, that his deed was inflicted on him
> rather than committed by him.
> GEORGE ELIOT *The Mill on the Floss* 1860

> I hit him where I wanted, plug in his right eye . . . Demetriades stood like a
> parody of Oedipus with his hands over his eyes.
> JOHN FOWLES *The Magus* 1966

> The last time I saw you, when I was passing through from Mississippi, you were
> in pretty bad shape. You've probably regressed completely by now living in that
> substandard old house with only your mother for company. Aren't your natural
> impulses crying for release? A beautiful and meaningful love affair would
> transform you, Ignatius. I know it would. Great Oedipus bonds are encircling
> your brain and destroying you.
> JOHN KENNEDY TOOLE *A Confederacy of Dunces* 1980

> Her younger brother, Basil, in his final year of Modern Greats at Oxford, spoke
> of going into the City when he graduated, but Robyn considered this was just
> talk, designed to ward off hubris about his forthcoming examinations, or an
> Oedipal teasing of his academic father.
> DAVID LODGE *Nice Work* 1989

Scarlett O'Hara Scarlett O'Hara is a beautiful and egotistical Southern belle,
the heroine of Margaret Mitchell's novel *Gone with the Wind* (1936), set during
the American Civil War. The hugely successful 1939 film starring Vivien
Leigh and Clark Gable further popularized the story of Scarlett and her
stormy and ultimately unhappy love affair with the handsome Rhett Butler.
See also RHETT BUTLER, GONE WITH THE WIND.

> I found myself whistling Mozart under my breath as I got dressed. The Scarlett
> O'Hara syndrome. Rhett comes and spends the night and suddenly you're
> singing and happy again.
> SARA PARETSKY *Guardian Angel* 1992

> 'I need you to come with me.' His voice was clipped and anything but
> apologetic. 'I believe you were informed I'm busy. And you haven't been invited
> into this room.' 'Save it Scarlett.' He grabbed her hand and pulled.
> NORA ROBERTS *Sanctuary* 1997

> I took another look at my hair and decided it needed some help, so I did the
> gel, blow-dry, hair spray routine. When I was done I was several inches taller. I
> stood in front of the mirror and did the Wonder Woman thing, feet spread, fists

on hips. 'Eat dirt, scumbag,' I said to the mirror. Then I did the Scarlett thing, hand to my heart, coy smile. 'Rhett, you handsome devil, how you do go on.'
JANET EVANOVICH *Four to Score* 1998

Old Harry Old Harry is another name for the Devil or Satan. *See* DEVIL, SATAN.

The old mill 'ud miss me, I think, Luke. There's a story as when the mill changes hands, the river's angry—I've heard my father say it many a time. There's no telling whether there mayn't be summat *in* the story, for this is a puzzling world, and Old Harry's got a finger in it—it's been too many for me, I know.
GEORGE ELIOT *The Mill on the Floss* 1860

The thing is, Con, don't you see, he's old? I think he *minds* not being able to do things the way he used to. He's always been—well, I've gathered he's a pretty domineering type, and now his property and his money's the only kind of power he's got left. That's why he won't commit himself; I don't think he realises just how unfair he's being to younger people . . . to you anyway. He just thinks—quite rightly—that it's his property, and he'll play Old Harry with it if he wants to.
MARY STEWART *The Ivy Tree* 1964

Old Man of the Sea The Old Man of the Sea is a character in 'Sinbad the Sailor', one of the tales in *The Arabian Nights*. He persuades Sinbad to carry him on his shoulders, whereupon he entwines his legs round him, so that Sinbad cannot dislodge him. Sinbad is forced to carry him on his shoulders for many days and nights, until at last he gets the Old Man drunk with wine and manages to shake him off. The term can be used to denote a tiresome, heavy burden or allude to irritating persistence. *See also* ARABIAN NIGHTS.

He is the bore of the age, the old man whom we Sinbads cannot shake off.
ANTHONY TROLLOPE *Barchester Towers* 1857

Well, we can't have it, so don't let us grumble but shoulder our bundles and trudge along as cheerfully as Marmee does. I'm sure Aunt March is a regular Old Man of the Sea to me, but I suppose when I've learned to carry her without complaining, she will tumble off, or get so light that I shan't mind her.
LOUISA M. ALCOTT *Little Women* 1868

Old Nick Old Nick is another name for the Devil or Satan. *See* DEVIL, SATAN.

Olive Oyl In Elzie Segar's comic strip *Thimble Theater*, which started in 1919, Olive Oyl is the very skinny girlfriend of Popeye the Sailor Man. *See also* POPEYE.

The nice thing about leggings is they fit anybody from Olive Oyl to a lapsed Weightwatcher.
SARAH LACEY *File under: Arson* 1995

She stood tall, straight and thin, like a tense Olive Oyl gone blonde.
LINDA MATHER *Gemini Doublecross* 1995

She was rarely between films—I hadn't seen her for almost a year. She still looked like a gorgeous Olive Oyl, all long, gangly limbs and droopy skirts—albeit an Olive Oyl who had finally hit the hay with Popeye.
LINDSAY MARACOTTA *Playing Dead* 1999

Olympus Mount Olympus, in Greece, is traditionally held to be the home of the Greek gods. The adjective 'Olympian' can refer to anyone or anything that is superior to or more important than lesser mortals.

I think I shall have a lofty throne for you, godmamma, or rather two, one on the lawn and another in the ballroom, that you may sit and look down upon us like an Olympian goddess.
GEORGE ELIOT *Adam Bede* 1859

It was Mrs Heeny who peopled the solitude of the long ghostly days with lively anecdotes of the Van Degens, the Driscolls, the Chauncey Ellings and the other social potentates whose least doings Mrs Spragg and Undine had followed from afar in the Apex papers, and who had come to seem so much more remote since only the width of the Central Park divided mother and daughter from their Olympian portals.
EDITH WHARTON *The Custom of the Country* 1913

'Indeed!' Mr Barbecue-Smith smiled benignly, and looking up at Denis with an expression of Olympian condescension, 'And what sort of things do you write?'
ALDOUS HUXLEY *Crome Yellow* 1921

Ruth can hardly keep still and Philip Drummond has to tell her to sit down and await her turn, and when her turn comes she tears Molteno to pieces for his equivocal espousal of justice. Molteno looks at her as though she were some Olympian Judge of Appeal, astonished and mystified that a lawyer could exhibit such passion.
ALAN PATON *Ah, But Your Land Is Beautiful* 1981

Aristotle Onassis Aristotle Socrates Onassis (1906–75) was a Greek shipowner who built up an extensive independent shipping empire and founded the Greek national airline, Olympic Airways. His name can stand for great wealth.

Chilcott rubbed his hands together. 'Wickham's something in the City and as rich as Onassis, according to Sir Peter. Could do me a lot of good, business-wise, if I play my cards right.'
SUSAN MOODY *Grand Slam* 1994

Eugene Onegin and Tatiana In Pushkin's novel in verse form *Eugene Onegin* (1823–31), Tatiana, a young country girl, falls in love with Eugene Onegin, the friend of her sister Olga's fiancé, Lensky. Onegin, who, though young, is cynical, disillusioned, and easily bored, is dismissive when Tatiana pours out her feelings to him in a letter. The following winter, Onegin flirts with Olga and Lensky challenges him to a duel in which Lensky is killed.
Some years later Tatiana meets and marries the middle-aged Prince

Gremin. Onegin meets her at a ball, falls in love with her, and is subject to the same fevered passion as she had earlier experienced for him. Eventually he calls on her and manages to wring from her the admission that she does still love him. But she holds to her marriage and dismisses him.

Pushkin's poem is also the subject of Tchaikovsky's opera of the same name.

> I felt like Eugene Onegin listening to that tiresome Prince hymn his Tatyana.
> JULIAN BARNES *Talking It Over* 1991

Ophelia In Shakespeare's *Hamlet* (1604), Ophelia, the daughter of Polonius, is in love with Hamlet but rejected by him. Her grief after her father's fatal stabbing at Hamlet's hands sends her into a state of madness. During her famous 'mad scene' in the play, she sings several bawdy and death-obsessed songs. Later it is reported that, while making garlands of flowers by the side of a stream, she fell in and drowned. Ophelia's death scene is the subject of a famous painting (1851–2) by John Everett Millais, which depicts her floating face-upwards in the stream, surrounded by flowers, and about to slip beneath the water. According to theatrical tradition, she is often portrayed on stage with flowers entwined in her hair. *See also* POLONIUS.

> How do you know that Hetty isn't floating at the present moment in some star-lit pond, with lovely water-lilies round her, like Ophelia?
> OSCAR WILDE *The Picture of Dorian Gray* 1891

> She is an accomplished actress and a most practised liar. While among us, she amused herself with a number of supposed fits, hallucinations, caperings, warblings and the like, nothing being lacking to the impersonation but Ophelia's wild flowers entwined in her hair.
> MARGARET ATWOOD *Alias Grace* 1996

> I just hoped there was no way he could trace back to my connection with Tim. Otherwise my lifeless corpse would probably be found floating down the river on Sunday evening after the river cruise, an Ophelia in polluted waters.
> LAUREN HENDERSON *The Black Rubber Dress* 1997

Ophir Ophir was an unidentified region in the Bible, perhaps in south-east Arabia, famous as the source of the gold and precious stones brought to King Solomon (1 Kgs. 9: 28, 10: 10). *See also* NINEVEH.

Oracle *See* DELPHI.

Orestes In Greek mythology, Orestes was the son of Agamemnon and Clytemnestra, and the brother of Electra. On reaching manhood in exile, he returned to Argos and killed his mother and her lover Aegisthus in revenge for the murder of Agamemnon. Pursued and driven mad by the avenging Furies for the crime of matricide, he fled to the shrine of Apollo at Delphi, where ultimately he was pardoned by Athene. *See also* FURIES, PYLADES AND ORESTES.

In some places there were nagging clouds of black flies, so that I climbed
through the trees like a new Orestes, cursing and slapping.
JOHN FOWLES *The Magus* 1966

Orion In Greek mythology, Orion was a giant and hunter who at his death
was changed into a constellation by Artemis.

Orphan Annie Little Orphan Annie is the heroine of a US comic strip *Little
Orphan Annie* created by Harold Gray and first appearing in 1925. Annie is a
self-reliant, plucky, 11-year-old orphan girl with curly red hair. Her life is
eased by the intervention of the wealthy Daddy Warbucks. *See also* DADDY
WARBUCKS.

As he eased his way around the screen door, trying not to let in any more flies,
he could see her head bent over the typewriter, a mare's nest of Orphan Annie
curls that made him long to duck her head in a bucket of water.
SHARYN MCCRUMB *If Ever I Return* 1990

Decker shook her hand noticing long, slender fingers. Her face was grave, but
childlike—waifish with big brown eyes. Her hair was auburn and bushy. Little
Orphan Annie had grown up to be a doctor.
FAYE KELLERMAN *Prayers for the Dead* 1996

Orpheus According to Greek mythology, Orpheus was a poet who sang and
played his lyre so beautifully that he could charm wild beasts. He married
Eurydice, a dryad, and when she died from a snake bite Orpheus went down
to the underworld to try to recover her. He used his music to persuade the
goddess Persephone to let Eurydice return with him, to which Persephone
agreed on condition that Orpheus should not look back as he left the
underworld. Violating this condition to assure himself that Eurydice was still
following him, Orpheus did look back, whereupon she vanished for ever.

'What do you think of our modern Orpheus?' 'If you're referring to Tolley, I
don't think he can conduct Beethoven.'
ALDOUS HUXLEY *Point Counter Point* 1928

But we were shadows, like the dead after Orpheus passes them on his way
through the Underworld, after this living man vanishes and the last sound of his
music is lost to the incoming silence. All my life I've made friends and lost lovers
and talked about these two activities as though they were very different,
opposed; but in truth love is the direct and therefore hopeless method of
calling Orpheus back, whereas friendship is the equally hopeless because
irrelevant attempt to find warmth in other shades.
EDMUND WHITE *A Boy's Own Story* 1982

If I give in to this passion, my real life, the most solid, the best known, will
disappear and I will feed on shadows again like those sad spirits whom Orpheus
fled.
JEANETTE WINTERSON *The Passion* 1987

Orwell George Orwell was the pseudonym of Eric Arthur Blair (1903–50). He was a novelist and essayist. In Orwell's novel *Nineteen Eighty-Four* (1949), the character referred to as Big Brother is a dictator whose portrait with the caption 'Big Brother is watching you' can be found everywhere. Orwell's own name can now be used to allude to the power and omnipresence of a dictatorial state. The related adjective is 'Orwellian'. *See also* BIG BROTHER, THOUGHT POLICE.

> Parliament contains MPs and Ministers who know about the necessity for openness. They can be aware that security cameras and interlinked computers raise the Orwellian prospect that everything about their constituents, from their phone calls to what they buy on credit cards, can now be discovered with relative ease. *The Observer* 1997

Ossa *See* PELION ON OSSA.

Ossian Ossian is the Anglicized form of Oisin, the name of a legendary Irish warrior and bard, the son of Finn MacCool. He travelled to Tír na nÓg, the land of perpetual youth, and returned 300 years later. Ossian's name became well known in 1760–3 when the Scottish poet James Macpherson published what was later discovered to be his own verse as an alleged translation of 3rd-century Gaelic tales. Ossian's wanderings are the subject of a poem by W. B. Yeats.

Othello In Shakespeare's play *Othello* (1622), Desdemona marries Othello, a Moor, who is asked to command the Venetian forces fighting the Turks in Cyprus. Othello's ensign Iago convinces Othello that Desdemona is unfaithful to him. Othello, in a state of acute jealousy, smothers Desdemona in her bed. Desdemona is subsequently proved innocent, and Othello, in despair, kills himself, having described himself as 'one that lov'd not wisely, but too well'. Othello can be referred to as the epitome of sexual jealousy. *See also* DESDEMONA, IAGO, SHAKESPEARE.

> Mr Pontifex is the exact likeness of Othello, but with a difference—he hates not wisely but too well.
> SAMUEL BUTLER *The Way of All Flesh* 1903

> But it is when jealousy turns into pathological jealousy, or the Othello syndrome as it is now called, that problems begin to surface and treatment becomes necessary. *The Independent* 1998

Outer Mongolia Mongolia, in eastern Asia, bordered by Russia and China, was known formerly as Outer Mongolia and thought of as the epitome of a remote, inaccessible place.

Olive Oyl *See under* OLIVE.

Oz Oz is the name of the fictional land and city (also called the Emerald City) in L. Frank Baum's children's story *The Wizard of Oz* (1900). The name can be applied to any place thought to resemble Baum's city, especially any fantastic or ideal domain. *See also* WIZARD OF OZ.

> The boxcar doors were opened, and the doorways framed the loveliest city that most of the Americans had ever seen. The skyline was intricate and voluptuous and enchanted and absurd. It looked like a Sunday school picture of Heaven to Billy Pilgrim. Somebody in the box car said 'Oz.'
> KURT VONNEGUT *Slaughterhouse-Five* 1969

> Fundamentalist religion is very big out there, and getting bigger. You have to do things and do them right, and if you don't you're gonna suffer terrible consequences. If you do them right, you're gonna enter Emerald City. You'll be Dorothy and Toto running down the yellow brick road to Oz.
> STUDS TERKEL *American Dreams: Lost and Found* 1980

Ozymandias Ozymandias is the name of the imaginary ancient king in Shelley's poem of the same name (1819). The poem describes how the shattered remains of parts of a statue of the king are found lying in the empty desert and on the pedestal are carved the ironic words:
'My name is Ozymandias, king of kings:
Look on my works, ye Mighty, and despair!'
Ozymandias can be used to represent hubris and the trap of having too much pride in earthly achievements which will crumble to dust after death.

> Wield gave what Pascoe had once described as his Ozymandias sneer and made a gesture which took in the car-packed garage.
> REGINALD HILL *A Killing Kindness* 1980

> Maybe he [Orson Welles] suffered from an Ozymandias complex—he wanted to bequeath the world a vast, scattered ruin in order to imply a lost glory. It's true that no ruins were ever so magisterially bewildering. *The Guardian* 1997

Ozzie and Harriet *The Adventures of Ozzie and Harriet* was a long-running US television comedy series (1952–66) about a middle-class American family in which Ozzie and Harriet Nelson and their sons David and Ricky played fictional versions of themselves. The names Ozzie and Harriet came to epitomize wholesome and happy family life.

> I came through here once, a long time ago, and liked the look of the town. It looked like a nice place to live. An Ozzie and Harriet sort of place, I guess.
> SHARYN MCCRUMB *If Ever I Return* 1990

> The hardest part was keeping the brutality of the job separate from your home life. Police marriages often fell apart for that reason. How do you go home and talk about how you spent your day after something like the scene in that house? Rose had been understanding about it. She'd lived most of her life in a war-torn country. She hadn't been raised to expect an Ozzie and Harriet life in the 'burbs. Still, it hadn't been easy.
> JOHN MADDOX ROBERTS *A Typical American Town* 1995

Kerry Packer Kerry (Francis Bullimore) Packer (b. 1937) is an Australian media tycoon who became famous for creating World Series Cricket in 1977, a series of unofficial one-day matches in Australia for which he paid top cricketers high fees to play. He obtained exclusive television rights for his own TV channel to cover the series.

> 'I wouldn't worry,' Margin told Delaney. 'It's probably only a box number somewhere, and no one can watch a box number twenty-four hours a day. You'd have to be Kerry Packer to afford it.'
> THOMAS KENEALLY *A Family Madness* 1985

Pacolet In the early French romance *Valentine and Orson*, Pacolet is a dwarf messenger whose winged horse, made of wood, carries him instantly wherever he wishes.

> 'And pray how long, Miss Ashton,' said her mother, ironically, 'are we to wait the return of your Pacolet—your fairy messenger—since our humble couriers of flesh and blood could not be trusted in this matter?'
> WALTER SCOTT *The Bride of Lammermoor* 1819

Paddington Bear First appearing in 1958, Paddington is the hero of a series of children's books by Michael Bond. He is a bear 'from Darkest Peru' who is found by the Brown family at London's Paddington Station (hence his name) with a label saying 'Please look after this bear'. Paddington wears a duffle coat, wellingtons, and a sou'wester hat with an upturned brim. He has a fondness for marmalade sandwiches and for giving people a long, hard stare to express disapproval.

> Unfortunately, Tube carriage windows are reflective when the train is in a tunnel, so she noticed I was looking, gave me a Paddington Bear hard stare and left to sit opposite. *Big Issue* 1994

Pan In Greek mythology, Pan was a god of nature, fecundity, flocks, and herds, and usually represented as having a human torso and arms but the legs, ears, and horns of a goat. He lived in Arcadia and was said to be responsible for sudden, irrational fears (the origin of our word 'panic'). On one occasion he pursued the nymph Syrinx, who escaped him by turning into a reed. As he could not distinguish her from all the other reeds, he cut several and made them into the pan pipes which still bear his name. News of

Pan's death is said to have been brought by a divine voice shouting across the sea to a sailor, Thamus: 'When you reach Palodes, take care to proclaim that the great god Pan is dead!' His name can denote general commotion and disorder, he can be alluded to as a player of sweet music, and he is often portrayed as lecherous.

> He could cut cunning little baskets out of cherry-stones, could make grotesque faces on hickory nuts, or odd-jumping figures out of elder-pith, and he was a very Pan in the manufacture of whistles of all sizes and sorts.
> HARRIET BEECHER STOWE *Uncle Tom's Cabin* 1852

> They coughed as they danced, and laughed as they coughed. Of the rushing couples there could barely be discerned more than the high lights—the indistinctness shaping them to satyrs clasping nymphs—a multiplicity of Pans whirling a multiplicity of Syrinxes; Lotis attempting to elude Priapus, and always failing.
> THOMAS HARDY *Tess of the D'Urbervilles* 1891

> Mr Beebe . . . was bidden to collect the factions for the return home. There was a general sense of groping and bewilderment. Pan had been amongst them—not the great god Pan, who has been buried these two thousand years, but the little god Pan, who presides over social contretemps and unsuccessful picnics.
> E. M. FORSTER *A Room with a View* 1908

> She sank down on to her knees, on to the carpet of golden leaves, and Gordon ran off through the trees, wildly, like a mad disciple of the great god Pan.
> KATE ATKINSON *Human Croquet* 1997

Peter Pan *See under* PETER.

Pandemonium Pandemonium, meaning 'All the Demons', was the name given by John Milton to the capital of Hell in his poem *Paradise Lost* (1667). The word 'pandemonium' is usually applied to a place of utter confusion and uproar, but is sometimes used to suggest a place of vice and wickedness.

> It presented to me then as exquisite and divine a retreat as Pandemonium appeared to the devils of hell after their sufferings in the lake of fire.
> MARY SHELLEY *Frankenstein* 1831

> It was dreadful to be thus dissevered from his dryad, and sent howling back to a Barchester pandemonium just as the nectar and ambrosia were about to descend on the fields of asphodel.
> ANTHONY TROLLOPE *Barchester Towers* 1857

Pandora's box In Greek mythology, Pandora, the first mortal woman, created out of clay by Hephaestus, was given by the gods a jar (or box) that she was forbidden to open. Out of curiosity she disobeyed, and released from it all the evils and illnesses that have afflicted mankind ever since, with only Hope remaining at the bottom. The phrase 'a Pandora's box' is thus used for a source of many unforeseen and unmanageable problems.

> Hardy was the first to try to break the Victorian middle-class seal over the supposed Pandora's box of sex.
> JOHN FOWLES *The French Lieutenant's Woman* 1969

> The anthropic principle opens a Pandora's box of smart worlds when it tries to explain just one.
> BART KOSKO *Fuzzy Thinking* 1993

Pangloss In Voltaire's *Candide* (1759), Dr Pangloss is the tutor who imbues Candide with his guiding philosophy that all is for the best in the best of all possible worlds. No matter what misfortunes they each suffer on their travels—disease, shipwreck, earthquake, flogging, and even attempted hanging and dissection—Pangloss confidently and complacently assures Candide that things could not be otherwise. *See also* CANDIDE.

> Of course it would be naive to expect the Chancellor to draw attention to the failings of government policy. None the less, the rest of us notice them, and find them hard to reconcile with the distinctly Panglossian tone that Mr Clarke adopted yesterday. *Daily Telegraph* 1996

> Nor do the proposals even address the preoccupations of economic underperformance, poor training, underinvestment and growing inequality. Instead there is an explicit Panglossian view that all in the economic garden is flourishing. *The Observer* 1997

Pantagruel Pantagruel (whose name means 'All-Thirsty') is the son of Gargantua in Rabelais's satire *Pantagruel* (1532). A giant like his father, Pantagruel has a similarly enormous appetite, especially for wine. *See also* GARGANTUA, RABELAIS.

> Don Emmanuel, with his rufous beard, his impressive belly, and his flair for ribaldry, made pantagruelian quantities of guarapo, involving hundreds of pineapple skins, which he served with a gourd and his usual good humour.
> LOUIS DE BERNIÈRES *Señor Vivo and the Coca Lord* 1991

> Diana had produced not the embroidered silk in which she had swathed Pia the previous day, but a night-gown of enormous proportions made out of thick country-woven linen. 'Who could have worn this? Only a giant.' 'A stout farmer or his huge wife perhaps.' 'Pantagruel, certainly.'
> ELIZABETH IRONSIDE *Death in the Garden* 1995

Pantheon Pantheon means, in Greek, 'all the gods' (from *pan* meaning 'all' and *theion* meaning 'god'), and can be used to refer to a group of distinguished people or people who wield considerable influence.

> But his true fighting weight, his antecedents, his amours with other members of the commercial Pantheon—all these were as uncertain to ordinary mortals as were the escapades of Zeus. While the gods are powerful, we learn little about

them. It is only in the days of their decadence that a strong light beats into heaven.
E. M. FORSTER *Howards End* 1910

Sancho Panza *See* DON QUIXOTE.

Paolo and Francesca Paolo and Francesca were lovers whose story was immortalized in Dante's *Inferno*. Francesca da Rimini was married to Giovanni Malatesta but fell in love with his brother Paolo. When their affair was discovered, they were both put to death in 1289.

> But it was no ordinary passion that seized them; it was something so overwhelming that they felt as if the whole long history of the world signified only because it had led to the time and place that had brought them together. They loved as Daphnis and Chloe or as Paolo and Francesca.
> SOMERSET MAUGHAM *The Judgment Seat* 1951

Papa Doc François Duvalier (1907–71), known as Papa Doc, was president of Haiti in 1957–71. His regime was noted for its brutality and oppressiveness. Many of his opponents were either assassinated or forced into exile by his security force, known as the Tontons Macoutes.

> As for the people, many are afraid of him and the rest admire him, not for his behaviour, you understand, but because he can get away with it. They see this as power and they admire a big man here. He spends their money on new cars and so forth for himself and his friends, they applaud that. . . . It's the old story, my friend. We will have a Papa Doc and after that a revolution or so. Then the Americans will wonder why people are getting killed.
> MARGARET ATWOOD *Bodily Harm* 1981

p

Paracelsus Paracelsus (c.1493–1541) was a Swiss physician who introduced a more scientific approach to medicine and saw illness as having an external cause rather than arising as a result of an imbalance in the body's humours.

> A recipe that an Indian taught me, in requital of some lessons of my own, that were as old as Paracelsus.
> NATHANIEL HAWTHORNE *The Scarlet Letter* 1850

Paradise Paradise is the Garden of Eden described in the book of Genesis, the place of perfect happiness enjoyed by Adam and Eve before their Fall and expulsion. The term is more commonly used, however, to refer not to the biblical Eden but rather to Heaven, 'the second Eden', and to a place or state of complete happiness. *See also* ADAM AND EVE, EDEN.

> Not a river at all, just a trickle of water choked with reeds, and mosquitoes in the evenings, and a caravan park full of screaming children and fat barefoot men in shorts braising sausages over gas cookers. Not Paradise at all.
> J. M. COETZEE *Age of Iron* 1990

> The sun was shining and every stone of the wall seemed as clear as glass and

lighted up like a lamp, it was like passing through the gates of Hell and into Paradise.
MARGARET ATWOOD *Alias Grace* 1996

Parcae Sisters 'The Parcae Sisters' was the Roman name for the Fates, the three goddesses who presided over the birth, life, and death of humans. *See also* FATES.

Octavian saw his daughter slowly disappearing in the engulfing slush, her smeared face further distorted with the contortions of whimpering wonder, while from their perch on the pigsty roof the three children looked down with the cold unpitying detachment of the Parcae Sisters.
SAKI 'The Penance' in *The Toys of Peace* 1919

Paris In Greek mythology, all the gods and goddesses were invited to the wedding of Peleus and Thetis except Eris, the goddess of discord. Angered by this, Eris threw a golden apple inscribed with the words 'for the fairest' at the feet of the wedding guests, causing disagreement between three goddesses, Hera, Athene, and Aphrodite, who each claimed the prize for herself. When Zeus appointed the Trojan prince Paris, the son of King Priam, to judge them, each goddess in turn tried to bribe him. Athene promised him wisdom and victory in war; Hera promised him dominion over mankind; Aphrodite promised him the most beautiful woman on earth as his wife. Paris chose Aphrodite as the winner of the contest. His reward was to be Helen of Troy. *See also* APPLE OF DISCORD, HELEN, TROJAN WAR.

Parnassus In Greek mythology, Parnassus was a mountain a few miles north of Delphi associated with Apollo and the Muses. On its slopes was the Castalian spring, whose waters were believed to give inspiration to those who drank of them. *See also* MUSES.

If the world of literary critism knew nothing but, say, her twelve finest poems, she would have an unquestioned, uncategorized place on anyone's Parnassus.
VICTORIA GLENDINNING *Edith Sitwell* 1981

Parsifal Parsifal (or Perceval) is a legendary figure found in French, German, and English poetry from the late 12th century onwards. He is the father of Lohengrin and the hero of a number of legends, some of which are associated with the Holy Grail. Parsifal is often portrayed as a guileless innocent, a 'holy fool'. In some versions of the story, he witnesses a procession of the Grail in the castle of his uncle the Fisher King, a wounded king who is the guardian of the Grail and who will only be healed when the right question about the Grail is asked. Despite his curiosity, Parsifal fails to ask the required question (about the significance of the Grail, or, in other versions, about the cause of his uncle's pain) and his silence prevents his uncle from being restored to health. Parsifal eventually becomes the guardian of the Grail himself. Wagner's opera *Parsifal* (1882) is based on the legend. *See also* HOLY GRAIL, LOHENGRIN.

> Unlike Parsifal I did not fear to ask questions. 'What's wrong with Ma?'
> ROBERTSON DAVIES *The Cunning Man* 1994

> She considered what she knew about the former Olivia Grahame. Born and married into a class she had rejected. One child she obviously saw as a cross between Sir Parsifal and a pearl above rubies.
> SUSAN MOODY *Grand Slam* 1994

> As statistic after depressing statistic passed before my eyes, the eccentric crusade to which my uncle had dedicated his life seemed more and more heroic. The White Knight had metamorphosed into Parsifal.
> MICHÈLE BAILEY *Haycastle's Cricket* 1996

Parthian The Parthians lived and ruled in an area of western Asia in ancient times and were governed by a military aristocracy. They held out against the encroaching Romans until the 2nd century AD and were famous for their cavalry, who had perfected the art of shooting backwards at an enemy from whom they were in retreat, the 'Parthian shot'. The term has come to be applied to a hostile remark delivered by someone at the moment of departure.

> 'I command you to leave this room at once.' 'Very well. Since all I have ever experienced in it is hypocrisy, I shall do so with the greatest pleasure.' With this Parthian shaft Sarah turned to go.
> JOHN FOWLES *The French Lieutenant's Woman* 1969

Pasiphae In Greek mythology, Pasiphae was the wife of Minos, king of Crete. When Minos refused to sacrifice a bull to Poseidon, Poseidon punished him by inflicting on Pasiphae a passion for the bull. Helped by Daedalus to gratify her passion, she became the mother of the Minotaur, half-man and half-bull. Pasiphae can be alluded to in the context of an unnatural sexual union, or as the victim of a cruel punishment by the gods. *See also* MINOS, MINOTAUR.

> He smiled bitterly at the thought of them together. Here was the cruel and antique malice of the gods, such as they once sent forth against Pasiphae. Centuries of aspiration and culture—and the world could not escape it.
> E. M. FORSTER *Where Angels Fear to Tread* 1905

Passchendaele The battle of Passchendaele (1917) was a period of prolonged and indecisive trench warfare during the First World War near the village of Passchendaele in western Belgium. The battle, also known as the third battle of Ypres, involved appalling loss of life in a sea of mud, for no eventual strategic gain. *See also* YPRES.

> I spent much of the day in Panama watching two teeming colonies of leaf-cutter ants fighting, and my mind irresistibly compared the limb-strewn

battlefield to pictures I had seen of Passchendaele. I could almost hear the guns and smell the smoke.

RICHARD DAWKINS *The Blind Watchmaker* 1986

Patroclus *See* ACHILLES AND PATROCLUS.

General Patton George Smith Patton (1885–1945) was an American general who commanded US forces in the Second World War. Known as 'Old Blood and Guts', he pursued an aggressive military strategy, taking the 3rd Army across France and Germany as far as the Czech border.

Paul In the Bible, Paul was initially named Saul of Tarsus, and was a committed persecutor of Christians. After his dramatic conversion to Christianity on the road to Damascus, he became known as Paul. He subsequently saw it as his mission to preach the gospel to the Gentiles and his letters form part of the New Testament. A dramatic change of mind or heart can be referred to as a Pauline conversion. *See also* DAMASCUS.

> I remember a dramatic scene. I was Paul on the road to Damascus . . . I was walking towards the museum along Fifth Avenue, thirty blocks, because there was a victory parade . . . I kept walking, and there was a long-haired kid, nearer the bleachers, being assailed by this guy. The guy was yelling from the top of the bleachers: 'You guys ought to be eliminated. In a democracy like this, you're not fit.' I stopped and thought: If this is what Vietnam is doing to us, it's time it was over. I was anti-war from that day on.
>
> STUDS TERKEL *American Dreams: Lost and Found* 1980

> Like most Italians of his age and background, Vianello had always believed himself immune to statistical probability. Other people died from smoking, other people's cholesterol rose from eating rich food, and it was only they who died of heart attacks because of it. . . . This spring, however five precancerous melanomas had been dug out from his back and shoulders, and he had been warned to stay out of the sun. Like Saul on the road to Damascus, Vianello had experienced conversion, and, like Paul, he had tried to spread his particular gospel.
>
> DONNA LEON *The Anonymous Venetian* 1994

> 'I appreciate your feelings. But I felt I must come to tell your wife that I now believe her to be innocent and want to do what I can to put the record straight.' He did not unbend. 'It would certainly have been welcome if you had experienced this Pauline conversion at the time. Now, when my wife is trying to put it all behind her, I cannot see that disinterring the past will serve any useful purpose.'
>
> ALINE TEMPLETON *Last Act of All* 1995

Paul and Virginia Paul and Virginia are two children in the pastoral romance *Paul et Virginie* (1788) by Jacques Henri Bernardin de Saint-Pierre.

The tale, inspired by Longus' *Daphnis and Chloe*, relates how the two are brought up by their respective mothers on a tropical island (Mauritius) as if brother and sister, under a regime designed to be in accordance with the laws of nature. They grow to adolescence in happy if frugal circumstances. Then Virginia moves to Paris to stay with a wealthy maiden aunt. On her return, some years later, she is shipwrecked off the Mauritian coast. She refuses to remove her clothing in order to save herself and drowns. In the shock and pain of bereavement, Paul and both mothers then also die.

> She had recovered from her emotion, and walked along beside him with a grave, subdued face. Bob did not like to assume the privileges of an accepted lover and draw her hand through his arm; for, conscious that she naturally belonged to a politer grade than his own, he feared lest her exhibition of tenderness were an impulse which cooler moments might regret. A perfect Paul-and-Virginia life had not absolutely set in for him as yet, and it was not to be hastened by force.
> THOMAS HARDY *The Trumpet Major* 1880

Pavlov Ivan Petrovich Pavlov (1849–1936) was a Russian physiologist and director of the Institute of Experimental Medicine in St Petersburg, winning a Nobel Prize for work on digestion in 1904. He is best known for his later work on conditioned reflexes using dogs. He showed that, by linking food with the sound of a bell over a period of time, the salivation response associated with food could become a conditioned response to the sound of the bell alone. Pavlov's dogs have come to stand for automatic or unconscious obedience to a signal, while a Pavlovian response is any automatic unthinking response.

> The shop-bell rang and, behaving exactly like a Pavlov dog, Stamp got up and began, elaborately, to put on his coat.
> KEITH WATERHOUSE *Billy Liar* 1959

> Obviously continual response to the music had developed within them an almost Pavlovian response to the noise, a response which they believed was pleasure.
> JOHN KENNEDY TOOLE *A Confederacy of Dunces* 1980

> I've obviously got some sort of Pavlov reflex to men. . . . If a bloke asks me the time of day often enough, after a while I only have to look at my watch to imagine myself saying 'I do' and driving a Volvo estate filled with children dressed in Baby Gap clothes.
> ARABELLA WEIR *Does My Bum Look Big in This?* 1997

Pavlova Anna Pavlova (1881–1931) was a Russian ballerina who became famous for her roles in Fokine's ballets, in particular in his solo dance for her *The Dying Swan*. She lived in Britain from 1912 and formed her own company, with which she toured Europe and the world.

> Her office was hardly larger than the interior of my car . . . and she had to

squeeze between the edge of her desk and the wall to get up to greet me. It was a maneuver that would have looked clumsy performed by Pavlova and Margaret Dopplemeier turned it into a lurching stumble.
JONATHAN KELLERMAN *When the Bough Breaks* 1992

Johnnyboy draped himself across the workbench like Pavlova in the closing moments of the 'Dying Swan'.
JOYCE HOLMS *Bad Vibes* 1998

Pax In classical times, Pax was the allegorical figure personifying peace. She was represented by the Athenians as holding Plutus, the god of wealth, in her lap to demonstrate that peace gives rise to prosperity and opulence. The Romans represented her with the horn of plenty and carrying an olive branch in her hand. *See also* CORNUCOPIA, PLUTUS.

Norman Vincent Peale (1898–1993) Norman Vincent Peale, also known humorously as Normal Vincent Peale, was an American clergyman and author, best known for his 1952 work entitled *The Power of Positive Thinking*, which argues that the only thing necessary for success is a positive attitude: 'Empty pockets never held anyone back. Only empty heads and empty hearts can do that.' His name can evoke excessive and unrealistic optimism.

'We don't emphasize anything being out of our kids' reach. We want them to feel that the only thing limiting them is their own lack of motivation. That they must take responsibility for themselves. That they can reach the sky—that's the name of a book written for children by Reverend Gus. *Touch the Sky*. It's got cartoons, games, coloring pages. It teaches them a positive message.' It was Normal Vincent Peale spiced up with humanistic psychological jargon.
JONATHAN KELLERMAN *When the Bough Breaks* 1992

Pecksniff Seth Pecksniff is a character in Dickens's *Martin Chuzzlewit* (1844). An architect by profession, Pecksniff is an arch-hypocrite with a 'soft and oily' manner, who uses an outward appearance of virtue and morality to win the affection and respect of old Martin Chuzzlewit, in an attempt to inherit his money. He fails in this attempt and is exposed as the hypocrite that he really is. *See also* DICKENSIAN.

Sad for once, as Hayes had struck me as the only exception to the rule that 'decent Tory' is an oxymoron. Accuser looks like a pasty-faced, hard-eyed, sharp-toothed, back-stabbing, nausea-inducing, pocket-lining Pecksniff, who says he is acting in the public interest. *The Observer* 1997

Peeping Tom According to legend, Tom the tailor was said to have peeped at Lady Godiva when she rode naked through the streets of Coventry, as a result of which he was struck blind. He was thereafter known as Peeping Tom. A peeping Tom is thus someone who spies on someone else, or a voyeur. *See also* LADY GODIVA.

Most of us, at one time and another, have been tempted to play the Peeping Tom on other people's souls.
CHRISTOPHER J. KOCH *The Year of Living Dangerously* 1978

Eventually, he's reduced to lying in wait in the lane opposite her cottage, like a Peeping Tom.
ROBERT HARRIS *Enigma* 1995

He lived in a row house and that made surveillance difficult because we couldn't creep round the entire house and do our Peeping Tom thing.
JANET EVANOVICH *High Five* 1999

Pegasus In Greek mythology, Pegasus was a winged horse which sprang from the blood of the Gorgon Medusa when Perseus cut her head off. Pegasus was ridden by Perseus in his rescue of Andromeda, and by Bellerophon when he fought the Chimera. The name Pegasus can represent a means of escape. *See also* ANDROMEDA, BELLEROPHON, MEDUSA, PERSEUS.

Bertie, in short, was to be the Pegasus on whose wings they were to ride out of their present dilemma.
ANTHONY TROLLOPE *Barchester Towers* 1857

I opened them to see the deer as stunned as I was, peering at me through the glass, standing utterly still, unable to move. But standing. After an interminable moment, he lifted his head and took off like Pegasus across the turnpike.
CAROL BRENNAN *Chill of Summer* 1995

Pelion on Ossa In Greek mythology, Mount Pelion in Thessaly was held to be the home of the centaurs, and the giants were said to have piled Pelion on top of Mount Ossa (or sometimes Ossa on Pelion) in their attempt to scale Mount Olympus and destroy the gods. To 'pile Pelion on Ossa' is to add difficulty to difficulty.

Whether one thinks the relevant ministers should have gone or stayed, these have been abject performances. Their effect has been to make mountains of molehills (except in the case of the ERM, where it was more a case of piling Pelion on Ossa). *Sunday Telegraph* 1994

That was final enough in itself, but within minutes a fax arrived from Capitaine Lapollet. If such a thing was possible, it made things worse by rubbing salt into Timberlake's near-mortal wounds. It said the late Comte de Gaillmont's group was A, which meant that he could be Jean-Louis's father. It didn't mean he was his father, but this last blow was piling Pelion upon Ossa.
MAX MARQUIS *Written in Blood* 1995

Pelléas and Mélisande The story of Pelléas and Mélisande was initially told in the poetic drama by Maurice Maeterlinck (1892) and later in Debussy's opera of the same name (1902). Golaud, the grandson of King Arkel, marries Mélisande, despite the fact that he knows little about her. They move to his father's gloomy, cold castle, where his younger half-brother Pelléas is staying, whereupon Pelléas and Mélisande fall in love. Golaud, on discovering them together, becomes jealous, even to the extent of trying to use his own infant son by his previous marriage to spy on them. Pelléas, who is planning to leave the castle, is forbidden to see Mélisande, but he feels that he must see her once more before leaving, and meets her outside the castle in the shadow of a tree. Golaud, on finding them again together, stabs and kills Pelléas and wounds himself and Mélisande. The latter dies giving birth to a child while Golaud is still torturing himself over whether or not the lovers had slept together or were innocent of anything but embraces.

> Last night Gillian started quizzing me about one of the girls at the School. Talk about wide of the mark. Might as well accuse Pelléas of leg-over with Mélisande. (Though I suppose they must have done it, mustn't they?)
> JULIAN BARNES *Talking It Over* 1991

Penelope In Greek mythology, Penelope was the wife of Odysseus who waited patiently and faithfully for her husband to return home after the end of the Trojan War. She put off her many suitors by saying that she would marry only when she had finished the piece of weaving that she had started. Each night she unravelled the work that she had done during the day. *See also* ODYSSEUS, TROJAN WAR.

> 'There is always about you', he said, 'a sort of waiting. Whatever I see you doing, you're not really there: you are waiting—like Penelope when she did her weaving.' He could not help a spurt of wickedness. 'I'll call you Penelope,' he said.
> D. H. LAWRENCE *Sons and Lovers* 1913

> She feared in her heart that back home he would dismiss her, . . . that she would be left forever, faithful and forgotten, waiting like Penelope for a man who never came.
> LOUIS DE BERNIÈRES *Captain Corelli's Mandolin* 1994

> She had always resented the male characterization of war: that man the warrior would go off to perilous shores and have adventures, while the Penelopes of the world waited at home, safely tending the garden, mending clothes, and putting their lives on hold until the heroes returned.
> SHARYN MCCRUMB *The Hangman's Beautiful Daughter* 1996

Samuel Pepys Samuel Pepys (1633–1703) is chiefly remembered for his diary (1660–9) in which he vividly describes life in the early Restoration period and records such contemporary events as the Great Plague, the Fire of London, and the sailing of the Dutch fleet up the Thames.

Perceval *See* PARSIFAL.

Pericles Pericles (c.495–429 BC) was an influential Athenian statesman who expanded the Athenian Empire and was responsible for the Parthenon and other great buildings. He was noted for his oratory.

Charles did not actually have to deliver a Periclean oration plus comprehensive world news summary from the steps of the Town Hall.
JOHN FOWLES *The French Lieutenant's Woman* 1969

Peripatetic The word 'Peripatetic' (literally 'walking around') came to be applied to Aristotle's school at the Lyceum on account of his habit of walking up and down while teaching his students. *See also* ARISTOTLE.

A large group of buyers stood round the auctioneer, or followed him when, between his pauses, he wandered on from one lot of plantation-produce to another, like some philosopher of the Peripatetic school delivering his lectures in the shady groves of the Lyceum.
THOMAS HARDY *The Woodlanders* 1887

Reginald Perrin Reginald Perrin was the main character in a British TV series entitled *The Fall and Rise of Reginald Perrin*, which ran from 1976 to 1979. Based on the book *The Death of Reginald Perrin* by David Nobbs (1975), the series follows the life of Reginald Perrin, a middle-aged sales executive combating a mid-life crisis as he attempts to escape his mundane and unfulfilling life by faking his own suicide, leaving a pile of clothes on a beach and walking off into the sunset.

It appears that, in true Reggie Perrin fashion, he carefully planned his disappearance. *Ten O'Clock News, BBC Radio 4* 1999

Persephone In Greek mythology, after Persephone had been abducted by Hades (also known as Pluto or Dis) to be his queen in the underworld, she was granted the opportunity to return to the earth on condition that no food had passed her lips in the underworld. However, while wandering in the gardens she had eaten some pomegranate seeds from a tree, and this fact was revealed by Ascalaphus. Persephone was ordered by Zeus to remain six months with Hades and to spend the rest of the year on the earth with her mother, Demeter. *See also* ASCALAPHUS, DEMETER, HADES.

It must just be a question of what you're used to, she thought, picturing Persephone, resolutely anorexic in the Halls of Dis until the pomegranate proved too much for her will power.
ALICE THOMAS ELLIS *The 27th Kingdom* 1982

Perseus In Greek mythology, Perseus was the son of Zeus and Danae, a hero celebrated for many accomplishments. Helped by the gods, he killed the gorgon Medusa by cutting off her head. On his return, flying on Pegasus, he rescued Andromeda, who had been chained to a rock and left to be devoured by a monster. Perseus slew the sea-monster, rescued Andromeda, and married her. *See also* ANDROMEDA, MEDUSA, PEGASUS.

He seemed to see her like a lovely rock-bound Andromeda, with the devouring monster Society careering up to make a mouthful of her; and himself whirling down on his winged horse—just Pegasus turned Rosinante for the nonce—to

cut her bonds, snatch her up, and whirl her back into the blue.
EDITH WHARTON *The Custom of the Country* 1913

Peter Pan Peter Pan is the hero of J. M. Barrie's play of the same name (1904), a boy with magical powers who never grew up. He takes Wendy Darling and her brothers on an adventure to Never-Never Land, where they encounter Captain Hook and his pirate gang. The term 'Peter Pan' can be applied to a man who never seems to grow older or who is immature. Peter is traditionally played on stage by an actress, and so a 'Peter Pan haircut' is a short boyish one worn by a woman or girl. *See also* NEVER-NEVER LAND, TINKER BELL, WENDY.

I could see why my mother was fascinated by the music. It was being pounded out by a little Chinese girl, about nine years old, with a Peter Pan haircut. The girl had the sauciness of a Shirley Temple.
AMY TAN *Two Kinds* 1989

Only Rainger would want to dance and skylark in the shadow of the prison door. He wasn't really wicked, he was Peter Pan. He simply could not cope with the responsibilities of the adult world, could not connect his actions in the drug trade with the human wreckage that floated in its wake, nor begin to comprehend why his light-hearted infidelities had brought his wife to the edge of serious mental disorder.
RICHARD HALEY *Thoroughfare of Stones* 1995

Britain's music industry was toasting more than the knighthood for Cliff Richard, the pop world's Peter Pan, following the release of figures yesterday which showed that sales have powered ahead by more than a fifth in the first six months of the year. *The Guardian* 1995

The computer games industry never grows up. This does not mean an idyllic Peter Pan-style childhood but rather a perpetual adolescence. *The Independent* 1998

Petra Petra is an ancient ruined city in Jordan. It was the capital of the Nabataeans from 312 BC until 63 BC, when they became subject to Rome. The city's extensive ruins include temples and tombs carved in the sandstone cliffs. The poet John Burgon famously described Petra as 'A rose-red city—"half as old as time" '.

Think of it. Of a Sunday, Wall Street is deserted as Petra; and every night of every day it is an emptiness.
HERMAN MELVILLE *Bartleby* 1856

Petrarch and Laura Petrarch (1304–74) was an Italian Renaissance poet whose father had been expelled from Florence and with whom he moved to Avignon. He met Laura, the woman who was the inspiration for his love poetry, in Avignon in 1327. Her identity is not known.

His love was as chaste as that of Petrarch for his Laura.
THOMAS HARDY *The Return of the Native* 1880

Though he could not declare his doubts, he thought it more than probable that this Laura of the voiceless Petrarch was unworthy of such constancy, and that she had no intention whatever of rewarding it, even if the opportunity arrived.
GEORGE GISSING *Born in Exile* 1892

Petruchio In Shakespeare's comedy *The Taming of the Shrew* (1623), Petruchio is the suitor for Katherina, the ill-tempered shrew of the title. After marrying Katherina, Petruchio tames her by devising a series of humiliations, including preventing her from eating or sleeping. At the end of the play, he is able to win a bet on who is the most submissive of three wives.

In truth, Mrs Proudie was all but invincible; had she married Petruchio, it may be doubted whether that arch wife-tamer would have been able to keep her legs out of those garments which are presumed by men to be peculiarly unfitted for feminine use.
ANTHONY TROLLOPE *Barchester Towers* 1875

Phaethon In Greek mythology, Phaethon, the son of Helios, the sun god, asked to drive his father's sun chariot for a day. However, he did not have the strength to control the horses and the chariot rose so high above the earth that human beings on the ground nearly froze, then plunged so close to the earth that it was scorched. Zeus intervened to save the world and killed Phaethon with a thunderbolt.

The sun rose higher on its journey, guided, not by Phaethon, but by Apollo, competent, unswerving, divine.
E. M. FORSTER *A Room with a View* 1908

Pharaoh Pharaoh was the title of a king of ancient Egypt, most associated with those mentioned in the Old Testament and Hebrew Scriptures in whose time the oppression and Exodus of Israel took place. During the time when Joseph was in prison in Egypt, Pharaoh had troubling dreams, including one in which seven fat kine (cows) were followed by seven lean kine which ate the fat ones. On hearing that Joseph was able to interpret dreams, he sent for him. Joseph interpreted the dreams as meaning that seven years of plenty would be followed by seven years of famine, advising Pharaoh to store grain for the future famine (Gen. 41: 1–40). At a later period, when Moses was born, Pharaoh had decreed that all male babies born to the Israelites should be thrown into the Nile. Moses' mother hid the baby and then placed him in a basket in the reeds of the river. He was discovered by Pharaoh's daughter, who felt sorry for him and decided to raise him as her own son, using his mother for a nurse (Exod. 1: 22 – 2: 10). *See also* JOSEPH, MOSES.

Listen here . . . I have dreams like a Pharaoh. When I was fourteen and asleep in Fowey, I was here on this exact shore. I saw Will Bryant—it's none of a surprise

to me. These days and night, I have dreams I cannot utter. . .
THOMAS KENEALLY *The Playmaker* 1987

I suppose he is interested in my dreams because a dream can mean something,
or so it says in the Bible, such as Pharaoh and the fat kine and the lean kine,
and Jacob with the angels going up and down the ladder.
MARGARET ATWOOD *Alias Grace* 1996

Pharisee The Pharisees were members of an ancient Jewish sect who strove
to ensure that the state was ruled according to strict Jewish law. According to
the Bible, they were denounced by Jesus for their hypocrisy in maintaining
an outward appearance of morality and virtue while acting only out of self-
interest: 'Woe unto you, scribes and Pharisees, hypocrites! For ye are like
unto whited sepulchres, which indeed appear beautiful outward, but are
within full of dead men's bones, and of all uncleanness' (Matt. 23: 27).

They who only strive for this paltry prize, like the Pharisees, who prayed at the
corners of streets, to be seen by men, verily obtain the reward they seek.
MARY WOLLSTONECRAFT *A Vindication of the Rights of Women* 1792

Conventionality is not morality. Self-righteousness is not religion. To attack the
first is not to assail the last. To pluck the mask from the face of the Pharisee, is
not to lift an impious hand to the Crown of Thorns.
CHARLOTTE BRONTË *Preface to Jane Eyre* 1848

'Useless relatives!' he was saying. 'Thieves and gossips. Pharisees!
Troublemakers! Hypocrites!'
BEN OKRI *Dangerous Love* 1996

Pheidias Pheidias (or Phidias) was a 5th-century BC Athenian sculptor
celebrated for his colossal gold-and-ivory Athena Parthenos at Athens and for
his vast statue of Zeus at Olympia. He also designed many of the sculptures
of the Parthenon and Acropolis.

In Clym Yeobright's face could be dimly seem the typical countenance of the
future. Should there be a classical period to art hereafter, its Pheidias may
produce such faces.
THOMAS HARDY *The Return of the Native* 1880

Pheidippides Pheidippides (5th *c.* BC) was an Athenian messenger who was
sent from Athens to Sparta to ask for help after the Persian landing at
Marathon in 490. He is said to have covered 150 miles on foot in two days.
The long-distance race known as the marathon derives its name from a later
story that, after the Greeks had defeated the Persians, a messenger ran the
22 miles from Marathon to Athens with news of the Greek victory, but fell
dead on arrival.

Philistines The ancient Philistines were the traditional enemies of the
Israelites, regarded by them as hostile barbarians. Their name has come to be
applied to people who are indifferent to culture and the arts and have

uncultivated tastes. When in the biblical story the Philistines arrived to take Samson captive, Delilah said, 'The Philistines be upon you, Samson!' (Judg. 16). These words can be used when people regarded as the enemy suddenly arrive. *See also* SAMSON.

'The Philistines be upon us,' said Liddy, making her nose white against the glass.
THOMAS HARDY *Far from the Madding Crowd* 1874

When I was a young man, though his books sold but little and one or two were banned by the libraries, it was very much a mark of culture to admire him. He was thought boldly realistic. He was a very good stick to beat the Philistines with.
W. SOMERSET MAUGHAM *Cakes and Ale* 1930

Five hundred copies of *The Voice of Youth* were on sale in the dinner hall today. Five hundred copies were locked in the games cupboard by the end of the afternoon. Not one copy was sold! My fellow pupils are nothing but Philistines and Morons!
SUE TOWNSEND *The Secret Diary of Adrian Mole Aged 13¾* 1982

Philoctetes Philoctetes was a Greek hero of the Trojan War. His father was with Hercules when he died and received from him Hercules' bow and arrows, which Philoctetes inherited. On his way to the war Philoctetes was bitten by a serpent and abandoned by his companions on the island of Lemnos owing to a foul-smelling wound on his foot. On the island he was able to use the bow and arrows to keep himself fed. When in the tenth year of the war the Greeks were informed by an oracle that only with Hercules' arrows could Troy be taken, Odysseus and Diomedes came back to fetch him to Troy, where he killed Paris. *See also* TROJAN WAR.

Arresting for a moment the wave of memories, Roberto realized he had evoked his father's death not with the pious intention of keeping open that Philoctetes' wound, but by mere accident.
UMBERTO ECO *The Island of the Day Before* 1994

Philosopher's Stone The Philosopher's Stone was an imaginary substance, sought after by alchemists, that was supposed to have the power of changing base metals into gold and sometimes of curing all diseases and prolonging life indefinitely. The term can be used to describe a universal cure or solution that proves elusive.

Any opiate that relieves pain is habit forming, and the more effectively it relieves pain the more habit forming it is. The habit forming molecule, and the pain killing molecule of morphine are probably identical, and the process by which morphine relieves pain is the same process that leads to tolerance and addiction. Non habit forming morphine appears to be a latter day Philosopher's Stone.
WILLIAM BURROUGHS *The Naked Lunch* 1959

Phlegethon In Greek mythology, Phlegethon, literally 'the Fiery One', was one of the rivers of Hades. As with other aspects of Hades, its name can evoke evil or unpleasantness. *See also* HADES.

Phobos In Greek mythology, Phobos, one of the sons of Aphrodite and Ares, was the god of dread and alarm. He was often represented with a lion's head.

Phoebe In Greek mythology, Phoebe ('the Bright One') was a daughter of the Titans Uranus and Gaia, whose name became associated with the moon.

> Like Phoebe breaking through an envious cloud . . .
> PHILIP MASSINGER *Bashful Lover* 1655

Phoebus Phoebus ('the Bright One') was an epithet of the Greek god Apollo, used in contexts where the god was identified with the sun. *See* APOLLO.

> He would never have survived the lash of Phoebus.
> UMBERTO ECO *The Island of the Day Before* 1994

Phoenix The Phoenix was a mythical bird of gorgeous plumage, the only one of its kind. After living for five or six centuries in the Arabian desert, it burnt itself on a funeral pyre ignited by the sun and fanned by its own wings, and rose from the ashes with renewed youth to live through another lifespan. Anything that has been restored to a new existence after apparent destruction can be said to be like the Phoenix. It has come to symbolize resurrection.

> The house's character had changed much with the fire that had wrecked it and the several stages of reconstruction that renewed it; phoenix-like, the place seemed reborn of itself.
> RUSSELL HOBAN *The Mouse and his Child* 1967

> Here in person was a sign, Alexander thought, if a hard sign to interpret, female by sex, male by gender, undergoing a positively Attic self-mutilation to become an analogue of the first Elizabeth's emblem, the renewed Phoenix.
> A. S. BYATT *The Virgin in the Garden* 1978

> 'I've left Carl,' Lucy said, and my heart lurched. 'This evening, in fact, just before the film started, during that speech when the Chairman of Britmovie was telling us that the phoenix of British film had risen from the ashes.'
> BEN ELTON *Inconceivable* 1999

Phryne Phryne was a celebrated Greek courtesan of the 4th century BC, said to have been the model for such beautiful statues as the *Cnidian* Venus of Praxiteles and the Venus Anadyomene of Apelles. Phryne became so wealthy that she offered to pay for the rebuilding of the walls of Thebes.

> Her underclothes are positively Phrynean.
> ALDOUS HUXLEY *Point Counter Point* 1928

Picasso Pablo Picasso (1881–1973) was a Spanish painter, sculptor, and graphic artist, one of the most versatile and influential artists of the 20th century. His melancholy 'blue period' (1901–4), depicting the poor and suffering, gave way to his 'rose period' (1904–6), depicting circus life. Among Picasso's masterpieces are *Les Demoiselles d'Avignon* (1907), an important work in the development of Cubism, and *Guernica* (1937), which expresses the artist's condemnation of the bombing of civilians in the Spanish Civil War. In the early 1920s Picasso went through a classical period, in which he painted monumental figures inspired by antique sculpture.

> For all his size and shape, he looked neither strong nor fertile. He was like one of Picasso's great sterile athletes, who brood hopelessly on pink sand, staring at veined marble waves.
> NATHANAEL WEST *The Day of the Locust* 1939

Mr Pickwick Mr Samuel Pickwick is the central character of Charles Dickens's novel *The Pickwick Papers* (1836–7). Founder of the Pickwick Club, he is jovial, generous, and unworldly in character and short, plump, and bespectacled in appearance. *See also* DICKENSIAN.

> His face was round and shiny, like Mr Pickwick's.
> JOHN BUCHAN *The Thirty-Nine Steps* 1915

> He was a little man, considerably less than of middle height, and enormously stout; he had a large, fleshy face, clean-shaven, with the cheeks hanging on each side in great dew-laps, and three vast chins; his small features were all dissolved in fat; and, but for a crescent of white hair at the back of his head, he was completely bald. He reminded you of Mr. Pickwick. He was a grotesque figure of fun, and yet, strangely enough, not without dignity.
> W. SOMERSET MAUGHAM *Mackintosh* 1951

> Upright, he looked like Mr Pickwick, with a chubby rubicund face and a fringe of long white hair around a gleaming pink scalp.
> ANABEL DONAL *The Glass Ceiling* 1994

Pied Piper The Pied Piper is the subject of Robert Browning's narrative poem *The Pied Piper of Hamelin* (1842). The Piper undertakes to rid the town of Hamelin of the rats that have been plaguing its citizens. The Mayor and Corporation agree to pay 1 000 guilders for this service. The Piper plays his pipe and the rats follow him to the river, where all but one perish. The Mayor then reneges on the payment; in revenge, the Piper starts to play his pipe again and this time is followed by all the children. He marches to the mountain where a portal opens and leads the children inside, whereupon it closes. One child, lame and unable to keep up, remains outside. He explains his subsequent lifelong sadness and solitude towards the end of the poem:
'And just as I became assured
My lame foot would be speedily cured,
The music stopped and I stood still,
And found myself outside the hill,

deserted, Piranesi perspectives of the station, discoloured by

Fireworks 1974

ypt In the book of Exodus, when Pharaoh refused to allow
he Israelites out of Egypt, God sent ten plagues to afflict the
d. 7–12). The plagues were: turning the Nile to blood; frogs;
th of cattle; boils; hail; locusts; darkness; and death of the
orn in every family. As a result of these plagues, Pharaoh
lites from bondage. *See also* GOSHEN, MOSES, NINTH PLAGUE OF

's so ready to take farms under you, it's a pity but what he should
d see if he likes to live in a house wi' all the plagues o' Egypt
e cellar full o' water, and the frogs and toads hoppin' up the steps
—and the floors rotten, and the rats and mice gnawing every bit o'
d runnin' over our heads as we lie i' bed till we expect 'em to eat us

Adam Bede 1859

reek philosopher Plato (*c*.429–*c*.347 BC) was a pupil of Socrates
r of Aristotle. He founded the Academy school of philosophy in
set out his views in the dialogues, in which Socrates is the
acter who conducts the discussions. His *Republic* explores his
rfect and just society. His name has become a byword for
rfection. Platonic love is love that is purely spiritual and not
a Platonic vision or idea is a perfect, idealized one.

Julie was lost in the photo-painter's Platonic idea of childhood; her
anity was smothered somewhere back of gobs of pink and white.
Goodbye, Columbus 1959

reek mythology, Pluto was an alternative name for Hades, lord of
orld. It was considered unwise to mention Hades by his true
he name Pluto, meaning literally 'the Rich One', was often used
he realm of Pluto is therefore the underworld, a land of perpetual
nd gloom. *See also* HADES.

grim, and ancient Raven, wandering from the nightly shore,
what thy lordly name is on the night's Plutonian shore?
LLEN POE *The Raven* 1845

vine now expandingly descends into a great, purple, hopper-shaped
v, far sunk among many Plutonian, shaggy-wooded mountains.
N MELVILLE *The Paradise of Bachelors and the Tartarus of Maids* 1856

t want to die on the Sicilian plains—to be snatched away, like Proserpine
same locality, to the Plutonian shades.
JAMES *Portrait of a Lady* 1881

Left alone against my will,
To go now limping as before,
And never hear of that country more!'
The citizens of Hamelin never see their children again.

> We passed the first houses, and children began to follow us, scampering along
> the banks till I felt like the Pied Piper.
> WILFRED THESIGER *The Marsh Arabs* 1974

> Some fall in behind her, and follow her to the lecture theatre, so that she
> appears to be leading a little procession, a female Pied Piper.
> DAVID LODGE *Nice Work* 1988

> It is a thought that has occurred to Rio di Angelo, a former member of Heaven's
> Gate, the suicide cult whose membership checked out en masse in March after
> announcing their departure on the Internet. Like the last child, too lame to
> follow the Pied Piper into the mountain, di Angelo was left behind. *The
> Observer* 1997

Pieria In Greek mythology, Pieria was a district on the slopes of Mount
Olympus associated with the Muses. The Pierian spring was located there,
believed to give poetic inspiration to those who drank its waters.

> A little learning is a dangerous thing;
> Drink deep, or taste not the Pierian spring.
> ALEXANDER POPE *An Essay on Criticism* 1711

> 'This is no time for blasphemy!' 'A little learning goes to the heads of fools.'
> 'Yes, drink deep of the Pierian spring or . . .'
> NATHANAEL WEST *The Dream Life of Balso Snell* 1931

Miss Piggy Miss Piggy is a puppet creation of Jim Henson that has appeared
in the television series *The Muppet Show* and *Sesame Street*. She is a large pink
pig with long blonde hair.

> I just know I've put on at least half a pound. The bus driver's going to notice
> and give me a pitying look, sort of saying, 'Well, hello, Miss Piggy, how do you
> expect to get a seat on the bus with that fat arse?'
> ARABELLA WEIR *Does My Bum Look Big in This?* 1997

Pontius Pilate Pontius Pilate was the Roman procurator of Judaea (AD
26–36) before whom accusations against Jesus were brought. The Jews, under
the direction of the high priest, Caiaphas, wanted Jesus executed, which
required him to be tried under Roman rather than Jewish law. After
questioning Jesus, Pilate could find no basis for a charge against him. The
Jews were insistent that Jesus be crucified and eventually Pilate gave in to
them: 'When Pilate saw that he could prevail nothing, but that rather a
tumult was made, he took water and washed his hands before the multitude,
saying, I am innocent of the blood of this just person: see ye to it' (Matt. 27:
24). Pontius Pilate is alluded to as someone who colludes in a crime or
dishonest act but tries to distance himself from it and assume no

responsibility for it. Pilate's gesture proclaiming his innocence has given us the phrase 'to wash one's hands of something', meaning to take no further responsibility for it. *See also* JESUS.

> 'I know Hosnani was a friend of yours, sir.' Mountolive felt himself colouring slightly. 'In matters of business, a diplomat has no friends,' he said stiffly, feeling that he spoke in the very accents of Pontius Pilate.
> LAWRENCE DURRELL *Mountolive* 1958

> The day will come when we and the British Empire will stand together and say to the world, 'It was we who made you free,' and the Americans and the Russians and the other Pontius Pilates like them will hang their heads and feel ashamed that all the glory came to us.
> LOUIS DE BERNIÈRES *Captain Corelli's Mandolin* 1994

> 'I think I know why she left the money to Dr Blakeney.' 'Why?' 'I reckon it was a Pontius Pilate exercise. She'd done a lousy job herself bringing up her daughter and granddaughter, knew they'd destroy themselves with jealous infighting if she left the money to them, so passed the buck to the only person she'd ever got on with or respected. Namely Dr Blakeney.'
> MINETTE WALTERS *The Scold's Bridle* 1994

> Chief Ranger Hull crossed the clearing, wiping his hands carefully on a clean white pocket hanky. . . . Hull never looked up from his hands while he talked, but continued to rub meticulously between each finger with the square of cotton. . . . Finally Norman Hull pocketed the handkerchief and Anna breathed a sigh of relief. Till it stopped she'd not realized how much his Pontius Pilate routine was getting on her nerves.
> NEVADA BARR *Endangered Species* 1997

Pilate's wife In the New Testament, when Jesus was brought before Pontius Pilate for judgement, Pilate's wife reported to her husband the distress she had suffered in a dream on account of Jesus, and urged him: 'Have thou nothing to do with that just man: for I have suffered many things this day in a dream because of him.' *See also* PONTIUS PILATE.

> 'All dreams mean something.' 'For Joseph and Pharaoh, or Pilate's wife, perhaps. You will have to work very hard to convince me that they mean anything here and now.'
> ROBERTSON DAVIES *The Manticore* 1972

Pilgrim's Progress *The Pilgrim's Progress* (1678, 1684) is the religious allegory by John Bunyan in which Christian undertakes a pilgrimage to the Celestial City encountering various allegorical characters on the way. *See also* APOLLYON, BEULAH, CELESTIAL CITY, CHRISTIAN, DELECTABLE MOUNTAINS, MR FACING-BOTH-WAYS, GIANT DESPAIR, GREATHEART, SLOUGH OF DESPOND, VALLEY OF THE (SHADOW OF) DEATH, VALLEY OF HUMILIATION.

Pillars of Hercules The Pillars of Hercules are the two promontories at the sides of the Straits of Gibraltar, one in Europe and one in North Africa,

known in ancient times as Calpe [...] Gibraltar and Mount Acho in Ceut[...] were either erected by Hercules or[...] island of Erytheia to complete the [...] the oxen of the three-bodied mons[...] regarded in ancient times as marki[...]
HERCULES.

Pinkerton's Pinkerton's National D[...] in 1850 by Allan Pinkerton, a Scottisl[...] American private detective agency, w[...] series of train robberies. During the *A*[...] chief of the secret service on the Unio[...] Confederate lines.

> 'And you don't happen to have a frier[...] held up my hand in submission. 'The l[...] Bradshaw, yes?' 'Yes.' It was obvious th[...] career move for me.
> MALCOLM HAMER *Dead on Line* 1996

Pinocchio Pinocchio is the puppet hero [...] (1883) by G. Lorenzini, who wrote under [...] According to the story, the puppet Pinocc[...] Geppetto from a piece of wood that magic[...] Once created, Pinocchio has many strange [...] becoming a real boy. During one of his adv[...] longer every time he tells a lie. Allusions to [...] context of someone telling lies or being pu[...]

> Also, the characters can be transformed or [...] when Mario tells lies to a viewer, his nose ca[...]
> *New Scientist* 1993

> 'Madonna Maria, Dottore, please tell me som[...] truth will make us free. We overcome by look[...]
> LOUIS DE BERNIÈRES *Captain Corelli's Mandolin* 19[...]

> 'I promise you, it's not a problem, it's been so l[...] interested in a woman, it's a relief in a way.' Pir[...] glad to see him happy. I've never seen him this[...] for him.' But you'd be even better for me.
> LISA JEWELL *Ralph's Party* 1999

Piranesi Giovanni Battista Piranesi (1720–78) w[...] architect famous for his views of the ruins of Ro[...] imaginary prisons (1745–61).

> When it was time for the first train in the mornin[...]

> mysteriously [...]
> dawn.
> ANGELA CARTER[...]

plagues of Eg[...]
Moses to lead t[...]
Egyptians (Exo[...]
gnats; flies; dea[...]
Egyptian first-[...]
freed the Israe[...]
EGYPT.

> If Mr Thurle[...]
> take this, a[...]
> in't—wi' th[...]
> by dozens—[...]
> cheese, an[...]
> up alive.
> GEORGE ELIOT[...]

Plato The G[...]
and a teache[...]
Athens. Plat[...]
central char[...]
ideas of a pe[...]
idealized po[...]
sexual, and [...]

> Poor littl[...]
> tiny hum[...]
> PHILIP ROT[...]

Pluto In G[...]
the under[...]
name, so t[...]
instead. T[...]
darkness [...]

> Ghastl[...]
> Tell me[...]
> EDGAR [...]

> The ra[...]
> hollow[...]
> HERMA[...]

> I don[...]
> in the[...]
> HENRY[...]

Plutus Plutus was the son of Demeter and the god of wealth in Greek mythology. The Greeks represented him as blind because he distributed riches indiscriminately, as lame because riches come slowly, and with wings because riches disappear more quickly than they come.

> It would be difficult for the most jealous and eager devotee at the shrine of Plutus to devise any securities for property. *Harper's Monthly* 1880

Pocahontas Pocahontas (*c*.1595–1617) was a beautiful American Indian princess who is alleged to have saved the life of the English colonist John Smith when he was captured by her father, Powhatan.

> Then go to America, and drown your sorrows on the bosom of some charming Pocahontas.
> JOHN FOWLES *The French Lieutenant's Woman* 1969

Podsnap Mr Podsnap is a character in Dickens's *Our Mutual Friend* (1864–5) who is self-satisfied and complacent, and has a high opinion of his own importance: 'Mr Podsnap . . . stood very high in Mr. Podsnap's opinion.' *See also* DICKENSIAN.

> Masochists may get their kicks from national self-denigration, but for the rest of us there is neither much fun nor much enlightenment in such bouts of inverted Podsnappery. *The Independent* 1992

Edgar Allen Poe Edgar Allen Poe (1809–49) was an American short-story writer and poet, best known for his macabre tales of mystery and the supernatural, including 'The Fall of the House of Usher' (1839), set in an eerie crumbling mansion. *See also* HOUSE OF USHER.

> The Wilberforce place looked a lot better for its conversion. Around the turn of the century some local bigwig had let a similarity of names go to his head and in a spirit of philanthropy had built and endowed an orphanage. The idea itself was good but it was a shame he hadn't picked a better architect. A mix of Wuthering Heights and Edgar Allen Poe is not somewhere I would willingly opt to spend my childhood.
> SARAH LACEY *File under: Arson* 1995

Hercule Poirot Hercule Poirot is the Belgian detective in many novels by Agatha Christie. He has a waxed moustache, drinks tisanes, and uses 'the little grey cells' to deduce the identity of the murderer.

> It was well after midnight before Jamieson got back to the residency and heard Sue gasp when she saw the state of him. Jamieson sat down slowly in the only armchair and asked her to pour him a drink while he told her what had happened. 'So you didn't even find out what Thelwell was up to?' said Sue. There was a suggestion of 'I told you so' in her voice, but she didn't actually say it. Jamieson agreed with a shake of the head and said, 'More Clouseau than Poirot.'
> KEN MCCLURE *Chameleon* 1994

Pollock Jackson Pollock (1912–56) was a US abstract expressionist painter, the foremost exponent of 'action painting'. In 1947 he abandoned the use of brushes, adopting a technique in which he vigorously dribbled or hurled the paint straight onto the canvas. These works, sometimes referred to as his 'drip paintings', are made up of complicated laceworks of swirling coloured lines.

> The ENT Man treated his victims' blood like it was paint and he was Jackson Pollock.
> PAUL JOHNSTON *Body Politic* 1997

> With one headlight missing, the other dangling from its socket, the van looks like a mutilated monster. A mangled front bumper, lashed to the grille with pieces of twine, bounces wildly. Slashes of assorted paints crisscross the chassis—Jackson Pollock on wheels.
> SUSAN SUSSMAN with SARAJANE AVIDON *Cruising for Murder* 2000

Pollux *See* CASTOR AND POLLUX.

Pollyanna The heroine of stories for children written by the American author Eleanor H. Porter (1868–1920), Pollyanna is a perpetually cheerful girl who teaches everyone she meets to play the 'just being glad' game: 'the game was to just find something about everything to be glad about—no matter what 'twas'. The name Pollyanna has come to stand for an unflagging (and often excessively saccharine) cheerfulness, an ability to find apparent cause for happiness in the most unpromising situations. The term often seems to be accompanied by a sense of apology, a recognition that such optimism may seem to others rather naive.

> Hadn't they been happy here? After all the bedsits and borrowed apartments and shitty pensiones, hadn't this been the dream place? . . . Had he lived in some Pollyanna blur all this time? Was he missing something? Was she miserable and bored? And worse?
> TIM WINTON *The Riders* 1994

> Alison sulked while Anna dragged the canoe up on shore and unloaded it. Anna tried to keep up her end of the day but she felt a childish resentment that her plans had been disrupted. 'I'm the ranger,' she said peevishly. 'That and a dollar won't even get you a cup of coffee here,' Chris returned. She excused herself to find the 'ladies' room' and left Anna and Ally sitting with their legs dangling over the edge of the dock, both steadfastly refusing to play the Pollyana Glad Game.
> NEVADA BARR *A Superior Death* 1994

> I don't want to sound too Pollyanna-ish, but anyone getting autumn state-of-the-world blues might tune in to BBC Radio's 1995 Young Writers' Festival, First Bite, which has just ended its first week. If the pieces I heard are any gauge of the creativity to come, then the grounds for optimism are abundant. *The Guardian* 1995

Marco Polo Marco Polo (*c.*1254–*c.*1324) was a Venetian traveller and writer. Between 1271 and 1275 he accompanied his father and uncle on a trading expedition east into central Asia, eventually reaching China and the court of Kublai Khan. After entering diplomatic service with the emperor and travelling widely in the empire for a decade and a half, Polo returned home to Venice (1292–5) via Sumatra, India, and Persia. His written account of his travels was the West's primary source of knowledge of the Far East until the 19th century, though doubt has subsequently been cast on its veracity.

> The commonest ailment experienced by modern-day Marco Polos is an intestinal attack known as gyppy tummy. *New Scientist* 1970

Polonius In Shakespeare's play *Hamlet* (1604), Polonius is the court chamberlain who hides behind an arras (a tapestry screen) in Gertrude's bedchamber to eavesdrop on Hamlet's conversation with the queen. Hamlet, believing it is the king, Claudius, he can hear behind the arras, runs his sword through it and mistakenly stabs Polonius to death. *See also* SHAKESPEARE.

Polycrates Polycrates was the ruler of Samos and was extraordinarily lucky. So much luck put him in danger of retribution from Nemesis, and in order to appease her he threw away a very valuable ring. The ring was subsequently found in the belly of a fish which a fisherman had presented to Polycrates. He was killed in *c.*522 BC.

Polydamas In Greek legend, Polydamas was a celebrated athlete who imitated Hercules in whatever he did. He killed a lion with his fist and is said to have stopped a speeding chariot with his hand. He died attempting to catch a falling boulder.

Polyhymnia Polyhymnia was one of the nine Muses in Greek mythology, associated especially with songs to the gods. *See also* MUSES.

Polyphemus In Greek mythology, Polyphemus was one of the Cyclopes, huge one-eyed monsters, who fell in love with Galatea, a sea-nymph. She did not love him, but did have a lover by the name of Acis. In a jealous rage, Polyphemus hurled a rock at Acis, crushing him to death. *See also* CYCLOPS.

Pomona Pomona was the Roman goddess of fruit, married to Vortumnus, the god of orchards and fruit.

> Down in the heart of the apple-country nearly every farmer kept a cider-making apparatus and wring-house for his own use, building up the pomace in great straw 'cheeses', as they were called; but here, on the margin of Pomona's plain, was a debatable land neither orchard nor sylvan exclusively, where the apple-produce was hardly sufficient to warrant each proprietor in keeping a mill of his own.
> THOMAS HARDY *The Woodlanders* 1887

Pompeii Pompeii was an ancient city in western Italy, south-east of Naples. Following an eruption of Mount Vesuvius in AD 79, the city was completely buried beneath volcanic ash. Excavations of the site, which began in 1748, have revealed that the ruins had been extremely well preserved, giving a detailed insight into the everyday life in Roman times.

> He was rather glad that they were all out; it was amusing to wander through the house as though one were exploring a dead, deserted Pompeii.
> ALDOUS HUXLEY *Crome Yellow* 1921

> I picked up the waste-paper basket and found, among ash to equal the destruction of Pompeii, a large number of old cigar butts, and a handful of unopened bills . . . and an unopened cablegram.
> JOHN MORTIMER *Rumpole's Return* 1980

> Then, just for a second, Ferrera's eyes lifted and he caught a glimpse of Mark, standing some fifty yards away. He froze completely, his foot drawn back for the shot, looking for all the world like a victim at Pompeii, covered in ash for ever. Finally he completed the shot and Sergovich dived to his left and caught the ball in triumph.
> MEL STEIN *White Lines* 1997

Pony Express The Pony Express was a system of mail delivery in the United States in 1860–1. Relays of horse-riders covered a total distance of 1 800 miles between St Joseph in Missouri and Sacramento in California.

Pooh *See* WINNIE THE POOH.

Pooh-Bah Pooh-Bah is the Lord-High-Everything-Else, a character in Gilbert and Sullivan's *The Mikado* (1885). His name can be applied to a self-important person or to a person holding many offices at once.

> *None is too many*, is what some Canadian government pooh-bah said about the Jews, during the war.
> MARGARET ATWOOD *The Robber Bride* 1993

> 'Ben, look at this . . . What do you see?' Same thing I had seen at our earlier viewing, a shot of King and four former State Department poohbahs exiting a helicopter at a luxurious Aspen, Colorado non-profit think-tank mountain ranch maintained by our tax dollars.
> JUSTIN SCOTT *Frostline* 1997

Popeye The cartoon character Popeye the Sailor Man was created by Elzie Segar for the comic strip *Thimble Theater* in 1929, ten years after the first edition. Eating a can of spinach gave Popeye prodigious strength. He was depicted with hugely bulging forearms, one eye, and a pipe clenched between his teeth. His girlfriend was the skinny Olive Oyl and his arch-enemy Bluto. *See also* OLIVE OYL.

> The overall impression was of a powerhouse. Lennie had been a seaman for

years, and he still had the rolling gait. In fact, with his muscular build he resembled a pumped-up Popeye.

NORMAN PARKER *Parkhurst Tales* 1994

Mary Poppins Mary Poppins is the name of the Edwardian nanny with magical powers who appears in a series of children's books by P. L. Travers. It is probably Julie Andrews's portrayal of the character in the film musical *Mary Poppins* (1964) that has caused the character's name to become a byword for unfailing cheerfulness and somewhat saccharine wholesomeness.

> We were never happy. Gavin was a public schoolboy who never grew up. Like many men with that background, he was uneasy with women. Some end up treating us like whores, others decide we're madonnas. Gavin was the madonna type. Unfortunately I'm not. I found the strain of playing Mary Poppins just too much. In the end I told him to bugger off and be done with it.
> KEN MCCLURE *Requiem* 1992

> Phyllis put her crocks in the dishwasher, shrugged into a beige raincoat, checked her umbrella and keys and made a rush for the door. Mary Poppins she was not and a malicious old trout to boot.
> VIVEN ARMSTRONG *Fly in Amber* 2000

Sir Joseph Porter KCB Sir Joseph Porter KCB is a character in Gilbert and Sullivan's *HMS Pinafore* (1878) who boasts that he has achieved the exalted status of 'ruler of the Queen's Navee' by his industry as an office boy, junior clerk, articled clerk, lawyer and MP, without any experience in the Navy. His song ends with the instruction that if you want to 'rise to the top of the tree', you should
'Stick close to your desks and never go to sea,
And you all may be rulers of the Queen's Navee!'

Porthos *See* THREE MUSKETEERS.

Portia In Shakespeare's play *The Merchant of Venice* (1600), Portia, a rich heiress, disguises herself as a male lawyer to save Antonio, a friend of her betrothed, Bassanio. Antonio had borrowed money from Shylock to help Bassanio and later, unable to pay it back, is faced with paying the bond of a pound of his flesh instead. Portia saves Antonio's life by arguing that, although Shylock has the right to take a pound of Antonio's flesh, he has no right to shed any of his blood, making it impossible for Shylock to exact his due. *See also* SHAKESPEARE, SHYLOCK.

> He growled savagely at witnesses, he shouted and reduced young male barristers to stammering jellies and made lady barristers weep (Miss Trant, the Portia of our Chambers, once fled in tears from Bullingham's Court, saying that the cause of justice there would be advanced if they brought back trial by ordeal).
> JOHN MORTIMER *Rumpole's Return* 1980

Poseidon Poseidon, the son of Cronus and Rhea, was the Greek god of the sea, water, earthquakes, and horses, often depicted with a trident in his hand. Poseidon was frequently portrayed as both irritable and vengeful. He corresponds to the Roman god Neptune.

> Mandras was too young to be a Poseidon, too much without malice. Was he a male sea-nymph, then? Was there such a thing as a male Nereid or Potamid?
> LOUIS DE BERNIÈRES *Captain Corelli's Mandolin* 1994

Flora Poste Flora Poste is the heroine of the novel *Cold Comfort Farm* by Stella Gibbons (1932) who visits her relatives the Starkadders in Sussex and finds herself in a household full of gloom, seething emotion, dark secrets, and rural intrigue. She cheerfully sets about reforming the characters and sorting out their personal lives.

> 'Oh Ma!' Michael said, when I told him. 'You interfering old busybody!'
> 'Nonsense,' I said. 'I prefer to think of myself as a sort of Flora Poste, tidying up people's lives and making them happy.'
> HAZEL HOLT *Lilies that Fester* 2000

Potiphar's wife Joseph was a Hebrew patriarch, son of Jacob. In Egypt, Joseph was bought by Potiphar, an Egyptian officer, in whose house he was soon made overseer. Potiphar's wife tried to seduce him but Joseph repeatedly refused her advances because of his loyalty to his master. Finally when Potiphar's wife found herself alone in the house with Joseph, she grabbed hold of him, saying 'Lie with me'. Joseph fled from the house, leaving a piece of his clothing in her hand. She subsequently made a false accusation that he had attempted to rape her (Gen. 39). *See also* JOSEPH.

> So pressing an issue is it [the sexual harassment of men by women] . . . that the European Union considered it necessary to produce a 93-page booklet on what it described as 'the Potiphar's wife syndrome'. *The Guardian* 1994

pottage *See* JACOB.

pound of flesh *See* SHYLOCK.

Praxiteles Praxiteles (4th c. BC) was an Athenian sculptor. Although only one of his works survives, a sculpture of Hermes carrying the infant Dionysus, he is considered to be one of the foremost Greek sculptors. One of his most famous works was a statue of Aphrodite, which is known through later copies.

> She had bared her plump neck, shoulders, and arms to the moonshine, under which they looked as luminous and beautiful as some Praxitelean creation.
> THOMAS HARDY *Tess of the D'Urbervilles* 1891

> He stood up slowly and went over to close the curtains. His silhouette against the window was like something Praxiteles might have knocked up for personal consumption.
> LAUREN HENDERSON *The Black Rubber Dress* 1997

Pre-Raphaelite The Pre-Raphaelite Brotherhood was a group of English 19th-century artists founded by Dante Gabriel Rossetti, John Everett Millais, and Holman Hunt. Their aim was to emulate the vivid use of colour and meticulously detailed fidelity to nature of Italian painting from before the time of Raphael. The term 'Pre-Raphaelite' is often applied to a woman who resembles the models painted by this school, especially in having wavy auburn hair and a pale complexion. The faces of these models, notably Elizabeth Siddal, Fanny Cornforth, and Jane Morris, appear in a great many of the paintings.

> Some would say her hair is her finest feature, though Robyn herself secretly hankers after something more muted and malleable, hair that could be groomed and styled according to mood—drawn back in a severe bun like Simone de Beauvoir's, or allowed to fall to the shoulders in a Pre-Raphaelite cloud.
> DAVID LODGE *Nice Work* 1988

> Beneath the wide, full mouth, the arrogant stare of the eyes, the dark, crimped, Pre-Raphaelite hair streaming in the wind.
> P D. JAMES *Devices and Desires* 1989

> She has narrow sloping shoulders, and in those days a soulful pre-Raphaelite look.
> FAY WELDON *Life Force* 1992

Prester John In a European legend dating from the 12th century, Prester John (meaning 'Priest John') was a Christian priest–king who ruled over a fabulously wealthy empire in Asia. In 14th-century versions of the legend, he was believed to be the king of Ethiopia. Another theory identifies him with a Chinese prince who defeated the sultan of Persia in 1141.

> By this good wine, I'll ride to the end of the world—the very gates of Jericho, and the judgment-seat of Prester John, for thee!
> WALTER SCOTT *The Bride of Lammermoor* 1818

Priapus In Greek mythology, Priapus was a god of fertility and procreation, represented as an ugly human figure with enormous genitals. He was also a god of gardens and vineyards. His name is sometimes used in the context of male libido; the adjective derived from his name, 'priapic', means 'phallic'.

> Then she touched him. King Priapus, he who had been scared to death, now rose up from the dead.
> TOM WOLFE *The Bonfire of the Vanities* 1987

Prince Charming Prince Charming is the hero of the fairy story *The Blue Bird* (*L'Oiseau bleu*) by Mme d'Aulnoy. Having fallen in love with a king's daughter, he falls foul of her wicked stepmother and is condemned to spend seven years in the form of a blue bird. At the end of the seven years, he regains his proper shape and all turns out well. The name, which has come to be erroneously associated with other fairy stories, particularly with the prince in the Cinderella story, can also be applied to any idealized young lover or suitor. *See also* CINDERELLA.

> You have made me understand what love really is. My love! my love! Prince Charming! Prince of life!
> OSCAR WILDE *The Picture of Dorian Gray* 1891

> It always happens this way. The right bridegroom turns up verily like the Prince Charming all of a sudden when the time comes.
> R. K. NARAYAN *Under the Banyan Tree* 1985

> Darling John, I know I'm not exactly Cinderella but you really have come into my life like Prince Charming and I just can't bear the thought—I won't bear it! I know I'm an old silly, doubting you like this, but you've no idea how lonely it is without you!
> JOAN SMITH *Full Stop* 1995

Prince of Darkness The Prince of Darkness is another name for the Devil or Satan. *See* DEVIL, SATAN.

Princes in the Tower The Princes in the Tower were Edward, prince of Wales (b. 1470), and Richard, duke of York (b. 1472), the two young sons of Edward IV. When Edward IV died in 1483, the young Edward reigned briefly as Edward V, but soon afterwards he and his brother were sent to the Tower of London by their uncle, the future Richard III. It is generally assumed that they were murdered in the tower at the instigation of Richard, although some argue that the culprit was his successor, Henry VII. Two skeletons discovered in the Tower in 1674 are thought to be theirs.

Prisoner of Chillon *The Prisoner of Chillon* is the title of a poem by Byron, published in 1816, which describes the imprisonment of François de Bonnivard (1496–1570) in the castle of Chillon, on Lake Geneva.

Prisoner of Zenda *The Prisoner of Zenda* is the title of a book by Anthony Hope, published in 1894. The novel follows the adventures of Rudolf Rassendyll, an Englishman who bears a striking resemblance to the king of Ruritania. When the king is kidnapped, Rassendyll impersonates him, helps to rescue him from his imprisonment in the castle of Zenda, and thwarts a plot to usurp him. *See also* RURITANIA.

> Edna: Oh, I'm dead chokka! Cook, wash, clean—that's all I do—I never go anywhere. I'm like the bleeding Prisoner of Zenda.
> TERENCE DAVIES *A Modest Pageant* 1992

Procrustes In Greek mythology, Procrustes was a brigand who forced travellers who fell into his hands to lie on an iron bed. If they were longer than the bed, he cut off the overhanging length of leg; if they were shorter than the bed, he stretched them until they fitted it. He was eventually killed by Theseus, who attached him to his own bed and then, as he was too long for it, cut off his head. References to Procrustes usually suggest someone who attempts to enforce uniformity or conformity by forceful or ruthless methods. The adjective 'Procrustean' is sometimes used to describe the process of cutting something large down to size.

> I do not say that people don't judge their neighbours' conduct, sometimes, doubtlessly, unfairly. But I do say that there is no unvarying conventional set of rules by which people are judged; no bed of Procrustes to stretch or cramp their minds and lives.
> WILLIAM MORRIS *News from Nowhere* 1886

> Procrustes in modern dress, the nuclear scientist will prepare the bed on which mankind must lie.
> ALDOUS HUXLEY *Brave New World* 1946

> Given the Procrustean dimensions of film, the director and writer, Curtis Hanson and Brian Helgeland, have simplified the plot, timeline and character.
> JOHN SUTHERLAND *The Guardian* 1997

Prodigal Son In a parable told by Jesus, a young man squandered the property his father gave him 'with riotous living'. He is traditionally known as the Prodigal Son, meaning one who is spendthrift or recklessly extravagant. When, repenting his behaviour, the son returned home, he was received with compassion and forgiveness by his father: 'Bring forth the best robe, and put it on him; and put a ring on his hand, and shoes on his feet: And bring hither the fatted calf, and kill it; and let us eat, and be merry: For this my son was dead, and is alive again; he was lost, and is found' (Luke 15: 11–32). The terms 'prodigal' and 'prodigal son' are now generally used to refer to a repentant sinner or a returned wanderer. *See also* FATTED CALF.

> 'Aye, she'll git tired of deh life atter a while an' den she'll wanna be a-comin' home, won' she, deh beast! I'll let 'er in den, won' I?' 'Well, I didn't mean none of dis prod'gal bus'ness anyway,' explained Jimmie. 'It wa'n't no prod'gal dauter, yeh fool,' said the mother. 'It was prod'gal son, anyhow.'
> STEPHEN CRANE *Maggie: A Girl of the Streets* 1893

> The wicked wolf that for half a day had paralysed London and set all the children in the town shivering in their shoes, was there in a sort of penitent mood, and was received and petted like a sort of vulpine prodigal son.
> BRAM STOKER *Dracula* 1897

> 'Two eggs,' she commanded, rapping out her solicitude. 'Two, I insist. They were made especially for you.' 'You treat me like the prodigal son,' said Burlap. 'Or the fatted calf while it was being fattened.'
> ALDOUS HUXLEY *Point Counter Point* 1928

> He waved to Atwood. 'Hello, Frank. Look who's back! The prodigal returns!'
> ROBERT HARRIS *Enigma* 1995

Prometheus In Greek mythology, Prometheus was a Titan, the brother of Atlas, seen in many legends as the champion of humankind against the gods. In some stories he actually made the first men by making figures of clay which, with the help of Athene, he brought to life. He first angered Zeus when he was asked to arbitrate in a dispute between men and gods over which portion of a sacrificial bull should be given to the gods and which portion should be kept by men. Prometheus divided the carcass into two bags, one containing the flesh, which he made unappealing by covering it with the bull's stomach, the other containing the bones, which he covered with fat to make it look like meat. He thus tricked Zeus into choosing the bag containing the bones, which would thereafter be the gods' portion. In anger Zeus withheld fire from men, saying that they could eat their flesh raw. Prometheus responded by going to Olympus himself and stealing some fire hidden in a stalk of fennel, which he gave to men. He also improved their lives by teaching them arts and sciences. As a punishment for his disobedience to the gods, Zeus had Prometheus chained to a rock, where each day an eagle tore out his liver, which grew again each night. He was eventually rescued by Hercules, who shot the eagle with his bow and arrow. Prometheus is the archetype of the courageous rebel who dares to challenge the power of the gods and of fate. The Promethean spark or fire is the spark of life or vitality.

White necks, carmine lips and cheeks, clusters of bright curls, do not suffice for me without the Promethean spark which will live after the roses and lilies are faded, the burnished hair grown grey.
CHARLOTTE BRONTË *The Professor* 1857

Moreover to light a fire is the instinctive and resistant act of man when, at the winter ingress, the curfew is sounded throughout Nature. It indicates a spontaneous, Promethean rebelliousness against the fiat that this recurrent season shall bring foul times, cold darkness, misery and death.
THOMAS HARDY *The Return of the Native* 1880

She sees the victimized character. She sees one long set of attacks on him. She would never take account of the self-inflicted wrong—the chap who breaks his own arm to avoid going back to school, then says some big bully has done it for him; the chap who lashes himself to his bedroom chair so as not to have to go and cope with the burglar—oh, she'd think he was Prometheus.
ELIZABETH BOWEN *The Death of the West* 1938

He remembered Holy Week in the old days when a stuffed Judas was hanged from the belfry and boys made a clatter with tins and rattles as he swung out over the door. Old staid members of the congregation had sometimes raised objections: it was blasphemous, they said, to make this guy out of Our Lord's betrayer; but . . . it seemed to him a good thing that the world's traitor should be made a figure of fun. It was too easy otherwise to idealise him as a man who fought with God—a Prometheus, a noble victim in a hopeless war.
GRAHAM GREENE *The Power and the Glory* 1940

Promised Land In the Bible, Canaan is described as the Promised Land, promised by God to Abraham and his descendants as their heritage (Gen. 12: 7). When the Israelites left Egypt, led by Moses, (Exod. 12: 31–42) they wandered through the Sinai desert for 40 years until they finally reached the borders of Canaan (Num. 34). Moses was not allowed to cross the river Jordan into Canaan but was allowed a glimpse of the Promised Land from Mount Pisgah before he died. The term can be applied to any desired place of expected happiness, especially heaven. *See also* MOSES.

> Years ago, when we were in trouble, we thought we could one day go north. Well, we are north now. We are at that Promised Land.
> STUDS TERKEL *American Dreams: Lost and Found* 1980

Prospero In Shakespeare's *The Tempest* (1623), Prospero is the usurped duke of Milan, marooned on a remote enchanted island with his daughter Miranda. His knowledge of magic enables him to raise the storm at the beginning of the play and gives him power over the airy spirit Ariel. He finally resolves to renounce his 'rough magic', breaking his staff and burying his books, the sources of his powers. *See also* ARIEL, MIRANDA, SHAKESPEARE.

> You were Prospero enough to make her what she has become.
> HENRY JAMES *Portrait of a Lady* 1881

Proteus In Greek mythology, Proteus, the son of Oceanus and Tethys, was given by Poseidon the power to prophesy the future. He also had the power to change his shape, which he would exploit in order to escape those seeking his predictions. In an episode recounted in the *Odyssey*, Proteus changes himself in rapid succession into a lion, a serpent, a panther, a wild boar, a torrent of water, and a tree. The name Proteus has come to refer to changeability, along with the adjective 'protean'. Proteus was sometimes depicted as emerging from the sea, almost like a male Venus, and resting on the seashore.

> So might I, standing on this pleasant lea,
> Have glimpses that would make me less forlorn;
> Have sight of Proteus rising from the sea;
> Or hear old Triton blow his wreathed horn.
> WILLIAM WORDSWORTH 'The World is too much with us' 1807

> Donald appeared not to see her at all, and answered her wise little remarks with curtly indifferent monosyllables, his looks and faculties hanging on the woman who could boast of a more Protean variety in her phases, moods, opinions, and also principles, than could Elizabeth.
> THOMAS HARDY *The Mayor of Casterbridge* 1886

> And suddenly, like a crew-cut Proteus rising from the sea, Ron Patimkin emerged from the lower depths we'd just inhabited and his immensity was before us.
> PHILIP ROTH *Goodbye, Columbus* 1959

> Well, it was a virtuoso performance, and obscured for those few hours all shadows of the other Lennys, the cold, the cruel, the distant ones. And so I learnt a lesson for times to come. That my battle was not so much with a

dragon breathing fire, as with Proteus changing shapes, and that whatever magic was woven around me, I should always be on my guard.
SARAH DUNANT *Snow Storms in a Hot Climate* 1988

Proust Marcel Proust (1871–1922) was a French novelist, whose masterpiece, *À la recherche du temps perdu* (1913–27), is usually translated into English with the title *Remembrance of Things Past*. In exploring its theme of recovery of the lost past, the novel repeatedly describes how a sensory stimulus in the present, such as the taste of a madeleine cake dipped into tea, can act as the unconscious trigger for a flood of memories from the past, especially from childhood.

Sam stood stropping his razor, and steam rose invitingly, with a kind of Proustian richness of evocation—so many such happy days, so much assurance of position, order, calm, civilization, out of the copper jug he had brought with him.
JOHN FOWLES *The French Lieutenant's Woman* 1969

Settle for the cordite. That I am certain of. My nose tells the truth. I am the Proust of filth.
JOHN LAWTON *Black Out* 1995

Hester Prynne Hester Prynne is the adulteress in Nathaniel Hawthorne's novel *The Scarlet Letter* (1850) set in 17th-century Boston. Hester is sent by her ageing English husband to Boston, where he joins her two years later. He arrives to find her in the pillory, with her illegitimate baby in her arms. She refuses to name her lover and is sentenced to wear a scarlet 'A', for 'adulteress', on her bosom. Her husband, taking on the assumed name of Roger Chillingworth, sets out to discover the identity of her lover and eventually identifies him as Arthur Dimmesdale, a young and much-respected church minister. Hester, ostracized by the community, brings up her child on the outskirts of the town, and eventually wins back the respect of the townsfolk by her good works.

'You would have surely seen . . . I mean, you were . . .' Tristan was finding it difficult to meet Hannah's eyes. He glanced away from her. 'Weren't you and Lucas . . . I mean, that's what I assumed from what you—' 'That I was sleeping with Lucas, do you mean?' A kind of cold embarrassment dropped over Hannah, as though she were the woman taken in adultery, a latter-day Hester Prynne.
SUSAN MOODY *The Italian Garden* 1994

Psycho *Psycho* is the title of an Alfred Hitchcock thriller, released in 1960. The film centres on Norman Bates, a murderous psychopath who is the owner of the Bates Motel, and includes a famously shocking murder scene in which a woman is stabbed repeatedly by Bates in her shower.

The owner, whom I roused from a backroom television den, didn't look anything like Norman Bates, and treated the whole transaction as if it was just

his job. It made me wonder if we Europeans are the only ones to conjure up an instant vision of *Psycho* on journeys into the unknown. Americans at least had experience of motels long before that particular highway was removed and Norman's mother slept once too often with her new lover.
SARAH DUNANT *Snow Storms in a Hot Climate* 1988

But there was something too intimate in this, something stealthily domestic something she had to fight against. It was one of the reasons why she had turned down Giles Laughton's proposals of marriage. Coping with the trivia of daily living was bad enough one on one: scuffed heels, stray hairs, crumbs on the table, dirty knickers. To choose voluntarily to assimilate someone else's trivia as well, made about as much sense as booking into Norman Bates's motel.
SUSAN MOODY *Grand Slam* 1994

Puck Puck, also called Robin Goodfellow, is a mischievous sprite or goblin of popular folklore believed to roam the English countryside playing pranks. He appears as a character in Shakespeare's *A Midsummer Night's Dream* (1600), where he is described as a 'shrewd and knavish sprite' who delights in frightening village girls, preventing butter from being churned, and leading people off the right path at night. *See also* SHAKESPEARE.

But I have Puckish news for you. I read in the paper this morning that if you smoke you're less likely to develop Alzheimer's disease than if you don't. A hit, a veritable hit? Go on, have one, kipper your lungs and keep your brain intact.
JULIAN BARNES *Talking It Over* 1991

She couldn't tell if he was smiling, or if his face always wore that puckish grin.
DOUG BEASON and KEVIN J. ANDERSON *Assemblers of Infinity* 1993

pumpkin Turn into a pumpkin. *See* CINDERELLA.

Punch and Judy Punch (also called Punchinello) and Judy are characters in a traditional English seaside puppet show presented to children on a stage in a collapsible booth. Punch strangles his baby, is beaten by his wife, whom he then beats to death, and has various violent encounters with other characters including a doctor and a policeman. Both Punch and Judy talk in strained, high-pitched voices.

That was how they came to find themselves together on a journey which threw up a sort of ludicrous shadow-image of a love-relationship, like a clever magic-lantern picture of a landscape, created by, strangely—not Justine at all—but a worse mischief-maker—the novelist himself. 'It was Punch and Judy all right!' said Pursewarden ruefully afterwards.
LAWRENCE DURRELL *Balthazar* 1958

Yakimov's normal voice was thin, sad and unvarying, the voice of a cultured Punchinello.
OLIVIA MANNING *The Great Fortune* 1960

Edie Iden . . . was built on the same substantial lines as her husband. She came through from the shut public bar to take up position leaning on the bar beside Charlie, and rest her bosom on her forearms. Jonathan Cade, drinking his coffee a yard away in the empty lounge, pictured Mr Punch bobbing up beside them to crack a cudgel across their heads. Edie even sounded, with her breathy squeak, like someone in a puppet show.

STAYNES AND STOREY *Dead Serious* 1995

Purgatory In the Roman Catholic religion, Purgatory is a place of spiritual cleansing after death for the souls of people who have died in the grace of God but have to expiate venal sins before they may enter Heaven. It can describe any place or situation in which a person is waiting to move on.

I was in a strange condition which could be described as neither life nor death but something in between; a kind of air-conditioned purgatory. Not to put too fine a point on it, I had retired and gone to live in America.

JOHN MORTIMER *Rumpole's Return* 1980

Now Roberto had only to think of Her at the side of Ferrante, and lo, his marine Purgatory was transformed into a Hell.

UMBERTO ECO *The Island of the Day Before* 1994

Pygmalion

ancient Greek king In Greek legend, Pygmalion was the king of Cyprus who created a statue of a beautiful woman, according to Ovid, and then fell in love with it. He prayed to Aphrodite for a wife who resembled the statue, and Aphrodite responded by bringing it to life. The woman, whom Pygmalion married, has come to be called Galatea. *See also* GALATEA.

How many lovers since Pygmalion have been able to build their beloved's face out of flesh, as Amaril has?

LAWRENCE DURRELL *Balthazar* 1958

If Brocky had a fault, as a friend, it was just the tiniest assumption that he had created me out of some unlikely assemblage of oddments, as the young Frankenstein had created his Monster. I said so. 'Not a bit of it,' he said; 'keep your shirt on. No, no; I was, in so far as I was anything, the Pygmalion who released you, alive and talking, from the marble block.'

ROBERTSON DAVIES *The Cunning Man* 1994

phonetics teacher In Bernard Shaw's play *Pygmalion* (1913), Professor Henry Higgins, a phonetician, bets that he can take a cockney flower-seller and train her to speak standard English and fit into an upper-class social life. He succeeds, but she rebels against his relentless coaching and tyrannical behaviour. Eventually, they come to a truce. The play was made into a musical, *My Fair Lady*, which was filmed in 1964. *See also* ELIZA DOOLITTLE, HENRY HIGGINS.

He had taught her about books, not condescendingly, not seeing himself as some kind of Pygmalion, but wanting to share with someone he loved the

things that he loved. And now the time had come for that, too, to end.
P. D. JAMES *Original Sin* 1994

'But will any woman want to . . . it's not like you're going to be keeping it a
secret, who and what you were before . . . how will you, um . . . That's one
place Armsman Pygmalion over there,' Ivan waved at Szabo, 'won't be able to
coach you.'
LOIS MCMASTER BUJOLD *A Civil Campaign* 1999

Pylades and Orestes In Greek mythology, Pylades and Orestes were
constant friends, whose names have become synonymous with the idea of
strong and loyal friendship.

What animal magnetism drew thee and me together I know not; certainly I
never experienced anything of the Pylades and Orestes sentiment for you, and I
have reason to believe that you, on your part, were equally free from all
romantic regard to me.
CHARLOTTE BRONTË *The Professor* 1857

Pyramus and Thisbe Pyramus and Thisbe are next-door neighbours in
Babylon who are in love with each other. Their parents forbid them to marry,
but they are able to talk to each other through a hole in the wall that divides
their homes. Eventually they arrange to meet outside the city. Thisbe,
arriving first, sees a lion fresh from the kill and flees, dropping her cloak.
When Pyramus arrives and sees the cloak, now blood-stained having been
mauled by the lion, he assumes that Thisbe has been killed by the lion and
stabs himself to death. Thisbe returns as he is dying and also kills herself.
Their story is told by Ovid and also, comically, by Bottom and his fellow
workers in Shakespeare's *A Midsummer Night's Dream* (1600).

Why Pia's brother had volunteered Jono was never clear; Jono had done so
because he loved Charles and could not let him go alone. In the end they were
parted early on, sent off to different regiments. Charles had fallen distressingly
in love with Diana whom he met on his last leave before his departure for
France in 1915. She had kissed him and given him a photograph which he
carried until his death four weeks later. Jono, too, had kissed her, chastely, as
Pyramus had kissed the Wall, which she still represented for him, dividing him
from and uniting him with the golden Charles who had ridden off to war like
one of Edith's troubadours, carrying Diana's favour in his breast.
ELIZABETH IRONSIDE *Death in the Garden* 1995

Pyrrhic victory Pyrrhus (*c.*318–272 BC) was king of Epirus *c.*307–272. In
defeating the Romans at Asculum in 279, he sustained heavy losses,
commenting, 'Such another victory and we are ruined.' Hence a 'pyrrhic
victory' is one gained with terrible loss of life or at too great a cost.

Pythias *See* DAMON AND PYTHIAS.

Quasimodo Quasimodo is the ugly, deaf, hunchbacked bell-ringer of the Cathedral of Notre Dame in Victor Hugo's novel *Notre-Dame de Paris*, usually translated as *The Hunchback of Notre Dame* (1831). The popular image of the character has been largely formed by Charles Laughton's 1939 film portrayal in which a hauntingly pitiful Quasimodo finds comfort and solace in the bell tower of the cathedral with his beloved bells. Though grotesque in appearance, Quasimodo is gentle and tender-hearted and becomes devoted to Esmeralda, a gypsy dancer.

> Birchfield Place had relied, like most stately homes, on a state-of-the-art mix of hard-wired detectors on doors and windows, passive infrared detectors at all key points and pressure-activated alert pads in front of any items of significance. Given the fail-safes I'd put in place, I couldn't for the life of me see how anyone could have got through my system undetected without setting off enough bells to drive Quasimodo completely round the bend.
> VAL MCDERMID *Clean Break* 1995

> Close beside the bed, a bed Kudzuvine had never been in before and in a room he didn't begin to recognize, there sat the most malevolent creature he had ever seen since Quasimodo in a reshowing of *The Hunchback of Notre Dame*.
> TOM SHARPE *Grantchester Grind* 1995

Allan Quatermain Allan Quatermain is a principal character in several of Rider Haggard's adventure stories, including *King Solomon's Mines* (1885) and *Allan Quatermain* (1887). In the former novel, Quatermain sets off with two other men to find George Curtis, who has gone missing while looking for the treasure of King Solomon's mines in the lost land of the Kukuanas. After a perilous journey across deserts and over freezing mountains, they find the missing man and return safely home with enough of the lost treasure to make them wealthy men. Their servant also turns out to be the rightful king of the Kukuanas and, after a battle, they restore him to his throne.

Mistress Quickly In Shakespeare's *Henry IV Part 1*, *Henry IV Part 2*, and *Henry V*, Mistress Quickly, or Dame Quickly, is the colourful hostess of the Boar's Head tavern frequented by Falstaff and his companions. *See also* SHAKESPEARE.

> Dame Honeyball was a likely, plump, bustling little woman, and no bad substitute for that paragon of hostesses, Dame Quickly.
> WASHINGTON IRVING *The Sketch Book* 1820

quixotic *See* DON QUIXOTE.

Ra In ancient Egyptian mythology, Ra was the sun god and supreme deity, worshipped as the creator of all life and often portrayed with a falcon's head bearing the solar disc. He appears travelling in a ship with the other gods, crossing the sky by day and passing through the underworld, the land of the dead, by night.

rabbit-hole In Lewis Carroll's children's story *Alice's Adventures in Wonderland* (1865), Alice's adventures begin when she follows a white rabbit down a rabbit-hole and finds herself tumbling down a very deep well, ending up at the bottom in a strange world where she meets a succession of outlandish characters and experiences some bizarre adventures. Allusions to the rabbit-hole can evoke either entry to a strange or upside-down world, or the action of falling steeply downwards. *See also* ALICE IN WONDERLAND.

> 'I should think you'd like to see it [Nashville] again.' 'Never—I've kept away for fifteen years. I hope I'll never see it again.' But he would – for the plane was unmistakably going down, down, down, like Alice in the rabbit hole.
> F SCOTT FITZGERALD *The Last Tycoon* 1941

Rabelais The French writer François Rabelais (*c.*1494–1553) is chiefly known for his two satires *Pantagruel* and *Gargantua*, which, through their larger-than-life characters, express an exuberantly bawdy humour combined with a biting satirical wit and a philosophy of enjoying life to the full. *See also* GARGANTUA, PANTAGRUEL.

> Married or not, I could fancy Paula, were I prepared to wave goodbye to a modestly successful career. Early thirties, unmarried, generous curves and a sense of humour that could have stopped Rabelais in his tracks.
> RAYMOND FLYNN *A Public Body* 1996

> What disturbs us is ageing *women* having children. There's something ribald, Rabelaisian, about old fathers—'a man is as old as the woman he feels,' as Groucho Marx put it—while old mothers are seen as selfish and unnatural. *The Observer* 1997

Rachel Rachel was the second wife of Jacob, and the mother of Joseph and Benjamin. In the book of Jeremiah, she is described as weeping for her children who were taken away in captivity to Babylon: 'Thus says the Lord: A voice is heard in Ramah, lamentation and bitter weeping. Rachel is weeping for her children; she refuses to be comforted for her children, because they are not' (Jer. 31: 15). *See also* JACOB, JOSEPH.

> She was like Rachel, 'mourning over her children, and would not be comforted.'
> WASHINGTON IRVING *The Sketch-Book of Geoffrey Crayton, Gent.* 1820

> But by her still halting course and winding, woeful way, you plainly saw that this ship that so wept with spray, still remained without comfort. She was Rachel, weeping for her children, because they were not.
> HERMAN MELVILLE *Moby Dick* 1851

Rachman Peter Rachman (1919–62) was a London landlord whose exploitation and intimidation of his tenants became legendary. His name, and the related noun 'Rachmanism', have come to represent such practices.

> His dream is to banish forever the nightmare of Rachmanism, which still haunts the rented sector over 30 years after the worst excesses of the west London racketeer who gave landlords such a bad name. *The Observer* 1996

Arthur Rackham Arthur Rackham (1867–1939) was a British illustrator. Because he is best remembered for his illustrations of well-known children's books, his name has become associated with the idea of childhood innocence and simplicity.

> How could this Arthur Rackham nymph, his English Alice, be Pete Curtis's 'very good lay'?
> CHRISTOPHER J. KOCH *The Year of Living Dangerously* 1978

> The girls watched mesmerised as Kate wiped the make-up off her face. And Kate watched them in the mirror. Maisie, tall now, with pale translucent skin, narrow limbs, and an aureole of reddish fair hair, an Arthur Rackham girl. Alison, even taller, a Nefertiti head and an easy athletic grace.
> MAUREEN O'BRIEN *Dead Innocent* 1999

Raffles Raffles is a debonair, cricket-loving gentleman burglar created by the novelist E. W. Hornung (1866–1921). The character of Raffles first appeared in *The Amateur Cracksman* (1899), in which the story is narrated by Raffles's admiring assistant and ex-fag Bunny.

> While he was thinking, Signora Pianta told him in no uncertain terms that Argyll and his confederates—she still clearly saw him as some sort of latter-day Raffles, which seemed to Bottando one of the most unlikely comparisons he had ever heard—must have come here in the dead of night, loaded the pictures up and sailed off to hide them.
> IAIN PEARS *The Titian Committee* 1991

Raft of the Medusa *The Raft of the Medusa* (1819) is the most famous work by the French painter Theodore Géricault. It depicts with harrowing realism the sufferings of survivors of an actual shipwreck who had been cut adrift and left to drown. Some of the figures are based on Géricault's study of corpses and sickness.

Raggedy Ann Raggedy Ann is a rag doll in books by the American author Johnny Gruelle (1880–1938), the first of which, *Raggedy Ann Stories*, was published in 1918.

> She turned and raised a sleep-bleared Raggedy Ann face, shoe-button eyes peering, cobweb hair afloat. 'Whumya timezit?' she mumbled.
> J. D. MACDONALD *The Quick Red Fox* 1964

Ragnarok In Norse mythology, Ragnarok (literally 'Destined End of the Gods' or 'Twilight of the Gods') is the final battle between the gods and the forces of evil that will result in the destruction of the world, the Scandinavian equivalent of the Götterdämmerung.

> An all-out race war would be triggered, a final, bloody Ragnarok of the races. *Time* 1993

rainbow *See* END OF THE RAINBOW

Rambo Rambo is the hero of David Morrell's novel *First Blood* (1972), a Vietnam War veteran characterized as macho and bent on violent retribution, and popularized in three films in which the character is played by Sylvester Stallone. The name can be applied to any man who displays a great deal of physical violence or aggression. *See also* SYLVESTER STALLONE.

> Times like that a mini fire-extinguisher isn't near as comforting as a sub-machine-gun, but it was the best I could do. I got ready to ram the button and kneed open the door—that's about the only advantage lever handles have, you don't need hands to use them. I felt a little silly crouching there like Rambo when there was no one in the place but me.
> SARAH LACEY *File under: Jeopardy* 1995

> He's got Howard's big ol' Buck knife strapped to his belt and has been swaggering around like Rambo saying he's got to defend himself.
> NEVADA BARR *Firestorm* 1996

> Dressed from head to toe in camouflage gear—the kind that so many fathers and sons wear on hunting expeditions in the surrounding countryside at weekends—they were firing Rambo-style with an array of weapons, including high-velocity rifles and handguns. *The Independent* 1998

Raphael Raphael (Italian name Raffaello Sanzio; 1483–1520) was an Italian painter and architect known especially for his Madonnas, usually shown seated with a child on their knee and a beautifully serene expression.

> I have often wondered whether those early Madonnas of Raphael, with the blond faces and somewhat stupid expression, kept their placidity undisturbed

when their strong-limbed, strong-willed boys got a little too old to do without clothing.

GEORGE ELIOT *The Mill on the Floss* 1860

Rapunzel In the fairy story, Rapunzel is a beautiful long-haired girl who is locked at the top of a tall tower by a witch. The witch, and subsequently a handsome prince, are able to climb up to her after calling out 'Rapunzel, Rapunzel, let down your long hair'.

As I understand it, a gazebo is an open structure. I spent fifteen minutes searching for something resembling a park bandstand before coming upon a round building made of piled rock, like an old New England stone fence gone berserk. The rocks rose high, into a miniature fairy-tale tower, complete with turret. Huddled by the shore of a dark lake, it looked like an illustration from a children's book. If I waited till sunrise perhaps Rapunzel would cast down hair even longer than Marissa's.

LINDA BARNES *Cold Case* 1997

Vicky had the hair for it, yards of beautiful Rapunzel tresses curled and heaped and framing her delicate features like a baroque picture frame carved of chestnut.

JUSTIN SCOTT *Frostline* 1997

Rasputin Grigori Rasputin (1871–1916) was a Russian monk, notorious for his debauchery, who came to exert great influence over the tsarina Alexandra, wife of Nicholas II, by claiming miraculous powers to heal the heir to the throne, who suffered from haemophilia. Rasputin was eventually assassinated by a group of Russian noblemen loyal to the tsar.

Believe me, I'd much rather be by your side than poolside, where I spend most of my time these days. Which is what a 'development deal' seems to entail. . . . I develop a tan while the studio develops cold feet on the project. Happily, thanks to my beloved agent, Rasputin, they still have to pay oodles of money either way, but I have to stick around awhile, just in case it's a go.

JANE DENTINGER *Death Mask* 1988

As far as I could tell from the results of the audit so far, Future Assurance's income was still insufficient to cover the pared-down overheads and the inconsiderate claims of its policy-holders. Another year of loss rather than profit. Future Assurance was a corporate haemophiliac, without a Rasputin standing in the wings ready to weave magic spells to stem the fatal loss of blood.

PAUL BENNETT *False Profits* 1998

Reading Gaol Oscar Wilde spent time in Reading Gaol (1895–7) for homosexual offences, and wrote his poem *The Ballad of Reading Gaol* based on his experiences there. The poem highlights the harsh conditions in the prison and the despair of the prisoners. *See also* OSCAR WILDE.

And by the end of the evening, Reading Gaol would have felt like the George V.
<small>JULIAN BARNES</small> *Talking It Over* 1991

Edwin Reardon Edwin Reardon is a character in George Gissing's novel *New Grub Street* (1891), a gifted writer whose literary ambitions are nonetheless thwarted by poverty and by the lack of sympathy of his materialistic wife. Unable to succeed as a writer and deserted by his wife, Reardon is driven to an early grave.

Rebel Without a Cause *See* <small>JAMES DEAN.</small>

Red Cross Knight In Edmund Spenser's *The Faerie Queen*, the Red Cross Knight, almost certainly meant to be St George, is sent by the queen to slay a dragon that is ravaging the country of the princess Una. The Red Cross Knight does indeed destroy the dragon and marries Una. *See also* <small>SPENSER.</small>

> He himself isn't quite what Simon has been expecting; no heroic delivering Perseus, no Red Cross Knight.
> <small>MARGARET ATWOOD</small> *Alias Grace* 1996

Red Queen In an episode in Lewis Carroll's *Through the Looking-Glass* (1871), Alice finds herself running hand in hand with the Red Queen, who repeatedly urges them on with the words 'Faster! Faster!' But 'however fast they went, they never seemed to pass anything'. As the Queen observes to Alice: 'it takes all the running you can do to keep in the same place'.

> The principle of zero change in success *rate*, no matter how great the evolutionary progress in *equipment*, has been given the memorable name of the 'Red Queen effect' by the American biologist Leigh van Valen. In *Through the Looking Glass*, you will remember, the Red Queen seized Alice by the hand and dragged her, faster and faster, on a frenzied run through the countryside, but no matter how fast they ran they always stayed in the same place.
> <small>RICHARD DAWKINS</small> *The Blind Watchmaker* 1986

Red Riding Hood In the fairy story *Little Red Riding Hood*, first recorded by Perrault in 1697, Little Red Riding Hood, a young girl who earns her name from her red cloak and hood, sets off one day to visit her sick grandmother. Walking through a wood on her way, she meets a wolf, who asks where she is going. On hearing the answer, the wolf runs on ahead, imitates Red Riding Hood's voice to gain entry to the grandmother's cottage, and devours the grandmother. It then puts on the grandmother's clothes and gets into the grandmother's bed to await Red Riding Hood. When she arrives, the wolf talks to her kindly, trying to disguise its voice, but Red Riding Hood is struck by the strange appearance of her grandmother, and comments on the size of her ears, eyes, and finally teeth: 'What big teeth you have, grandmother', at which point the wolf, responding 'All the better to eat you with!', leaps up and devours Red Riding Hood. The wolf can be alluded to in the context of someone disguising themselves in order to win another's confidence and hide their own dishonest or evil intentions.

> The animal itself was as peaceful and well-behaved as that father of all picture-wolves, Red Riding Hood's quondam friend, whilst seeking her confidence in masquerade.
> BRAM STOKER *Dracula* 1897

> Carl May smiled and it seemed to Bethany that his teeth were fangs and growing as long as the wolf's ever were in 'Red Riding Hood'.
> FAY WELDON *The Cloning of Joanna May* 1989

Red Sea According to the Old Testament book of Exodus, God led Moses and the Israelites out of Egypt and through the Red Sea. Pharaoh, having given them permission to leave Egypt, changed his mind and took his army after them. God parted the waters to let the Israelites cross. 'But the children of Israel walked upon dry land in the midst of the sea; and the waters were a wall unto them on their right hand, and on their left' (Exod. 14: 28). The pursuing Egyptians were drowned when the waters closed on them. *See also* MOSES.

> They hurry after the Plenipo. Moses going through the Red Sea, thinks Gideon of Elliott's progress through the crowd.
> TIMOTHY MO *An Insular Possession* 1986

Red Shoes *The Red Shoes* was a Powell and Pressburger film released in 1948 starring Moira Shearer as a student, Victoria Page, who becomes a famous ballerina. She falls in love with Julian Craster, the composer of the ballet *The Red Shoes*, which her teacher, Boris Lermontov, is staging for her to star in, and has to choose between love and career. She commits suicide. The story of *The Red Shoes*, a fairy tale by Hans Christian Andersen (1845), is of a little girl called Karen whose impious thoughts in church about her beautiful red shoes lead to her being cursed to dance all day and night when she is wearing the shoes, the shoes taking over her feet. Eventually, she has her feet cut off in order to escape from the shoes, and after much repentance is eventually forgiven.

Donna Reed Donna Reed (b. Donna Mullenger; 1921–86) was a US film actress, closely identified with wholesome girl-next-door roles in such films as Frank Capra's *It's a Wonderful Life* (1946). In her long-running television series *The Donna Reed Show* (1958–66), she personified the perfect and devoted wife and mother.

> Janie, Trish, and Kay had graduated from Dobbs High School together and had then married Cotton Grove boys within two years of each other, which brought them back into the same social orbit where two incomes weren't a necessity quite yet. The 'Donna Reed' syndrome lasted a bit longer in the South than elsewhere, and none of the three had held down real jobs back then.
> MARGARET MARON *Bootlegger's Daughter* 1992

> Poor Luis! she thought. Sitting at home in front of the television, he had

invented just the kind of Donna Reed mother a lonely little boy would invent.
ROBERT B. PARKER *Thin Air* 1995

So far, they had not. She had visions of an eternally smiling Donna Reed gliding among the congregation like a ministering angel, but she still found herself standing awkwardly at Will's side, wondering if she was overdressed and trying without notable success to think of something she could possibly discuss with these people who seemed neither to read nor travel.
SHARYN MCCRUMB *The Hangman's Beautiful Daughter* 1996

Rembrandt Rembrandt Harmenszoon van Rijn (1606–69) was the greatest Dutch painter of the 17th century, particularly celebrated for his portraits and self-portraits and for his subtle use of light and shadow, or chiaroscuro, contrasting highlights and half-lights with deep shadows. He is especially remembered for the obscure lighting and brown-and-black palette of his later paintings. Rembrandt is the artist whose name is most often used as shorthand for the idea of 'a great painter'.

The interior was shadowy with a peculiar shade. The strange luminous semi-opacities of fine autumn afternoons and eves intensified into Rembrandt effects.
THOMAS HARDY *Far from the Madding Crowd* 1874

Now a man's head was lit as with a light of Rembrandt.
G. K. CHESTERTON *The Man Who Was Thursday* 1908

The dim gold lamplight and the restless firelight made Rembrandt shadows in the remoter corners of the kitchen.
STELLA GIBBONS *Cold Comfort Farm* 1932

Paul Revere Paul Revere (1735–1818) was an American patriot, one of the demonstrators involved in the Boston Tea Party of 1773. In 1775 he rode through the night from Boston to Lexington to warn American revolutionaries of the approach of British troops.

Mrs Louderer drove, and Tam O'Shanter and Paul Revere were snails compared to us.
ELINORE PRUITT STEWART *Letters of a Woman Homesteader* 1914

Reynolds Joshua Reynolds (1723–92) was an English painter who was regarded as the leading portraitist of his day and became the first president of the Royal Academy in 1768. Many of his portraits consciously borrow poses from classical statues and Renaissance paintings.

Her youngest brother was only five. He was a frail lad, with immense brown eyes in his quaint fragile face—one of Reynolds's 'Choir of Angels', with a touch of elf.
D. H. LAWRENCE *Sons and Lovers* 1913

Rhadamanthus Rhadamanthus was the son of Zeus and Europa, and brother of Minos, who, as a ruler and judge in the underworld, was renowned for his justice. The term 'Rhadamanthine' has come to mean stern and incorruptible in judgement. *See also* MINOS.

> But Tom, you perceive, was rather a Rhadamanthine personage, having more than the usual share of boy's justice in him—the justice that desires to hurt culprits as much as they deserve to be hurt, and is troubled with no doubts concerning the exact amount of their deserts.
> GEORGE ELIOT *Mill on the Floss* 1860

> Women at forty do not become ancient misanthropes, or stern Rhadamanthine moralists, indifferent to the world's pleasures—no, even though they be widows.
> ANTHONY TROLLOPE *The Small House at Allington* 1862

Cliff Richard Cliff Richard (b. Harry Webb, 1940) is a British pop singer whose many successful recordings include 'Living Doll' and 'The Young Ones'. He became a born-again Christian in the 1970s and since then has combined his pop career with evangelism. Cliff Richard is sometimes mentioned with reference to his clean-living image and his youthful looks.

> 'And I suppose you got nowhere at Brown's?' 'Squeaky clean.' 'Same here, this pair. They've got Cliff Richard in the front office and Mother Theresa doing the books.'
> ALEX KEEGAN *Kingfisher* 1995

Cardinal Richelieu Armand Jean du Plessis (1585–1642), known as Cardinal Richelieu, was the chief minister of Louis XIII from 1624 to 1642 and dominated the French government. He is remembered as a clever, calculating, and scheming politician.

> But we tried to do these pieces intelligently and with wit and we tried to do a few serious-minded pieces too. That had been harder to do once Investigative Reports, headed by former foreign correspondent Reb 'Rambo' Ryan and his shrewd and sneaky Cardinal Richelieu, Solange Stevenson, came on the scene and stole every good hard news story out from under us, leaving us with the fillers and the features.
> SPARKLE HAYTER *The Last Manly Man* 1998

Rip Van Winkle Rip Van Winkle is the hero of Washington Irving's story *Rip Van Winkle* (1820). During a walk in the Catskill Mountains, Rip falls asleep, and wakes some 20 years later to find that the world has changed considerably. His wife has died, his daughter has married, and he has completely missed the War of American Independence.

> Having been incarcerated for most of the last forty-five years, he was probably feeling like Rip van Winkle, marveling at all the changes in the world at large.
> SUE GRAFTON *L Is for Lawless* 1995

> A political Rip van Winkle who had never watched television and read neither newspapers nor books until the last years of his term, Kim cannot believe, even

less comprehend, this changed world. His only reading material until 1990 had been the Bible.
ANDREW HIGGINS *The Observer* 1997

She led him to the window and swung the panel so that it acted as a mirror. 'See that antique wreck standing next to that gorgeous woman? That's you. If Rosie opens her eyes and sees you first, she'll think she's done a Rip Van Winkle and slept for fifty years.'
REGINALD HILL *On Beulah Height* 1998

Lots of people commented on how long it had been, and Trish began to feel as though she were Rip van Winkle, coming alive again to a world she had not seen for decades.
NATASHA COOPER *Fault Lines* 1999

Rivera Diego Rivera (1886–1957) was a Mexican painter whose monumental murals for public buildings in the 1920s and 1930s were influenced by Aztec art and deal with political and revolutionary subjects.

'Ms Ochoa?' The face that looked up was out of a mural by Rivera. Reddish-brown skin stretched tightly over sharply defined but delicately constructed bones; liquid lips and melting black eyes gabled by full, dark brows. Her hair was long and sleek, parted in the middle, hanging down her back. Part Aztec, part Spanish, part unknown.
JONATHAN KELLERMAN *When the Bough Breaks* 1992

rivers of Babylon Psalm 137, which commemorates the exile of the Jews in Babylon, opens with the words 'By the rivers of Babylon, there we sat down, yea, we wept, when we remembered Zion.' The phrase 'the rivers of Babylon' has come to be associated with the idea of mourning for the dead. *See also* BABYLON.

road to Damascus *See* DAMASCUS.

Roadrunner Roadrunner is an American cartoon character, a bird that can run extremely fast and always manages to outrun its arch-enemy, a coyote called Wile E. Coyote. The characters were created for Warner Brothers by Chuck Jones and the first was shown in 1949. The films always take place along the highways of the south-west American desert and are seen from the perspective of the coyote.

Dennis grinned like Wile E. Coyote. My heart sank. I was well past a convincing impersonation of the Roadrunner.
VAL MCDERMID *Star Struck* 1998

Robben Island A small island off the coast of South Africa, Robben Island is the site of a prison in which political prisoners, including Nelson Mandela, were formerly held.

Robert the Bruce Robert I (1274–1329), known as Robert the Bruce, was a Scottish king who led the campaigns against Edward I and Edward II, culminating in the Scottish victory at Bannockburn in 1314. According to tradition, Robert spent some time hiding in a cave after suffering a defeat at the hands of the English. After watching a spider fail many times in its attempt to spin a web but persevere until it finally succeeded, he was inspired to fight on against the English.

Robin Hood The legend of Robin Hood probably began in the 12th or 13th century and was well established by the 14th. According to the stories, he was the leader of a band of outlaws living in Sherwood Forest in Nottinghamshire who robbed the rich (most notably the sheriff of Nottingham) and gave the spoils to the poor. As well as invoking the idea of taking from the rich and giving to the poor, his name is used in the more general context of someone who stands up against tyranny and oppression. *See also* FRIAR TUCK.

> The idea that she was among thieves prevented her from feeling any comfort in the revival of deference and attention towards her—all thieves, except Robin Hood, were wicked people.
> GEORGE ELIOT *The Mill on the Floss* 1860

> I supposed it was too much to hope that the primitive mind would see it as anything other than a sort of Robin Hood gesture of bravery. To the peasant the hashish brought pleasure, and money. If an unreasonable Government chose to forbid its growth for private purposes, why then the Government must be fooled. It was as simple as that. It was the same mentality which, in more sophisticated societies, assumes that the tax and speed laws are made to be broken.
> MARY STEWART *The Gabriel Hounds* 1967

> I sit by the River Shannon near the dry docks sipping Mrs. Finucane's sherry. Aunt Aggie's name is in the ledger. She owes nine pounds. It might have been the money she spent on my clothes a long time ago but now she'll never have to pay it because I heave the ledger into the river. I'm sorry I'll never be able to tell Aunt Aggie I saved her nine pounds. . . . I wish I could tell them, I'm your Robin Hood.
> FRANK MCCOURT *Angela's Ashes* 1997

> Lula repeated the word. 'Vigilante.' 'Someone who takes the law into his own hands,' I said. 'Hunh. I guess I know what it means. You're telling me Mo is like Zorro and Robin Hood.'
> JANET EVANOVICH *Three to Get Deadly* 1997

Mr Rochester Edward Fairfax Rochester is the hero of Charlotte Brontë's novel *Jane Eyre* (1847), a handsome man but silent, brooding, and grim of temperament. *See also* JANE EYRE AND MR ROCHESTER, MRS ROCHESTER.

Caroline put on a face of modesty, and then said she thought Mr Ramsay was

handsome in a kind of scary way, like Mr Rochester in Jane Eyre.
ROBERTSON DAVIES *Fifth Business* 1970

Talk to me. Don't sit there looking gloomy and enigmatic like Mr Rochester.
What's bothering you?
BARBARA MICHAELS *Search the Shadows* 1988

Mrs Rochester The deranged wife of Edward Rochester in Charlotte
Brontë's *Jane Eyre* (1847) is kept in seclusion at Thornfield Hall. Her existence
is only revealed when Jane's marriage to Rochester is about to take place.
The early life of Bertha Rochester is imagined by Jean Rhys in her novel *Wide
Sargasso Sea* (1966). Allusions to Mrs Rochester are often to a strange or mad
person who is kept locked or hidden away in an attic. *See also* JANE EYRE AND
MR ROCHESTER.

You saw her once, didn't you?' said Nancy. 'That's right. I just happened to look
up and caught her peering at me from an upper window, like the first Mrs
Rochester or something, though she kept well back from the window.'
SUSAN MOODY *The Italian Garden* 1994

Dropped at the comfy, modern entrance of St Pat's, the psychiatric hospital
where Professor Anthony Clare does his day job, I had no choice but to make
my way through the entire building to reach Clare's Georgian lair on the far
side. It was oddly quiet—the Mrs. Rochesters of Dublin obviously have good
sound-proofing in their attics. *Sunday Telegraph* 1999

Rockefeller John Davison Rockefeller (1839–1937) was an American oil
magnate who founded the Standard Oil Company, gaining increasing control
of all aspects of the oil industry in the 1870s. He later used his money for
philanthropic projects, giving money for medical research and educational
institutions and establishing the Rockefeller Foundation in 1913 'to promote
the well-being of mankind'.

No worthy charity ever knocked and found him absent. In his limited way,
having only half a million at his disposal instead of the customary millions, he
was as much of a philanthropist as Rockefeller. He gave substantially to the
Community Fund, aside from which he donated his time and services to many
civic enterprises.
CHESTER HIMES *A Modern Fable* 1939

The agent says, There's plenty of work for willing men. You can work overtime
till you drop and if you save it up, mate, you'll be Rockefeller at the end of the
war.
FRANK MCCOURT *Angela's Ashes* 1997

If Edward's hours were billable, she thought, he'd be as rich as Rockefeller.
NORA KELLY *Old Wounds* 1998

Norman Rockwell Norman Rockwell (1894–1978) was a US illustrator and
cartoonist best known for his covers for the magazine the *Saturday Evening*

r

Post. These were typically idealized scenes of everyday small-town American life of the kind described in the Elizabeth Peters quotation below.

> The charm was more than visual, however. It was equally compounded of nostalgia for a way of life that had not so much vanished as never really existed. Freckle-faced boys riding bikes and healthy, pink-cheeked nuclear families dressed in their Sunday best, walking hand in hand toward a white, steepled church . . . A Norman Rockwell cover, flimsy as the paper on which it was printed, with ugly things hidden behind the pretty facade.
> ELIZABETH PETERS *Naked Once More* 1989

> He reminded me of a Norman Rockwell *Saturday Evening Post* cover, the rural general practitioner about to remove a splinter from a tearful boy's finger. Kindly, gentle, wise, competent.
> WILLIAM G. TAPPLY *Tight Lines* 1992

> By 1788, when the lost state of Franklin was reabsorbed by North Carolina and Tennessee, Jonesborough's brief flicker of glory was over, and it reverted to a paintbox-pretty mountain town where Norman Rockwell would have felt at home.
> SHARYN MCCRUMB *The Rosewood Casket* 1996

> 'A dislocated collar bone. The father's story was that it happened during a game of catch. The boy had run to catch a wild throw and knocked himself into the side of the garage.' She glanced meaningfully at me. I tried to picture this frisky Norman Rockwellesque game of catch between Seth and his son. The image wouldn't jell. The picture that did sketch itself in my mind was Seth, in a mindless fit of fury, slamming the little boy up against the garage and dislocating his collarbone.
> LINDSAY MARACOTTA *Playing Dead* 1999

Buck Rogers The US cartoon hero Buck Rogers first appeared in the comic strip *Buck Rogers in the 25th Century* in 1929. Originally the hero of the short story *Armageddon 2419* by Philip Nowlan, he is a 20th-century airforce pilot who is trapped down a mine filled with a strange radioactive gas and kept in suspended animation until the 25th century. When he awakes, he has numerous space adventures in which he performs deeds of great daring to save the world from the evil Killer Kane and Ardala, aided by his companion Wilma Deering.

> But he was free, and considered that the roundabout up-and-down-about was going slow enough to make a getaway. No need to wait until it really stops, was his last thought. It was like Buck Rogers landing from a space ship without due care, though a few minutes passed before he was able to think this.
> ALAN SILLITOE *The Loneliness of the Long Distance Runner* 1959

Ginger Rogers Ginger Rogers (1911–95), born Virginia Katherine McMath, was an American actress and dancer. Best known for her dancing partnership with Fred Astaire, she also won an Oscar for her performance as an actress in *Kitty Foyle* (1940). *See also* FRED ASTAIRE.

I put my hand in his and followed. He was one of those men who can make you feel like Ginger Rogers on the dance floor, conveying an entire set of suggestions in the way he applied pressure to the small of my back.
SUE GRAFTON *H Is for Homicide* 1991

Roy Rogers Known as the King of the Cowboys, Roy Rogers (1912–98) was a clean-cut American singing cowboy hero who began his career as a country-and-western singer and went on to appear in several films. He later appeared in his own television series, *The Roy Rogers Show*, first broadcast in 1951. Riding his trusty stallion Trigger, he maintained law and order in the contemporary West with the help of his bumbling sidekick Pat Brady and his wife, Dale Evans.

The playwright laughed. He hadn't heard the Yank using bad language until now. It didn't fit with the suit. could it be that Mr Whiz Kid might be human after all? 'Yes. I'll do the other thing myself. Kilmacud, is it?' 'Yes. No Roy Rogers stuff now. Think of it as a part. Imagine yourself as a gangster.'
JOHN BRADY *A Stone of the Heart* 1988

Roland and Oliver Roland was the legendary nephew of Charlemagne and was one of his paladins, the twelve peers of Charlemagne's court. He is the hero of the *Chanson de Roland*, a 12th-century medieval romance, and of Ariosto's *Orlando Furioso* (1532). Roland is said to have become a close friend of Oliver, another paladin, after engaging him in a prolonged single combat which was so evenly matched that neither ever won. The expression 'a Roland for an Oliver' denotes a well-balanced combat or an effective retort or retaliation.

He gave my termagant kinsman a *quid pro quo*—a Rowland for his Oliver, as the vulgar say.
WALTER SCOTT *Antiquary* 1816

Romeo and Juliet The young lovers in Shakespeare's *Romeo and Juliet* (1599) are the offspring of two warring families, the Montagues and the Capulets. They meet at a feast given by the Capulets, are instantly attracted, and marry in secret. Juliet's family, unaware of her marriage, plan to marry her to Count Paris. Juliet takes a potion on the eve of the wedding which will make her appear dead for 24 hours. A message to Romeo goes astray. Romeo, hearing of Juliet's death, returns to Verona and to Juliet's body, takes poison, and dies. Juliet awakes, sees his body, and stabs herself. Romeo's name alone can be used to denote a young man in love, though it is now frequently, and somewhat unjustly, applied to a womanizer, as in the phrase 'the office Romeo'. See also MONTAGUES AND CAPULETS, SHAKESPEARE.

His personal feeling that loving Phoebe Wilson was a thing beyond the scope of the most determined Romeo he concealed. It could, apparently, be done.
P G. WODEHOUSE *Cocktail Time* 1958

It's that middle stretch of the night, when the curtains leak no light, the only

street-noise is the grizzle of a returning Romeo, and the birds haven't begun their routine yet cheering business.
JULIAN BARNES *A History of the World in 10½ Chapters* 1989

I watched Duncan clipping his hedge this afternoon and could barely remember the handsome man he was. If I had been a charitable woman, I would have married him forty years ago and saved him from himself and Violet. She has turned my Romeo into a sad-eyed Billy Bunter who blinks his passions quietly when no one's looking.
MINETTE WALTERS *The Scold's Bridle* 1994

Fleur's in love, I understand, with Phil Merrick—a Romeo-and-Juliet affair disapproved of by his grandfather; though his grandfather already has an Olympic bronze in disapproval.
STAYNES AND STOREY *Dead Serious* 1995

Romulus and Remus According to Roman mythology, Romulus and Remus were the twin sons of Mars by the vestal virgin Rhea Silvia. Custom dictated that, because they had been born to a vestal, the twins had to be abandoned in infancy in a basket on the river Tiber, but they were found and suckled by a she-wolf and later raised by a shepherd family. They subsequently undertook to build a city on the banks of the Tiber; after a quarrel, however, Romulus killed his brother. He went on to found Rome, naming the city after himself.

Roscius Quintus Roscius Gallus (d. 62 BC), known as Roscius, was the most celebrated of Roman comic actors, who later became identified with all that was considered best in acting. Many great actors, notably David Garrick, were nicknamed after him. The child actor William Betty (1791–1874) was known as the Young Roscius.

I put my hands in my pocket. A folded piece of paper in one of them attracting my attention, I opened it and found it to be the playbill I had received from Joe relative to the celebrated provincial amateur of Roscian renown.
CHARLES DICKENS *Great Expectations* 1860

Rosencrantz and Guildenstern In Shakespeare's *Hamlet* (1604), Rosencrantz and Guildenstern are two messengers sent with Hamlet to England with sealed orders from the King that Hamlet should be killed on arrival. Hamlet escapes back to Denmark, where the rest of the action of the play unfolds. The fate of Rosencrantz and Guildenstern is reported right at the end of the play, when an ambassador enters and announces that 'Rosencrantz and Guildenstern are dead.' This line was used as the title of a play by Tom Stoppard (1966), in which he places these two characters at the centre of a drama. The names of Rosencrantz and Guildenstern can be used in the context of someone who has managed to miss all the action.

'And you, as I remember, were such a self-absorbed girl that other people didn't quite register.' I couldn't protest that one; I remembered the same thing.

I was about to learn, apparently, I'd been Rosencrantz or Guildenstern, submerged up to the eyes in the utterly absorbing drama of my own life, and completely out of the loop about the real goings-on with Prince Hamlet at Elsinore.
CAROL BRENNAN *Chill of Summer* 1995

Rosinante Rosinante (or Rozinante) is the name of Don Quixote's scrawny old horse in Cervantes' romance. The name can be applied to any worn-out or emaciated horse. *See also* DON QUIXOTE.

Plump and naked . . . they [the camels] were a great contrast to our shaggy, Rosinantine beasts.
PETER FLEMING *News from Tartary* 1936

Up Boyes Drive the car was labouring now, willing but old, like Rocinante.
J. M. COETZEE *Age of Iron* 1990

Rothko Mark Rothko was a Russian-born US painter (1903–70), an abstract expressionist. His most characteristic works are enormous canvases consisting of rectangles or horizontal bands of subtly related colour with blurred edges.

Rothschild Meyer Amschel Rothschild (1743–1812), a German Jew, founded a banking house in Frankfurt and a dynasty. His five sons set up banks throughout Europe. His third son, Nathan (1777–1836), who founded the London bank, made a £1 million profit on the Stock Exchange having staked his fortune on the outcome of the battle of Waterloo.

If she wanted a new hat, he'd say hadn't he bought her a hat only five or six years ago and get off nasty cracks about women who seemed to think they'd married into the Rothschild family.
P G. WODEHOUSE *Cocktail Time* 1958

'I said I was your housekeeper,' replied that lady . . . 'Oh good,' said Aunt Irene. 'He'll think I'm Rothschild.'
ALICE THOMAS ELLIS *The 27th Kingdom* 1982

Rousseau
artist Henri Rousseau (1844–1910), known as Le Douanier ('the Customs Officer'), was a French naive painter. Self-taught, he is best known for his paintings of exotic jungle landscapes and haunting, dreamlike scenes, including *Tiger in a Tropical Storm* (1891), *The Sleeping Gypsy* (1897), and *The Snake Charmer* (1907). These pictures are bold and colourful, and painted with a painstakingly detailed technique.

An island with a happy name lay opposite, and on it stood a row of prim, tight buildings, naive as a painting by Rousseau.
DOROTHY PARKER *The Custard Heart* 1944

philosopher and author Jean-Jacques Rousseau (1712–1778) was a philosopher and writer. Born in Switzerland, he left home at the age of 15 to move to Italy and during his life he moved often, living in various parts of France, Italy, Switzerland, and, later, England. He developed the philosophy that 'primitive' man, the 'noble savage' was naturally innocent and that the effect of civilization was to corrupt people. His *Du Contrat social* (The Social Contract, 1762) begins with the famous sentence 'Man is born free; and everywhere he is in chains', and he coined the phrase 'Liberty, Equality, Fraternity'. His name can be used to refer to an intellectual thinker or writer. *See also* NOBLE SAVAGE.

> To be yearning for the difficult, to be weary of that offered; to care for the remote, to dislike the near; it was Wildeve's nature always. This is the true mark of the man of sentiment. Though Wildeve's fevered feeling had not been elaborated to real poetical compass, it was of the standard sort. He might have been called the Rousseau of Egdon.
> THOMAS HARDY *The Return of the Native* 1880

> Somehow I pictured myself a sort of celebrity, kept apart from the other prisoners in a special wing, where I would receive parties of grave, important people and hold forth to them about the great issues of the day, impressing the men and charming the ladies. What insight! they would cry. What breadth! We were told you were a beast, cold-blooded, cruel, but now that we have seen you, have heard you, why—! And there am I, striking an elegant pose, my ascetic profile lifted to the light in the barred window, fingering a scented handkerchief and faintly smirking, Jean-Jacques the cultured killer.
> JOHN BANVILLE *The Book of Evidence* 1989

Rubens Peter Paul Rubens (1577–1640) was the foremost Flemish painter of the 17th century, an exuberant master of the baroque. Rubens painted portraits and religious works but is perhaps best known for his mythological paintings featuring voluptuous female nudes, such as *Venus and Adonis* (*c*.1635). These sumptuous paintings display the artist's love of rich colour, sensual feeling for the tactile, and sheer delight in fleshy women. Indeed, the word 'Rubenesque' can be used to describe a woman's attractively plump and rounded figure.

> She had none of that dazzling brilliancy, of that voluptuous Rubens beauty.
> ANTHONY TROLLOPE *Barchester Towers* 1857

> Upstairs, I took off all my clothes and had a full view of myself in the wardrobe mirror. I was getting fat all right. I turned sideways, and looked round so that I could see the reflection of my hip. It was nicely curved and white like the geranium petals in the dressmaker's window-ledge. 'What's Rubenesque?' I asked Baba. 'I don't know. Sexy, I suppose. Why?' 'A customer said I was that.'
> EDNA O'BRIEN *The Country Girls* 1960

> The old couple in the room next door moved out and were replaced by two plump Rubensian nymphs whose life was a permanent party for all manner of local Romeos.
> LOUIS DE BERNIÈRES *Señor Vivo and the Coca Lord* 1991

> She put down the paper. 'An artist's model?' 'Right.' 'With your figure?' 'My

figure is simply crying out to be captured in charcoal, according to my new friend. I have a Rubenesque form and challenging contours.'
PETER LOVESEY *The Summons* 1995

Rubicon In 49 BC Julius Caesar, having defeated the Gauls in the Gallic Wars, brought his troops south to fight a civil war against Pompey and the Roman Senate. When he crossed the Rubicon, a stream marking the boundary between Italy and Gaul, he was committed to war, having violated the law that forbade him to take his troops out of his province. To 'cross the Rubicon' is to commit oneself to changing to a new course, leaving no possibility of turning back. *See also* CAESAR.

He had crossed his Rubicon—not perhaps very heroically or dramatically, but then it is only in dramas that people act dramatically.
SAMUEL BUTLER *The Way of All Flesh* 1903

'We're going too fast again,' Quade said. 'It's really impossible to discuss the matter until we've had a chance to evaluate the letter. Have you any idea how that might be brought about, Mr Vermont? 'This was my Rubicon. After it there could be no turning back, no denial of the story I had told them, no depending on a brilliant barrister to shred their case against me. I would have convicted myself.
PALMA HARCOURT *The Vermont Myth* 1994

Another depressing development for Laurence is that his children know about the split now. I think that's a kind of Rubicon as far as he's concerned. As long as they didn't know, there was always the possibility that he and Sally might get back together again with no serious damage done, no embarrassment, no loss of face.
DAVID LODGE *Therapy* 1995

Rudolph According to the popular song, Rudolph the Red-Nosed Reindeer, despite being ridiculed by the other reindeer because of his shiny red nose, is chosen to pull Santa Claus's sledge.

Rumpelstiltskin In the Grimms' fairy story, a miller claims that his daughter can spin straw into gold. The king locks the girl into a room with a pile of straw and a spinning wheel, promising to marry her if she can accomplish the task. Rumpelstiltskin appears and spins the straw into gold, asking for her necklace in payment. He performs this feat for the girl twice more, requiring in payment first her ring and then, when she has no more jewellery, her first child. She becomes queen, and when her first child is born, Rumpelstiltskin says that she may keep the child if she can discover his name within three days. She sends out messengers to find all the strange names they can collect, and one messenger comes across the little man dancing round a fire and chanting a rhyme that ends with the line: 'Rumpelstiltskin is my name!' When the queen confronts him with his name, Rumpelstiltskin becomes so angry that he stamps his foot into the ground and tears himself in two when he tries to pull it out. *See also* GRIMM.

At such times they fell out over anything which came handy, from the day's work and the morrow's commitments to the points of spaniels or the quality and proof of beer; but never over Claire Falchion. Her name was protected by as exact a taboo as Rumpelstiltskin.

EDITH PARGETER *By Firelight* 1948

He always arrived fifteen minutes ahead of the agreed time because he knew she'd be early. It didn't matter which time he'd chosen, she'd turn up ahead of schedule because she was convinced he was Rumpelstiltskin, the man who could spin twenty-four-carat gold out of the dry straw of her life.

VAL MCDERMID *The Wire in the Blood* 1997

Sir Ian McKellen, who can't appear on the stage without doing something interesting, is a complicated mixture of rage, precision and desperation. When he performs his impassioned dance he is at first a model of military precision, and later as enraged as Rumpelstiltskin.

SUSANNAH CLAPP *The Observer* 2003

Ruritania Ruritania is an imaginary central European kingdom used as the setting for Anthony Hope's novels of courtly intrigue and romance, such as *The Prisoner of Zenda* (1894) and *Rupert of Hentzau* (1898). The name has become synonymous with political scheming. *See also* PRISONER OF ZENDA.

The singing had gathered strength again, but everyone watched the English party as it went. 'Well,' said Clarence out in the square, 'this may be Ruritania, but it's no longer a joke.'

OLIVIA MANNING *The Spoilt City* 1962

Rutebeuf The French trouvère Rutebeuf (*c.*1230–1286) was the author of *Le Dit de l'herberie*, a comic monologue by a quack doctor.

'Yes,' said the doctor and he was smiling, 'you will be disappointed! . . . I am no herbalist, I am no Rutebeuf, I have no panacea.'

DJUNA BARNES *Nightwood* 1936

Ruth The book of Ruth in the Old Testament relates the story of Ruth, a widow who refuses to leave her mother-in-law after the death of her husband, saying 'whither thou goest, I will go; and where thou lodgest, I will lodge: thy people shall be my people, and thy God my God' (Ruth 1: 16). Ruth is the epitome of loyalty and devotion.

Then listen to me again, once more, my heart's own darling, my love, my husband, my lord! If I cannot be to you at once like Ruth, and never cease from coming after you, my thoughts to you shall be like those of Ruth—if aught but death part thee and me, may God do so to me and more also.

ANTHONY TROLLOPE *The Small House at Allington* 1862

Dr Ruth Born in Germany but later emigrating to the United States, Dr Ruth Westheimer (b. 1928) is a popular psychosexual therapist who has appeared in several US radio and television shows in which she talks about sexuality and tries to resolve people's sexual difficulties.

> Angela bestowed on Jonathan a look of maternal understanding to rival Dr. Ruth, but he was past consoling.
> JANE DENTINGER *Death Mask* 1988

Sabine women According to (unhistorical) legend, Romulus, the founder of Rome, secured wives for his citizens by inviting the neighbouring Sabines to witness games in the city. While the games were proceeding Romans carried off and raped the Sabine women.

> At the finish of the meal he broke suddenly into a radiant smile, thanked his hostess for a charming repast, and kissed her hand with deferential rapture. Miss Huddle was unable to decide in her mind whether the action savoured of Louis Quatorzian courtliness or the reprehensible Roman attitude towards the Sabine women.
> SAKI *Short Stories* 1904

Sadduccee The Sadducees were a Jewish sect at the time of Christ, who accepted only the written law, not oral tradition, denied the existence of angels and demons, and did not believe in the resurrection of the dead. A Sadduccee is therefore someone who refuses to believe things that are readily accepted by others.

> No, he was not at all angry; he was very friendly to me. I was quite drawn out to speak to him; I hardly know how, for I had always thought of him as a worldly Sadducee. But his countenance is as pleasant as the morning sunshine.
> GEORGE ELIOT *Adam Bede* 1859

> 'Law, mother! I don't doubt he thought so. I suppose he and Cack got drinking toddy together, till he got asleep, and dreamed it. I wouldn't believe such a thing if it did happen right before my face and eyes. I should only think I was crazy, that's all.' 'Come, Lois, if I was you, I wouldn't talk so like a Sadduccee,' said my grandmother.
> HARRIET BEECHER STOWE *The Ghost in the Mill* 1872

Marquis de Sade Donatien Alphonse François, comte de Sade (1740–1814), known as the Marquis de Sade, was a French writer and soldier. He was frequently imprisoned for sexual offences. While in prison he wrote a number of sexually explicit works, which include *Les 120 Journées de Sodome* (1784), *Justine* (1791), and *La Philosophie dans le boudoir* (1795). Sadism, the deriving of sexual pleasure from inflicting pain or suffering on others, is named after him.

> 'We sort of got talking. And we sort of got on.' Ah, that's my Stuart. Do I hear

Tristan? Don Juan? Casanova? Do I hear the unspeakably naughty Marquis?
No, I hear my mate and mucker Stuart Hughes. 'We sort of got talking. And we
sort of got on.'
JULIAN BARNES *Talking It Over* 1991

sage *See* SEVEN SAGES OF GREECE.

the Saint The Saint is the name used by Simon Templar, the hero of a
popular British television series first broadcast in 1963 starring Roger Moore.
Based on a series of novels by Leslie Charteris, the Saint is a reformed British
gentleman crook, described by Charteris as 'a dashing daredevil,
imperturbable, debonair, preposterously handsome, a pirate or a
philanthropist as the occasion demands'. In the television shows he battles
against crime and international espionage, drives fast cars, and falls for
beautiful women.

'What, go straight? Me, the local successor to Raffles and the Saint and all
those other debonair, gallant British adventurers?'
ELIZABETH PETERS *Street of the Five Moons* 1978

St Agnes, St Augustine, St Bartholomew, etc. *See under* AGNES,
AUGUSTINE, BARTHOLOMEW, etc.

Saladin Saladin (Arabic name Salah-ad-Din Yusef ibn-Ayyub) (1137–93) was a
sultan of Egypt and Syria who invaded the Holy Land and reconquered
Jerusalem from the Christians in 1187, and fought against the Christians in
the Third Crusade. He earned a reputation not only for military skill but also
for honesty and chivalry.

Saddam Hussein, once hailed as a latter-day Saladin who would right Arab
wrongs and 'liberate' Palestine from the Israelis, commands little love or
admiration in the Arab world these days. *The Observer* 1997

Salome According to the Bible (Matt. 14: 6–9), Salome, the stepdaughter of
King Herod Antipas, danced for her stepfather the king and 'pleased him'. He
then 'promised with an oath to give her whatsoever she would ask' and
Salome, instructed by her mother, demanded the head of John the Baptist.
See also HEROD AND SALOME.

I'm no tumbler, neither a friar, nor yet a thirteenth-century Salome dancing arse
up on a pair of Toledo blades—try to get any lovesick girl, male or female, to do
that today!
DJUNA BARNES *Nightwood* 1936

John Major's head is back on the wish list for a small but determined bunch of
Salomes on the back benches. *The World at One, BBC Radio 4* 1994

Samaritan *See* GOOD SAMARITAN.

S

Samarra The ancient Middle Eastern fable of the 'Appointment in Samarra' relates how a servant, having been sent to market by a merchant, returned home trembling, saying that he had seen Death in the market, and Death had threatened him. The servant asked to borrow the merchant's horse so that he could leave Baghdad and ride to Samarra, where Death would not find him. Later the merchant went to the market and saw Death in the crowd. He asked Death why he had threatened his servant, to which Death replied, 'I did not threaten your servant. It was merely that I was surprised to see him here in Baghdad, for I have an appointment with him tonight in Samarra.' The story is retold by Somerset Maugham in his play *Sheppey* (1933), and is also the title of a novel (1934) by John O'Hara. Allusions to Samarra evoke the idea that one cannot escape one's destiny or death.

'I don't know what Val died of. I don't think anyone knows yet.' . . . 'Such a nice lady too,' went on Mrs Kinver. 'She should have got away.' It wasn't clear what she meant by this remark, although Stella could guess. Got away before her fate, whatever it was to be, caught up with her. An appointment in Samarra, she thought. You can't run from what gets there before you.
GWENDOLINE BUTLER *Coffin and the Paper Man* 1990

He was silent for a few seconds more, peering down into the darkness: 'The trouble with men like me, John, is we have natures that tend to shape our destinies. I have dark and dreadful days when I feel that however often I switch roads they all eventually end up in Samarra.'
RICHARD HALEY *Thoroughfare of Stones* 1995

Samson In the Bible, the book of Judges (16: 4–22) relates how Samson, an Israelite leader (probably 11th *c.* BC) known for his great strength, fell in love with Delilah. The Philistines asked her to discover the secret of his great strength. On three occasions when she asked him for the secret he lied to her. She continued to ask him, telling him that he could not love her as he claimed to if he did not tell her the truth. Eventually, Samson explained that the secret of his strength was in his hair, which had never been cut. Delilah arranged to have his hair shaved while he slept. Delilah delivered Samson up to the Philistines, who 'put out his eyes, and brought him down to Gaza, and bound him with fetters of brass' (Judg. 16: 21). During his captivity, his hair grew back and, being brought out to make sport for the Philistines during a religious celebration, he called on God for strength and pulled down the pillars supporting the temple, destroying himself and a large number of Philistines. Samson's hair can be alluded to when referring to a strong or powerful person rendered weak and vulnerable. *See also* DELILAH, PHILISTINES.

Like imprisoned Samson, I would rather remain all my life in the mill-house, grinding for my very bread, than be brought forth to make sport for the Philistine lords and ladies.
WALTER SCOTT *The Bride of Lammermoor* 1819

Arabella ascended the stairs, softly opened the door of the first bedroom, and peeped in. Finding that her shorn Samson was asleep she entered to the

bedside and started regarding him.
THOMAS HARDY *Jude the Obscure* 1895

I fell to plotting ways of short-circuiting the machine. Perhaps if I shifted my body about so that the two nodes would come together—No, not only was there no room, but it might electrocute me. I shuddered. Whoever else I was, I was no Samson. I had no desire to destroy myself even if it destroyed the machine; I wanted freedom, not destruction.
RALPH ELLISON *Invisible Man* 1952

This is the very dilemma that once confronted a young Hick. Hailed as great before he'd achieved it, he lost the glow of youth with frightening rapidity. With the erosion of innocence went his power, weakened like Samson at the barber's shop. *The Observer* 1998

Samuel In the Bible, Saul, son of Kish, went looking for some donkeys of his father that had gone missing. After much searching, Saul was about to give up and return home when his servant told him that there was a man of God in the town whose prophecies always came true. Saul was concerned that he would not have enough food with which to reward the holy man, Samuel. When Saul found Samuel, Samuel had meat already set aside to feed Saul (1 Sam. 9: 22–4).

'May be so, Mr Henchard,' said the weather-caster. 'Ah—why do you call me that?' asked the visitor with a start. 'Because it's your name. Feeling you'd come I've waited for 'ee; and thinking you might be leery from your walk I laid two supper plates—look ye here.' He threw open the door and disclosed the supper-table, at which appeared a second chair, knife and fork, plate and mug, as he had declared. Henchard felt like Saul at his reception by Samuel.
THOMAS HARDY *The Mayor of Casterbridge* 1886

Sancho Panza *See* DON QUIXOTE.

Sandman In children's stories, the Sandman is a man who makes children feel sleepy by sprinkling sand in their eyes.

Now if you're a good little girl and sleep sound so the Sandman won't have to throw sand in your eyes, Santa Claus will bring you something nice for Christmas.
CHESTER HIMES *Christmas Gift* 1944

Most people find it easy to sleep on trains, but for me it's particularly easy. In fact, I find it almost impossible to stay awake. I grew up in a house that backed on to a train line and night-time was when you'd notice the trains most. My version of the Sandman is the 12:10 from Euston.
ALEX GARLAND *The Beach* 1996

Santa Claus In the modern tradition, Santa Claus (or Father Christmas, as he is usually called in Britain) lives at or near the North Pole, where he is aided by elves in making presents for children. He is represented as wearing

S

a red robe and having a long white beard. On the night of Christmas Eve, he sets forth in his sleigh pulled by reindeer to visit all good children, coming down the chimney of each family's house to leave the children their presents. The name Santa Claus derives from St Nicholas, honoured in Holland as the patron saint of children, and the origin of the figure of Father Christmas.

> 'Don't be any dafter than you can help. I've a proposition for you. Anyway—' he gave me one of his unexpectedly charming smiles, the hanging judge becoming a Santa Claus who would send absolutely every item on the list—'you might as well have lunch first.'
> JOHN BRAINE *Room at the Top* 1957

> 'When I give, I give to all,' Mrs Tulsi said. 'I am poor, but I give to all. It is clear, however, that I cannot compete with Santa Claus.'
> V. S. NAIPAUL *A House for Mr Biswas* 1961

> And here I am as poor as a bowl of yak—me. What do they think I am? Some kind of Sandy Claus? Well, they can just take they stocking down, 'cause it *ain't* Christmas.
> TONI MORRISON *The Bluest Eye* 1970

Sappho Sappho, born in Lesbos, was a celebrated Greek lyric poet of the early 7th century BC. The poetry that survives consists mainly of love poems, many expressing her passionate friendships with women. This explains her association with female homosexuality and the derivation of the word 'Sapphic'. *See also* LESBOS.

> She was one of the group known as the 'Dorm 5 Co' who were suspected of active homosexual relations which, if the stories were true, left the school's more normal Sapphic romances looking almost Christian.
> PETER CAREY *Illywhacker* 1985

> Ralph remembered how Brenham had ranged around the tent, ticking off the rhymes on the fingers of her left hand. Mile, style, file, smile. A lesser Sappho making line endings for a clever poetaster.
> THOMAS KENEALLY *The Playmaker* 1987

Sarah Sarah was the wife of Abraham, who, according to the Old Testament, remained childless for many years. God promised her that she would bear a child to Abraham, which she did at the age of 90. The child was Isaac. Sarah can be alluded to as someone whose prayers are finally answered. *See also* ISAAC.

SAS The Special Air Service, or SAS, is a specialist British army regiment trained in commando techniques of warfare. It was formed during the Second World War and is used in clandestine operations, especially against terrorists and most dramatically in several high-profile rescues of hostages.

Satan According to Christian tradition, Satan (meaning 'the Adversary'), also known as Lucifer or the Devil, rebelled against God and as punishment was cast out from heaven. He is characterized as the arch-tempter in the Bible. At the end of Jesus' 40-day fast in the wilderness he challenged Jesus with a series of temptations: to relieve his hunger by turning stones into loaves of bread; to prove his divine power by throwing himself from the temple-top; to gain absolute earthly power 'if you will fall down and worship me'. Jesus rejected each of these temptations (Matt. 4: 1–11). Satan is traditionally depicted with sharp features and a V-shaped hairline in the middle of his forehead and his name is used to suggest utter evil or wickedness. *See also* DEVIL, JESUS, LUCIFER.

> O my poor old Harry Jekyll, if ever I read Satan's signature upon a face, it is on that of your new friend.
> ROBERT LOUIS STEVENSON *The Strange Case of Dr Jekyll and Mr Hyde* 1886

> But the deeper the depression of the rest, young Rupert went about Satan's work with a smile on his eye and a song on his lip.
> ANTHONY HOPE *The Prisoner of Zenda* 1894

> The V motif was picked up again by thickish brows rising outward from twin creases above a hooked nose, and his pale brown hair grew down—from high flat temples—in a point on his forehead. He looked rather pleasantly like a blond Satan.
> DASHIELL HAMMETT *The Maltese Falcon* 1930

> Charles felt himself, under the first impact of this attractive comparison, like Jesus of Nazareth tempted by Satan. He too had had his days in the wilderness to make the proposition more tempting.
> JOHN FOWLES *The French Lieutenant's Woman* 1969

Saturn In Roman mythology, Saturn was an ancient god identified with the Greek Cronus, the father of Zeus. Because he knew that he would eventually be supplanted by one of his children, he swallowed them all at birth.

> Suddenly, and after all these years, she has no appetite for politics. Vergniaud's dying words keep running through her head: 'The revolution, like Saturn, is devouring its own children.'
> HILARY MANTEL *A Place of Greater Safety* 1992

Saturnalian The ancient Roman festival of Saturn in December, called the Saturnalia, was characterized by general unrestrained merrymaking. The term is often applied to a scene of wild revelry or an orgy.

Satyr In classical mythology satyrs were lustful woodland spirits associated with Dionysian revelry. In Greek art they were represented with the tail and ears of a horse, whereas Roman sculptors represented them with the ears, horns, tail, and legs of a goat. *See also* DIONYSUS.

> The looseness of his lower lip and the droop of his upper eyelids combined with

the V's in his face to make his grin lewd as a satyr's.
DASHIELL HAMMETT *The Maltese Falcon* 1930

It was hard to imagine H.E. sniffing after some other country woman, or being discovered mounting one of the milking girls. H.E., even when he was twenty-seven, would not have made a credible farmyard satyr.
THOMAS KENEALLY *The Playmaker* 1987

Behind her the bedroom door was open and a large movable mirror had been specially positioned, reflecting the bed and its satyr's heaven of throttled sheets and twisted pillows.
MARTIN AMIS *London Fields* 1989

Saul Saul of Tarsus, a persecutor of the Christians, became known as Paul after his conversion to Christianity on the road to Damascus. *See also* DAMASCUS, PAUL.

'You start Saul, and end up Paul,' my grandfather had often said. 'When you're a youngun, you Saul, but let life whup your head a bit and you starts to trying to be Paul—though you still Sauls around on the side.'
RALPH ELLISON *Invisible Man* 1952

Savonarola Girolamo Savonarola (1452–98) was a Dominican monk and ascetic and a zealous religious and political reformer. A puritanical opponent of the Renaissance, he gained power in Florence, where he preached against immorality, vanity, and corruption in the religious establishment. This led the Pope to excommunicate him, and he was hanged and burnt as a heretic.

That evening, as they ate a rather nasty potato salad and some sour canned cherries, he had raged like a Savonarola against the vanities of female dress.
ROBERTSON DAVIES *Tempest-Tost* 1951

He followed me. 'When you were in the library, did you notice if all the books in the locked sections were still there?' 'There again, I wouldn't know without the catalogue. I didn't notice any gaps.' We clattered down the schoolroom stairs. 'Perhaps you'd better leave that job for us, anyway,' he suggested. 'Like hell I will. I'm of age, and in any case probably all the worst ones have gone. Don't forget Emma Ashley burned a few of them.' Grandmamma Savonarola. So she did. Pity,' he said cheerfully.
MARY STEWART *Touch Not the Cat* 1976

There was something in his manner as absolute as that of Lord Beaverbrook requiring women at war to hurl aluminium, zinc baths and iron railings onto scrap mountains for national munitions, or Savonarola calling the ladies of Florence to repent, save their souls, and cast their false hair and jewels into his bonfire.
A. S. BYATT *The Virgin in the Garden* 1978

Meanwhile, up at the mill, I was slogging away and trying to earn an honest bob or two in conference with the book-seller, who was describing the difficulties which face an honest vendor of adult reading material in the town

of Grimble. There was, it seemed, a local Savonarola or Calvin who was a particular thorn in Mr Meacher's flesh.
JOHN MORTIMER *Rumpole's Return* 1980

Tom Sawyer Tom Sawyer is the hero of Mark Twain's novel *The Adventures of Tom Sawyer* (1876). Tom is a bold, independent, mischievous boy who rejects the conventional values of hard work, honesty, and cleanliness. In a famous episode, Tom is asked by his Aunt Polly to whitewash a fence, a monotonous chore. When one by one his friends come along, Tom pretends to be enjoying the work so much that his friends beg to be allowed to have a go. Tom therefore has 'a nice, good, idle time all the while—plenty of company—and the fence had three coats of whitewash on it!'

> I was the winner, Miss Illinois. All I could do was laugh. I'm twenty-two, standing up there in a borrowed evening gown, thinking: What am I doing here? This is like Tom Sawyer becomes an altar boy.
> STUDS TERKEL *American Dreams: Lost and Found* 1980

> At other times, Tom Sawyer-like, she led the way in mischief, as when she decided that they should have a dog, despite a school rule prohibiting pets.
> LEONARD S. MARCUS *Margaret Wise Brown* 1992

scapegoat In the Bible, the scapegoat was a goat which was sent into the wilderness after a priest had symbolically laid all the sins of the Israelites upon it so that the sins would be taken away (Lev. 16: 8–22). The word 'scapegoat' has now come to refer to any person who takes the blame for the wrongdoings or failings of others.

> Last night I had looked into the heart of darkness, and the sight had terrified me. What part should I play in the great purification? Most likely that of the Biblical scapegoat.
> JOHN BUCHAN *Prester John* 1910

Scaramouch Scaramouch (literally 'Skirmish') was a stock character in old Italian farce, portrayed as a cowardly braggart. He was usually represented as a Spanish don, wearing a black costume.

> He swore no scaramouch of an Italian robber would dare to meddle with an Englishman.
> WASHINGTON IRVING *Tales of a Traveller* 1824

Scarecrow In L. Frank Baum's children's story *The Wizard of Oz* (1900), the Scarecrow is one of the companions, along with the Cowardly Lion and the Tin Woodman, who joins Dorothy on the Yellow Brick Road on her journey to find Oz. He does not have, and wants to find, a brain. *See also* COWARDLY LION, TIN MAN, WIZARD OF OZ.

scarlet letter In Nathaniel Hawthorne's novel *The Scarlet Letter* (1850), Hester Prynne is sentenced to wear a scarlet 'A', for 'adulteress', on her bosom when she gives birth to an illegitimate child and refuses to name the child's father. *See also* ARTHUR DIMMESDALE, HESTER PRYNNE.

> It was the nineties. No one believed dinner—even a late dinner—with a member of the opposite sex doomed a woman to wear the scarlet 'A'.
> NEVADA BARR *Mountain of Bones* 1995

Scarlet Pimpernel 'The Scarlet Pimpernel' is the name assumed by the English nobleman Sir Percy Blakeney, the hero of a series of novels by Baroness Orczy, including *The Scarlet Pimpernel* (1905). Apparently a lazy fop, Blakeney uses ingenious disguises to outwit his opponents and rescue French aristocrats from the guillotine during the French Revolution. He reveals his true identity to no one, not even to those he rescues, but leaves the sign of a small red flower, the scarlet pimpernel, as his calling-card whenever he has effected a rescue. The Scarlet Pimpernel's exploits inspire the famous rhyme
'We seek him here, we seek him there,
Those Frenchies seek him everywhere.
Is he in heaven?—Is he in hell?
That demmed, elusive Pimpernel?'
His name can be applied to anyone who is difficult to find or catch.

> I'm asking Wilson, but he's gone away—to Lagos for a week or two. The damned elusive Pimpernel. Just when I wanted him.
> GRAHAM GREENE *The Heart of the Matter* 1948

> One fifteen-year-old was kept isolated for three years in her bedroom. Sometimes all they want is higher education. Legends keep them going. Like the true story of a runaway who is now a graduate and successful businesswoman. Philip Balmforth, Bradford Police's community officer, is the indefatigable local scarlet pimpernel who rescues these girls and who arranges new lives, new identities. *The Independent* 1998

Scheherazade Scheherazade is the narrator of *The Arabian Nights*, the bride of King Shahriyar, who, after discovering his first wife's infidelity, has sworn to marry a new wife each day and execute her the next morning. Scheherazade escapes this fate by telling him stories in instalments, always breaking off at an interesting point, promising to resume the story the next night. After 1 001 nights of her storytelling, King Shahriyar cancels his threat. *See also* ARABIAN NIGHTS.

> At my next appointment, feeling rather like Scheherazade unfolding one of her never-ending, telescopic tales to king Schahriar, I took up where I had left off.
> ROBERTSON DAVIES *The Manticore* 1972

> 'Lying,' says Mackenzie. 'A severe term, surely. Has she been lying to you, you ask? Let me put it this way—did Scheherazade lie? Not in her own eyes.'
> MARGARET ATWOOD *Alias Grace* 1996

> Her voice fills in the intervals between nurses and consultant's rounds, visitors and sleep. After days, possibly weeks, maybe years, I realize that she's telling

me a story. She is my own Scheherazade, she knows everything, she must be
the storyteller from the end of the world.
KATE ATKINSON *Human Croquet* 1997

Oskar Schindler Oskar Schindler (1908–74) was a German industrialist who,
during the Second World War, employed jewish workers in his factory in
Poland and managed to save many of them from certain death in
concentration camps by having them relocated to a new armaments factory
in Czechoslovakia. His life and role in rescuing Polish Jews are celebrated in
Thomas Keneally's novel *Schindler's Ark* (1982) and the film *Schindler's List*
(1993), directed by Steven Spielberg.

He eventually reached New York in 1940, with the help of a Japanese Schindler
figure called Chiune Sugihara, a vice-consul in Lithuania, who gave him a
transit visa and later helped some 10,000 desperate Jews. *The Observer* 1997

Schopenhauer Arthur Schopenhauer (1788–1860) was a German
philosopher whose pessimistic philosophy, embodied in his chief work *The
World as Will and Idea* (1819), argued that attempts to understand the world
rationally are doomed to failure.

So we should not go around moping, looking as miserable as Schopenhauer
when the toast has landed marmalade-down in the Wilton. *The Guardian* 1998

Arnold Schwarzenegger The Austrian-born American actor Arnold
Schwarzenegger (b. 1947) began his career as a bodybuilder, becoming Mr
Universe on seven occasions. As a film actor, he is best known for his role as
an impassive killer in *The Terminator* (1984) and its sequel. He was elected
Governor of California in 2003. *See also* TERMINATOR.

It felt erotic the moment she poured the warm oil down his back. It stopped
feeling erotic when she started working on his neck and shoulders. Goddamn!
She was brutal!'You so skinny,' she said. 'Sometimes hurt bony guy. No meat.
Bones hurt.''Yeah, yeah,' he said. 'I didn't know you had to be Arnold
Schwarzenegger to get a massage.'
WAMBAUGH JOSEPH *The Glitter Dome* 1981

'Nowt better than a bit of exercise,' said Dalziel, patting his gut with all the
complacency of Arnold Schwarzenegger flexing his biceps.
REGINALD HILL *On Beulah Height* 1998

Ranger was waiting under the canopy. He was dressed in a black T-shirt and
black assault pants tucked into black boots. He had a body like
Schwarzenegger, dark hair slicked back off his face and a two-hundred-watt
smile.
JANET EVANOVICH *Four to Score* 1998

Albert Schweitzer Albert Schweitzer (1875–1965) was a Franco-German
medical missionary, theologian, and musician, born in Alsace. In 1913 he

qualified as a doctor and went as a missionary to Lambarene in FrenchEquatorial Africa (now Gabon), where he established a hospital and spent most of his life. Schweitzer was awarded the Nobel Peace Prize in 1952. His philosophy was founded on 'reverence for life' and he can be referred to as the epitome of goodness.

> This is the guy who killed my mother, Reverend. And he's going to kill again, that's a fact. He's out there laughing at me, and laughing at the cops, and laughing at you for protecting him, and I would knock down Mother Theresa, run over Albert Schweitzer and shoot the Pope to get at this guy. Do you understand me now?
> STEPHEN BOGART *Play It Again* 1994

> Was it guilt that had transformed him from a trust-fund kid in dress whites to a would-be Schweitzer?
> JONATHAN KELLERMAN *The Web* 1995

Scott of the Antarctic Robert Falcon Scott (1868–1912) was an English explorer and naval officer who led two expeditions to Antarctica. On the second expedition (1910–12) Scott and four companions reached the South Pole by sled, only to discover that the Norwegian explorer Amundsen had beaten them to their goal by a month. Scott and his companions died on the return journey. Scott's name can be associated with very cold weather.

> 'You're making it sound as though I was out for an evening stroll,' Cassie said. 'I don't think you understand what conditions were like out there.' 'Tough, was it?' said Walsh. . . . 'It was hell,' said Cassie. 'I mean, we're talking Scott of the Antarctic.'
> SUSAN MOODY *Grand Slam* 1994

> With low pressure sweeping in from the Bay of Biscay, you'd have to be Scott of the Antarctic to go out collecting conkers. *The Observer* 1998

Walter Scott The Scottish poet and novelist Sir Walter Scott (1771–1832) is sometimes mentioned in connection with the romantic heroes and heroines of many of his poems and novels. During his lifetime and for nearly a century after his death he was a hugely popular writer. *See also* GURTH, LOCHINVAR.

> 'Oh, I know all about that old quarrel with this fellow's father. But it was never as bad as you pretended.' 'I think I am the best judge of that. And this young man has offered me insults which I cannot brook.' 'Listen, Wally, stop talking like a novel by Sir Walter Scott. You should have some thought for Liz and Pearlie.'
> ROBERTSON DAVIES *Leaven of Malice* 1954

> The truth is, he mistook me for a knight out of Walter Scott, because I once fished him out of a scrape in a gaming hell.
> KATE ROSS *Cut to the Quick* 1993

Scrooge The miserly Ebenezer Scrooge is a character in Dickens's *A Christmas Carol* (1843), whose parsimony and lack of charity are mostapparent at Christmas. On the night of Christmas Eve he is visited by the ghost of his late partner, Marley, and sees three spirits, the Ghost of Christmas Past, the Ghost of Christmas Present, and the Ghost of Christmas Yet to Come. These three ghosts allow Scrooge to revisit his childhood and to discover how he is now perceived by other people and the uncharitable response to his own death that the future holds. The experience shocks him into generous behaviour on Christmas Day. His name has come to denote any mean or tight-fisted person. *See also* DICKENSIAN, MARLEY'S GHOST.

He felt moved but helpless, like Scrooge watching the tableaux unfolded by the spirits of Christmas.
DAVID LODGE *The British Museum Is Falling* 1965

Our genetic makeup permits a wide range of behaviours—from Ebenezer Scrooge before to Ebenezer Scrooge after. I do not believe that the miser hoards through opportunistic genes or that the philanthropist gives because nature endowed him with more than the normal complement of altruist genes.
STEPHEN JAY GOULD *Ever Since Darwin* 1978

When, earlier this year, I decided finally to put my foot down and to ban party bags from my younger son's fifth birthday, there was a certain amount of agonising in the household over whether or not I would go down in local lore as the Scrooge of the reception class. *The Independent* 1996

Scylla and Charybdis In Greek mythology, Scylla was a ferocious sea-monster whose cave was situated in the Straits of Messina opposite Charybdis, a whirlpool. Sailors had to navigate their way between these two dangers. If they steered too hard to avoid one, they would become victims of the other. Someone who is 'between Scylla and Charybdis' is in a predicament in which avoiding one of two dangers or pitfalls increases the risk of the other.

Between the Scylla of Skullion and the Charybdis of Lady Mary, not to mention the dangers of the open sea in the shape of the Fellows at High Table, the Bursar led a miserable existence.
TOM SHARPE *Porterhouse Blue* 1974

Goodenough did not answer immediately but concentrated on finding a spot as equidistant as possible from the Scylla of the roaring fire and the Charybdis of the pulsating radiator.
REGINALD HILL *Child's Play* 1987

But none of them has soothed us, held our hands, led us past the Scylla and Charybdis of cookery cock-ups, better than Delia. *The Guardian* 1995

St Sebastian St Sebastian was a Roman martyr of the 3rd century. According to legend, he was a soldier who was shot with arrows on the orders of Diocletian, and, after surviving this ordeal, was then clubbed to death. The scene of St Sebastian being shot by archers was a popular subject among Renaissance painters.

> Here self-defence was impossible, and individual drops stuck into her like the arrows into Saint Sebastian.
> THOMAS HARDY *The Return of the Native* 1880

> He was so preoccupied with an inner life that he took little notice of the humiliations and slights that pushed and jabbed at him the moment he ventured outside the community. If, like the rest of his kind, he was a Sebastian, the arrows did not penetrate his sense of self.
> NADINE GORDIMER *My Son's Story* 1990

Selene In Greek mythology, Selene was the moon goddess, the daughter of the Titans Hyperion and Theia.

Sennacherib Sennacherib (d. 681 BC) was king of Assyria in 705–681 BC, devoting much of his reign to suppressing revolts in various parts of his empire. He sacked Babylon in 689. According to the account in the Bible, when he invaded Palestine in the reign of Hezekiah, his army was destroyed by a pestilence brought by the Angel of Death: 'And the Lord sent an angel, who cut off all the mighty warriors and commanders and officers in the camp of the king of Assyria' (2 Chr. 32: 21). This episode is the subject of Byron's poem 'The Destruction of Sennacherib'.

> Max felt his suave sophistication return with the rush of elation that an ailing diva must have when she finds her voice again. A touch here, a word there, and the guests disappeared like the hosts of Sennacherib.
> SARA PARETSKY *V.I. for Short* 1995

Sermon on the Mount In the Bible, the Sermon on the Mount is the long sermon given by Jesus to his disciples on a mountain, recorded in Matthew 5–7, in which he preached love, humility, and charity. It contains the Beatitudes:

> 'Blessed are the poor in spirit: for theirs is the kingdom of heaven.
> Blessed are they that mourn: for they shall be comforted.
> Blessed are the meek: for they shall inherit the earth.
> Blessed are they which do hunger and thirst after righteousness: for they shall be filled.
> Blessed are the merciful: for they shall obtain mercy.
> Blessed are the pure in heart for they shall see God.
> Blessed are the peacemakers: for they shall be called the children of God.
> Blessed are they which are persecuted for righteousness' sake for theirs is the kingdom of heaven.' (Matt. 5: 3–10)

It also includes the Lord's Prayer. *See also* JESUS.

> They listened to the words of the man in their midst, who was preaching, while they abstractedly pulled heather, stripped ferns, or tossed pebbles down the slope. This was the first of a series of moral lectures or Sermons on the Mount,

which were to be delivered from the same place every Sunday afternoon as long as the fine weather lasted.
THOMAS HARDY *The Return of the Native* 1880

Serpent In the book of Genesis, the Serpent, which was 'more subtil than any beast of the field which the Lord God had made', persuaded Eve to eat the forbidden fruit from the Tree of Knowledge of good and evil in the Garden of Eden, saying that 'in the day ye eat thereof, then your eyes shall be opened, and ye shall be as gods, knowing good and evil' (Gen. 3). She in turn tempted Adam to eat and as a result of this disobedience they were banished from the Garden of Eden. A serpent can therefore be something that is a source of problems in an otherwise happy situation. *See also* ADAM AND EVE.

> By his original constitution aided by the co-operating influences of his lot, Billy in many respects was little more than a sort of outright barbarian, much such perhaps as Adam presumably might have been ere the urbane Serpent wriggled himself into his company.
> HERMAN MELVILLE *Billy Budd* 1924

> The fresh hill air had exhilarated my mind, and the aromatic scent of the evening gave the last touch of intoxication. Whatever serpent might lurk in it, it was a veritable Eden I had come to.
> JOHN BUCHAN *Prester John* 1910

> Nothing sends you straight back to childhood quicker than getting an unexpected insight into how things—relationships—really were when you lived in Eden, a child oblivious to the Serpent.
> MARGARET MARON *Shooting at Loons* 1994

> It is necessary . . . to be innocent as the dove with Monsieur de Toiras, but also sly as the serpent in the event that his king wishes them to sell Casale.
> UMBERTO ECO *The Island of the Day Before* 1994

Seven against Thebes In the tragedy *The Seven Against Thebes* by Aeschylus, seven heroes lead the attack by the Argive army on the town of Thebes, one at each of the seven gates of Thebes. They can be alluded to as examples of heroic courage.

Seven Sages of Greece The Seven Sages was the name given in ancient times to the following wise men: Solon of Athens, Thales of Miletus, Bias of Priene, Chilo of Sparta, Cleobulus of Lindus, Pittacus of Mitylene, and Periander of Corinth. They lived in the 7th and 6th centuries BC and were, variously, philosophers, scientists, lawmakers, and statesmen. *See also* SOLON.

Seven Sleepers In early Christian legend, the Seven Sleepers were seven Christian youths of Ephesus who, while fleeing persecution, entered a cave and fell asleep. They slept for almost 200 years. The legend is also told in the Koran.

I wonder by my troth, what thou and I
Did, till we loved? Were we not weaned till then,
But sucked on country pleasures, childishly?
Or snorted we in the seven sleepers' den?
JOHN DONNE 'The Good Morrow' in *Songs and Sonnets* 1633

We shouted back loud enough to wake the seven sleepers.
JEROME K. JEROME *Three Men in a Boat* 1889

Shadrach, Meshach, and Abednego The Bible relates a famous episode
during Nebuchadnezzar's reign, in which the king set up a golden idol and
commanded all to worship it. When three Jews, Shadrach, Meshach, and
Abednego, refused to do so, the king ordered some of his soldiers to throw
them into a 'fiery furnace'. Although the soldiers were consumed by the
flames, Shadrach, Meshach, and Abednego miraculously came out
unharmed: 'these men, upon whose bodies the fire had no power, nor was an
hair of their head singed, neither were their coats changed, nor the smell of
fire had passed on them'. *See also* DANIEL.

Left to its own devices, the class tied Eunice Ann Simpson to a chair and placed
her in the furnace room. We forgot her, trooped upstairs to church, and were
listening quietly to the sermon when a dreadful banging issued from the
radiator pipes, persisting until someone investigated and brought forth Eunice
Ann saying she didn't want to play Shadrach any more—Jem Finch said she
wouldn't get burnt if she had enough faith, but it was hot down there.
HARPER LEE *To Kill a Mockingbird* 1960

Shakespeare William Shakespeare (1564–1616), was a great English
dramatist and poet. He was born in Stratford upon Avon in Warwickshire. As
an adult, he moved to London, where he made his career as a writer and
actor in the theatre company the Lord Chamberlain's Men, later to become
the King's Men. The company built the Globe theatre in south London.
Shakespeare lived in London during the theatrical seasons while his wife and
family remained in Stratford. He retired back to Stratford in his late forties.
He is habitually cited as the epitome of the literary or theatrical genius. *See
also* ANTONY AND CLEOPATRA, ARIEL, SIR TOBY BELCH, CALIBAN, CAPULET,
CLEOPATRA, CORDELIA, CORIOLANUS, GLOUCESTER, HAMLET, IAGO, MACBETH, LADY
MACBETH, MALVOLIO, MIRANDA, MONTAGUES AND CAPULETS, OPHELIA, OTHELLO,
POLONIUS, MISTRESS QUICKLY, ROMEO AND JULIET, SHYLOCK, SYCORAX, TROILUS AND
CRESSIDA.

The appointed day came. . . . Rampion presented himself. . . . Mrs Felpham
tried to rise to the occasion. The village Shakespeare, it was obvious, must be
interested in the drama.
ALDOUS HUXLEY *Point Counter Point* 1928

'Cole would have regarded her as the mistress of the house, certainly,' Abner
said, 'and as a woman to be trusted. He must have been close to her in the hall.
He could have handed it to her and whispered to her to keep it for him.' 'Your

imagination is quite Shakespearean,' Sylvia Daisy said.
JOHN MASEFIELD *The Box of Delights* 1935

'What did you want to write it out again for?' 'There were some mistakes in it. I just thought it would stand a better chance if it was better written, that's all.' I was beginning to feel annoyed with her for picking at trivialities at a time like this. 'Yes, well we can't all be Shakespeares, can we,' she said, in a way that was supposed to shame me.
KEITH WATERHOUSE *Billy Liar* 1959

Wilkie went Shakespearean. He asked what was love, and answered himself there was no such thing, nor honour either.
A. S. BYATT *The Virgin in the Garden* 1978

Shangri-La Shangri-La is a Tibetan utopia depicted in James Hilton's novel *Lost Horizon* (1933), frequently used as a type of an earthly paradise, a place of retreat from the worries of modern civilization.

He gave a quick, nervous cough. 'Jesus. You can run but you can't hide. I figured that place was Shangri-la. But it's getting as bad up there as it is in the city.'
TED WOOD *A Clean Kill* 1995

Becky Sharp Becky Sharp and Amelia Sedley are the main characters in Thackeray's satirical novel *Vanity Fair* (1847–8). Becky starts out penniless and orphaned, unlike the comfortably off Amelia. However, she harnesses her charm and wits in her relentless pursuit of her own comfort and wealth.

But there was a minute tilt at the corner of her eyelids, and a corresponding tilt at the corner of her lips . . . that denied, very subtly but quite unmistakably, her apparent total obeisance to the great god Man. An orthodox Victorian would perhaps have mistrusted that imperceptible hint of a Becky Sharp; but to a man like Charles she proved irresistible.
JOHN FOWLES *The French Lieutenant's Woman* 1969

She In the novel *She: A History of Adventure* (1887) by Sir Henry Rider Haggard, the underground tombs of Kor are ruled over by a mysterious queen known as Ayesha, or She-Who-Must-Be-Obeyed. She possesses the secret of eternal life, but when she tries to demonstrate to the heroes of the book how to gain immortal life by passing through the fire of Life, she herself becomes instantly old and dies. The name of She, or She-Who-Must-Be-Obeyed, can invoke absolute power over others, mysterious youthful beauty, or a rapid descent into old age and death. *See also* RIDER HAGGARD.

He could feel his face wrinkling and his hair greying as they spoke, like She after the ill-advised second bath.
CYNTHIA HARROD-EAGLES *Shallow Grave* 1998

queen of Sheba In the Bible, the queen of Sheba, having heard about the famous Solomon, went to visit him, taking with her a magnificent caravan 'with camels that bare spices, and very much gold, and precious stones' (1 Kgs. 10: 2). The name can be used to typify a woman or girl who is conscious of her own superiority, or she can be associated with privilege and wealth.

> If Undine . . . took no care, it was not because her wants were as few as but because she assumed that care would be taken for her by those whose privilege it was to enable her to unite floral insouciance with Sheban elegance.
> EDITH WHARTON *The Custom of the Country* 1913

> 'They was all on thorns to do it; they all paid their shares, all except the Queen of Sheba.' The Queen of Sheba was Clara. 'And wouldn't she join?' Paul asked. 'She didn't get the chance; we never told her; we wasn't going to have *her* bossing *this* show. We didn't *want* her to join.'
> D. H. LAWRENCE *Sons and Lovers* 1913

> The very first night he insisted on having Lind and his gang join us for what he called a snack on our drawing-room. Snack! Solomon and the Queen of Sheba would have been happy with such a snack.
> ROBERTSON DAVIES *The Deptford Trilogy* 1975

> Not really knowing what to do with all their new-found wealth, they decided, well before any of their neighbours, to invest in the kind of palace only the Queen of Sheba or the builder of the Taj Mahal could dream up.
> ANDRÉ BRINK *Imaginings of Sand* 1996

Jack Sheppard Jack Sheppard (1702–24) was a notorious thief who was famous for his prison escapes, including one in which he escaped from Newgate prison through a chimney. He was later captured and hanged.

> He is safe now at any rate. Jack Sheppard himself couldn't get free from the strait-waistcoat that keeps him restrained.
> BRAM STOKER *Dracula* 1897

Sherlock Holmes *See under* HOLMES

shirt of Nessus *See* NESSUS.

Shylock Shylock is the Jewish moneylender in Shakespeare's *The Merchant of Venice* (1600). He lends the sum of 3 000 ducats to the merchant Antonio on condition that if the sum is not repaid by the agreed date, Antonio will forfeit a pound of his flesh. When the time to pay falls due, Antonio is unable to refund Shylock, who insists on being paid his pound of flesh. Portia, the wife of Bassanio for whom Antonio has borrowed the money, disguises herself as a lawyer and conducts Bassanio's defence. When a plea for mercy fails, she outwits Shylock by insisting that, although he can take his pound of flesh, he must not spill a drop of blood in the process, since the bond allows only for flesh, not blood. Someone demanding or extorting repayment can be described as a Shylock, and 'a pound of flesh' has come to mean an agreed payment or penalty which is strictly due but which is harsh or inhuman to demand. *See also* PORTIA, SHAKESPEARE.

'You want paying, that's what you want,' she said quietly, 'I know.' She produced her purse from somewhere and opened it. 'How much do you want, you little Shylock?'
L. P HARTLEY *The Go-Between* 1953

'Your prejudices are showing, sir,' Llewellyn remarked laconically. 'Have you forgotten the Superintendent's politeness programme? I suspect that when he finally realizes the descriptive qualities of that acronym with which you provided him, like Shylock he'll be satisfied with nothing less than his pound of flesh. Your flesh. If you don't want to supply him with an extra knife, it might be wise to keep such opinions to yourself.'
GERALDINE EVANS *Death Line* 1995

Siberia Siberia, the vast region of northern Russia noted for its severe winters, was traditionally used as a place of banishment and exile. Its name typifies an inhospitable place of exile.

She and her family are still living in the projects—exiled to an urban Siberia where shops, banks, and other amenities of city living are few and far between. *Washington City Paper* 1992

In the grim Siberian wastes of the Brighton Conference Centre . . . not one pro-Mandelson joke was to be heard. *The Observer* 1997

Sibyl The Sibyls were prophetesses in ancient Greece. They included the Cumaean Sibyl, who guided Aeneas through the underworld. Sibyls gave their prophecies in an ecstatic state, when they were believed to be possessed by a god, and their utterances were often ambiguous and riddle-like. *See also* AENEAS, CUMAEAN SIBYL.

She would lie with far-seeing eyes like a sibyl, stroking my face and repeating over and over again: 'If you knew how I have lived you would leave me. I am not the woman for you, for any man. I am exhausted.'
LAWRENCE DURRELL *Justine* 1957

You know, Mother Shipton lived in a house cut out of the rock. Like the Sibyl at Cumae, and the Pythian priestess.
A. S. BYATT *The Virgin in the Garden* 1978

When Ken Cracknell asked me about our strategy, I would utter such Sibylline phrases as 'I propose to play it largely by ear', or 'Sufficient unto the day, my dear fellow', or 'Let's just deny everything and then see where we go from there'.
JOHN MORTIMER *Rumpole's Return* 1980

Siegfried In Germanic legend, Siegfried (equivalent to the Sigurd of Norse legend) was a prince of the Netherlands and the hero of the first part of the *Nibelungenlied*. Having obtained a hoard of treasure by killing the dragon Fafner, Siegfried helped Gunther to win Brunhild. He was treacherously slain by Hagen, who discovered that Siegfried was vulnerable in only one spot on his back. Siegfried had become invulnerable after being bathed in the hot blood of a dragon he had slain, but a linden leaf had fallen between his shoulder-blades, preventing that part from being covered in the blood. Siegfried's story is also told in the opera of the same name in Wagner's *Ring Cycle*. *See also* ALBERICH'S CLOAK, NIBELUNG, WAGNER.

Silas Marner *See under* MARNER.

Silenus In Greek mythology, Silenus was an old woodland spirit who was a teacher of Dionysus. He is generally represented as a fat and jolly old man, riding an ass, intoxicated, and crowned with flowers. *See also* DIONYSUS.

> 'My wife didn't like Spain, she went back to Camberwell, she was more at home there.' 'Oh, I'm sorry for that.' His black eyes flashed a bacchanalian smile. He really had somewhat the look of a young Silenus. 'Life is full of compensations,' he murmured.
> SOMERSET MAUGHAM *The Happy Man* 1951

> She wriggled away and stared with cold judgment at his white Silenus-paunch and rosy appendages on the sheets.
> A. S. BYATT *The Virgin in the Garden* 1978

> But now, of all inappropriate beings, who should appear but Silenus? Brocklebank, perhaps a little recovered or perhaps in some extraordinary trance of drunkenness, reeled out of his cabin and shook off the two women who were trying to restrain him.
> WILLIAM GOLDING *Rites of Passage* 1980

silly walks *See* MINISTRY OF SILLY WALKS.

St Simeon Stylites *See under* STYLITES.

Simple Simon Simple Simon is a character in a children's nursery rhyme and the name can be applied to any foolish person or simpleton.

Sinai, Voice from According to the Bible, God spoke to Moses on Mount Sinai and gave him the Ten Commandments (Exod. 19–34). The Voice from Sinai is thus the voice of God, giving moral instruction. *See also* MOSES.

> To all who have been born in the old faith there comes a time of danger, when the old slips from us, and we have not yet planted our feet on the new. We hear the voice from Sinai thundering no more, and the still small voice of reason is not yet heard.
> OLIVE SCHREINER *The Story of an African Farm* 1883

Sinbad Sinbad the Sailor is the hero of one of the tales in the *Arabian Nights*. He is a rich young man of Baghdad who undertakes seven extraordinary sea voyages during which he meets with various fantastic adventures, including encounters with the Old Man of the Sea and the Roc, a giant bird. *See also* ARABIAN NIGHTS, OLD MAN OF THE SEA.

> He delighted the rustics with his songs, and, like Sinbad, astonished them with his stories of strange lands, and shipwrecks, and sea-fights.
> WASHINGTON IRVING *The Sketch-Book* 1819–20

> 'I don't know how soon I be goin' to settle down,' proclaimed the rustic sister of Sinbad.
> SARAH ORNE JEWETT *'The Flight of Betsey Lane' (1893)* in *Stories* 1896

Sirens In Greek mythology, the Sirens were sea-creatures, usually portrayed as bird-women, whose singing had the power to lure sailors to their deaths on dangerous rocks. In the *Odyssey*, when Odysseus had to sail past the island of the Sirens, he ordered his crew to plug their ears with wax so that they would not hear the singing of the Sirens. He had himself lashed to the mast of his ship so that he would not be able to respond to their call. The word is now used to suggest someone or something that lures a person away from a safe course to danger or uncertainty, especially a seductive woman who lures men to their doom. *See also* ODYSSEUS.

> Charles and his father sometimes disagreed. But they always parted with an increased regard for one another, and each desired no doughtier comrade when it was necessary to voyage for a little past the emotions. So the sailors of Ulysses voyaged past the Sirens, having first stopped one another's ears with wool.
> E. M. FORSTER *Howards End* 1910

> Of course such a marriage was only what Newland was entitled to; but young men are so foolish and incalculable—and some women so ensnaring and unscrupulous—that it was nothing short of a miracle to see one's only son safe past the Siren Isle and in the haven of a blameless domesticity.
> EDITH WHARTON *The Age of Innocence* 1920

> She will always be the odd Japanese artist who stole Britain's greatest rock'n'roller, the wife of John Lennon, the woman who split the Beatles, the siren on whose rock the mythical innocence of the Sixties was wrecked. *The Independent* 1996

> Faces flashed in front of me. I made out Caro's and Katherine's, then they were both replaced by the flawless mask of the murderess, her lips moving as she spoke. I opened my eyes with a start and she disappeared. But her voice still rang in my ears, sweeter and more deadly than any siren's song.
> PAUL JOHNSTON *Body Politic* 1997

Sisyphus In Greek mythology, Sisyphus was a king of Corinth, punished in Hades for his misdeeds in life by being condemned to the eternal task of rolling a huge stone to the top of a hill. Every time he approached the summit, the stone slipped and rolled down to the bottom again. His name can allude to efforts to achieve or finish something that constantly fails or to a seemingly endless ordeal. *See also* HADES.

> Trinity College had undertaken the Sisyphean task of repairing all of its historic Front Square.
> JOHN BRADY *A Stone of the Heart* 1988

> Is that the only future humanity has, to push the boulder, like Sisyphus, up to the top of a hill, only to see it roll to the bottom again?
> ISAAC ASIMOV *Forward the Foundation* 1994

> The team gets hot, threatens to win the Championship, blows it. The players move on, the side rebuilds, then it happens all over again. The club's official historians compared its existence to that of Sisyphus. Now yet again the boulder has gone all the way uphill and rolled straight back over all our toes.
> *The Guardian* 1994

> Ralph glanced round at a profusion of books and papers equalling that of the front room, and shrugged eloquently. 'You can see how things are. I feel like Sisyphus trying to keep up with the projects and my assistant only keeps the stone from backsliding a bit.'
> DEBORAH CROMBIE *Dreaming of the Bones* 1996

Skid Row Skid Row is believed to be derived from 'skid road', originally a track for hauling logs and later used to refer to a part of town frequented by loggers. The term is now used to refer to a part of town where the poorest people live, the haunt of drunks and vagrants.

> What in fact I did was to . . . go into the downstairs men's room and vomit and gag and retch until I was on the floor with my head hanging into the toilet bowl, in a classic Skid Row mess.
> ROBERTSON DAVIES *The Deptford Trilogy* 1972

> Harry's father had died when Harry was five, leaving his family not exactly on Skid Row, but certainly much less well-provided for than might have been expected.
> SUSAN MOODY *Dummy Hand* 1998

Luke Skywalker Luke Skywalker is the young hero of the initial trilogy of *Star Wars* films, the first of which, *Star Wars*, was released in 1977. The films portray a classic struggle between good and evil, in which Luke Skywalker fights against the evil Empire and its general, Darth Vader. *See also* STAR WARS.

> Labour's chief whip versus an amiable rebel—it sounds like a battle between Torquemada and Luke Skywalker. *The Observer* 1997

Sleeping Beauty The fairy tale of Sleeping Beauty is told in its most famous version by Perrault (1696). A princess is born to a childless king and queen who invite fairies to her christening. One fairy, who is mistakenly not invited, takes offence and curses the princess, prophesying that she will pierce her hand with a spindle and die. Another fairy ameliorates the curse, saying that rather than die she will sleep. As a result of this spell, Sleeping

Beauty and all those in her palace fall asleep for 100 years. A forest grows up around the sleeping palace. The instant Sleeping Beauty is finally wakened from her slumber by a prince's kiss, all life and bustle returns to the palace.

> Edith came in from the back drawing-room, winking and blinking her eyes at the stronger light, shaking back her slightly-ruffled curls, and altogether looking like the Sleeping Beauty startled from her dreams.
> ELIZABETH GASKELL *North and South* 1854–5

> The front door was opened. They entered. In the silent, empty hall three and a half centuries of life had gone to sleep . . . 'Like the Sleeping Beauty,' she said. but even as she spoke the words, the spell was broken. Suddenly, as though the ringing glass had called the house back to life, there was sound and movement.
> ALDOUS HUXLEY *Point Counter Point* 1928

Sleepy Hollow Washington Irving's short story 'The Legend of Sleepy Hollow' is set in an isolated valley called Sleepy Hollow, described as 'one of the quietest places in the whole world'. The name has come to represent any rural backwater. *See also* BROM BONES, ICHABOD CRANE.

> 'This place is what I call Sleepy Hollow.' 'Oh yes.' 'Most of the people are so old they've retired from their retirement.'
> FRANK PARRISH *Voices from the Dark* 1993

Sleipnir In Scandinavian mythology, Sleipnir was Odin's eight-legged horse, which could outrun the wind on water or land, or through the air.

Slough of Despond The Slough of Despond is a bog into which Christian and his fellow traveller Pliable fall because they were not paying attention to the path, in Bunyan's religious allegory *The Pilgrim's Progress* (1678, 1684). Christian sinks deeply into the mire because he carries a burden on his back but manages to struggle through to the other side, where he is helped out. Pliable is quickly discouraged, manages to struggle out of the bog on the side he entered, and gives up the journey. The term 'Slough of Despond' is sometimes used for a state of utter hopelessness and despondency. *See also* PILGRIM'S PROGRESS.

> We were in the Slough of Despond tonight, and Mother came and pulled us out as Help did in the book.
> LOUISA M. ALCOTT *Little Women* 1868

> Burdens fell, darkness gave place to light, Marjorie apocalyptically understood all the symbols of religious literature. For she herself had struggled in the Slough of Despond and had emerged; she too had climbed laboriously and without hope and had suddenly been consoled by the sight of the promised land.
> ALDOUS HUXLEY *Point Counter Point* 1928

> Brussels he sees as 'utterly complacent, and a negative force of great influence', but not quite the Slough of Despond. *The Observer* 1996

Samuel Smiles Samuel Smiles (1812–1904) was a Scottish doctor who wrote several works of advice. His books include *Self Help* (1859) and *Thrift* (1875). The name can be used to allude to financial prudence and hard work.

> Work may be prayer; but it's also hiding one's head in the sand, it's also making such a din and a dust that a man can't hear himself speak or see his own hand before his face. It's hiding yourself from yourself. No wonder the Samuel Smiles and the big business men are such enthusiasts for work. Work gives them the comforting illusion of existing.
> ALDOUS HUXLEY *Point Counter Point* 1928

> British banks and finance houses, their fingers so badly burnt by colossal debt write-offs, have behaved with the caution of Samuel Smiles in their lending policies.
> WILL HUTTON *The Observer* 1997

Snark In Lewis Carroll's nonsense poem *The Hunting of the Snark* (1876), the Snark is a fabulous animal, the quarry of the expedition undertaken by the Bellman and his crew. The word can be applied to an elusive goal.

> If Truth is the Snark of Westminster, it is most effectively pursued by those ambitious journalists who will seek to scoop each other and make their names by peddling the spin, delivered to favoured trusties by spokespeople, spin-doctors, sources and 'friends'.
> SHEENA MCDONALD *The Guardian* 1998

Snow Queen *The Snow Queen* is a fairy story by Hans Christian Andersen in which Kai, a young boy, is carried off by the cold and cruel Snow Queen after two splinters of glass become lodged in his eyes and heart, making him unable to feel any human emotions. He is rescued by his sister Gerda, who melts his frozen heart with her tears. The Snow Queen has come to represent a person, especially a woman, who seems incapable of human emotions. *See also* HANS CHRISTIAN ANDERSEN.

> I was so young I thought it didn't matter. Infatuated! His unhappiness had to be loaded on to me; that was what it was. He denied life, made me deny it too. He turned me into some sort of snow queen and when I made just one small attempt to thaw myself out he used it as an excuse to throw me out of his life.
> FAY WELDON *The Cloning of Joanna May* 1989

> It started by describing Alice's beauty as 'a fatal thing'. It wondered if 'like Daphne she will get so tired of it, she will pray to be turned into a hedge'. It said nothing about Valentina's own fantastic snow-queen beauty.
> ROSE TREMAIN *The Way I Found Her* 1998

Snow White The heroine of the traditional fairy tale *Snow White and the Seven Dwarfs* is 'as white as snow, as red as blood and had hair as black as ebony'. Her stepmother is proud and vain, and regularly demands of her magic mirror:
'Mirror, mirror on the wall,

Who is the fairest of them all?'

When Snow White grows to be more beautiful than her, the stepmother orders that her stepdaughter be taken into the forest and killed so that she will once again be 'the fairest of them all'. The men charged with Snow White's murder take pity on her and simply abandon her in the forest, where she lives for a while in the house of the Seven Dwarfs and eventually marries a handsome prince.

> 'She didn't look very dangerous,' I said, bristling. 'She just seemed like a silly young girl.' 'Yeah, a regular Snow White. Who just happened to be packing a gun.'
> LINDSAY MARACOTTA *Playing Dead* 1999

Socrates Socrates (469–399 BC) was a Greek philosopher concerned with the search for truth and reason in questions of morality and ethics. His method of inquiry (the Socratic method) was based on debating moral issues with those around him: he systematically questioned his pupils and then cross-examined them to expose inconsistencies and errors. Through this discourse and careful questioning, he challenged accepted beliefs and attempted to expose foolishness, irrationality, and error. He wrote nothing himself, but is known through the works of one of his pupils, Plato, who recorded his dialogues and teachings. Socrates was charged with impiety and corrupting the young, and was condemned to die by taking hemlock. *See also* PLATO.

> 'I do, as it happens,' said Philip and, still skirmishing . . . in the realm of dialectic, went on like a little Socrates, with his cross-examination.
> ALDOUS HUXLEY *Point Counter Point* 1928

> I hope that you will be glad to know that I have decided to make my own dowry. I think that my father has no sense of shame, and sometimes I feel very angry with him for refusing the very thing that is normal for every other girl. He is not fair because he is too rational. He thinks that he is a Socrates who can fly in the face of custom.
> LOUIS DE BERNIÈRES *Captain Corelli's Mandolin* 1994

> As far as Cassandra Swann was concerned, Charlie Quartermain, gross, unbuttoned, sphisciform, might be St Francis of Assisi and the Angel Gabriel rolled into one, with a touch of Paul Newman on the one hand and a dollop of Socrates on the other, but that still wouldn't make up for the fact that basically she just didn't fancy him.
> SUSAN MOODY *King of Hearts* 1995

Sodom and Gomorrah Sodom and Gomorrah were towns in ancient Palestine, probably south of the Dead Sea. According to Genesis 19: 24, they were destroyed by fire and brimstone from heaven as a punishment for the depravity and wickedness of their inhabitants. In particular 'the sin of Sodom' is traditionally taken to refer to buggery. Lot, the nephew of Abraham, was allowed to escape from the destruction of Sodom with his family. His wife disobeyed God's order not to look back at the burning city and was turned into a pillar of salt. *See also* LOT'S WIFE.

> 'The village,' she said in her quiet voice, 'the village grows worse and worse
> every day.' 'What has happened now?' asked Mr Bodiham, feeling suddenly
> very weary. 'I'll tell you.' She pulled up a brown varnished chair and sat down.
> In the village of Crome, it seemed, Sodom and Gomorrah had come to a
> second birth.
> ALDOUS HUXLEY *Crome Yellow* 1921

> 'Be serious. It's not just the wife. Dunny, we have to face it. You're queer.' 'The
> sin of Sodom, you mean? If you knew boys as I do, you would not suggest
> anything so grotesque. If Oscar Wilde had pleaded insanity, he would have
> walked out of court a free man.'
> ROBERTSON DAVIES *Fifth Business* 1970

> The landslip had swept away a whole Sodom and Gomorrah of private
> fantasies and unacted desires. He felt a new man in the calm, initially sexless
> atmosphere of Desiree Zapp's luxurious eyrie high up on the peak of Socrates
> Avenue.
> DAVID LODGE *Changing Places* 1975

> In front of me is the Pacific, which sends up sunset after sunset, for nothing; at
> my back are the improbable mountains, and beyond them an enormous
> barricade of land. Toronto lies behind it, at a great distance, burning in thought
> like Gomorrah.
> MARGARET ATWOOD *Cat's Eye* 1988

Solomon Solomon, the son of David and Bathsheba, was the king of ancient
Israel *c.*970–*c.*930 BC. He was famed for his wisdom and justice. The phrase
'the Judgement of Solomon' refers to his arbitration in a dispute about a
baby claimed by each of two women (1 Kgs. 3: 16–28). Solomon proposed
dividing the baby in half with his sword, and then gave it to the woman who
showed concern for its life: 'And all Israel heard of the judgement which the
king had rendered; and they stood in awe of the king, because they perceived
that the wisdom of God was in him, to render justice.'

> I, who am all-powerful, I, whose loveliness is more than the loveliness of that
> Grecian Helen, of whom they used to sing, and whose wisdom is wider, ay, far
> more wide and deep than the wisdom of Solomon the Wise.
> H. RIDER HAGGARD *She* 1887

> 'All women are thus.' Kim spoke as might have Solomon.
> RUDYARD KIPLING *Kim* 1900

> It was beginning to dawn on me that I am the member of the public to whom
> the public interest requirement refers. In effect, the police are saying, 'You were
> there. Was it bad? Do you think that person deserves to be punished?' But this
> requires the judgement of Solomon. *The Independent* 1995

> I phoned my condolences to a couple of Danbury Hospital patients recovering
> from a River Road head-on. Ollie, it seemed, had proved Solomonic in an

attempt to hasten the investigation, slapping both colliders with 'excessive speed for conditions'.
JUSTIN SCOTT *Frostline* 1997

Solomon's temple In 957 BC King Solomon built the Israelites' first temple on Mount Zion, Jerusalem (1 Kgs. 5–7 and 2 Chr. 3–4). The magnificence of this temple became legendary. Each room had walls panelled with cedar wood, carved with palm trees and cherubim, and overlaid with gold.

> In this process the chamber and its furniture grew more and more dignified and luxurious; the shawl hanging at the window took upon itself the richness of tapestry; the brass handles of the chest of drawers were as golden knockers; and the carved bed-posts seemed to have some kinship with the magnificent pillars of Solomon's temple.
> THOMAS HARDY *Tess of the D'Urbervilles* 1891

Solon Solon (*c.*630–*c.*560 BC) was an Athenian statesman and lawgiver noted for his economic, constitutional, and legal reforms. He was one of the supposed Seven Sages of Greece. A wise statesman can be described as a Solon. *See also* SEVEN SAGES OF GREECE.

> Are you Socrates or Solon, always right?
> BARBARA MICHAELS *The Wizard's Daughter* 1980

Somme The battle of the Somme was one of the major battles of the First World War, fought in northern France from July to November 1916. The British soldiers were ordered up out of their trenches to face, on foot, the German machine guns opposite. Over a million men on both sides were killed or wounded. Going 'over the top' at the Somme was seen as going to certain death.

Somnus Somnus was the Roman god of sleep, father of Morpheus. *See also* MORPHEUS.

sorcerer's apprentice *The Sorcerer's Apprentice* is the title of an orchestral composition by Paul Dukas (1897), after a ballad by Goethe (1797). It was one of the pieces used in the 1940 Disney animated film *Fantasia*. According to the story on which Dukas's work is based, the sorcerer's apprentice finds a spell to make objects do work for him but is then unable to cancel it. In the Disney version, Mickey Mouse is the apprentice and the spell causes a broom to keep fetching buckets of water from a well. The term is used to describe a person who instigates but is unable to control a process.

> How would Emily put what she felt into words? She would describe this, perhaps, in terms of that image of her sweeping, sweeping, the sorcerer's apprentice put to work in a spiteful garden against floods of dying leaves that she could never clean away no matter how hard she tried.
> DORIS LESSING *Memoirs of a Survivor* 1974

The giant deer had evolved from small forms with even smaller antlers.

Although the antlers were useful at first, their growth could not be contained and, like the sorcerer's apprentice, the giant deer discovered only too late that even good things have their limits.
STEPHEN JAY GOULD *Ever Since Darwin* 1978

South Sea Bubble The South Sea Bubble is the name given to a fever of speculation in 1720 in shares of the South Sea Company, a company formed in 1711 to trade with South America. The boom was followed by the company's failure and a general financial collapse. The South Sea Bubble can be alluded to in the context of something that appears to be successful and stable, but could fail suddenly.

Sam Spade Sam Spade is the American private investigator in *The Maltese Falcon* (1930) and in other stories written by Dashiell Hammet in the 1930s. Spade was the first in a long line of tough, hard-boiled American private detectives. Essentially an honourable man, he is willing to break the law on occasion to see justice done.

The downtown office buildings were just sparkling on their lights; it made you think of Sam Spade.
JACK KEROUAC *On the Road* 1957

I inquired. He said that when they got ready to roll out and make an arrest, I'd know about it. Translation: 'We are no longer buddies, Sam Spade, so you can go fuck yourself.'
CAROL BRENNAN *Chill of Summer* 1995

Spartan The Spartans were the inhabitants of an ancient Greek city state in the southern Peloponnese. They were known for their austerity and self-discipline and their toughness in enduring pain and hardship.

Pearl and he ate heartily upon these occasions, not knowing what Spartan nastiness the preoccupied Mrs. Vambrace might have left in the refrigerator for them at home.
ROBERTSON DAVIES *Tempest-Tost* 1951

A Spartan matron, iron-hearted, bearing warrior-sons for the nation.
J. M. COETZEE *Age of Iron* 1990

The water temperature would have struck even a Spartan as low and the soap was as carbolic as Hamilton's temper, but I felt better afterwards.
PAUL JOHNSTON *Body Politic* 1997

Spartan boy The story of the Spartan Boy and the Fox, told by the Roman writer Plutarch (*c*.46–*c*.120), relates how a Spartan boy, having stolen a young fox and hidden it under his cloak, let it tear out his guts with its teeth and claws and died, rather than let it be seen. The story can be alluded to in the context of someone who hides a secret and suffers as a result.

Willow did not say aloud the thought in her mind: 'And so you did not completely trust him. Did you feel that there was something wrong with him after all?' But she could tell that Caroline had thought the same thing. No wonder she looked just as the Spartan boy with the fox gnawing at his vitals must have looked.

NATASHA COOPER *Poison Flowers* 1990

Speedy Gonzalez Speedy Gonzalez is a Mexican mouse in a series of Warner Brothers cartoons, noted for his ability to run very fast. The first cartoon appeared in 1953 and the second, *Speedy Gonzalez* (1955), won an Oscar.

Frank Spencer The character of Frank Spencer, played by Michael Crawford, appeared in the BBC television comedy series *Some Mothers Do 'Ave 'Em*, first broadcast in 1973. The well-intentioned Frank is hopelessly incompetent and accident-prone, and causes chaos and mayhem all around him.

Spenser Edmund Spenser (*c.*1552–1599) was an English poet best known for his allegorical romance *The Faerie Queene* (1590, 1596). In book III of this work, Spenser celebrates the courtly virtue of chastity, 'that fairest virtue, far above the rest', as embodied in the character of Britomart, the female knight of chastity. *See also* ARCHIMAGO, BELPHOEBE, BRITOMART, DUESSA, RED CROSS KNIGHT.

I get the impression that Trevor believes in a version of Mediaeval Chastitie, sort of Spenserian you know.

MARGARET ATWOOD *The Edible Woman* 1969

Sphinx In Greek mythology, the Sphinx was a winged monster with a woman's head and a lion's body. It lay outside Thebes and asked travellers a riddle, killing anyone who failed to solve it. When Oedipus gave the right answer, the Sphinx killed itself. The Sphinx asked what animal walked on four legs in the morning, two legs at noon, and three in the evening. Oedipus correctly answered that man crawls on all fours as a child, walks on two legs as an adult, and is supported by a stick in old age. In ancient Egypt, a sphinx was a stone figure with a lion's body and the head of a man, ram, or hawk. An enigmatic or mysterious person can be described as a sphinx or as sphinx-like.

This human mind wrote history, and this must read it. The Sphynx must solve her own riddle.

RALPH WALDO EMERSON 'History' in *Essays* 1841

'Men have educated us.' 'But not explained you.' 'Describe us as a sex,' was her challenge. 'Sphynxes without secrets.'

OSCAR WILDE *The Picture of Dorian Gray* 1891

Ian persevered, hauling the rib cage up and down, trying to get air into the lungs mechanically. Stephen and I watched in silence for what seemed a very

long time. I didn't try to stop him. Stopping had to be his own decision. And I suppose some quality in Malcolm's total lack of response finally convinced him, because he reluctantly laid the arms down to rest, and turned to us a blank and Sphinx-like face.
DICK FRANCIS *Trial Run* 1978

He was without doubt the Raj's most sphynxian figure, the guardian of the secret of its final and most decisive deed. *The Observer* 1997

Spock In the original series of the television science fiction series *Star Trek* (1966–9), Mr Spock, played by Leonard Nimoy, is the ultra-logical science officer on the USS *Enterprise*. He has a human mother and a Vulcan father, and it is the Vulcan side of his nature that causes his actions to be governed by logical reasoning rather than by intuition or emotion. Mr Spock has large, sharply pointed ears. *See also* STAR TREK.

We would like to believe we reasoned with Aristotle's logic. That's why Sherlock Holmes and Star Trek's Mr. Spock are heroes and not fictional commoners.
BART KOSKO *Fuzzy Thinking* 1993

If you were doing OK, you'd be sitting in the posh downstairs office in that place of yours, dumping the unpromising cases on someone else and clipping off part of their fee, 'stead of that pint-sized smart aleck with the Mr. Spock ears.
LIZ EVANS *Who Killed Marilyn Monroe?* 1997

Jack Sprat According to the traditional nursery rhyme,
'Jack Sprat could eat no fat,
His wife could eat no lean:
And so betwixt them both, you see,
They lick'd the platter clean.'
Jack Sprat is usually pictured as extremely thin, and his wife as very plump.

The Galls, thought Solly, might have posed for a picture of Mr. and Mrs. Jack Sprat. Alfred Gall was thin to the point of being cadaverous, stooped, pale and insignificant. His wife was covered with that loose, liquid fat which seems to sway and slither beneath the skin.
ROBERTSON DAVIES *A Mixture of Frailties* 1951

Jerry Springer Jerry Springer (b. 1944) is a London-born US talk show host. His show, *The Jerry Springer Show*, was first broadcast in the United States in 1991 and became known for guests expressing extreme views, fighting on stage, and shouting foul language. Since 1999 his shows have adhered to a no-violence rule.

But argument is crucial. It should be encouraged not hidden or denied or even quashed. It's such an elementary point that it should not, here of all places, need to be made. But any deviation from consensus is depicted now—and by people who should know better, and indeed who do know better but cynically

pretend otherwise—as some sort of Jerry Springer free-for-all.
NIGELLA LAWSON *The Observer* 1998

Wackford Squeers Wackford Squeers is the ignorant headmaster of the Yorkshire school Dotheboys Hall in Dickens's *Nicholas Nickleby* (1839). Squeers presides over a cruel regime, starving and bullying his miserable pupils under pretence of education. *See also* DICKENSIAN.

Trembling first-formers (secretaries) huddled over their work like Dickensian pupils, fearing the inevitable moment when a toothy, strigine, six-foot Wackford Squeers of a Headmistress would come screaming into the room. *Time Out* 1991

Stakhanov Aleksei Grigorievich Stakhanov (1906–77) was a Russian coalminer who started an incentive scheme in 1935 for exceptional output and efficiency by individual steelworkers, coalminers, etc. Prize workers became known as Stakhanovites.

Now, as the only female among the four partners in a small City law firm specialising in patents and intellectual property, her Stakhanovite capacity for work could only be applauded.
ELIZABETH IRONSIDE *Death in the Garden* 1995

Leicester's work-rate makes Comrade Stakhanov look like a clock-watcher and nowhere more so than in midfield. *The Guardian* 1998

Stalin Joseph Stalin (1879–1953) was born Iosif Vissarioniovich Dzhugashvili and changed his name to Stalin ('Man of Steel') in 1912. He became a Bolshevik in 1903 and general secretary of the Communist Party in 1924. After Lenin's death in 1924, he became increasingly powerful and was leader of the party by 1926. Stalin's attempts to collectivize agriculture led to the death of up to 10 million peasants, and his purges against anyone thought to oppose him were ruthless. After the Second World War he gained power over eastern Europe and imposed the iron curtain which divided Europe until 1989. His name is often associated with the idea of authoritarianism.

At the same time Clemmow was addressing the massed ranks of the BBC *Newsnight* operation facing, ashen-faced, allegations of 'editorial Stalinism' and 'centralised control'. *The Observer* 1997

Sylvester Stallone The American actor Sylvester Stallone (b. 1946) is best known for his lead roles in the Rambo films, the first of which, *First Blood*, was released in 1982. He also played the lead role in the Rocky series, the first of which appeared in 1976. In these and other films he plays tough, muscle-bound, monosyllabic heroes. *See also* RAMBO.

I pulled on jogging pants and a sweatshirt without showering and drove over to the Thai boxing gym in South Manchester where I punish my body on as regular a basis as my career in crime prevention allows. It might not be the Hilton, but it meets my needs. It's clean, it's cheap, the equipment is well

maintained and it's mercifully free of muscle-bound macho men who think they've got the body and charm of Sylvester Stallone when in reality they don't even have the punch-drunk brains of Rocky.
VAL MCDERMID *Crack Down* 1994

Stanislavsky Stanislavsky (1863–1938), the great Russian actor, director, and teacher, was born Konstantin Sergeevich Alekseev. He founded the Moscow Art Theatre in 1898 and was known for his productions of Chekhov and Gorky. His theories about technique, in particular in paying attention to the characters' backgrounds and psychology, eventually formed the basis for the US movement known as 'method acting'.

'What? I didn't! That's absurd!' he protested, emoting surprise and shock in a sub-Stanislavskian style.
REGINALD HILL *Child's Play* 1987

Sir Henry Morton Stanley Sir Henry Morton Stanley (1841–1904) was the Welsh explorer and journalist who, sent by the *New York Herald*, 'found' Dr Livingstone at Ujiji in 1871, and, according to the popular account, greeted him with the words 'Doctor Livingstone, I presume?'. *See also* DR. LIVINGSTONE.

It would take a Stanley to find Dr. Livingstone on board. I presume. Even with the aid of one of Grandma Belle's hand-drawn maps, I could never do this on my own.
SUSAN SUSSMAN with SARAJANE AVIDON *Cruising for Murder* 2000

Starship Enterprise In the television science fiction series *Star Trek*, and the subsequent films, the Starship USS *Enterprise* is the spaceship captained by Captain Kirk and, later, Captains Picard and Janeway. The bridge is dominated by computer monitors and other futuristic technology. *See also* STAR TREK.

Christ, the office will look like the Starship Enterprise by the time you've finished with it. Didn't we leave Maher and Malcolm to escape the tyranny of computers?
MARTIN EDWARDS *Yesterday's Papers* 1994

She patted the whale-sized flank of the Buick. 'This car is absurd. I feel as if I'm driving the Starship *Enterprise*.'
NORA KELLY *Old Wounds* 1998

Star Trek The American television science fiction series *Star Trek*, first broadcast in 1966, depicts the adventures of the Starship USS *Enterprise* as it explores space, the 'final frontier', and overcomes evil aliens under the direction of Captain James T. Kirk and his first officer, Mr Spock. One of the most memorable features of the series is the ship's transporter system, by which crew members can be made to dematerialize from one place and then rematerialize elsewhere, leading to the often repeated request to Chief Engineer Scott to 'Beam me up, Scottie' from crew members in danger. The

S

mission of the *Enterprise*, with its famously split infinitive, 'to boldly go where no man has gone before', has also become a catchphrase. *See also* MR SPOCK.

> One became aware of [Knebworth] manifesting rather than entering. Bone compared it to *Star Trek*. He and Grizel had become hilarious over the idea of Mrs Knebworth beaming Knebworth up from a console in the kitchen, his molecules assembling where he was wanted.
> STAYNES AND STOREY *Bone Idle* 1993

Star Wars The initial trilogy of *Star Wars* films, directed by George Lucas, *Star Wars* (1977), *The Empire Strikes Back* (1980), and *Return of the Jedi* (1983), portrays a classic struggle between good and evil set in space, with the hero, Luke Skywalker, battling against the evil Empire and its general, Darth Vader. The name Star Wars was later given informally to the Strategic Defense Initiative, a proposed US defence system based partly in space and intended to protect the United States from nuclear attack by intercepting intercontinental ballistic missiles before they reached their targets. The name Star Wars can evoke any battle on a huge scale. *See also* DARTH VADER, LUKE SKYWALKER, YODA.

Steen Jan Steen (1626–79) was a Dutch painter of humorous subjects, especially crowded tavern scenes and social gatherings in middle-class households. His prolific output includes such works as *The World Upside-Down* (*c.*1663), *Interior of a Tavern with Cardplayers and a Violin Player* (1665–8), and *The Wedding Party* (1667). The term 'Jan Steen household' is still used today by the Dutch to describe a boisterous and chaotic family.

> As I went past, a drunk stumbled out, and for a second, before the door swung shut again, I had a glimpse inside. I walked on without pausing, carrying the scene in my head. It was like something by Jan Steen: the smoky light, the crush of red-faced drinkers, the old boys propping up the bar, the fat woman singing, displaying a mouthful of broken teeth.
> JOHN BANVILLE *The Book of Evidence* 1989

Stentor Stentor was a Greek herald in the Trojan War, supposed to have the voice of 50 men combined. He was unwise enough to challenge Hermes to a shouting match and when he lost paid the penalty for his presumption by being put to death. His name, and the word 'stentorian', can be used to describe a person with a powerful voice.

> And his voice rang out into the night like that of Stentor as he bawled.
> RICHARD BUTLER *Against Wind* 1979

Stepford Wives *The Stepford Wives* is the title of a film made in 1974, based on a book by Ira Levin, which tells the story of a young couple who move into the commuter village of Stepford, near New York. The wife is shocked that the other wives she meets are interested only in trivial domestic issues and in serving their husbands' needs, to the point that they seem incapable of even thinking about anything else. It gradually emerges that the men of the village, in their chauvinistic search for ideal wives, have in fact killed their real wives and replaced them with androids programmed to behave in this way. A 'Stepford wife' is therefore a dutiful wife who is mindlessly devoted to the minutiae of domestic life and blindly obeys her husband, seeming to have no mind or wishes of her own. More generally, the term can be applied to anyone who unthinkingly supports another person or behaves according to a set pattern.

> She went off without a word, as obedient and unquestioning as a Stepford wife.
> RICHARD HALEY *Thoroughfare of Stones* 1995

> He leaned over and kissed me. 'Mmmmmm, you smell nice,' then offered me a cigarette. 'No thank you, I have found inner poise and given up smoking,' I said, in a pre-programmed, Stepford Wife sort of way, wishing Daniel wasn't quite so attractive when you found yourself alone with him.
> HELEN FIELDING *Bridget Jones's Diary* 1996

> Rafe's turning her into a little Stepford wife. He's joined that horrible bunch of hypocrites called Family Matters, you know, where men get together and learn to be men again, praying God to smite all the evil feminists in their midst and pick out Christian spouses for their children.
> SARA PARETSKY *Ghost Country* 1998

St Stephen St Stephen (d. *c*.35) was the first Christian martyr, stoned to death in Jerusalem.

> It was so kind and tender of you to give up half a day's work to come and see me! . . . You are Joseph the dreamer of dreams, dear Jude. And a tragic Don Quixote. And sometimes you are St. Stephen, who, while they were stoning him, could see Heaven opened.
> THOMAS HARDY *Jude the Obscure* 1895

> Illidge sat down and recounted his adventure, boastfully and with embellishments. He had been, according to his own account, a mixture of Horatius defending the bridge and St Stephen under the shower of stones.
> ALDOUS HUXLEY *Point Counter Point* 1928

Dink Stover John Humperdink (Dink) Stover is the hero of a series of boys' novels by the American novelist Owen Johnson (1878–1952). The best known, *Stover at Yale* (1911), follows the adventures of the young Dink as he goes through Yale University, working hard and becoming a successful athlete and respected student.

> The client can always take a walk in estate planning, my lawyer had said, so estate lawyers, especially estate lawyers for the very rich, tend to be a cross between Dink Stover and Uriah Heep, unless of course they're very rich themselves.
> MAX BYRD *Finders Weepers* 1983

Struldbrug In Jonathan Swift's *Gulliver's Travels* (1726), the Struldbrugs are inhabitants of Luggnagg, a race endowed with immortality but who become increasingly infirm and decrepit. After the age of 80 they are regarded as legally dead. The term can be used to describe a person who is incapacitated by age or infirmity. *See also* GULLIVER'S TRAVELS.

> Yet which of us in his heart likes any of the Elizabethan dramatists except Shakespeare? Are they in reality anything else than literary Struldbrugs?
> SAMUEL BUTLER *The Way of All Flesh* 1903

Stygian *See* STYX.

St Simeon Stylites St Simeon Stylites (*c.*390–459) was a Syrian monk who is said to have become the first to practise an extreme form of asceticism which involved living for 30 years on top of a tall pillar.

> In Saint Stylites, the famous Christian hermit of old times, who built him a lofty stone pillar in the desert and spent the whole latter portion of his life on its summit, hoisting his food from the ground with a tackle; in him we have a remarkable instance of a dauntless stander-of-mast-heads; who was not to be driven from his place by fogs or frosts, rain, hail, or sleet; but valiantly facing everything out to the last, literally died at his post.
> HERMAN MELVILLE *Moby Dick* 1851

> At Boulogne, Patrick was usually to be found, like Simeon Stylites, on the top of a purpose-built pillar.
> JEANETTE WINTERSON *The Passion* 1987

Styx In Greek mythology, the river Styx was the main river of Hades, the underworld, across which the souls of the dead were said to be ferried by Charon. Any deep, gloomy, or foggy darkness can be described as 'Stygian'. *See also* HADES.

> A beam from the setting sun pierced the Stygian gloom.
> H. RIDER HAGGARD *She* 1887

> The report Dr. Fraker had dictated effectively reduced Rick's death to observations about the craniocerebral trauma he'd sustained, with a catalogue of abrasions, contusions, small-intestine avulsions, mesenteric lacerations, and sufficient skeletal damage to certify Rick's crossing of the River Styx.
> SUE GRAFTON *C is for Corpse* 1990

> It was a Stygian night. Outside the rain drifted in drapes and an east wind was gusting.
> LOUIS DE BERNIÈRES *Captain Corelli's Mandolin* 1994

> Research had assured Jonathan that although some of these intruders from the past were not fussy about requiring darkness or any particular ambiance in

which to operate, some of them appeared to work to a species of timetable not discernible from this side of the Styx.
STAYNES AND STOREY *Dead Serious* 1995

Sun City Sun City was the name given by political prisoners to Diepkloof Prison, near Johannesburg in South Africa. Sun City is actually a South African casino resort.

It's a better place than Sun City. Better conditions.
NADINE GORDIMER *My Son's Story* 1990

Sun King Louis XIV (1638–1715), known as the Sun King (Le Roi Soleil), whose palace, Versailles, was richly furnished, surrounded himself with wealth. He can stand for the embodiment of rich, lavish, and sumptuous splendour. *See also* LOUIS XIV.

These two small tables were surrounded and bedecked by a buildup of objects, fabrics, and bibelots so lush it would have made the Sun King blink.
TOM WOLFE *The Bonfire of the Vanities* 1987

Superman Superman is a US comic-book superhero who possesses prodigious strength, the ability to fly, X-ray vision, and other powers which help him to battle against crime and evil. His alter ego is Clark Kent, a shy, bespectacled reporter for the *Daily Planet* newspaper. He is invulnerable except when exposed to pieces of the green rock kryptonite, fragments of the planet of his birth, Krypton. Superman was first created by the writer Jerry Siegel and the artist Joe Shuster, both aged 17, in 1938. *See also* CLARK KENT, KRYPTONITE.

Kent was the TV heartthrob of the Gulf War, his Superman good looks gilding his newshawk reputation. *Chatelaine* 1992

'You haven't met Zach Ralston. He's one man in a million, Jacob.' 'Well, he damn well better be Superman, to drag me all the way out here to the doggamned *tundra*.'
DEANNIE FRANCIS MILLS *The Trap Door* 1995

You're mixing me up with Superman. I just do what I can to hold the tide back a bit. I leave saving planets to the Met.
LIZ EVANS *Who Killed Marilyn Monroe?* 1997

Superwoman
comic book heroine Superwoman is a US comic-book heroine, a female version of Superman who uses her superhuman powers to fight against evil. Like Superman, she wears a cloak and can fly.

'That's when it started. They told me to lay off, to stop being a troublemaker. And I don't think I'm very good at being diplomatic, Kat.' I nodded. That thought had crossed my mind a time or two. I drove past the big blue and white Louden Industries sign and pulled into the company lot and up to the plant. I looked over at Amanda, looked for a Superwoman cape. No. No hero statement—just ironed blah beige and pearls. Maybe she'd left her cape at home.

KAREN KIJEWSKI *Wild Kat* 1994

professional woman *Superwoman* is the title of a book by Shirley Conran(1975), which gives tips to women on how to pursue a successful career and be a good mother at the same time. The book has been criticized for establishing an unrealistic role model for working women.

She's a sort of grim Superwoman type: runs a home and x children plus dog, makes them cakes for their birthdays and incidentally manages a business as well.

LINDA MATHER *Gemini Doublecross* 1995

Susanna Susanna is the central character in the book of Susanna, one of the books of the Apocrypha in the Bible. She was a beautiful young woman who aroused the lust of two of the elders, who secretly spied on her when she was bathing naked in a garden. The two elders threatened her that unless she slept with them they would accuse her of adultery with a young man, which would mean her certain death. Susanna chose the latter, saying that she preferred to suffer death than to 'sin in the sight of the Lord'. Susanna was tried and condemned to death, but, in answer to her prayer, God 'raised up the spirit of a young youth, whose name was Daniel'. Daniel cross-examined the two elders and showed that they were lying, upon which they were condemned to death and Susanna was released. Susanna is alluded to as someone who is falsely accused.

Well, we are playing rough, aren't we? And the virtuous Val presenting herself like Susannah, she who suffered from the horny-pawed Elders.

JULIAN BARNES *Talking It Over* 1991

'I went for a walk. It was warm and I was aching to be outside.' 'Did you leave the island?' 'No. I hiked to the pond and wound up skinny-dipping.' 'Anybody see you?' 'You mean paddling around in my birthday suit like Susanna and the Elders?'

MICHAEL MEWSHAW *True Crime* 1991

Svengali Svengali is a musician in George du Maurier's novel *Trilby* (1894), who trains Trilby's voice and makes her a famous singer. His control over her is so great that when he dies, she loses her ability to sing. The name Svengali has come to be used of someone who establishes considerable or near-total influence over someone else.

The idea of the hypnotist as an all-powerful demon, like Svengali, who could make anybody do anything, he pooh-poohed.

ROBERTSON DAVIES *World of Wonders* 1975

Suddenly the spirit of that evil man is haunting this house. He has become your Svengali!

JOHN KENNEDY TOOLE *A Confederacy of Dunces* 1980

Academics like myself are labelled as trendy progressives, not believing in

structure, the Svengali figures to whom thousands of poor dears in the teaching profession are in ideological thrall, a patronising and laughable view.
The Observer 1997

Just over two years of marriage to a man twice her age, and she seemed to have wholeheartedly embraced the philosophy along with the man himself. Svengali and Trilby? Or a slavish acceptance of the good old fashioned motto, money talks?
RAYMOND FLYNN *Busy Body* 1998

Swaffham tinker According to a traditional story, John Chapman, a tinker from Swaffham in Norfolk, dreamt that if he went to London Bridge he would hear news greatly to his advantage. Having gone there, he was accosted by a man who asked him what he wanted, to which he explained his errand based on his dream. The man replied, 'Alas, good friend, if I had heeded dreams I might have proved myself as very a fool as thou hast, for 'tis not long since I dreamt that at a place called Swaffham, in Norfolk, dwells John Chapman, a peddler, who hath a tree at the back of his house, under which is buried a pot of money.' The tinker hurried home, found the pot of money, and lived the rest of his life a wealthy man.

That night was an eventful one to Eustacia's brain, and one which she hardly ever forgot. She dreamt a dream; and few human beings, from Nebuchadnezzar to the Swaffham tinker, ever dreamt a more remarkable one.
THOMAS HARDY *The Return of the Native* 1880

Swineherd In Hans Andersen's fairy story *The Swineherd*, a prince, having failed to win an emperor's daughter by presenting her with a beautiful rose and a nightingale, disguises himself and obtains a job at her father's palace as a swineherd in order to try to win her attention. Although there is no equivalent traditional story of a princess disguising herself as a swine-girl, D. H. Lawrence uses this idea in the quote below. *See also* HANS CHRISTIAN ANDERSEN.

The girl was romantic in her soul. Everywhere was a Walter Scott heroine being loved by men with helmets or with plumes in their caps. She herself was something of a princess turned into a swine-girl in her own imagination. And she was afraid lest this boy, who, nevertheless, looked something like a Walter Scott hero, who could paint and speak French, and knew what algebra meant, and who went by train to Nottingham every day, might consider her simply as the swine-girl, unable to perceive the princess beneath; so she held aloof.
D. H. LAWRENCE *Sons and Lovers* 1913

sword of Damocles Damocles was a legendary courtier of Dionysius I of Syracuse, who had talked openly of how happy Dionysius was. To show him how precarious this happiness was, Dionysius invited Damocles to a sumptuous banquet, and seated him under a sword which was suspended by a single thread. 'The sword of Damocles' thus refers to a danger that is always present and might strike at any moment.

True, in old age we live under the shadow of Death, which, like a sword of Damocles, may descend at any moment.
SAMUEL BUTLER *The Way of All Flesh* 1903

A reduction in international armaments is impossible; by virtue of any number of fears and jealousies. The burden grows worse as science advances, for the improvements in the art of destruction will keep pace with its advance and every year more and more will have to be devoted to costly engines of war. It is a vicious circle. There is no escape from it—that Damocles sword of a war on the first day of which all the chartered covenants of princes will be scattered like chaff.
FAY WELDON *Darcy's Utopia* 1990

Daphne took another call. I knew even before I had registered her hushed and respectful tone that the sword of Damocles was suspended above me.
BEN ELTON *Inconceivable* 1999

Sybaris Sybaris was a Greek colony in southern Italy, founded in around 720 BC. It was an important trading centre, and its wealth and luxury became proverbial, giving us the word 'sybaritic' in English.

'It's very nice,' said Jennifer. 'We certainly didn't have vast open fires at St Hilda's.' She sniffed. 'Mmm. Smells like apple logs. And look at those rugs. For a women's college this is a veritable Sybaris.'
RUTH DUDLEY EDWARDS *Ten Lords A-Leaping* 1995

Sycorax In Shakespeare's play *The Tempest* (1623), Sycorax is a witch, the mother of Caliban, who enchanted the island and imprisoned the spirit Ariel for disobedience. *See also* ARIEL, CALIBAN, SHAKESPEARE.

Dame Gourlay's tales were at first of a mild and interesting character . . . Gradually, however, they assumed a darker and more mysterious character, and became such as, told by the midnight lamp, and enforced by the tremulous tone, the quivering and livid lip, the uplifted skinny forefinger, and the shaking head of the blue-eyed hag, might have appalled a less credulous imagination, in an age more hard of belief. The old Sycorax saw her advantage, and gradually narrowed her magic circle around the devoted victim on whose spirit she practised.
SIR WALTER SCOTT *The Bride of Lammermoor* 1819

Symplegades In Greek mythology the Symplegades, literally 'Clashing Ones', were rocks at the north end of the Bosporus which were believed to clash together, crushing ships that passed between them. When Jason and the Argonauts had to pass between them, a bird was released to fly ahead of the ship. The rocks came together and nipped off the bird's tail feathers, and as they recoiled again the Argonauts rowed through with all speed and lost only the ornament on the stern of the ship. After this, in accordance with a prophecy, the rocks remained still. *See also* JASON AND THE ARGONAUTS.

Taliesin Taliesin was a 6th-century Welsh bard, to whom a considerable quantity of poetry has been ascribed. He is the supposed author of *The Book of Taliesin* (14th c.), a collection of heroic poems.

> It was quite impossible—recounting tales in the presence of people who knew them already. She wondered how Taliesin, Demodocus and all the other storytellers had coped.
> ALICE THOMAS ELLIS *The 27th Kingdom* 1982

> If the Obie thing broke, the famed cottage (therapeutic oratory, refuge and sacrarium, Brentwood's own confessional Taliesin of above-the-line tears, fears and renewal) would be the sudden locus of *Hard Copy* helicopters, *Vanity Fair* layouts and O.J.ish lookie-loos.
> BRUCE WAGNER *I'm Losing You* 1997

Tamerlane Tamerlane or Tamburlaine (1336–1405) was born Timur Lenk and was the Mongol ruler of Samarkand from 1369 to 1405. With his force of Mongols and Turks he conquered a large area of Persia, northern India, and Syria and established his capital at Samarkand. Marlow's play about Tamerlane (1590) is entitled *Tamburlaine the Great*.

> Gina made it clear that Anstice . . . had consistently portrayed Richard as a Lionheart, a Tamburlaine, a veritable Xerxes in the sack.
> MARTIN AMIS *The Information* 1995

Tammany Hall Tammany Hall was the headquarters of a US Democratic Party organization that was very influential in New York City during the 19th and early 20th centuries. The organization was notorious for corruption and for maintaining power by the use of bribes, and the name Tammany Hall can now be used to denote any place of political corruption.

> He had been a legendary President of the Union, succeeding in getting elected in spite of being at Magdalen, a college with little or no history of involvement in the Union. He did this by creating what became known as 'the Magdalen Machine', a ruthless Tammany Hall-style operation that propelled several other Magdalen students to the presidency, including a hardline Communist called Malcolm Bull. *The Observer* 1997

Tannhäuser Tannhäuser (*c.*1200–*c.*1270) was a German lyric poet who became a legendary figure as a knight enamoured of a beautiful woman. She takes him into the grotto of Venus, where he spends seven years in revelry and debauchery. He then repents and goes to the Pope to ask for forgiveness. The Pope answers that it is as impossible for Tannhäuser to be forgiven as it is for his dry staff to burgeon. Tannhäuser leaves in despair, but after three days the Pope's staff does in fact blossom. The Pope sends for Tannhäuser, but he has returned to the grotto of Venus. The story is the subject of an opera by Wagner.

> Her Tannhäuser still moved on, his plodding steed rendering him distinctly visible yet.
> THOMAS HARDY *The Woodlanders* 1887

Tantalus In Greek mythology, Tantalus was the king of Phrygia who was punished for his misdeeds (including killing his son Pelops and offering his cooked flesh to the gods) by being condemned in Hades to stand up to his chin in water which receded whenever he tried to drink it and under branches of fruit which drew back when he tried to reach them. *See also* HADES.

> It may condemn us, Tantalus-like, to reach evermore after some far-off, unattainable good. *Harper's Monthly* 1858

> That must be it, it was all planned from the beginning, I was never to have her, always to be tormented, mocked like Tantalus.
> JOHN FOWLES *The Magus* 1977

> This is not the first time ill luck has befallen one of her projects: in fact her career has been punctuated by similar misfortunes. It's an architectural version of the torments of Tantalus: a competition is held; against all the odds Hadid wins; the photographers, the 15 minutes of fame ensue; then before one spade of earth can be turned, fate intervenes and kills the thing off. *Independent on Sunday* 1996

Tara's halls The Hill of Tara, to the north of Dublin, was the seat of the Irish god–kings in Irish mythology, and later associated with the historical high kings of Ireland until the 6th century AD. In the buildings there, 'Tara's halls', were held a national assembly and also gatherings for music and games. The idea of Tara's halls being empty and abandoned comes from Thomas Moore's poem 'The harp that once through Tara's halls' (1807):
'The harp that once through Tara's halls
The soul of music shed,
Now hangs as mute on Tara's walls
As if that soul were fled.'

> Now the vast press rooms were empty; as silent as Tara's halls.
> MICHAEL MOLLOY *Dogsbody* 1995

tar baby In one of Joe Chandler Harris's stories of Uncle Remus (pub. 1881-1910), Brer Fox, in one of his many attempts to catch Brer Rabbit, makes a baby out of tar and places it by the side of the road. When Brer

Rabbit comes along, he tries to talk to the tar baby and, receiving no reply, becomes angry and hits out at it, whereupon he sticks fast. A tar baby is something that is to be avoided, because it will cause problems for anyone who touches it.

> Turning to Salinas, she smiled again. 'No matter how you play him, Victor, Ricardo's sort of a tar baby. I suggest that you consider him more carefully before you imagine the jury weeping.'
> RICHARD NORTH PATTERSON *Eyes of a Child* 1995

> The trouble is that both men are tar babies, contaminating anyone who deals with them. *The Observer* 1996

Tardis The Tardis (Time and Relative Dimensions in Space) is the time machine in which Doctor Who travels around the galaxy in the BBC's long-running children's television series. From the outside it looks like an old-fashioned police box, and its most surprising feature is the fact that it is significantly larger on the inside than it is on the outside. *See also* DOCTOR WHO.

> The club at Hawaiian Gardens is like Dr Who's Tardis: from the outside it looks like a windowless brick box dumped between a liquor store, a discount petrol station, a health centre and an empty plot of land. Inside it is a hive of concentrating humanity, a sea of numbers. *The Observer* 1997

Tarentine Tarentum was an ancient city and seaport in southern Italy, now named Taranto. Lying in very fertile country, it became renowned for its wealth and luxury. Its honey, olives, and other products were praised by Horace.

> That Royal port and watering-place, if truly mirrored in the minds of the health-folk, must have combined, in a charming and indescribable manner, a Carthaginian bustle of building with Tarentine luxuriousness and a Baian health and beauty.
> THOMAS HARDY *The Return of the Native* 1880

Tarquin Tarquinius was the name of two semi-legendary kings of ancient Rome. According to legend, Sextus, the son of Tarquinius Superbus, raped Lucretia (or Lucrece), which led to the expulsion of the Tarquins from Rome by a rebellion under Brutus, and the introduction of republican government. The story is told in Shakespeare's poem *The Rape of Lucrece* (1594). *See also* LUCRETIA.

> There was but little of the Roman about Mr Harding. He could not sacrifice his Lucretia even though she should be polluted by the accepted addresses of the clerical Tarquin at the palace.
> ANTHONY TROLLOPE *Barchester Towers* 1857

Tartarus In Greek mythology, Tartarus was the lowest region of Hades, which was reserved for the punishment of the wicked for their misdeeds, especially those such as Ixion and Tantalus, who had committed some outrage against the gods. *See also* HADES.

> Down, downward they went, and yet farther down—their descent at each step seeming to outmeasure their advance. Their skirts were scratched noisily by the furze, their shoulders brushed by the ferns, which, though dead and dry, stood erect as when alive, no sufficient winter weather having as yet arrived to beat them down. Their Tartarean situation might by some have been called an imprudent one for two unattended women.
> THOMAS HARDY *The Return of the Native* 1880

> Your soul gets judged, then it's punishment or reward. Tartarus or the Elysian fields.
> CHARLES HIGSON *Getting Rid of Mr Kitchen* 1996

Tartuffe Tartuffe is the main character of Molière's play *Le Tartuffe; ou, L'Imposteur*, first performed in 1664. Tartuffe is a religious hypocrite who uses the sly pretence of virtue and religious devotion to win the admiration and friendship of an honest but foolish man, Orgon. Tartuffe cleverly persuades the wealthy Orgon to sign over all his property to him, while behind Orgon's back he makes advances to his wife and mocks his gullibility.

> 'I see it all,' said the archdeacon. 'The sly *tartufe*! He thinks to buy the daughter by providing for the father.'
> ANTHONY TROLLOPE *Barchester Towers* 1857

> That a figure such as Godwin Peak, a young man of vigorous intellect, preparing to devote his life to the old religion, should excite Mr Warricombe's interest was of course to be anticipated; and it seemed probable enough that Peak, exerting all the force of his character and aided by circumstances, might before long convert this advantage to a means of ascendency over the less self-reliant nature. But here was no instance of a dotard becoming the easy prey of a scientific Tartufe.
> GEORGE GISSING *Born in Exile* 1892

Tarzan Tarzan is a character in novels by Edgar Rice Burroughs and subsequent films and television series. *Tarzan of the Apes* (1914) is the first of Burroughs' tales. Tarzan is an English aristocrat, Lord Greystoke, who is abandoned as a small child in the African jungle and reared by apes. He is a very strong and fearless hero, often depicted as wrestling with wild animals or using liana vines to swing through the trees of the jungle. The name can be applied to any man of great physical strength and agility.

> 'The other side now, viejo,' he shouted up to Anselmo and climbed across through the trestling, like a bloody Tarzan in a rolled steel forest.
> ERNEST HEMINGWAY *For Whom the Bell Tolls* 1941

> Putting me to silence by brute strength? Okay, Tarzan. Then you'll never hear the rest—which is also the best.
> ROBERTSON DAVIES *The Manticore* 1972

I thought I recognized one of his buddies looking fetching in greasy styled hair and a stained T-shirt under a sports shirt he'd unbuttoned, son of an urban-Tarzan-gone-to-seed look.
KAREN KIJEWSKI *Wild Kat* 1994

Jeremy Taylor Jeremy Taylor (1613–67) was an Anglican clergyman and theologian. On the royalist side during the Civil War as chaplain to Charles I, he stayed true to his faith despite three periods of imprisonment.

Well, if I were so placed, I should preach Church dogma, pure and simple. I would have nothing to do with these reconciliations. I would stand firm as Jeremy Taylor; and in consequence should have an immense and enthusiastic congregation.
GEORGE GISSING *Born in Exile* 1892

Teflon Teflon® is a material used as a non-stick coating for pans and kitchen utensils. Its name can be used in connection with criminals who always manage to avoid having criminal charges 'stuck' on them, or with politicians who seem able to shrug off scandal or misjudgement so that nothing 'sticks'.

In their periods of melancholy, such as the day he walked from court after beating a charge of importing 1.4 tonnes of pure cocaine, they called him the 'Teflon criminal'. *The Observer* 1997

I've tried to learn other languages, can 'pretend talk' authentic-sounding Spanish, French, Italian, Russian, German and Swedish. But my Teflon mind won't hold real words and grammar.
SUSAN SUSSMAN with SARAJANE AVIDON *Cruising for Murder* 2000

Teletubbies The Teletubbies are characters created for a British children's television programme aimed at pre-school children and first broadcast in 1997. The four characters, Tinky Winky, Laa-Laa, Dipsy, and Po, look like lifesize dolls and speak in simplified babylike language.

Turok is a lucid champion of his discipline and is thoughtful enough to give me what I suspect is the Teletubbies' version of events. *The Observer* 1997

Shirley Temple Shirley Temple (b. 1928) won fame as an American child star, appearing in a succession of films in the 1930s, including *Curly Top* (1935) and *Dimples* (1936), in which she sang and danced. She is remembered for her sweet, innocent good looks, especially her mop of golden curls.

I felt a need for someone to want the black baby to live—just to counteract the universal love of white baby dolls, Shirley Temples, and Maureen Peals.
TONI MORRISON *The Bluest Eye* 1970

He made a chirping noise and patted his knee invitingly, and Hortense immediately leapt on his lap and starting rubbing her head against his chest, purring like mad. He tickled her under the chin, murmuring idiotic blandishments into her black velvet ears. 'Don't be fooled by the Shirley Temple

routine,' I said sourly. 'That cat is four kilos of cunning in a black fur coat.'
MICHÈLE BAILEY *Haycastle's Cricket* 1996

Beside McConnachie's massive bulk, Fizz looked like a kitten smiling up at a Rottweiler. Sun-bleached tendrils of hair framed a face that made Shirley Temple look depraved and her denim-blue eyes rested on Duncan with absolute faith and affection.
JOYCE HELM *Foreign Body* 1997

Mother Teresa Mother Teresa (1910–97) was a Roman Catholic missionary, born Agnes Gonxha Bojaxhiu of Albanian parents in what is now Macedonia. She became a nun in 1928 and went to India, where she devoted herself to helping the destitute. She founded the order of Missionaries of Charity, which became noted for its work among the poor and dying in Calcutta. Mother Teresa was awarded the Nobel Peace Prize in 1979. She is often referred to as the model of saintly compassion.

Or maybe she could go in for superhuman goodness, instead. Hair shirts, stigmata, succouring the poor, a kind of outsized Mother Teresa.
MARGARET ATWOOD *The Robber Bride* 1993

Then Hawkeye said, 'Shame about Jasper Moon. I rather liked him. He might have put his pecker in peculiar places, but his heart was in the right spot. Ever since I caught those young tearaways who'd been vandalizing his street door he always gave a good Christmas bung to the Widows and Orphans fund.' Rafferty frowned as yet another witness depicted Moon as aspiring to sainthood. What was it about the man? Their child-abuser seemed to be turning into a veritable Father Teresa.
GERALDINE EVANS *Death Line* 1995

'Bruises on your face hurt?' he asked, crouching down and lightly tapping his fingertips against my cheek, over the bridge of my nose. . . . 'Roz,' he said, 'could you bring me a clean towel?' 'There's one in the bathroom,' she snapped. 'Right through the kitchen, Mother Teresa.'
LINDA BARNES *Hardware* 1995

termagant Termagant was the name given in medieval morality plays to an imaginary deity of violent and turbulent character. The name now denotes an overbearing or shrewish woman.

Terminator In the film *The Terminator* (1984) and its sequel, *Terminator 2: Judgment Day* (1991), Arnold Schwarzenegger plays an almost indestructible android sent from the future. Both films are extremely violent, and the Terminator destructively deploys an arsenal of massive weaponry. *See also* ARNOLD SCHWARZENEGGER.

'I need you to help me take down a skip.' This meant Ranger either needed a good laugh or else he needed a white female to use as a decoy. If Ranger needed serious muscle he wouldn't call me. Ranger knew people who would

take on the Terminator for a pack of Camels and the promise of a fun time.
JANET EVANOVICH *Four to Score* 1998

Terpsichore Terpsichore (literally 'Delighting in Dance') was one of the nine Muses in Greek mythology, associated with dancing, particularly choral dancing and its accompanying song. The adjective derived from her name is 'Terpsichorean'. *See also* MUSES.

The old-fashioned fronts of these houses . . . rose sheer from the pavement, into which the bow-windows protruded like bastions, necessitating a pleasing *chassez-déchassez* movement to the time-pressed pedestrian at every few yards. He was bound also to evolve other Terpsichorean figures in respect of door-steps, scrapers, cellar-hatches, church buttresses.
THOMAS HARDY *The Mayor of Casterbridge* 1886

He offended her by refusing to go into a dance-hall on the grounds that the music was so bad that it was a sacrilege against St Cecilia and Euterpe and Terpsichore, when she just wanted to go in and lose her unhappiness in dancing.
LOUIS DE BERNIÈRES *Señor Vivo and the Coca Lord* 1991

Thais Thais was an Athenian courtesan, mistress of Alexander the Great, who accompanied Alexander on his Asiatic expedition. She was the subject of the novel *Thais* (1890) by Anatole France, which was made into an opera by Massenet (1894). Her name has become a byword for a prostitute.

A thousand taxis would yawn at a thousand corners, and only to him was that kiss forever lost and done. In a thousand guises Thais would hail a cab and turn up her face for loving. And her pallor would be virginal and lovely, and her kiss chaste as the moon.
E SCOTT FITZGERALD *The Beautiful and the Damned* 1922

Thalia Thalia was one of the nine Muses in Greek mythology, associated especially with comedy and bucolic poetry. *See also* GRACES, MUSES.

Call me the Great Escapologist. Call me Harry Houdini. Hail Thalia, Muse of Comedy. Oh boy I need a round of applause.
JULIAN BARNES *Talking It Over* 1991

Thermopylae Thermopylae was a narrow pass in ancient Greece which was along the main route into southern Greece taken by armies invading from the north and consequently an important site for defence. The most famous battle fought at the pass was between invading Persians, commanded by Xerxes, and an army of approximately 6 000 Greeks, including 300 Spartans, under the leadership of Leonidas, king of Sparta. The Persians found an alternative mountain pass and were able to come upon the Greeks from behind. Many of the Greek allies departed before the battle, but Leonidas, his Spartans, and many Thespians and Thebans died in defence of the pass. Simonides' epitaph on the battle read:

'Go, tell the Spartans, thou who passest by,
That here obedient to their laws we lie.'
See also XERXES.

> He would much prefer not to die. He would abandon a hero's or a martyr's end gladly. He did not want to make a Thermopylae, not be Horatius at any bridge, nor be the Dutch boy with his finger in that dyke.
> ERNEST HEMINGWAY *For Whom the Bell Tolls* 1941

> He shivered and then stood erect. He had made a decision; it would be another Thermopylae. If three hundred Spartans could hold out against five million of the bravest Persians, what could he not achieve with twenty divisions against the Italians?
> LOUIS DE BERNIÈRES *Captain Corelli's Mandolin* 1994

Theseus In Greek mythology, Theseus was the son of Aegeus, king of Athens, who volunteered to be one of the seven youths sacrificed annually to the Minotaur, a creature with a man's body and a bull's head, in the labyrinth at Knossus. He managed to kill the Minotaur and escaped from the labyrinth using a ball of thread given to him by Ariadne, which he unravelled as he went in and followed back to find his way out again. *See also* ARIADNE, LABYRINTH, MINOTAUR.

> Now I really was Theseus; somewhere in the darkness Ariadne waited; and perhaps the Minotaur.
> JOHN FOWLES *The Magus* 1966

Thespis Thespis was a Greek dramatic poet of the 6th century BC and is generally regarded as the founder of Greek tragedy, having introduced the role of the actor in addition to the traditional chorus. The word 'Thespian', which derives from his name, means 'relating to drama or acting'.

> If Mrs. Caesar Augustus Conquergood's name might appear, alone, at the top of an otherwise double column of patrons of the Salterton Little Theatre then, in Nellie's judgment, the drama had justified its existence, Thespis had not rolled his car in vain.
> ROBERTSON DAVIES *Tempest-Tost* 1951

thirty pieces of silver Thirty pieces of silver was the payment made to Judas Iscariot for betraying Jesus in the Bible. *See* JUDAS.

> His only direct contact with Bellegarde was when Sir Robert sent him the hundred pounds reward that had been posted for solving the murder. To Julian it seemed more like thirty pieces of silver.
> KATE ROSS *Cut to the Quick* 1993

Thor In Scandinavian mythology, Thor, the son of Odin and Frigga, was the god of thunder and war. He was also the god of the weather, agriculture, and the home. He was usually represented as a man of enormous strength armed with a hammer called Mjollnir, which returned to his hand after he had thrown it. Thor also wore iron gloves to help him grasp his hammer and belt, which doubled his strength. *See also* ODIN.

> But Arthur never faltered. He looked like a figure of Thor as his untrembling arm rose and fell, driving deeper and deeper the mercy-bearing stake, whilst the blood from the pierced heart welled and spurted up around it.
> BRAM STOKER *Dracula* 1897

Thoth In Egyptian mythology, Thoth was the god of the moon, wisdom, writing, and the sciences. He is usually represented with the head of an ibis.

> He was an important man. He wielded power: power of appointment, power of disappointment, power of the cheque book, power of Thoth and the Mercurial access to the Arcana of the Stant Collection.
> A. S. BYATT *Possession* 1990

Thought Police In George Orwell's novel *Nineteen Eighty-Four* (1949), the Thought Police are the secret police whose job is to control and change the thoughts of anyone who dares to think independently, using brainwashing and torture. *See also* ORWELL.

Thraso Thraso is a boastful soldier in the Roman writer Terence's comedy *Eunuchus* (first performed in 161 BC). His name, and the related adjective 'Thrasonical', can be used to denote someone who is vain and boastful.

> Mr O'Rourke, surely you are not so Thrasonical as to declare yourself a genius?
> TIMOTHY MO *An Insular Possession* 1986

Three Musketeers Athos, Porthos, and Aramis are the three friends whose adventures with D'Artagnan are celebrated in Alexandre Dumas's novel *The Three Musketeers* (1844). They declare their comradeship with the famous rallying-cry 'All for one, and one for all!'

> And then Weary tied in with two scouts, and they became close friends immediately, and they decided to fight their way back to their own lines. They were going to travel fast. They were damned if they'd surrender. They shook hands all around. They called themselves 'The Three Musketeers'.
> KURT VONNEGUT *Slaughterhouse-Five* 1969

> Finchley and Rawlings were active together in an African-American police fraternity. Each took a D'Artagnan-Athos view of slights towards the other.
> SARA PARETSKY *Guardian Angel* 1992

> Hawk leaned down and fed sticks into the woodstove. Anna guessed that whatever gnawed at Holly was eating him. Once more she had the sense that they were two aspects of one person. This night it was the Holly aspect that spoke. Hawk stood back, a reservoir of strength for her to draw on. 'Porthos and Aramis,' Anna said aloud. Watching the two faces, so alike, she had put the allusion together. 'How long have the three of you been diving together?'
> NEVADA BARR *A Superior Death* 1994

Three Stooges The Three Stooges were an American comedy act of the 20th century known for their physical and sometimes cruel brand of slapstick comedy. The original three stooges were Larry Fine (Louis Feinberg), Moe Howard (Harry Moses Horwitz), and Curly Howard (Jerome Lester Horwitz). They starred in over 200 short films from the 1930s to 1960s, and several feature-length films, including *Snow White and the Three Stooges* (1961) and *The Three Stooges Meet Hercules* (1962).

> It was great, Vic. God, I wish I'd brought my camera. It took 'em about an hour to get out of here and all the time we're boo-hoo-hooing like we're the Three Stooges and can't help ourselves.
> SARA PARETSKY *Guardian Angel* 1992

Thule *See* ULTIMA THULE.

Thumbelina Thumbelina is a tiny girl in a fairy tale by Hans Christian Andersen who, after being rescued by a swallow, marries the equally tiny king of the Angels of the Flowers.

Thyestes In Greek mythology, Thyestes was the brother of Atreus, with whose wife he committed adultery. In revenge, Atreus invited him to a banquet and served him the flesh of Thyestes' own children to eat. Thyestes fled in horror, laying a curse on the house of Atreus. *See also* ATREUS.

Tigger Tigger is the cheerful bouncy tiger in A. A. Milne's children's book *The House at Pooh Corner* (1928). *See also* WINNIE THE POOH.

> I'd just finished a second piece of toast when Greg, like Tigger in mid-bounce, made his entrance.
> JUDITH CUTLER *Dying for Power* 1998

Timbuktu Timbuktu (or Timbuctoo) is a town in northern Mali, thought of as a very faraway place.

> And he yelled at us to get out of the station before he kicked our arses to Timbuctoo.
> CHRISTOPHER HOPE *Darkest England* 1996

Tinker Bell In J. M. Barrie's play *Peter Pan* (first performed in 1904), Tinker Bell is a fairy and a friend of Peter's. It is said in the play that every time someone says that they do not believe in fairies, a fairy dies. When Tinker Bell herself is close to death, members of the audience are invited to clap their hands to show that they do believe in fairies, and thus save Tinker Bell's life. Tinker Bell can be alluded to for her diminutive size. *See also* PETER PAN.

> Since that first glimpse from the road, he had worked his way much nearer the headwall, passing the first of the ridges and reaching a point just below the middle crest. In the low, ruddy light from the west his big-featured face and

bright hair moved from place to place like a coin of light in a lens. Tinker Bell. Tinker Bell with cord trousers and boots and a check shirt with a brilliant yellow silk scarf at the neck which he hadn't even removed.

DOROTHY DUNNETT *Moroccan Traffic* 1991

She wondered about it. But only for a second. The lorries from W Crisp were due in an hour to take away one hundred thousand. She looked at herself backed by all this moving product. A small, a fragile, young thing achieving, magnifying. Tinkerbell with a mobile phone.

MICHAEL CARSON *Dying in Style* 1998

Tin Man In L. Frank Baum's children's story *The Wizard of Oz* (1900), the Tin Woodman is one of Dorothy's companions on her journey to find Oz. When Dorothy and the Scarecrow first meet the Tin Woodman, he is frozen in position, having been caught in the rain while chopping wood. He is freed by Dorothy, who locates his oil can and oils his joints. The Tin Woodman is now more popularly known as the Tin Man, as the character was called in the 1939 film of the book starring Judy Garland. *See also* WIZARD OF OZ.

Lucy had a gift for making me feel like the Tin Man rusting in the forest. Was I becoming the rigid, serious adult I would have disliked when I was her age?

PATRICIA CORNWELL *Cruel and Unusual* 1993

He stood from a crouched position, his knees cracking as he rose. He and the Tin Man—they needed oil.

FAYE KELLERMAN *Sanctuary* 1994

After he'd been taken off the ventilator and was no longer being fed immobilising drugs that 'turned me into the Tin Man, forcing open one eye, twitching one little finger', and after he knew that he was, after all, going to live, the psychological reactions set in. *The Observer* 1996

I froze. I understand now why rape victims say that they didn't do anything—you know, scream or try to fight the man off—because I seized up like the Tin Man in *The Wizard of Oz*.

LAURA WILSON *Dying Voices* 2000

Tin Pan Alley Tin Pan Alley is the name given to a district in New York (28th Street, between 5th Avenue and Broadway) where many songwriters, arrangers, and publishers of popular music were based. The district gave its name to the American popular music industry between the late 1880s and the mid-20th century.

All this litter lies amid the desert's natural untidiness, the endless scatter of bony apparently lifeless scrub that speckles it from horizon to horizon. The only clear spaces are the tracks along which wind the occasional line of trucks or armoured cars, the 'Tin-Pan Alleys' defined by petrol cans.

PENELOPE LIVELY *Moon Tiger* 1988

Tiresias In Greek mythology, Tiresias was a blind soothsayer from Thebes who was renowned for his wisdom. In one legend, he was blinded as a young man by Athene as a punishment for seeing her bathing naked. Later, relenting somewhat, she gave him the gift of prophecy in compensation.

> The eyes of Lucian Freud's sitters as they stare out from his pictures suggest that, like the blind Tiresias, they 'have foresuffered all'. *New York Review of Books* 1993

Titan The Titans were the older gods of Greek mythology who preceded the Olympians and were the children of Uranus (Heaven) and Gaia (Earth). They rebelled against and overthrew Uranus and were in turn defeated by their own children, the Olympians, led by Zeus. A person of very great strength and size can be described as a Titan.

> Laputa was in truth a Titan, who in the article of death could break down a bridge which would have taken any three men an hour to shift.
> JOHN BUCHAN *Prester John* 1910

> They respected him because he spoke English, though they could scarcely believe he had actually been to England. England they held to be a sort of paradise, the abode of titans.
> OLIVIA MANNING *The Spoilt City* 1962

> He let out a howl and stayed where he was, face down on the ground. He looked just as big prone as he had upright; a fallen Colossus, a toppled Titan.
> ELIZABETH PETERS *Silhouette in Scarlet* 1983

> However thin and bedraggled he had become since he had gone to the front, Velisarios was still the biggest man that anyone had ever seen, and Carlo, despite his equivalent experiences on the other side of the line, was also the biggest man that anyone had ever seen. Both of these Titans had become accustomed to the saddening suspicion within themselves that they were freaks.
> LOUIS DE BERNIÈRES *Captain Corelli's Mandolin* 1994

Titania In Shakespeare's *A Midsummer Night's Dream* (1600), Titania is the queen of the fairies, and wife of Oberon. While she sleeps in her 'flow'ry bed', Oberon drops on her eyelids the juice from a magic flower which will make her fall in love with the first creature she sees when she wakes. This turns out to be Bottom the weaver, who has been given an ass's head by the mischievous sprite Puck. *See also* SHAKESPEARE.

> She lay curled up on the sofa in the back drawing-room in Harley Street, looking very lovely in her white muslin and blue ribbons. If Titania had ever been dressed in white muslin and blue ribbons, and had fallen asleep on a crimson damask sofa in a back drawing-room, Edith might have been taken for her.
> ELIZABETH GASKELL *North and South* 1854–5

> I'm going to rescue your wife, selfish man. She's an exquisite little Titania.
> KATHERINE MANSFIELD *Marriage à La Mode* 1920–4

Titanic The *Titanic* was a British passenger liner which was claimed to be unsinkable. On her maiden voyage in 1912, the ship struck an iceberg in the North Atlantic and sank with the loss of 1 490 lives. The scale of the loss of life, mainly men, was a consequence of the over-confidence of the owners of the liner, the White Star Line. The company was so sure of the ship's design and engineering they provided only a few lifeboats, believing that they would never be needed. The *Titanic* is often alluded to as an example of a foolish belief in the ability of modern science to eliminate danger, or more frequently as an unavoidable disaster.

> Jane Collingswood looked at Rachel for a second, then said, 'I think you're being very brave. I don't know how I'd hold up if I were in your shoes.' I did. Jane Collingswood could survive the sinking of the *Titanic*.
> STEVEN WOMACK *Dead Folks' Blues* 1992

> Janey had it right, Ben. Booze. Dope. Just different seats on the *Titanic*.
> JUSTIN SCOTT *Stone Dust* 1995

Tithonus In Greek mythology, Tithonus was a Trojan prince who was so beautiful that the goddess Aurora fell in love with him. She asked Zeus to grant him immortality but forgot to ask for eternal youth, and he became very old and decrepit although he talked perpetually. Tithonus pleaded with Aurora to remove him from this world and she changed him into a grasshopper.

Titian Titian (1477–1576), whose Italian name was Tiziano Vecellio, was a Venetian painter and one of the greatest artists of the high Renaissance. He is known particularly for his sumptuous mythological works, such as *Bacchus and Ariadne* (1522–3) and *Diana Surprised by Actaeon* (1556–9), noted for their brilliant colours, especially glowing reds and deep blues.

> Miss Templeman deposited herself on the sofa in her former flexuous position, and throwing her arm above her brow—somewhat in the pose of a well-known conception of Titian's—talked up at Elizabeth-Jane invertedly across her forehead and arm.
> THOMAS HARDY *The Mayor of Casterbridge* 1886

> How odd that bones, reminders of old mortality, should be considered essential to beauty in this perverse age. What of Titian and Rubens?
> ALICE THOMAS ELLIS *The 27th Kingdom* 1982

Tityus Tityus was a giant of Greek mythology, punished with eternal torture in the underworld for attempting to rape Leto, the mother of Apollo and Artemis. Vultures continually devoured his liver.

Mr Toad In Kenneth Grahame's story for children *The Wind in the Willows* (1908), Mr Toad of Toad Hall is passionately devoted in turn to boats, gypsy caravans, and then the motorcar. He buys 'a shiny new motor-car, of great size, painted a bright red (Toad's favourite colour)'. Because of his inability to resist the lure of fast driving, Badger and Rat take his car and try to keep him off the road, deeming him unsafe, but he steals a car and sets off again. He 'was only conscious that he was Toad once more, Toad at his best and highest, Toad the terror, the traffic queller, the Lord of the lone trail, before whom all must give way or be smitten into nothingness and everlasting night'.

> Crouching over the wheel, a cross between Jehu and Mr Toad of Toad Hall, Crosby bent his mind to covering the distance, while Detective Inspector Sloan addressed himself over the car radio to every police officer in 'F' division.
> CATHERINE AIRD *After Effects* 1996

> A few months ago he would have been hunched forward on one of the straight-backed dining chairs, glued to the screen of his computer. But Norman, like Mr Toad, flits in and out of hobbies, changing corresponding identities with a fickleness that belies his constancy when it comes to the two things that matter to him: money and friends.
> PAUL BENNETT *False Profits* 1998

Sweeney Todd Sweeney Todd was a fictional barber who murdered his customers with a razor and then had his lover serve up the remains in a meat pie. He was the central character in several plays by George Dibdin Pitt (1799–1855), including *Sweeney Todd: The Demon Barber of Fleet Street*.

Tom Thumb Tom Thumb was the hero of an English folk tale, the son of a ploughman and his wife who was only as tall as his father's thumb. After many adventures he was knighted by King Arthur. General Tom Thumb was the name given to Charles Stratton (1838–83), an American midget exhibited in the Barnum and Bailey shows.

Tonto Tonto, a Native American, is the trusty companion and friend of the masked law-enforcer the Lone Ranger in the radio and television series (1956–62). *See also* LONE RANGER.

> Come on Mark. The days of the Lone Ranger are far behind. Everybody needs their Tonto.
> MEL STEIN *White Lines* 1997

Tophet Tophet was the name of a place in the Valley of Hinnom to the south of Jerusalem. Hinnom was known as the Valley of Slaughter (Jer. 7: 31-2), and was used for idolatrous worship, with children being burnt alive as sacrifices to the idol Moloch. Later Tophet was used for burning refuse, and bonfires were kept burning there for this purpose. Hence there is a strong association between the name and the fires of Hell.

> It seemed the great Black Parliament sitting in Tophet. A hundred black faces turned round in their rows to peer; and beyond, a black Angel of Doom was beating a book in a pulpit.
> HERMAN MELVILLE *Moby Dick* 1851

> The careless sergeant smiled within himself, and probably too the devil smiled

from a loop-hole in Tophet, for the moment was the turning-point of a career.
THOMAS HARDY *Far from the Madding Crowd* 1874

Topsy Topsy is the mischievous little black slave girl in Harriet Beecher
Stowe's novel *Uncle Tom's Cabin* (1852), whose 'woolly hair was braided in
sundry little tails, which stuck out in every direction'. She has been kept in
complete ignorance by her owners, and knows nothing about her family.
When asked who she is and who were her parents, Topsy replies, 'Never was
born, never had no father, nor mother, nor nothin'. I 'spect I grow'd. Don't
think nobody never made me.' *See also* UNCLE TOM.

Black women in terrycloth robes with their faces greased and their straightened
hair done in small tight plaits like Topsy.
CHESTER HIMES *Blind Man with a Pistol* 1969

Torquemada Tomás de Torquemada (1420–98) was a Dominican monk and
the first inquisitor-general of Spain, remembered for his pitiless cruelty.
Anyone who questions a person persistently can be described as a
Torquemada.

He brought up Rosemary's loss of faith almost at once, and at every subsequent
opportunity thereafter. He was very dissatisfied with Rosemary's explanation
that 'it just went', but he failed to get much more out of her. He clearly had
ambitions to be a Torquemada, without any of the necessary skills.
ROBERT BARNARD *The Bad Samaritan* 1995

tortoise Aesop's fable 'The Hare and the Tortoise' relates how a hare,
jeering at the slow pace of a tortoise, challenged the latter to a race. On the
day of the race the hare, confident of his greater speed, lay down to rest and
fell asleep. The tortoise plodded on and won the race, leading to the moral
that 'Slow but steady wins the race'. The tortoise can be alluded to as an
example of patient perseverance. *See also* AESOP'S FABLE.

Toulouse-Lautrec Henri Marie Raymonde de Toulouse-Lautrec (1864–1901)
was a French painter and lithographer. His reputation largely rests on his
colour lithographs from the 1890s depicting scenes of Parisian low life,
actors, music-hall singers, circus artists, prostitutes, and waitresses in
Montmartre. The Moulin Rouge series of posters (1894) is particularly well
known. His work is characterized by strong silhouettes, large areas of flat
garish colour, and theatrical lighting. The artist broke both his legs in
childhood, as a result of which he was stunted in growth, and the
appearance of Toulouse-Lautrec himself is sometimes alluded to.

My mother arrived in the kitchen barefoot. The sight of her bunions and her big
yellow toenails annoyed me. She had wrapped herself in an impossible, shot-
silk tea-gown. She had the florid look of one of Lautrec's ruined doxies.
JOHN BANVILLE *The Book of Evidence* 1989

Tower Hill The scaffold on Tower Hill was the place where traitors imprisoned in the Tower of London, often high-ranking state prisoners, were executed by beheading. The first such execution there was in 1388 and the last in 1747, though the site was also used for public hangings until 1783.

> His execution was a hole-and-corner affair. There was no high scaffolding, no scarlet cloth (did they have scarlet cloth on Tower Hill? They should have had), no awe-stricken multitude to be horrified at his guilt and be moved to tears at his fate—no air of sombre retribution.
> JOSEPH CONRAD *Lord Jim* 1900

Tower of Babel According to the book of Genesis, the descendants of Noah decided to build a city and a tower, the Tower of Babel, 'whose top may reach unto heaven' (Gen. 11: 4). On seeing the tower, God was concerned that man was becoming too powerful and so decided to thwart him by introducing different languages: 'Go to, let us go down, and there confound their language, that they may not understand one another's speech' (Gen. 4: 6–7). Having caused the people to be mutually incomprehensible, God then dispersed and scattered them. The story can be mentioned in the context of linguistic diversity, particularly when this severely hampers communication, or can refer to the confused noise of several or many voices.

> I take it, that the earliest standers of mast-heads were the old Egyptians; because, in all my researches, I find none prior to them. For though their progenitors, the builders of Babel, must doubtless, by their tower, have intended to rear the loftiest mast-head in all Asia, or Africa either; yet (ere the final truck was put to it) as that great stone mast of theirs may be said to have gone by the board, in the dread gale of God's wrath; therefore, we cannot give these Babel builders priority over the Egyptians.
> HERMAN MELVILLE *Moby Dick* 1851

> 'This is the original Tower of Babel,' Harris said. 'West Indians, Africans, real Indians, Syrians, Englishmen, Scotsmen in the office of Works, Irish priests, French priests, Alsatian priests.'
> GRAHAM GREENE *The Heart of the Matter* 1948

> Shanghai is the biggest building site since the Tower of Babel. *Correspondents Look Ahead, BBC Radio 4* 1997

t

Tower of London The Tower of London is a fortress in central London, built by William the Conqueror, used as a royal residence and later as a state prison.

Tower of Siloam In the New Testament book of St Luke, Jesus tells the story of the collapse of the Tower of Siloam, which killed eighteen people, saying that we should not assume that because these eighteen suffered this fate they were more wicked than others. 'Or those eighteen, upon whom the tower in Siloam fell, and slew them, think ye that they were sinners above all men that dwelt in Jerusalem? I tell you, Nay: but, except ye repent, ye shall all likewise perish' (Luke 13: 14–15).

> How did their household differ from that of any other clergyman of the better
> sort from one end of England to the other? Why then should it have been upon
> them, of all people in the world, that this tower of Siloam had fallen?
> SAMUEL BUTLER *The Way of All Flesh* 1903

Town Mouse and Country Mouse In Aesop's fable 'The Town Mouse and
the Country Mouse', the town mouse visits the country mouse and is
unimpressed by the food that he has to offer. He invites the country mouse
to visit him in town and the country mouse is amazed at the quality and
variety of the food available. But they are interrupted by people and have to
flee, terrified. Eventually the country mouse retires back to the country
where the food might be plain but at least he can eat it in safety. *See also*
AESOP'S FABLE.

> But now those old feelings were rising to the surface again, the feelings of
> inadequacy, of being the country mouse, the poor relation, the social misfit, the
> butt of someone's joke.
> LISA JEWELL *Ralph's Party* 1999

Dick Tracy Dick Tracy was one of the first American comic-strip detectives,
drawn by Chester Gould and first appearing in 1931. Tracy joins forces with
the police to find the criminals who have kidnapped his girlfriend and
murdered her father, and goes on to become a tireless fighter for justice,
pursuing criminals at great risk to himself.

> The work I do for nonprofits is limited to writing the occasional check. Anyway,
> I never wanted to be Dick Tracy, running around town with a gun.
> SARA PARETSKY *Tunnel Vision* 1994

Trafalgar The battle of Trafalgar, one of the decisive naval battles of the
Napoleonic Wars, was fought on 21 October 1805 off the Cape of Trafalgar on
the south coast of Spain. The British fleet under Nelson won a victory over
the combined fleets of France and Spain, and Napoleon was never again able
to mount a serious threat to British naval supremacy. Nelson was killed
during the battle. *See also* NELSON.

Tree of Knowledge According to the book of Genesis, the Tree of
Knowledge of good and evil grew in the Garden of Eden and bore the
forbidden fruit which Eve was tempted by the serpent to eat. 'The woman
saw that the tree was good for food, and that it was a delight to the eyes, and
that the tree was to be desired to make one wise, she took of its fruit and ate;
and she gave some to her husband, and he ate. Then the eyes of both were
opened, and they knew that they were naked' (Gen. 3: 6–7). To 'eat from the
Tree of Knowledge' is to obtain knowledge at the cost of a loss of innocence.
See also ADAM AND EVE.

> I do not actually remember the curtains of my room being touched by the
> summer wind although I am sure they were; whenever I try to bring to mind

this detail of the afternoon sensations it disappears, and I have knowledge of the image only as one who has swallowed some fruit of the Tree of Knowledge—its memory is usurped by the window of Mrs Van der Merwe's house and by the curtains disturbed, in the rainy season, by a trifling wind, unreasonably meaning a storm.

MURIEL SPARK 'The Curtain Blows by the Breeze' in *The Collected Stories* 1961

Captain Tripps Captain Tripps is the name given to a deadly flu virus which is accidentally released from a laboratory in Stephen King's science fiction novel *The Stand* (1978), killing over 90 per cent of the population. The book was made into a successful film in 1994.

A plague: the American version of the Black Death, an antiquated form of Captain Tripps, killing two out of every three people. The survivors abandoning a desolated community, carting thousands and thousands of dead bodies with them? Not bloody likely.

NEVADA BARR *Mountain of Bones* 1995

Tristram and Iseult In the medieval legend, Tristram (or Tristan, or Tristrem) is sent to seek the hand of Iseult (or Isolde) on behalf of his uncle King Mark of Cornwall. During the voyage in which Tristram escorts Iseult to Cornwall, the couple mistakenly drink a love potion which had been intended for Iseult and Mark on their wedding night. Tristram and Iseult fall hopelessly in love, although Iseult is contracted to marry Mark. In one version of the story, King Mark finds the pair lying in the forest with a sword between them. In another version, Tristram marries another woman but, when dying, sends for Iseult. He arranges a signal from the boat in which she would be travelling to let him know whether she is on board. If she is, a white flag will be flown; a black flag will be flown if she is not. When the boat arrives, the white flag is flying, but his wife tells him it is black and he dies in despair, believing that Iseult has not come. The relationship is the subject of Wagner's opera *Tristan and Isolde*, which ends after Tristan has died in Isolde's arms. Tristram was an exceptional hunter from an early age.

There hasna been a better hunter since Tristrem's time.
WALTER SCOTT *The Bride of Lammermoor* 1819

I longed to sleep with her, I longed to be joined to her. But always my dreadful secret lay between us, like the sword between Tristan and Isolde.
JOHN FOWLES *The Magus* 1966

Passion is destructive. It destroyed Antony and Cleopatra, Tristan and Isolde.
W. SOMERSET MAUGHAM *The Razor's Edge* 1944

Triton Triton was the son of Poseidon and Amphitrite, in Greek mythology. He was half-man and half-fish, having a fish's tail.

Sometimes diving under her and merging the other side, spouting water like a Triton.
PATRICK O'BRIAN *Treason's Harbour* 1983

t

Troilus and Cressida Troilus and Cressida are characters from Greek mythology, mentioned in Homer's *Iliad* although not as lovers. The main post-classical sources for their story, which is set against the background of the Trojan War, are Chaucer's *Troilus and Criseyde* (*c.*1385) and Shakespeare's play *Troilus and Cressida* (1609). Troilus, a son of the Trojan king Priam, falls in love with Cressida, and she is persuaded to start a love affair with him by Pandarus, her uncle. Cressida is then required to move to the Greek camp, either because her father has defected to the Greeks or as part of the war negotiations. Once in the Greek camp, she betrays Troilus by falling in love with the Greek commander, Diomedes. *See also* SHAKESPEARE.

> In such a night
> Troilus methinks mounted the Troyan walls
> And sighed his soul toward the Grecian tents,
> Where Cressid lay that night.
> WILLIAM SHAKESPEARE *The Merchant of Venice* 1600

> 'Troilus loved and was fooled,' said the more manly chaplain. 'A man may love and yet not be a Troilus. All women are not Cressids.'
> ANTHONY TROLLOPE *Barchester Towers* 1857

Trojan The Trojans, the inhabitants of ancient Troy, had a reputation for working hard without complaining.

> And before long he was weeding away by moonlight like a Trojan—just as though the garden were his own and no danger threatened him within a thousand miles.
> HUGH LOFTING *Dr Dolittle's Circus* 1924

Trojan Horse In Greek mythology, the Trojan Horse, also known as the Wooden Horse of Troy, was a device used by the Greeks after the death of Achilles to capture the city of Troy. The Greek craftsman Epeius constructed a large wooden horse and left it outside the walls of the city. The Greeks then sailed out of sight, leaving behind just one man, Sinon, who pretended to be a Greek deserter. Sinon reported to the Trojans that the horse was an offering to Athene, which, if brought within the city walls, would render Troy impregnable. The horse was in fact full of Greek soldiers, and once it had been brought into Troy and night had fallen, these soldiers came out and took the city. *See also* GREEKS BEARING GIFTS, LAOCOÖN, TROJAN WAR.

Trojan War The legendary Trojan War is described in Homer's *Iliad*. It took place when Agamemnon put together a fighting force of Greeks to travel to Troy and recover his wife, Helen, who had been abducted by Paris. The first nine years of the war were taken up by a siege of the city of Troy. After the Trojans drove the Greeks back to the shore, there was a period of fighting; then the Greeks devised the ruse of the Trojan Horse, which enabled them to enter and take the city. Troy was sacked and razed by fire.

Many of the incidents and characters who are associated with the Trojan War are covered in more detail in other entries in this book. *See* ACHILLES,

ACHILLES AND PATROCLUS, AGAMEMNON, AJAX, APPLE OF DISCORD, ATREUS, EPEIUS, HECUBA, HELEN, LAOCOÖN, NESTOR, PARIS, PHILOCTETES, TROJAN HORSE.

> Max had got into conversation with a Welshman about some detail of trade union politics that sounded as complicated as the Trojan war and would probably go on as long.
> GILLIAN LINSCOTT *Blood on the Wood* 2003

Friar Tuck Friar Tuck is the jolly, rotund friar who forms part of Robin Hood's band of outlaws in the legend of Robin Hood. As well as for his large size, he can be alluded to for his characteristic tonsure. *See also* ROBIN HOOD.

> Rosie is about eighteen inches long, she has got a big head with fuzzy black hair in a Friar Tuck style.
> SUE TOWNSEND *The Growing Pains of Adrian Mole Aged 13¾* 1984

Turner Joseph Mallord William Turner (1775–1851) was an English painter who became interested in capturing the effects of atmospheric light in his pictures. His best-known paintings, such as *The Fighting Téméraire* (1838), depict dramatic skies using yellows, oranges, and reds in an impressionistic style.

> 'Look . . .' Barton nodded up towards the slope and the wood, to where they could just see Queronne in the lemon-white light. 'It's like a Turner canvas.'
> SUSAN HILL *Strange Meeting* 1971

Dick Turpin Dick Turpin (1705–35) was a famous English highwayman who started his career as a smuggler and cattle- and horse-thief. He was hanged at York for horse-stealing and murder.

Tutankhamun The tomb of Tutankhamun, in the Valley of the Kings in Egypt, was discovered by Howard Carter (1874–1939) and the earl of Carnarvon (1866–1923) in November 1922. Carnarvon died in Luxor shortly after the discovery from a mosquito bite which led to a blood infection and pneumonia. Carter died seventeen years later but before he was able to provide a final report on the find, having spent the intervening years conserving the contents of the tomb and sending them to the Cairo Museum. The association of the two deaths gave rise to a popular tradition that the tomb was cursed.

t

Archbishop Tutu Desmond Mpilo Tutu (b. 1931) is a South African clergyman. He served as general secretary of the South African Council of Churches in 1979–84, and during this time he became a leading figure in the struggle against the country's apartheid policies, advocating non-violent opposition. He was awarded the Nobel Peace Prize in 1984. Tutu became Johannesburg's first black Anglican bishop in 1985 and was archbishop of Cape Town from 1986 to 1996, when he retired. He was made head of the Truth and Reconciliation Commission in 1995.

> And I'm telling you, when Bacon gets hold of something, things happen. He's

not Martin Luther King or Bishop Tutu. Okay? He's not gonna win any Nobel
Prize. He's got his own way of doing things, and sometimes it might not stand
close scrutiny.
TOM WOLFE *The Bonfire of the Vanities* 1987

There were agonized decisions about who should appear where, when public
occasions demanded a presence if the movement were to retain its popular
power. He was no Tutu or Boesak or Chikane, and he could have been blacker,
but as one of the best speakers, bloodied by prison, he had to be used only
where he would be most effective with least risk.
NADINE GORDIMER *My Son's Story* 1990

Tweedledum and Tweedledee Tweedledum and Tweedledee were
originally names applied to the rival composers Handel and Bononcini in a
1725 satirical poem by John Byrom, making the point that the differences
between them were so small as to be negligible. The names were later
popularized when Lewis Carroll used them for two identical characters in
Through the Looking-Glass (1872). They are fat, quarrelsome twin brothers who
fight a ridiculous battle with one another. Two people or things that are so
alike that they are practically indistinguishable can be referred to as
Tweedledum and Tweedledee.

Weary looked like Tweedledum or Tweedledee, all bundled up for battle. He
was short and thick. He had every piece of equipment he had ever been issued,
every present he'd received from home.
KURT VONNEGUT *Slaughterhouse-Five* 1969

The two heads turned like Tweedledum and Tweedledee, and nodded solemnly
in tempo.
ELIZABETH PETERS *Silhouette in Scarlet* 1983

Coffin studied them, then drew the interview to an end. Won't get much more
out of Tweedledum and Tweedledee just now, he thought.
GWENDOLINE BUTLER *A Dark Coffin* 1995

Twiggy Twiggy (b. Lesley Hornby, 1949) was an English fashion model of the
1960s. She began her modelling career in 1966, becoming famous for her
short-haired, thin-bodied boyish look. Twiggy later appeared in films such as
The Boyfriend (1971) and *The Blues Brothers* (1980).

He looked over at waiflike Louise, a Twiggy lookalike with her cropped hair and
miniskirt.
EILEEN GOUDGE *Such Devoted Sisters* 1992

Twilight Zone *The Twilight Zone* was an American television series (1959–65)
that told a different supernatural or science fiction story every week. The
title of the series is sometimes alluded to in the context of a seemingly
supernatural occurrence or a highly improbable coincidence.

Oliver Twist In Charles Dickens's novel *Oliver Twist* (1837–8), Oliver is born a pauper in a workhouse and suffers the cruel and restrictive conditions of the regime under the parish beadle, Mr Bumble. Inadequately fed, he infuriates the authorities by asking for more food. He later runs away to London, where he falls into the hands of a gang of pickpockets led by Fagin. *See also* DICKENSIAN, FAGIN.

> This is the worst Christmas Day I have ever spent. . . . I feel like Oliver Twist in the workhouse.
> V. S. NAIPAUL *A House for Mr Biswas* 1961

> Poor Davey! How you have starved! A real little work-house boy, an Oliver Twist of the spirit!
> ROBERTSON DAVIES *The Manticore* 1972

> He turned and looked down at me. The big, ugly face showed new signs of fatigue. 'I'm depressed, Alex.' He held out his empty cup like some overgrown, slack-jawed Oliver Twist. 'Which is why I'll tolerate more of this disgusting swill.'
> JONATHAN KELLERMAN *When the Bough Breaks* 1992

> The parliament will fuel high expectations that cannot be met under the Government's current spending plans. Scots would pretty soon come to see London as a hindrance and would act like little Oliver Twists, asking for more and more. *The Observer* 1997

Tyburn Tyburn was a place in London, near Marble Arch, where public hangings were held from 1388 to 1783. The triangular gallows there were often referred to as Tyburn Tree.

> She didn't deserve to die. Perhaps none of us do, not like that. We don't even hang the Whistler now. We've learned something since Tyburn, since Agnes Poley's burning.
> P. D. JAMES *Devices and Desires* 1989

Typhoid Mary Typhoid Mary was the name given to Mary Mallon (d. 1938), an Irish-born American cook who transmitted typhoid fever in the United States. Her name can be used to suggest someone whose presence can instantly empty a place of people, or whom nobody wants to know or be near.

> He's dying, man, and what do they do? The assholes wear surgical masks and stand back ten feet from his bed like he's Typhoid Mary while they're asking him shit.
> PATRICIA CORNWELL *Body of Evidence* 1991

> Archie Young looked round the canteen which was almost empty, all the tables near them had cleared with speed. It was like being Typhoid Mary, he thought.
> GWENDOLINE BUTLER *The Coffin Tree* 1994

> 'Deirdre?' The Head of Sixth Form forced his vocal cords into action. 'You

threaten me—my sixth form—with Deirdre Lessing, the Typhoid Mary of West Sussex?'

M. J. TROW *Maxwell's Flame* 1995

Few of my old friends were around any longer and the two who were both had girlfriends to whom the sound of my voice was less welcome than that of Typhoid Mary.

LAUREN HENDERSON *The Black Rubber Dress* 1997

Tyr In Scandinavian mythology, Tyr was the god of battle, corresponding to the Roman Mars.

Udolpho Ann Radcliffe's *The Mysteries of Udolpho* (1794) is a gothic novel set at the end of the 16th century. Most of the action takes place in the sinister castle of Udolpho in which the sliding panels, secret passages, and apparently supernatural occurrences are all typical of the genre.

> Was there a 'secret' at Bly—a mystery of Udolpho or an insane, an unmentionable relative kept in unsuspected confinement?
> HENRY JAMES *The Turn of the Screw* 1898

Ugly Duckling In Hans Christian Andersen's fairy story *The Ugly Duckling* (1846), a cygnet in a brood of ducklings is mocked by the other ducks and hens for his drab appearance. He runs away, struggles through the winter, and in the spring meets three swans. Looking at his reflection in the water, he discovers that he too has turned into a beautiful swan. The term 'ugly duckling' can be applied to an ugly person, or a person initially thought ugly who turns out to be extremely beautiful.

> She was a fairy princess who had taken a fancy to a little boy, clothed him, petted him, turned him from a laughing stock into an accepted member of her society, from an ugly duckling into a swan.
> L. P HARTLEY *The Go-Between* 1953

> All you Ugly Ducklings out there, take heart; you are better off than you realize. When people love you, they love the important things about you, the things that endure after wrinkles and middle-aged spread have set in—your brains and your personality and your sense of humor. When people look at me, all they see is a blown-up centerfold. Nobody takes me seriously. When I was younger, I wanted to be little and cuddly and cute. Now I'd settle for being flat-chested and myopic.
> ELIZABETH PETERS *Street of the Five Moons* 1978

Ugly Sisters In the children's fairy story, Cinderella has two ugly stepsisters who despise and ill-treat her. The stepsisters are invited to the prince's ball and spend days fussing over what they are going to wear to the ball and how beautiful they are going to look. In pantomime versions of the tale, the stepsisters are presented as the Ugly Sisters, played by men, and made grotesquely ugly so that their vanity becomes ridiculous and comical. *See also* CINDERELLA.

'Ma's got this cousin with a flat near the Colosseum.' 'And is this cousin young, male, gorgeous and loaded?' 'As a matter of fact, she's ninety-two and looks like a cross between the Hunchback of Notre Dame and one of the ugly sisters.'
SUSAN MOODY *The Italian Garden* 1994

Ultima Thule Thule was a land first described by the ancient Greek explorer Pytheas as being six days' sail north of Britain, thought to be Iceland, Norway, or the Shetland Islands. To the Romans it was the northernmost extremity of the world, described by Virgil as Ultima Thule, literally 'Farthest Thule'. It has come to denote any distant unknown region or, figuratively, the limit of what is attainable.

Forget Marat, and the black distress he bred; he's going to create a new, Ultima Thule atmosphere, very plain, very bright, every word translucent, smooth. The air of Paris is like dried blood; he will (with Robespierre's permission and approval) make us feel that we breathe ice, silk and wine.
HILARY MANTEL *A Place of Greater Safety* 1992

After a brief crawl he reached the end, striking his head against hard larch, the Ultima Thule of the *Daphne*, beyond which he could hear the water slapping against the hull.
UMBERTO ECO *The Island of the Day Before* 1994

Ulysses Ulysses is the Roman name for Odysseus. *See* ODYSSEUS. *See also* ODYSSEY.

Her father was a romantic wanderer—a sort of Greek Ulysses.
THOMAS HARDY *The Return of the Native* 1880

Her hair blew forward, clouding her face a little. I wanted to brush it back, or to shake her hard; I wasn't quite sure which. In the end I stared out to sea, a little on the same principle as Ulysses when he tied himself to the mast.
JOHN FOWLES *The Magus* 1966

Many older and wiser heads have been enmeshed in her toils, and you would do well to stop your ears with wax, as Ulysses made his sailors do, to escape the Sirens.
MARGARET ATWOOD *Alias Grace* 1996

Uncle Tom Uncle Tom is a loyal and ever-patient black slave, the main character of Harriet Beecher Stowe's anti-slavery novel *Uncle Tom's Cabin* (1852). The term can be applied to a black man whose behaviour to white people is regarded as submissively servile, and by extension can refer to anyone regarded as betraying his or her cultural or social allegiance.

'Ignore his lying tongue,' Ras shouted. 'Hang him up to teach the black people a lesson, and theer be no more traitors. No more Uncle Toms. Hang him up theer with them blahsted dummies!'
RALPH ELLISON *Invisible Man* 1952

'Mary Lou's being modest. She had them rolling in the aisles with her tour de

force called "Black Studies as a Floating Signifier".' Amiss seized the claret.
'What's the female equivalent of an Uncle Tom?'
RUTH DUDLEY EDWARDS *Matricide at St Martha's* 1994

Undine Undine was the spirit of water created by Paracelsus. She had no soul, but if she married a mortal and bore him a child, she could obtain a soul along with all the pains of the human race.

'You looked like Undine.' And so she had, with all the brilliant colour of her eyes, fern-green and pebble-brown, caught into the sudden light, and the quivering reflections of rain upon the window staining the whiteness of her face with greenish gleams.
EDITH PARGETER *By Firelight* 1948

She seemed to him to possess a sort of Undine beauty.
GRAHAM GREENE *The Heart of the Matter* 1948

Urania Urania was one of the nine Muses in Greek mythology, associated especially with astronomy. *See* MUSES.

Uriah Uriah the Hittite was an officer in David's army, the husband of Bathsheba. David slept with Bathsheba, whom he had seen bathing, and when she became pregnant, sent Uriah to his death in the front line of battle so that he could marry her. Uriah was given a letter to carry to his commanding officer, Joab, which was in fact Uriah's own death warrant: 'Set Uriah in the forefront of the hardest fighting, and then draw back from him, that he may be struck, and die' (2 Sam. 11: 15). *See also* DAVID.

Usher *See* HOUSE OF USHER.

Utopia Utopia (literally 'No-Place') is an imaginary place or condition of ideal perfection. The word was first used as the name of an imaginary island, governed on a perfect political and social system, in the book *Utopia* (1516) by Sir Thomas More. The name has given us the adjective 'utopian', meaning 'idealistic'.

The founders of a new colony, whatever Utopia of human virtue and happiness they might originally project, have invariably recognized it among their earliest practical necessities to allot a portion of the virgin soil as a cemetery, and another portion as the site of a prison.
NATHANIEL HAWTHORNE *The Scarlet Letter* 1850

Oh, is it, then, Utopian
To hope that I may meet a man
Who'll not relate, in accents suave,
The tales of girls he used to have?
DOROTHY PARKER 'De Profundis' in *Enough Rope* 1926

Their education had taught them to judge civilization entirely by material progress and they were, in consequence, ashamed of their background and

anxious to forget it. A suburbia covering the length and breadth of Iraq was the Utopia of which they dreamed.
WILFRED THESIGER *The Marsh Arabs* 1964

We got talking about the permissive sexual mores of the ancient Polynesians, which Yolande described as 'the kind of sexual Utopia we were all pursuing in the sixties—free love and nudity and communal child-rearing'.
DAVID LODGE *Paradise News* 1992

u

Vale of Tempe The Vale of Tempe is a narrow valley between Mount Olympus and Mount Ossa in north-eastern Thessaly, Greece. The ancient Greeks dedicated Tempe to the cult of Apollo, so it became associated with music and beauty. Because of its proximity to Mount Olympus, the home of the gods, it can also represent earthly life rather than divine.

> Marty said no more, but occasionally turned her head to see if she could get a glimpse of the Olympian creature who, as the coachman had truly observed, hardly ever descended from her clouds into the Tempe-vale of the parishioners.
> THOMAS HARDY *The Woodlanders* 1887

> He had meant to state his passion from the past, to provide pipes, timbrels, wild ecstasy, Tempe, and the Vale of Arcady.
> A. S. BYATT *The Virgin in the Garden* 1978

Valhalla In Norse mythology, Valhalla was the great banqueting hall in Asgard in which heroes who had been slain in battle feasted with Odin eternally. *See also* NIFLHEIM, ODIN.

> It was an admirable commentary on the deliberations of the afternoon and underneath the frenetic licence and fervour of the singing he seemed to catch the drift of older undertones— passages from Tacitus, perhaps? Or the carousings of death-dedicated warriors heading for valhalla?
> LAWRENCE DURRELL *Mountolive* 1958

> Her pale eyes glittered and her face was deathly pale. With her colourless eyelashes and blonde hair she presented a strange sight, almost like a carved marble head. He thought she looked terrifying, like a Valkyrie come to escort him to some icy-halled Valhalla, whether he wanted to go or not.
> ANN GRANGER *Candle for a Corpse* 1995

> 'Then why didn't you just live there happily ever after?' 'Because there's a snake in every paradise, even if it is Valhalla, or Nirvana, or whatever it was they called it in Persia.'
> ANDRÉ BRINK *Imaginings of Sand* 1996

Valkyrie In Scandinavian mythology, the Valkyries (literally 'Choosers of the Slain') were Odin's twelve handmaidens who hovered over battlefields, selected the most valiant warriors to die in battle, and escorted them to

Valhalla, the hall of heroes. They appear in Wagner's opera *Die Walküre* (1854–6). *See also* ODIN, WAGNER.

> Dorothy Thompson seemed to me an overpowering figure in a Wagnerian opera, a Valkyrie, deciding with careless pointing of her spear who should die on the battlefield.
> JOHN HERSEY 'Sinclair Lewis' in *Life Sketches* 1987

> Martya ducked the tub aimed at her; the second exploded at Kareen's feet. Muno's attempt to lay down a covering fire for his party's retreat backfired when Enrique dropped to his knees and scrambled away down the hall toward his screaming Valkyriesque protectors.
> LOIS MCMASTER BUJOLD *A Civil Campaign* 1999

Valley of (the Shadow of) Death The phrases 'the Valley of the Shadow of Death' and 'the Valley of Death' have various literary sources. Psalm 23 contains the lines 'Yea, though I walk through the valley of the shadow of death, I will fear no evil.' In John Bunyan's allegory *The Pilgrim's Progress*, Christian passes through the Valley of the Shadow of Death, with a dangerous bog on one side and a deep ditch on the other, and the mouth of Hell close by. Alfred, Lord Tennyson's poem *The Charge of the Light Brigade* (1854) contains the famous refrain
'Into the valley of Death
Rode the six hundred.'
See also PILGRIM'S PROGRESS.

> But after a time he fell silent, and there was only the sound of Charley's hooves on the road, and the rustling of the slight wind. I thought I might jump down from the wagon, and run off into the woods; but knew I would not get far, and even if I did, I would then be eaten by the bears and wolves. And I thought, I am riding through the Valley of the Shadow of Death, as it says in the Psalm; and I attempted to fear no evil, but it was very hard, for there was evil in the wagon with me, like a sort of mist.
> MARGARET ATWOOD *Alias Grace* 1996

Valley of Humiliation The Valley of Humiliation is one of the places that Christian and Christiana pass through in John Bunyan's allegory *The Pilgrim's Progress*. To enter the Valley of Humiliation is to be humbled or humiliated. *See also* PILGRIM'S PROGRESS.

> Melbury had entered the Valley of Humiliation even further than Grace. His spirit seemed broken.
> THOMAS HARDY *The Woodlanders* 1887

Vandal The Vandals were a Germanic people that overran part of Roman Europe in the 4th and 5th centuries AD. Of the various invading peoples of this period (Goths, Visigoths, Huns, etc.), it is the Vandals whose name is most closely associated with the idea of mass invasion and wanton destruction. In modern usage, a vandal is a person who maliciously destroys or damages property. *See also* GOTHS.

> For too long, Scotland has measured itself against England and contented itself that things aren't so bad. Exiles, ironically, return with their gold with tales of a society and civilisation inhabited by Vandals and Goths. *The Observer* 1997

Vanderbilt Cornelius Vanderbilt (1794–1877) was a US businessman and philanthropist who amassed a fortune from shipping and railroads. Subsequent generations of his family increased the family wealth and continued his philanthropy.

> The word 'mural' suggests to most people either the wall spaces of Rockefeller Center or the wealth of a Vanderbilt. *American Home* 1936

Van Dyck Sir Anthony Van Dyck (also Vandyke; 1599–1641) was a Flemish painter chiefly famous for his portraits of the English aristocracy and royalty, including a number of Charles I. Van Dyck's refined and languidly elegant portrait style determined the course of English portraiture for at least 200 years. The term 'Vandyke' is also applied to a broad white collar which has the edge cut into deep points and to a neat pointed beard, both of which commonly appear in Van Dyck's portraits. Vandyke brown is a deep, rich brown colour.

> One was a young man, in the Vandyke dress common to the time of Charles I.
> WALTER SCOTT *The Bride of Lammermoor* 1819

> Well, I see this rather like a portrait by Van Dyck, with a good deal of atmosphere, you know, and a certain gravity, and with a sort of aristocratic distinction.
> W. SOMERSET MAUGHAM *Cakes and Ale* 1930

Van Gogh Vincent (Willem) Van Gogh (1853–90) was a Dutch Post-Impressionist painter. The bright colours (especially the vivid yellows) and thick, frenzied, swirling brushwork give his paintings a passionate intensity. Among his best-known works are several studies of sunflowers and landscapes such as *A Starry Night* (1889). Van Gogh suffered from depression, and after a violent quarrel with Gauguin he cut off part of his own ear. He eventually committed suicide. Among his portraits is *Self-Portrait with Bandaged Ear* (1889).

> I went in search of Randolph. He wore a large lint pad pressed to the left side of his head, held in place by a rakishly angled and none-too-clean bandage. . . . he bore a striking resemblance to poor, mad Vincent in that self-portrait made after he had disfigured himself for love.
> JOHN BANVILLE *The Book of Evidence* 1989

Dolly Varden In *Barnaby Rudge* (1841) by Charles Dickens (1812–70), Dolly Varden is the daughter of Gabriel Varden, who marries Joe Willet. She is a pretty, lively girl, but somewhat proud and wilful, qualities which she comes to regret. *See also* DICKENSIAN.

> What I needed was not one of those stuck-up Dolly Vardens but a good sensible girl with her head screwed on straight who would do what she was told.
> ROBERTSON DAVIES *Fifth Business* 1970

Vashti The Old Testament book of Esther relates how King Ahasuerus ordered that his wife, Queen Vashti, should come before him, 'But the queen Vashti refused to come at the king's commandment by his chamberlains: therefore was the king very wroth, and his anger burned in him' (Esther 1: 12). As a result of this disobedience, Vashti was banished and the king married Esther in her place. *See also* AHASUERUS, ESTHER.

> Rumour, for a wonder, exaggerated little. There threatened in fact, in Grace's case as in thousands, the domestic disaster, old as the hills, which, with more or less variation, made a mourner of Ariadne, a by-word of Vashti, and a corpse of Amy Dudley.
> THOMAS HARDY *The Woodlanders* 1887

veil of Isis Isis was an ancient Egyptian nature and fertility goddess, wife and sister of Osiris and mother of Horus. She is usually depicted as a woman with cow's horns, between which was the disc of the sun. Statues of her often carried the inscription 'I am all that is, has been, and shall be, and none among mortals has lifted my veil'. Hence the phrase 'to lift the veil of Isis' means to penetrate a great mystery. *See also* ISIS AND OSIRIS.

> That Fitzpiers would allow himself to look for a moment on any other creature than Grace filled Melbury with grief and astonishment. In the simple life he had led it had scarcely occurred to him that after marriage a man might be faithless. That he could sweep to the heights of Mrs. Charmond's position, lift the veil of Isis, so to speak, would have amazed Melbury by its audacity if he had not suspected encouragement from that quarter.
> THOMAS HARDY *The Woodlanders* 1887

Velázquez Diego Rodríguez de Silva y Velázquez (1599–1660) was the foremost Spanish artist of the 17th century. In 1623 he was appointed court painter to Philip IV in Madrid, where he painted many notable portraits of the royal family. He produced several portraits of the king's daughter, the doll-like Infanta Margareta Teresa, including *Las Meninas* (1656), which portrays her with her retinue of maidservants and dwarfs, and *The Infanta Margareta in Blue* (1659). Velázquez's works also include a number of impressive equestrian portraits.

> Style? Why, she had the style of a little princess; if you couldn't see it you had no eye. It was not modern, it was not conscious, it would produce no impression in Broadway; the small, serious damsel, in her stiff little dress, only

looked like an Infanta of Velazquez.
HENRY JAMES *Portrait of a Lady* 1881

He was a beautiful horse that looked as though he had come out of a painting by Velasquez.
ERNEST HEMINGWAY *For Whom the Bell Tolls* 1941

Rosa crossed the living room and sat next to Terri, folding her hands. Somewhere between Terri's childhood and now, her mother had lost the habit of smiling; her face often seemed as somber as a Velázquez oil.
RICHARD NORTH PATTERSON *Eyes of a Child* 1995

Venus Venus was the Roman goddess identified with the Greek Aphrodite, the goddess of beauty, fertility, and sexual love. She was supposed to have been born from the sea-foam, though she is sometimes depicted (as in Botticelli's painting *The Birth of Venus*) emerging from a large seashell. She was the mother of Eros. *See also* APHRODITE.

She ducked gracefully to slip into the lacy fabric which her mother held above her head. As she rose Venus-like above its folds there was a tap on the door, immediately followed by its tentative opening.
EDITH WHARTON *The Custom of the Country* 1913

Here was beauty. It silenced all comment except that of eager praise. A generation that had admired piquante women, boyish women, ugly, smart, and fascinating women was now confronted by simple beauty, pure and undeniable as that of the young Venus whom the Greeks loved to carve.
STELLA GIBBONS *Cold Comfort Farm* 1932

I have already said that I am not much of an actor, but I gave a powerful, if crude impersonation of the hero who is tremendous on the field of Mars but slighted in the courts of Venus.
ROBERTSON DAVIES *Fifth Business* 1970

'I mean give us a hand!' snapped Cutangle, rising from the wavelets like a fat and angry Venus.
TERRY PRATCHETT *Equal Rites* 1987

Venus de Milo The Venus de Milo is a classical marble statue of the goddess Aphrodite (*c.*100 BC), now in the Louvre in Paris. The statue, missing its arms, was discovered on the Greek island of Melos in 1820. Aphrodite's short wavy hair is tied back with a ribbon.

She had crisp white hair which she wore like the Venus of Milo.
W. SOMERSET MAUGHAM *Cakes and Ale* 1930

Veronese Paolo Veronese (*c.*1528–1588) was an Italian painter, born in Verona as Paolo Caliari and later named after his birthplace. He specialized in biblical, allegorical, and historical subjects, and is particularly known for his richly coloured feast and banquet scenes such as *The Marriage at Cana* (1562) and *The Feast in the House of Levi* (1573). The latter, originally entitled *The*

Last Supper, was the subject of a trial by the Inquisition, which objected to Veronese's habit of inserting profane details (dogs, soldiers, drunkards, etc.) into his sacred pictures.

> Let me set the scene. There were ten of us . . . at the back of the restaurant, at a long table in a slight alcove—a touch Last Supper after Veronese.
> JULIAN BARNES *Talking It Over* 1991

Amerigo Vespucci Amerigo Vespucci (1451–1512) was an Italian-born navigator in whose honour the Americas were named. He made two voyages to the New World, in which he discovered the mouth of the Amazon and explored the north-east coast of South America. His distorted and embroidered account of his travels, *Four Voyages*, was published in 1507, and, based on this, the Latin version of his name, 'Americus', was given to the two American continents.

> She first reached Wildeve's Patchs, as it was called, a plot of land redeemed from the heath, and after long and laborious years brought into cultivation. The man who had discovered that it could be tilled died of the labour: the man who succeeded him in possession ruined himself in fertilizing it. Wildeve came like Amerigo Vespucci and received the honours due to those who had gone before.
> THOMAS HARDY *The Return of the Native* 1878

Vesuvius Vesuvius is an active volcano near Naples, in southern Italy. It erupted violently in AD 79, burying the towns of Pompeii and Herculaneum.

> She also became more and more irascible and violent, something of a terror in the neighbourhood; and visitors had to keep a safe distance. Her eruptions were vesuvian.
> ANDRÉ BRINK *Imaginings of Sand* 1996

> Senoritas are the wear this season in Hell, and I am tired with the long climb to a pulsing Vesuvius of alien pricks.
> WILLIAM BURROUGHS *Naked Lunch* 1959

Via Dolorosa The Via Dolorosa, Latin for 'Sorrowful Way', is another name for Jesus Christ's route to Calvary to be crucified. It can be used to describe any difficult or distressing experience. *See also* JESUS.

> Edna came in with a tea tray, taking in her sister's distress with a knowing look. It would be a long, perhaps endless, via dolorosa for Phyllis.
> VIVIEN ARMSTRONG *Fly in Amber* 2000

Vicar of Bray The Vicar of Bray is the subject of an anonymous 18th-century song in which he boasts that he has been able to adapt to the differing religious regimes of, successively, Charles II, James II, William III, Anne, and George I. 'The Vicar of Bray' stands for someone who will change their opinions in order to retain power.

> The Ashleys have always had a talent for retaining just what they wanted to

retain, while adapting immediately and without effort to the winning side. The Vicar of Bray must have been a close relation. We were Catholics right up to Henry VIII, then when the Great Whore got him we built a priest's hole and kept it tenanted until we saw which side the wafer was buttered, and then somehow there we were under Elizabeth, staunch Protestants and bricking up the priest's hole, and learning the Thirty-nine Articles off by heart, probably aloud.
MARY STEWART *Touch Not the Cat* 1976

Inevitably, his success had encouraged sniping and his detractors claimed that, amongst political turncoats, he made the Vicar of Bray look like a model of constancy.
MARTIN EDWARDS *Yesterday's Papers* 1994

Queen Victoria The famous line 'We are not amused' is attributed to Queen Victoria (1819–1901) in Caroline Holland's *Notebooks of a Spinster Lady* (1919), though whether she actually uttered these words is not at all certain. The quotation is so well known, though, that Queen Victoria can be alluded to in the context of a lack of a sense of humour or an inability to see the funny side of a situation.

His smile was wide, about three-quarters of an inch. 'I don't amuse easy,' he said. 'Just like Queen Victoria,' I said.
RAYMOND CHANDLER *The High Window* 1943

Vietnam The Vietnam War was a lengthy conflict between South Vietnam and the communist North Vietnam. The United States became militarily involved on the side of the South in the 1960s, but the war became unpopular and the United States withdrew its troops in 1973 under the presidency of Richard Nixon, ceding victory to the North. References to Vietnam often suggest the idea of a worsening disaster.

Anderson Country is Forgan's Vietnam: she's committed to it and can't get out.
The Independent 1994

St Vitus St Vitus (d. *c.*300) was a Christian martyr said to have died during the reign of Diocletian. He was the patron of those who suffered from epilepsy and certain nervous disorders, including St Vitus's dance (Sydenham chorea). St Vitus is sometimes alluded to in the context of violent physical movement.

Not a limb, not a fibre about him was idle; and to have seen his loosely hung frame in full motion, and clattering about the room, you would have thought Saint Vitus himself, that blessed patron of the dance, was figuring before you in person.
WASHINGTON IRVING *The Legend of Sleepy Hollow* 1819–20

Vivien *See* NIMUE.

Vlad the Impaler Vlad the Impaler (c.1431–1476) was a Romanian prince. Although little is known about his life or brief period of rule, he is remembered as a cruel tyrant, whose punishments included impaling victims on stakes. Because of his legendary cruelty, including rumours that he drank the blood of his victims, he is believed by some to be the inspiration behind the Dracula legend and Bram Stoker's novel *Dracula* (1879).

> 'Yes,' she said. The final sibilant came out in a long hiss. 'You were everything I ever wanted, but you had her!' The way she said *her* sounded like she might have been speaking of Vlad the Impaler.
> ROBERT B. PARKER *Walking Shadow* 1994

Volpone Volpone is the main character in Ben Jonson's comedy of the same name (printed 1607). Volpone, a childless man, lures potential heirs to his bedside, where he pretends he is about to die imminently. His sidekick, Mosca, persuades each of these suitors that a suitable expensive present will confirm that he is the heir, and Volpone gloats gleefully over the gifts. Eventually Mosca engineers a position in which he can blackmail Volpone. Rather than lose his wealth to him, Volpone confesses to the authorities and the two are punished for their scheme.

Voltaire Voltaire was the pseudonym of François-Marie Arouet (1694–1778). A French writer, dramatist, and poet, Voltaire was a leading figure of the Enlightenment. He condemned intolerance and superstition and was an outspoken critic of religious and social institutions, his radical views earning him several periods of imprisonment and banishment. His name is particularly associated with mocking scepticism.

> 'Sue, you are terribly cutting when you like to be—a perfect Voltaire!'
> THOMAS HARDY *Jude the Obscure* 1895

Vulcan Vulcan was the Roman god of fire and metalworking, corresponding to the Greek Hephaestus. He was lame as a result of having interfered in a quarrel between his parents (Juno and Jupiter). Ugly in appearance, he was married to the most beautiful of the goddesses, Venus (who had many affairs). He is said to have made Pandora (the first woman on earth), the thunderbolts of Zeus, and the armour of Achilles. Vulcan is often depicted at the forge.

> The picture you have just drawn is suggestive of a rather too overwhelming contrast. Your words have delineated very prettily a graceful Apollo: he is present to your imagination,—tall, fair, blue-eyed, and with a Grecian profile. Your eyes dwell on a Vulcan,—a real blacksmith, brown, broad-shouldered: and blind and lame into the bargain.
> CHARLOTTE BRONTË *Jane Eyre* 1847

> She considered the name her personal affair. She had arrived at it first purely on the basis of its ugly sound and then the full genius of its fitness had struck her.

She had a vision of the name working like the ugly sweating Vulcan who stayed in the furnace and to whom, presumably, the goddess had to come when called.
FLANNERY O'CONNOR *Good Country People* 1955

A Vulcan guarding the flames, he gives us instructions about which doors to keep closed or opened for proper distribution of heat, lays kindling by, discusses qualities of coal, and teaches us how to rake, feed, and bank the fire.
TONI MORRISON *The Bluest Eye* 1970

At Lord's Smith was the smith whose Vulcan hammer-blows beat out and shaped England's victory. *Sunday Telegraph* 1995

Wagner The German composer Richard Wagner (1813–83) developed an operatic genre which he called music drama, combining music, drama, verse, legend, and spectacle. His cycle of four operas known as the *Ring Cycle* (*Das Rheingold*, *Die Walküre*, *Siegfried*, and *Götterdämmerung*) are based loosely on ancient German sagas. The adjective 'Wagnerian' is applied to anything that evokes the dramatic music, storms, and strong emotions depicted in Wagner's operas. *See also* BRYNHILD, FLYING DUTCHMAN, GÖTTERDÄMMERUNG, LOHENGRIN, SIEGFRIED, VALKYRIES.

> The vroom and whoosh of the storm created an atmosphere of Wagnerian drama in a city now almost deserted, the usual late-night ravers keeping their heads down until the tempest blew itself out.
> VIVIEN ARMSTRONG *Fly in Amber* 2000

Waltons *The Waltons* was a popular US television series (1972–81) based on the life of its creator, Earl Hamner, Jr. Set in a poor area of Virginia during the Depression and the Second World War, the stories, often fairly sentimental, concerned the struggles and trials of a good-natured, honest family. The usual closing sequence, in which each member of the family called goodnight to the others, is much parodied. The Waltons can be alluded to in the context of a family that seems just too good to be true.

> Stewart's early life, I learnt, was rather sweet and Waltons-like. He loved his father and mother. He went to church.
> WILLIAM LEITH *The Observer* 1997

Wandering Jew In medieval legend, the Wandering Jew was a man condemned to roam the earth until the Day of Judgement, as a punishment for having taunted Christ on the way to the Crucifixion, urging him to go faster. In some versions of the legend he is given the name Ahasuerus.

> He would slouch out, like Cain or the Wandering Jew, as if he had no idea where he was going and no intention of ever coming back.
> CHARLES DICKENS *Great Expectations* 1861

> But her thoughts soon strayed far from her own personality; and, full of a passionate and indescribable solicitude for one to whom she was not even a

name, she went forth into the amplitude of tanned wild around her, restless as
Ahasuerus the Jew.
THOMAS HARDY *The Return of the Native* 1880

Warbucks *See* DADDY WARBUCKS.

V. I. Warshawski V. I. Warshawski is the Chicago-based private investigator
heroine of a series of novels by Sara Paretsky. Feisty, tough, and feminist, she
is, in the American tradition, not above breaking the law herself when
necessary.

> She knew as well as I that a million people pass through Heathrow every week.
> That London's a big place. That without a point of contact, not even V. I.
> Warshawski would have a hope in hell of locating Claire.
> MICHELLE SPRING *Running for Shelter* 1994

George Washington George Washington (1732–99) was the first president
of the United States, serving from 1789 to 1797. An early biographer of
Washington, Mason Weems, recounted a fanciful story of how Washington
as a boy, on receiving a new hatchet, chopped down his father's prized
cherry tree. When his father asked how the tree had fallen, Washington was
tempted to tell a lie, but then, 'looking at his father with the sweet face of
youth brightened with the inexpressible charm of all-conquering truth, he
bravely cried out, "I can't tell a lie. I did cut it with my hatchet." ' George
Washington is often mentioned as an example of someone who tells the
truth and admits to wrongdoing.

> 'You must have looked like George Washington or something.' 'If that was the
> old darling who never told a lie,' I had to admit, 'well really, not much.'
> JOHN MORTIMER *Rumpole's Return* 1980

> She didn't trust him any more. He'd had sex with her neighbour, impregnated
> her, he'd lied to her, he wasn't the man she'd thought he was, the honest
> George Washington, incapable of telling a lie.
> LISA JEWELL *Ralph's Party* 1999

Waterloo The battle between the French on one side and the British under
Wellington, the Dutch, and the Prussians on the other near the village of
Waterloo (now in Belgium) in 1815 was the final battle in the Napoleonic
Wars and marked the end of Napoleon's rule in Europe. The name can allude
to a decisive defeat from which recovery is impossible. *See also* WELLINGTON.

> He frowned and flipped the cigaret against the wall at the back of the cell. He
> was conscious of a dull burning resentment at having been sold by a lousy frail.
> He didn't claim to be smart but he didn't usually act that dumb. Well, a jane
> had been many a con's Waterloo, but that didn't ease the choking, self-
> contemptuous intensity of the chagrin.
> CHESTER HIMES *His Last Day* 1933

> So it was woe to the boulevard denizens for the next few weeks while

W

Buckmore Phipps and Gibson Hand worked at exorcising the memory of their Waterloo at the hands of Jukebox Johnson and a future corpse who called himself Harvey H.
JOSEPH WAMBAUGH *The Glitter Dome* 1981

As Stephen Fay meticulously details in his volume, *The Collapse of Barings*, the failure of the bank which manages the Queen's personal assets was in effect a Waterloo for British banking. *The Guardian* 1996

John Wayne John Wayne, born Marion Michael Morrison (1907–79), was a US film actor nicknamed the Duke and chiefly associated with his roles in such classic westerns as *Stagecoach* (1939), *Red River* (1948), *The Searchers* (1956), and *True Grit* (1969). He was known for his portrayals of tough but honest gunfighters or lawmen.

'Don't threaten me, McGraw,' Thayer growled. John Wayne impersonation.
SARA PARETSKY *Indemnity Only* 1982

A mythical John Wayne America, a land of free, rugged individualists that has been progressively undermined by federal laws and regulations. *The Independent* 1996

wedding guest *See* ANCIENT MARINER.

Wee Willie Winkie Wee Willie Winkie is a nursery rhyme character who makes sure that all children are in bed and asleep:
'Wee Willie Winkie runs through the town
Upstairs and downstairs in his night gown,
Rapping at the window, crying through the lock,
Are the children all in bed, for it's past eight o'clock?'

Wellington The first duke of Wellington (1769–1852) was a British soldier and statesman. His military victories included those against the French during the Peninsular War (1808–14) and in particular the defeat of Napoleon at the battle of Waterloo (1815). *See also* WATERLOO.

Well, I don't want to be a soldier, he thought. I know that. So that's out. I just want us to win this war. I guess really good soldiers are really good at very little else, he thought. That's obviously untrue. Look at Napoleon and Wellington. You're very stupid this evening, he thought.
ERNEST HEMINGWAY *For Whom the Bell Tolls* 1941

H. G. Wells H. G. Wells (1866–1946) was an English novelist best remembered for his science fiction novels, including *The Time Machine* (1895) and *the War of the Worlds* (1898).

He'd already established a business in Tehran. Cables, satellites, mobile phones, they were all a dream of the future when he started out, but he anticipated them all. When they were still close Yasmin had described him proudly as 'my own H. G. Wells'.
MEL STEIN *White Lines* 1997

Wells Fargo Wells Fargo was the name of a US transportation company, founded in 1852, which carried mail to and from the newly developed West, founded a San Francisco bank, and later ran a stagecoach service.

Wendy In J. M. Barrie's *Peter Pan* (1904), Wendy Darling is the girl who is taken with her brothers to the magical Never-Never Land and offers to become a mother to the Lost Boys there. When the Darling children finally return home, Wendy is allowed to go back once a year to Never-Never Land to do Peter's spring cleaning for him. Wendy represents an idealized vision of motherhood. *See also* PETER PAN.

> Oh, you know, she makes everything seem so snug and homey; she wants to be a dear little Wendy-mother to us all. Not being a Peter Pan myself, I don't like it.
> ROBERTSON DAVIES *Tempest-Tost* 1951

Werther In Goethe's romance *The Sorrows of Young Werther* (1774), Werther falls in love with Charlotte, who is betrothed to Albert, and gives himself up to a few weeks' happiness in Albert's absence. Then he tears himself away. Albert and Charlotte are married, and despair gradually comes over Werther, who finally takes his own life. 'Wertherian' can be used to describe morbidly sentimental, emotional distress.

> He should have spent this afternoon among the poor at St Ewold's, instead of wandering about at Plumstead, an ancient love-lorn swain, dejected and sighing, full of imaginary sorrows and Wertherian grief.
> ANTHONY TROLLOPE *Barchester Towers* 1857

> Only one thing was clear. Even if Maud would never again consider marrying him—which was no more than he deserved—he must get down on his knees and beg her pardon for the monstrous things he had said. After that, it did not matter what became of him. And he went away to dress for dinner, with the air of young Werther on his way to his suicide chamber.
> KATE ROSE *Cut to the Quick* 1993

John Wesley John Wesley (1703–91) was an English preacher and one of the founders of Methodism. He travelled throughout Britain, preaching and gaining converts.

West Side Story Bernstein and Sondheim's film musical *West Side Story* (1961) relocates the story of Romeo and Juliet to 20th-century New York. Shakespeare's feuding families the Montagues and the Capulets are represented as rival gangs, the Jets and the Sharks. Among several memorable dance sequences featuring fast, aggressive, athletic movements in the film is the 'rumble', danced as a stylized gang fight.

> The sweating, red-faced cops in their blue uniforms and white helmets slashed the hot night air with their long white billies as though dancing a cop's version of West Side Story.
> CHESTER HIMES *Blind Man with a Pistol* 1969

Mary Whitehouse Mary Whitehouse (1910–2001) was a British schoolteacher who founded the National Viewers and Listeners Association (now Mediawatch-UK) to campaign against bad language and immorality on television and radio.

> It is an absorption, as Foucault has noted, which links prudes and libertines. The Mary Whitehouses of this world are as preoccupied with sexuality as those they oppose. *The Observer* 1996

White Rabbit In Lewis Carroll's *Alice's Adventures in Wonderland* (1865), Alice follows the White Rabbit down a rabbit-hole and into Wonderland as he hurries along, constantly muttering to himself 'Oh dear! Oh dear! I shall be so late!' and 'Oh my ears and whiskers, how late it's getting!' *See also* ALICE IN WONDERLAND.

> 'Look, a student!' my friend cried, and we watched as he rolled by, wearing khaki shorts, a Stanford logo T-shirt and baseball hat, muttering like the white rabbit about being late for class. *The Independent* 1997

Whore of Babylon The Whore of Babylon is referred to in the book of Revelation. She is described as a woman sitting on a scarlet beast with seven heads and ten horns: 'The woman was arrayed in purple and scarlet colour, and decked with gold and precious stones and pearls, having a golden cup in her hand full of abominations and filthiness of her fornication.' On her forehead was written, 'Babylon the great, mother of harlots and abominations of the earth' (Rev. 17: 3–5). The term was applied to the Roman Catholic Church by the early Puritans, and could also be used to represent sexual immorality. *See also* BABYLON.

> I'd marry the W——of Babylon rather than do anything dishonourable!
> THOMAS HARDY *Jude the Obscure* 1895

> Here he was: leading foreigners over in hordes to places that were not theirs, to cause disputes, to uproot niggers, to plant the Whore of Babylon in the midst of the righteous!
> FLANNERY O'CONNOR *The Displaced Person* 1953

> Now there was Valentine—toute belle—and Mrs O'Connor, who at her best mightily resembled the Whore of Babylon.
> ALICE THOMAS ELLIS *The 27th Kingdom* 1982

Wicked Witch of the East In L. Frank Baum's story for children *The Wizard of Oz* (1900), the heroine, Dorothy, destroys the Wicked Witch of the East inadvertently when her house, carried to the land of Oz by a cyclone, falls on the witch, killing her and leaving only her feet sticking out. *See also* WIZARD OF OZ.

Wicked Witch of the West In L. Frank Baum's story for children *The Wizard of Oz* (1900), the heroine, Dorothy, destroys the Wicked Witch of the West, who has imprisoned her, by throwing a bucket of water over her, causing the witch to 'melt away to nothing'. *See also* WIZARD OF OZ.

> I dreamed I was taking a shower with Brandon, my wet skin slithering erotically against his. Then Paul Lynch was pressing his face against the streaming glass of the stall, contorting it like a stretched rubber mask. 'You're out of shampoo again,' he clucked. 'Such filthy habits.' I wanted Brandon to defend me, but when I looked back at him, the water was melting him away like the Wicked Witch of the West.
> LINDSAY MARACOTTA *Playing Dead* 1999

Wife of Bath In Geoffrey Chaucer's *The Canterbury Tales* (*c.*1343–1400), the Wife of Bath is one of the characters who tells a tale to the other travellers. She is a domineering, licentious, pleasure-seeking woman who has had five husbands and is on the lookout for her sixth. Her tale, *The Wife of Bath's Tale*, develops the theme of women's mastery over men. *See also* CHAUCER.

Wild Boy of Aveyron The Wild Boy of Aveyron was an 11-year-old boy who was found running wild and naked in a wood near Aveyron in the south of France in the early part of the 19th century. The French physician Jean Itard tried to train and educate him, and published an account of his experiences in *Rapports sur le sauvage d'Aveyron* (1807). 'The Wild Boy of Aveyron' can be used to describe someone who has absolutely no experience of the ways of the world, society, or people.

> 'People divide writers into two categories,' she went on, deeply embarrassed by his silence. 'Those who are preternaturally wise, and those who are preternaturally naïve, as if they had no real experience to go on. I belong in the latter category,' she added, flushing at the truth of what she said. 'Like the Wild Boy of the Aveyron.'
> ANITA BROOKNER *Hotel du Lac* 1984

Oscar Wilde The Irish writer Oscar Wilde (1854–1900) was imprisoned for two years in Reading Gaol (1895–7) for homosexual offences. His poem *The Ballad of Reading Gaol* (1898), concerning the trial and execution of the murderer Charles Thomas Wooldridge, is based on his experiences there and criticizes the prison's harsh conditions. His name can stand for being gay.

> 'Your brother Roderick, I think,' Colefax continued, 'had a fiancée and was engaged to be married?' 'Oh yes. They'd both dined with me that night at my club. There was absolutely none of the Oscar Wildes about Rory.'
> JOHN MORTIMER *Rumpole's Return* 1980

> Should I extend the week's grace to a fortnight? Convince myself that the poor woman would need more than a week to prepare for the biggest culture-shock since Oscar Wilde had gone inside?
> RICHARD HALEY *Thoroughfare of Stones* 1995

W

Lord Peter Wimsey Lord Peter Wimsey is the eccentric amateur sleuth created by Dorothy L. Sayers in a series of detective novels beginning with

Whose Body? (1923). A perfect gentleman with a degree from Oxford, he solves crimes with the aid of his loyal retainer Bunter.

windmill Tilt at windmills. *See* DON QUIXOTE.

Winnie the Pooh Winnie the Pooh is Christopher Robin's teddy bear in A. A. Milne's books *Winnie the Pooh* (1926) and *The House at Pooh Corner* (1928). He is a rather plump bear who is not particularly intelligent (he describes himself as 'a Bear of Very Little Brain') and has a constant craving for honey, often suggesting that it is 'time for a little something'. In one episode, he enters a rabbit's burrow, eats a considerable amount of honey, and then becomes stuck when trying to get out of the hole again. *See also* EEYORE, TIGGER.

> Charlie as crime preventer was like Winnie the Pooh as honey warden.
> SARAH LACEY *File under: Deceased* 1992

> It had been a long day. First, there had been the inspection of the roof-space at the Chavanacs' villa: an undignified episode, in which he had almost got stuck in a very small trapdoor (like Pooh Bear wedged in a window, Hugo said later).
> HILARY WHELAN *Frightening Strikes* 1995

Wise Men *See* MAGI.

Wise Men of Gotham Gotham is a village in Nottinghamshire which is associated with the English folk tale 'The Wise Men of Gotham', in which the inhabitants of the village demonstrated cunning by feigning stupidity. Gotham was proverbial in the Middle Ages for folly, and the phrase 'wise man of Gotham' used to mean a fool.

witches In Shakespeare's *Macbeth* (1623), the three weird sisters, or witches, encountered by Macbeth and Banquo on the blasted heath are described as 'So wither'd, and so wild in their attire,
That look not like th'inhabitants o'th'earth'
and later as 'you secret, black, and midnight hags'.

> She stood there, by that beech trunk—a hag like one of those who appeared to Macbeth on the heath of Forres.
> CHARLOTTE BRONTË *Jane Eyre* 1847

Witch of Endor In the book of Samuel, the Witch of Endor was the medium consulted by Saul when he was threatened by the Philistine army. At his request she summoned up the ghost of the prophet Samuel, who prophesied the death of Saul and the destruction of his army by the Philistines.

> Conjuration, sleight of hand, magic, witchcraft, were the subjects of the evening. Miss Pole was slightly sceptical, and inclined to think there might be a scientific solution found for even the proceedings of the Witch of Endor.
> ELIZABETH GASKELL *Cranford* 1853

Wizard of Oz In L. Frank Baum's *The Wizard of Oz* (1900), Dorothy journeys with her companions to see the Wizard of Oz in the hope that he will help her return home. Though he initially appears intimidatingly powerful, he turns out to be a fraud, not a wizard at all, but an old man who was blown to Oz from Omaha in a balloon. *See also* COWARDLY LION, END OF THE RAINBOW, MUNCHKIN, OZ, SCARECROW, TIN MAN, WICKED WITCH OF THE EAST, WICKED WITCH OF THE WEST, YELLOW BRICK ROAD.

> Suddenly, as if by magic, like something from the *Wizard of Oz*, the huge doors behind Gayfryd start to open by themselves, very slowly.
> IRENE DARIA *Fashion Cycle* 1990

> She squinted out the window some more, then came back to the table and picked up her glass. 'How can he see at night while he's wearing those sunglasses?' I gave her a little shrug. There are some things even the great and wonderful Oz does not know.
> ROBERT CRAIS *Lullaby Town* 1992

> 'You could say he was three parts mighty tycoon to one part Wizard of Oz.' 'What do you mean?' 'Just that. I think he was a bit of a charlatan in some ways.'
> LAURA WILSON *Dying Voices* 2000

wolf *See* BIG BAD WOLF, RED RIDING HOOD.

wolf in sheep's clothing The wolf in sheep's clothing is one of the fables of Aesop, a Greek storyteller who lived in the 6th century BC. The fable relates how a wolf decides to disguise himself as a sheep in an attempt to obtain an easy meal. He spends the day with a flock of sheep, fooling sheep and shepherd alike, and in the evening is shut into the fold with the other sheep. However, when the shepherd gets hungry later in the evening he comes to the fold to choose a sheep to eat and chooses the wolf, which he proceeds to eat on the spot. A 'wolf in sheep's clothing' is anyone who uses an outward appearance of friendship or kindness to conceal underlying hostility or cruelty. *See also* AESOP'S FABLE.

> I'm ordinarily the sweet soul, too good for this world, too kind for my own good, too gentle, a little lamb. To discover the wolf cub in lamb's skin doesn't suit my mother's preconceptions.
> EDMUND WHITE *A Boy's Own Story* 1982

Woman in White The novel *The Woman in White* (1860) by Wilkie Collins (1824–89) tells the story of a mysterious Woman in White, Anne Catherick, who has escaped from a mental asylum having been locked up there because she knows a discreditable secret about the past of the book's villain, Sir Percival Glyde. The term is used more generally about any woman dressed all in white. *See also* WILKIE COLLINS.

> She was a woman in white, being dressed in white silk, with white lace over it,

and with no other jewels upon her person than diamonds.
ANTHONY TROLLOPE *The Small House at Allington* 1862

Wonderland *See* ALICE IN WONDERLAND.

Wonder Woman Wonder Woman was a US comic-book heroine created in the 1940s by Charles Moulton and later developed into a television series. She was one of a race of lost Amazon women who had found a magic substance, Feminum, which gave them superhuman powers. Having travelled to the United States, Wonder Woman led an ordinary life as Yeoman Prince, but, when trouble threatened, could transform herself into Wonder Woman, clad in tights and a cape that looked something like the American flag.

> I stepped out of the shower and shook my head by way of styling my hair. I dressed in my usual uniform of spandex shorts and halter-style sports bra and topped it off with a Rangers hockey jersey. I took another look at my hair and decided it needed some help, so I did the gel, blow-dry, hair spray routine. When I was done I was several inches taller. I stood in front of the mirror and did the Wonder Woman thing, feet spread, fists on hips. 'Eat dirt, scumbag,' I said to the mirror.
> JANET EVANOVICH *Four to Score* 1998

Woody Woodpecker Woody Woodpecker is a cartoon character with a tall comb of red hair. He was created in 1940 by Ben Hardaway and has a raucous laugh.

> He has red hair that stands up at the top like Woody Woodpecker's.
> MARGARET ATWOOD *Cat's Eye* 1988

Bertie Wooster Bertie Wooster is the amiable but vacuous young man about town in *The Inimitable Jeeves* (1924) and the subsequent series of novels by P. G. Wodehouse. He relies on his resourceful valet, Jeeves, to rescue him from the predicaments his dim-wittedness lands him in. *See also* JEEVES.

> At the time the Tory press was portraying Tony Blair as a sort of upper-class twit, a Bertie Wooster figure with an idiotic grin. *The Observer* 1997

Lady Would-Be Lady Would-Be and her husband, Sir Politic Would-Be, are characters in Ben Jonson's comedy *Volpone* (1606), both pompous, foolish, and, as their name suggests, socially ambitious.

> And whomsoever you are to go to, will excuse you, when they are told 'tis *I* that command you not to go; and *you* may excuse it too, young Lady *Would-be*, if you recollect, that 'tis the unexpected arrival of your late lady's daughter, and your master's sister, that requires your attendance on her.
> SAMUEL RICHARDSON *Pamela* 1740

Wreck of the Hesperus 'The Wreck of the Hesperus' is the title of a poem by H. W. Longfellow (1840), which tells of the destruction of a schooner, the

Hesperus, which was caught in a storm and wrecked on the reef of Norman's Woe, off the coast of Massachusetts, in 1839.

> When he went back to the room it was filled with the slight but offensive smell of face powder and there were clothes everywhere. Miserably, he dressed. 'The wreck of the blasted Hesperus,' he said.
> V. S. NAIPAUL *A House for Mr Biswas* 1961

> And he would certainly have said I looked like the Wreck of the Hesperus; it was one of his few literary allusions.
> ROBERTSON DAVIES *The Manticore* 1972

Frank Lloyd Wright Frank Lloyd Wright (1869–1959) was an American architect whose early work, with its use of new building materials and cubic forms, was particularly significant for the development of modernist architecture.

> The house I'd been directed to looked more Frankenstein than Frank Lloyd Wright. It had more turrets and crenellations than Windsor Castle, all in bright red Accrington brick.
> VAL MCDERMID *Clean Break* 1995

writing on the wall *See* BELSHAZZAR.

W

Xanadu Xanadu is the name of the ancient city in south-east Mongolia where Kublai Khan (1216–94), the Mongol emperor of China, had his residence. Coleridge's poem 'Kubla Khan' (1816) begins with the famous words
'In Xanadu did Kubla Khan
A stately pleasure-dome decree.'
The name can be applied to a place of dreamlike magnificence, beauty, and luxury. *See also* KUBLAI KHAN.

> Levy's Lodge—that was what the sign at the coast road said—was a Xanadu of the senses; within its insulated walls there was something that could gratify anything.
> JOHN KENNEDY TOOLE *A Confederacy of Dunces* 1980

> [The film] is *Hoop Dreams*, a three-hour documentary about two black inner city kids who dream of playing in the NBA, the professional basketball league and Xanadu to every deprived teenager who can dribble 20 yards. *The Guardian* 1995

Xerxes Xerxes (*c*.519–465 BC) was the king of Persia, son of Darius I. He led the invasion of Greece, building a bridge from boats to allow his army to cross the Hellespont (now the Dardanelles) and winning the battles of Artemisium and Thermopylae. He was later defeated at the battle of Salamis and had to withdraw from Greece. *See also* THERMOPYLAE.

> Gina made it clear that Anstice had consistently portrayed Richard as a Lionheart, a Tamburlaine, a veritable Xerxes in the sack.
> MARTIN AMIS *The Information* 1995

X-Files The successful television series *The X-Files* (1993–2002) relates the adventures of the FBI special agents Dana Scully and Fox Mulder as they encounter various preternatural and extra-terrestrial phenomena. The X-Files are often alluded to in the context of strange or surprising coincidences.

> 'Missing kids, every sod old enough to have a stiff cock ends up in the frame. He'd be eighteen or thereabout. Bad age. And all the kids who went missing were blonde and he wed himself a blonde . . .' 'Come on!' said Pascoe. 'You reach any further and you'll be in the X-files.'
> REGINALD HILL *On Beulah Height* 1998

Yahoo The Yahoos are an imaginary race of brutish creatures, resembling human beings, in Jonathan Swift's *Gulliver's Travels* (1726). They embody all the baser vices and instincts of the human race. The word 'yahoo' has become a part of the language, referring to a coarse, loutish, or rowdy person, or one who engages in wanton vandalism. *See also* GULLIVER'S TRAVELS.

> In the main the animals would have walked along quietly enough; but the Casterbridge tradition was that to drive stock it was indispensable that hideous cries, coupled with Yahoo antics and gestures, should be used.
> THOMAS HARDY *The Mayor of Casterbridge* 1886

> Hens were in attendance, quietly and unquestioningly supportive, among all the dust and rubbish. As for the two pigs, they were yahoos even by the standards of the yard.
> MARTIN AMIS *London Fields* 1989

Dornford Yates Dornford Yates was the pseudonym of the English novelist Cecil William Mercer (1885–1960). His novels featuring the hero Richard Chandos are adventure thrillers and include the titles *Blind Corner* (1927) and *Perishable Goods* (1928).

> At other times, Mary would have enjoyed the circumstances of their departure: they had elements of romantic adventure, as if lifted from a novel by John Buchan or Dornford Yates.
> ANDREW TAYLOR *Mortal Sickness* 1995

Yellow Brick Road In L. Frank Baum's children's story *The Wizard of Oz* (1900), Dorothy follows the Yellow Brick Road to Oz in the hope that the Wizard will help her to get home. She is joined on her journey by three companions she meets on the way: the Scarecrow, who wants a brain; the Cowardly Lion, who wants courage; and the Tin Woodman, who wants a heart. *See also* WIZARD OF OZ.

> For this group of divers their 'yellow brick road' will take them along a professional route towards the PADI Divemaster and PADI Open Water Scuba Instructor ratings. *Sport Diver* 1999

Yoda In the *Star Wars* films, Yoda is a small, scrawny-looking creature with pointed ears who instructs Luke Skywalker on how to become a Jedi knight and battle against the evil Empire. *See also* STAR WARS.

> An elfin woman bustles in and heads straight for the sewing machines. With a wiry frizz of gray-black hair atop a Yoda body, she is the spitting image of my Tante Leah.
> SUSAN SUSSMAN with SARAJANE AVIDON *Cruising for Murder* 2000

Yogi Bear Yogi Bear is an American animated-cartoon character who appeared on television in the 1950s and 1960s. Living in Jellystone Park, Yogi Bear considers himself 'smarter than the average bear' and with his companion Boo Boo spends his time trying to outwit the park ranger and steal picnic baskets from visitors to the park.

Ypres The battle of Ypres is the name given to each of three battles of the First World War that took place near the town of Ypres in north-west Belgium. As with the battle of the Somme, going 'over the top' at Ypres was seen as going to certain death. *See also* PASSCHENDAELE, SOMME.

> The realization that one day he himself was going to have to rent or buy a house of some sort would fill him with dismay and despair, like the thought of going over the top at Ypres or the Somme without any prospect of a medal.
> KINGSLEY AMIS *The Riverside Villas Murder* 1973

y

Zapata Emiliano Zapata (1879–1919) was a Mexican revolutionary leader who fought successive federal governments to repossess expropriated village lands. Probably because of the appearance of Marlon Brando in the film *Viva Zapata* (1952), the term 'Zapata' can be used to describe a type of moustache in which the two ends extend downwards to the chin.

> 'What's happened to your gaucho moustache?' 'I . . . I shaved it off.' 'Why?' 'In view of certain comments, your Honour, passed in the Station. It wasn't a gaucho. More a Viva Zapata, actually.'
> JOHN MORTIMER *Rumpole of the Bailey* 1978

> He knew—he even hoped—this was probably false (and felt the formation, across his upper lip, of a Zapata moustache of sweat).
> MARTIN AMIS *London Fields* 1989

> Gonzago and Tomas looked so much alike that Gonzago grew a Zapata moustache so that people could distinguish them.
> LOUIS DE BERNIÈRES *The War of Don Emmanuel's Nether Parts* 1990

Zarathustra Zarathustra is another name for Zoroaster (*c.*628–*c.*551 BC), a Persian prophet and founder of Zoroastrianism. Friedrich Nietzsche's book *Thus Spake Zarathustra* (1885) chronicles the wanderings and teachings of Zarathustra and develops the idea that human beings are a transitional form between apes and what Nietzsche calls the *Übermensch*, or Superman.

> In truth I am deafened by the pomposity of my own utterances. They echo in my skull like the reverberating eructations of Zarathustra, like the wind whistling through Montaigne's beard.
> LAWRENCE DURRELL *Clea* 1960

Zeboiim *See* ADMAH AND ZEBOIIM.

Zenobia Zenobia (3rd c. AD) was a queen of Palmyra who succeeded her murdered husband as ruler and then conquered Egypt and much of Asia Minor. She can be alluded to as a powerful and aloof woman.

> She has been very farouche with me for a long time; and is only just beginning to thaw a little from her Zenobia ways.
> MRS GASKELL *North and South* 1854–5

Zeus The supreme ruler of the Olympian gods in Greek mythology, identified by the Romans with Jupiter, Zeus was the protector and ruler of mankind, the dispenser of justice, and the god of weather (whose most famous weapon was the thunderbolt). Although he was the husband of Hera, he had many amorous liaisons with goddesses, nymphs, and mortal women. He often disguised himself to accomplish seductions, encountering Danae in the form of a shower of gold, Leda as a swan, and Europa as a bull.

> But his true fighting weight, his antecedents, his amours with other members of the commercial Pantheon—all these were as uncertain to ordinary mortals as were the escapades of Zeus. While the gods are powerful, we learn little about them. It is only in the days of their decadence that a strong light beats into heaven.
> E. M. FORSTER *Howards End* 1910

> 'You never slept with Oupa?' I repeat, inanely. 'Yet you had six children.' 'Nine. Three died.' 'So the Holy Ghost got going on you too?' I say sarcastically. 'Like Zeus, the Holy Ghost has been known to assume many shapes.'
> ANDRÉ BRINK *Imaginings of Sand* 1996

Zeuxis Zeuxis (5th c. BC) was a Greek painter known for creating extremely lifelike paintings. One anecdote relates how birds flew to his painting of a bunch of grapes, taking them to be real.

> Is she pretty? More—beautiful. A subject for the pen of Nonnus, or the pencil of Zeuxis.
> THOMAS LOVE PEACOCK *Crotchet Castle* 1831

Zorba In the 1964 film of Nikos Kazantzakis's novel *Zorba the Greek* (1946), Anthony Quinn plays Zorba, a larger-than-life Cretan much given to exuberant solo dancing.

> Michael was already imagining the scenario. Ol' frizzy-haired Mona, sullen and horny in some smoky taverna. Mrs Madrigal holding court in her oatmeal linen caftan, doing that Zorba dance as the spirit moved her.
> ARMISTEAD MAUPIN *Sure of You* 1990

Zorro Zorro is the masked hero of Hollywood films of the 1930s to 1960s who first appeared in a comic strip in 1919. In reality he is Don Diego de la Vega, a member of a wealthy Spanish family, but his true identity remains a secret, and in his disguise as Zorro (the Fox) he rights wrongs and protects the weak, leaving as his calling card a letter 'Z' cut into the clothing or body of his enemies. He can be alluded to in the same way as Robin Hood, as someone who defies unjust rulers and stands up for the weak and helpless.

> These ideas were swimming around in my mind, not quite as coherently as I have expressed them, as I went loping across the roofs of Trastevere like Zorro or the Scarlet Pimpernel or somebody of that ilk.
> ELIZABETH PETERS *Street of the Five Moons* 1978

> Milo knocked softly just before midnight. He was carrying a hard-shell case the

size of an attaché and had on a polo shirt, twill pants, and windbreaker. All in black. Regular-guy parody of the L.A. hipster ensemble. I said, 'Trying to fade into the night, Zorro?'
JONATHAN KELLERMAN *Devil's Waltz* 1993

'You'll have to talk to the police,' said Robin with sudden decision, reaching for the telephone. 'Dammit, Sarah, who else knew she called you her scold's bridle? Surely it's occurred to you that the message is directed at you.' 'What message?' 'I don't know. A threat, perhaps. You next, Dr Blakeney.' She gave a hollow laugh. 'I see it more in terms of a signature.' She traced a line on the desk with her fingertip. 'Like the mark of Zorro on his victims.'
MINETTE WALTERS *The Scold's Bridle* 1994

Thematic Index

Montagues and Capulets
Philistines

Envy
Calchas
Iago
Joseph

Escape and Survival
Artful Dodger
Bunbury
Deucalion
Houdini
Isaac
Jonah
Lot
Noah
Pegasus
Jack Sheppard
Teflon
Tinker Bell

Evil
Ahab
Big Bad Wolf
Cesare Borgia
Lucrezia Borgia
Borgias
Caliban
Cruella de Vil
Darth Vader
Eve
Fu Manchu
Herod
Hitler
Mr Hyde
Iago
Hannibal Lecter
Loki
Lady Macbeth
Manson
Moloch
Rasputin
Tarquin
Whore of Babylon

Explorers
Balboa
St Brendan
Columbus
Captain Cook
Cortés
Sir Francis Drake

Dr Livingstone
Sir Henry Morton
Stanley
Star Trek
Amerigo Vespucci

Failure
Canute
Casey
Chappaquiddick
Clouseau
Edsel
Icarus
Willy Loman
Lucifer
Phaethon
Edwin Reardon
Sisyphus
South Sea Bubble
Frank Spencer

Fatness
Billy Bunter
Falstaff
Fat Controller
Mr Pickwick
Miss Piggy
Rubens
Silenus
Friar Tuck

Fear
Norman Bates
Deimos
Grimm
Hansel and Gretel
Alfred Hitchcock
Freddy Krueger
Christopher Lee
Nightmare on Elm Street
Phobos
Psycho

Fertility
Abraham
Aphrodite
Ashtoreth
Astarte
Bacchus
Demeter
Dionysus
Flora

Freyja

Fierce Women
Amazon
Norma Desmond
harpy
termagant

Food and Drink
Amalthea
ambrosia
Bacchanalia
Bacchante
Bacchus
Belshazzar
Cornucopia
Betty Crocker
Falernian
fatted calf
Horn of Plenty
Jacob's pottage
Lucullus
manna
nectar
Prodigal Son
Samuel
Saturnalian
Silenus

Forgiveness
Jesus
Prodigal Son
Tannhäuser

Freedom
John Brown
Patrick Henry
Jim
Abraham Lincoln
Messiah
Moses

Friendship
Achates
Achilles and Patroclus
Damon and Pythias
David and Jonathan
Don Quixote and Sancho
Panza
Man Friday
Pylades and Orestes
Three Musketeers
Tonto

Helicon
Hippocrene
Laura
Melpomene
Muses
Parnassus
Pieria
Polyhymnia
Terpsichore
Thalia
Urania

Intelligence
Aristotle
St Augustine
Professor Challenger
Darwin
Einstein
Stephen Hawking
Sherlock Holmes
Houyhnhnms
Hypatia
Jesuit
Mozart
Isaac Newton
Plato
Socrates
Spock

Invisibility
Alberich's cloak
Bilbo Baggins
Gyges
Harvey
Invisible Man
Mambrino's helmet

Jealousy
Cephalus
Deianira
Leontes
Medea
Oedipus
Othello
Polyphemus

Judgement and Decision
Aristeides the Just
Judge Jeffreys
Minos
Paris

Rhadamanthus
Solomon

Knowledge
Argus
Charlie Chan
Chingachgook
GCHQ
Janus
Sibyl
Topsy
Tree of Knowledge

Large Size
Anak
Brobdingnagian
Buckingham Palace
Colossus
Gargantua
Goliath
Gulliver
Jotun
King Kong
Leviathan
Mutt and Jeff
Procrustes
Tardis
Titan

Leaders
Abraham
Alfred the Great
Napoleon Bonaparte
Boudicca
Caesar
Charlemagne
Cleopatra
Oliver Cromwell
Fagin
Garibaldi
Hippolyta
Joan of Arc
Pantheon
Saladin
Tamerlane
Xerxes
Zenobia

Life: Generation of Life
Adam and Eve
Frankenstein
Galatea

Pinocchio
Prometheus
Pygmalion

Light
Apollo
Balder
Celestial City
Goshen
Helios
Mithras
Phoebe
Phoebus
Ra
Selene

Love and Marriage
Aphrodite
Arthurian
Barbara Cartland
Cordelia
Cupid
Doris Day
Eros
Gone with the Wind
Gretna
Miss Havisham
Hymen
Mills and Boon
Ruth
Swineherd
Venus
Wendy

Lovers
Abelard and Héloïse
Antony and Cleopatra
Aucassin and Nicolette
Beatrice and Benedick
Cinderella
Cupid and Psyche
Dante and Beatrice
Daphnis and Chloe
Darby and Joan
David and Bathsheba
Dido and Aeneas
Hero and Leander
Isis and Osiris
Jacob and Rachel

Sweeney Todd

Music
Aeolian
Apollo
Arcadia
Beethoven
Blondel
St Cecilia
David
Euterpe
Gabriel
Minerva
Miriam
Mozart
Orpheus
Pan
Quasimodo
Roy Rogers
Vale of Tempe
Terpsichore
Tin-Pan Alley
Wagner

Mystery
Agatha Christie
Wilkie Collins
Eleusinian mysteries
Kaspar Hauser
House of Usher
Mona Lisa
Edgar Allen Poe
Sphinx
Udolpho
Veil of Isis
X-Files

Naivety
Arcadia
Babes in the Wood
Enid Blyton
Candide
Dickensian
Happy Hooligan
Daisy Miller
Miranda
noble savage
Arthur Rackham
Rousseau
Shirley Temple
Waltons
Wild Boy of Aveyron

Nakedness
Actaeon
Adam and Eve
Lady Godiva
Susanna

Nonconformity
Bohemia
Holden Caulfield
James Dean
Huckleberry Finn
Galileo
Rebel Without a Cause
Tom Sawyer
Socrates

Noses
Bardolph
Cyrano de Bergerac
Jimmy Durante
Pinocchio
Rudolph

Old Age
Cumaean Sibyl
Elli
Father Time
Father William
Jared
Mahalalel
Methuselah
She
Struldbrug
Tithonus

Optimism
Aunt Chloe
Mr Micawber
Pangloss
Norman Vincent Peale
Pollyanna

Oratory
Cato
Winston Churchill
Cicero
Demosthenes
Hamlet
John the Baptist
Abraham Lincoln
Pericles
Sermon on the Mount

John Wesley

Outdatedness
Ark
Dark Ages
Forth Bridge
Jurassic
Noah's Ark
Rip Van Winkle

Outlaws
Billy the Kid
Bonnie and Clyde
Butch Cassidy
Jesse James
Ned Kelly
Robin Hood
Dick Turpin

Past
Adam and Eve
King Arthur
Beowulf
Caesars
Creation
Cyclopean
Flood
Merlin
Noah

Patience
Enoch Arden
Estragon
Godot
Griselda
Jacob
Job
Man of Uz
Penelope
Vladimir

Peace
Abraham's bosom
Buddha
Neville Chamberlain
Concordia
Gandhi
Irene
Madonna
Pax

Perseverance
Ancient Mariner